S0-FQX-983

SAP® Cloud Platform Integration

John Mutumba Bilay, Peter Gutsche, Mandy Krimmel,
Volker Stiehl

SAP® Cloud Platform Integration

The Comprehensive Guide

Editor Will Jobst
Acquisitions Editor Hareem Shafi
Copyeditor Julie McNamee
Cover Design Graham Geary
Photo Credit iStockphoto.com/518857661/© gregobagel
Layout Design Vera Brauner
Production Hannah Lane
Typesetting SatzPro, Krefeld (Germany)
Printed and bound in the United States of America, on paper from sustainable sources

ISBN 978-1-4932-1706-9
© 2018 by Rheinwerk Publishing, Inc., Boston (MA)
2nd edition 2018

Library of Congress Cataloging-in-Publication Data
Names: Bilay, John Mutumba, author.
Title: SAP cloud platform : the comprehensive guide / John Bilay, Peter Gutsche, Mandy Krimmel, Volker Stiehl.
Other titles: SAP HANA cloud integration
Description: 2nd edition. | Bonn ; Boston : Rheinwerk Publishing, 2018. | Revised edition of: SAP HANA cloud integration / John Mutumba Bilay, Peter Gutsche, Volker Stiehl. 2016. | Includes index.
Identifiers: LCCN 2018024335 (print) | LCCN 2018026190 (ebook) | ISBN 9781493217076 (ebook) | ISBN 9781493217069 (alk. paper)
Subjects: LCSH: Cloud computing. | SAP HANA (Electronic resource)
Classification: LCC QA76.585 (ebook) | LCC QA76.585 .B55 2018 (print) | DDC 004.67/82--dc23
LC record available at https://lccn.loc.gov/2018024335

Contents at a Glance

Dear Reader,

On the cover of this book is a modern, futuristic-looking suspension bridge. Against a striking sky, this engineering marvel combines form and function, providing something that is used daily, even by members of the SAP PRESS team! As all of us live in the greater Boston area, we commute to the same place, to create and refine books that cater to the SAP audience, covering SAP from every direction. Cables connecting to a singular hub.

Like the bridges getting us to our jobs, SAP Cloud Platform Integration connects your cloud and on-premise applications! Even more, this star author team of John Mutumba Bilay, Peter Gutsche, Mandy Krimmel, and Volker Stiehl all came together to provide you the be-all, end-all guide to SAP Cloud Platform Integration. In these pages is the information that you need, as solid as a suspension bridge.

What did you think about Controlling with *SAP Cloud Integration: The Comprehensive Guide*? Your comments and suggestions are the most useful tools to help us make our books the best they can be. Please feel free to contact me and share any praise or criticism you may have.

Thank you for purchasing a book from SAP PRESS!

Will Jobst
Editor, SAP PRESS

willj@rheinwerk-publishing.com
www.sap-press.com
Rheinwerk Publishing · Boston, MA

Contents

11 Productive Scenarios Using SAP Cloud Platform Integration 737

12 Summary and Outlook 755

Appendices 765

Foreword by Björn Goerke

Undoubtedly, the rapid succession of innovations we see in the field of information technology is fundamentally changing how we do business, how we communicate with each other, even how we live. Software is increasingly driving the world and everything is digitizing. Self-driving cars, refrigerators that order food on their own, robots that take over complex tasks previously only performed by humans–just a few years ago, this would have sounded like science fiction, but now these things are discussed seriously and debated publicly. The future of enterprise IT has to be agile, yet robust. Distributed, while interconnected. Open, yet secure. Simple, but intelligent.

When the world's master of the Go game, the Chinese Ke Jie, was defeated by Google's AlphaGo algorithm in 2017, software capable of learning without being explicitly programmed for every eventuality clearly moved from the realm of theory to practical reality, highlighting the fact that such technological changes will inevitably shape all our futures.

In times such as these, it is no longer an option for enterprises to simply keep pace with new technology. Instead it is imperative to forge ahead, embrace innovations and build new businesses and processes that maximize the advantages they offer. A new IT era is upon us.

No IT company "knows" business processes better than SAP, the world's largest vendor of business software. And no one knows better how crucial it is to have a reliable, experienced and responsive partner to help you make the most of every innovation and opportunity. Agility will be key to winning in this new era. With SAP Cloud Platform (SAP CP), you can benefit from THE agile platform-as-a-service that provides you with the capabilities to develop, extend, and build intelligent applications using SAP's cloud infrastructure.

This new era will lead to new competitive dynamics and business models, and will introduce new disruptive players, who will be quick to harness innovation. To supercharge our continuous journey to innovate the future, we will have to embrace extreme openness in our technology stack and culture.

Of course, *integration* was and still is a key challenge facing forward-looking enterprises. Companies must be able to run, monitor, and control business processes distributed over heterogeneous system landscapes–both in the cloud and on premise.

Integration will only become more significant as technological developments bring new software systems to connect to and integrate.

SAP Cloud Platform Integration–Cloud Integration–as SAP's integration service on top of SAP CP, is the way to go. It comes with a rich set of tools that enable you to design, build, and operate integration scenarios based on the exchange of messages within distributed landscapes. It supports various protocols and standards to connect SAP and non-SAP systems securely, in the cloud and on premise. Cloud Integration is a unique platform that enables you to adopt the cloud world. Furthermore, it provides you with a rich variety of predefined integration content that supports out-of-the-box integration of SAP systems with each other as well as with third-party systems.

The platform is continuously innovating, with updates released every two weeks with zero downtime for your business. Therefore, since the release of the first edition of this book, the Cloud Integration team has enhanced the portfolio of the product by many new features.

Curious to find out more? This new edition explains all these innovations in detail, along with an in-depth introduction to the product portfolio and the architecture underlying it. However, like the first edition, the book is suited for the beginner who wants to dive in and get started with the product, with easy-to-follow instructions on how to set up and run your first integration scenario. At the same time, this second edition offers a deeper look into the details of integration design and touches on more sophisticated scenarios. As a result, the advanced user also can rely on it as a valuable reference.

This book is sure to be a good companion on your way to becoming an integration expert. Enjoy reading!

Björn Goerke
Chief Technology Officer at SAP and President of SAP Cloud Platform

Preface

The IT landscapes in today's companies are getting more complex every day. With the advent of cloud computing, the need for integration between on-premise applications and cloud solutions, or between cloud applications, becomes apparent. By reading this book, you will learn how SAP Cloud Platform Integration can help you solve your integration challenges.

Enterprise application integration (EAI) has a long history. The need for easy data exchange came up early, with the first computer systems. Whether it was the transfer of master data, such as customer or product data, or the transmission of transactional data, such as orders or invoices, systems of importance always required some sort of communication and integration. Interestingly, this communication wasn't restricted to systems and applications *within one company*. The demand for intercompany data transfer increased the integration challenge even further.

With the arrival of cloud computing, we face a new dimension to the integration domain, as on-premise and cloud applications need to work seamlessly with each other. Companies selling standard software for both worlds, on-premise and on-demand, face an additional challenge: their customers expect seamless data exchange between their applications out of the box. As SAP's strategy clearly focuses on becoming *the* cloud-company for business software, the need to supply an easy-to-use integration solution running in the cloud became apparent. SAP had already gathered experience in building integration software with SAP Process Integration. However, for this new integration era, the good old SAP Process Integration solution wasn't suitable, as it didn't support typical cloud qualities such as multi-tenancy, data isolation, rolling software updates, zero downtime, or cloud elasticity. Instead of further investing in SAP Process Integration and trying to make it "cloud-ready," SAP decided to deliver a completely new integration solution called SAP Cloud Platform Integration. SAP Cloud Platform Integration was developed from scratch on top of the SAP Cloud Platform, with typical cloud integration scenarios in mind. With this approach, SAP is combining the best of both worlds: on-premise integration with its rock-solid SAP Process Integration product and cloud-based integration with SAP Cloud Platform Integration. With this separation, customers have the freedom of choice when considering their particular needs.

Structure of the Book

This book introduces SAP Cloud Platform Integration and covers a wide range of topics. We will begin with **Chapter 1** and a discussion of how SAP Cloud Platform Integration, as the prime integration point between disparate cloud and on-premise systems, fits into SAP's overall strategy to become *the* cloud-company for business software. In addition, we will present the main use cases of SAP Cloud Platform Integration, such as cloud-to-cloud or cloud-to-on-premise integration. Chapter 1 closes with an explanation of SAP Cloud Platform Integration's major capabilities.

As we wanted to deliver a practical book with lots of examples, **Chapter 2** dives directly into the hands-on experience. After introducing the architecture of SAP Cloud Platform Integration and the new vocabulary you need to get used to, we guide you step-by-step through a very simple scenario. You will work with the *Web UI* as the central SAP Cloud Platform Integration tool used to model, deploy, run, and monitor your integration scenarios, or *integration flows* in Cloud Integration's nomenclature. This chapter lays the foundation upon which all further chapters and exercises will be built.

Besides modeling integration scenarios from scratch, SAP Cloud Platform Integration also comes with prepackaged integration content. Remember, SAP's customers expect a smooth message exchange between SAP's on-premise and cloud solutions, as a single vendor ships both types of products. This data exchange can only work if SAP delivers pre-configured integration content running on top of SAP Cloud Platform Integration out-of-the-box. The delivered integration flows seamlessly glue the systems together without running costly integration projects, which were once a necessity. This prepackaged integration content is already available in the *Integration Content Catalog*. **Chapter 3** explains how you can benefit from the Integration Content Catalog and describes in detail, for example, the integration content for seamlessly connecting SAP SuccessFactors and SAP ERP Human Capital Management. At the end of the chapter, we will also explain how you can develop your own integration content and make it available in the Integration Content Catalog—an offering that is of special interest for SAP's partner ecosystem.

Chapter 4, **Chapter 5**, and **Chapter 6** focus on developing custom integration flows in case the prepackaged content provided in the Integration Content Catalog isn't sufficient for your business needs. In particular, we'll use step-by-step guides on how to apply the various step types that are part of SAP Cloud Platform Integration's web-based modeling environment. Over the course of these three chapters, you will learn how to:

- Work with SAP Cloud Platform Integration's data model.
- Enrich incoming data with data from an external OData source.
- Map data between different message interfaces.
- Route messages to the right receiver depending on the message's content (i.e., *content-based routing*).
- Influence the evaluation sequence of conditions for the content-based router.
- Handle messages comprising a list of items (such as order items); splitting and merging the individual list items are of particular interest in this section.
- Influence the execution of synchronous and asynchronous scenarios.
- Use Java Message Service (JMS) queues to temporarily store messages on the Cloud Integration platform and, that way, to asynchronously decouple inbound from outbound communication.
- Schedule timer-based integration flows, which run at pre-defined times and/or at pre-defined intervals.
- Dynamically configure integration flow parameters using headers and properties.
- Structure large integration scenarios based on modularization and the usage of local integration flows.
- Exchange data between parent and child integration flows.
- Directly connect integration flows by using the ProcessDirect adapter.
- Understand the versioning concept of the cloud-based integration flow modeler and migrate integration flows to another version.
- Transport integration content across tenants.
- Develop your own adapters by using the *Adapter Development Kit* (ADK).
- Last but not least, get an overview of some best practices for integration flow design to make sure to optimize reliability and performance of message processing.

Chapter 7 covers the capabilities of SAP Cloud Platform Integration to support business-to-business (B2B) integration. SAP has developed various new components to support such use cases, such as the Integration Content Advisor, the Partner Directory, and various new adapters and integration flow step types. This chapter guides you along one end-to-end scenario through the usage of these components and tools.

Chapter 8 continues our journey with the operational aspects of SAP Cloud Platform Integration. As the previous chapters have shown you how to design integration flows to cover use cases with increasing complexity, you—the integration developer—like to monitor how these integration flows actually process messages on your SAP Cloud Platform tenant. Monitoring messages is one task. But there are additional tasks you can accomplish using the Monitor section of the Web UI, such like managing security artifacts (for example, the keys and certificates contained in the tenant keystore), and data storages on your tenant. This chapter covers all these aspects in detail.

So far, we have in detail described how people can work with the user interface of SAP Cloud Platform Integration (basically, the Web UI) to perform tasks such like integration flow development or monitoring messages. However, SAP Cloud Platform Integration provides also the option to access integration-related artifacts based on an application programming interface (API). The available APIs are described in detail in **Chapter 9**. This chapter also shows you how you can use Cloud Integration APIs together with SAP Cloud Platform API Management, a dedicated service of SAP Cloud Platform that helps you to develop, manage, and publish your own APIs.

So far, we have completely left out security aspects from our discussion. However, when it comes to cloud computing, security is one of the top-ranked requirements from customers, whether they are addressing the service provider hosting SAP Cloud Platform Integration or the integration developer running scenarios on top of it. We have decided to collect all security-relevant topics in one chapter, rather than spread them across the book. Therefore, **Chapter 10** will be your one-stop shop for all security-related questions. The chapter summarizes the measures taken by SAP to protect your data at the highest level and shows what you can do to maximize the security level of your integration scenarios. Keeping with our habit of providing hands-on examples, this chapter also contains guides that show you how to build simple integration flows that contain features such as digital encryption or authentication.

We now approach the end of the book. **Chapter 11** looks at already-running productive scenarios using SAP Cloud Platform Integration. We will mainly focus on the specifics of the following scenarios:

- Integration of SAP Cloud for Customer and SAP ERP
- Integration of SAP Cloud for Customer with SAP S/4HANA Cloud
- Integration of SAP Marketing Cloud and various applications
- Integration of SAP SuccessFactors and SAP ERP
- Integration of SAP applications with the Ariba Network

Once finished with this chapter, you will understand how of SAP Cloud for Customer plays a crucial role as part of SAP's classical and new business applications.

Finally, **Chapter 12** concludes the book with an outlook comprising the roadmap for SAP Cloud Platform Integration. By reading this chapter, you will receive an impression of how of SAP Cloud for Customer will evolve over time and how of SAP Cloud for Customer grows even more important for SAP's overall company strategy.

Sample Applications

Over the course of this book, we will be developing many sample applications that demonstrate the key concepts of of SAP Cloud for Customer in context. Some of these applications require certain artifacts such like files that contain web service descriptions. To make it easy for you to set up these applications, we provide these files ready-to-download in the supplemental materials of this book. You can download them at *www.sap-press.com/4650*.

You can generally find instructions for installing and deploying these applications within the chapters that cover them. If you run into any problems with the examples, you can email the authors directly at: *johnbilay@rojoconsultancy.com*, *mandy.krimmel@sap.com*, and *peter.gutsche@sap.com*.

The downloaded archive—when unpacked—will have a directory structure which is oriented along the chapters where the associated files are required:

- **Chapter 2:** The file **SendOrder_Async.wsdl** contains the Web Services Description Language (WSDL) file that defines an input message (asynchronous interface) used in various sample integration flows.

- **Chapter 4:** The file **GetOrderShipDetails_Sync.wsdl** contains the Web Services Description Language (WSDL) file that defines an input message (synchronous interface) used in a sample integration flow.
- **Chapter 5:** The file **SendOrderList_Async.wsdl** contains the Web Services Description Language (WSDL) file that defines an input message (asynchronous interface) used in a sample integration flow.
- **Chapter 7:** The following files are required to set up the B2B scenario:
  - The archive **EDI_IDoc_Template.zip** is the template to be used to create the integration flow.
  - The folder **ASC_X12_to_SAP_IDOC_Purchase_Order_Mapping** contains *.xsd and *.xsl files generated from Integration Content Advisor.
  - The file **GroovyScript.txt** contains the coding for the groovy script flow step to retrieve configuration data from partner directory.
  - File **850 - Purchase Order.txt** contains the test payload for the scenario.
  - File **850 - Purchase Order - Technically incorrect.txt** contains an incorrect payload for the scenario to test the error case.
- **Chapter 10:** The file **SendOrder_Async.wsdl** (same file as used for Chapter 2) contains the Web Services Description Language (WSDL) file that defines an input message (asynchronous interface) used in various sample integration flows.

Who This Book Is For

This book addresses a broad audience, from integration architects, integration consultants, and integration developers, to technical-oriented business users, project leaders, and managers who want to understand how SAP Cloud Platform Integration can support either their journey into the cloud or how it can solve integration challenges related to integrating cloud solutions (on-premise-to-cloud or cloud-to-cloud). The reader, ideally, should be familiar with basic concepts regarding enterprise application integration and messaging, as this book will not cover those concepts. In addition, a basic understanding of Java, scripting languages, and enterprise integration patterns is beneficial. However, note that no knowledge of SAP Cloud Platform Integration or SAP Process Integration is required. You will receive everything you need to begin productive work with Cloud Integration, from designing and running a simple integration flow, up to implementing complex integration patterns from this book.

Now that you have an understanding of the book's contents, and for whom the book was written, we don't want to lose any more time getting started. We wish you an enjoyable ride!

Acknowledgments

Writing a book is always a challenging task. And it would be close to impossible without the help of many good friends and colleagues. This chapter is for those who supported us in one way or another.

We would like to start by thanking the team at Rheinwerk Publishing for all their support throughout the project. We are very thankful for your support and your team spirit. You have made it all possible. We would like, in particular, to thank Hareem Shafi from Rheinwerk Publishing for encouraging us to take up the task of writing a second edition of the book and for helping us set up the project. We would like to sincerely thank Will Jobst for accompanying us throughout the whole project. Will was always there when we needed support and quickly answered our many questions. Without his help during the whole writing process, it would not have been possible to bring the project to a successful end. Thank you for that!

We would like to thank Björn Goerke for recognizing this book with his foreword.

Sindhu Gangadharan encouraged us to take over the task to write a second edition of the book and, like she did for the first edition, supported our project.

Anette Asmus and Anita Riegel critically read some text passages and helped us to refine them at the final stage of writing this book.

We would like also to thank Volker Stiehl, coauthor of the first edition of the book, for his dedication in shaping the initial version of the book and for his insights into the topic of integration. Unfortunately, you couldn't join us in working on the second edition, Volker, but your contributions were invaluable in making the book what it is today.

We would also like to sincerely thank all the people who have contributed and reviewed different chapters of this SAP Cloud Platform Integration book. We would also like to acknowledge many others that we did not mention their name for their direct and indirect support and interest on the book.

John Mutumba Bilay

I have enjoyed the teamwork and collaborative spirit during this book project. It has been a true honor to work alongside Peter and Mandy. Your detailed and critical look at every topic made a difference. Thank you for that.

I would like to personally thank and express my gratitude to the many people who contributed to this book in different ways:

- Sabarish T. S. and Deepak Govardhanrao Deshpande for their support with questions related to OData provisioning. Your contribution is highly appreciated.
- Sujit Hemachandran for his valuable contribution and review of prepackaged content.
- Sandra Voges for her valuable inputs and review of Chapter 9.
- My gratitude also goes to the entire team of Rojo Consultancy B.V. for their help and consideration during the book writing process.

Finally, a big thank you to my wife Hermien and my boys Ralph, Luc, and Ruben for their loving support, patience and encouragement. You have made me stronger, better and more fulfilled than I could have ever imagined. During the process of writing this book, you have allowed me to skip some playtime to work on the book instead! I love you all to the moon and back.

Peter Gutsche

Like when writing for the first edition of this book, I experienced continuous and professional support from my colleagues in the SAP Cloud Platform Integration development teams, the user assistance team, and the product management team. Without the support of all of you this project would have not been possible. However, listing all your names would go beyond the scope of this section.

I would like in particular to thank the following colleagues who were involved in discussions or text reviews directly related to the book project:

- Peter Goebel helped me for any technical question related to the SAP Cloud Platform Integration system.
- I would like to thank Gunther Stuhec for sharing his knowledge of business-to-business integration in a couple of inspiring coffee corner chats.
- Franz Forsthofer, Christian Becker, Frantisek Deglovic, and Martin Matejcek helped my clarifying questions related to SAP Cloud Platform Integration security.
- Aurelian Stratica was a critical reader of the first edition of the book and shared his feedback.
- Finny Babu reviewed Chapter 6 and provided valuable input and feedback, in particular, for the topic of versioning and migration.

- Ralf Belger, Boris Zarske, VishnuPrasath Dhayanithi, Sabarish T. S., and Dimitar Aleksandrov helped me to find my way through the topic of integration content transport. I could count on your professional support when setting up a scenario using the beta version of the SAP Cloud Platform Transport Management Service.
- For the adapter development topic, I got input and support from Kumar Amar, Gopalkrishna Kulkarni, Appala Naidu Uppada, and Sharath Sasi.
- Markus Beier and Stephan Siano helped my clarifying some questions related to Camel headers and properties.
- Udo Paltzer and Andreas Quenstedt were there for all my questions about the product strategy and sharing their perspective on the outlook of the product.
- Divya Mary provided valuable feedback to Chapter 12. Thank you!
- Abinash Nanda helped clarifying questions related to integration scenarios including SAP Cloud for Customer.

I would like to thank my co-authors for this second book edition, Mandy and John, for their continuous support and team spirit. It was always possible to contact you and get your feedback in time when I came over a question. Your input and feedback to the individual chapters I wrote were invaluable. It was a real pleasure to work with you!

My manager Stefanie Schmitt supported me throughout the whole time of writing this book. Thank you for that!

Sherry Föhr was always there when I had questions related to the nuances of the English language and helped out with her expertise.

Finally, and of capital importance: I would like to thank Isabelle Krys for her encouragement and forbearance throughout the process of writing. Without you, it would have been hard for me to keep up with the project. Thank you!

Mandy Krimmel

Working on a book project like this requires helpful colleagues and understanding friends in the background. Working at SAP, I have the advantage of having many experienced, helpful and motivated people around to drill with questions. I would like to express my special thanks to the following colleagues for their support:

- The B2B chapter would not have been possible without the help of the development team of the Integration Content Advisor. Special thanks to Prashantha Halmuttur Lakshminarayana for helping to get the EDI template running. Jörg

Ackermann, Gunther Stuhec, and Marton Luptak supported me in understanding and describing the features of the Integration Content Advisor.

- Appala Naidu Uppada supported me with his expert knowledge of the AS2 adapter and the EDI flow steps. He helped me getting the Mendelson AS2 tool setup and running and had to answer lots of B2B-specific questions.
- Franz Forsthofer contributed with his comprehensive blogs about the partner directory and reviewed the respective section in the book.
- Stephan Siano and Jörg Kessler answered countless questions about the JMS functionality and JMS resources.
- Ines Ahrens and Maik Keller supported me with their expert knowledge in the operations area of Cloud Integration.
- Peter Göbel often saved my day by helping me with the setup and maintenance of my test cluster.

Gabriela Vittek, my manager, encouraged me to bring my knowledge into this book project. She supported me throughout the whole project and always had open ears and constructive suggestions when something did not run as planned.

Not to forget my two co-authors: Peter and John! It was a pleasure working with you! I enjoyed the constructive and goal-oriented discussions and the helpful attitude. I'm proud that I was part of this team!

Above all, none of this would have been possible without my husband Stefan and my daughter, who supported me throughout, even when deprived of my time and attention. Thank you!

Finally, we want to thank you, our readers, for choosing and purchasing this book. You want to learn more about SAP Cloud Platform Integration, and we hope you receive all the information needed in the following chapters to drive your personal education forward. Enjoy reading, and we hope you benefit from SAP Cloud Platform Integration in your next cloud integration project.

John Mutumba Bilay, **Peter Gutsche**, and **Mandy Krimmel**

Chapter 1
Introduction to SAP Cloud Platform Integration

This chapter explains how SAP Cloud Platform Integration fits into SAP's overall cloud strategy and its main use cases.

It's no secret anymore: the world is going digital! The convergence of trends, such as cloud computing, social networks, mobility, the Internet of Things, blockchain, hashgraph, and the resulting big data, is changing how we conduct business. We're increasingly experiencing this change in our personal lives, but these trends are quickly moving into the enterprise world, as well. Just take a look at how software is consumed today: more and more businesses are choosing to have their software delivered as a service and hosted in huge data centers. While on-premise environments aren't going anywhere soon, the industry is definitely seeing a shift to increased cloud adoption. Subscription-based licensing and central hosting are simply how people want to receive software these days. In this changing world of software delivery, the importance of simplicity can't be understated. All of these converging technological forces are creating a much more complex world. Hence, the drive to simplify experiences for software users is of paramount importance.

SAP, the world's largest provider of business software, has recognized the technological shift and is continuously expanding its offering of cloud software. However, SAP customers who have invested in on-premise landscapes in recent years can't be expected to immediately abandon their solutions and move to the cloud. This is where SAP Cloud Platform Integration comes into play, as the solution of choice for companies that are looking to bring their cloud and on-premise technologies together.

That brings us to the topic of the upcoming section: the role SAP Cloud Platform Integration plays in a company's cloud strategy. We'll also discuss the main use cases of SAP Cloud Platform Integration and provide an introduction to its various capabilities in this chapter.

Note

SAP Cloud Platform Integration is the new name for a product which was previously known as SAP HANA Cloud Integration (SAP HCI). The product was renamed in the beginning of 2017 as part of a general rebranding of SAP's cloud offering.

1.1 The Role of SAP Cloud Platform Integration in a Cloud-Based Strategy

As SAP moves to the cloud, hybrid deployments are going to play an increasingly major role in businesses. Most customers who run businesses today must, without a doubt, maintain existing IT landscapes. It's simply unreasonable to assume that cloud deployments will completely replace current environments. Consequently, successful companies look for solutions that will help them combine their current environments, which are typically on premise, with cloud-based applications (where it makes sense). Hybrid deployments will be the solution of choice for most companies in the years to come. This is where the market is heading, and this is where SAP sees investments in IT while moving to the cloud. However, hybrid landscapes automatically mean integration needs: on-premise and cloud applications need to exchange data with each other. This is exactly where an integration platform such as SAP Cloud Platform Integration fills the gap: it's responsible for reliable message exchange between systems. However, before we dive into the details of SAP Cloud Platform Integration and its strategic role in SAP's future plans, let's understand what motivates companies to implement cloud strategies.

The move to the cloud is made for good reasons. Figure 1.1 summarizes key business benefits of cloud computing, categorized into four major pillars.

When we talk about the cloud, we're actually thinking about the benefits shown in Figure 1.1. First and foremost, it's all about faster deployments. By deployment, we mean the first setup and customizing of the software that makes it ready for productive usage. Deployment in the old days used to take months, even years. With cloud solutions, deployment time is reduced drastically, sometimes to weeks or days. This trend is accompanied by a mobile user experience. The cloud is consumer-grade, it's beautiful, and it's flexible. Today's users expect to use software instantly and find it easy to adapt to without yesterday's long-lasting training sessions and expensive courses.

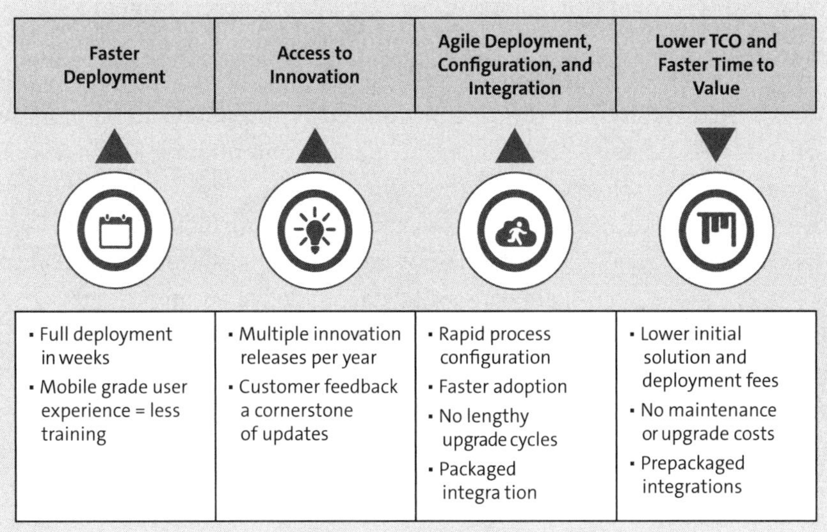

Faster Deployment
Access to Innovation
Agile Deployment, Configuration, and Integration
Lower TCO and Faster Time to Value
▪ Full deployment in weeks
▪ Mobile grade user experience = less training
▪ Multiple innovation releases per year
▪ Customer feedback a cornerstone of updates
▪ Rapid process configuration
▪ Faster adoption
▪ No lengthy upgrade cycles
▪ Packaged integra tion
▪ Lower initial solution and deployment fees
▪ No maintenance or upgrade costs
▪ Prepackaged integrations

Figure 1.1 Business Benefits of Cloud Computing

Access to innovation, the second pillar in Figure 1.1, is another important benefit of cloud computing. We're moving away from upgrade cycles that once took years, to at least quarterly upgrade cycles with most of today's software-as-a-service (SaaS) offerings. In many solutions, the innovation cycle may even be reduced to a monthly update. This results in the delivery of quarterly (or monthly) innovations to all users of a solution at the same time, and allows the software to always remain up to date. Consequently, all users are consistently working with the latest version of their software.

This leads directly to the next advantage of cloud computing: because all users are working with the same software at the same time, a short feedback cycle is ensured. Potentially millions of people are working with the software and will report their experiences directly to the vendor. This regular feedback cycle helps the software become better and better each day, as the vendor can react to issues almost immediately. Compare this cycle to the old days: after the vendor sold the solution, the deployment, as well as the upgrade, depended on the customer's planning, and the vendor never really received feedback about the software's usage. Today, cloud solutions allow innovations to be implemented faster, driving the quality of the software forward.

In summary, deployment and upgrade processes are becoming more and more agile, resulting in rapid configurations for faster adoption of the software without lengthy upgrade cycles. However, one problem needs to be solved in this new world of cloud-based software delivery: How do the systems residing in the cloud and on premise talk to each other? Fortunately, prepackaged integration content comes to the rescue. As the vendors of these solutions know their software best, they also know how to best connect them with each other. This is the home turf of SAP Cloud Platform Integration, as we'll see in a moment. Integrations between cloud systems, or between cloud and on-premise systems, are increasingly being delivered prepackaged. This means, in essence, the way those systems communicate and exchange data with each other can be defined in advance by the software vendor so that the consumer needs just a few configuration steps to make them executable: plug and play at its best. Customers have the choice of moving only certain functionality to the cloud. Out-of-the-box integrations are then used to allow for a smooth transition from the on-premise world to the cloud world at the speed the customer chooses.

Finally, we've heard a lot about lower total cost of ownership (TCO) and faster time to value of cloud solutions. This is the result of the advantages pointed out before: customers don't have to spend money on hardware and software hosted in their own data centers anymore. They can now outsource these tasks to the solution provider. Customers optimize their TCO due to lower initial solution and deployment fees, as well as no longer needing to shoulder the maintenance and upgrade costs. So, if you think about TCO, typically cloud solutions do very well in that regard.

The advantages are obvious: these benefits of cloud deployments free up time, money, and energy that can be spent on new innovations and new engagement models with your customers, partners, suppliers, and employees. You can now dedicate more time to serving your customers best. So remember, when you think about the cloud, it's not only about functional benefits but also about further innovations that become possible because you have more resources to dedicate to what really matters for your business.

Now that we understand the advantages that the cloud brings to the table, the need for an integration platform weaving together the loose ends between various combinations of cloud and on-premise solutions becomes even more obvious. SAP Cloud Platform Integration is itself a cloud solution based on the SAP Cloud Platform. It benefits from all of the advantages just outlined and manages reliable message exchanges between all participants. Whether we're talking about SAP on-premise/

cloud applications, non-SAP on-premise/cloud solutions, or business-to-business integrations (B2B), SAP Cloud Platform Integration is the solution of choice to connect them. In other words: a cloud strategy without SAP Cloud Platform Integration would be impossible. The solution is therefore SAP's strategic integration platform on the road to becoming a successful cloud company.

SAP Cloud Platform Integration has another big advantage when compared to the competition: because SAP knows its own applications better than any other vendor, SAP Cloud Platform Integration is shipped with preconfigured integration content that just needs a few configuration steps to become productive for most businesses. This approach reduces time and money for integration projects to the absolute minimum.

But what does a typical integration scenario look like? To sharpen the picture of a universal integration platform, let's take a look at some concrete use cases.

1.2 Use Cases

Business processes, in many cases, require different applications and software systems to exchange data with each other. For example, clicking on the **Buy an article** button in a seller's web catalog typically triggers subsequent processes that involve complex data flows in a landscape of software systems, often distributed across the boundaries of different organizations. Such landscapes are usually heterogeneous in the sense that the systems that communicate with each other use different technical communication protocols and store data in different individual formats and data structures.

An integration expert who is in charge of implementing such complex distributed processes faces the challenge of cross-linking a large number of systems and data sources in the right way, and of making sure that the relevant data is exchanged during the operation of a business process correctly.

In the following sections, we'll first discuss how such integration challenges can be addressed by SAP Cloud Platform Integration. In this context, we'll introduce the concept of mediated communication. We'll then describe the various use cases that are covered by SAP Cloud Platform Integration in general. Over the course of this discussion, we'll also briefly touch on another integration solution provided by SAP, called SAP Process Orchestration.

1.2.1 Point-to-Point versus Mediated Communication

Let's first assume that our integration expert solves the integration challenge by implementing direct connections between each of the components that are to exchange data with each other. The resulting method these components use to exchange data with each other is referred to as *point-to-point communication*.

For example, if the components are different SAP systems, *point-to-point connections* can be implemented by remote function calls (RFCs). In this case, all components are tightly coupled with each other, as illustrated in Figure 1.2, on the left. This setup has a number of disadvantages. For example, if one component, A, is upgraded, all connections where A is involved also have to be adapted. In the case of a large number of components, upgrade and maintenance tasks could easily spiral out of control, because the number of connections grows to the square of the number of components.

A more reliable and efficient approach to solving this integration challenge is to use a central integration platform—or an *integration bus*—that is interconnected between the involved systems. This setup is illustrated in Figure 1.2, to the right. All integration-related tasks are managed by the integration bus. This approach is called *mediated communication*, and it ensures that the number and arrangement of connections remains manageable.

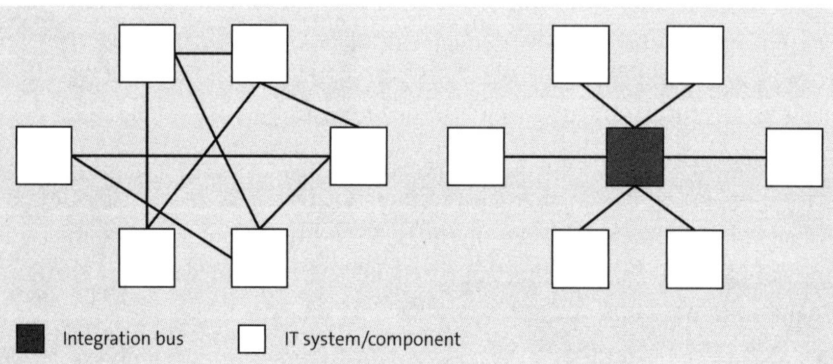

Figure 1.2 Point-to-Point Communication (Left) with a "Spaghetti-like" Arrangement of Connections, Compared to Mediated Communication (Right)

1.2.2 Message-Based Process Integration

Mediated communication is typically based on the exchange of messages. Let's examine what this means with the help of a few simple examples.

The integration bus makes sure, for example, that a message sent from system A to system B in a certain process step is transformed in a way that system B can interpret and further process the data contained in the message. If a message is to be forwarded from system A to more than one receiver, the integration platform manages proper routing of the message. Other process steps, in turn, might require that messages are split into smaller chunks, each of which might be forwarded to a different receiver, and so forth.

The integration bus approach makes sure that integration-related information and processes are centrally maintained and that tasks such as maintaining and updating the integration software are kept separate from integrated business applications.

An additional paradigm is to design the integration in a way that the applications to be integrated are loosely coupled with each other; that is, each individual application runs independently. This approach makes the overall business process less error-prone and reduces dependencies.

By addressing such integration challenges and approaches, SAP Cloud Platform Integration enables you to integrate processes that span different applications, organizations, or enterprises. This includes systems and applications of any kind, including non-SAP systems.

It's evident that different kinds of business processes require different means of exchanging messages between connected components. SAP Cloud Platform Integration supports a large number of these *Enterprise Integration Patterns*.

The term enterprise integration pattern—also referred to as *messaging pattern*—has been shaped and made popular by Gregor Hohpe and Bobby Woolf in their book *Enterprise Integration Patterns* (Addison-Wesley, 2004). The book defines and documents a number of integration patterns and how robust integration solutions can be designed. Each of the 65 patterns are illustrated in an intuitively understandable visual notation. The description is general enough to allow for an implementation with many different integration technologies.

A key capability of SAP Cloud Platform Integration—if not the most important one—is that it supports the implementation of enterprise integration patterns. As we'll explain in detail in Chapter 2, SAP Cloud Platform Integration uses the integration framework Apache Camel for this.

Integration Pattern Examples

One example of an Enterprise Integration Pattern is the *content-based router*. Imagine that a sender is connected to multiple receiver systems, and the business process requires that a message from the sender is forwarded to a particular receiver system depending on the content of the message (e.g., a customer ID). The content-based router makes such forwarding possible.

Another example is the *splitter*, which defines that a single message is split into multiple partial messages that can be processed individually.

To support different integration patterns, SAP Cloud Platform Integration offers a wide range of integration capabilities and connectivity options, as described in Section 1.3. However, let's first go into the different use cases that are supported by SAP Cloud Platform Integration.

1.2.3 Cloud-to-Cloud Integration

SAP Cloud Platform Integration is a cloud-based integration platform that provides on-demand process integration services (see Figure 1.3). Customers can use the platform's resources flexibly by paying a monthly fee. They don't need to install any integration middleware in their own landscape. All software processes that deal with message exchange run fully on SAP servers.

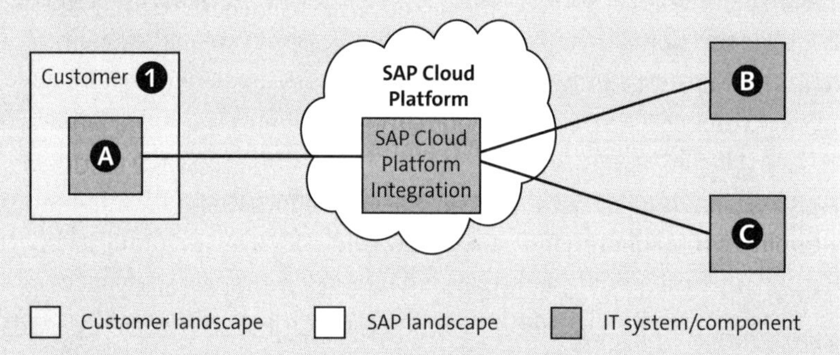

Figure 1.3 SAP Cloud Platform Integration as the Integration Platform Based on the SAP Cloud Platform

To run an integration scenario that requires message exchange between the three IT systems outlined in Figure 1.3, connections between these systems and SAP Cloud

Platform Integration are required. All integration-related processes run in the SAP landscape (as part of SAP Cloud Platform).

Figure 1.3 doesn't specify which kind of component or systems can be connected with each other. As our example, let's assume that component Ⓐ belongs to the system landscape of customer ❶. The other components to be connected aren't further specified.

Components or applications that are subject to an integration scenario can, in principle, be differentiated according to the following criteria:

- **On premise**
  The component or application is installed and maintained in the landscape of an integration solution customer, on the premises, or locally, in the customer landscape.
- **Cloud**
  The component or application runs in the cloud—for example, in SAP's cloud—and can be used by the customer on demand.

SAP Cloud Platform Integration, first and foremost, is suitable for the integration of cloud applications, that is, for cloud-to-cloud integration.

1.2.4 Cloud-to-On-Premise Integration

More and more cloud applications appear on the market and replace, in part, applications that until recently have only been available as on-premise solutions. However, large enterprises have invested much in their on-premise landscape and want to keep this investment. They only want to source out a part of their business into the cloud. These enterprises look for integration solutions that support the integration of their existing on-premise applications with new cloud applications.

SAP Cloud Platform Integration also supports this cloud-to-on-premise integration use case, whether you're using SAP or non-SAP systems.

Predefined Integration Content

SAP allows SAP Cloud Platform Integration customers to quickly implement a range of integration solutions out of the box. For this, customers can choose among a set of predefined integration packages in the Integration Content Catalog. The available integration packages cover the integration with a number of SAP solutions. We'll go into more detail on this in Chapter 3.

1.2.5 On-Premise-To-On-Premise Integration

SAP has successfully distributed SAP Process Orchestration for a number of years and continues to do the same today. SAP Process Orchestration is a combined package of SAP Process Integration and SAP Business Process Management (SAP BPM) capabilities that allow you to design business processes.

Note

Refer to *SAP Process Orchestration: The Comprehensive Guide* (SAP PRESS, 2017) for a comprehensive introduction to SAP Process Orchestration.

The SAP Process Integration part of SAP Process Orchestration is an on-premise integration middleware that, like SAP Cloud Platform Integration, can be used as an integration bus and that addresses the integration challenges mentioned in Section 1.2.1 and Section 1.2.2. In this context, we only refer to these integration bus capabilities and therefore don't consider the overall SAP Process Orchestration solution.

From a use case perspective, and having introduced SAP Cloud Platform Integration as the solution of choice for cloud-based integration, we want to emphasize that SAP Process Integration is the recommended solution for pure on-premise-to-on-premise integration.

Note that SAP Process Integration itself is an on-premise middleware that requires customers to install the integration software within their own landscape.

Figure 1.4 outlines the differences between a cloud-based integration solution and an on-premise integration solution by providing a high-level comparison of the general technical landscapes for SAP Process Integration and SAP Cloud Platform Integration. In the example, two customers run integration scenarios that involves message exchanges between three IT systems (Ⓐ, Ⓑ, and Ⓒ), where system Ⓐ is part of the customer's landscape. Systems Ⓑ and Ⓒ aren't further specified. On the left side of Figure 1.4, SAP Process Integration is installed in the landscape of customer ❶. This means that, at runtime, the message exchange among systems Ⓐ, Ⓑ, and Ⓒ is performed by an integration bus hosted *within* the customer's landscape. On the right side of Figure 1.4, customer ❷ is using SAP Cloud Platform Integration as an integration bus to facilitate message exchange among IT systems Ⓐ, Ⓑ, and Ⓒ. Here SAP Cloud Platform Integration is *outside* the customer's landscape (i.e., in the cloud).

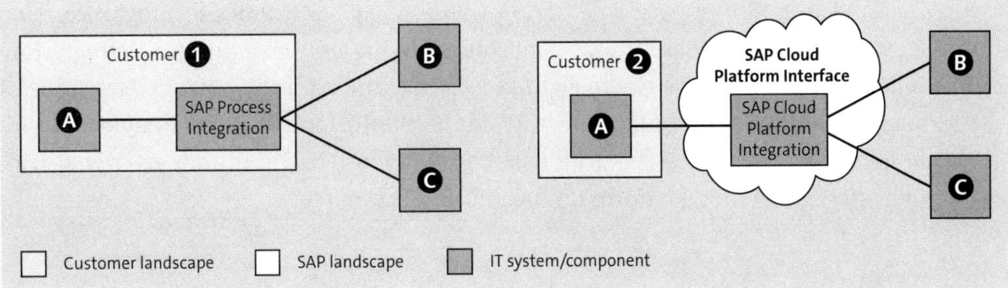

Figure 1.4 General Use Case and Component Setup for SAP Process Integration (Left) and SAP Cloud Platform Integration (Right)

Federated Process Integration

In more complex integration scenarios that span different enterprises, entire landscapes of various customers need to communicate with each other. Such cases typically require the installation of several SAP Process Integration instances at the site of each involved customer. Such federated scenarios fall outside the scope of this book.

Although SAP Cloud Platform Integration and SAP Process Integration are both integration platforms, note that SAP Cloud Platform Integration doesn't replace SAP Process Integration. SAP Cloud Platform Integration is a new solution that runs on SAP Cloud Platform, and it's designed as an integration platform-as-a-service (PaaS). We'll explain this in more detail in Section 1.3.1.

1.2.6 Hybrid Usage of Cloud and On-Premise Integration Solutions

From a use case perspective, SAP Cloud Platform Integration is suitable for those business cases where customers like to outsource their integration-related processes—or parts of them—into the cloud.

Obviously, SAP Cloud Platform Integration is the solution of choice when you need to integrate processes that run within a landscape of cloud applications. As such, SAP Cloud Platform Integration is a complementary solution, as compared to SAP Process Integration. In many cases, the best strategy for customers might be to use SAP Cloud Platform Integration in combination with an already existing SAP Process Integration installation. For example, let's assume that you, the customer, have already invested in an *on-premise integration solution* (e.g., SAP Process Integration) and would like to keep these investments, outsourcing only parts of your integration-related processes to the cloud. Figure 1.5 shows schematically how the landscape of such a *hybrid* scenario could appear. To connect SAP Cloud Platform Integration with SAP Process Integration, you can use the SAP Cloud Platform Connectivity service (hereafter, SAP Cloud Platform Connectivity) (Section 1.3.3).

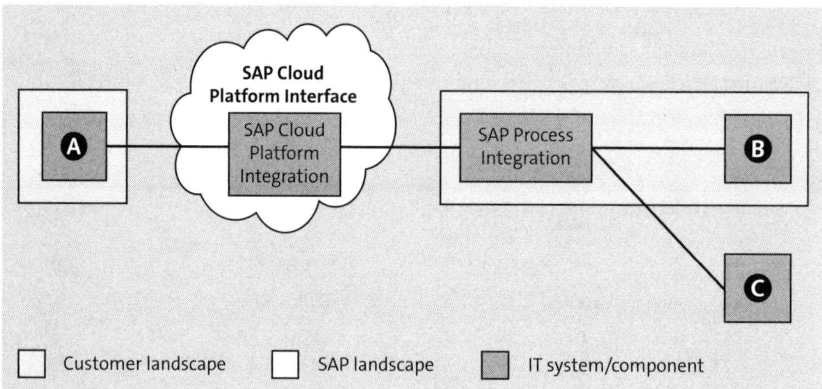

Figure 1.5 Hybrid Use Case Where Parts of the Landscape Are Integrated with SAP Cloud Platform Integration and Other Parts by SAP Process Integration

In this section, we've given an overview of the general use cases that can be addressed with SAP Cloud Platform Integration. To show how such use cases are implemented in practice, Chapter 11 will describe a few examples of how SAP Cloud Platform Integration is used in real life.

1.3 Capabilities

Now that you understand how SAP Cloud Platform Integration can be used to benefit your business, let's delve deeper into the solution's capabilities. In this section, we provide a high-level overview of SAP Cloud Platform Integration's main features. We'll briefly touch on the aspect that SAP Cloud Platform Integration is an integration platform that is operated in the cloud and summarize the benefits of this setup. We'll then give an overview of the different ways messages can be processed by SAP Cloud Platform Integration and of the connectivity options supported by the platform. We'll also succinctly discuss integration content, security, and high availability, and, finally, introduce the tools that come with SAP Cloud Platform Integration, as well as the different editions of the software that can be purchased.

In the subsequent chapters of the book, all these features will be discussed at length.

1.3.1 Integration Platform-as-a-Service

SAP Cloud Platform Integration is designed as an integration PaaS. What does that mean?

First, SAP Cloud Platform Integration helps you integrate multiple independent applications with each other in the context of a business process. This is the *integration platform* or *integration bus* aspect.

SAP Cloud Platform Integration allows you to integrate processes based on the exchange of messages. Similar to SAP Process Integration—the integration bus part of SAP Process Orchestration—SAP Cloud Platform Integration acts as an integration bus that is interconnected between the components that are connected in the context of a business process. All processes that manage data transfer and message routing run on the integration platform. SAP Cloud Platform Integration supports various methods of processing messages and offers many connectivity options that allow several software systems and applications to communicate with each other. These capabilities are described in more detail in Section 1.3.2 and Section 1.3.3.

Secondly, in contrast to SAP Process Integration, SAP Cloud Platform Integration provides integration services in the cloud. This is the *integration-as-a-service* (IaaS) aspect. The resources of the integration platform can be used on demand. Furthermore, you can flexibly adapt resource consumption according to changed business requirements. The latter capability is also referred to as *horizontal scaling*; that is, whenever you require more processing capacity, additional resources can be allocated quickly.

Customers don't need to care for the maintenance and upgrade of the integration software. SAP provides monthly updates of the software without any need for customers to schedule any downtime of their business processes that are based on SAP Cloud Platform Integration.

A key characteristic of the cloud-based integration platform is *multitenancy*: although different components and organizations (participants) connected to SAP Cloud Platform Integration share the same physical resources, these resources are strictly isolated per participant. This means that data owned by a participant is strictly separated from data owned by other participants.

1.3.2 Message Processing Step Types (Integration Capabilities)

SAP Cloud Platform Integration supports various integration patterns, or means of integrating applications with each other. Each pattern requires a specific set of processing steps. At the time of this book's publication, SAP Cloud Platform Integration supports the following types of message processing steps:

- **Participants**
  Contains objects that represent participants of an integration scenario, for example, a sender and receiver system.
- **Mapping**
  Contains mapping steps that transforms the data structure or format used by the sender into a structure or format the receiver can consume.
- **Message Transformers**
  Transforms the content of a message. Such transformation steps include content modifier, convertor, encoder, and many others.
- **Persistence**
  Stores the message content in the database. Storage steps may be required when the message content is needed for later processing steps or if the message content should be analyzed in a later step.
- **Security elements**
  Includes steps that enable you to digitally encrypt or sign (or both) the content of a message to ensure maximum protection of the exchanged data. It's also possible to decrypt signed messages. SAP Cloud Platform Integration supports a number of security standards, as will be described in detail in Chapter 10.
- **Message routing**
  Forwards a message to multiple receivers. Routing can also be defined to depend on the content of the message (content-based routing).
- **Events**
  Contains different types of events, including end event, end message, error end event, and many others. Refer to Chapter 2 for the complete list.

- **Process**
  Enables you to define subprocesses and exception processes.
- **Call**
  Enables you to perform calls to local or external services.
- **Message Validator**
  At the time this book was published, this section contains the XML validator, which enables you to validate an XML message based on a specific XML schema.

We'll discuss the complete list of integration patterns and involved processing steps in Chapter 2 and Chapter 5.

1.3.3 Connectivity Options

The variety of integration scenarios that can be designed and operated with SAP Cloud Platform Integration depends on the kinds of systems that can be technically connected to it. These *connectivity options* are implemented by SAP Cloud Platform Integration adapters.

Figure 1.6 illustrates various connectivity options.

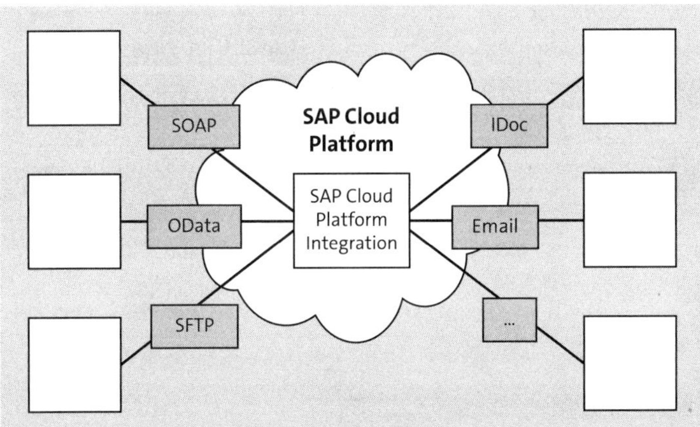

Figure 1.6 Connectivity Options That Allow You to Integrate Systems with Different Technical Characteristics with Each Other

At the time of this book's publication, the adapter types in Table 1.1 are available for use.

Adapter Type	Description
SOAP adapter	Allows you to connect SAP Cloud Platform Integration to a system that communicates based on the Simple Object Access Protocol (SOAP). There are currently two flavors available: ■ **SOAP (SAP RM) adapter:** Connects SAP Cloud Platform Integration to systems based on SAP Reliable Messaging (SAP RM), which is a simplified communication protocol for one-way asynchronous communication. ■ **SOAP 1.x adapter:** Connects SAP Cloud Platform Integration to systems based on SOAP 1.1 or SOAP 1.2.
IDoc (SOAP) adapter	Allows systems to exchange an IDoc through SAP Cloud Platform Integration.
HTTP adapter	Allows you to connect SAP Cloud Platform Integration to receiver systems using HTTP.
Mail adapter	Allows you to connect SAP Cloud Platform Integration to mail servers and send out encrypted emails.
SFTP adapter	Allows you to connect SAP Cloud Platform Integration to a system through the Secure Shell File Transfer Protocol (SFTP).
SuccessFactors adapter	Allows you to connect SAP Cloud Platform Integration to an SAP SuccessFactors system through the SOAP, Representational State Transfer (REST), or Open Data Protocol (OData) message protocol.
Ariba adapter	Connects SAP Cloud Platform Integration to the Ariba Network.
OData adapter	Allows you to connect SAP Cloud Platform Integration to OData service providers.
Twitter adapter	Allows you to connect SAP Cloud Platform Integration to Twitter and to extract Twitter content.
Facebook adapter	Allows you to connect SAP Cloud Platform Integration to Facebook and to extract Facebook content.

Table 1.1 SAP Cloud Platform Integration Adapter Types

Adapter Type	Description
ODC	Enables you to connect SAP Cloud Platform Integration to a SAP Gateway OData Channel. Note that it uses the HTTPS transport protocol. The following operations are currently supported: create (POST), read (GET), update (PUT), delete (DELETE), merge (MERGE), and query (GET).
AS2	Allows you to exchange business-specific data securely and reliably with a partner through the Applicability Statement 2 (AS2) protocol. Security is achieved using digital certificates and encryption.
JMS	Allows you to exchange asynchronous messaging using message queues with the Java Message Service (JMS). Note that a license for SAP Cloud Platform Integration, Enterprise Edition, is required to use this feature. Refer to Chapter 5 for more details.
RFC	Enables you to connect SAP Cloud Platform Integration to a SAP ABAP system using an RFC destination.
LDAP	Connects SAP Cloud Platform Integration to a Lightweight Directory Access Protocol (LDAP) directory service (through TCP/IP).
XI	Enables connectivity to handle communication using the SAP Exchange Infrastructure (XI) protocol.

Table 1.1 SAP Cloud Platform Integration Adapter Types (Cont.)

It's important to mention that there are additional adapters for SAP Cloud Platform Integration provided by different SAP partners. An up-to-date list of these adapters can be found via the **Discover** section in the Web UI of SAP Cloud Platform Integration. Note that some adapters are only available for one side of the communication, either to connect to a sender system or to a receiver system. For the actual available capabilities, refer to the SAP Cloud Platform Integration product documentation (see Appendix B for resources).

Several adapter types (e.g., the HTTP adapter and the OData adapter) support SAP Cloud Platform Connectivity, which can be used as a link between SAP Cloud Platform components and on-premise landscapes. SAP Cloud Platform Connectivity supports the simple configuration of on-premise systems that are to be connected with the SAP Cloud Platform.

You can also build your own adapters using the Adapter Development Kit (ADK), as described in detail in Chapter 6.

A concrete integration scenario is specified by combining a set of processing steps and adapters from Table 1.1 in this section. For more information, read on to Chapter 2.

1.3.4 Prepackaged Integration Content

SAP provides predefined integration content that allows you to implement a number of integration scenarios out of the box.

Integration Content and Integration Packages

The term *integration content* summarizes integration flows, interfaces, mapping programs, and other objects that define how messages are exchanged through SAP Cloud Platform Integration in the context of an integration scenario. A collection of such objects that addresses the integration challenges of a specific business case is referred to as an *integration package*.

For a definition of what an integration flow is, see Chapter 2.

In the public Integration Content Catalog, you can select integration packages that facilitate the integration of applications with SAP SuccessFactors applications, SAP Cloud for Customer, and the Ariba Network.

The Integration Content Catalog is available at *https://api.sap.com/shell/integration*.

For more information on the available integration content in the SAP Integrated Content Catalog, see Chapter 3.

1.3.5 Security Features

SAP Cloud Platform Integration is designed in a way that ensures maximum protection of customer data during the operation of an integration scenario. Physical protection of relevant data is ensured by the fact that the SAP Cloud Platform Integration is hosted in SAP data centers located in different countries, which provide a maximum level of protection, for example, through the usage of surveillance cameras at the data center location.

Although different participants connected to SAP Cloud Platform Integration share the same physical resources, data that is processed and stored on the platform is strictly separated per participant (multitenancy).

Each customer can define dedicated permissions for different people working on the customer-related account and tenant.

The connections between SAP Cloud Platform Integration and other components can be secured using standard transport-level security options, such as HTTPS and Secure Shell (SSH). On top of that, SAP Cloud Platform Integration provides many options to protect the exchanged messages with digital signatures and encryption.

These are only a few key security features. More details on the topic can be found in Chapter 10, which thoroughly describes the security features of SAP Cloud Platform Integration.

1.3.6 High Availability

SAP Cloud Platform Integration is available for customers to process messages at any time, and productive business processes that use SAP Cloud Platform Integration as their integration bus will continue operation even if one component of the integration platform fails.

SAP Cloud Platform Integration's architecture supports horizontal scaling in the sense that additional runtime components can be flexibly added when required (e.g., in the case of component failure). If a node fails, another node starts immediately.

Regular health checks are also performed to make sure that exceptions are detected quickly and that the responsible administrator at SAP can take immediate measures to resolve the issue.

In addition, the SAP Cloud Platform Integration platform is hosted redundantly in different SAP data centers at different locations, and SAP provides monthly software updates without any downtime of productive scenarios.

All of these measures ensure that SAP Cloud Platform Integration customers aren't left in the lurch should component failure ever occur.

1.3.7 Integration Design and Monitoring Tools

Customers using SAP Cloud Platform Integration have the option to design or enhance integration content by themselves and to monitor message exchange at runtime. The following tools are available:

- A browser-based web application called the *Web UI* is available for these tasks, and it's the central tool that you'll deal with throughout this book.
- Various Eclipse add-ons are available for adapter developments.
- The SAP Cloud Platform cockpit can be used by customers to perform user management tasks on their account.

1.4 Editions

SAP Cloud Platform Integration comes in different editions that are tailored to different customer requirements. You can find the different editions and their descriptions listed in Table 1.2.

Edition	Description
SAP Cloud Platform Integration for SAP cloud applications	Can be used as a dedicated integration solution in combination with at least one specific SAP cloud application, such as SAP SuccessFactors. When you have an integration use case with at least one connection to an SAP cloud application, this edition is the solution of choice.
SAP Cloud Platform Integration, DI edition	Geared toward data integration. It therefore includes data integration capabilities but excludes other components such as SAP Process Integration.
SAP Cloud Platform Integration, PI edition	Can be used as standalone, general-purpose integration platform with no restriction on the types of connected systems. This edition allows any-to-any system integration. A determined number of connections can be used, and a maximum bandwidth (in terms of transferred data volume per time) is available. Note that this edition doesn't include data integration. It's possible to extend this edition.

Table 1.2 SAP Cloud Platform Integration Editions

Edition	Description
SAP Cloud Platform Integration, Enterprise Edition	This is a fully featured version of SAP Cloud Platform Integration that includes the following features: ■ Data integration ■ SAP Process Integration ■ Unlimited connections ■ API management ■ OData Provisioning ■ SAP Enterprise Messaging
Partner Edition	The edition is specially tailored for SAP partners to develop their own custom integration scenarios. This includes, for instance, integration content or adapter development. The edition includes a determined number of connections and a maximum bandwidth. Additional connections and bandwidth can be purchased according to customer requirements. Note that this edition isn't intended for productive use.

Table 1.2 SAP Cloud Platform Integration Editions (Cont.)

For more details on the number of connections, bandwidth, and included components in the editions mentioned in Table 1.2, go to *https://cloudplatform.sap.com/support/service-description.html#section_11.*

For each edition, SAP remains fully in charge of providing, maintaining, and upgrading SAP Cloud Platform Integration on a regular basis. SAP sets up the account and tenant for the customer and operates the customer-specific integration runtime.

In general, however, the customer is responsible for integration content design and deployment on the tenant, as well as for monitoring the message exchange at runtime.

1.5 Summary

In this chapter, we introduced SAP Cloud Platform Integration as *the* integration solution that supports companies on their journey of digital transformation. We've shown that SAP Cloud Platform Integration's use cases cover both cloud-to-cloud and cloud-to-on-premise integration, and that SAP Cloud Platform Integration can also be used together with SAP's on-premise integration solution SAP Process Orchestration. Finally, we provided you with an overview of the capabilities of the product and introduced the available editions of SAP Cloud Platform Integration.

In the next chapter, we'll set our focus even more on SAP Cloud Platform Integration, introduce you to its main concepts, and disclose the architecture and setup of components. Furthermore, we'll show how you can quickly set up and run your first integration scenario.

Chapter 2
Getting Started

This chapter provides an introduction to the main concepts and the architecture of SAP Cloud Platform Integration. In addition, a tutorial shows you how to set up and run a simple integration scenario.

In this chapter, we'll answer the following main questions: How does SAP Cloud Platform Integration work, what are the building blocks it's composed of, and how do you get started using it?

Section 2.1 allows you to glance behind the scenes of SAP Cloud Platform Integration with a detailed look at the solution's architecture. It also explains the main components of the integration platform and how they interact with each other. We then discuss the basic mechanisms that are in action when a cloud-based integration scenario is executed. Section 2.2 outlines the typical sequence and the main phases of an integration project and points out how the tools provided by SAP Cloud Platform Integration fit into the sequence. Finally, Section 2.3 describes, step-by-step, how to set up and run your first simple integration scenario.

By the end of this chapter, you'll have the foundational knowledge needed to start working with SAP Cloud Platform Integration.

2.1 Architecture Overview

In this section, we show you how SAP Cloud Platform Integration's architectural design makes it a cloud-based integration platform that can be shared by many participants, allows for flexible resource allocation for different participants, and ensures that resources belonging to different participants are strictly separated from each other.

We begin with the following questions:

- What are the runtime components in charge of message processing during the operation of an integration scenario?
- Which components are in action when messages are passed through SAP Cloud Platform Integration?

We'll then see how the integration platform is structured in more detail and, finally, provide a complete bird's eye view of the solution's architecture.

2.1.1 Virtual and Clustered Integration Platform

As we discussed in Chapter 1, SAP Cloud Platform Integration is a cloud-based integration platform that allows you to integrate processes by enabling them to exchange messages with each other. It's built on the SAP Cloud Platform.

SAP Cloud Platform

SAP Cloud Platform is SAP's platform-as-a-service (PaaS) offering that provides a development environment in the cloud which enables customers to develop, deploy, and manage applications.

SAP Cloud Platform Integration is designed as a virtualized and clustered integration platform in the cloud. In this context, *virtualized* means that the fundamental entities of the integration platform are virtual machines, rather than physical ones, and *clustered* means that the platform is modularized and composed of smaller, more or less independent entities that, as a whole, make up a cluster.

To illustrate this, consider a simple landscape with only a few IT systems participating in an integration scenario and SAP Cloud Platform Integration interconnected between them, as shown in Figure 2.1. Let's further assume that, in a dedicated process step within the integration scenario, data is sent from system Ⓐ to system Ⓒ. Another process step triggers system Ⓑ to send data to system Ⓓ and other systems not specified here. It's not important now if system Ⓐ and Ⓑ belong to the same organization or to different ones, or if the two process steps are part of the same integration scenario or different ones.

Figure 2.1 illustrates the following aspects of SAP Cloud Platform Integration: first, all systems (or participants) connected to SAP Cloud Platform Integration share the same physical resources of SAP Cloud Platform. You can assume that the required hardware that takes care of processing the messages is located on one, or a few, of SAP's data centers. Secondly, each participant can access and use only a part of the commonly shared resources. Furthermore, the resources allocated to individual participants are strictly separated from each other.

In Figure 2.1, a platform resource assigned to participant Ⓐ processes messages received by Ⓐ and forwards them to participant Ⓒ, whereas a resource assigned to another participant processes messages from that participant.

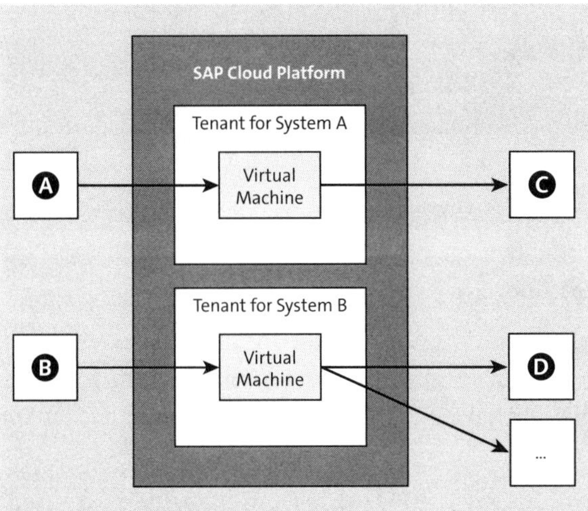

Figure 2.1 Partitioning of the SAP Cloud Platform Integration Runtime into Individual Virtual Environments

To explicate the aspect of resource isolation, let's first discuss the terms *account* and *tenant*.

Account

An account is the basic entry point to SAP Cloud Platform. It represents a hosted environment provided by SAP to a customer and defines a set of authorizations and platform resources allocated to the customer. There are two types of accounts on SAP Cloud Platform: global accounts and subaccounts.

A global account represents the functional scope of the platform you're entitled to use based on your license. It can contain one or more subaccounts.

A subaccount is associated with a certain physical location where applications, data, or services are hosted.

Tenant

A tenant is a logical entity that represents the physical resources of SAP Cloud Platform allocated to a specific participant and within an application context. SAP Cloud Platform Integration is multitenant-capable, meaning that although all customers using SAP Cloud Platform Integration share the same physical resources, their tenants can't interfere with each other. They are isolated from each other with regard to memory, data storage, and CPU. Tenant isolation means that physical resources allocated by tenant Ⓐ can't be accessed by tenant Ⓑ.

Although different tenants of SAP Cloud Platform Integration might physically share one common database, different database schemas per tenant are used. This ensures that data is strictly separated per tenant.

Participants or customers subscribing to SAP Cloud Platform Integration receive exactly one tenant per subaccount. The tenant is the foundational entity of SAP Cloud Platform Integration and is important topic throughout this book.

For each tenant, a separate virtual integration runtime operates. Messages sent from one participant to SAP Cloud Platform Integration are processed on a virtual machine—to be precise, on a Java virtual machine (JVM)—that is assigned to the tenant.

Basic Constituents of the Virtual Integration Platform

For each tenant, one or more virtual machines are operated. The term *virtual machine* (VM) is used in the sense that a VM is a software implementation that executes a program in the same way as a physical computer.

To be more precise, the SAP Cloud Platform Integration runtime environment is based on *Java virtual machine (JVM)*, specified by the Java Platform, Standard Edition (Java SE). A JVM is a virtual environment used to execute Java applications.

The actual processing of messages at runtime is accomplished on a Java instance that is referred to as JVM instance.

An expert—such as an integration developer—can specify the way messages are to be processed on a tenant in an intuitive manner using a graphical editor. The corresponding models are referred to as *integration flows*. We'll explain this term and the related concepts in more detail in Section 2.1.4. Here, we simply want to point out that an integration flow is deployed on a JVM of the SAP Cloud Platform Integration platform, enabling the JVM to process messages exactly as specified by the integration flow model. As soon as a JVM instance (the runtime process) has been started, and an integration flow has successfully been deployed on it, the JVM instance is ready to process incoming messages in the intended way.

JVM instances constitute the basic *parts* into which the SAP Cloud Platform Integration runtime is split. As you'll see in Section 2.1.2, the platform is implemented as a cluster of such virtual processes, which are referred to as *nodes* of the cluster.

Note that each node doesn't live only during the time a message is being processed by it. It's ready to process incoming messages from the moment it has been started by an administrator of SAP Cloud Platform Integration, and it lives until it's stopped either by failure or manually by the administrator.

Note that the resources provided by one VM aren't restricted to one integration flow. An integration developer can deploy multiple integration flows on the same JVM.

To recap, the SAP Cloud Platform Integration runtime is designed as a clustered virtual platform. Messages received from different connected participants are processed on separate JVM instances on the platform. The organizing entity is the tenant. All virtual machines belonging to different tenants are isolated from each other with regard to memory, data storage, and CPU.

Figure 2.2 presents all entities that shape the SAP Cloud Platform Integration platform and shows how they relate to each other.

On the left side of Figure 2.2, you can see that each customer subscribes to one or more subaccounts of SAP Cloud Platform. For customers who subscribed to SAP Cloud Platform Integration, exactly one tenant is assigned to each subaccount.

As we'll explain in Section 2.1.2, Figure 2.4, the virtual runtime environment of a tenant in general is composed of different nodes, and there are two different node types, each responsible for a different kind of task:

- Tenant management node
- Runtime node

For each tenant, one or more tenant management nodes, as well as one or more runtime nodes, can be started. Each node (independent of whether it's a tenant management node or a runtime node) is an instance of a virtual process running on SAP Cloud Platform (a SAP Cloud Platform process). Technically, each such process is a virtual machine. As the SAP Cloud Platform Integration runtime environment is based on a JVM, each VM running on the SAP Cloud Platform is realized as a JVM and can execute applications written in Java. We'll explain this in more detail in Section 2.1.4.

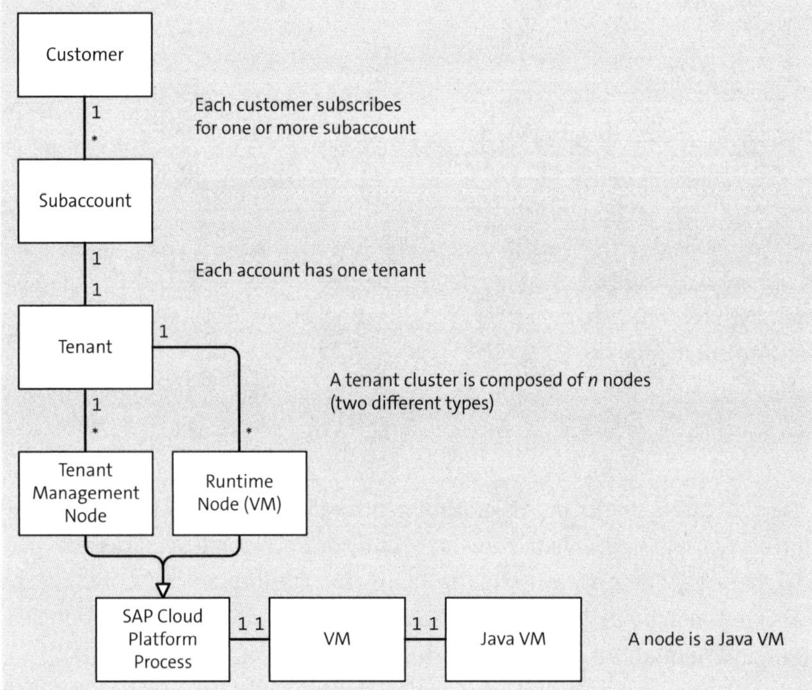

Figure 2.2 Entity Diagram of the Virtual SAP Cloud Platform Integration Runtime

HTTPS is often used as the transport protocol for remote connections, which implies Transport Layer Security (TLS) mechanisms. We'll go into more detail about the security aspects of SAP Cloud Platform Integration in Chapter 10. At this stage, we only want to point out that the load balancer in the case of Figure 2.3 terminates the inbound TLS connection and establishes a new connection to call the tenant.

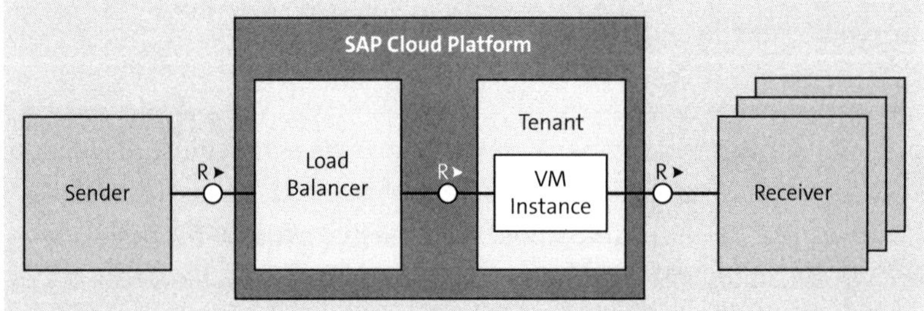

Figure 2.3 Incoming Messages Processed by the Tenant and Forwarded to One or More Receivers

Figure 2.3 shows how a tenant is related to the sender and receiver systems exchanging messages through that tenant (when the sender connects to SAP Cloud Platform Integration through HTTPS).

The processing of a sender's message is performed on a VM instance (which is the runtime node) on the *tenant*. Note, however, that the sender isn't directly connected to the tenant. A *load balancer* is interconnected that accepts all inbound requests and dispatches them to the right tenants.

The actual processing of messages is performed on the runtime node of the tenant. If routing steps are specified, the message is forwarded to multiple receiver systems, as illustrated in Figure 2.3.

You may have noticed the **R>** notation in Figure 2.3. This notation will also occur in many other figures throughout this book. **R>** indicates the direction of a request. In Figure 2.3, a sender system sends a message to SAP Cloud Platform Integration, where it's processed and forwarded to a receiver system. In other words, the direction of the message flow is from the sender to the receiver. In this same example (and in many other cases), the direction of the message flow is identical to the direction of the request. For the sake of simplicity, we assume that the sender initiates the message flow by sending a request message to SAP Cloud Platform Integration. Note, however, that there are also other cases where the directions of the request and of the message flow are opposite (e.g., in cases where a sender sends a request to a server to read, or *pull*, data from it).

2.1.2 Detailed Structure of a Cluster

In the previous section, you learned that each SAP Cloud Platform Integration tenant comprises a cluster of VMs (nodes). A cluster operated for a tenant is also referred to as *tenant cluster*. In this section, we'll shed more light on how a tenant cluster is structured.

A tenant cluster is composed of nodes of different types. Figure 2.4 shows the structure of a tenant cluster. It depicts how the different node types relate to each other. Furthermore, it points out the main data storage areas and user access points.

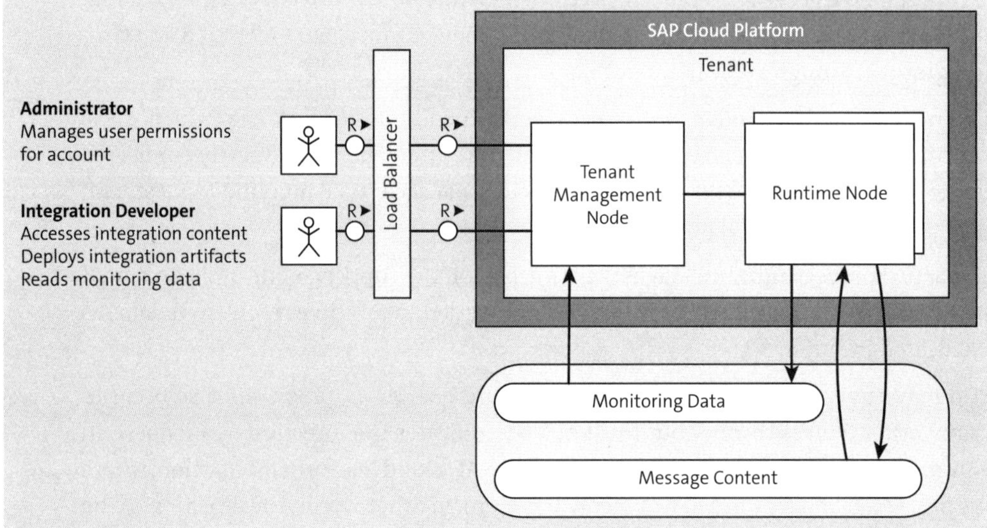

Figure 2.4 Structure of a Tenant Cluster, Indicating the Data Storage Areas and User Access Points

Table 2.1 summarizes the node types that constitute a tenant cluster.

Node Type	Tasks
Tenant management node	Acts as agent between the human user and the runtime components of SAP Cloud Platform Integration. As illustrated by the direction of the request in Figure 2.4 (**R>**), the tenant management node manages the runtime nodes; in other words, it starts or stops runtime nodes. This node type interacts with human users (e.g., integration developers) who perform tasks such as deploying integration artifacts (Section 2.1.4 and Section 2.1.5). At the request of an integration developer, the tenant management node also reads message content and monitoring data from the database and makes it available for the monitoring application accessed by the user.
Runtime node	Processes messages that are exchanged through the tenant. Integration flows run on this node type. This node type interacts with the external systems and the load balancer.

Table 2.1 Different Node Types Responsible for Different Kinds of Tasks

A tenant cluster is typically composed of one tenant management node with multiple runtime nodes associated to it.

High Availability

For simplicity, only one tenant management node is depicted in Figure 2.4. However, SAP Cloud Platform Integration allows you to set up multiple tenant management nodes per tenant. Operating multiple nodes of the same type allows you to configure failover scenarios where, in case of a node failure, the redundant node can take over the tasks of the original one. This way, high availability is supported by the architecture of SAP Cloud Platform Integration.

At the time of this book's publication, SAP Cloud Platform Integration doesn't yet support elasticity in the sense that resources are automatically adapted to the needs of consumers of the integration platform. However, additional nodes can be easily and flexibly started in a tenant cluster. The option to flexibly add additional virtual resources is also referred to as *horizontal scaling*.

This architecture ensures that SAP Cloud Platform Integration is highly available; integration scenarios can be operated without the risk of any downtime.

Persistence

During the processing of a message (by a runtime node), there can be various steps where data is stored in a database (as indicated in Figure 2.4).

Table 2.2 summarizes which kind of data can be stored at runtime.

Type of Stored Data	Description
Monitoring data	Monitoring data records what happens to a message during the message processing. In particular, all involved processing steps are stored in a structure called a *message processing log* (MPL). This feature enables administrators to monitor message flow during the operation of an integration scenario. You can find more information on this in Chapter 8. As indicated in Figure 2.4, monitoring data is written to the database by the runtime node and read by the tenant management node, where it can be requested by the user.

Table 2.2 Different Kinds of Data Stored at Runtime

<table>
<tr><th>Type of Stored Data</th><th>Description</th></tr>
<tr><td>Message content</td><td>Message content contains business data (in the payload of the message) and the message header.

Where in the processing sequence such data is to be stored can be configured per scenario.

Message content can be stored long-term for purposes such as error analysis, audit logging, and archiving. In such a case, the storage duration is, by default, 90 days. This data is written by the runtime node to the database, but the runtime node can't read it from the database.

Message content can also be stored temporarily to make it available for later processing steps in the same sequence. Temporarily stored message content, consequently, can be read by the runtime node during message processing.

In all cases, the data can be stored encrypted.

JMS Queues

A specific, temporary persistence option is storing messages in Java Message Service (JMS) queues. You can use this option to asynchronously decouple inbound from outbound processing in scenarios where you like to enable the integration platform (rather than the sender system) to retry message processing in case an error occurs. When an integration flow has been configured to use JMS resources, it's also the runtime node that temporarily stores message content in JMS queues. This option is available with the SAP Cloud Platform Integration, Enterprise Edition.

As indicated in Figure 2.4, message content is stored and (if temporarily persisted) accessed in the database and in JMS queues by the runtime node during message processing. For monitoring purposes, it's read by the tenant management node.</td></tr>
</table>

Table 2.2 Different Kinds of Data Stored at Runtime (Cont.)

Software Update

The software running on the various subsystems of SAP Cloud Platform Integration is updated on a monthly basis by SAP in a process that doesn't require any downtime of productive scenarios running on SAP Cloud Platform Integration.

2.1.3 Secure Communication

A fundamental requirement for a cloud-based integration platform is that the data exchanged through it is protected from misuse. To that end, the remote systems and nodes of an integration platform should only communicate with each other through secure channels.

There are various options to set up secure connections between SAP Cloud Platform Integration and the involved remote systems. A common security measure is to use transport protocol HTTPS and to enforce mutual authentication of the communicating components based on digital certificates.

On top of transport-level security (e.g., HTTPS), SAP Cloud Platform Integration allows you to set up scenarios in a way that the exchanged messages are digitally encrypted and signed for increased security. All of these security options will be explained in detail in Chapter 10.

At this point, we want to mention that each security option requires the implementation of digital keys of a certain kind, as well as the setup of storage locations for digital keys. To activate a certain security option for a tenant (and the integration scenarios deployed on it), these keys or key storages have to be deployed on the tenant as *integration artifacts*. In Chapter 10, you'll learn about the complete set of security-related integration artifacts.

Integration flows, which have been introduced in Section 2.1.1 (and will be described in more detail in Section 2.1.4), constitute another kind of integration artifact that can be deployed on a tenant.

2.1.4 Implementation of Message Flows

In this section, we'll discuss how a tenant cluster is enabled to process messages as defined in an integration flow.

We'll also briefly touch on additional, *specific* approaches that are supported by SAP Cloud Platform Integration, namely, first, specifying integration content for business-to-business (B2B) scenarios using the Integration Content Advisor (ICA), and, secondly, designing OData service artifacts. These options are described in detail in dedicated sections (in Chapter 7 and Chapter 4, respectively).

An integration flow, however, is the basic design artifact to define message flows, and it's of fundamental importance that you understand the concept of an integration flow before going into the details of more sophisticated integration design tasks.

Therefore, we focus on the basics of integration flow design in this beginner's chapter.

Integration Flows as Models to Specify Message Flows

An integration developer can intuitively define the way a message should be processed with a graphical modeling environment. The corresponding models are *integration flows*. They use a notation related to Business Process Model and Notation (BPMN).

Figure 2.5 shows a schematic sketch of an integration flow model (for the case when message routing is configured).

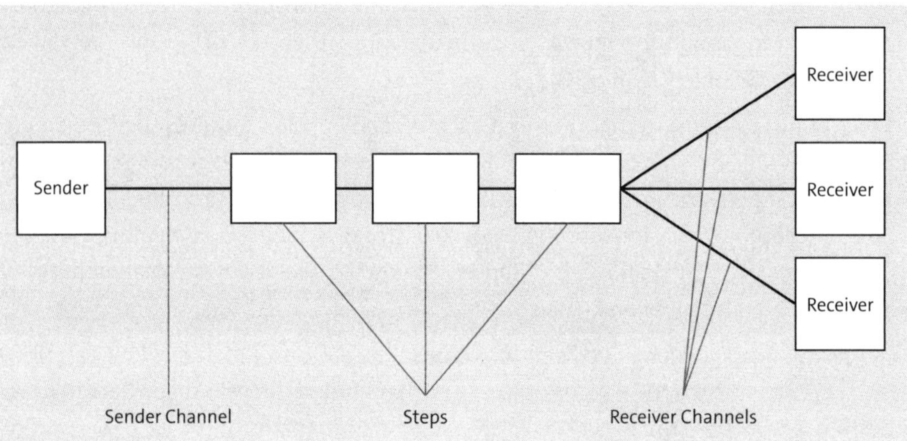

Figure 2.5 Schematic Illustration of the Integration Flow Elements

First of all, in an integration flow, you specify the sender and receiver systems of a message flow. The details of the technical connection between a sender/receiver and the tenant are configured within a channel. A channel allows you to specify an *adapter*, according to the technical protocol of the connected sender or receiver.

The way a message is processed by the integration bus and how it's transformed, routed, or enriched with additional data (to mention a few examples) are all specified within different *integration flow steps*.

Integration Flow

An integration flow specifies how a message is to be processed on a tenant. It's a BPMN-like model that can be intuitively specified by an integration developer as a graphical model. To make an integration flow available for the runtime node (which is in charge of processing the message at runtime), it must be deployed on the corresponding tenant.

OData Services

A specific modeling option is provided by *OData service* artifacts. You can use such an artifact to expose various data sources as OData endpoints. It provides a simple and intuitive way to convert different kinds of protocols to the OData protocol. In technical terms, when an OData service is created, the system generates an integration flow out of it that contains an OData sender adapter by default. For more information, check out the information box in Section 2.3.4 or Chapter 4, Section 4.5.

Apache Camel as an Integration Framework

The information specified by an integration developer in an integration flow is made accessible to the runtime node, which is in charge of actually processing a message, via Apache Camel (*http://camel.apache.org*). Apache Camel is a Java-based open-source integration framework that allows developers to easily specify how a message is to be processed. Chapter 4 provides a detailed introduction of Apache Camel's message model. In this section, we focus on those aspects that are required to get a first understanding of the concept behind an integration flow.

An elementary sequence of message processing steps is implemented as a *Camel route*. A Camel route specifies a message flow from one source endpoint to one or more target endpoints. The message flow can be subject to several processing steps such as data transformations and content-based routing.

As we mentioned before, as an integration expert in charge of designing integration scenarios, you don't need any Java programming skills or knowledge about Apache Camel to get the full functionality out of integration flows. You simply design the integration flow with a graphical tool and then deploy it on the tenant with a single click. With this second activity, you trigger a process that generates the corresponding Apache Camel objects out of the integration flow and makes them available for the runtime node associated with the tenant.

How the Integration Framework Relates to the Virtual Runtime

In Section 2.1.2, you learned how the virtual runtime of SAP Cloud Platform Integration is structured, and what its properties are. In this section, we introduced the Apache Camel integration framework, and the associated design-time models, known as integration flows. Now let's discuss how the entities of the integration framework relate to those of the virtual runtime.

For this purpose, we've enhanced Figure 2.2 by adding the entities that define how message processing is implemented on the runtime components. Figure 2.6 shows the result.

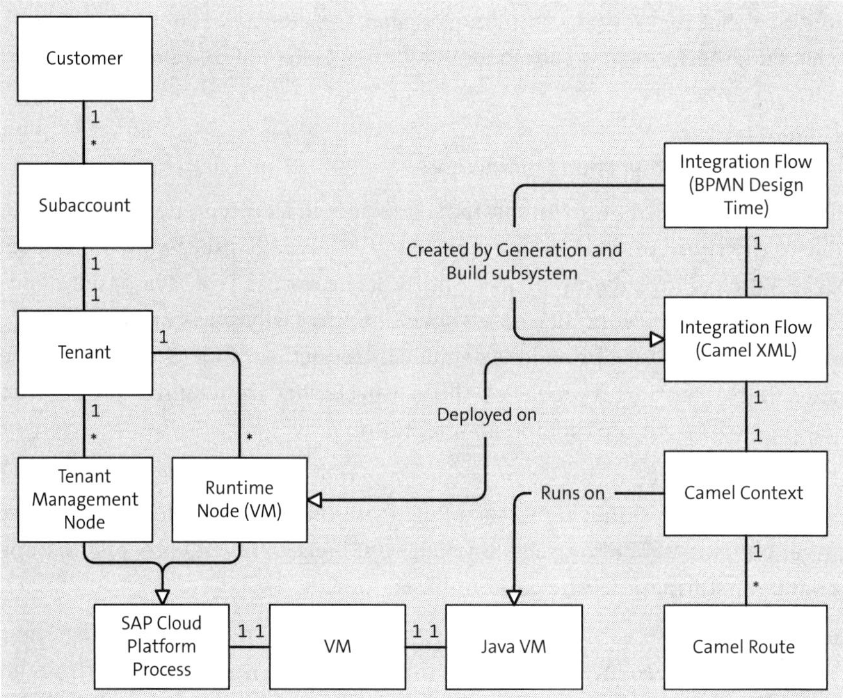

Figure 2.6 Runtime Resources and Artifacts That Define a Message Flow

The entities on the left side have already been explained in Section 2.1.1 (also refer to Figure 2.2). These are the entities that make up the virtual runtime.

The right side of Figure 2.6 depicts each entity that is relevant to specify message flows. The integration flow is a BPMN-like model created or edited by an integration developer with the support of a graphical tool. With an integration flow model, you can fully specify how a message should be processed on a tenant. When the integration developer has finished modeling and deploys the integration flow on a tenant, the model is transformed into an XML structure, which is compatible with the Apache Camel specification. This XML structure is deployed on all runtime nodes assigned to the tenant. Looking into how message flows are implemented in Java, a Camel context defines the container of Camel components for a specific integration flow. Depending on the complexity of the integration flow, for each Camel context, one or more Camel routes are specified. A Camel route defines (on the level of the Java programming model) a message flow from one source endpoint to one or more target endpoints. In many cases, one integration flow finally leads to exactly one Camel route. However, complex integration flows can result in multiple Camel routes.

When you've finished the integration flow design and your integration scenario is up and running, you can monitor the runtime components with the monitoring application. Chapter 8 covers these aspects in detail. Here, we would like to state that you can also monitor the status of all integration flows that have been deployed on your tenant. We refer to an integration flow as one kind of *integration artifact*. We introduced this term in Section 2.1.3. With the monitoring tool, you can quickly check if the required integration flows are available for your integration runtime components.

Microservices

Before we wrap up this detailed walkthrough of the architecture of SAP Cloud Platform Integration, let's point out that the introduced cluster architecture implements the concept of microservices to a large extent.

A *microservice*, within a complex architecture, is considered a small and highly decoupled part of a software or service, which covers a specific task or a specified set of tasks. In other words, microservices allow you to modularize complex applications and help avoid monolithic systems by decomposing an architecture into smaller, independent services. They are small, easy to replace, organized around capabilities, and complete.

The presented cluster design implements this pattern: it's designed in a way that different node types are responsible for different tasks. The tasks related to message processing are accomplished by runtime nodes, whereas tasks related to the operation of a cluster and monitoring the message processing are accomplished by tenant management nodes. The nodes of a cluster are independent, in the respect that the availability of one node doesn't have any impact on that of others. Therefore, for example, tasks like monitoring (on a tenant management node) are still possible when an associated runtime node fails.

The current design of SAP Cloud Platform Integration, however, shows one important difference from the microservices paradigm: runtime nodes and tenant management nodes can't (yet) be deployed independently.

2.1.5 Architecture Summary

So far in this section, you've learned that the SAP Cloud Platform Integration runtime is designed as a clustered virtual platform. Messages received from different connected participants are processed on separate JVM instances on the platform. The organizing entity is the tenant. All VMs belonging to different tenants are isolated from each other with regard to memory, data storage, and CPU. You also learned how message flows can be designed by a user and made available to the platform.

Now, let's pause for a moment and provide an overview of SAP Cloud Platform Integration's architecture to show how all the components described in the previous sections work together. Figure 2.7 shows a high-level view of the overall architecture.

Let's start with the user access points in the left part of Figure 2.7. First, user interaction takes place when a customer is provided with one or more SAP Cloud Platform subaccounts by SAP, each subaccount providing access to one SAP Cloud Platform Integration tenant.

The corresponding role involved in the first user interaction is the administrator. The administrator receives the initial information about the subaccount from SAP, accesses the subaccount through the SAP Cloud Platform cockpit, and defines authorizations for all additional users of the subaccount. Consider these additional users as representing the people who are—on the customer side—involved in tasks such as integration flow design or monitoring. In larger organizations, these tasks are typically performed by different persons who have separate permissions.

Figure 2.8 shows the dialog box in the SAP Cloud Platform cockpit where the administrator can manage the authorizations of single users (arrow) or user groups (right side). For more information on the tools, Section 2.2.1.

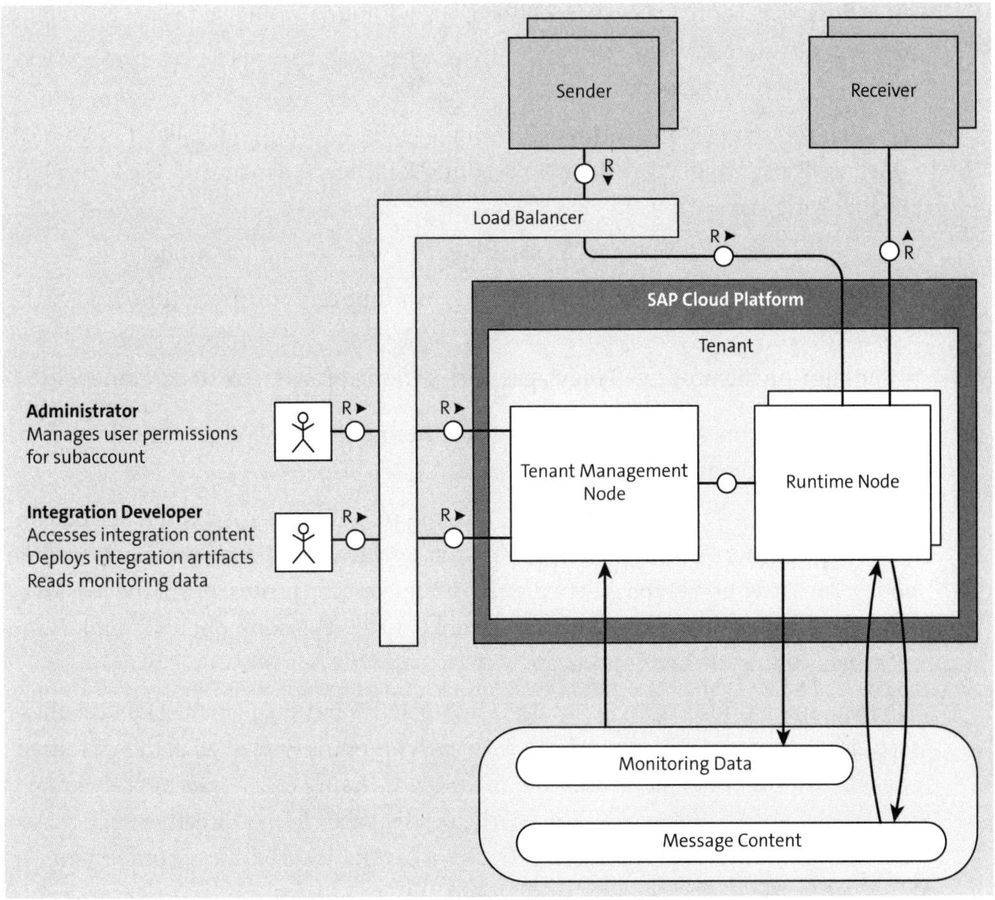

Figure 2.7 Bird's-Eye View of the SAP Cloud Platform Integration Architecture

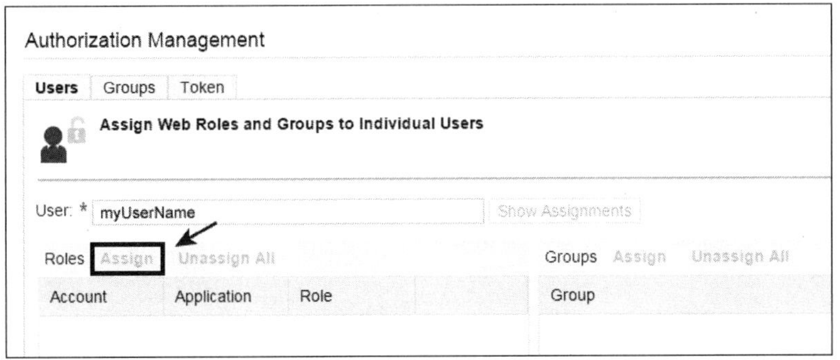

Figure 2.8 Authorization Management Page in the SAP Cloud Platform Cockpit

After the permissions have been defined, the additionally enabled users come into play and can start working with SAP Cloud Platform Integration. The role in focus is the integration developer.

The integration developer will work with a web-based frontend, called the Web UI, which we'll explain in more detail in Section 2.2.1. The developer uses the Web UI for the following tasks:

- Designing integration flows or OData services with a graphical modeler
- Deploying integration artifacts (security content and integration flows) on the tenant
- Monitoring the processed messages, integration artifacts, stored data, and logs

The Web UI is connected to the tenant management node and is accessible by the user through a tenant-specific URL.

For the tenant assigned to the subaccount, the tenant cluster is started, which consists of one or more tenant management nodes, each managing one or more runtime nodes. The latter node type is actually responsible for the processing of the messages and, therefore, is connected to the external technical components (sender and receiver systems) that communicate with each other.

When an integration scenario has been set up and is in the operational phase, these technical systems can communicate with each other. As explained earlier, a tenant-specific runtime node is responsible for the processing of messages received by a sender system. As shown in Figure 2.7, the sender system isn't directly connected to the tenant but is rather interconnected by a central load balancer component. All inbound traffic is managed by this component and dispatched to the appropriate tenants.

The runtime node processes the message according to the steps specified in the integration flow and forwards it to one or more receiver systems.

During the operation of the integration scenario, data is stored at various steps. This includes data that is required for monitoring purposes but also the message content itself for archiving purposes. The separation of data belonging to different customers is achieved by using different database schemas (respectively, JMS instances when JMS queues are used) per tenant (refer to Table 2.2).

Integration Content Advisor

If you have an SAP Cloud Platform Integration, Enterprise Edition, license, you additionally get access to the ICA. This application allows you to easily specify integration content for B2B scenarios in an intuitive way (see also Section 2.2.1). It comes with additional components and a database that stores the required B2B content.

In this chapter, we focus on the basic building blocks of SAP Cloud Platform Integration to introduce you to the key principles. Therefore, we didn't add the additional components related to the ICA in the architecture overview (refer to Figure 2.7).

ICA is described in detail in Chapter 7.

Now that you're familiar with the architecture of SAP Cloud Platform Integration, we'll provide an overview of the tools related to SAP Cloud Platform Integration and of the processes relevant to integration developers.

2.2 Tools and Processes

This section provides an overview of the tools and main processes required to set up and run a SAP Cloud Platform Integration scenario.

2.2.1 Tools

Different tools are available for different kinds of user interactions in SAP Cloud Platform Integration.

SAP Cloud Platform Cockpit

This application provides access to SAP Cloud Platform and allows administrators to perform user management tasks for the account and tenant. The administrator can specify individual permissions for people who are supposed to work on the tenant cluster in different roles, such as integration developers (refer to Figure 2.8).

Customers with SAP Cloud Platform Integration, Enterprise Edition, also use SAP Cloud Platform cockpit to subscribe to ICA and to set up a JMS Message Broker for scenarios using JMS queues.

Public Integration Content Catalog

The Integration Content Catalog provides access to predefined integration packages provided by SAP that can be used out of the box. You can browse through the content at *https://api.sap.com/shell/integration* (see Figure 2.9).

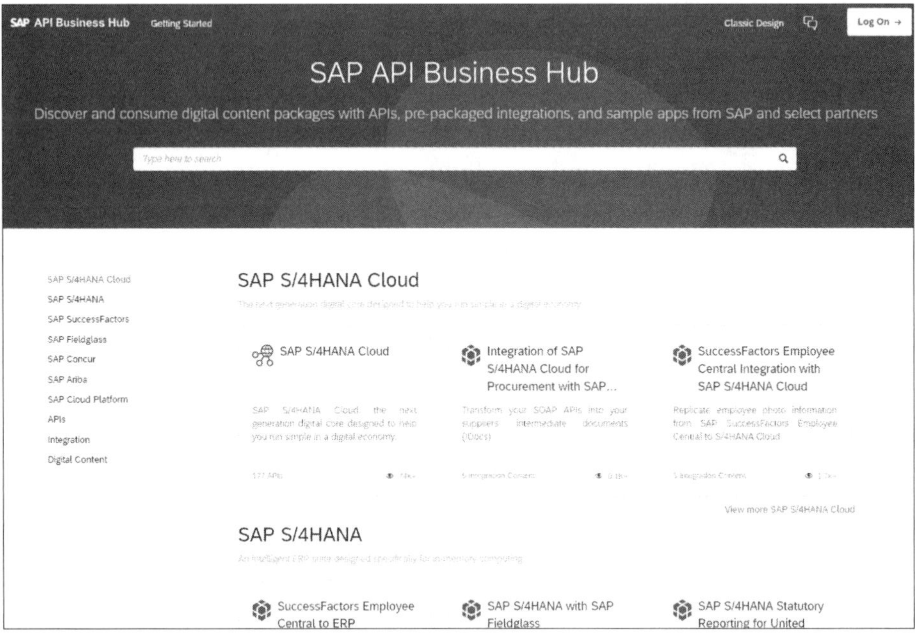

Figure 2.9 The Integration Content Catalog

You may notice this content is published on the SAP API Business Hub (as you'll see in Chapter 9). The packages are stored in read-only mode. Customers who would like to use an integration package have to copy it into their own design workspace before they can start modifying it according to their requirements.

For more information on the Integration Content Catalog, see Chapter 3.

Integration Content Advisor for SAP Cloud Platform Integration

As mentioned already in Section 2.1.5, the ICA is available with SAP Cloud Platform Integration, Enterprise Edition. It facilitates the development of B2B scenarios because it allows you to easily design interfaces (referred to as *message implementation guidelines*) that best fit to your own and your partners' business requirements. Additionally, the tool allows you to create mappings between those interfaces. A key feature of the ICA is that it assists the user in defining message implementation guidelines and mappings by using an intelligent, crowd-based machine learning approach.

When you've finished the specification of message implementation guidelines and mappings, runtime artifacts are generated out of them that can be used in integration flows.

For more information on ICA for SAP Cloud Platform Integration, read Chapter 7.

Web UI for Integration Design and Monitoring

The Web UI is the most important tool used by integration developers. You can open the Web UI through a URL, although the specific URL depends on the customer tenant and is communicated to you in an email from SAP, along with the details of the tenant.

The Web UI comprises four tabs: **Discover**, **Design**, **Monitor**, and **Settings**. Figure 2.10 shows how to access the tabs in the Web UI.

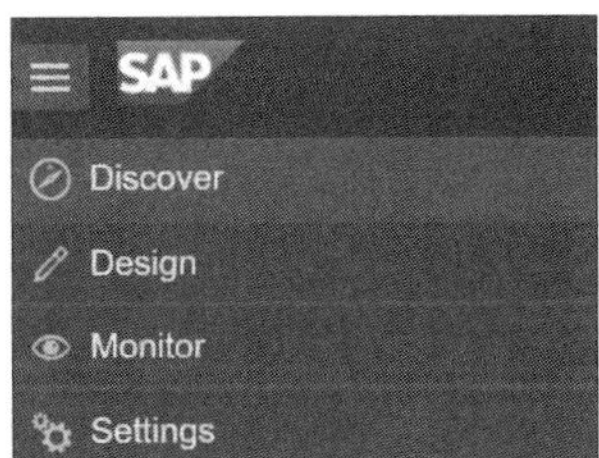

Figure 2.10 Tabs of the Web UI

Table 2.3 provides an overview of the task areas covered by each tab. For more information, Section 2.3.4, and the following *Basic Artifact Types* information box.

Tab	Allows You To...
Discover	Access the Integration Content Catalog. You can select already available content from this catalog and add it to your own workspace where you can further edit the content and adapt it to your own integration challenges. It also includes a list and details of third-party adapters provided by SAP partners. The Integration Content Catalog will be discussed further in Chapter 3.

Table 2.3 Main Sections (Tabs) of the SAP Cloud Platform Integration Web UI

Tab	Allows You To...
Design	Design the following kinds of artifacts: ■ **Integration Flow** This is the key topic of this book. In Section 2.3, you'll learn how to create and run your first integration flow. The subsequent chapters cover the various aspects of integration content design in detail. ■ **OData Service** We'll introduce this design option in Chapter 4, Section 4.3. ■ **Value Mapping** We'll briefly touch on this topic in Chapter 4, Section 4.4. ■ **Data Integration** We won't cover this artifact type in this book because it isn't related to process integration. For more information on these artifact types, see the *Basic Artifact Types* information box in Section 2.3.4.
Monitor	Monitor the message flow at runtime and check the status of deployed artifacts. Using this tab, you can also create and deploy security-related artifacts such as user credentials, keys, and certificates, and manage message stores and locks. Chapter 8 will cover this topic in detail.
Settings	Configure personal settings. In particular, this tab allows you to select a *product profile*. But what are product profiles good for? In this book, we only cover scenarios where the integration content designed with the Web UI is executed on your cloud-based SAP Cloud Platform Integration tenant cluster. However, you can also decide that your integration content is to be executed, for example, on an on-premise integration bus of SAP Process Integration (the integration bus that is available as part of SAP Process Orchestration). As the features that are supported by the SAP Process Integration runtime (of a specific release) slightly differ from those supported by the SAP Cloud Platform Integration runtime, the Web UI also provides a slightly different set of integration flow design features in case you select the corresponding product profile related to the target runtime SAP Process Integration. In other words, a product profile defines the target integration platform for the content designed with the Web UI. Chapter 6, Section 6.5.3, will touch on this topic.

Table 2.3 Main Sections (Tabs) of the SAP Cloud Platform Integration Web UI (Cont.)

2

Tab	Allows You To...
Settings (Cont.)	Whether or not you have several profiles present on the **Settings** tab depends on the basic configuration of your tenant provided initially by the SAP Cloud Platform Integration operations team. Select the profile for which you intend to develop the integration flows.

Table 2.3 Main Sections (Tabs) of the SAP Cloud Platform Integration Web UI (Cont.)

Figure 2.11 shows an integration flow opened in the **Design** tab of the Web UI.

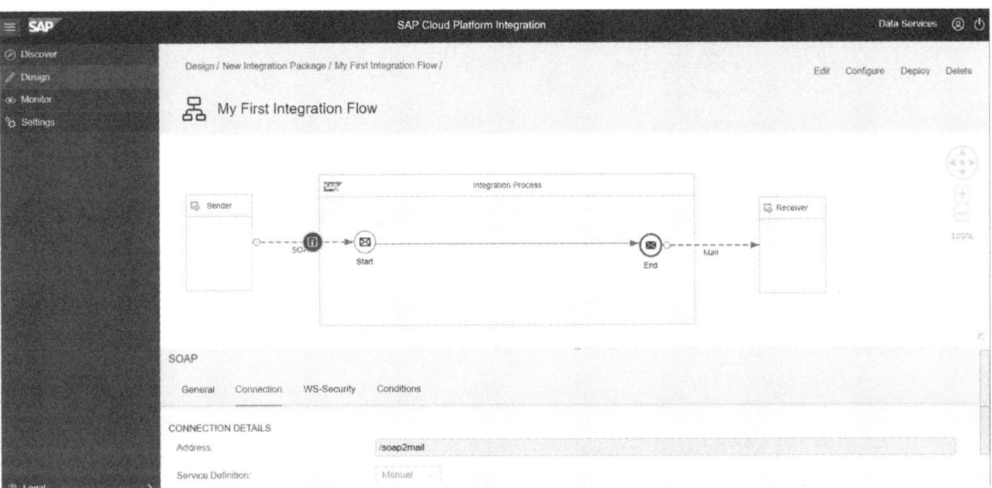

Figure 2.11 Modeling of an Integration Flow in the Design Tab of the Web UI

When designing an integration flow, you add elements (e.g., integration flow steps) to it and integrate them in a specific order to specify how messages are to be processed on the tenant. We provide an overview of the elements that can be added to an integration flow later in Table 2.4.

When designing OData services, the procedure is slightly different. We'll introduce this option in Chapter 4, Section 4.3.

Figure 2.12 shows the **Monitor** tab page from Figure 2.10.

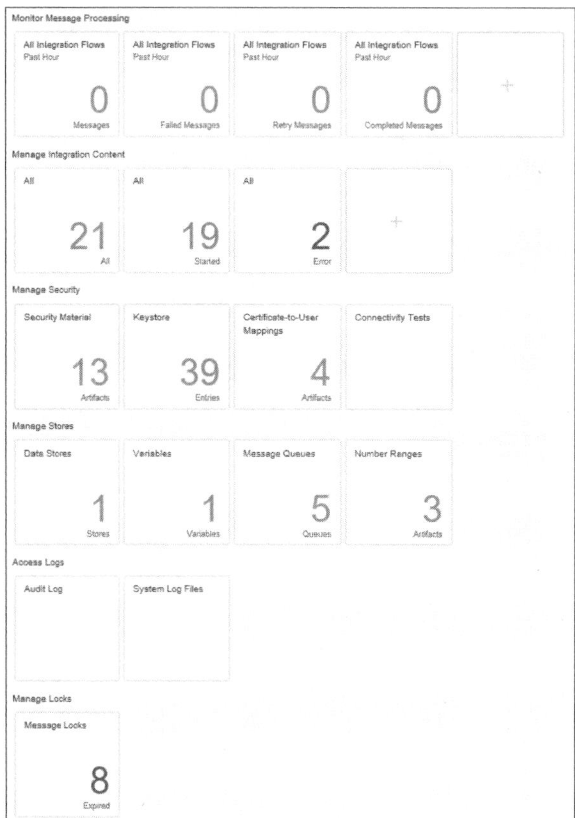

Figure 2.12 The Monitor Tab Page of the Web UI

The monitoring application is divided into the following main sections (not all are shown in the figure):

- **Monitor Message Processing**
  This section allows you to monitor messages that are exchanged by your tenant based on the integration flows that are deployed.
- **Manage Integration Content**
  This section allows you to monitor the status of the deployed integration content artifacts (integration flows).
- **Manage Security**
  This section allows you to manage artifacts that are required when setting up secure connections between your tenant and remote systems. The **Security Material** tile allows you to manage specific security-related artifacts such as user

credentials, Pretty Good Privacy (PGP) keyrings, known hosts (required when using SFTP), or OAuth credentials. The **Keystore** tile allows you to manage keys and certificates that are required when using TLS. Using this tile, you can also manage the lifecycle of keys (renewing expired keys). The **Certificate-to-User Mappings** tile allows you create and manage certificate-to-user mappings. You need such an artifact to configure inbound authentication based on a digital client certificate and to map this certificate to a user (for which you can then define permissions based on user roles). For more information on the concepts behind these artifacts types and how to use them, go to Chapter 10. Finally, the **Connectivity Tests** tile allows you to test the outbound connection (for different protocols such as TLS, SSH, SMTP, IMAP, and POP3). We'll briefly show this tool in Section 2.3.6 and explain it in detail in Chapter 8, Section 8.3.4.

- **Manage Stores**
  This section allows you to handle storages on the tenant that are used to temporarily persist data during message processing. The **Data Stores** tile allows you to manage data stored temporarily by an integration flow (to make it available for later processing steps). You can view the content of the data store or delete entries. The **Variables** tile allows you to monitor variables used in integration flows.

  When you've purchased SAP Cloud Platform Integration, Enterprise Edition, this section also shows a **Message Queues** tile that allows you to monitor queues that come into play when using the JMS or the AS2 adapter (for more information on the JMS adapter, go to Chapter 5, Section 5.4). For the different kinds of data stored during message processing, see Table 2.2.

  Finally, the **Number Ranges** tile allows you to get an overview of number ranges which are relevant when running B2B scenarios. In scenarios using Electronic Data Interchange (EDI) messages, a unique interchange number is added to each business document. The **Number Ranges** tile allows you to configure and monitor the interchange number (only available for SAP Cloud Platform Integration, Enterprise Edition).

- **Access Logs**
  This section allows you to monitor system changes, such as integration flow deployment events (**Audit Log** tile), and to get access to information related to errors that occurred during HTTP inbound processing (**System Log Files** tile). In case of inbound processing errors, the **System Log Files** tile might be the only information source available for administrators to analyze the cause of the error, as in such situations typically no MPL is created.

- **Manage Locks**
  This section allows you to manage lock entries that are created to prevent the same message from being processed more than once in parallel. In certain situations (e.g., when a runtime node shuts down unexpectedly), the system tries to reprocess a message, however, a lock entry is still in the database and blocks processing of subsequent messages. The **Manage Locks** section enables you to resolve such situations.

For more information on the **Monitor** application, see Chapter 8.

In Section 2.3, we'll introduce you to the Web UI and show how to create your first integration flow using this tool.

Eclipse Tools

The Web UI is the central tool that supports developers throughout the lifecycle of an integration project. However, over the course of this book, we'll also talk about an additional SAP Cloud Platform Integration-specific tool that requires an Eclipse installation. You'll need this tool to develop adapters (as explained in Chapter 6, Section 6.7).

2.2.2 Processes

In this section, we offer a brief overview of the main phases of an integration project before we walk you through your own first integration project in Section 2.3.

The main phases of any SAP Cloud Platform Integration project are as follows:

1. **Browsing the Integration Content Catalog**
   First-time users and decision makers can browse the Integration Content Catalog to find out which integration scenarios can be used out of the box with minimum implementation effort. We'll provide more details on this in Chapter 3.
2. **Requesting a tenant and administering the account**
   Customers who intend to use SAP Cloud Platform Integration need to contact SAP and request a tenant. After the customer has been provided with an account and a tenant, an administrator on the customer's side uses the SAP Cloud Platform cockpit to perform user management tasks on the account. In this phase, the administrator defines who else is allowed to work on the account and defines permissions for individual users.

3. **Provisioning a JMS Message Broker**
   If you like to use JMS queues, you need to perform an additional step to set up a JMS Message Broker (only for users with SAP Cloud Platform Integration, Enterprise Edition). This is also done using the SAP Cloud Platform cockpit.
4. **Setting up a secure connections between remote systems and the tenant**
   In this phase, secure communications with SAP Cloud Platform Integration are enabled for sender/receiver systems. This phase is divided into the following tasks (typically performed by different people):
   - *Configuring the sender/receiver systems*
     This task is usually performed by administrators of the sender/receiver system and comprises all steps to set up the technical connection between the sender/receiver system and SAP Cloud Platform Integration.
   - *Configuring the tenant*
     Users performing this task enable the tenant to securely communicate with the related sender and receiver systems.

   In Chapter 10, we'll explain how to set up a secure connection between SAP Cloud Platform Integration and remote systems.
5. **Designing integration flows**
   In this phase, an integration developer designs integration flows to specify how messages should be processed on the tenant. When the design has been finished, the integration flows are deployed on the tenant.

   To perform these tasks, the integration developer uses the **Discover** and **Design** tabs on the Web UI (refer to Figure 2.10).

   Designing integration flows is the core topic of this book. After you've learned how to create, deploy, and run your first integration flow, you can find more details on integration flow design in Chapter 4, Chapter 5, and Chapter 6. Chapter 7 and Chapter 10 also contain tutorials that show how to develop specific integration flows.

   The process of designing an OData service is described in Chapter 4, Section 4.3.
6. **Operating and monitoring SAP Cloud Platform Integration**
   In this phase, you monitor the integration artifacts on the tenant cluster and the processed messages. To perform these tasks, the integration developer uses the **Monitor** tab on the Web UI.

For more details, consult Chapter 8.

2.3 Running Your First Integration Scenario

In this section we'll show you how to set up and run a simple integration flow. By following these steps, you'll learn how to use the Web UI to create and edit an integration flow and how to deploy the integration flow on your tenant. Finally, when you've started the integration flow, you'll be able to monitor the resulting messages and the involved integration artifacts.

2.3.1 Demo Scenario and Landscape

For the sake of illustration, a simple integration flow has been chosen for our demo scenario. It will do nothing more than receive a Simple Object Access Protocol (SOAP) message (with a simple structure) from a SOAP client and forward it to an email receiver. In addition to having access to a SAP Cloud Platform Integration tenant, you only need a publicly accessible email account to set up and run this scenario.

The scenario intuitively shows one basic capability of SAP Cloud Platform Integration: exchanging messages between different systems. SAP Cloud Platform Integration supports connectivity with a large number of different systems, as shown in Section 1.3.3. Such a system can be, for example, a complex SAP business system, a file system, or, as in our first example, an email server (to mention only a few examples).

This first integration flow might give you an idea of how SAP Cloud Platform Integration can be used as a message broker in heterogeneous system landscapes. Imagine that you, as an integration expert, are asked to build up an IT solution for your enterprise that accepts incoming messages (e.g., orders) and mails them automatically to the relevant departments within your organization. The first challenge to solve is to set up the message exchange between the sender system(s) and the mail server. This is where the various adapters (namely, the SOAP sender and the mail receiver adapter) come into play. For simplicity, in this first tutorial, we exclusively cover the connectivity aspect of SAP Cloud Platform Integration. The integration flow won't impose any further processing of the message on the SAP Cloud Platform Integration platform: it does nothing more with the received message than simply hand it over to an email server. Chapter 4 and the subsequent chapters will then successively show you how a message can further be processed in various ways on its path between sender and receiver.

The following tutorial also provides you with a simple method of checking whether your tenant cluster works properly: You can simply check in your email account (and with the **Monitor** application) to see if SAP Cloud Platform Integration delivered the message as expected.

Figure 2.13 visually depicts the target integration flow already in the notation that is used by the Web UI's integration flow design application.

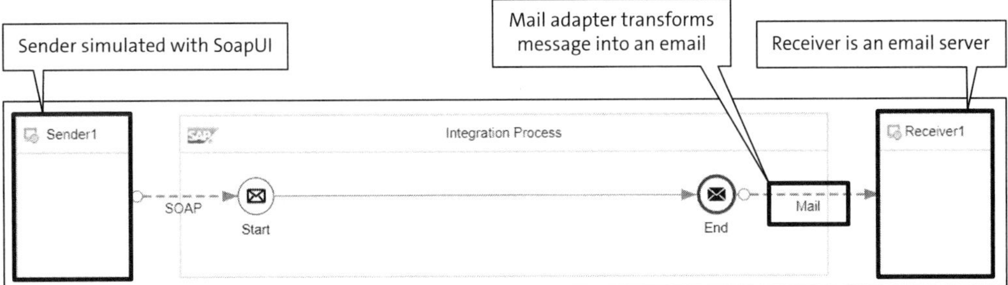

Figure 2.13 Your First Integration Flow

To simulate a SOAP Sender, you can use SoapUI (*www.soapui.org*). This software allows you to set up a SOAP client and send a SOAP message to an endpoint with a few clicks. The SOAP endpoint is a service on the runtime node where the integration flow is deployed.

Let's get started!

2.3.2 Prerequisites

Our first step is to make sure that the following prerequisites are met:

- Request a SAP Cloud Platform Integration tenant from SAP (*www.sap.com*). You'll receive an email from SAP with information on how to access the tenant and the Web UI.
- Install the SoapUI from *www.soapui.org*.
- Register an email account. For simplicity, we recommend using Gmail (*www.google.com/gmail*), and, in this tutorial, we show how to connect the tenant to a Gmail server.

2.3.3 Set Up the Landscape and the Technical Connections

To keep it simple, we assume that the SOAP sender calls the SAP Cloud Platform Integration system using basic authentication (with your user credentials). This way, you don't need to generate and install client certificates and have them signed by a certification authority (this process will be explained in Chapter 10). Nevertheless, a keystore with specific content must be deployed on the tenant because even when inbound authentication is accomplished based on a username and password, a TLS-based authentication of the server (SAP Cloud Platform Integration in our case) is enforced (as explained in Chapter 10). SAP will provide the required keystore with the tenant, so you don't need to perform any additional steps related to this. Depending on the mail server that should be used as receiver, it might be required to import additional certificates into the keystore as explained in Section 2.3.6.

Install and Configure SoapUI

Prepare the SOAP sender, and specify the format of the message that is to be sent to SAP Cloud Platform Integration. The data structure of the message is specified in the Web Services Description Language (WSDL). For your convenience, you can download the WSDL file from *www.sap-press.com/3979*. The name of the file is *SendOrder_Async.wsdl*.

After you've downloaded the WSDL file and installed SoapUI, perform the following steps:

1. Open SoapUI and create a new SOAP project by clicking on **File** and then selecting **New SOAP Project** in the menu.
2. Specify a **Project Name**, and click on the **Browse** button, located to the right of the **Initial WSDL** field (Figure 2.14).

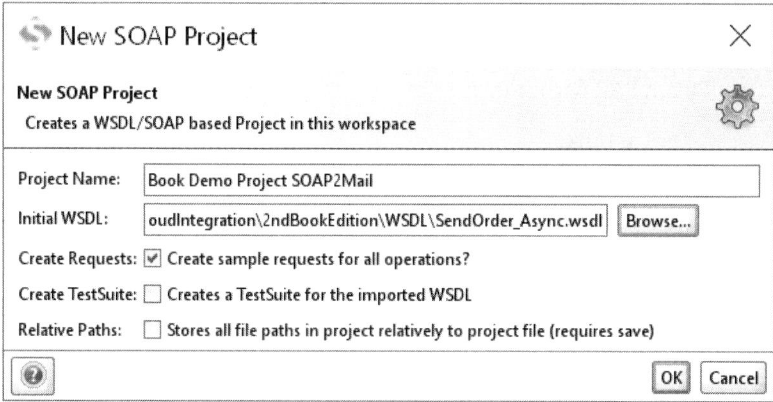

Figure 2.14 Required WSDL File Upload When Creating a Project

3. Navigate to the WSDL file on your computer, and click **Open**. The project appears in the left navigation bar.

When you open the request, you can find the structure of the message to be sent (see Figure 2.15).

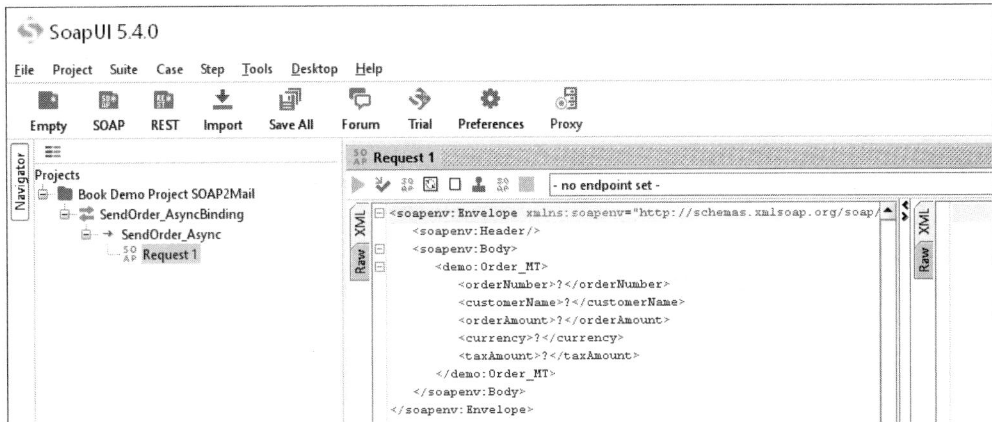

Figure 2.15 The Demo SOAP Project Consisting of One Request with a Simple Message Structure

Assign Role for Inbound Call to Runtime Node

The following scenario uses basic authentication as a simple option to authenticate the sender of the message (which is the SOAP client configured with SoapUI). The SAP Cloud Platform Integration runtime evaluates the authorization of the sending system (the SOAP client) based on permissions defined for the role associated with the sender. The permission to process messages on the SAP Cloud Platform Integration platform is defined in the role `ESBMessaging.send`. You'll encounter this role several times in the course of this book.

To authorize the user (associated with the inbound call) to process messages on the tenant, perform the following steps:

1. Access the SAP Cloud Platform cockpit through the URL provided to you by SAP with the email that contains the details of your tenant.
2. Select your subaccount.
3. Go to **Security • Authorizations**.

4. As **User**, enter the user that should be associated with the SOAP call.
5. In the next screen, for the **Application** field, select the entry from the dropdown list that ends with **iflmap** (Figure 2.16).

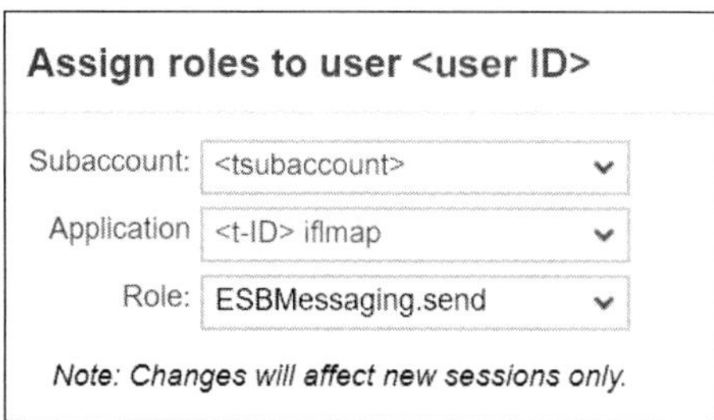

Assign roles to user <user ID>
Subaccount: <tsubaccount>
Application <t-ID> iflmap
Role: ESBMessaging.send
Note: Changes will affect new sessions only.

Figure 2.16 Assigning ESBMessaging.send to the Runtime Node in the SAP Cloud Platform Cockpit

The entry in the **Application** field that ends with **tmn** identifies the tenant management node. Roles with regard to permissions of human users in the integration team are assigned to the tenant management node (for more details on this, check out Chapter 10, Section 10.3).

6. For **Role**, the entry **ESBMessaging.send** should be preselected.
7. Choose **Save**.

Compare with Figure 2.40 later in this chapter to check out how to specify the user credentials of the sender.

2.3.4 Develop the Integration Flow

Now it's time to develop your first integration flow. You'll begin by creating an integration flow, after which you'll design the integration flow using a number of available elements.

Create an Integration Flow

1. Open the Web UI using the **Web UI URL** provided in the email from SAP.
2. Choose the **Design** tab (refer to Figure 2.10).
3. Choose **Create** to create a new integration package (at the bottom of the left pane, see Figure 2.17).

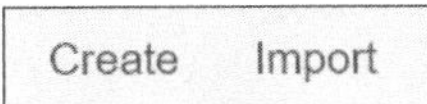

Figure 2.17 Create Button for Integration Packages

4. In the next dialog box (shown in Figure 2.18), provide a name for the integration package and a short description.

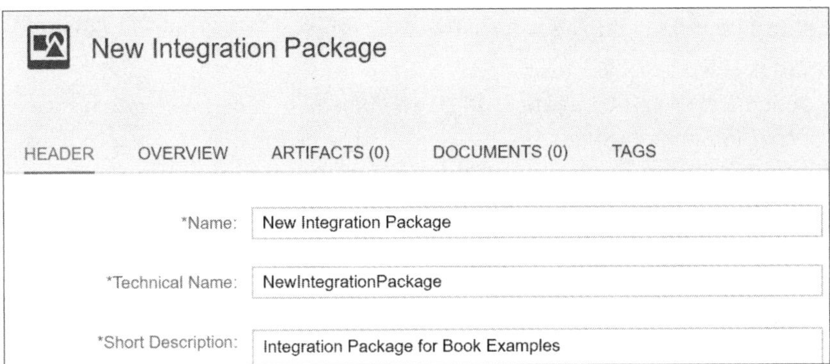

Figure 2.18 Specifying a Name for the New Integration Package

5. Select the **Artifacts** tab, click on **Add,** and select **Integration Flow** (see Figure 2.19). As a result, the **Add process integration flow artifact** dialog box shown in Figure 2.20 opens.

   This selection makes sure that, with the next steps, you can create and edit an integration flow. Before proceeding, let's briefly take a look at the other artifact types you can create in the following *Basic Artifact Types* information box.

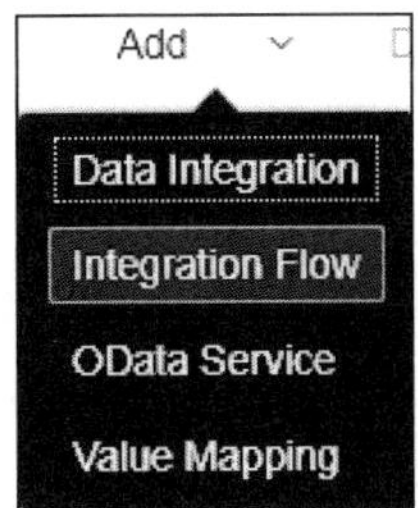

Figure 2.19 Artifact Types You Can Select When Creating Integration Content

Basic Artifact Types

Let's briefly talk about the three options that you'll encounter when you want to add an artifact to an integration package.

- **Data Integration**
  This option allows you to create artifacts to set up *data integration scenarios* that implement extract, transform, and load (ETL) processes. ETL processes commonly integrate data from multiple systems. This topic is beyond the scope of this book.
- **Integration Flow**
  This option allows you to create artifacts to implement *process integration scenarios* that integrate business processes across the boundaries of organizations or enterprises. An integration flow does exactly what is required for such scenarios: it specifies how messages are exchanged within such a process integration scenario. Integration flow design will be covered in detail in this book.
- **Value Mapping**
  This option allows you to define value mappings. Those of you who are already familiar with SAP Process Orchestration or SAP Process Integration know this function very well. For those not yet familiar with value mappings, the basic idea is as follows: Data to be exchanged isn't always represented in the same manner in the sender and receiver systems involved in an integration scenario. System X could be using values such as "male" and "female" to represent an employee's gender, whereas system Y could be using numeric values instead, such as "1" for male and "2" for female. Typically, when a message containing employee data needs to be exchanged between systems X and Y, these two ways of representing the same data need to be translated. The value of "male" from the source system will need to become "1" in the target system. This form of translation is called value mapping. For more information, see Chapter 4, Section 4.4.4.
- **OData Service**
  This option allows you to develop an OData service from an existing data source (e.g., from a SOAP WSDL file). OData is an open standard that allows service providers to specify HTTP-based data access in a standardized manner. You can use an **OData Service** artifact, for example, when you like to expose data through OData to consume it in a frontend application. Note that there is also the option to create an **Integration Flow** artifact with an OData sender channel. In this case, however, you can only expose one OData entity and operation at a time, whereas the **OData Service** artifact allows you to expose multiple entities and operations

at a time. The topic of OData is covered several times within this book, for example, in the context of the SAP Cloud Platform APIs (Chapter 9) or when describing a scenario that includes an OData adapter (see Chapter 4, Section 4.3). Chapter 4, Section 4.5, finally, will explicitly introduce you to the topic of OData service design.

In the dialog box shown in Figure 2.20, make sure the **Create** radio button is selected, and enter a name for the integration flow in the **Name** field.

The **Upload** option (next to the **Create** option in Figure 2.20) allows you to upload an integration flow file from your computer to the Web UI.

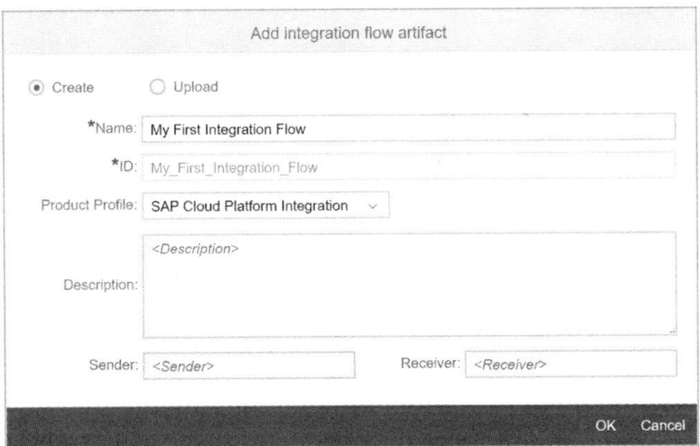

Figure 2.20 Creating an Integration Flow

6. Click **OK**. The specified integration flow is listed as a new artifact for your integration package (see Figure 2.21).

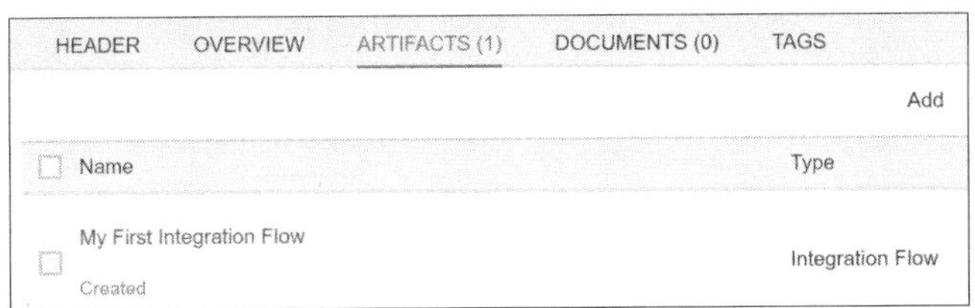

Figure 2.21 The Newly Created Integration Flow Listed as a New Artifact

7. Click the **Save** button (located above the **Artifacts** list) to save the integration package.

8. When you click the integration flow name (in the **Artifacts** list, see Figure 2.21), the editor opens and shows a template where you can begin modeling (Figure 2.22).
9. Click the **Edit** button shown in Figure 2.22 to start modeling the message flow. You'll notice that a palette becomes visible on the left side of the editing area. Behind this palette, you can select elements that can be added to an integration flow. Before we continue, let's briefly discuss the palette and the available modeling elements.

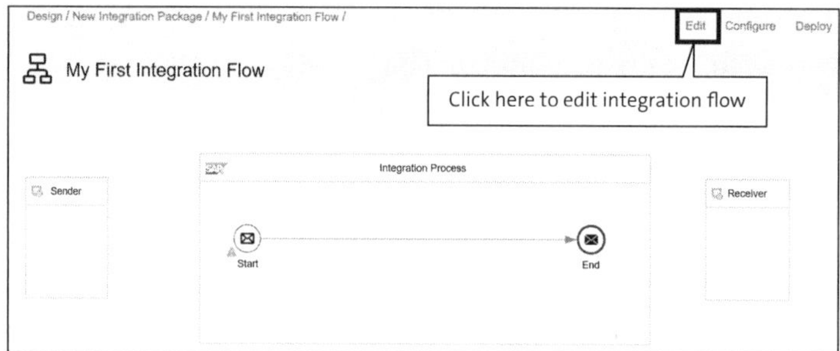

Figure 2.22 Integration Flow Template to Start Modeling

The Palette: Elements of an Integration Flow

The integration flow modeler's palette (together with the tooltips for each icon group) is shown in Figure 2.23.

Figure 2.23 Palette of the Integration Flow Modeler

Table 2.4 summarizes the modeling elements available at the time this book published, sorted by group.

Group	Description
Participants	Contains elements that represent the connected participants of an integration scenario: **Sender**, **Receiver**.
Process	Contains elements that can be used as containers for a whole integration flow (**Integration Process**), a subprocess (**Local Integration Process**), or a subprocess that handles exceptions that occur during message processing (**Exception Subprocess**). You can use **Local Integration Process** elements to source out parts of the process logic, which are invoked from the main process, into smaller chunks. That way, you can keep larger integration flows at a reasonable size. Local integration processes and exception subprocesses are introduced in Chapter 6, Section 6.3.
Events	Contains event elements to define the beginning or the end of message processing. You can select from the following step types: **End Message**, **End Event**, **Error End Event**, **Escalation**, **Start Message**, **Start Event**, **Terminate Message**, and **Timer** (see Chapter 6, Section 6.1).
Mapping	Allows you to insert a **Mapping** step to transform a source message into a target message. You can select from the following step types: **Message Mapping** and **XSLT Mapping** (see Chapter 4, Section 4.4).
Message Transformers	Contains elements to modify the message content by applying different operations, such as encoding (e.g., using Base64), conversion (e.g., from CSV to XML), or script functions. You can select from the following step types: **Content Modifier** (see Chapter 4, Section 4.1.4), **Converter**, **Decoder**, **Encoder**, **Filter**, **Message Digest**, or **Script**.

Table 2.4 Integration Flow Modeling Elements Offered in the Palette

Group	Description
Call	Contains elements to enable the tenant to call an external source or a local integration process. ■ **External Call** Enables the tenant to call an external source (e.g., to retrieve data from external sources, such as SOAP or OData, and to enrich the message with it). You can select from the following step types: **Content Enricher**, **Request Reply** (see Chapter 6, 6.2.1), or **Send** (see Chapter 5, Section 5.3.3). ■ **Local Call** Calls a local integration process either once (**Process Call**) or in a loop (**Looping Process Call**) (see Chapter 6, Section 6.3.2).
Message Routing	Contains elements to forward the message to different receivers, to split larger messages, or to combine multiple messages into a larger one. You can select from the following step types: **Gather** (see Chapter 5, Section 5.2.1), **Router** (see Chapter 5, Section 5.1.1), **Splitter** (see Chapter 5, Section 5.2.1), **Join**, **Multicast** (see Chapter 5, Section 5.3.3), or **Aggregator**.
Security Elements	Contains elements to decrypt/verify incoming messages, or to encrypt/sign outbound messages. You can select from the following step types: **Decryptor**, **Encryptor**, **Signer**, or **Verifyer** (see Chapter 10).
Persistence	Contains elements to store message content at specific steps within the message processing. You can select from the following step types: **Data Store Operations**, **Persist Message**, or **Write Variables**.
Message Validators	Allows you to add an **XML Validator** step.

Table 2.4 Integration Flow Modeling Elements Offered in the Palette (Cont.)

Furthermore, it's also possible to use the **Select** and **Sort** options, which allow you to rearrange elements in an integration flow model but don't offer additional elements. The **Delete** option allows you to delete a selected element from the graphical editor.

Design the Integration Flow

Let's start designing our first integration flow using the **Sender** element. In the palette, navigate to **Participants • Sender**. After selecting and adding the sender element, follow these steps:

1. Position the cursor on the **Sender** shape. You'll notice that an information icon, a recycle bin symbol, and an arrow icon appear (as shown in Figure 2.24).

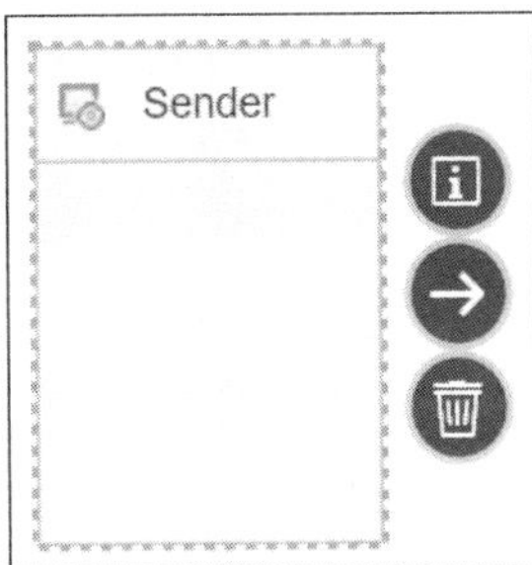

Figure 2.24 Information, Recycle Bin, and Arrow Icons for an Element

The arrow icon is used to connect elements of an integration flow (as shown in the next step). The recycle bin symbol is self-explanatory.

> **Information Icon**
>
> The information icon shows technical information about the selected integration flow element, namely, the ID and the version of the element. The ID is important to relate the information provided in the MPL (see Chapter 8, Section 8.2) to a certain integration flow shape (when monitoring the integration flow); you'll learn more about the version of an element in Chapter 6, Section 6.5.

2. Select the arrow icon, and drag and drop it to the integration flow start event (an orange dashed line will track your path) (see Figure 2.25).
3. A dialog box opens where you can select the sender **Adapter Type** (see Figure 2.26).

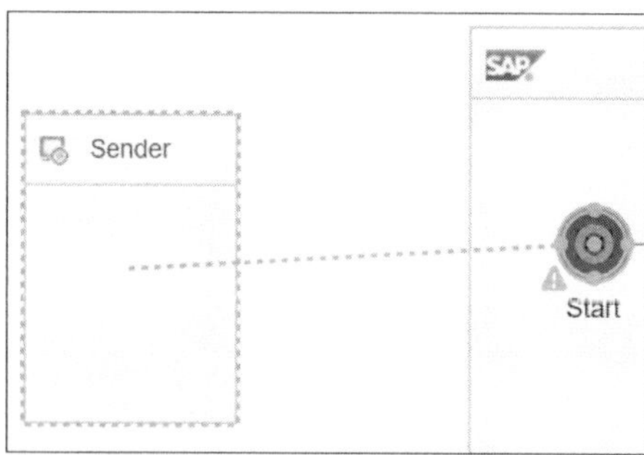

Figure 2.25 Creating a Connection between Sender and Start Event

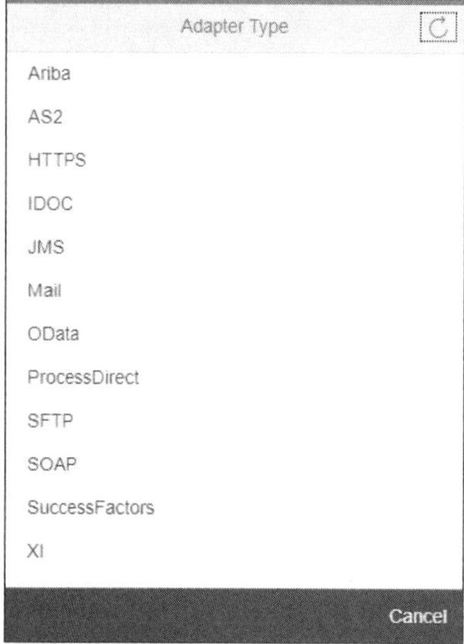

Figure 2.26 Offered Sender Adapter Types

4. Select **SOAP**. In the next dialog box that appears, select **SOAP 1.x**.
5. After this step, in the section below your model, a sheet appears where you can specify the properties of the adapter in different tabs.
6. Leave the settings under **General** as they are and choose the **Connection** tab. Here you specify settings as shown in Figure 2.27. These settings include:
   - **Address**: This is the specified string (including the forward slash at the beginning) necessary to generate the endpoint URL required by SoapUI. Here, enter "/soap2mail" in the field.

- **Service Definition**: With this parameter, you specify the source of the service definition to be used for the SOAP channel. We keep the default setting as **Manual**. We use the WSDL downloaded from the book's website only on the sender (SOAP client) side to specify the structure of the message.
- You can choose the alternative option **WSDL** if the SOAP sender adapter is supposed to use information contained in a dedicated WSDL file (to be specified) to determine how the message is to be processed. In the WSDL file, you can provide more information for the integration runtime to determine how the message is to be processed, for example, if a request is to be treated as a synchronous or asynchronous call, and the runtime node can treat the message accordingly. We go into the details of this in Chapter 5, Section 5.3.1.
- **Message Exchange Pattern**: With this parameter, you specify the communication type. Either keep the default setting as **Request-Reply** or set it to **One-Way**. In the first case, the adapter sends a reply message back to the sender; in the second case it doesn't. When you've selected **One-Way**, remember to keep the **Processing Settings** as **WS Standard**. Changing this setting to **Robust** would cause processing errors to be returned to the SOAP client.
- **Authorization**: This setting makes sure that for the user associated with the calling sender, the permissions are checked based on user-to-role assignments by the SAP Cloud Platform Integration framework. Here, keep the setting **User Role**. In the **User Role** field, keep the entry **ESBMessaging.send**. This role is predefined by SAP to authorize a sender (the SOAP client) to call your tenant. The **Select** option allows you to select a custom role if you've defined one (see Chapter 10, Section 10.3.3 for more details).

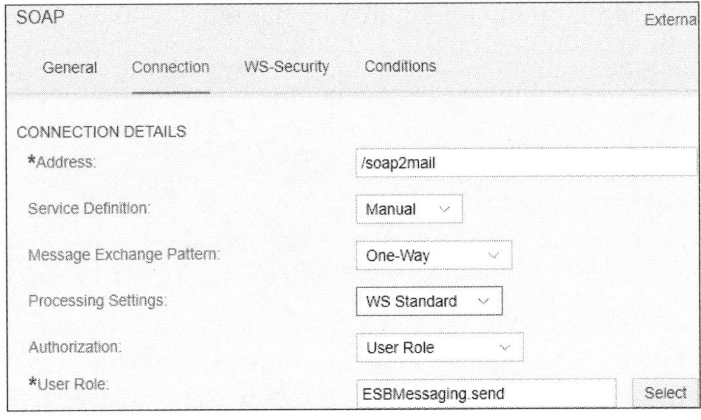

Figure 2.27 SOAP Adapter Settings

User Role Authorization

The **User Role** authorization option can be used along with *basic authentication* (among other authentication options, see the following *Inbound Authorization Options* information box). Using this authentication option, SAP Cloud Platform Integration expects credentials (username and password) to authenticate the user associated with the incoming call (compare the analog configuration of the SOAP client as shown later in Figure 2.40).

The integration flow model is again displayed. The only components missing in our integration flow model are the email receiver and the mail adapter. We explain how to configure the mail adapter in the next section.

Inbound Authorization Options

There are different options to combine inbound *authorization* with *authentication* methods. The two authorization options offered in the SOAP sender adapter (as well as in most HTTP-based adapters) can be combined with authentication in the following way:

- **User Role** authorization
  The permissions of the caller are checked based on roles defined for the user associated with the inbound call. Hereby, three *authentication options* are possible. First, the user can be authenticated based on credentials (which are provided in the HTTP header of the call), which is referred to as *basic authentication*. Second, the user can be evaluated by a *certificate-to-user mapping*. In this case, the sender authenticates itself against SAP Cloud Platform Integration based on a digital client certificate (which is mapped to a user in a subsequent step). To configure this option, an additional **Certificate-to-User Mapping** artifact needs to be defined for the scenario. As a third option, authentication can be established based on *OAuth*, an option to grant access to SAP Cloud Platform Integration without explicit credentials sharing.
- **Client Certificate** authorization
  Using this option, the permissions of the caller are checked by evaluating the distinguished name (DN) of the client certificate provided by the caller. Obviously, the caller is authenticated based on a client certificate.

This topic is covered in detail in Chapter 10. You can also check out the documentation of SAP Cloud Platform Integration at *https://help.sap.com/viewer/product/CLOUD_INTEGRATION/Cloud* by choosing **Connecting a Customer System to Cloud**

Integration • Concepts of Secure Communication • Basics • HTTPS-Based Communication • Authentication and Authorization Options (Inbound). You can find additional helpful information in the "Cloud Integration – How to Set Up Secure HTTP Inbound Connection with Client Certificates" blog (*https://blogs.sap.com/2017/06/05/cloud-integration-how-to-setup-secure-http-inbound-connection-with-client-certificates/*) published in SAP Community.

Adding and Configuring the Mail Adapter

To add and configure the mail receiver adapter, perform the following steps:

1. Click the **End** event so that the context buttons (the information, arrow, and recycle bin icons, from top to bottom) appear next to the shape, as seen in Figure 2.28.

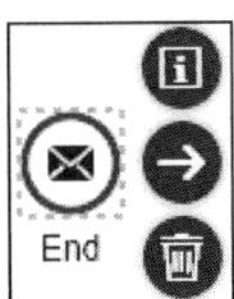

Figure 2.28 Context Buttons for the End Event

2. Connect the **End** event with the **Receiver** pool by clicking the arrow icon, dragging the cursor to the target shape (the **Receiver** pool in that case), and then releasing the mouse button (drop) (as seen in Figure 2.29).

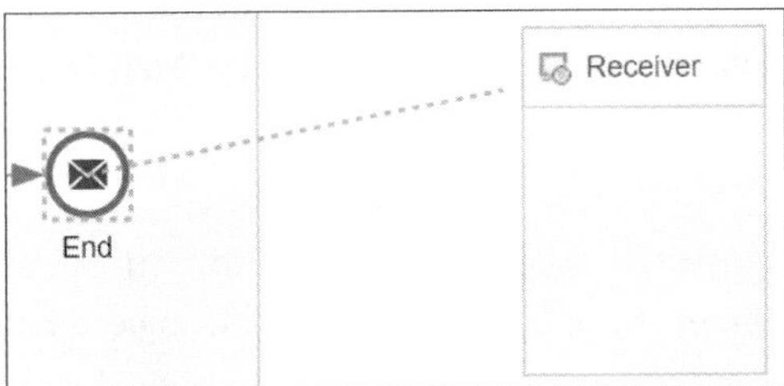

Figure 2.29 Connecting the End Event with the Receiver Pool

3. After releasing the mouse button, the **Adapter Type** dialog box will appear, which allows you to select the connection type you desire (Figure 2.30).
4. In the **Adapter Type** dialog, click on the **Mail** entry.

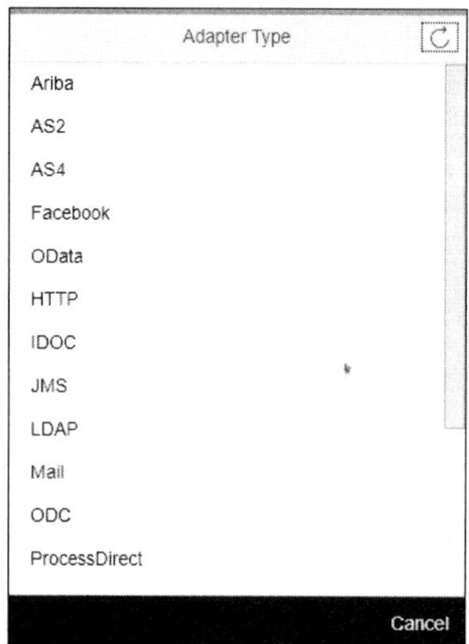

Figure 2.30 Adapter Type Dialog

5. After this step, in the section below your model, a sheet appears where you can specify the properties of the mail adapter in different tabs.

   In the **General** tab, you find the basic settings for your mail receiver:

   - Under **Channel Details**, you find information on the direction of the channel (directing from Cloud Integration to a receiver system) as well as the name of the connected system (**Receiver** in that case).
   - Under **Adapter Details**, the adapter type (Mail) is again shown as well as the supported transport protocol. For a mail receiver adapter, only Simple Mail Transfer Protocol (SMTP) is supported.

   You don't have to change anything here (Figure 2.31).

6. Click the **Connection** tab and configure the adapter according to your email account. The values shown in the screenshots (Figure 2.32) fit a Google email account. We briefly explain the parameters.

   In the mail channel under **Connection Details**, specify the settings as shown in Figure 2.32.

   In the **Address** field, specify the address of your mail server, in this case, Gmail. To find it in this example, check out the support information provided for Google at *https://support.google.com*. In this field, you also need to add the port, separated from the address by a colon. Which port to use follows from the other settings, as explained in the following paragraphs.

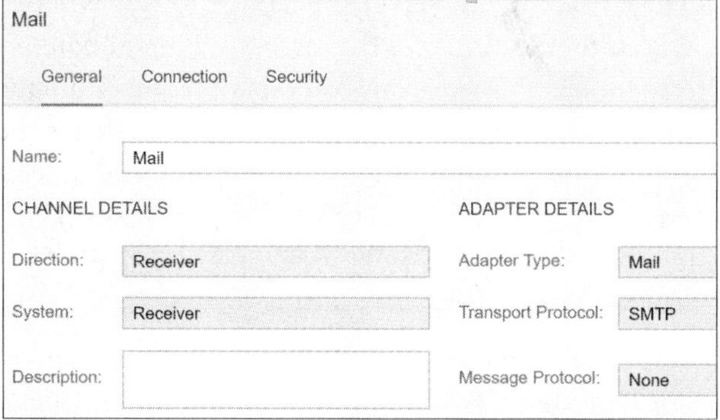

Figure 2.31 Configuring the Mail Adapter: General Tab

CONNECTION DETAILS

Address:	smtp.gmail.com:465
Proxy Type:	None
Timeout (in ms):	30000
Protection:	SMTPS
Authentication:	Plain User/Password
Credential Name:	FirstnameLastname

Figure 2.32 Configuring the Mail Adapter: Connection Tab/Connection Details

Allowed Ports for the Mail Receiver Adapter

Note that there are certain restrictions regarding the supported ports for the mail receiver adapter. In particular, you can use the following ports (for different **Protection** settings of the mail receiver adapter):

- 587 for SMTP+STARTTLS
- 465 for SMTPS

As we propose to choose **SMTPS** as **Protection**, port **465** must be also specified in the **Address** field, as shown in Figure 2.32.

The **Credential Name** field, as shown in Figure 2.32, contains a simple string that refers to a deployed credentials artifact on the SAP Cloud Platform Integration server. You can't define the username and password directly on the configuration screen of the mail adapter; instead, it's necessary to deploy the credentials containing the username and password on the server explicitly. This step is necessary for connections with basic authentication, as is the case for this email connection. When deploying the credentials on the server, you must provide a unique name (e.g., "FirstnameLastname", in our case) for reference purposes. This is the exact name you have to fill in the **Credential Name** field. If you have the rights for deploying (ask your tenant administrator), you can execute the steps described in Section 2.3.5.

7. In the **Connection** tab under **Mail Attributes**, most settings are self-explanatory (Figure 2.33). You specify the sender mail address (**From** field) and receiver address (**To** field) mail address (optionally, you can specify the mail's carbon copy [**CC** field] and blind carbon copy [**BCC** field] as well). Furthermore, add a text string which will then be written into the mail subject (**Subject** field).

Figure 2.33 Configuring the Mail Adapter: Connection Tab/Mail Attributes

Note

The default definition of the **Mail Body** field (`${in.body}`) makes use of Camel's Simple Expression Language. We're explicitly accessing the `in` message of the exchange and taking its body, which contains nothing but the message's payload and is exactly what we want to see in our email. The Camel data model is described in more detail in Chapter 4, Section 4.1.

With the **Body Mime-Type** setting, you specify the Internet Media Type of the message body, that is, the kind of data transferred with the message. Keep the default value **Text/Plain** because no other data format other than plain text (with the XML describing the message structure) is forwarded directly from the SOAP client. **Body Encoding** allows you to specify the character encoding of the incoming data. To ensure that data is passed unmodified, keep the default value **UTF-8** (Unicode encoding).

Finally, under **Attachments**, you can specify that the received mail should contain the outbound message as attachment. We don't define any attachment settings in the first integration flow.

For more details on how to configure the mail adapter, take a look at the online documentation of SAP Cloud Platform Integration. Go to *https://help.sap.com/viewer/product/CLOUD_INTEGRATION/Cloud*, and search for "mail adapter".

The final scenario should look similar to the one depicted earlier in Figure 2.13. You can easily identify the sender on the left (connected to the **Integration Process** shape by a SOAP channel), and the final receiver on the right (connected with the **Integration Process** shape by the mail channel configured just in the previous steps). The message invoked by the SOAP client (which simulates our sender system) is passed on without any further changes to the Mail adapter.

That's the advantage of a graphical environment: it clearly and intuitively describes how the message arrives at the server, how it's handled within the SAP Cloud Platform Integration server, and to which systems using which channels it's forwarded.

Save the integration flow, and click **Deploy**. You'll find the corresponding buttons for saving and deploying the integration flow on top of the integration flow editor (Figure 2.34).

Figure 2.34 Save and Deploy Buttons at the Bottom of the Editor

2.3.5 Creating and Deploying a User Credentials Artifact

To enable the tenant to connect to the email receiver using the credentials of the email account owner, you needed to add a **Credential Name** in the mail adapter of your integration flow, which at this point is little more than a placeholder for an artifact that we'll create using the following steps:

1. Choose the **Monitor** tab of the Web UI (refer to Figure 2.10).
2. Select the **Security Material** tile under **Manage Security**.
3. Choose **Add • User Credentials** (see Figure 2.35).

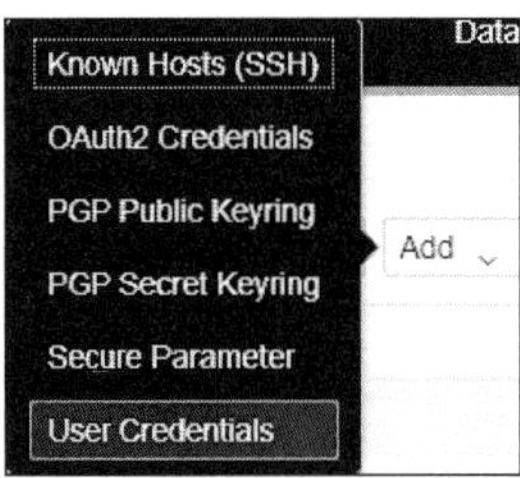

Figure 2.35 Adding a User Credentials Artifact

4. Specify the properties of the **User Credentials** artifact. For **Name**, enter the value that you entered in the **Credential Name** field in the mail adapter (refer to Figure 2.32). For **User**, enter your email box username, and as **Password/Repeat Password,** enter the associated password. Leave the **SuccessFactors** checkbox deselected. This setting is only relevant when you define credentials to be used when connecting to a SAP SuccessFactors system (see Figure 2.36).

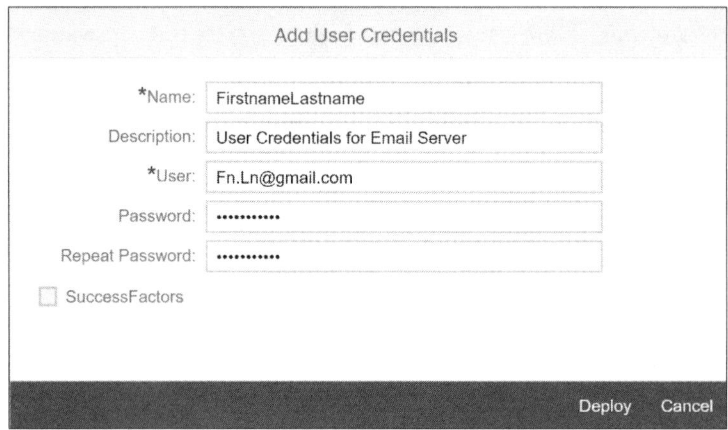

Figure 2.36 The Add User Credentials Dialog Contains the Properties of a User Credentials Artifact

5. Choose **Deploy**.

How Secure Are Your User Credentials?

You've now defined an artifact that contains the credentials used by the tenant to connect to your email account using the mail adapter. Configuring the integration scenario, it wasn't necessary to share these credentials (username and password) with anyone. In the mail adapter settings, only an alias (**Credential Name**) is specified, which the other participants of your integration team sharing the same tenant can see without any risk of a security leak.

Another artifact type, which is handled in the same way, is the **Secure Parameter** artifact required for scenarios that include social media adapters (for the Twitter adapter, see Chapter 10, Section 10.4.5) and when you use the Adapter Development Kit (ADK) (see Chapter 6, Section 6.7).

If you don't have deployment rights, ask the tenant administrator to take over the process for you.

You've almost reached the end of this first tutorial. However, there is one additional thing you have to do before you can successfully run your scenario and send the SOAP message: import certificates.

2.3.6 Import Certificate Required by the Mail Server into Keystore

The mail receiver adapter that you've configured specifies an outbound connection to an email server. To increase security, connections between an SAP Cloud Platform Integration tenant and remote systems can be protected by various methods, as you'll learn in Chapter 10. In our example integration flow, the tenant (as client) authenticates itself against the email server with the credentials (user and password). You've specified the required settings in the **User Credentials** artifact in the steps before.

However, in the other direction, SAP Cloud Platform Integration also needs to establish a trust relationship to the email server. When establishing the connection, the email server needs to authenticate itself against SAP Cloud Platform Integration to prove its trustworthiness. This is done based on a digital *server* certificate. SAP Cloud Platform Integration can only confirm trustworthiness of the email server when the keystore owned by SAP Cloud Platform Integration (deployed on the tenant) contains a root certificate that is also trusted by the email server. (For more information about certificates, see Chapter 10, Section 10.4.1.)

We'll now show you can get the required certificate into the tenant keystore (if not part of it already). Although you can find out which certificate needs to be in the tenant keystore from the organization that runs the email server (Google in our example at *https://pki.google.com/*), there is a smarter way (without needing to look it up online and download it): the outbound connectivity test tool. This tool is part of the **Monitor** application, which will be described in detail in Chapter 10. Therefore, we keep it short here.

1. Open the **Monitor** tab on the Web UI (refer to Figure 2.10).
2. Under **Manage Security**, click the **Connectivity Test** tile.
3. On the **Overview/Test Connectivity** screen, choose the **SMTP** tab to open the test options for the (outbound) connection to the email receiver (Figure 2.37).

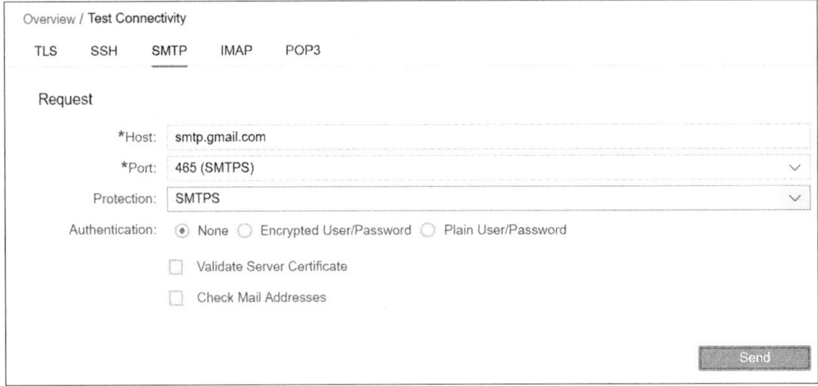

Figure 2.37 SMTP Outbound Connectivity Test

4. For **Host**, enter "smtp.gmail.com", and, for **Port**, select **465 (SMTPS)** (as these are the settings also specified in the mail receiver adapter, compare with Figure 2.32).
5. For **Authentication**, select **None**.
6. Deselect the **Validate Server Certificate** checkbox.
7. Choose **Send**.
8. As a response, you'll receive the message: **Successfully reached host at smtp. gmail.com:465**. Details of the server certificate are also displayed.
9. Choose **Download**.
10. The certificate is downloaded as a compressed file to your computer (*certificates.zip*).
11. Extract the certificate in a directory.

Next, you need to import the certificate into the tenant keystore, which has been provided to you by SAP together with the tenant by following these steps.

> **Note**
>
> If you don't have permissions for the following security-related steps, let the tenant administrator do it for you.

1. In the **Monitor** tab on the Web UI under **Manage Security**, click the **Keystore** tile. All certificates that are contained already in the tenant keystore are displayed in a table (Figure 2.38).

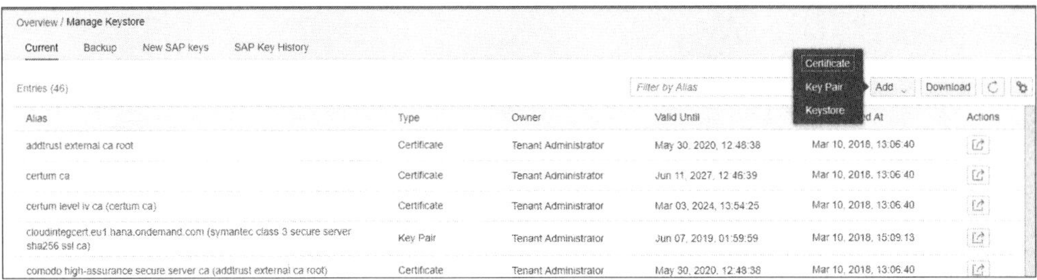

Figure 2.38 The Keystore Monitor

2. Click **Add** and then select **Certificate** as shown in Figure 2.38.
3. Select the extracted certificate from your computer. The list of certificates in the keystore monitor is refreshed and shows the imported certificate.

2.3.7 Send the SOAP Message

That's it! You've designed your first integration flow and finished the additional configuration settings. Now it's time to put this integration flow to use by sending a SOAP message.

Now that SAP Cloud Platform Integration is configured and prepared to process a message, let's send a SOAP message by following these steps:

1. Open SoapUI, and double-click **Request 1** in the expanded tree on the left side of the split screen (see Figure 2.39).
2. To tell SoapUI where to send the message, you need to specify an endpoint. In the dropdown list in the header of the **Request 1** window, select **[add new endpoint...]** (see Figure 2.39).

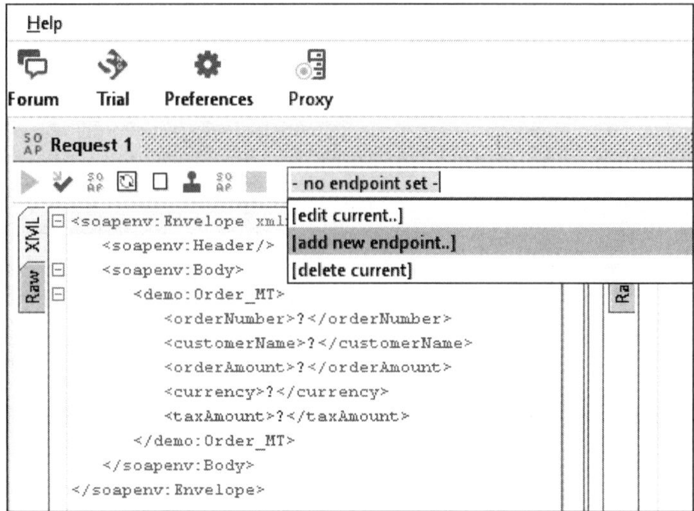

Figure 2.39 Adding a New Endpoint in SoapUI

3. In the next screen, enter the endpoint URL, and choose **OK**. The endpoint URL is composed of the runtime URL provided by SAP in the mail about your tenant, the string */cxf*, and the service address defined in the SOAP adapter (in the demo example, */soap2mail*) in the following way: *https://<Runtime URL provided by SAP>/cxf/soap2mail*.

   You can also find the endpoint URL by opening the **Monitor** tab of the Web UI and clicking on a tile under **Manage Integration Content**. In the list of deployed integration content, find your newly deployed integration flow, and click the corresponding entry. Copy the URL you find in the **Endpoint** field.

4. Now you need to enable the SOAP client to authenticate itself against SAP Cloud Platform Integration based on your user credentials. In SoapUI, click **Auth (Basic)**, and enter your credentials in the next screen (see Figure 2.40). Refer also to Figure 2.16 for the assignment of the corresponding role `ESBMessaging.send` to the user associated with the sending SOAP client.

5. Close the dialog box by clicking **Auth (Basic)** again. Make any entries for the elements in the **XML structure,** which can be found in the **Request 1** window. For example, enter your name between the opening and the closing tag for **CustomerName**, as shown in Figure 2.41.

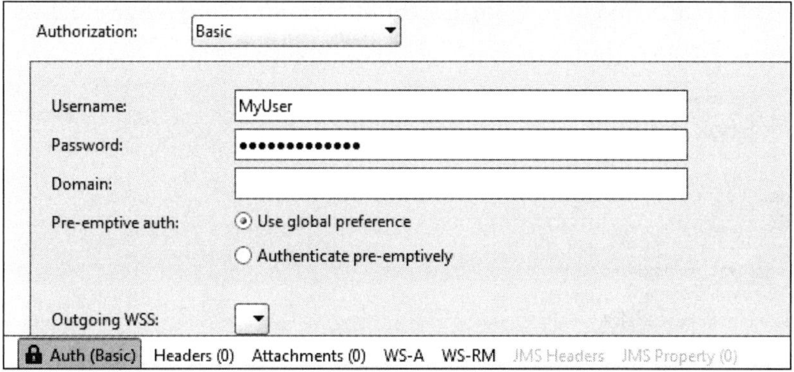

Figure 2.40 Specifying Username and Password to Enable the SOAP Client to Send Messages to SAP Cloud Platform Integration

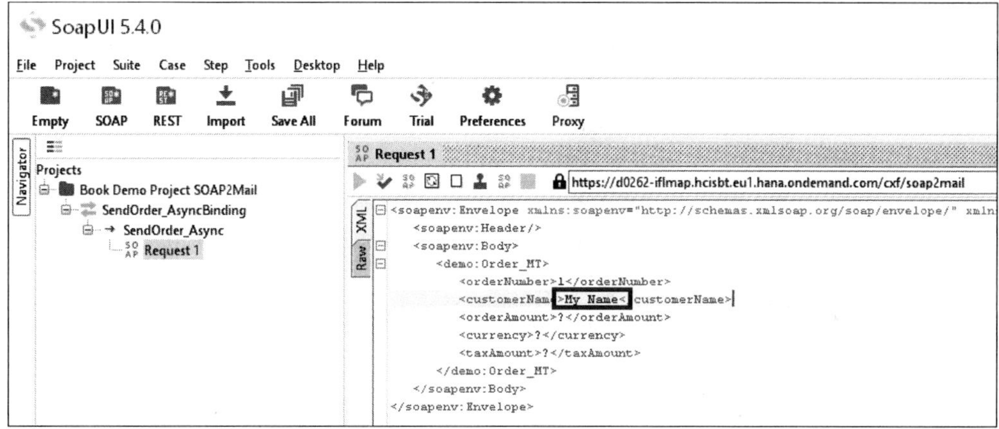

Figure 2.41 Entering Data in the XML Structure

6. To send the message, click on the green triangle icon (at top left corner of Figure 2.42; tooltip **Submit request to specified endpoint URL**), or press Alt+Enter.

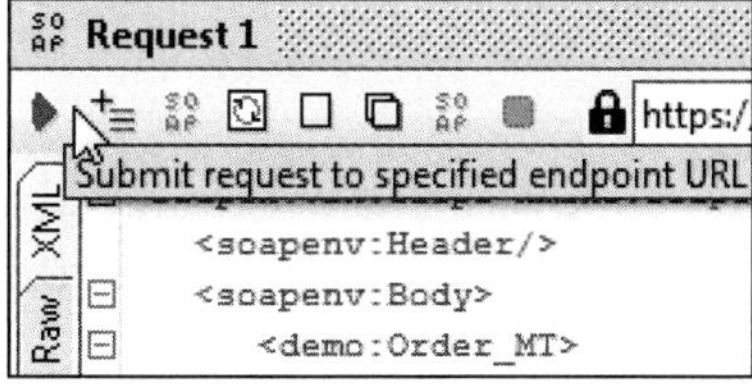

Figure 2.42 Clicking the Green Triangle Icon to Send the Message

The message will be delivered to your email account. You should receive an email like the one shown in Figure 2.43.

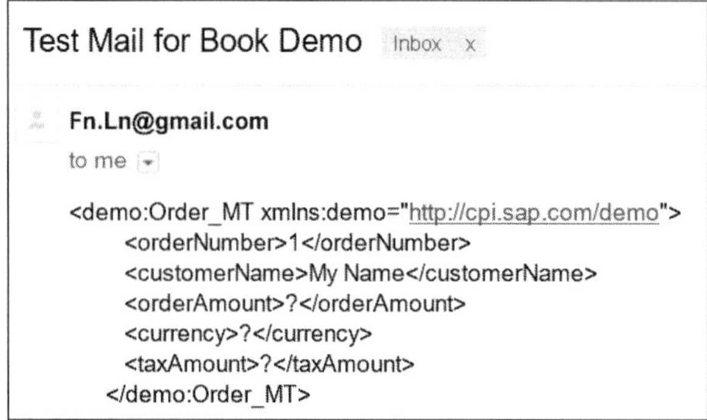
Test Mail for Book Demo
Inbox x
Fn.Ln@gmail.com
to me
<demo:Order_MT xmlns:demo="http://cpi.sap.com/demo">
<orderNumber>1</orderNumber>
<customerName>My Name</customerName>
<orderAmount>?</orderAmount>
<currency>?</currency>
<taxAmount>?</taxAmount>
</demo:Order_MT>

Figure 2.43 Email Content Shows Message Structure

Troubleshooting

If you're using a Google email account, as we've done in this exercise, consider the following:

- You might need to temporarily allow less secure apps to access your account. Otherwise, Google email will refuse your connection attempt via SAP Cloud Platform Integration. Note that this is just for test purposes. You should revert the settings in your Google email account after you've verified the sending of emails via SAP Cloud Platform Integration. More details can be found on the Internet. Search for "Google email allow less secure apps to access your account" or directly navigate to *https://support.google.com/accounts/answer/6010255*.
- If you receive an error message, such as **javax.net.ssl.SSLHandshakeException: unable to find valid certification path to requested target**, the reason is a missing certificate. You have to add the Google certificate to your keystore on your tenant (as explained in Section 2.3.6).

2.3.8 Monitor the Message

More information on the monitoring application, and the meaning of each section, will be provided in Chapter 8. For now, we'll only show you how to quickly check the processing status of your first integration flow.

1. Open the **Monitor** tab on the Web UI (refer to Figure 2.10).
2. To check for the message that you've just sent, select a tile with suitable filter criteria under **Monitor Message Processing** (see Figure 2.44).

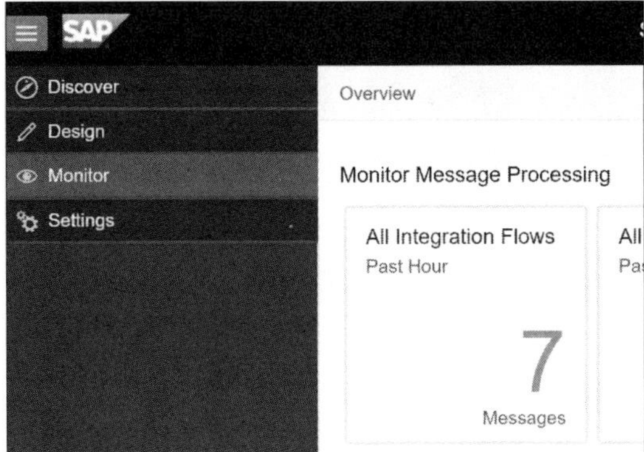

Figure 2.44 Monitor Message Processing Tile in the Monitoring Tab

A list of messages is displayed. Details about the processed message (for which the row is selected at the left side) are shown on the right side of the window (Figure 2.45).

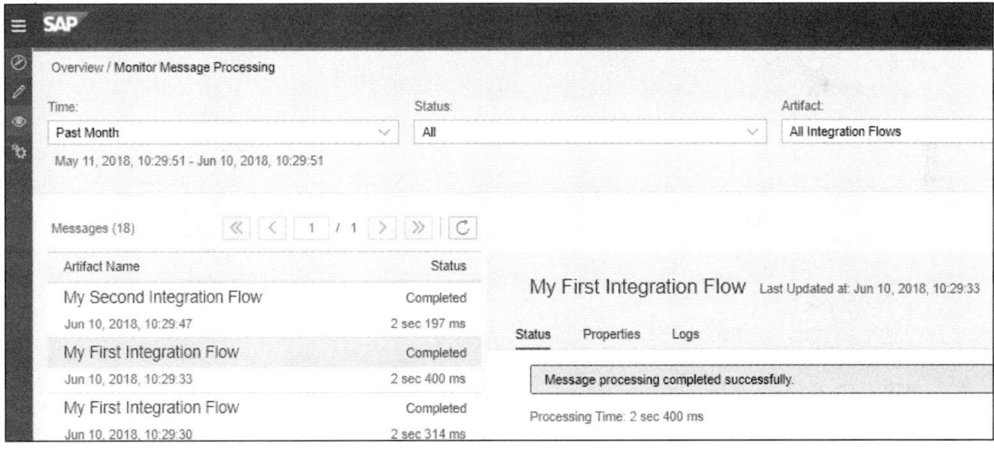

Figure 2.45 Detailed List of Processed Messages and MPL

3. The **Logs** tab shows a link to the MPL, which provides information on the processing of the message. Click **Open Text View** to display the processing steps of the selected message in a structured view (Figure 2.46).

You can configure different log levels to display information about the processing of the message on different detail levels. For more information on this and on the MPL, see Chapter 8.

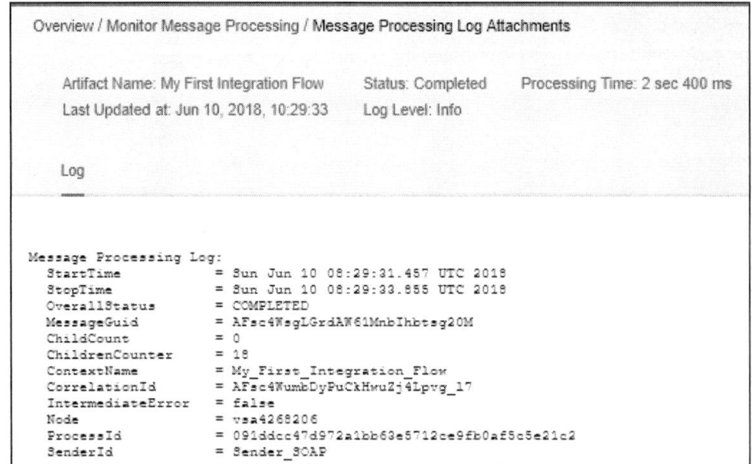

Figure 2.46 MPL

4. To check the status of the deployed integration flow, select a tile under **Manage Integration Content** (Figure 2.47).

Figure 2.47 Managing Integration Content Screen

The page in Figure 2.47 shows all integration artifacts (integration flows, value mappings, and OData services) that have been deployed on the tenant. This is a useful page for administrators who like to check the status of the integration artifacts. We'll provide more information on this in Chapter 8.

Congratulations! You've successfully processed your first message.

Mail Sender Adapter

SAP Cloud Platform Integration also offers the option to connect an email sender using a mail sender adapter. An integration flow with this adapter can read emails from a specified email account and further process them.

You can enhance your first integration flow by replacing the SOAP sender channel with a mail sender channel and trying out this feature. For simplicity, you can use the same Gmail account and email address you've specified for the mail receiver adapter. That way, you use SAP Cloud Platform Integration to send yourself an email.

You can quickly set up this scenario using the following steps and settings:

1. Remove the SOAP channel between **Sender** and **Start** event (by clicking the connection and selecting the recycle bin icon), as shown in Figure 2.48.

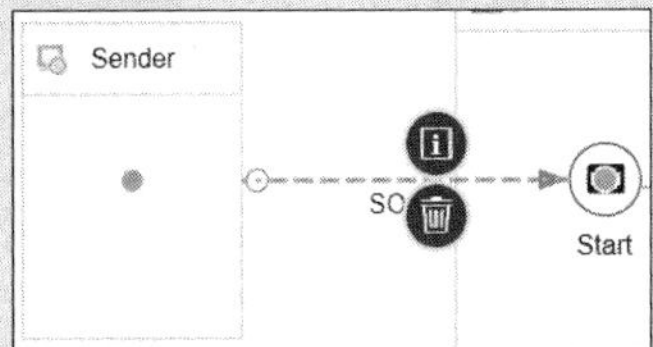

Figure 2.48 Removing an Existing Channel

2. Create a new channel, and select adapter type **Mail • IMAP4**.
3. In the **Connection** tab of the mail sender adapter, specify the following settings:
   - **Address**: Enter "imap.gmail.com:993". For more information on the allowed ports for the sender mail adapter, refer to the online documentation of SAP Cloud Platform Integration. For your convenience, we copy the list of allowed ports at the bottom of this box.
   - **Authentication**: Choose **Plain User/Password** to keep it simple, and use the same **Credential Name** as you did for the mail receiver adapter (i.e., "FirstnameLastname").
4. In the **Processing** tab, we recommend using the following settings:
   - **Selection**: Choose **Only Unread** (otherwise, the adapter would pick up all mails from the specified folder).
   - **Folder**: Specify a certain folder in your email account (other than the Inbox) so that SAP Cloud Platform Integration will take unread message from the Inbox and copy them to the specified folder.
   - **Post-Processing**: Specify what should happen with a mail once it has been processed by SAP Cloud Platform Integration.

5. Be careful with the settings in the **Scheduler** tab not to spam your inbox with your own mails after having deployed the integration flow. But as you've specified that only unread mails will be processed, you might be on the safe side (for **Selection**, you've chosen **Only Unread**).

Be aware of certain security risks when using mail sender channels, as SAP Cloud Platform Integration can't authenticate the sender of an email. For more information, check out the online documentation of SAP Cloud Platform Integration in the mail adapter section.

Allowed Ports for Mail Sender Adapter

In particular, you can use the following ports (for different **Protection** settings of the mail sender adapter):

- 143 for **IMAP+STARTTLS**
- 993 for **IMAPS**
- 110 for **POP3+STARTTLS**
- 995 for **POP3S**

A Simple Smoke Test Integration Flow

The described integration flow was quite simple: it didn't do anything further with the message than simply forwarding the content received by a sender component to an email receiver. However, even for this first flow, you needed to configure a receiver, which, in the context of this exercise means you needed to configure your email account in such a way that it accepts messages from SAP Cloud Platform Integration. The "Troubleshooting" box in Section 2.3.7 showed that even here, you can already run into errors.

If you like to quickly just check if your cluster works correctly, you can set up a "smoke test" integration flow without any receiver system involved. To find out how to do this, check out the online documentation of SAP Cloud Platform Integration at *https://help.sap.com/viewer/product/CLOUD_INTEGRATION/Cloud* (in the **Getting Started with SAP Cloud Platform Integration (Onboarding Guide)** section, select **Performing a Smoke Test**).

2.4 Summary

In this chapter, we provided you with a detailed introduction to the architecture of SAP Cloud Platform Integration. We explained its main components and showed you how messages are processed by the virtual runtime environment. We also introduced you to the available tools and processes, and we then finished up the chapter with a brief tutorial on how to design and run your first, very simple, integration flow. The tutorial showed you how to use SAP Cloud Platform Integration to exchange messages between different systems. Using a SOAP client and an email receiver system allowed you to set up a very simple system landscape without further technical prerequisites to meet. The first integration scenario, however, didn't impose any further processing of the message. If you can't wait to find out how to start modifying a message while processing it, you can proceed with Chapter 4 where step-by-step methods for processing a message will be introduced.

However, now that you're equipped with the basic knowledge required to dive further into the world of integration patterns, you might first want to find out what integration scenarios are provided by SAP out of the box. The next chapter provides you with an overview of the predefined integration content provided by SAP in the Integration Content Catalog.

Chapter 3
Integration Content Catalog

SAP provides prepackaged integration content that enables quick implementation of integration scenarios. These packages are found in the Integration Content Catalog. The chapter dives into the specifics of the Integration Content Catalog, presents its available features, and explores the prepackaged integration content currently available for customers.

In Chapter 1, we discussed the role that SAP Cloud Platform Integration plays within SAP's cloud strategy. We also discussed SAP Cloud Platform Integration's positioning within the SAP landscape and presented a number of use cases.

As the adoption of cloud-based applications keeps growing, the chance of more customers needing to build the same integration scenarios between these cloud-based applications will continue to increase. Why not build these common integration scenarios in advance and reduce the implementation cost for customers? With this approach, customers simply need to reuse existing integration scenarios, rather than build their own.

That is exactly what SAP has made available through its Integration Content Catalog. This chapter introduces the catalog and takes you through the different steps required to consume its prepackaged SAP-provided contents. The chapter further explores currently provided prepackaged content and then discusses some of their use cases.

3.1 Introduction to the Integration Content Catalog

Since the introduction of cloud computing technology, there has been a shift in the level of investment in software licenses by organizations. Organizations are rapidly moving from the concept of software ownership to software rental. As a result, SAP is also growing its cloud portfolio with standardized products in human resources (with SAP SuccessFactors), marketing, sales, service, procurement, supply chain management, and finance. We're convinced that this portfolio will continue to grow.

For most customers, the need might arise to integrate cloud-based applications with other on-premise or cloud-based applications to cover the total end-to-end business process. As explained in previous chapters, SAP Cloud Platform Integration is well positioned as the integration platform for such a use case.

Most capabilities provided by these cloud-based applications are standardized in terms of protocols, endpoints, and message structures. Therefore, integration scenarios built over SAP Cloud Platform Integration for these cloud-based applications have a good chance of being implemented and reused by many other customers and partners. That is exactly what SAP provides with its prepackaged integration content for the most frequently used SAP cloud-based applications. This integration content is available in the Integration Content Catalog.

The catalog covers templates with prebuilt integration flows, value mappings, and other integration artifacts that customers can reuse, enabling customers to significantly reduce implementation time, cost, and risk. The catalog presents and categorizes content in a simple manner, allowing customers to browse and discover content that might be relevant for their scenarios. The content of the Integration Content Catalog is bundled in packages. Each package contains artifacts and objects that logically belong together and support a particular integration scenario. The artifacts and objects bundled in a package relate to one of these categories: data integration, integration flow, OData service, or value mapping (see in the note box in Chapter 2, Section 2.3.4).

When dealing with the Integration Content Catalog, it's important to understand the different roles involved in consuming and publishing content. We generally distinguish the following roles:

- **Integration developer**
  A member of the partner or customer organization responsible for consuming the prepackaged content available in the Integration Content Catalog.
- **Content publisher**
  The person responsible for building and making the integration package available in the Integration Content Catalog.
- **Content reviewer**
  The person responsible for reviewing and ensuring the quality of the content delivered in the Integration Content Catalog by the publisher.

Separating roles during the publication process helps improve the correctness of the content published in the catalog. It's important to stress that at the time of this book's release, only SAP can publish content packages. Consequently, the content publisher and reviewer roles aren't yet relevant to customers. This chapter will therefore primarily focus on the *integration developer*, which is the role that you, as a reader of this book, will most probably play.

Accessing the Integration Content Catalog

You can access the Integration Content Catalog in two different ways:

- Via a publicly accessible URL
- Via your own tenant

We'll now explore both of these approaches.

Via a Publicly Accessible URL

The publicly (and freely) available Integration Content Catalog is a web-based application that you can access at *https://api.sap.com/shell/integration*. An impression of the page is shown in Figure 3.1.

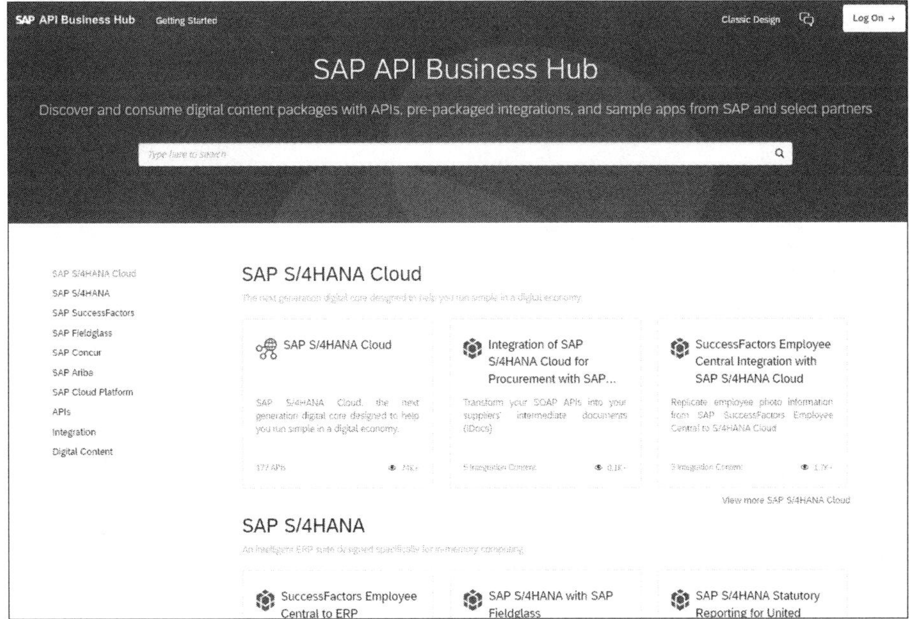

Figure 3.1 Publicly Accessible Integration Content Catalog

Note that the Integration Content Catalog is published on the SAP API Business Hub. You don't need an SAP Cloud Platform Integration tenant to use this web application. From this publicly available URL, only read access is available. If you need to reuse this content or have access to other features, you have to access a SAP Cloud Platform Integration tenant.

Via Your Own Tenant

You can access the Integration Content Catalog via the customer's tenant at *http://<server>:<port>/itspaces*.

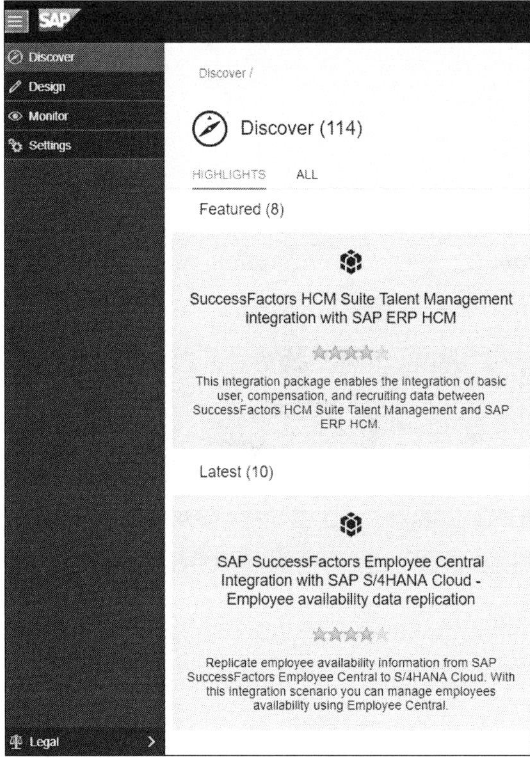

Figure 3.2 Landing Page of the Web UI

As shown on the left panel of Figure 3.2, the SAP Cloud Platform Integration Web UI is made of the following four main sections:

- **Discover**
- **Design**
- **Monitor**
- **Settings**

Refer to Chapter 2, Section 2.2.1, for more details about each section.

The **Discover** section is used to browse through the Integration Content Catalog. Let's dive deeper into the subject of consuming the available content, as shown in Figure 3.2.

3.2 Terms and Conditions of Using Prepackaged Integration Content

Terms and conditions, within the context of SAP Cloud Platform Integration, refer to usage restrictions that affect prepackaged content. The publisher of the content can decide on what and how the content in their package can be used. The terms and conditions mainly affect three aspects (at the time of this writing):

- **Quick configure versus content edit**
  Conditions that the publisher applies and that influence how the content can be consumed.
- **Notify about update (manual update)**
  Related to updating the prepackaged content included in the Integration Content Catalog.
- **Automatic update**
  Related to consumed prepackaged content automatically being updated.

We'll discuss these three aspects in the next sections.

3.2.1 Quick Configure versus Content Edit

One of the conditions that a publisher can apply to prepackaged content is the *quick configure versus content edit* condition. Quick configure or content edit conditions are used during the publication process to apply a usage restriction on the content. Let's explore these two conditions:

- **Quick configure (also called configure-only)**
  The user of the package can only configure the options already made available by the package artifacts. Depending on the specifics of the concerned package, this usually only includes configuring the different adapters used in the integration flow. The configure-only option also means that the integration content itself (e.g., the steps in an integration flow) can't be changed and are therefore use-only. This

option might be seen as restrictive because its consumers must stick to the provided content. However, one of the advantages of this approach is that it's easier for the content's publisher to manage the versions of the content and be certain that the content is being used the way it was intended. For example, you would be allowed to adjust the adapter's specific settings, including connection parameters and username/password, but you wouldn't be allowed to change the adapter type from, for instance, Simple Object Access Protocol (SOAP) to Java Message Service (JMS). The impact of new versions is, therefore, controllable and predictable. If your integration content has quick configure terms and conditions, the configure-only approach of configuration will apply, which will be discussed in Section 3.3.3.

- **Content edit**
  Consumers are free to modify the content as it suits them. This approach provides a lot of flexibility. However, with great power comes great responsibility. With content editing open to the user, it's possible for the integration developer to make changes to the content and fully deviate from the original intention of the content. For example, an integration developer might decide to add new steps to an integration flow or change the type of adapter used to communicate with the sender or receiver system. The changes brought to the content by its consumer might make future updates to the content more difficult. The resulting conflicts need to be manually resolved. At the time of this book's publishing, no automatic conflict resolution solution is available. Therefore, as the consumer, you must consider the impact of the changes you make to consumed content in relation to future updates of the content package. If your integration content uses the content edit terms and conditions, the content edit approach of configuration will apply, as will be discussed in Section 3.3.3.

Note that these options are only available to SAP at this moment because only SAP may publish content to the Integration Content Catalog.

3.2.2 Notify about Update (Manual Update)

During the publishing process, the **Notify about Update**, checkbox is available. If this option is selected, you'll be notified of any updates made to the integration package. Notifications are sent automatically to consumers using the integration content. As shown in Figure 3.3, a green **Update Available** link accompanies all updatable artifacts in the prepackaged content. In this way, the consumer is made aware that his content has an update available and can decide whether to perform the update.

Note

This type of notification is also called manual update. With manual update, the customer has the option to implement the update whenever it suits him. It's also possible to decide not to implement the changes. Not updating the content package doesn't create the danger that the deployed artifact will stop working. But the customer will obviously not benefit from the newly added features. Furthermore, it's also possible to revert back to an older version if necessary.

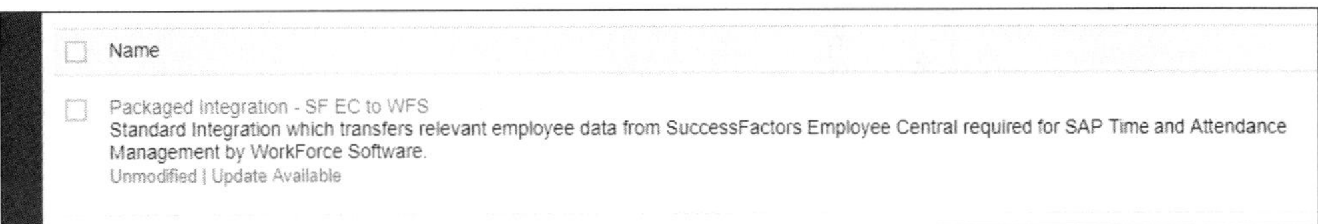

Name
Packaged Integration - SF EC to WFS
Standard Integration which transfers relevant employee data from SuccessFactors Employee Central required for SAP Time and Attendance Management by WorkForce Software.
Unmodified | Update Available

Figure 3.3 Notification of Updated Content in the Catalog

As a consumer, you can update your entire content package using the **Update package** button in the top-right corner of the screen (Figure 3.4). It's also possible to update single objects of the package instead of the entire package, by following these steps:

1. Select the content package whose object you would like to update.
2. Within the **Artifacts** tab of the package, select the artifacts that you want to update by checking the respective checkboxes. This tab lists all artifacts contained in the package and indicates which of them can be updated with the **Update Available** link, as shown in Figure 3.4.
3. Click on the **Update package** button.

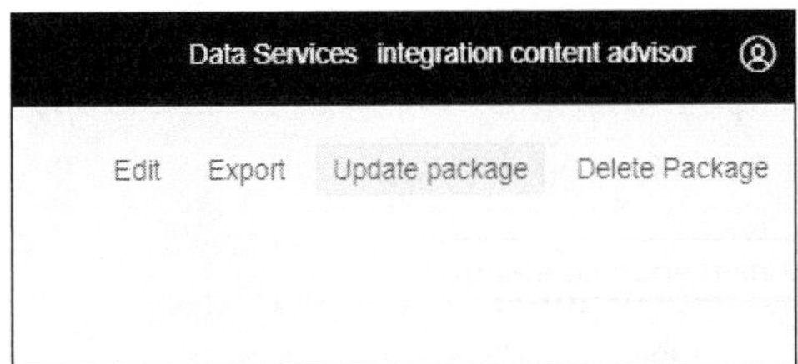

Figure 3.4 Updating Selected Items of the Content Package

Note that it's also possible to update a single integration flow by selecting the **Update** button in the **Actions** menu, as shown in Figure 3.5.

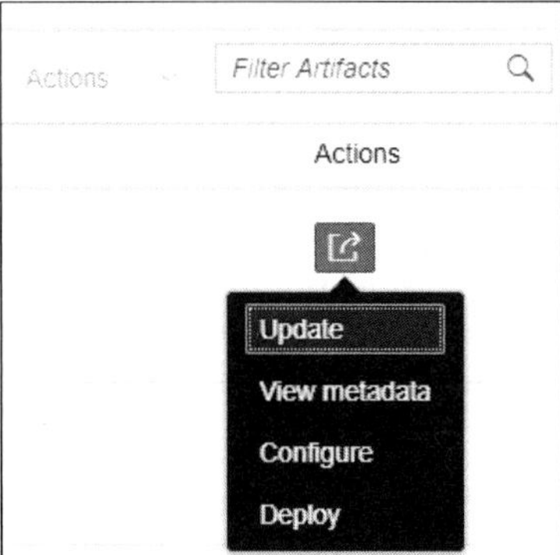

Figure 3.5 Updating a Particular Item of the Content Package

Note

In cases where the consumer modified integration content in the "modifiable" mode, a notification isn't sent when the content is updated by the publisher. The notification is only sent in the following cases:

- The consumed prepackaged content is in configure-only mode.
- The consumed prepackaged content is in modifiable mode but has only been configured and not modified. In other words, it has been used as if it was a configure-only package.

3.2.3 Automatic Update

As opposed to being notified of an update and being free to choose if or when to perform the actual update (as discussed in Section 3.2.2), there are cases when the publisher of the prepackaged content chooses automatic updating.

The main difference is that for manual update, the user explicitly has to perform the update operation, whereas no user interaction is required for automatic update. The updated content is automatically pushed to the tenant, and the deployed content is updated in one of two ways:

- **Immediate**
  If it's an immediate update, the customers have a window of up to 12 hours before the update is automatically applied to the corresponding deployed artifacts.
- **Scheduled**
  If it's a scheduled automatic update, the corresponding artifacts are marked with the date when the automatic update will be applied; for example, an artifact is marked with the message **Will be updated on . . .**, as shown in Figure 3.6.

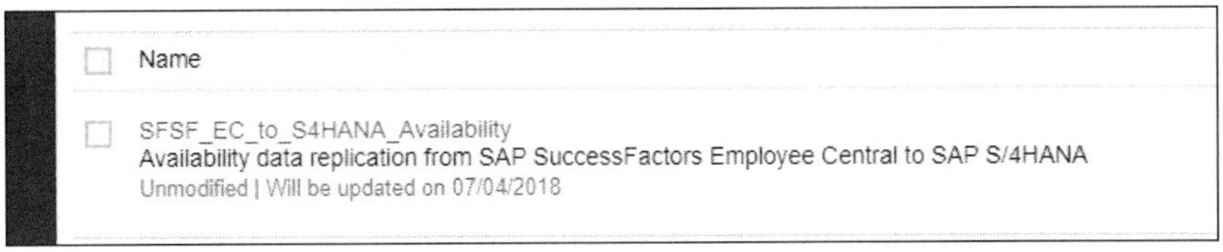

Name

SFSF_EC_to_S4HANA_Availability
Availability data replication from SAP SuccessFactors Employee Central to SAP S/4HANA
Unmodified | Will be updated on 07/04/2018

Figure 3.6 Artifacts Marked by the Scheduled Automatic Update

> **Note**
>
> Irrespective of whether the automatic update is immediate or scheduled, the customer has the option to apply the update before it's automatically done.
>
> Furthermore, an automatic update will always be applied, leaving the consumer without control.

Up to now, we've learned the steps involved in finding and consuming any prepackaged content. Let's now explore some of the content packages available in the Integration Content Catalog at the time of this book's publishing.

3.3 Consuming Prepackaged Content

We touched on the role of an integration developer in Section 3.1. In most cases, the integration developer is a member of the partner or customer organization and has the task of developing well-defined integration scenarios. Figure 3.7 shows the steps involved in consuming prepackaged content from the catalog.

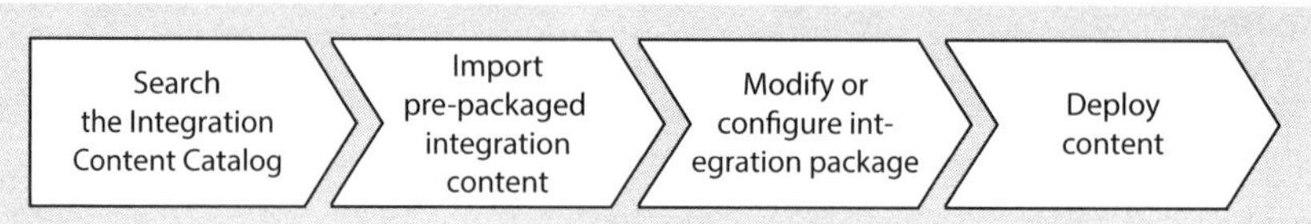

Figure 3.7 Process of Consuming Prepackaged Integration Content

We'll discuss these tasks in more detail in this section, with a hands-on, step-by-step guide.

3.3.1 Search in the Integration Content Catalog

It's a good practice to search through the Integration Content Catalog for existing content before attempting to develop your own content from scratch. To search the catalog, proceed as follows:

1. Navigate to your SAP Cloud Platform Integration tenant using the link provided by SAP on your browser. The link follows the format: *http://<server>:<port>/itspaces*.
2. Select the **Discover** menu item on the left side of the page to access the Integration Content Catalog, as shown in Figure 3.8.

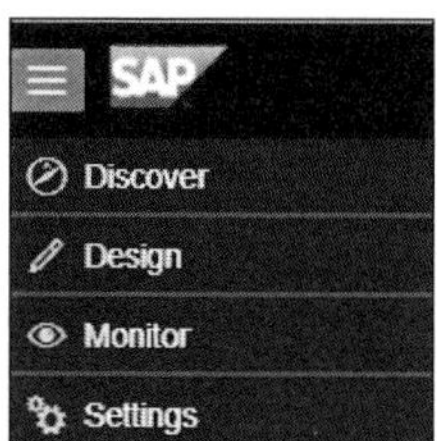

Figure 3.8 Accessing the Integration Content Catalog Main Page

3. In the Integration Content Catalog, you'll see a list of integration packages to choose from. By default, only the latest packages are listed. To view all existing packages, click on the **ALL** link on the top left of the page (see Figure 3.9). You then get a page similar to the one shown in Figure 3.10.

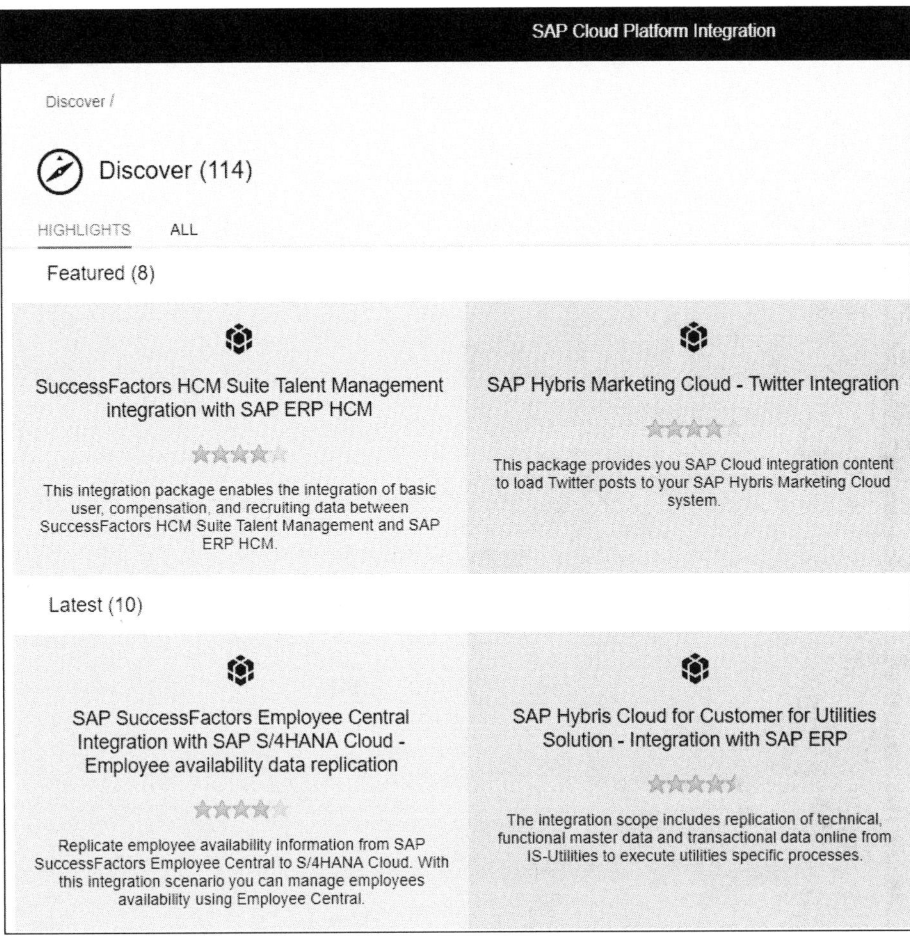

Figure 3.9 Discover Landing Page

4. A new screen appears with a variety of filtering categories. You have the option to filter using categories such as **Supported Platforms, Vendor, Countries, Industries, Line of Business, Products**, and **Keywords** (Figure 3.10). Note that you can also perform a keyword search on this screen.

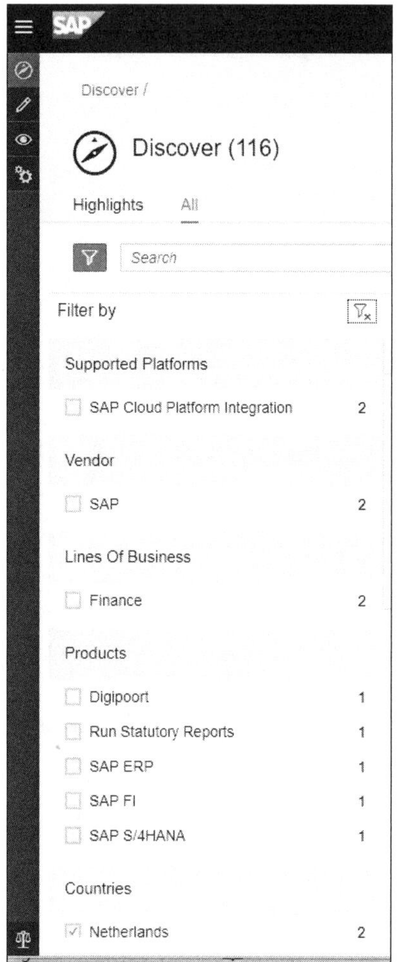

Figure 3.10 Filtering or Searching the Integration Content Catalog

The resulting list provides the name, high-level description of the package, published date, vendor, and version. Additionally, a user rating of the integration content is also available.

To view details of a particular package, select it from the list. As a result, you'll see a page similar to the one in Figure 3.11.

Figure 3.11 Viewing Details of an Integration Package

This Integration content detail page contains the following tabs:

- **Overview**
  Contains the description of the package and scenarios it covers.
- **Artifacts**
  Includes a list of integration flows, data integration flows, and other integration artifacts that make up the bundle.
- **Documents**
  Includes guides and links to provide more documentation and information about the integration content to assist the user further. It's common that integration guides are included among the documents. An integration guide provides step-by-step guidelines on how to set up and configure the integration scenario. Note that the corresponding contacts or components are mentioned in the release notes of the content. This is useful if there are issues with the artifacts, and you want to report the issue to SAP.
- **Tags**
  Provides different metadata to help classify content. The list of metadata includes industry, line of businesses, keywords, supported platforms, and so on.

- **Ratings**
  Contains details about consumer ratings as well as the logged-in user's own ratings.

Any of the items listed under the **Artifacts** tab, as shown in Figure 3.12, can be clicked to view. For instance, you can click on an integration flow's name to display it (see Figure 3.13).

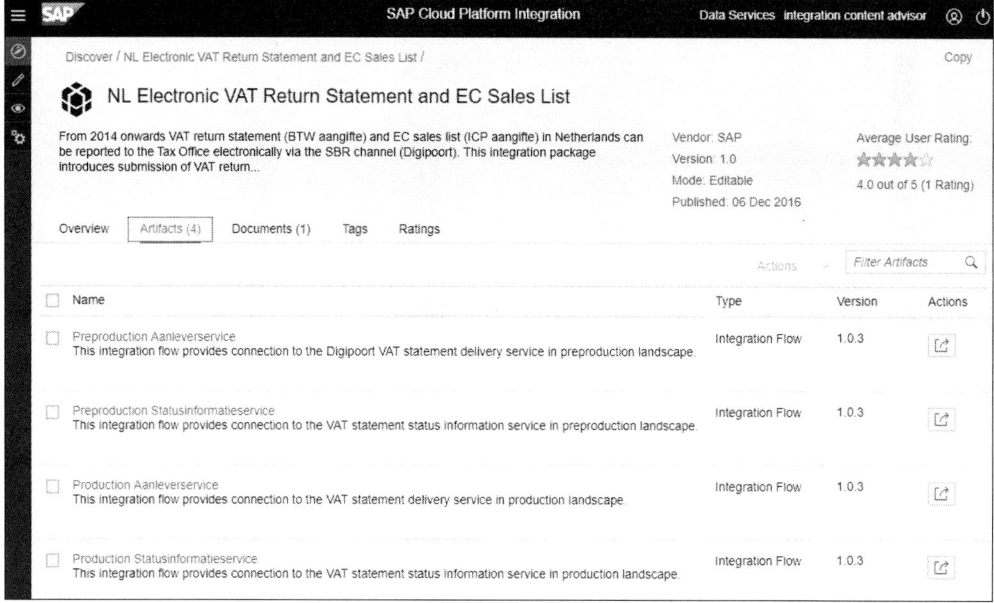

Figure 3.12 List of an Integration Package's Artifacts

After browsing around and finding the integration package that fits your needs, you're now ready to further modify and configure it according to your requirements. Note that the possibility to configure or modify depends on the mode of the prepackaged content, as we'll discuss in Section 3.3.3.

The next section will explore how to consume the content by copying it into your customer workspace.

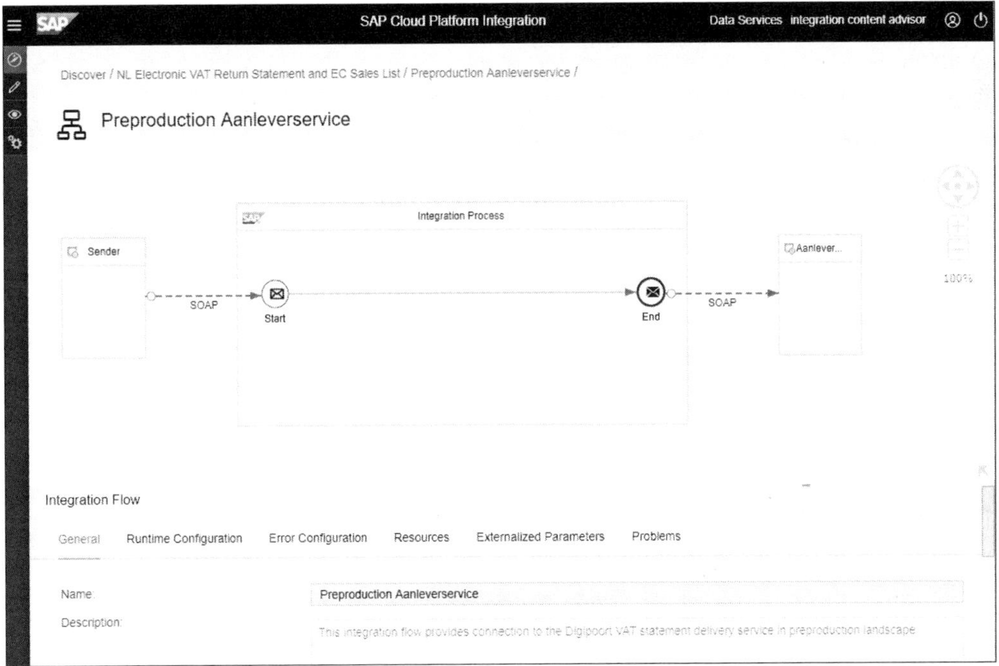

Figure 3.13 Details of the Integration Flow: Preproduction Delivery Service

3.3.2 Import Prepackaged Integration Content

You can copy the content available in the Integration Content Catalog into your own design workspace for further customer-specific configuration and enhancements. You can choose to use the template contained in the package as the basis upon which to make changes to suit your business requirements. To copy an integration package, perform the following steps:

1. After selecting the package that you want to copy (in our example, the **NL Electronic VAT Return Statement and EC Sales List** integration package), a **Copy** link appears in the top-right corner, as shown in Figure 3.14. This **Copy** link enables you to copy the integration package to your own customer workspace.

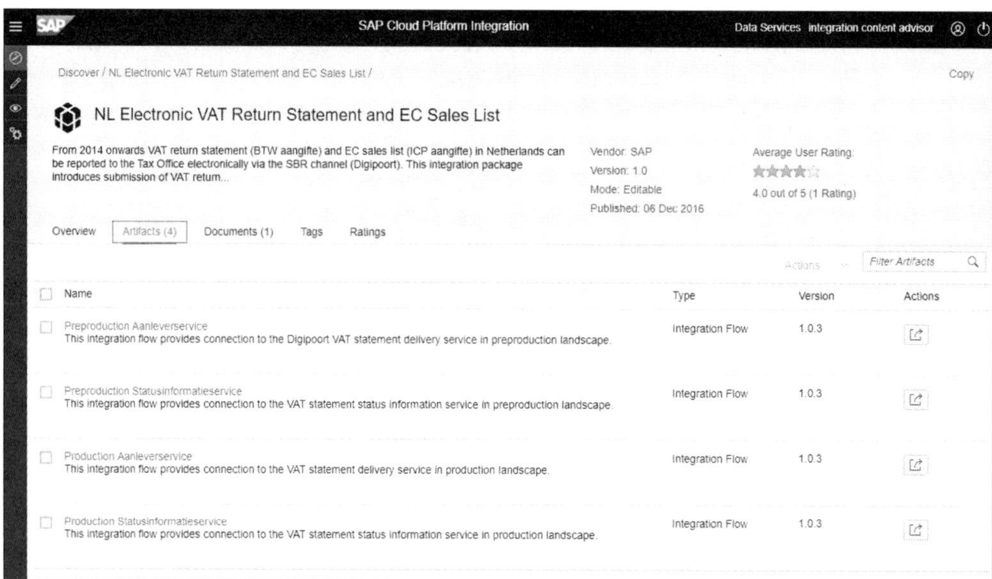

Figure 3.14 Copy Templates to Your Own Workspace

2. After performing the copy action, the copied package and its artifacts are displayed in your own design workspace. Click on the **Design** section (refer to Figure 3.8) to further enhance the copied content. Figure 3.15 shows that the copied package is now available in the customer's workspace, on the left.

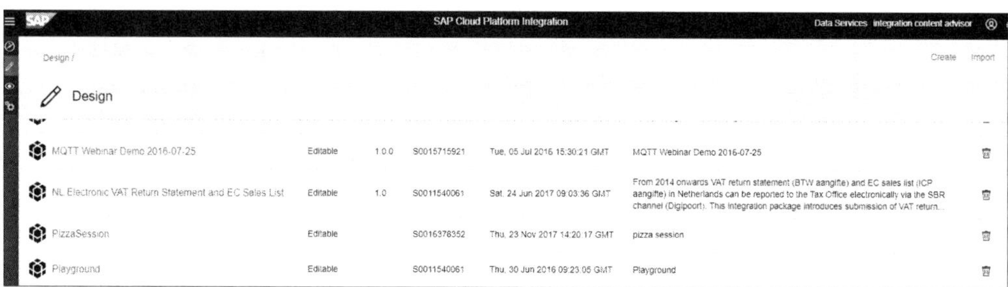

Figure 3.15 Design Component with Copied Templates

Note

As soon as you've copied a package from the **Discover** view to the **Design** view, a subscription is created in the background for each artifact contained in the package.

Having a subscription means that SAP Cloud Platform Integration knows that you're interested in any changes or planned updates on the concerned prepackaged integration content.

When anything changes on the package, you're informed via a tag next to the concerned artifacts. This subject is further discussed in Sections Section 3.2.2 and Section 3.2.3.

3.3.3 Modify or Configure the Integration Package

The content copied in the previous step is now ready for configuration. Such configuration steps might include adapter-specific endpoints. Depending on the customer-specific requirements, it's also possible to remodel and completely change the content. As stated previously, there are two approaches to configuring your integration package: content edit and configure-only. In the next sections, we'll explore each approach.

Content Edit Approach

This approach allows you to perform configuration steps to remodel and change the package content.

Notes

Being able to completely remodel and change the content of a copied package can be restricted by the terms and conditions of the integration package. When the package is restricted, use the configure-only approach, which we'll discuss further in the next section. The subject of terms and conditions was also discussed in Section 3.2.

The integration package copied to your tenant can be modified and configured to your own needs by following these steps:

1. Click on the desired package's name on the list of packages presented in the screen (refer to Figure 3.15).
2. A new page similar to the one presented earlier in Figure 3.12 loads. The page should display the full list of objects contained in the integration package. Note that the artifacts can be a mixture of integration flows, data integration, OData services, and value mappings. Furthermore, the **Documents** tab can contain files and URLs.

3. To display an integration flow, click on its name. You then get a detailed view of the flow as shown in Figure 3.16.

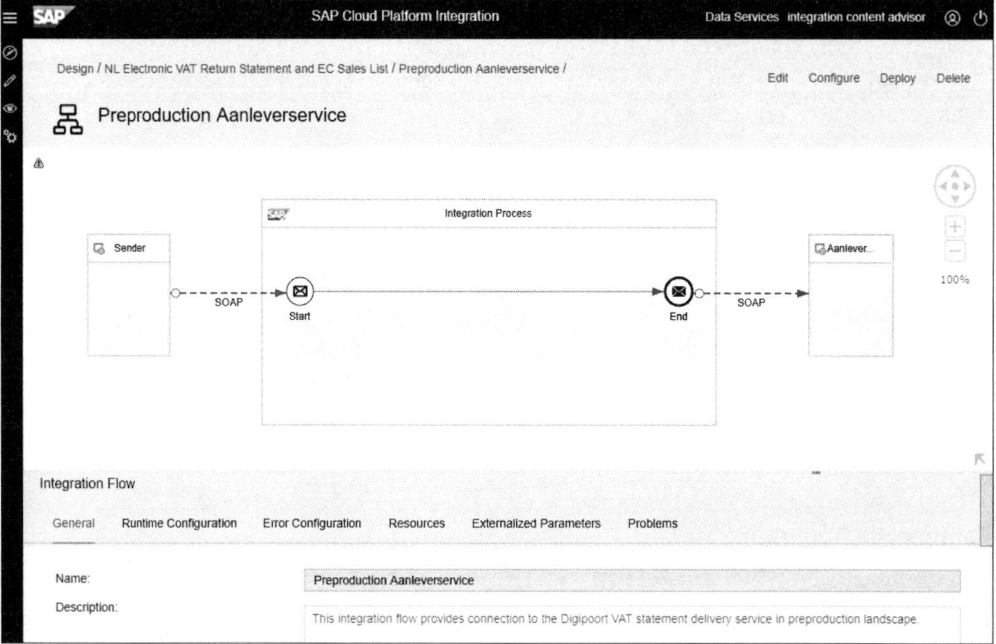

Figure 3.16 Details of the Integration Flow

4. To change an integration flow, click the **Edit** button in the upper-right corner of the screen. Note that, when in edit mode, the integration package editor locks the object and prevents any other user from changing it.
5. For most integration flows, connectivity details on the sender and receiver side need to be changed. Figure 3.17 for instance, shows that the SOAP receiver connection details can be filled in by selecting the respective connector and specifying the properties in the **Connection** tab.
6. After you've made the desired changes, you can click on the **Save** button on the top-right corner of the page (see Figure 3.17). Alternatively, click **Save as version** to save a new version of the integration flow. You're then asked to provide a comment for the new version. Note that the version number is also automatically incremented.

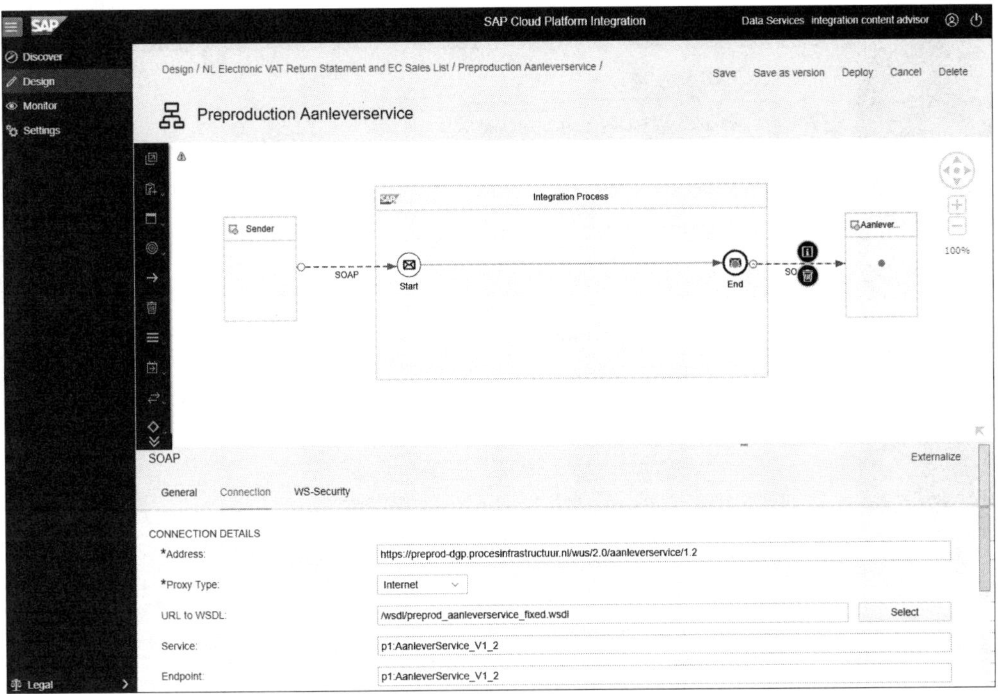

Figure 3.17 Adding Different Items to an Existing Integration Flow Template

7. After saving your work in the previous step, you can now choose to deploy the integration flow on the tenant by using the **Deploy** option (see Figure 3.17). If you attempt to deploy without saving, a popup message will warn you that there are unsaved changes. You'll also be asked if you want to save and deploy at the same time.

The integration flow can then be used at runtime to process actual messages.

Figure 3.18 shows that it's possible to download the content of an integration flow.

The content is downloaded to your local machine in a form of an archive file (e.g., ZIP file) containing the entire integration flow project. This integration flow's project ZIP file can then be imported into another package or deployed to run on a SAP Process Orchestration server as described in in Chapter 17 of *SAP Process Orchestration: The Comprehensive Guide* (SAP PRESS, 2017).

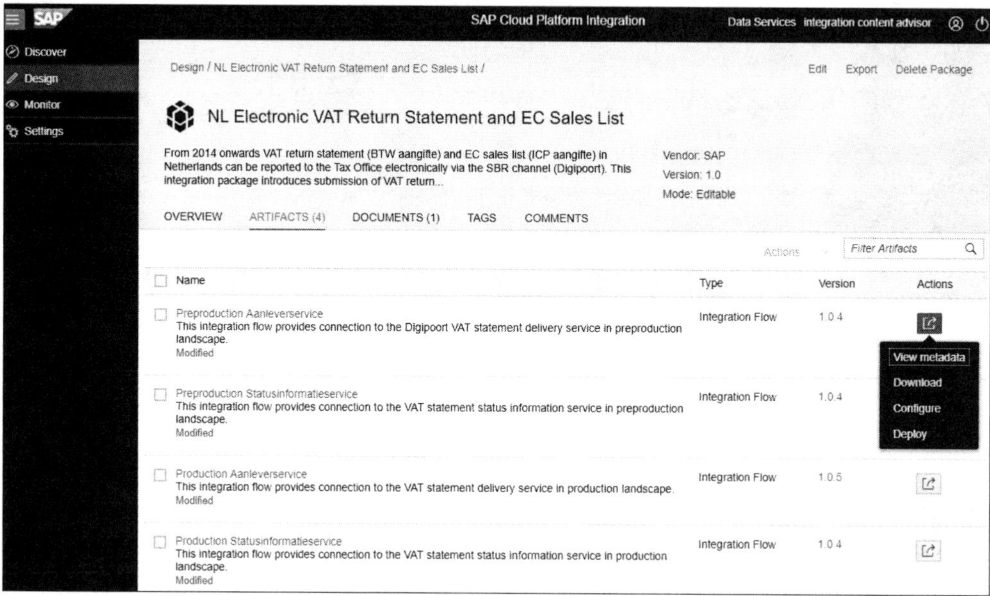

Figure 3.18 Overview of Updated Package

As shown in Figure 3.18, every integration flow contains a version number. After consuming a particular version of the integration flow, you have the option to revert to an older version by performing the following steps:

1. In the **Artifacts** tab (refer to Figure 3.18), click on the **Version** number of the integration flow. Note that this works in design mode only.
2. The next screen displays the history of the different versions of the integration flow (see Figure 3.19).

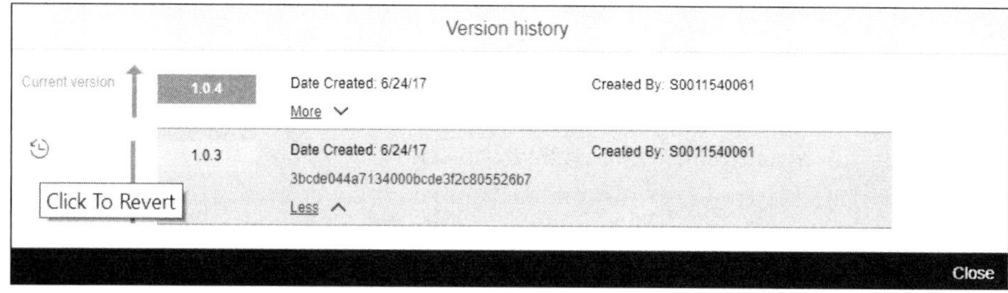

Figure 3.19 Reverting to a Different Version in the Version History

3. Hover over the version that you want to revert to, and click on the clock-like icon on the left side of the **Version history** screen, as shown in Figure 3.19.
4. A new screen pops up, from which you need to confirm your action by clicking the **Ok** button.

After the consumed prepackaged content is configured to suit your needs, it's time to deploy it and make it available in your tenant's runtime. We'll discuss this in Section 3.3.4.

Configure-Only Approach

The configure-only option provides an easy-to-use method of quickly adapting an integration flow to your requirements. It enables the user to perform only configuration activities, such as adding adapter-specific endpoints and assigning values to externalized parameters.

When you want to modify the content of the integration package, such as to add an extra step to the integration flow, you should use the content edit approach discussed earlier.

Following are the steps involved in using the configure-only approach:

1. Navigate to your design workspace by choosing the **Design** tab, as shown earlier in Figure 3.8.
2. Click on the package's name as shown earlier in Figure 3.15. The next screen displays a list of artifacts contained in the **Artifacts** tab.
3. Select the **Action** button on the row corresponding to the integration flow that you want to configure (see Figure 3.20), and then choose **Configure** from the dropdown menu.

   If the integration flow doesn't have configurable attributes, a warning pops up, as shown in Figure 3.21.

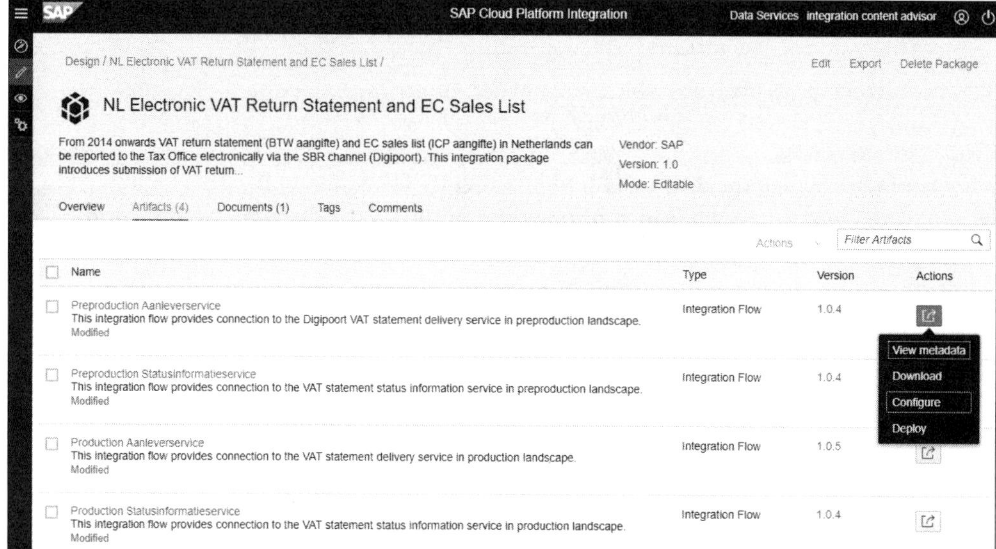

Figure 3.20 Accessing the Configure-Only Option

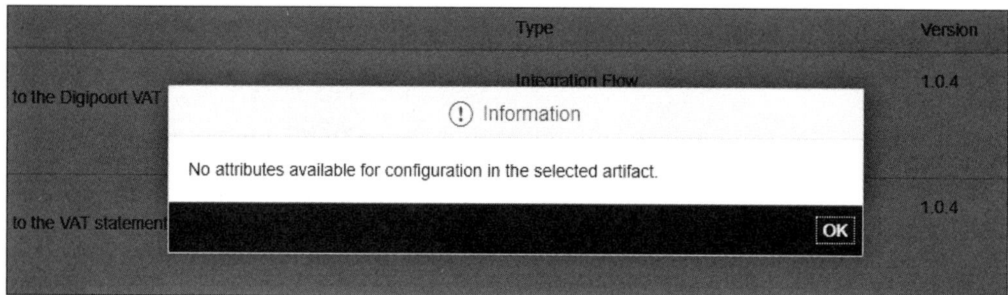

Figure 3.21 Warning for Missing Attributes in the Configure-Only Approach

4. If the integration flow does have configurable attributes, configure the details of each tab shown in Figure 3.22. Notice that in this screen, the **Time**, **Receiver**, and **More** tabs are displayed, but there are even more tabs available. A complete list of possible configuration tabs and their explanations are available in Table 3.1.

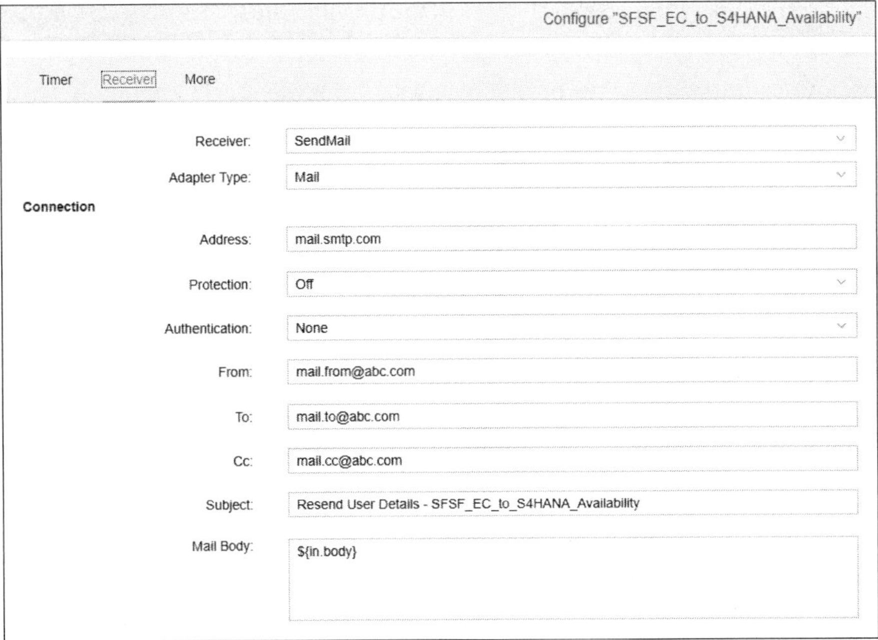

Figure 3.22 Configure the Receiver Connection Details of an Integration Flow

Configuration Tab	Description
Timer	If the integration flow uses a scheduler (a timer start event), its settings can be configured here. Possible options include **Run once**, **Schedule on Day**, or **Schedule to Recur**. We'll cover the topic of using a timer start event in an integration flow in Chapter 6, Section 6.1.2.
Sender	Configure the connectivity details of the sender adapter.
Receiver	Configure the connectivity details of the receiver adapter. See the example in Figure 3.22.
More	Provide a configuration feature for externalized parameters. Note that at the time of this book's publishing, all string fields can be externalized in all flow steps. Externalized parameters allow you to define variables and use them in an integration flow. The values of these variables can be assigned later in the configuration process. Parameters and externalization are further discussed in in Chapter 4, Section 4.2.

Table 3.1 Available Configuration Tabs for the Configure-Only Approach

5. After you've made the desired changes in the previous step, click on the **Save** button, as shown earlier in Figure 3.22.
6. Deploy the integration flow on the tenant by using the **Deploy** option (refer to Figure 3.22.)

Note

Note that the four tabs listed in Table 3.1 are available after you've clicked on the **Configure** option. However, the tabs are only populated with configurable properties under the following conditions:

- The presence of a sender adapter in the integration flow (**Sender** tab)
- The presence of a receiver adapter in the integration flow (**Receiver** tab)
- The presence of a timer start event (**Timer** tab)
- When you've externalized any string fields in any flow step (**More** tab)

For instance, when you have an integration flow beginning with a timer start event (i.e., no sender system is involved), the **Sender** tab won' be populated. If nothing has been externalized in the entire flow, you'll receive an error message stating, **No attributes available for quick configuration in the selected artifact.**

We'll explore the subject of externalizing parameters further in Chapter 4, Section 2.

3.3.4 Deploy Content

Your integration flow is now configured and ready to be deployed. You can deploy the integration flow by following these steps:

1. From within your customer workspace (**Design** tab), select the integration flow that you configured in Section 3.3.3.
2. Click on the **Deploy** button on the top right of Figure 3.23.

The deployed integration flow is now ready to reliably connect systems with each other through message exchange. Congratulations, you just learned to consume prepackaged integration content! Imagine how much time it would have taken to figure out the mapping requirements and build this entire integration flow from scratch.

Now it's time to explore the terms and conditions that might affect and restrict the way you consume prepackaged content.

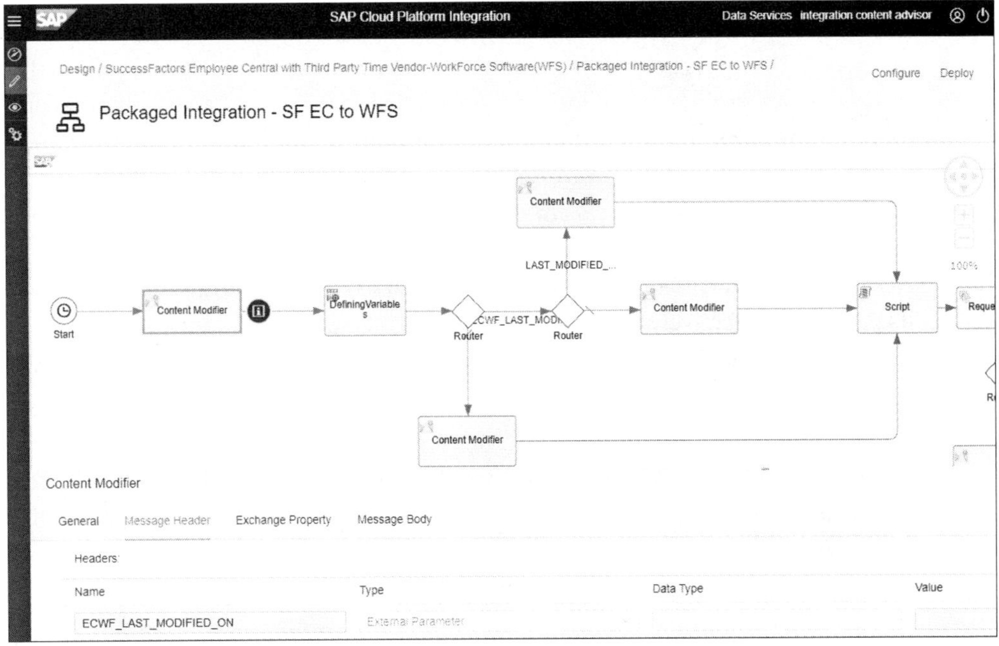

Figure 3.23 Deploying an Integration Flow

3.4 Prepackaged Content Provided by SAP

Let's showcase the Integration Content Catalog's content, which includes integration scenarios of SAP's most commonly used cloud-based applications:

- SAP SuccessFactors
- SAP Cloud for Customer
- SAP Ariba
- SAP C/4HANA
- Content for globalization scenarios

For each one of these categories, we'll explore their content and specify the use case under which the provided content can be leveraged.

3.4.1 Content for SAP SuccessFactors

SAP SuccessFactors is a cloud-based human capital management (HCM) solution that integrates onboarding, social business and collaboration tools, a learning management system (LMS), recruiting software, performance management, succession planning, applicant tracking software, talent management, and HR analytics to deliver business strategy alignment, team execution, and maximum people performance. SAP has another HR product called SAP ERP Human Capital Management (SAP ERP HCM), which provides an integrated set of modules to help an organization manage its people. It's effectively an on-premise HCM product.

Some customers have opted to use a hybrid approach, where SAP ERP HCM (on premise) and SAP SuccessFactors (cloud) work in tandem. In these cases, customers have to decide which part of an end-to-end HCM process runs on which system. One popular approach is to use SAP ERP HCM for core HR processes and use SAP SuccessFactors for one or more talent management processes. It's understood that with such a division of responsibilities between these two HCM systems, integration plays a critical part in linking and synchronizing them.

For illustration purposes, Figure 3.24 depicts a common onboarding process between SAP ERP HCM and SAP SuccessFactors. This process shows a requirement to export an employee's prehire data (information about candidates before they become employees) from SAP ERP HCM to SAP SuccessFactors Onboarding. Moreover, when the process is completed in SAP SuccessFactors Onboarding, you can export the employee data from SAP SuccessFactors Onboarding back to SAP ERP HCM and create employee master data. The complete use case is presented in Figure 3.24.

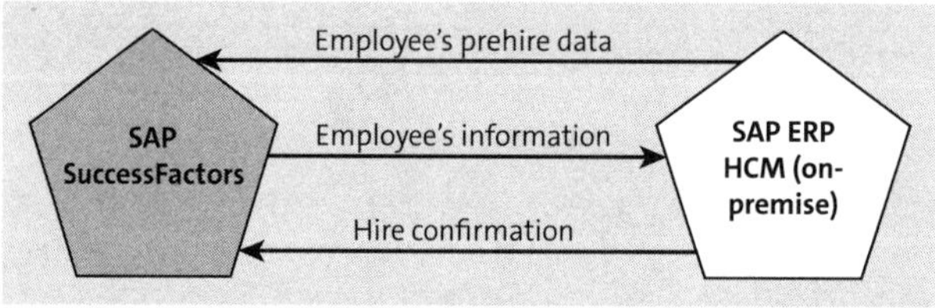

Figure 3.24 Use Case to Integrate SAP SuccessFactors Onboarding and SAP ERP HCM

By integrating and combining the functionalities of these two platforms, the customer can achieve a better end-to-end process result. The Integration Content Catalog provides a variety of packages to cover different integration scenarios, including for the use case presented in Figure 3.24. Refer to the Integration Content Catalog for the most up-to-date list of SAP SuccessFactors-related packages.

To discover all packages that relate to SAP SuccessFactors, you need to apply a filter on the main page of the Integration Content Catalog by selecting any entry with the word **SuccessFactors** as the value of the **Products** dropdown list. This filtering exercise is depicted in Figure 3.25.

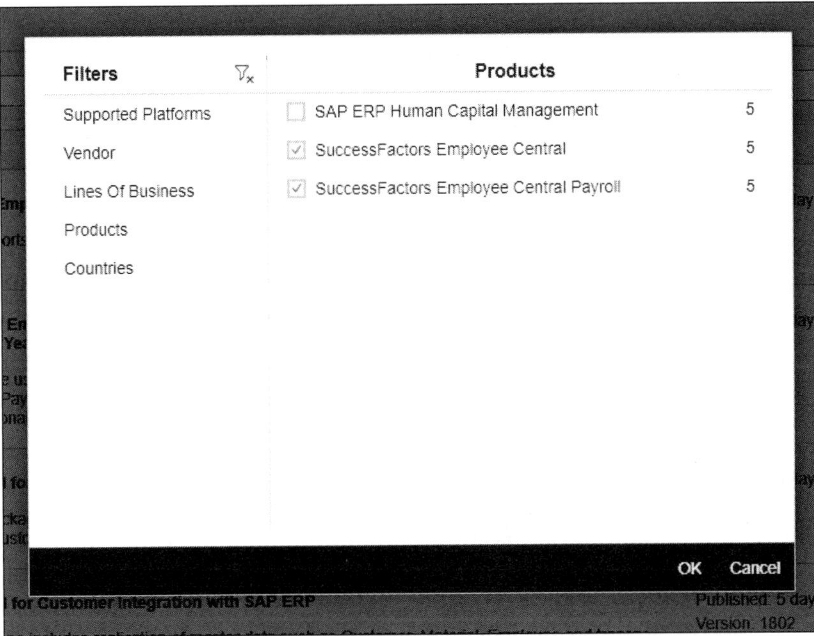

Figure 3.25 Filtering SAP SuccessFactors Packages

Most packages are self-explanatory based on their names. In addition, you can further explore and consume their content as already discussed in Section 3.2.

> **SAP SuccessFactors Adapter**
>
> Most of the integration flows included in this package make use of the SAP SuccessFactors adapter for SAP Cloud Platform Integration. This is a special adapter that has been developed to connect solely to SAP SuccessFactors applications. Refer to Chapter 1, Section 1.3.3, to read more about the SAP Cloud Platform Integration connectivity options.

3.4.2 Content for SAP Cloud for Customer

SAP Cloud for Customer is SAP's cloud customer relationship management (CRM) solution, which brings marketing, sales, commerce, and customer service together.

As a cloud-based CRM system, SAP Cloud for Customer needs to interact with a number of other systems to ensure that information such as accounts, materials, price conditions, and other master data are in sync.

Currently, the Integration Content Catalog provides three main content packages related to SAP Cloud for Customer. These packages include content that supports the following use cases:

- SAP Cloud for Customer integration with SAP ERP
- SAP Cloud for Customer integration with SAP CRM
- SAP Cloud for Customer integration with SAP Marketing Cloud

To further illustrate how the integration packages for SAP Cloud for Customer can be used, let's dig a bit deeper into the use case of integrating SAP Cloud for Customer with SAP ERP.

SAP Cloud for Customer Integration with SAP ERP

As stated in the previous section, SAP Cloud for Customer needs to exchange master and transactional data with SAP ERP. In terms of master data, in most use cases, SAP ERP acts as the master system. This means that master data is synchronized one-way, from SAP ERP to SAP Cloud for Customer. In addition, transactional data, such as opportunity, pricing, and quotes, is also exchanged between these platforms. An overview of the data exchanged between these two systems is depicted in Figure 3.26.

Through the Integration Content Catalog, SAP provides the needed integration flows to synchronize your on-premise SAP ERP and SAP Cloud for Customer systems. The integration flows cover the scope of business objects presented in Figure 3.26.

SOAP Adapter

From a technical perspective, the SOAP adapter is used to integrate SAP Cloud Platform Integration and SAP Cloud for Customer. The consumer of the integration package needs to perform configuration tasks in the **Adapter Specific** tab of the concerned integration flow, as explained in Section 3.3.3. Refer to Chapter 1, Section 1.3.3, to read more about SAP Cloud Platform Integration connectivity options.

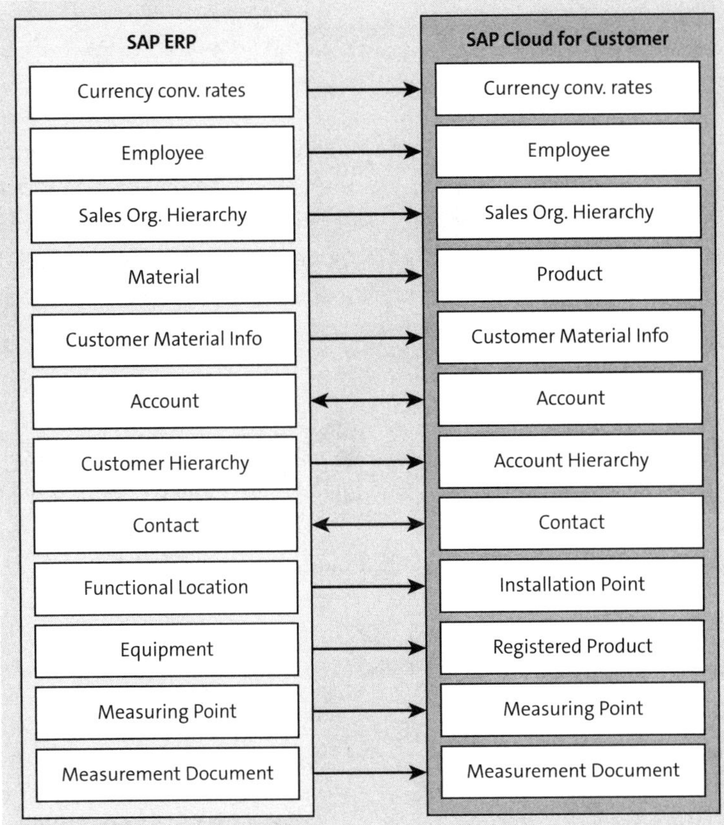

Figure 3.26 Master Data Synchronization between SAP Cloud for Customer and SAP ERP

To discover SAP Cloud for Customer-related integration packages, you need to apply a filter on the main page of the Integration Content Catalog by selecting the **SAP Hybris Cloud for Customer** entry from the **Product** dropdown list.

3.4.3 Content for Integrating with SAP C/4HANA

SAP C/4HANA is a family of cloud-based solutions that includes the following different products:

- SAP Commerce Cloud
- SAP Customer Data Cloud

- SAP Sales Cloud
- SAP Service Cloud
- SAP Marketing Cloud

In the preceding list of products, SAP Sales Cloud and SAP Service Cloud are included under the code name SAP Cloud for Customer. The integration content for SAP Cloud for Customer was already covered in Section 3.4.2. In the coming sections, we'll explore the content provided for SAP Commerce Cloud, SAP Marketing Cloud, SAP Subscription Billing, and SAP Billing and Revenue Innovation Management (formerly SAP Hybris Revenue and SAP Hybris Billing).

> **Note**
>
> For the most updated information of the current integration packages for SAP Commerce Cloud, SAP Subscription Billing or SAP Billing and Revenue Innovation Management, and SAP Marketing Cloud, refer to the **Documents** tab within each package. It generally contains integration guides and various informative documents. You can also refer to the SAP Community for more information. Please note that while the billing and revenue functionality was part of the old SAP Hybris suite, it is not part of the new SAP C/4HANA suite.

SAP Commerce Cloud

The integration content for SAP Commerce Cloud/SAP Cloud for Customer provides the possibility to do the following:

- Synchronize customer data from SAP Commerce Cloud to SAP Cloud for Customer.
- Synchronize customer service ticket data between the two systems to more efficiently connect customers with service or sales agents.

After SAP Commerce Cloud and SAP Cloud for Customer are connected, agents can provide service through the ticket or directly over the phone, all while accessing the same singular storefront as the customer, through the Assisted Service Module for SAP Commerce Cloud for exceptional service and sales assistance on the spot.

At the time of publishing this book, the integration package "SAP Customer Engagement Center Integration with SAP Commerce" is an example package used to synchronize data between SAP Commerce Cloud and SAP Customer Engagement Center integration. To illustrate common use cases, here are the business objects exchanged:

- Customer address replication from SAP Commerce Cloud to SAP Customer Engagement Center
- Customer replication from SAP Commerce Cloud to SAP Customer Engagement Center
- Basic sales order details replication from SAP Commerce Cloud to SAP Customer Engagement Center for indexing

SAP Subscription Billing and SAP Billing and Revenue Innovation Management

At the time of publishing this book, the integration package "Integration with SAP Subscription Billing" is an example package used to provide the capabilities to process bills originating from the SAP Subscription Billing in SAP S/4HANA for billing and revenue innovation management. Common use cases are listed here:

- Extract billing documents from SAP Subscription Billing to SAP S/4HANA.
- Send back Customer IDs from SAP S/4HANA to SAP Subscription Billing when customers are created or updated.
- Extract customers from SAP Subscription Billing and then replicate to SAP S/4HANA.
- Replicate customers from SAP S/4HANA to SAP Subscription Billing.

SAP Marketing Cloud

At the time of publishing this book, the available integration content covers many integration scenarios for SAP Marketing Cloud:

- **Master data and basic replication**
  The accounts, contacts, individual customers, leads activities, and opportunities are replicated from SAP Cloud for Customer to SAP Marketing Cloud.
- **Call center scenario**
  This scenario creates a call center campaign in SAP Marketing Cloud and executes the campaign in SAP Cloud for Customer.
- **Lead management scenario**
  Any lead that is converted into an opportunity further creates an opportunity interaction in SAP Marketing Cloud. These leads and opportunities in SAP Cloud for Customer also contain information about the corresponding campaigns from SAP Marketing Cloud.

Furthermore, several integration packages cover a number of use cases with SAP Marketing:

- SAP S/4HANA Enterprise Management on-premise – SAP Marketing Cloud integration
- SAP Marketing Cloud – SAP Customer Relationship Management (SAP CRM) integration
- SAP Cloud for Customer – SAP Marketing integration
- SAP Marketing Cloud – SAP Customer Attribution integration
- SAP Marketing Cloud – SAP ERP order and business partner integration
- SAP Marketing Cloud – Twitter integration
- SAP Marketing Cloud – Content Management System integration
- SAP Marketing – Google AdWords Paid Search integration
- SAP Marketing Cloud – Twitter integration admin
- SAP Marketing Cloud – Facebook integration admin
- SAP Marketing Cloud – Facebook integration
- SAP Marketing – Google Analytics integration

3.4.4 Content for Integrating with the Ariba Network

The Ariba Network is a cloud-based procurement solution that allows you to locate new suppliers, streamline transaction processes, and save costs. It's one of the largest trading partner communities that provides connectivity and online services to organizations engaged in business-to-business e-commerce.

With the Ariba Network, buyers and suppliers can do business with each other over the Internet and access each other's services. It contains additional functionality such as directory services, reporting tools, supplier tools, payment, and sourcing.

To illustrate a common use case, customers can create purchase orders, goods receipts, invoices, and so on, from the Ariba Network and have them synchronized back to their own (on-premise) SAP Business Suite operational purchasing or supplier-side processes. An overview of these common use cases between SAP ERP Materials Management (SAP MM) and SAP Supplier Relationship Management (SAP SRM) is depicted in Figure 3.27.

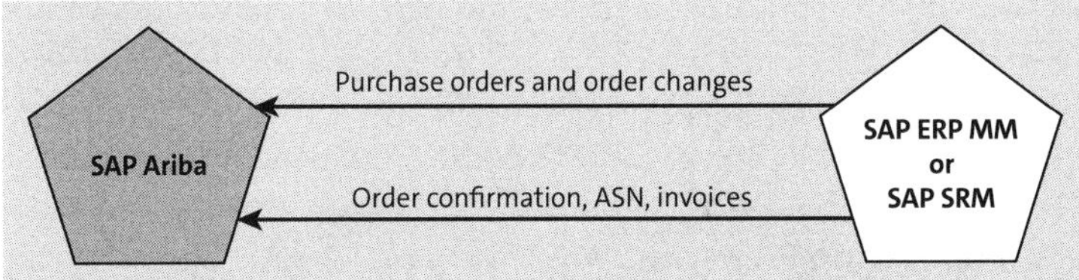

Figure 3.27 Integration Use Cases between SAP Ariba and SAP ERP or SAP SRM

Currently, one package is available to cover the need for integrating the Ariba Network with your existing SAP ERP using SAP Cloud Platform Integration. This content package integrates and automates your SAP Business Suite operational purchasing processes or supplier-side processes with the Ariba Network.

For buyers, the scope of this mediated connection based on the Ariba Network integration for SAP Business Suite Add-On 1.0 includes the following:

- Purchase order and invoice automation for MM and SAP SRM classic
- Discount management integration (optional)

The scope supports selected aspects of the following procure-to-pay end-to-end business scenarios:

- Self-service and indirect procurement
- Direct procurement
- Service procurement
- Invoice management
- Collaborative Supply Chain 1.0 with schedule agreement release order processing

For suppliers, the scope of this mediated connection, based on the Ariba Network integration with SAP Business Suite Add-On 1.0, includes the following:

- Sales order and billing integration with the Ariba Network for SAP ERP Sales and Distribution (SAP SD)

Notes

From a technical perspective, the SOAP adapter is used to integrate SAP Cloud Platform Integration with SAP Ariba. The consumer of the integration package needs to perform configuration tasks in the **Adapter Specific** tab of the concerned integration flow, as already explained in Section 3.3.3. Please refer to Chapter 1, Section 1.3.3, to read more about the SAP Cloud Platform Integration connectivity options.

To discover SAP Ariba-related integration packages, you need to apply a filter on the main page of the Integration Content Catalog by selecting the **Ariba Network with SAP Business Suite** entry from the **Product** dropdown list.

3.4.5 Content for Globalization Scenarios

Recently, many government agencies have been moving from traditional paper-based documents to digital or electronic documents. As such, businesses dealing with these government agencies (e.g., the tax office) must quickly adapt their internal processes to comply.

For multinational companies having, for instance, to report their taxes in many countries, this can be a challenge because documents need to be sent to the tax offices of different countries with different formats and standards from the same source application (SAP ERP system). Another aspect to consider is that, in most cases, the transmission of these government-related documents requires a high level of security.

The mapping of the source application's messages to the required government formats and the transmission thereof is a classic integration scenario. The need to transfer electronic documents to government agencies around the world is a use case SAP Cloud Platform Integration covers with its integration content for globalization. This content is also known as the eDocument Framework.

The eDocument Framework provides a generic approach to create, process, and manage electronic documents. The framework supports handling country-specific requirements for electronic documents with regard to the format of messages, security requirements, and processing steps in end-to-end integration scenarios. The source data for the documents may originate in any application that implements the web services available in the integration flows. At the time of this book's publication, a number of integration packages are provided in SAP Cloud Platform Integration to support eDocument for Chile, Italy, Spain, Peru, The Netherlands, Great Britain, Colombia, Germany, India, Mexico, United States, and Hungary.

With these packages, customers don't need to spend time trying to figure out how to perform mappings or find out which security levels are required to comply with these government electronic document formats. The customer can simply reuse the provided integration content and reduce implementation time and costs.

To discover a particular eDocument package for a specific country, you need to apply a filter on the main page of the Integration Content Catalog by selecting a country (e.g., **Netherlands**) from the **Country** dropdown list.

In this section, you learned about the prepackaged content delivered by SAP in the Integration Content Catalog. In the next section, we'll cover how to create your own content.

3.5 Creating Your Own Content Package

There might be cases when existing prepackaged content doesn't meet your business needs, and you would like to create a package that can be used and reused specifically by team members within your organization. In such a case, you may consider creating your own content package.

The first step of publishing your own content is to create the desired integration content. The process of creating your own content has been discussed when creating your first integration flow in Chapter 2. Furthermore, Chapter 4 will walk you through the process of creating different integration content artifacts. Therefore, we won't go into the development details here.

To create an integration package, follow these steps:

1. Open the **Design** menu item (refer to Figure 3.8).
2. Select the **Create** option to create an integration package, (see Figure 3.28).

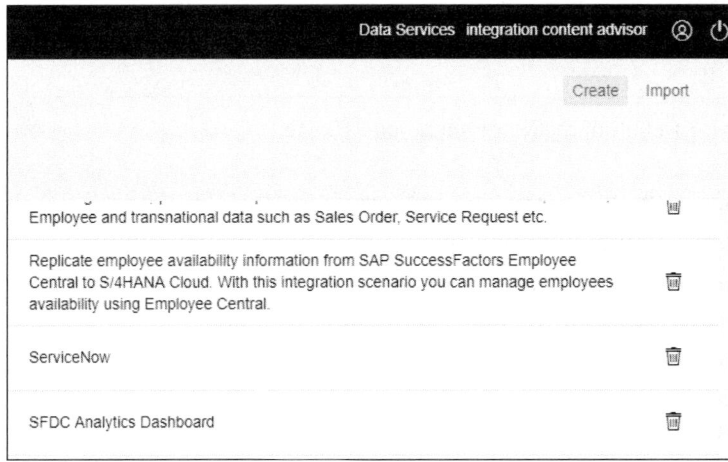

Figure 3.28 Creating an Integration Package

3. On the next screen, specify the name of the new integration package. Additional metadata details, such as the version, owner, mode, description, tags, products, industries, line of businesses, country, and keywords, can be provided. Some of this metadata is shown in Figure 3.29. You can maintain of these metadata details in tabs such as **Overview** and **Tags**. Bear in mind that this metadata is important to better classify content and allow consumers to find it easily. It's therefore important to provide as much detail as possible.

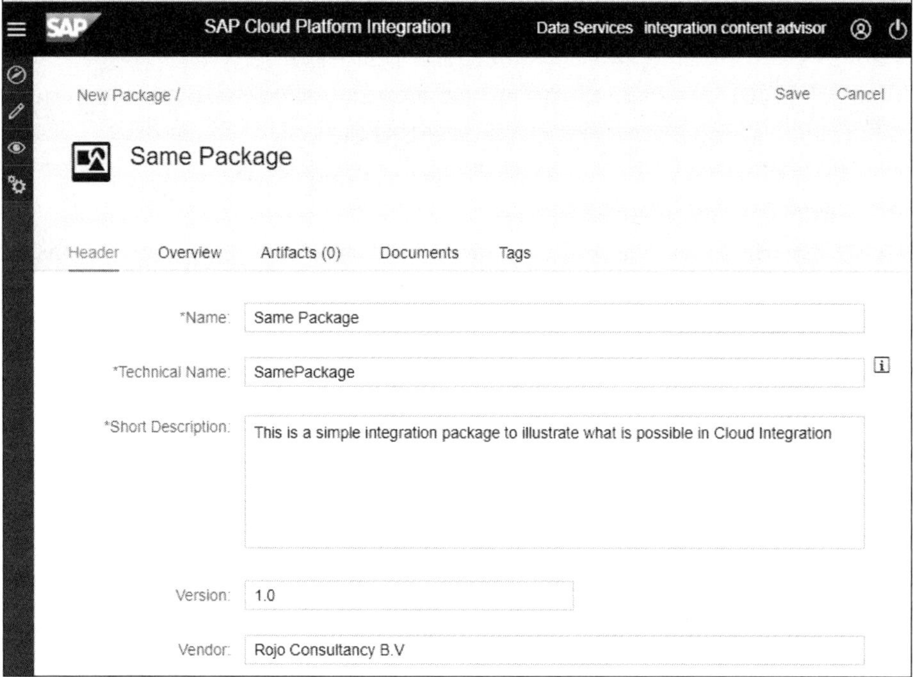

Figure 3.29 Specifying Details of the New Integration Package

4. Save the package using the **Save** button, as shown in Figure 3.29.
5. On the **Artifacts** tab, click **Add**, and choose an artifact of type **Data Integration**, **Process Integration**, **OData Service**, or **Value Mapping** to add it to the integration package (Figure 3.30).
6. Artifacts can be added to the newly created package by creating them from scratch if they don't already exist. Alternatively, the artifacts can also be imported if they already exist. These two options are made possible using the **Create** or **Upload** radio buttons, as shown in Figure 3.31.

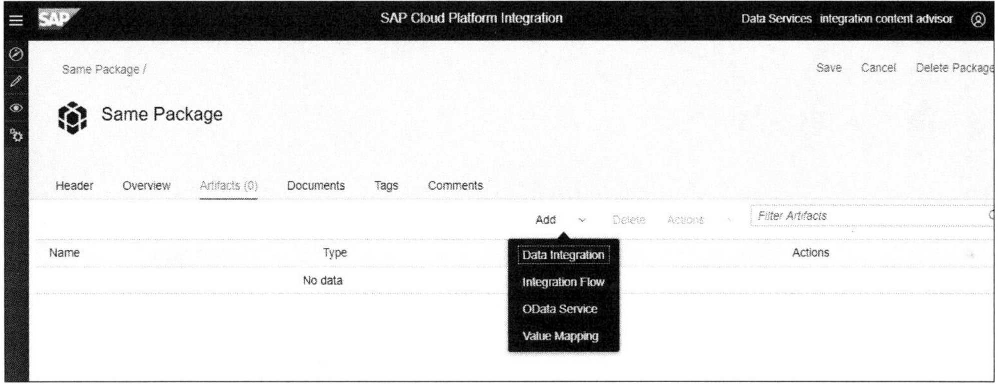

Figure 3.30 Adding Artifacts to an Integration Package

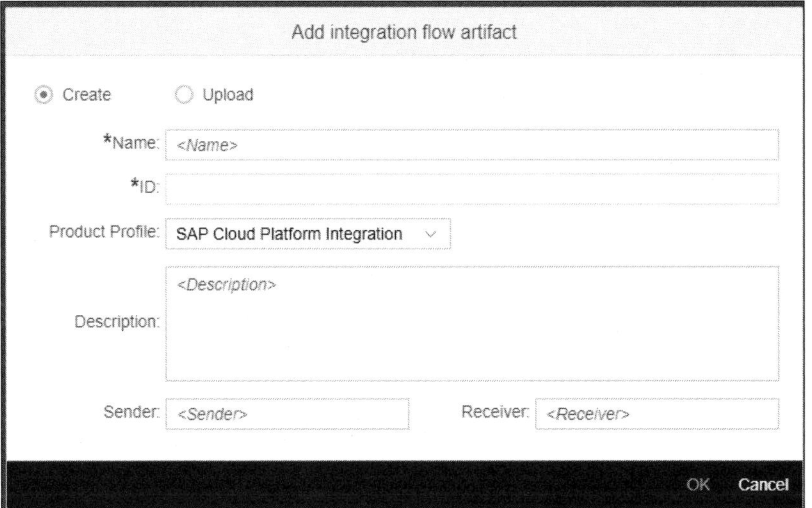

Figure 3.31 Creating or Importing a Process Integration Artifact

7. To provide documentation for the integration package, click on **Add** in the **Documents** tab, as shown in Figure 3.32. Documents of type **File** or **URL** can be added to this tab.

After packaging and saving the integration content, it becomes available in your own design space and can therefore be used by team members of your organization.

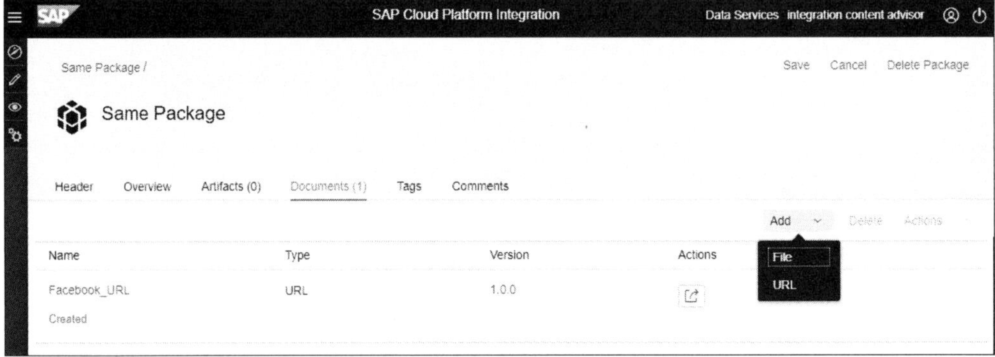

Figure 3.32 Adding a File or URL to a Content Package

> **Notes**
>
> A content package is automatically locked against modification from other users when someone is in the process of editing it. The package lock is only released for modification after it has been saved. If the session times out, or the browser closes while you're still working on your integration package, it remains locked until it's saved, canceled, or deleted by the lock owner.

Currently, only SAP is allowed to publish data to the Integration Content Catalog, so packages created by customers or partners are for their use only and can't be directly leveraged by other customers. Different SAP Partners have listed their prepackaged integration content on the Integration Content Catalog, but you'll need to contact the SAP Partners to purchase and obtain an archive of the package.

3.6 Summary

This chapter introduced you to the capabilities and features of the Integration Content Catalog in SAP Cloud Platform Integration. A systematic guide was used to demonstrate how to consume the contents of the catalog. You've also learned about the terms and conditions that can affect and restrict the way prepackaged content is consumed.

The chapter then explored the prepackaged content that SAP delivers in the Integration Content Catalog to speed up implementation time and save costs related to performing integration with the most-used SAP cloud-based applications. The Integration Content Catalog is expected to grow and see new packages added to it on a regular basis. It's therefore recommended that you first check the catalog before developing your integration scenarios from scratch.

In the next chapter, we'll further explore how SAP Cloud Platform Integration empowers developers to create their own basic integrations when prepackaged content won't suffice.

Chapter 4
Basic Integration Scenarios

If prepackaged integration content won't suffice, developers can use SAP Cloud Platform Integration to create their own integrations. This chapter explores these capabilities by taking a closer look at concrete integration challenges and how to solve them.

In the previous chapter, you learned how to configure prepackaged integration content. However, in many cases, you have individual integration needs that simply can't be fulfilled by an already existing package or that require too much effort to adjust a delivered scenario to the required functionality. Fortunately, SAP Cloud Platform Integration comes with a web-based development environment that allows you to model unique scenarios from scratch. We'll explore the options you have at your disposal in this chapter, followed by three more chapters drilling into topics that are more specialized. In this chapter, we'll take a close look at SAP Cloud Platform Integration's data model, how content enrichment works by invoking an OData service, and how to add mappings to an integration flow.

4.1 Working with SAP Cloud Platform Integration's Data Model

Before we dive into the details of a concrete modeling exercise, let's briefly discuss some terms and fundamental concepts of SAP Cloud Platform Integration's development and runtime environment. Figure 4.1 depicts a basic integration flow in SAP Cloud Platform Integration's web environment, showing the transfer of a message from a sender to a receiver via SAP Cloud Platform Integration.

The overall representation of integration flows is based on Business Process Model and Notation (BPMN), a widely adopted Object Management Group (OMG) standard for graphically depicting processes. Although the roots of BPMN are in the business process domain (as the name indicates), it's expressive enough to be useful for integration processes, as well. Hence, SAP decided to rely on BPMN as the lingua franca for all kinds of processes. BPMN is broadly used in SAP systems—for example, in SAP

Solution Manager, SAP Process Integration, and SAP Business Process Management (SAP BPM), to name a few.

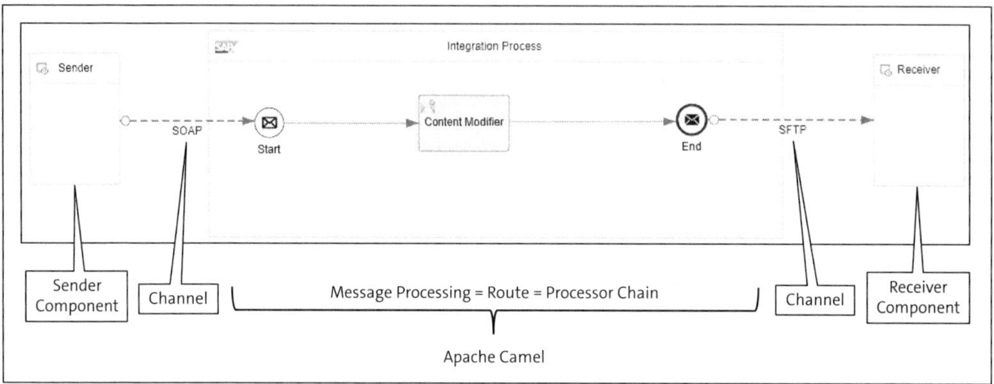

Figure 4.1 A Basic Integration Flow

On the left side of Figure 4.1, you can identify the sender component representing the sender of a message. The receiver is depicted on the far right. Both sender and receiver are represented by pools (the rectangles headlined with **Sender** and **Receiver**, respectively). A *pool* is a term taken from the BPMN standard and typically stands for a participant in collaborative scenarios in which several processes work together to fulfill a certain goal. A third pool, entitled **Integration Process**, shown in the middle of Figure 4.1, represents the SAP Cloud Platform Integration server where message processing actually happens.

The **Sender/Receiver** pools are connected via dashed arrows, or message flows, representing the technical connectivity between the respective participants. A dedicated label details how the two are connected: the sender and the integration flow via the Simple Object Access Protocol (SOAP) and the integration flow with the receiver via SSH File Transfer Protocol (SFTP). Dedicated channels take over the responsibility of implementing and speaking the respective protocols.

What's left is the integration flow in the middle, which contains details about the message processing steps. The circle on the left of the flow containing a white envelope is a *start event* (again, BPMN nomenclature). It expresses the start of the message processing sequence. The envelope indicates the start of the process caused by the reception of a message. After the flow has received the message, it continues with the content modifier step because they are connected with a directed solid arrow, also known as a *sequence flow*. The arrow indicates in which sequence steps are executed.

The rounded rectangle step is called a *task*, and indicates an activity that is executed during runtime. In our example, the content modifier changes the message content, as you'll see later in this chapter. After the task has finished its modifications, the process continues downstream. Again, just follow the sequence flow to the circle on the right, which contains a black envelope and represents an *end event* (circles in general stand for events in BPMN).

Black symbols and white symbols in events have a special meaning: white means waiting for the event to happen, and black means that the process itself initiates the event specified by the symbol inside the circle and immediately continues. In this example, the process waits for an incoming message at the beginning (white envelope) and sends a message after the process has reached the end of the flow (black envelope). The sent message is then transported via SFTP to the receiver. This is expressed by the message flow from the end event to the **Receiver** pool in Figure 4.1.

4.1.1 Message Processing: The Apache Camel Framework

Let's concentrate on the message processing part of SAP Cloud Platform Integration for a moment. As you now know, from a modeling perspective, the flow is based on BPMN. But how is the integration flow interpreted and executed during runtime? For this purpose, SAP Cloud Platform Integration relies on an open-source integration framework called Apache Camel (or Camel for short). To understand the inner workings of SAP Cloud Platform Integration, you should be familiar with the inner workings of Camel. That's why you find additional names for message processing in Figure 4.1, because, in Camel, the respective terms for the handling of messages are *route* or *processor chain*. It doesn't make sense to discuss the complete Camel framework in a chapter like this. We only concentrate on Camel's functions and features that are relevant for the respective scenario we're going to discuss. However, Claus Ibsen and Jonathan Anstey have written an excellent book about Camel called *Camel in Action* (Manning Publications Co., 2010). This book is a helpful reference for all detailed Camel questions you might have. Another valuable source of information for the Camel framework is the online documentation, found at *http://camel.apache.org/documentation.html.*

Note

Be aware that you can't just use any Camel feature, property, or header in SAP Cloud Platform Integration. You should only use the features, properties, and headers that are explicitly supported by SAP Cloud Platform Integration. Please refer to the SAP documentation found at *https://help.sap.com/viewer/product/CLOUD_INTEGRATION/Cloud.*

So, what exactly is Camel? It's a message routing and mediation engine. Interestingly enough, Camel is payload-agnostic, which means you can feed the engine with any data format, and Camel forwards it to the respective receivers depending on the modeled route. As long as there is no need to access the message's content (e.g., for routing purposes), Camel can handle any message format. However, some basic structure must also be available in Camel, as depicted in Figure 4.2.

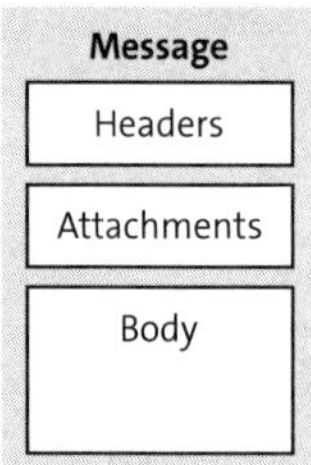

Figure 4.2 Camel's Message Model

Camel messages consist of headers, a body containing the raw data (the payload), and (optional) attachments. Messages are uniquely identified by an identifier of the type `java.lang.String` (not shown in Figure 4.2). The headers are additional values associated with the message, such as sender identifier, hints about content encoding, and authentication information. This information is added as headers in the form of name-value pairs. The name is a unique, case-insensitive string, whereas the value is of the type `java.lang.Object`. This is quite interesting, as almost anything can be added as an object to the header. The same is applicable for the body, which is also of the type `java.lang.Object`. Attachments are typically used for web service and email components and can transport additional data as separated items, if necessary.

During message processing, Camel requires a dedicated container for the message. The container is called an *exchange*, and it holds additional data besides the message. The exchange is passed along, step by step, in the processor chain, and every step has access to all the information the exchange carries. It can be seen as a global storage for the route as long as the message is being processed. The structure of the exchange is shown in Figure 4.3.

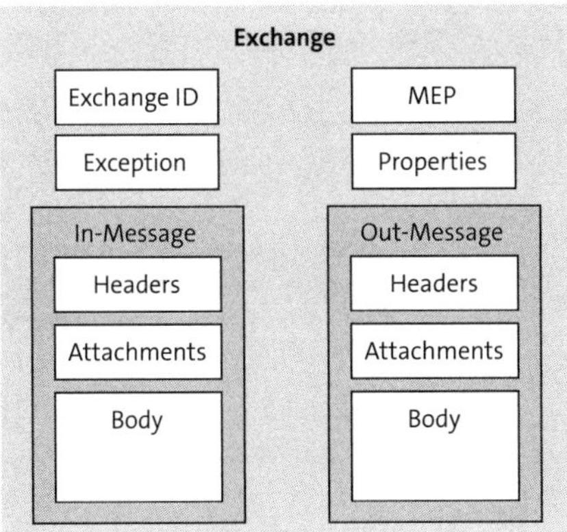

Figure 4.3 An Exchange

Let's briefly go over the parts that make up an exchange:

- **Exchange ID**
  A unique ID that identifies the exchange.
- **MEP**
  Short for message exchange pattern, field can contain two possible values: **InOnly** and **InOut**.
  - **InOnly**: The route handles a one-way message, where the sender doesn't wait for a reply from the receiver. Hence, the exchange carries an *in* message *only*. A scenario where a message travels in one direction only and where no response message is expected during the communication is also known as *asynchronous message handling*.
  - **InOut**: The route handles a request-response message. The sender expects a reply from the route, which will be stored as an out-message in the exchange. This behavior is also known as *synchronous message handling*. We'll revisit asynchronous and synchronous message handling in Chapter 5, Section 5.3.
- **Exception**
  If an error occurs during message processing, the reason for the error is stored in the **Exception** field of the exchange.
- **Properties**
  A form of temporary storage where process steps can store data in addition to the header area in the message. Properties can contain global-level information. Developers can store and retrieve properties at any point during the lifetime of an exchange.

Difference between Headers and Properties

Note that headers are part of a message and are propagated or transferred to a receiver. On the other side, properties last for the entire duration of an exchange but aren't transferred to a receiver.

A big difference regarding message handling within SAP Cloud Platform Integration, as compared to SAP Process Integration, is the flexible pipeline concept that stands behind Camel. In SAP Process Integration, you basically have three fundamental steps:

1. Receiver determination
2. Interface determination
3. Mapping

In addition, the sequence of these three steps is fixed. It's not possible to have, for example, a mapping step before an interface determination step. The result is a rather static message-processing environment. With SAP Cloud Platform Integration, this changes significantly. You have many more steps at your disposal, and you can use them in (almost) any sequence that your scenario requires. We'll demonstrate the benefits of this flexibility in later chapters when we address more complex integration scenarios.

Notice that we've also shown already in Chapter 2, Section 2.1, how the Camel framework fits into the overall architecture of SAP Cloud Platform Integration (also see Figure 2.6 in Chapter 2, Section 2.1.4).

4.1.2 Exercise: Working with Camel's Message Model

Now that you have a basic understanding of the data and message models that are used within Camel and SAP Cloud Platform Integration, let's see how you can benefit from this knowledge during message processing. To demonstrate how to access properties and headers when building a response message and to illustrate the consequences of storing data in the two locations, we'll use a simple scenario. In this example, we take an XML input message and store parts of the message in the properties/header area of the message model. To build the reply, you access the previously stored data from the properties/header areas and construct the response message. Let's get started!

1. We'll first create a new package for our exercise. After you connect to your SAP Cloud Platform Integration tenant with your Internet browser, switch to the **Design** view (Figure 4.4).
2. You'll see a list of available packages. Create a new package by clicking the **Create** button located beneath the package list. The **New** Integration **Package** dialog box opens (see Figure 4.5).

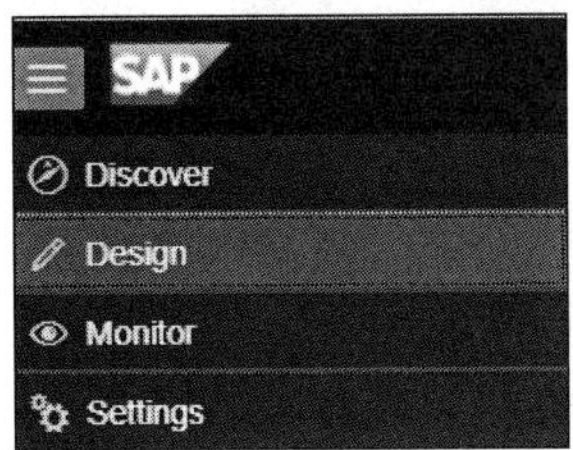

Figure 4.4 Switching to Design View

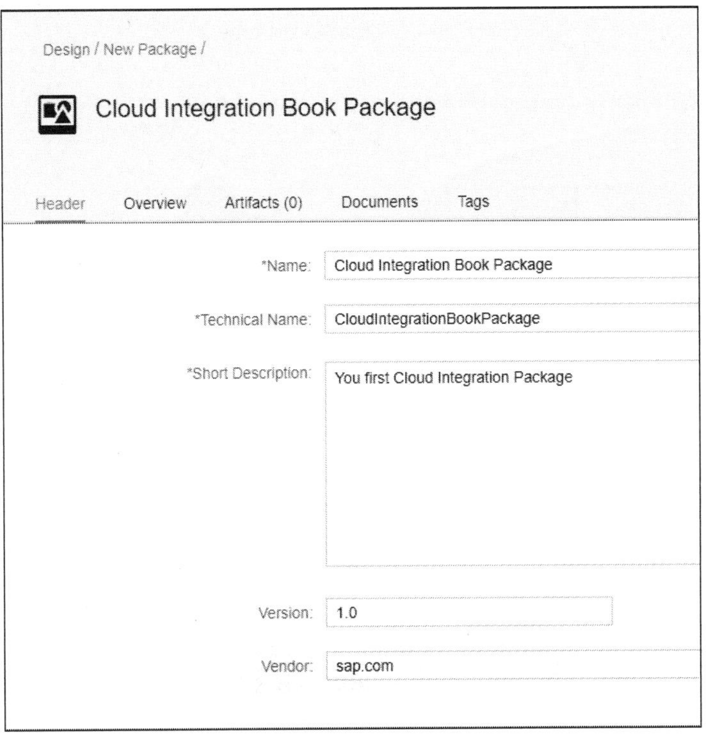

Figure 4.5 Creating a New Integration Package

3. Provide some basic information about the package, such as its name, version, and creator. Save it using the **Save** button.
4. From the resulting page, navigate to the **Artifacts** tab and add an integration flow to your package by choosing **Integration flow** from the **Add** dropdown list (see Figure 4.6).

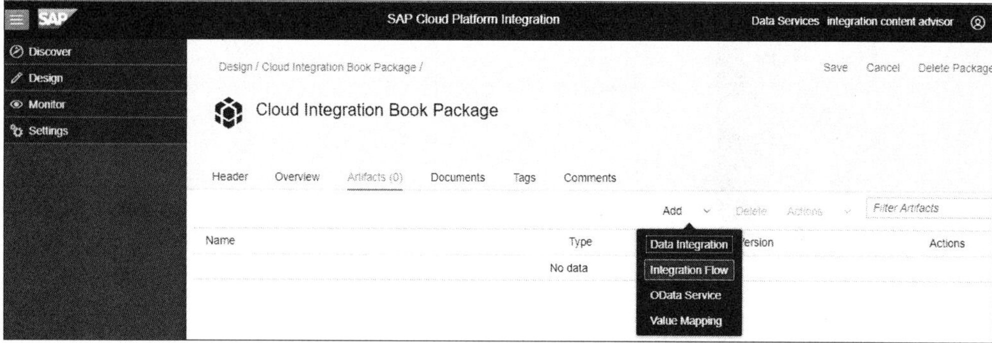

Figure 4.6 Adding an Integration Flow to the Newly Created Package

Another dialog box opens to provide some basic information about the integration flow (Figure 4.7).

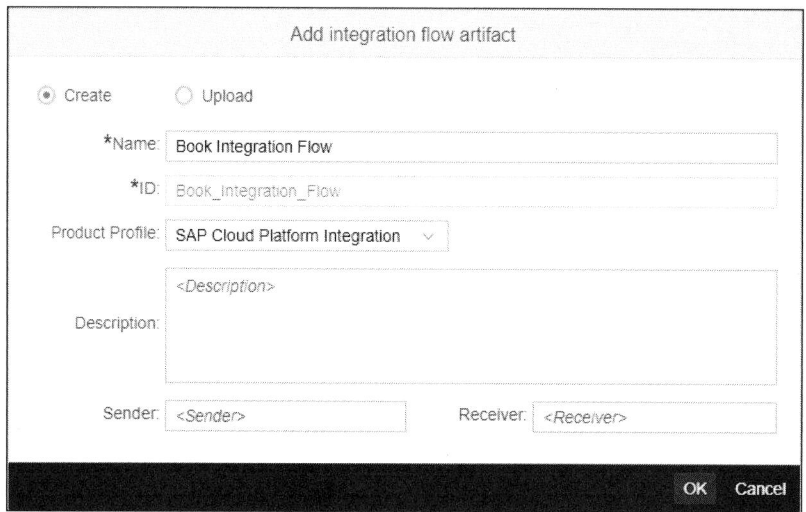

Figure 4.7 Creating an Integration Flow

5. Confirm the new integration flow by clicking the **Ok** button, and then store the new package by clicking on **Save**.
6. You've now created a package and an associated integration flow. Open the integration flow, which should look like the one depicted in Figure 4.8.

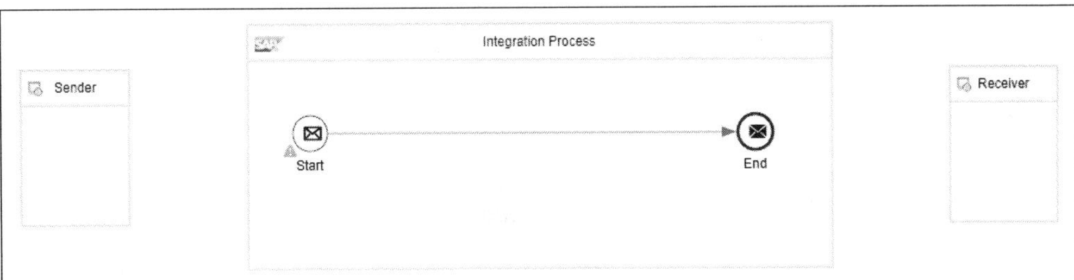

Figure 4.8 The Empty Integration Flow as a Starting Point for the Exercise

4.1.3 Connecting and Configuring a Sender with an Integration Flow

Switch to edit mode (the **Edit** button is in the top-right corner of the integration flow screen), and delete the **Receiver** pool, as we don't need the pool for this exercise. Start modeling the connection between the **Sender** pool on the left and the **Start** event by dragging a connection from the pool to the **Start** event via context buttons. Every time you select a shape in the model, context buttons appear on the right side of the shape to indicate what can be done with the shape at this moment. So, if you select the **Sender** pool, the context buttons shown in Figure 4.9 appear.

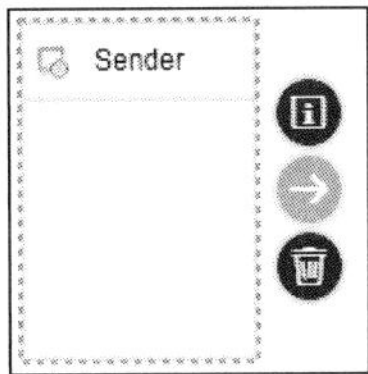

Figure 4.9 Context Buttons Next to the Selected Shape

Next click the connector icon ➔, drag the cursor to the target shape (the **Start** event in that case), and then release the mouse button (drop) (see Figure 4.10).

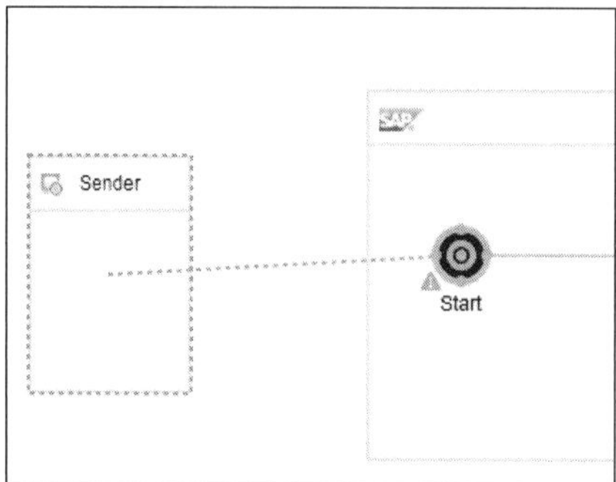

Figure 4.10 Connecting the Sender Pool with the Start Event

After dropping the mouse button on the **Start** event, a dialog box opens automatically that allows you to pick the connection type you want between the **Sender** and the SAP Cloud Platform Integration server. In this case, the connection should be a SOAP adapter and the message protocol SOAP 1.x. Simply pick the respective entries from the dialog boxes.

Finally, you have to maintain one parameter of the SOAP adapter: the address under which the service will be accessible. For this, select the message flow between the **Sender** component and the **Start** event so that it appears in orange (see the dotted line in Figure 4.11).

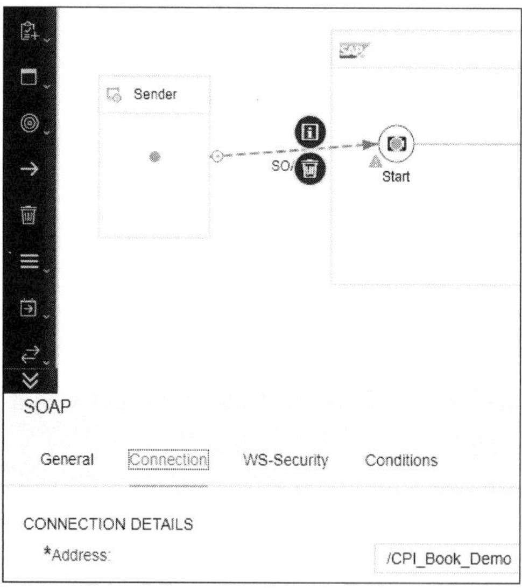

Figure 4.11 Configuration of the SOAP Channel

Beneath the process model, you should see the properties of the connection (in this case, the details of the channel). It's typical for the SAP Cloud Platform Integration modeling environment to select shapes in the graphical model and adjust properties in the area beneath the process model. The properties change depending on the selected component in the main area. In our example, click the **Connection** link and add "/CPI_Book_Demo" as the address in the **Address** field. That's all you have to do to configure the channel.

You also have to define the authentication type for the communication between the sender and the SAP Cloud Platform Integration server. We chose the SOAP adapter for our connection, so the most convenient authentication type is basic authentication, which requires the user's username and password. In SAP Cloud Platform Integration, the User Role authorization can be used either for username and password credentials or with a client certificate. To tell SAP Cloud Platform Integration that this type of authorization should be used, select the message flow between the **Sender** component and the **Start** event, and under the **Connection** tab, choose **User Role** from the **Authorization** dropdown list (see Figure 4.12).

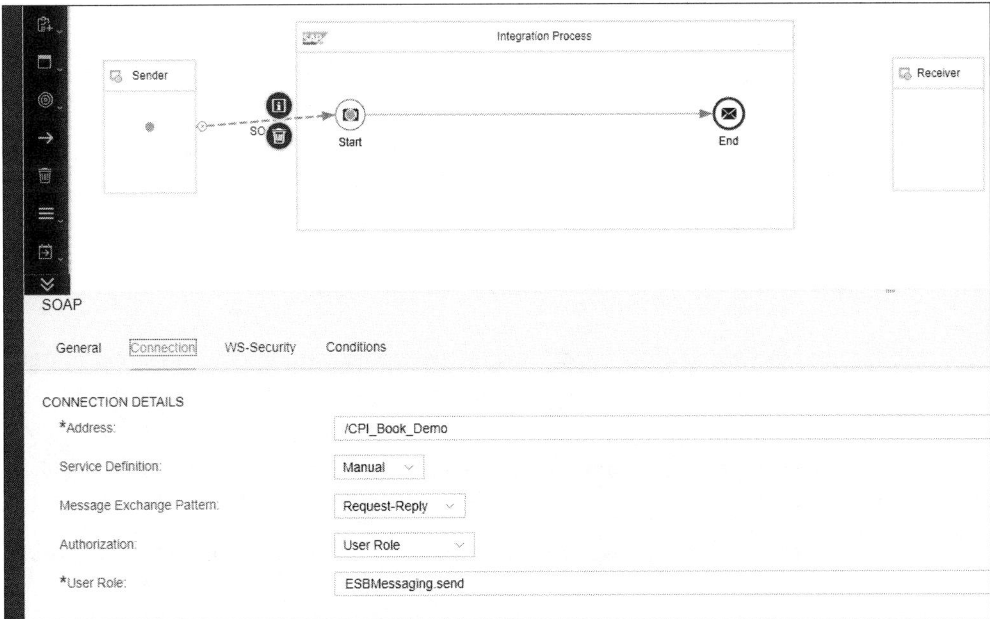

Figure 4.12 Setting the Authentication Type to Basic Authentication

As shown in Figure 4.12, the default value for the user role is **ESBMessaging.send**. This role authorizes a sender system to process messages on a tenant. For now, we'll leave the **Service Definition** and **Message Exchange Pattern** field to their default values.

4.1.4 Adding and Configuring Steps in the Integration Flow

Now, let's add and configure steps in our integration flow. We'll add two **Content Modifier** steps in the model. You can find them in the palette on the left as shown in Figure 4.13.

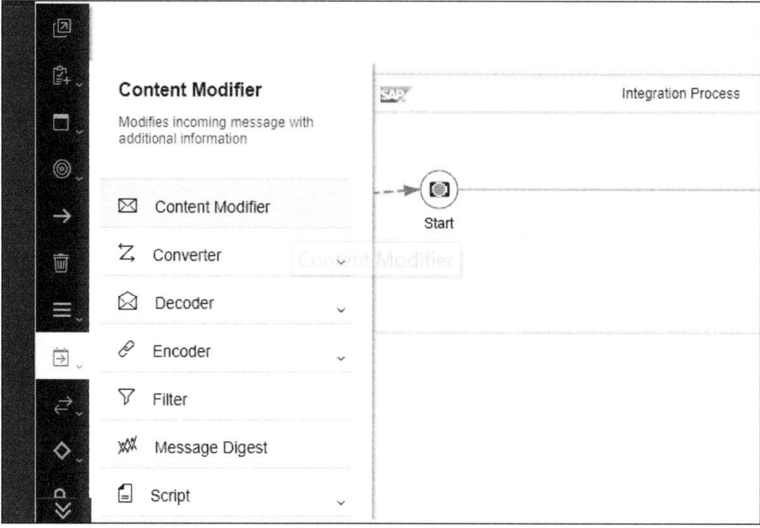

Figure 4.13 Selecting Content Modifier Steps from the Palette

Click the transformer icon in the palette. A submenu opens. Click the **Content Modifier** shape, which is the black envelope, and move the mouse pointer to the **Integration Process** pool. Click again to position the shape in the pool. Repeat the previous steps so that two **Content Modifier** shapes are added to the process model (see Figure 4.14).

Let's configure the first **Content Modifier**. Our goal is to write data with the first **Content Modifier** into the header of the message and into the properties area of the exchange. The second **Content Modifier** step retrieves the previously stored data from the respective locations and creates a new result message. By doing this, you prove that data can be stored in different locations and be available during future steps within the route.

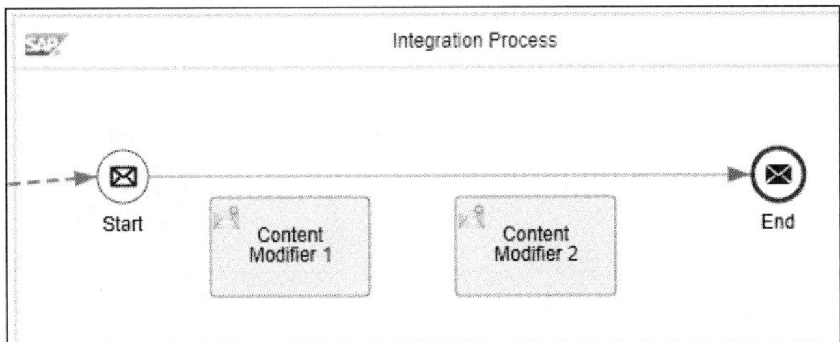

Figure 4.14 Process Model after Adding Two Content Modifier Steps

To retrieve data from the message, it must be clear what the incoming message looks like. We've defined the message structure used in this example for you, using a simple Web Services Description Language (WSDL) document called *GetOrderShipDetails_Sync.wsdl*. You can download the WSDL file from *www.sap-press.com/4650*. An example message following the WSDL's structure is depicted in Figure 4.15.

```
<soapenv:Envelope xmlns:soapenv="http://s
   <soapenv:Header/>
   <soapenv:Body>
      <demo:OrderNumber_MT>
         <orderNumber>10249</orderNumber>
      </demo:OrderNumber_MT>
   </soapenv:Body>
</soapenv:Envelope>
```

Figure 4.15 Example Message

Our first **Content Modifier** should retrieve the order number from the message and store it in the header of the message. In addition, it should take the complete message's body (the part between the Body tags in Figure 4.15) and store it in the properties area. By doing this, we demonstrate two important features:

- Single fields can be accessed, selectively retrieved, and stored in the header area.
- Complete complex structures, such as complete messages, can be retrieved and stored as properties.

Select the left **Content Modifier** by clicking it once so that its properties can be configured. Note that the configuration parameters of the **Content Modifier** distinguish between three locations: **Message Header**, **Message Body**, and **Exchange Property** (Figure 4.16).

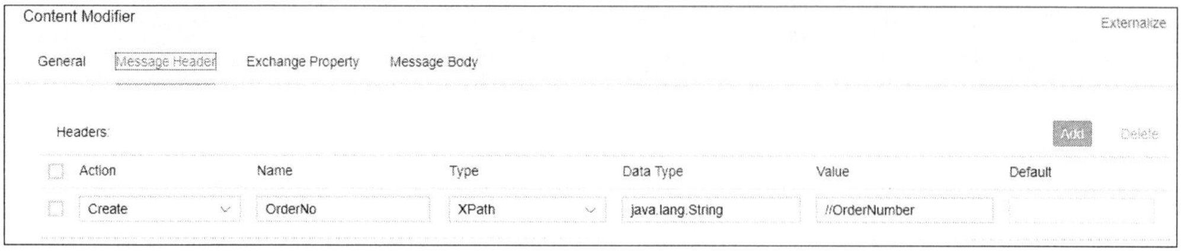

Content Modifier

Externalize

General | Message Header | Exchange Property | Message Body

Headers: Add Delete

Action	Name	Type	Data Type	Value	Default
Create	OrderNo	XPath	java.lang.String	//OrderNumber	

Figure 4.16 Writing Data into the Message's Header Area

The first **Content Modifier** uses the **Message Header** and the **Exchange Property** areas to write the data. The second **Content Modifier** uses the **Message Body** to create the response message. By selecting the appropriate link shown at the top of Figure 4.16, you always select the location where data is being stored. Figure 4.16 shows the correct configuration of the **Content Modifier** for writing data into the message's header.

Select the **Message Header** link in the top row. Continue by clicking the **Add** button to create a new row in the table underneath. Next, define the name under which the data should be stored in the message header. In our example, the name is (`OrderNo`). You can later access the value by using this exact name.

You now have to tell the integration engine how to access the value in the message and the type of data to retrieve. We chose **XPath** from the dropdown list, as we want to navigate inside an XML document, and **XPath** is the way to go to retrieve data from an XML document. The XPath expression is simply `//orderNumber`, as this is the information we're interested in, and the retrieved value is of type `String`. Here, a valid Java data type needs to be assigned—hence, the entry `java.lang.String`. That is all you need to do to store the order number in the message's header.

Figure 4.17 shows the configuration of the first **Content Modifier** for writing the complete body of the message into the property area of the exchange. As you can see, it's possible to have two (or more) write operations configured in a single **Content Modifier** step.

To achieve the result shown in Figure 4.17, click the **Exchange Property** link in the top row. Add a new row in the **Properties** table. The message will be stored under the name (`msg`) in the exchange's property area. This time, we want to store the complete message. Therefore, we aren't accessing a single field but the whole body. For this purpose, Camel provides the Simple Expression Language, which includes predefined variables as shortcuts that allow convenient access to certain parts of a message.

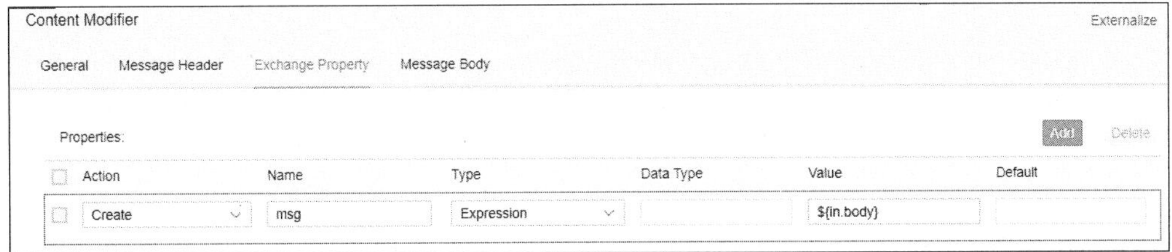

Figure 4.17 Writing Data into the Exchange's Property Area

In our case, we want to access the body of the incoming original message. The Camel variable to do so is `in.body` (as shown in Figure 4.17). The syntax requires the dollar sign and the curly brackets to actually access the variable's content. In the **Content Modifier** screen, choose **Expression** from the **Type** dropdown list, and add "${in.body}" to the **Value** field.

With that, you've completed the configuration of the first **Content Modifier**. If you want to learn more about Camel's expression language, we recommend checking out the Simple Expression Language documentation at *http://camel.apache.org/simple.html*.

We'll continue with the configuration of the second **Content Modifier** responsible for setting the body of the result message. The correct configuration is shown in Figure 4.18.

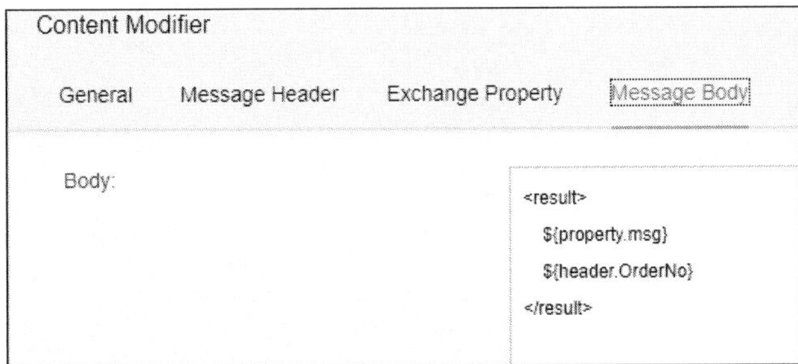

Figure 4.18 Defining the Content of the Reply Message as the New Message Body

Select the **Message Body** link in the top row of the **Content Modifier** screen. Next, fill the **Body** input field as shown in Figure 4.18. We defined a new opening and closing tag named `result`. In between those tags, we placed the contents of the two variables defined during the configuration of the first **Content Modifier**. You can see how to access the different storage areas: the properties in the exchange are accessible via the predefined Camel variable `property`, and the data is stored in the message's header via the predefined Camel variable `header`. In both cases, the actual data is accessed by adding the custom declared variable's name, separated by a dot: `property.msg` for the complete message and `header.OrderNo` for the order number.

Now that you've configured both **Content Modifier** shapes, you can add them to your model by dragging and dropping them on the sequence flow. As soon as the sequence flow changes its color to orange (Figure 4.19), you can release the mouse button, and the shape is inserted correctly. After adding both shapes, the result should look like the one shown in Figure 4.20.

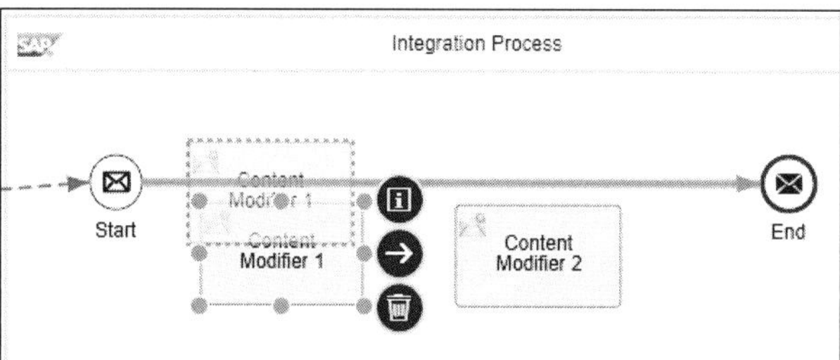

Figure 4.19 Adding the Content Modifier to Your Model

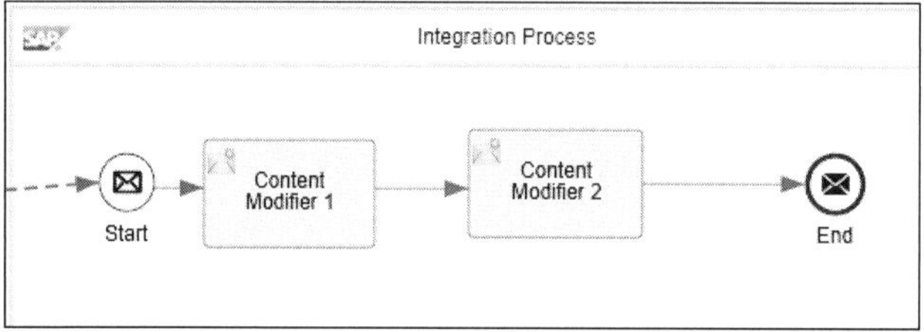

Figure 4.20 The Final Result of the Created Integration Flow

Finally, save your changes, and deploy the integration flow on your tenant.

4.1.5 Checking Configuration Using the Problems View

SAP Cloud Platform Integration supports the development process by performing validation checks each time you open, save, and deploy an integration flow. If these checks fail, warnings or problems are detected in the integration flow, and the concerned problematic step is visually marked with a red ✖ icon (for an error) or a yellow icon ⚠ (for a warning). Figure 4.21 shows that the integration flow model didn't pass the validation check and that there is a problem with the sender connector—as indicated by the red icon ⊗ on the integration flow.

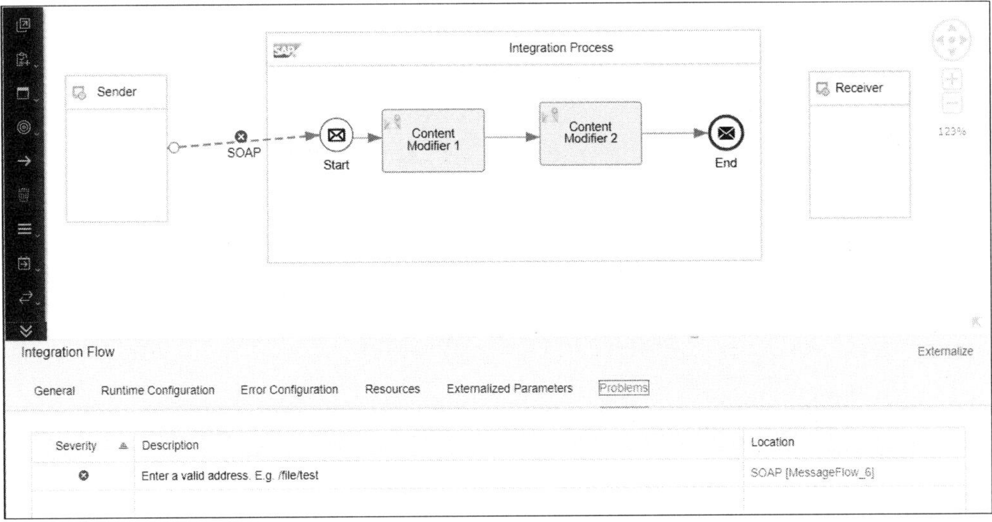

Figure 4.21 Overview of the Problems View Tab

As a developer of the integration flow, you can rely on two options to determine the exact problem causing the error:

- Hover your mouse over the error or warning icon in the integration flow to get a tooltip that describes the issue.
- Use the **Problems** view tab to obtain details about the error or warning.

Note

When a validations check is performed on the integration flow both warnings and errors can be detected and visually shown in the integration flow model and the Problems view tab. Errors are flagged by a red icon ⊗, whereas warnings are flagged with a yellow icon ⚠.

The **Problems** view tab helps you manage issues and problems in your integration flow by giving you specific details of the problem's root cause. It displays all design-time issues related to integration components and resources.

Table 4.1 provides a description of the columns available in the **Problems** view tab.

Column Name	Description
Severity	The severity status of an issue. This column is populated by icons that represent an error or a warning.
Description	A description of the problem. This column also often presents a tip or example of how to solve the issue.
Location	The location of the integration component or resource with the issue. The location is the name of the concerned integration component or resource, followed by the ID displayed in brackets. It's also possible to click the location ID to be redirected to the concerned step in the integration flow or to the affected resource.

Table 4.1 Attributes Available in the Problems View Tab

The visual representation of the warnings and errors can get quite cluttered if you have a lot of issues in the integration flow. Furthermore, having to hover over each problem icon before knowing the issues isn't always handy. Compared to the visual representation, the **Problems** view tab has a better overview and a consolidated list of issues in one glance. It's also possible to filter or sort the problems based on the different columns listed in Table 4.1.

4.1.6 Running the Integration Flow

After a successful deployment, you need the endpoint of your integration flow to actually invoke the integration flow via a SOAP client, such as SoapUI (*http://soapui.org*). You can find the endpoint's address using SAP Cloud Platform Integration's monitoring environment. Choose **Monitor** from the three-bar navigation icon ☰ in the upper-left corner of the screen (Figure 4.22).

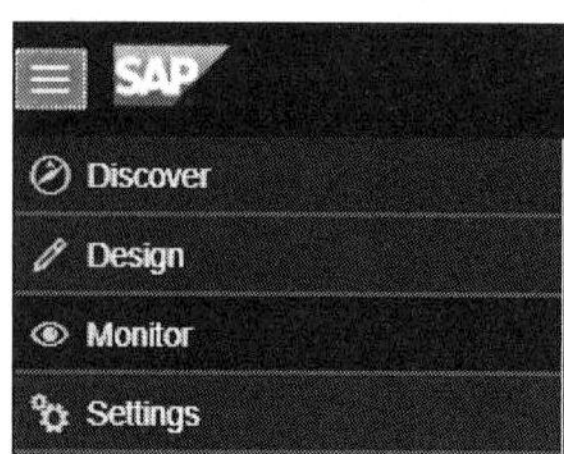

Figure 4.22 Switch to the Monitoring Environment of SAP Cloud Platform Integration

A screen with several tiles should appear. Click the **Started** tile, which is beneath the **Manage Integration Content** heading (Figure 4.23). This allows you to navigate to all of the already-started integration flows for your tenant.

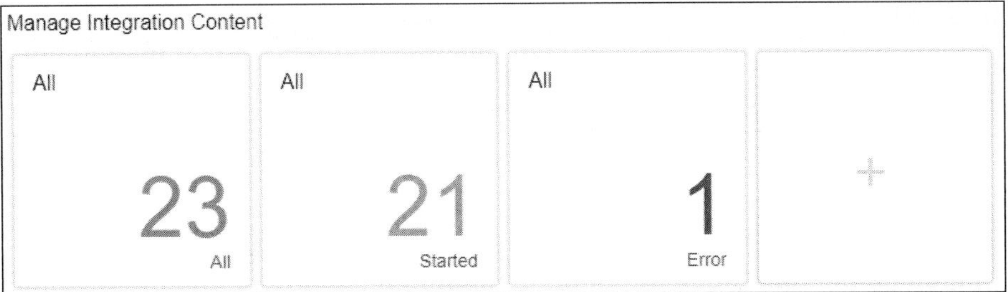

Figure 4.23 Tile for Already-Started Integration Flows on your Tenant

From the list of deployed and started integration content, find your newly deployed integration flow, and click its entry row (Figure 4.24). This takes you to the details of this particular integration flow.

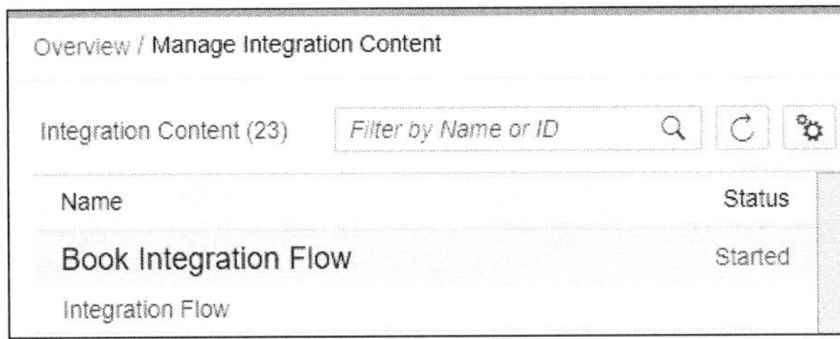

Figure 4.24 Navigate to the Details of a Selected Integration Flow

Besides other useful information, such as the integration flow's version number, the deployed state, and the deployment date/time, the endpoint's URL is of particular interest. It shows the URL by which the integration flow is invoked. Select the URL, and copy the address by clicking on the Copy icon shown in Figure 4.25. Additionally, depending on your needs, you can download the WSDL via one of these options: **WSDL**, **WSDL for ABAP Consumer**, or **WSDL without Policies**. The SOAP tool of your choice requires the URL as the invocation address.

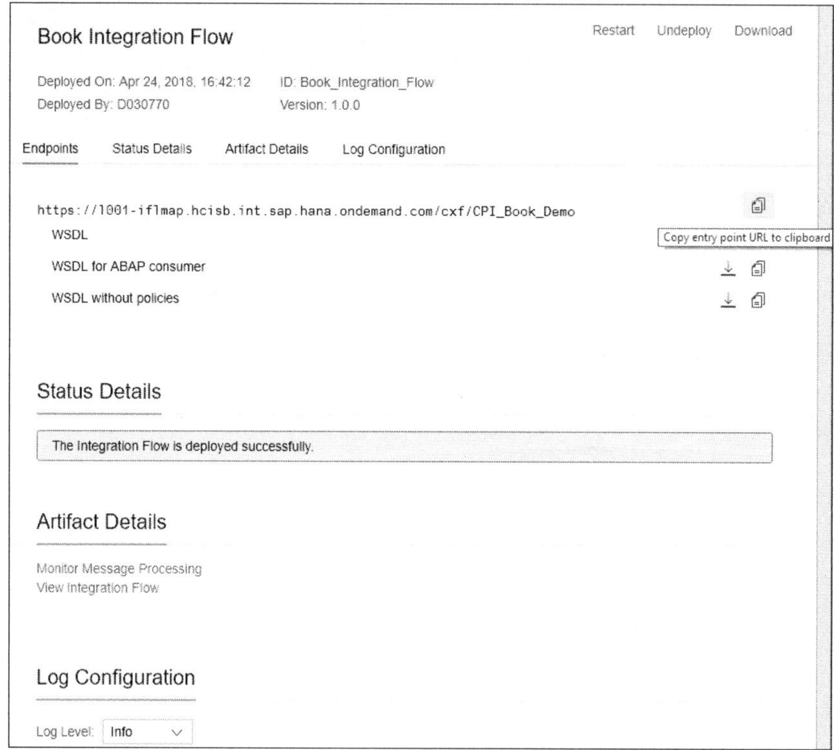

Figure 4.25 Copy the Endpoint's URL into the Clipboard

Now you have all information you need to run the integration flow. Open a SOAP client tool of your choice, such as SoapUI, and paste the copied URL as the invocation target. (We already discussed SoapUI in Chapter 2, Section 2.3.) Prepare a message that looks similar to the one shown earlier in Figure 4.15. Set the **Order Number** field accordingly (e.g., with **10249**), and don't forget to set the correct authentication type in your tool (**Basic Authentication** with the username and password provided by SAP operations for your SAP Cloud Platform Integration instance).

> **Note**
>
> Be aware that the user used in SoapUI needs to have the `ESBMessaging.send` role assigned for the service call to be authorized.

Finally, invoke the integration flow. As a result, you should receive an output comparable to the one shown in Figure 4.26.

```
<soap:Envelope xmlns:soap="http://schemas.xml
   <soap:Body>
      <result>
         <demo:OrderNumber_MT xmlns:demo="htt
            <orderNumber>10249</orderNumber>
         </demo:OrderNumber_MT>
         10249
      </result>
   </soap:Body>
</soap:Envelope>
```

Figure 4.26 Response after Invocation of Integration Flow

In Section 4.1.1, we made you aware of an important difference between storing data in the message's header and storing it in the exchange's property area: the data stored in the message's header will be forwarded to the receiver of the message, whereas the data in the exchange's properties area won't reach the receiver. How can you verify that? In your SOAP client tool, take a look at the headers of your response message. We've done this for SoapUI and created the screenshot shown in Figure 4.27.

Header	Value
Strict-Transport-Security	max-age=31536000; includeSubDomains; preload
OrderNo	10259
Date	Sun, 18 Mar 2018 22:01:57 GMT
Content-Length	348
#status#	HTTP/1.1 200 OK
SAP_MessageProcessingLogID	AFqu4dVFprmUt00JUG_yo10Vi0O
Set-Cookie	JSESSIONID=0F2399615D61B3296143F2E45A459F6892C02E19DB9B3622EBC3CEB4347EC57E; Path=/cxf; Secure; HttpOnly
Set-Cookie	JTENANTSESSIONID_ac965bd8f=eXvJACEI16VWrmqsmu5A5WZaLhl4AA4Q%2FAJkwrTQISM%3D; Domain=.hana.ondemand.com; Path=/; Secu...
Content-Type	text/xml;charset=UTF-8
Server	SAP

Figure 4.27 The Header Fields of the Response Message

In the second row of the table shown in Figure 4.27, you can identify the **OrderNo** field that was set during message processing. It reached the receiver, but as you can see, the data stored in the exchange's properties area didn't.

The fact that the data stored as header fields are returned in the message response means that we need to carefully use header fields. Storing large messages in header fields will be expensive in terms of resources and can create performance issues.

4.1.7 Troubleshooting

As with every development and runtime environment, errors can occur in SAP Cloud Platform Integration, and there are two main types to expect: errors that occur during deployment, and errors that occur during message handling. In both cases, the starting point for the error's root cause analysis is SAP Cloud Platform Integration's monitoring environment (refer to Figure 4.22 for details on how to open the monitoring environment). The monitoring environment's homepage consists of several areas, including **Message Processing Monitor**, **Integration Content Monitor**, **Manage Security**, **Manage Stores**, **Access Logs**, and **Manage Locks**. Some of these monitors can be seen in Figure 4.28. We'll discuss monitoring applications in more detail in Chapter 8.

If you're dealing with deployment errors, you'll find appropriate entries in the **Integration Content Monitor** area; the **Error** tile gives you an overview by displaying the number of erroneous artifacts. Click on the tile to learn more about the root cause of each error.

For runtime issues during message processing, the **Message Processing Monitor** section has the appropriate tiles to further analyze the errors. However, the tiles are useful for more than erroneous message handling routes. They also reveal a lot about the exact message processing steps within Apache Camel for successfully completed messages. To further illustrate this, perform the following steps:

1. Click on the **Completed Messages** tile in the **Message Monitor** section of Figure 4.28. Note that the tiles can be personalized and configured to your liking. If the tile has been modified in your tenant, there is a chance that it behaves differently than described here.

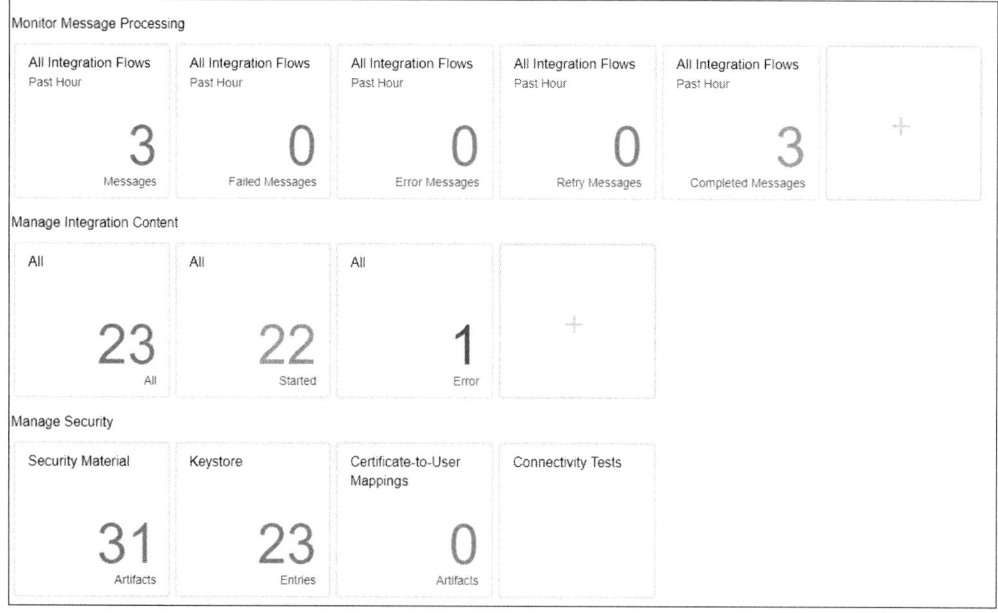

Figure 4.28 Monitoring Homepage

2. From the subsequent monitoring page, click on the concerned integration flow on the left side (see Figure 4.29). Then select the **Logs** tab on the right side to get a page similar to the one displayed in Figure 4.29.

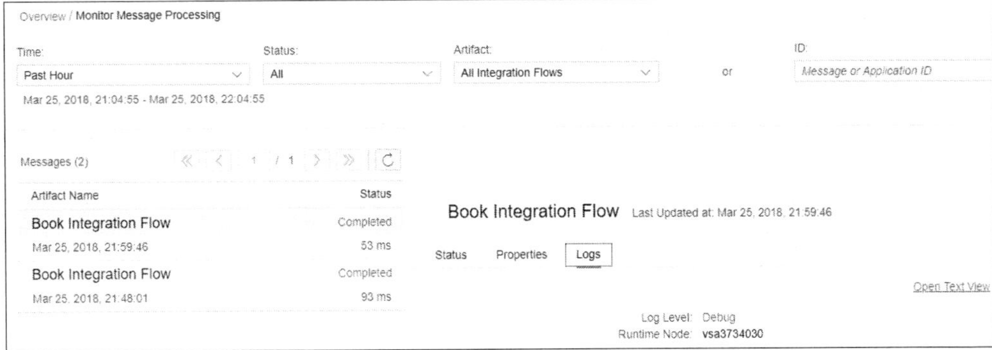

Figure 4.29 Details about Successfully Completed Messages

> **Note**
> Chapter 8, Section 8.2, discusses the various monitors in more detail.

In this section, you've learned a lot about the inner workings of SAP Cloud Platform Integration. Although we implemented a relatively simple scenario, doing so revealed many details about message handling within the underlying Apache Camel integration framework, including error analysis. This knowledge helps you work more consciously with messages, headers, and attachments. In the next section, we'll discuss how to use externalization in your integration flow.

4.2 Using Externalization to Enable Easy Reuse of the Integration Flow

When designing an integration scenario, it's important to take reusability into consideration. Following are some advantages brought by reusability:

- Reduces the overall cost of software development
- Reduces risks
- Saves time and cost while developing and testing interfaces
- Speeds delivery of software

When it comes to SAP Cloud Platform Integration, it practically means that for every step of your integration flow, you need to ask yourself the following questions:

- Is the concerned step likely to be repeated several times in your integration flow?
- Are there other steps in the integration flow which will reuse the same data?
- Does the step need a dynamic input coming from a variable or another step in the integration flow?
- Does the concerned integration flow need to be deployed in different tenants in the landscape, and do some of its steps need to be configured differently in other environments?
- Does it depend on the tenant which values are to be used for the adapters at runtime? (For example, the endpoint of a connected backend system might depend on whether you configure an integration flow on a test or on a productive tenant.)

Note that there are more potential questions that fit this category, but these are used for the sake of simplicity. If the answer to any of these questions is yes, consider generalizing the concerned step by making it more generic and configurable.

While working with SAP Cloud Platform Integration, one way to generalize and increase the reusability of data within an integration flow is known as externalization. In the next sections, we discuss externalization and explain how it can be used in an integration flow. We'll also discuss how the parameters used for externalization can be configured.

4.2.1 Externalize

If the integration content must be used across multiple landscapes or environments (e.g., development, test, acceptance, production), it can be assumed that the endpoints of the integration flow for each landscape will differ. In such a scenario, externalizing parameters can be used to declare a parameter as a variable at design time. The parameter can then be used later during configuration time to customize the attributes on the sender and receiver side or for a step in the integration flow.

Externalizing a parameter has the advantages of avoiding hard-coded values in your integration flow and providing the flexibility to change the parameter values at configuration time. *Configuration time* refers to a moment after an integration flow has been transported or imported in a tenant in your landscape (test, acceptance, or production). During this time, users might need to adapt some aspects of an integration flow, such as adding adapter-specific endpoints and assigning values to externalized parameters. The good news is that assigning a value to an externalized parameter during configuration doesn't involve changing the integration flow.

Let's now look at a practical use case by referring and extending the integration flow that we implemented in Section 4.1. We've built an integration flow that accepts a SOAP call. Imagine that you, as the integration developer, decide to have different addresses for calling the integration flow in the different environments (development, test, and production). As shown previously in Figure 4.11, we configured the flow to be called via the SOAP address */CPI_Book_Demo*. To externalize the address and make it configurable for each environment, follow these steps:

1. Open the concerned integration flow (in the Web UI design environment), click **Edit**, and select the SOAP adapter line, as shown in Figure 4.30.
2. Click on the **Externalize** button (see right corner of Figure 4.30).

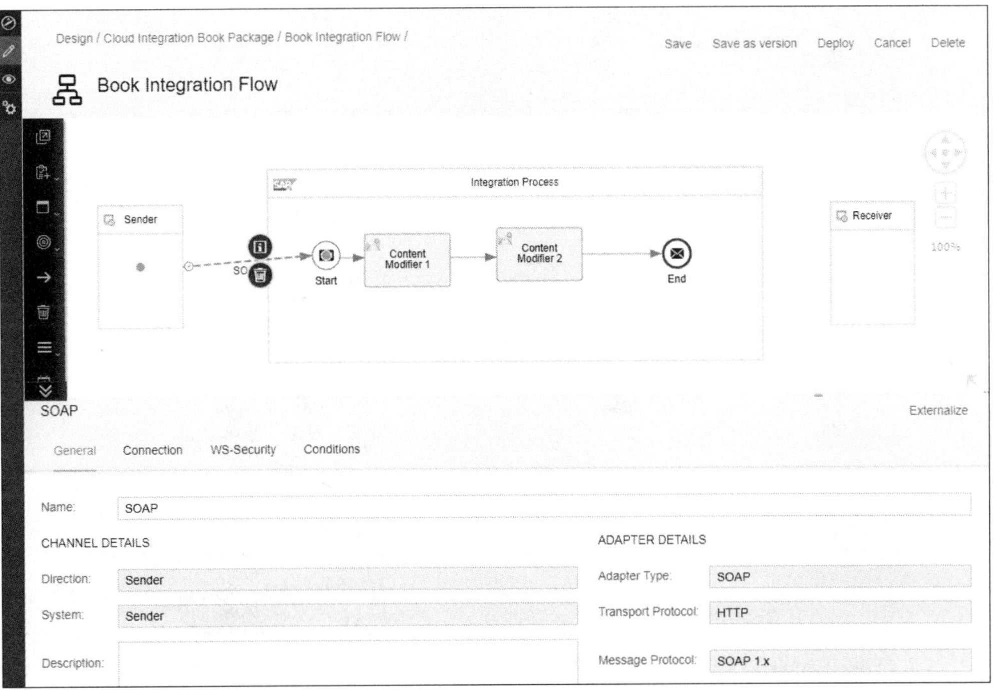

Figure 4.30 Selecting the SOAP Connector and the Externalize button

3. A new screen pops up with the **Externalization** editor, as shown in Figure 4.31. Note that the **Externalization** editor presents all possible configurations of the component that is selected. Let's now create a new parameter on the **Address** field. For

that, you'll need to select the **Connection** tab and remove the existing `/CPI_Book_Demo` value.

4. The parameter is defined using the format `{{<parameter>}}`. In our case, let's add a new parameter with the name `{{MY_ADDRESS>}}`, as shown in Figure 4.31.

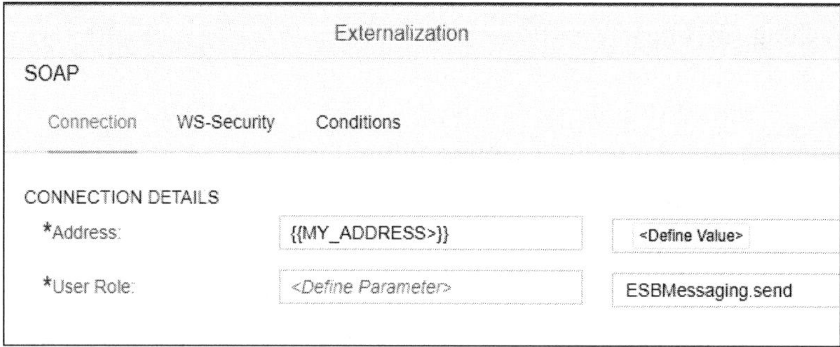

Figure 4.31 Creating a New Parameter in the Externalization Editor

> **Note**
>
> Not all components can be externalized. After selecting the component in the integration flow, the **Externalize** button only appears if the component contains at least one attribute that can be externalized.
>
> Note that the feature to create a parameter is only enabled when the integration flow is in edit mode. As soon as a parameter is created, it becomes available for various components (e.g., sender channel, receiver channel, timer, etc.) within the same integration flow. Furthermore, existing parameters can always be recalled by typing the double curly brackets `{{` in the parameter column. SAP Cloud Platform Integration will automatically suggest a list of parameters available in the integration flow.

5. The next step is to create a value for the externalized parameter by clicking on the `<Define Value>` tag shown in Figure 4.31. The **Define Value** option appears as soon as you've created an externalizable parameter. You then get a new popup screen with the possibility to define a value for the `{{MY_ADDRESS>}}` externalized parameter (see Figure 4.32). Fill in `/CPI_Book_Demo` as its new value.
6. Select the **Ok** button to return to the **Externalization** editor.
7. Once back in the **Externalization** editor, select **OK** again to return to the integration flow.

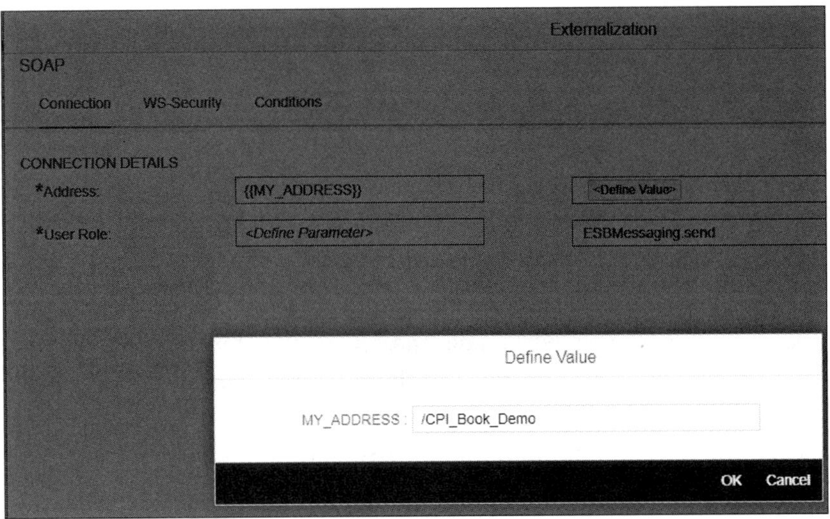

Figure 4.32 Defining a Value for an Externalized Parameter

Note

For some fields in SAP Cloud Platform Integration, it's possible to externalize many parameters at the same time and combine them together to achieve your requirement. Figure 4.33 shows multiple concatenated strings.

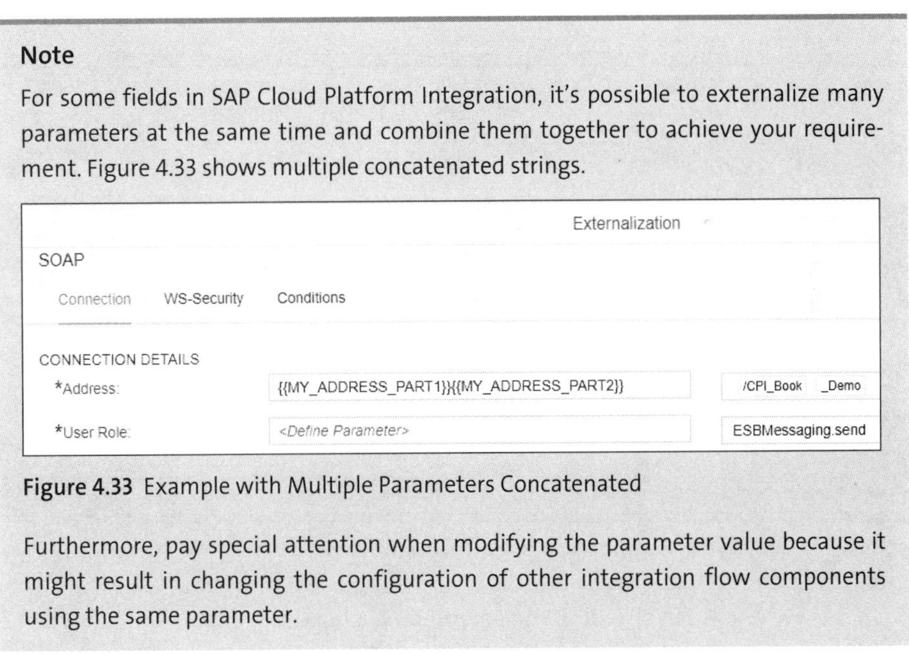

Figure 4.33 Example with Multiple Parameters Concatenated

Furthermore, pay special attention when modifying the parameter value because it might result in changing the configuration of other integration flow components using the same parameter.

You can also withdraw from externalizing a field by deleting it. Removing an externalization of a particular field doesn't remove it from the integration flow, however, because the parameter might be used in another component, step, or adapter. The parameter can completely be removed using the **Externalized Parameters** view, which enables you to manage all externalized parameters of the concerned integration flow.

Following are the steps necessary to manage externalized parameters in the **Externalized Parameters** view:

1. Click outside the integration flow model area to see the **Externalized Parameters** tab.
2. Open the integration flow in edit mode, and select the **Externalized Parameters** view, as shown in Figure 4.34. Note that this shows a list of all existing externalized parameters of the whole integration flow. These parameters aren't necessary for our example exercise; they have been added just for illustration sake.

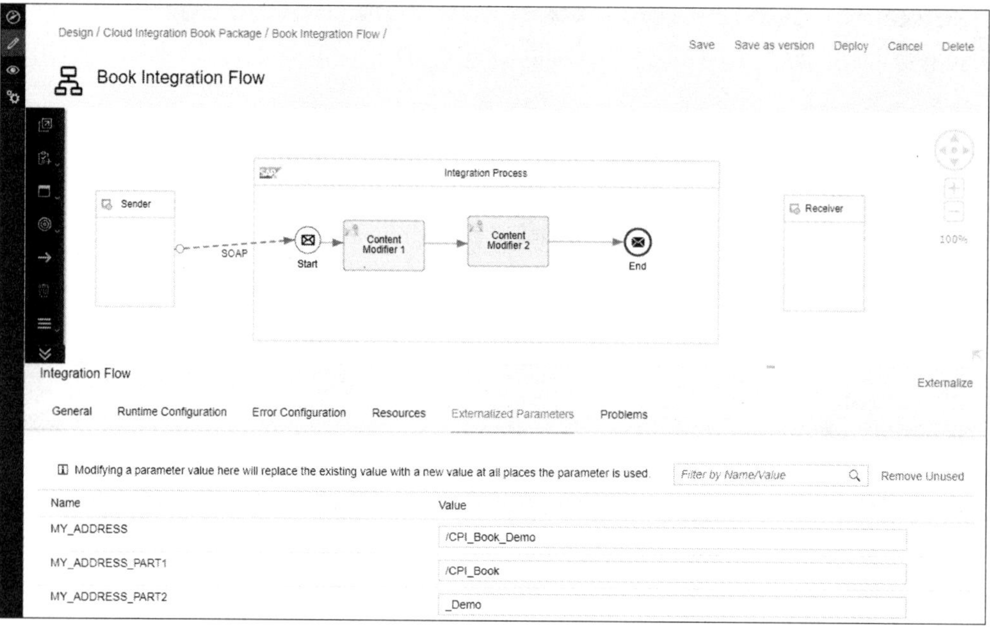

Figure 4.34 Externalized Parameters View in Design Time

3. In this view, you can also filter the parameters using their names or values via the **Filter by Name/Value** field (see right corner of Figure 4.34).
4. You can also update and adjust the values of any parameters from this central view.

5. Lastly, you can remove unused parameters using the **Remove Unused** link on the left side (see Figure 4.34). When you've done this, SAP Cloud Platform performs a check to identify unused parameters, and a screen appears with a request to confirm the removal of unused fields (see Figure 4.35). Upon confirmation, all unused parameters will be removed.

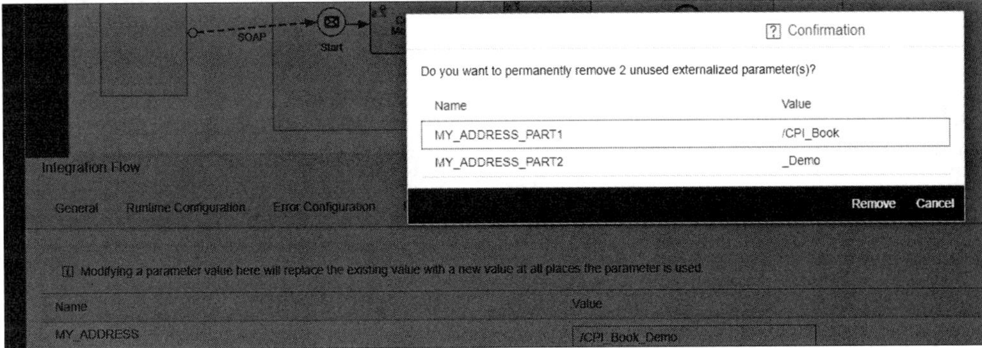

Figure 4.35 Removing Unused Externalized Parameters

6. Save and deploy the integration flow.

Now that you know how to add and manage externalized parameters, let's discuss how they can be configured and used for runtime.

4.2.2 Configure and Run the Scenario

As discussed in the previous section, externalization enables us to create a parameter in design time that can later be changed during configuration time, without the need to change the integration flow. Now that you've successfully developed your integration flow and imported it across other tenants in the landscape (e.g., test, acceptance, production), it's time to learn how to adapt the values of its existing externalized parameters to fit the requirements of the actual environment. Note that an integration flow can be transported across other tenants in the landscape (as will be addressed in Chapter 6).

In the example case that we've been building since Section 4.1, we added a parameter to specify a different SOAP address for each environment (Section 4.2.1). To change the SOAP address, proceed as follows:

1. Transport the integration flow to the other tenant you want to run the integration flow with different parameters.

2. Go to the desired tenant, navigate to the **Design** section, and open the concerned integration flow.
3. Click on the **Configure** link in the top-right corner (see Figure 4.36).

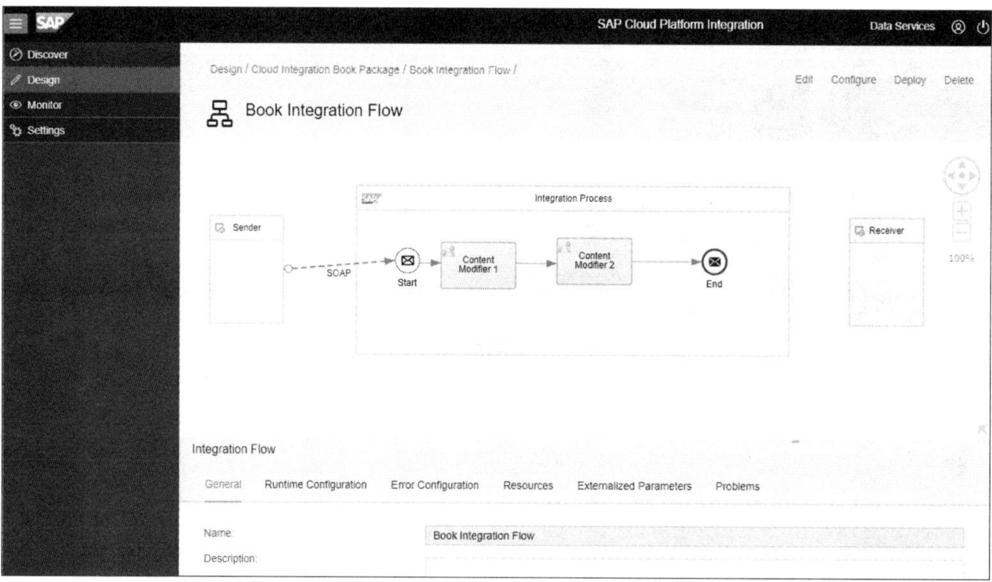

Figure 4.36 Configuring an Integration Flow

4. A **Configure** view is displayed that allows you to maintain values of externalized parameters. In our case, we can now replace the value of the **MY_Address** field with a new value. As illustrated in Figure 4.37, we'll now use the value `/CPI_Book_Demo_Test`.

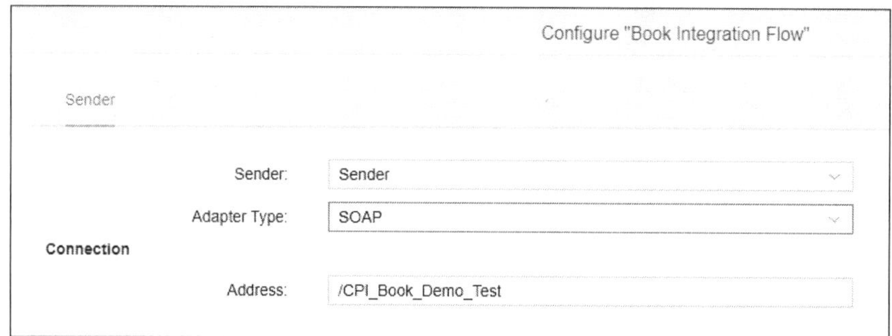

Figure 4.37 Changing an Externalized Parameter Value

5. Click **Save** and then **Deploy** (both buttons are located in the bottom-right corner as shown in Figure 4.37).

Now that our updated integration flow is deployed, we're ready to test it using SoapUI. Note that the steps to test with SoapUI were already described in Section 4.1.6. The main difference here is that we should now use the new invocation address instead. This new invocation address or endpoint can be found in the **Manage Integration Content** monitor, as shown in Figure 4.38.

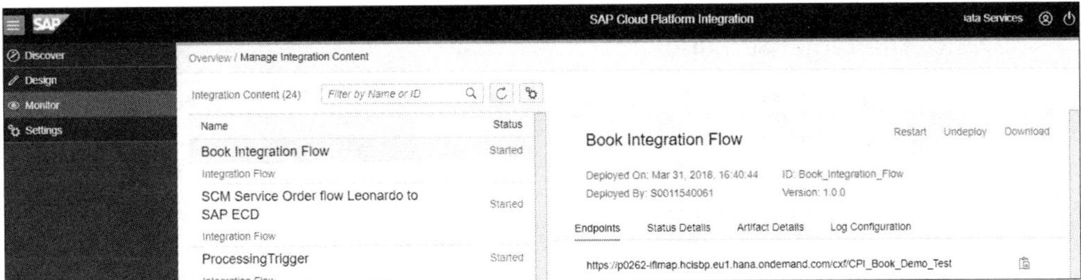

Figure 4.38 Finding the New Endpoint Address after Externalizing the SOAP Address

And voila! Congratulations, you're now equipped to define, manage, and configure externalized parameters.

4.3 Content Enrichment by Invoking an OData Service

SAP Cloud Platform Integration allows for the development of sophisticated integration scenarios. In this section, we provide an example of such a scenario: a synchronous call to an Open Data Protocol (OData) service to retrieve the details of an order for a given order number. The client sends the order number to SAP Cloud Platform Integration using a standard SOAP call.

Our example dives into the details of the communication with external data sources, as well as how to use them in synchronous scenarios. Finally, we explain the Query Editor, which is a tool that helps you generate the sometimes quite complex Representational State Transfer (REST) Uniform Resource Identifiers (URIs) for actually invoking the external OData sources.

Note

URI is a generic term to identify the name of a resource uniquely over the network. A URL is a concrete URI for a web address. In this book, when we talk about the OData service, we use the term URI. When talking about the invocation of the integration flow, which is reachable via SOAP using a concrete web address, we use the term URL.

4.3.1 The Target Scenario

The integration scenario in Figure 4.39 depicts the integration scenario we're going to build in the next section.

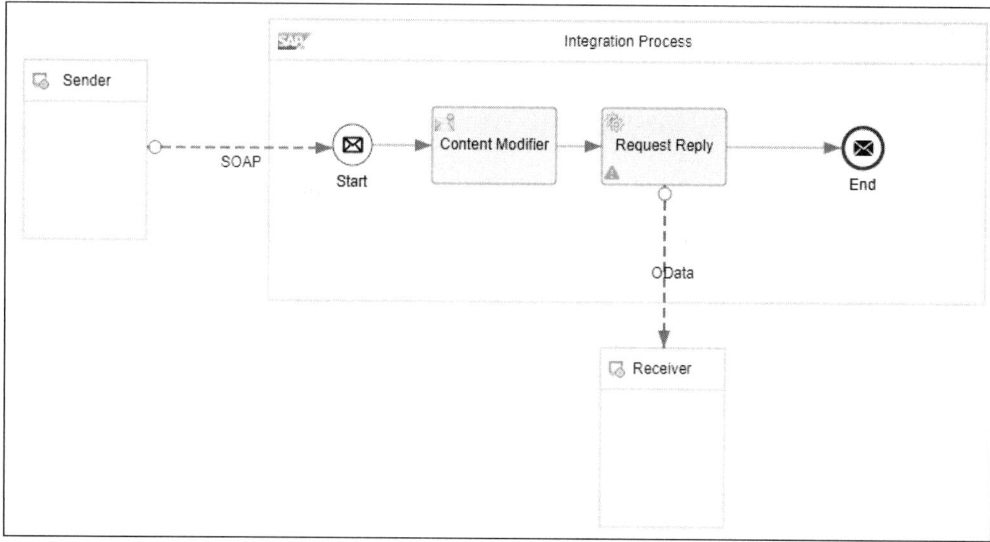

Figure 4.39 Invoking an OData Service

An integration flow covers the following aspects:

- Sending a SOAP request containing an order number from the **Sender** participant to SAP Cloud Platform Integration
- Retrieving the order number from the incoming message and storing it in the message's header field for later reference, using the **Content Modifier** step

- Invoking an OData service to retrieve the details of that particular order, implementing a **Request-Reply** pattern scenario
- Returning the received data to the client

The incoming message's structure is exactly the same as shown earlier in Figure 4.15. It contains the order number for which additional data should be retrieved from an external OData service. You can reuse most of the steps that we used in the previous exercise to create this new integration flow. The **Sender** pool is configured with **User Role** from the **Authorization** dropdown list and with **ESBMessaging.send** as the value for the user role (in the **Connection** tab).

For the message flow between the **Sender** pool and the **Start** event, the adapter-specific attribute **Address** should be set to **/CPI_Book_Demo_OData** (to define a different endpoint compared to the previous exercise). This string is later part of the URL under which the integration flow can be invoked. The **Content Modifier** step is responsible for storing the incoming order number in the message's header area. As a reminder, you can find its configuration in Figure 4.16. The **OrderNo** name was chosen as the storage's name to access it later. So far, the message has arrived at the integration flow, and an important piece of information, the order number, has been stored for later reference. Now the time has come to configure how to call the OData service.

4.3.2 Invoking an OData Service

The modeling environment of SAP Cloud Platform Integration provides a dedicated shape (or step) for accessing external sources synchronously. This shape is the **Request-Reply** step, located in the submenu of the **Call** icon ⇄ on the editor's palette (Figure 4.40).

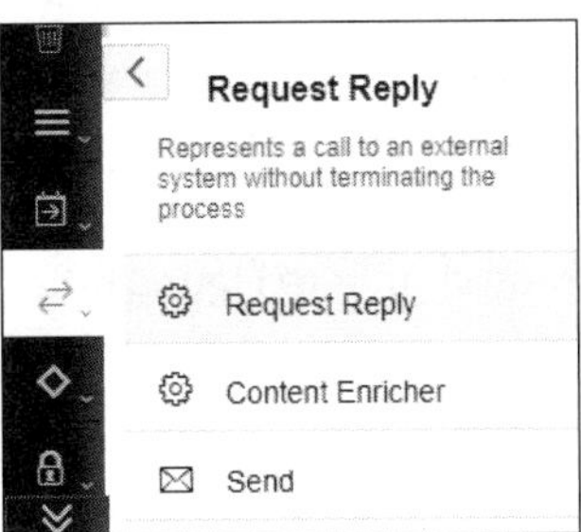

Figure 4.40 Modeling the Request-Reply Step

In the submenu, click the **External Call** entry, and then select the **Request-Reply** entry. Move the mouse pointer into the **Integration Process** pool, and click again to position the step on the canvas. Figure 4.41 shows the result.

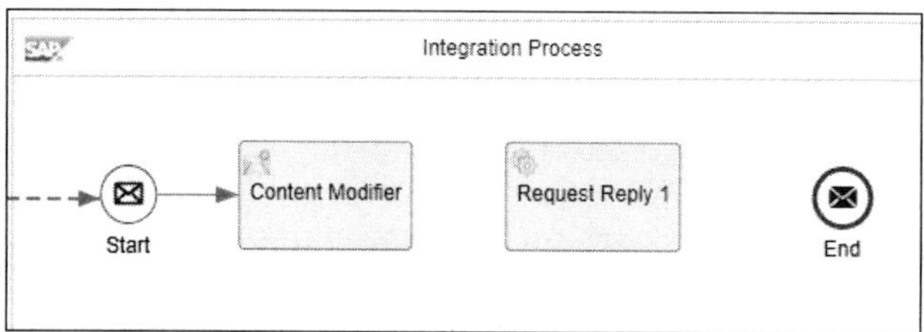

Figure 4.41 The Integration Process Pool with the Request-Reply Entry Added

Because the **Request-Reply** step needs access to an additional system, it's necessary to add the target system as an additional pool in the process model. You can find the respective **Receiver** shape in the submenu of the palette's main entry **Participants**. Figure 4.42 shows more details.

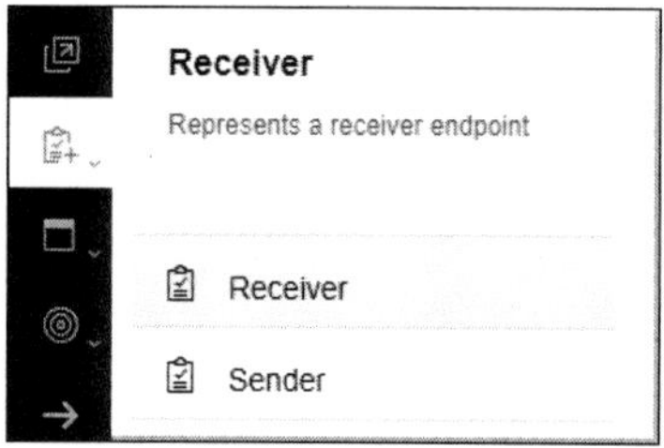

Figure 4.42 Picking an Additional Receiver from the Palette

This next step is important: Position **Receiver1** outside the **Integration Process** pool close to the **Request-Reply** step, as shown in Figure 4.43.

Next, connect the **Request-Reply** step with the **Receiver1** pool by using the connection icon from the **Request-Reply** step's context buttons. After dragging the connection to the **Receiver1** pool, a dialog box automatically opens asking you for the **Adapter Type**. Choose **OData**, and you should see something similar to Figure 4.44.

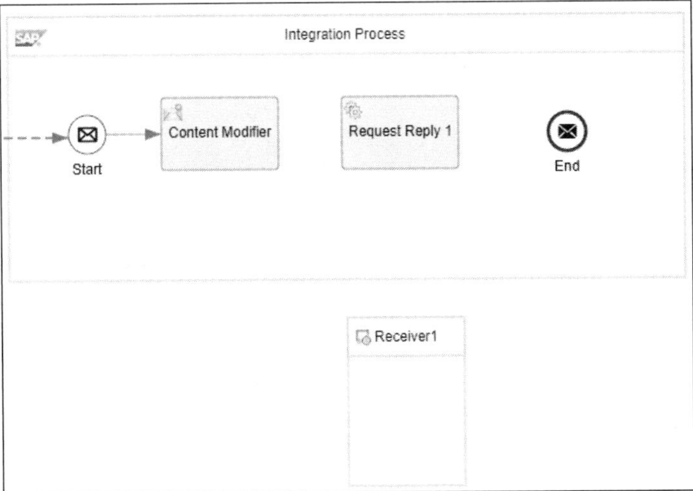

Figure 4.43 Positioning the Receiver1 Pool Close to the Request-Reply Step and Outside the Integration Process Pool

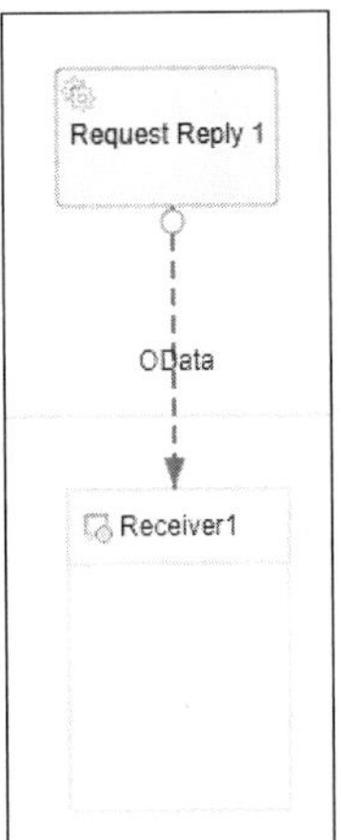

Figure 4.44 Connecting the Request-Reply Step with the Receiver1 Pool

4.3.3 Configuring the OData Connection

To actually invoke an external OData source, you need to configure several parameters. After selecting the message flow between the **Request-Reply** step and the **Receiver1** pool (the connection's color should switch from blue to blue with dotted orange), the parameters are depicted beneath the process diagram. They are shown in Figure 4.45 for the connection parameters and Figure 4.46 for processing parameters.

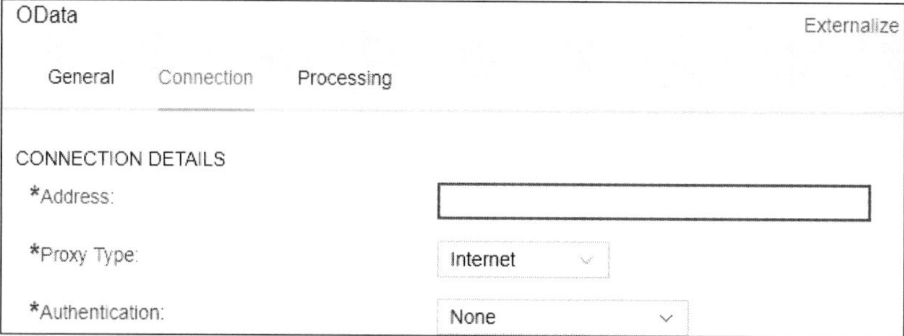

Figure 4.45 The Connection Parameters of the OData Connection to the External Source

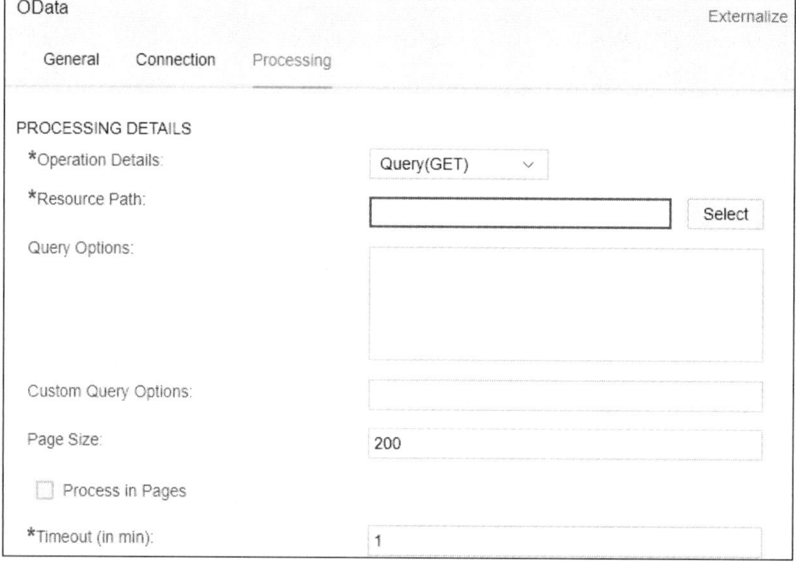

Figure 4.46 The Processing Parameters of the OData Connection to the External Source

Let's walk through the configuration fields of the **Connection** tab (see Figure 4.45) one by one:

- **Address**
  This field contains the service's root URI of the OData service provider to which you want to connect. In our example, we want to connect to a publicly available service on the Internet: one of the OData demo services available for trying out

OData connectivity and learning more about how to work with OData services. It's reachable under the URI *http://services.odata.org/Northwind/Northwind.svc.*

- **Proxy Type**
  This field defines whether you're connecting to a cloud system (**Internet**) or to an on-premise system via the SAP Cloud Platform Connectivity service (**on-premise**). Because we're connecting to a cloud-based OData service, we leave the field on the **Internet** entry.
- **Authentication**
  Depending on the OData service, you can choose different authentication types from the dropdown list. **Basic**, **Client Certificate**, **Principal Propagation** (only available for the **ON-PREMISE** proxy type), and **None** are currently supported. For our example, select **None**, as no authentication is required for the test service.

Let's now walk through the configuration fields of the **Processing** tab (see Figure 4.46) one by one:

- **Operation**
  OData is based on HTTP, which supports the following main operations: `GET`, for querying a set of entities or for reading one concrete entity (business object); `PUT`, for updating an entity; `POST`, for inserting data, `Merge` to merge entities; and `Delete`, for deleting an entity. Our requirement is to read exactly one order, so we're fine with the **GET** operation for this field.
- **Resource Path**
  In this field, you specify the URI that is appended to the OData service endpoint when connecting to the service provider. You may know this extension by heart (which is rarely the case because of the strict syntax you have to follow and the lengthiness of the string), but it's easier to let the SAP system's built-in Query Editor do the dirty work of creating the resource path for you. Later in this chapter, we'll explain how to work with the Query Editor to create the correct resource path.
- **Page Size**
  This final field specifies the total number of records that should be returned in the response from the OData service provider. We're leaving this field empty because we're defining a query that returns only one entry, so no limitation of the response is necessary.

From the preceding description, you can understand the importance of the **Resource Path** entry compared to the other fields of the **Processing** tab. That's why SAP provides the Query Editor to accurately formulate the string representing the resource path.

4.3.4 Creating the Resource Path Using the Query Editor

Click the **Select** button next to the **Resource Path** input field in Figure 4.46 to start the Query Editor. A wizard dialog box opens, asking you for details of the OData service provider to which the Query Editor should connect. Ensure that the **Connect to System** step is populated, as shown in Figure 4.47.

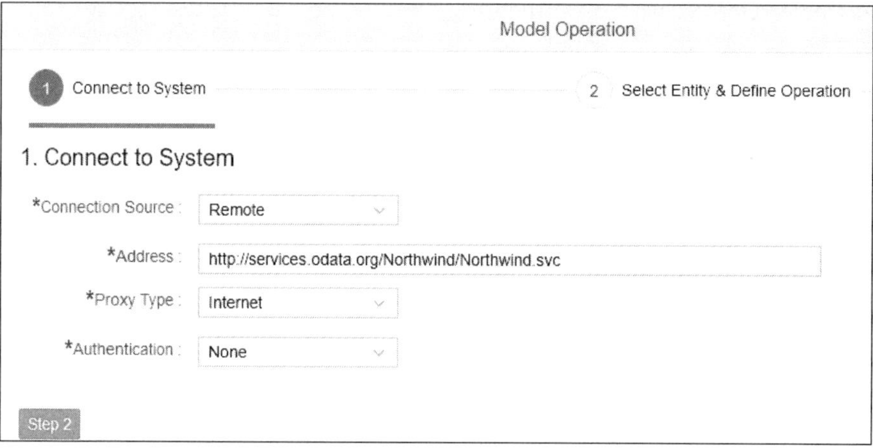

Figure 4.47 Providing Details about the OData Service Provider

Click on the **Step 2** button at the bottom of Figure 4.47 to proceed to the next step of the wizard.

The Query Editor connects to the service and retrieves its metadata information (Figure 4.48). Hence, it knows exactly which entities can be accessed and how.

Let's start with the entity and the operation. Because the Query Editor has read the details about the available entities, it can list them as part of the **Entity** dropdown list options (see Figure 4.48). To read exactly one concrete order, pick **Orders** from the list. For **Operation**, stick with the **Query (GET)** operation. Next, specify the fields that should be returned from the service. As you can imagine, an order can consist of hundreds of fields, but, most likely, you need just a handful for your concrete scenario. Therefore, pick just the fields relevant for you.

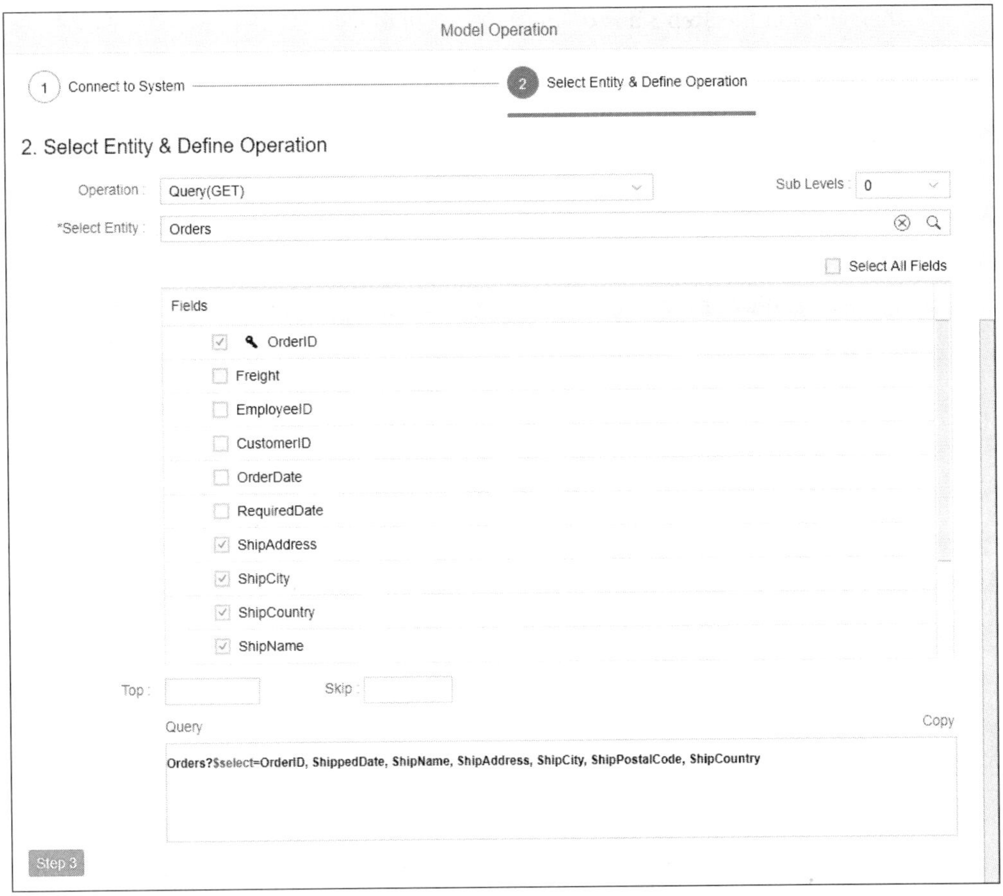

Figure 4.48 Defining the Entity, Operation, and Fields

From the **Fields** table list (Figure 4.48), select the required fields by checking their respective checkboxes. This information is again retrieved from the service's metadata information. For the sake of simplicity, choose the following fields: **OrderID**, **ShippedDate**, **ShipName**, **ShipAddress**, **ShipCity**, **ShipPostalCode**, and **ShipCountry**. After finishing your selections, the result should look like Figure 4.48.

Note the string being created for you above the circular icons and beneath the **Query Editor** title:

```
Orders?$select=ShippedDate,OrderID,ShipCountry,ShipPostalCode,ShipCity,
ShipAddress,ShipName
```

Then click on the **Step 3** button on the bottom of Figure 4.48 to proceed to the next step of the wizard.

As shown in Figure 4.49, the next screen enables you to configure how the data should be filtered and sorted:

- The `filter by` condition represents a condition to be used to select the entries that you're interested in. It works similarly to a `WHERE` clause in an SQL statement.
- The `order by` condition is used to sort data based on a particular field in ascending or descending order.

Note that to both filter by and order by area of Figure 4.49, it's possible to add as many entries as are required to specify your selection criterion. In our example, you just need one line because you're searching for an order with a concrete, well-defined order number. Check the **OrderID** field within the **Orders** object. This is the exact entry you find in the **Filter By** column of the screen shown in Figure 4.49.

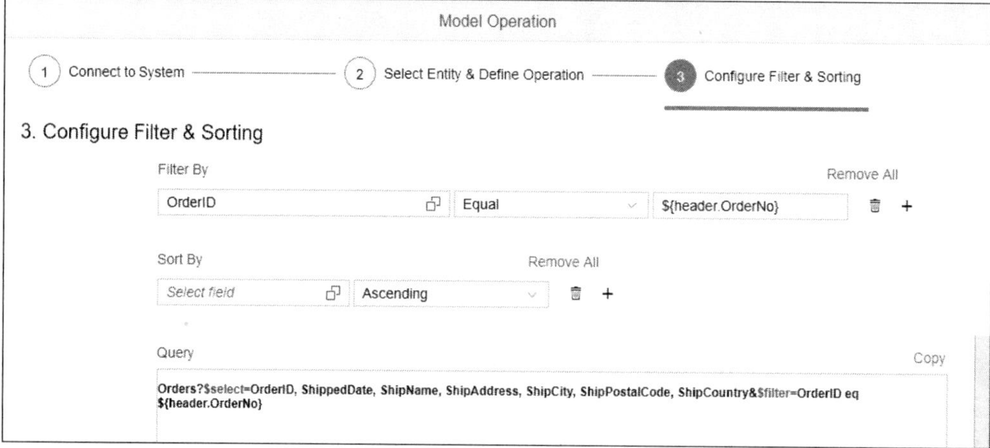

Figure 4.49 Defining the WHERE Clause in the Query Editor

Next, define the operator. Here, several logical operators are possible, but you only need the **eq** (equals) operator. Next, you need to decide which value you want to compare the entity's **OrderID** field against to find the right order. Presumably, you want to find the order whose number you received in the original incoming message, which you stored in the header area of the message under the variable name **OrderNo** (refer to Figure 4.16).

In this case, set the value to `${header.OrderNo}` to point to the value of **OrderNo**, which was stored in the header attributes. Now, hopefully you understand why you had to store the number in the message header and how to retrieve that number for the `where` clause. Notice, also, the additional string appended to the previous **Resource Path**. The Query Editor uses the Simple Expression Language to access Camel variables in the header area (`${header.OrderNo}`), which we introduced in Section 4.1.

Depending on your scenario, you can also complete the **Resource Path** by using the `Order By` condition.

The configuration is fairly straightforward: Enter the field's name by which the found entries should be sorted. Again, the Query Editor narrows down the fields after you start typing. You want the list (which later actually consists of exactly one entry) to be sorted by the **OrderID**. You could also define whether the list should be in ascending or descending order by selecting the **Ascending** or **Descending** in the dropdown, but this doesn't play a role in our scenario.

After finishing this step, you've finally completed the configuration of the OData Channel (ODC). Click the **Ok** button to close the Query Editor. You'll then see the message displayed in Figure 4.50.

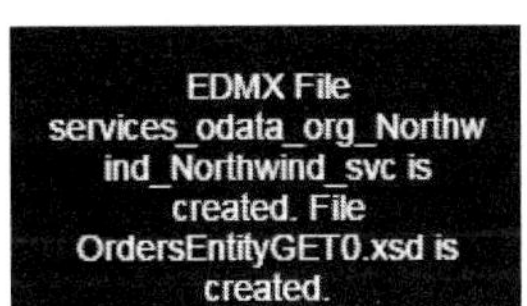

EDMX File services_odata_org_Northwind_Northwind_svc is created. File OrdersEntityGET0.xsd is created.

Figure 4.50 Query Editor Confirming That the EDMX and XSD Files Are Automatically Created

The message informs you that two files are automatically created: an Entity Data Model Designer (EDMX) file and an XML Schema Definition (XSD) file. The EDMX file contains the Entity Data Model, which stores the schema of the entities encapsulated in the OData service, including their fields and relationships (e.g., one-to-one, one-to-many, etc.). In our example, we selected an entity earlier in Figure 4.48 for a dropdown field named **Select Entity**.

But what is the XSD file good for? The OData service returns the found entity in the Atom format. However, SAP Cloud Platform Integration continues working with the result in the XML format. Hence, the runtime requires a description of the resulting XML message that fits the returned values of the newly configured query. As the Query Editor knows all of the details about the selected fields, as well as the format of each field (thanks to the EDMX file), it can generate an associated XSD file representing the returned data of the service in XML format. In the end, this helps the engine map the returned Atom format to the XML format.

The generated **Resource Path** is added to the **Query Options** field channel's configuration. The completed configuration of the connection to the OData service should look like Figure 4.51 for the **Processing** tab and Figure 4.52 for the **Connection** tab.

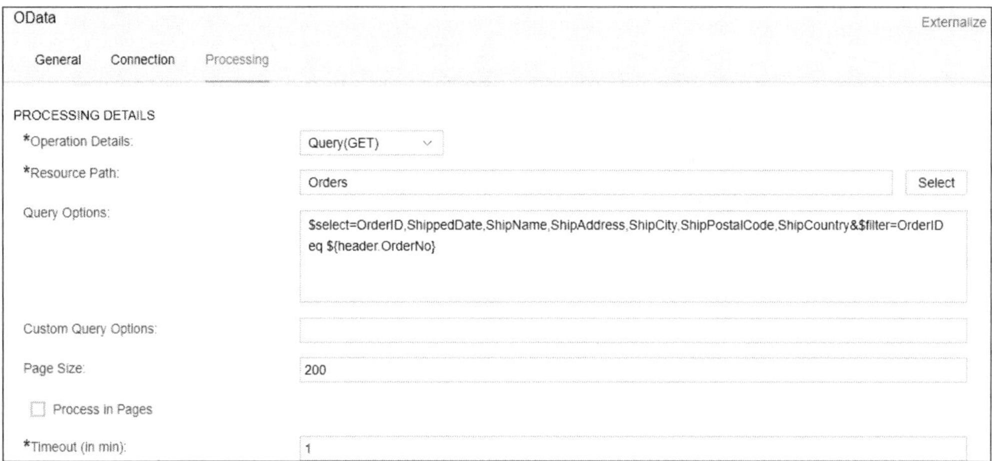

Figure 4.51 Completed Processing Configuration of the ODC

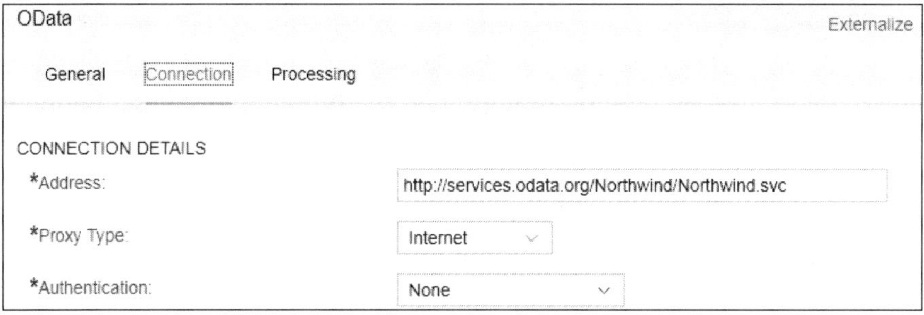

Figure 4.52 Completed Connection Configuration of the ODC

All that's left is to complete the integration flow itself by positioning the **Request-Reply** step in between the **Start** and **End** events. Figure 4.53 shows the end result.

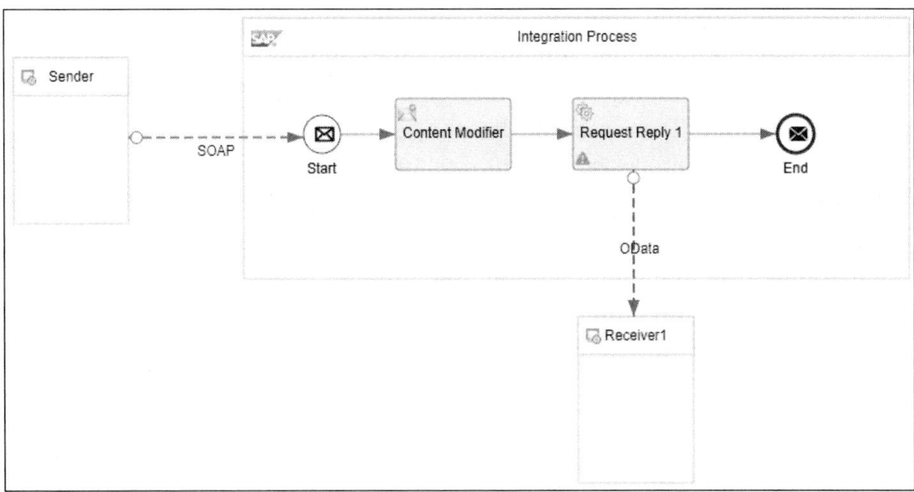

Figure 4.53 The Completed Configuration of the Integration Flow

Now, save and deploy your integration flow. After successful deployment, retrieve the integration flow's endpoint URL and invoke it via a SOAP client (with the order number 10249), such as SoapUI (see a detailed description of the invocation of integration flows in Section 4.1.6). As a result, you should see the response message displayed in Figure 4.54.

```
<soap:Envelope xmlns:soap="http://schemas.xmlsoap.org/soap/envelope/">
   <soap:Body>
      <Orders>
         <Order>
            <ShipPostalCode>44087</ShipPostalCode>
            <ShippedDate>1996-07-10T00:00:00.000</ShippedDate>
            <OrderID>10249</OrderID>
            <ShipCity>Münster</ShipCity>
            <ShipAddress>Luisenstr. 48</ShipAddress>
            <ShipCountry>Germany</ShipCountry>
            <ShipName>Toms Spezialitäten</ShipName>
         </Order>
      </Orders>
   </soap:Body>
</soap:Envelope>
```

Figure 4.54 Response Message from the OData Service Formatted in XML

4.3.5 Using the Content Enricher Step

An interesting variant on this scenario is the use of the **Content Enricher** step inside the route, instead of the **Request-Reply** step. Look at Figure 4.40 again, which shows the selection of **Request-Reply** from the palette. Below the **Request-Reply** entry, you'll find the **Content Enricher** step. In contrast to the **Request-Reply** activity, which simply returns the response message from the external data source to the caller, the **Content Enricher** merges the content of the returned external message with the original message. In other words, it converts the two separate messages into a single enhanced payload. You can try this scenario out yourself, as its configuration is pretty straightforward. All you need to do is replace the **Request-Reply** step with the **Content Enricher** step (Figure 4.55) and ensure that the OData adapter is selected.

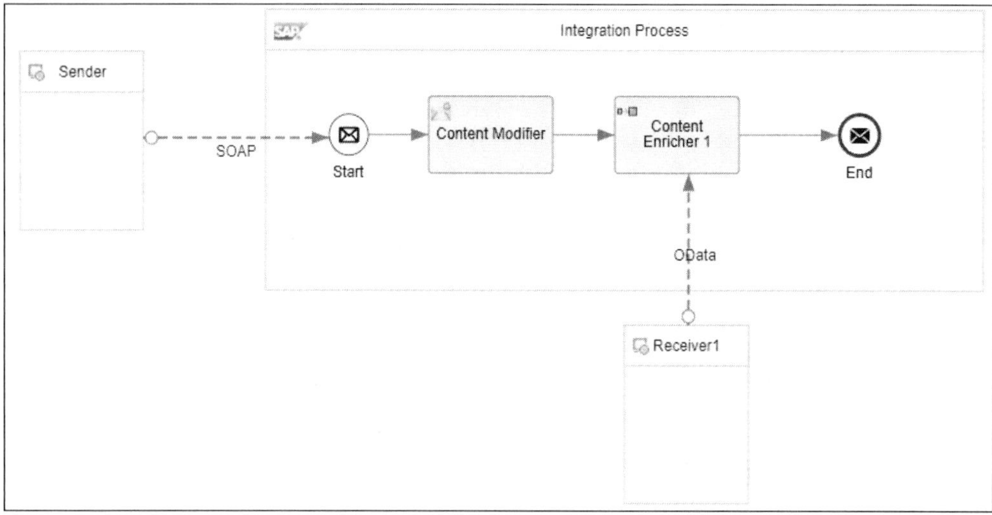

Figure 4.55 Replacing the Request-Reply Step with the Content Enricher Step

Note that there is one little, but very important, deviation from the configuration of the connection between the **Receiver1** pool and the **Content Enricher** activity: the arrow points from the **Receiver1** pool to the **Content Enricher** step. This is the opposite direction, as compared to the connection between the **Request-Reply** step and the **Receiver1** pool (refer to Figure 4.53 for a comparison). Ensure that you don't mix up the direction of the arrows. The **Content Enricher** step also includes a **Processing** tab with an **Aggregation Algorithm** field that should be left with its default value, namely **combine**. We'll revisit the **Aggregation Algorithm** field later in the section.

Once deployed, you can run the same input message against the newly configured integration flow. As a result, you'll see the output shown in Figure 4.56.

```xml
<soap:Envelope xmlns:soap="http://schemas.xmlsoap.org/soap/envelope/">
  <soap:Body>
    <multimap:Messages xmlns:multimap="http://sap.com/xi/XI/SplitAndMerge">
      <multimap:Message1>
        <demo:OrderNumber_MT xmlns:demo="http://hci.sap.com/demo">
          <orderNumber>10249</orderNumber>
        </demo:OrderNumber_MT>
      </multimap:Message1>
      <multimap:Message2>
        <Orders>
          <Order>
            <ShipPostalCode>44087</ShipPostalCode>
            <ShippedDate>1996-07-10T00:00:00.000</ShippedDate>
            <OrderID>10249</OrderID>
            <ShipCity>Münster</ShipCity>
            <ShipAddress>Luisenstr. 48</ShipAddress>
            <ShipCountry>Germany</ShipCountry>
            <ShipName>Toms Spezialitäten</ShipName>
          </Order>
        </Orders>
      </multimap:Message2>
    </multimap:Messages>
  </soap:Body>
</soap:Envelope>
```


Figure 4.56 Output after Running the Integration Flow with the Content Enricher Step

You can identify the original input message at the top of the reply, followed by the returned detailed message coming from the external OData call. This allows you to choose the pattern that best fits your needs.

Let's now revisit the **Processing** tab of the **Content Enricher** step (see Figure 4.57).

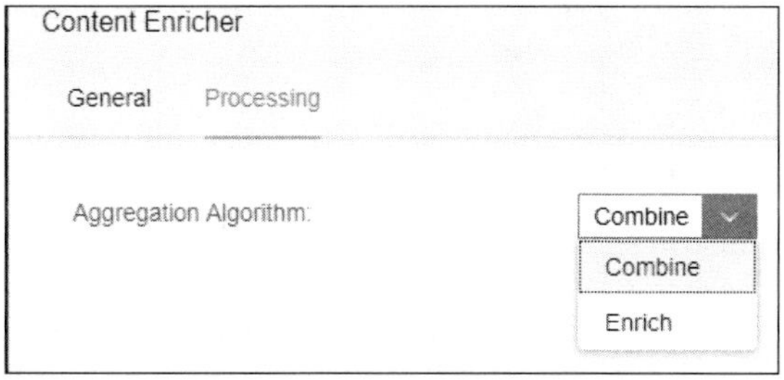

Content Enricher
General Processing
Aggregation Algorithm: Combine
Combine
Enrich

Figure 4.57 Processing Tab of the Content Enricher

As Figure 4.57 shows, the **Content Enricher** step has two different aggregation algorithms that it uses to combine two payloads as a single message: the **Combine** and **Enrich** aggregation algorithms. The next sections discuss both algorithms.

Combine

The **Combine** aggregation algorithm simply creates a new target message by adding two original messages next to each other. You don't have control to define how messages should be combined. This is the algorithm used in our previous example, which produced the response message shown in Figure 4.56. To better illustrate how the **Combine** algorithm differs from the **Enrich** algorithm, let's use a completely different example message (which doesn't relate to the example of Figure 4.56). Consider that you have an original message that looks like the one presented in Figure 4.58.

```
<StudentCollection>
    <Student>
        <id>100</id>
        <firstname>John</firstname>
        <lastname>Smith</lastname>
        <score_refid>a11</score_refid>
    </Student>
    <Student>
        <id>101</id>
        <firstname>Satoshi</firstname>
        <lastname>Nakamoto</lastname>
        <score_refid>a12</score_refid>
    </Student>
</StudentCollection>
```

Figure 4.58 Example of the Original Message

In addition, consider that the message presented in Figure 4.59 represents the response of the service called by the **Content Enricher** step. Note that this message is also sometimes referred to as a lookup message within the context of the **Content Enricher** step.

```
<StudentScores>
    <Score>
        <id>a11</id>
        <course>Mathematics</course>
        <score>70</score>
        <year>2018</year>
        <passed>true</passed>
    </Score>
    <Score>
        <id>a12</id>
        <course>Mathematics</course>
        <score>40</score>
        <year>2018</year>
        <passed>false</passed>
    </Score>
</StudentScores>
```

Figure 4.59 Example of the Response Message of the Content Enricher Step (Lookup Message)

Using the **Content Enricher** algorithm, the combination of the two messages shown in Figure 4.58 and Figure 4.59 results in a message similar to the one presented in Figure 4.60. Notice from Figure 4.60 that the two messages have been each wrapped by the nodes `message1` and `message2`, respectively. Another node named `messages` is used as the root of the message.


```
<multimap:messages xmlns:multimap="http://sap.com/xi/XI/SplitAndMerge">
 <message1>
    <StudentCollection>
        <Student>
                <id>100</id>
                <firstname>John</firstname>
               <lastname>Smith</lastname>
                <score_refid>all</score_refid>
        </Student>
        <Student>
                <id>101</id>
                <firstname>Satoshi</firstname>
              <lastname>Nakamoto</lastname>
                <score_refid>al2</score_refid>
        </Student>
    </StudentCollection>
 </message1>
 <message2>
    <StudentScores>
        <Score>
                <id>all</id>
                <course>Mathematics</course>
                <score>70</score>
                <year>2018</year>
                <passed>true</passed>
        </Score>
        <Score>
                <id>al2</id>
                <course>Mathematics</course>
                <score>40</score>
                <year>2018</year>
                <passed>false</passed>
        </Score>
    </StudentScores>
 </message2>
</multimap:messages xmlns:multimap="http://sap.com/xi/XI/SplitAndMerge">
```

Figure 4.60 Enriched Message Using the Content Enricher Combined Algorithm

Let's next look at how the result would have looked with the **Enrich** aggregation algorithm.

Enrich

The **Enrich** algorithm is used to provide you more control of how the original message and the one returned by the **Content Enricher** (lookup message) should be merged. You can specify the path to the node and key element based on which the original message is enriched with the lookup message.

Looking at the message presented earlier in Figure 4.58, and note that the element `<score_refid>` represents the reference ID to be used as a link to the lookup message (refer to Figure 4.59). While using the **Enrich** algorithm, you need a way to specify how the correct record should be retrieved from the lookup message. This is done with the help of the fields shown in Table 4.2. Note that these fields appear on the screen as soon as you select the **Enrich** value from the **Aggregator Algorithm** dropdown (see Figure 4.61).

Category	Field	Description	Example
Original Message	**Path to Node**	Path to the reference node in the original message	**StudentCollection/ Student**
	Key Element	Key element in the original message	**score_refid**
Lookup Message	**Path to Node**	Path to the reference node in the lookup message	**StudentScores/Score**
	Key Element	Key element in the lookup message	**id**

Table 4.2 Properties Available for the Enrich Aggregator Algorithm

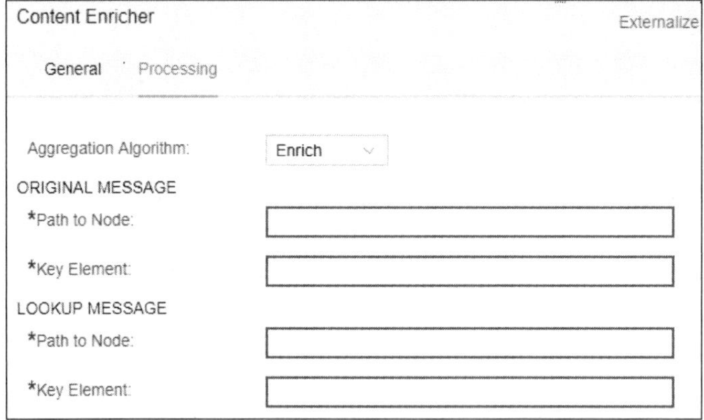

Figure 4.61 Example of Fields Required for the Enrich Algorithm

If you configure the **Enrich** properties with the values used in Table 4.2 (Example column), you'll get a result similar to the one depicted in Figure 4.62.

```
<StudentCollection>
      <Student>
            <id>100</id>
            <firstname>John</firstname>
            <lastname>Smith</lastname>
            <score_refid>all</score_refid>
            <Score>
                  <id>all</id>
                  <course>Mathematics</course>
                  <score>70</score>
                  <year>2018</year>
                  <passed>true</passed>
            </Score>
      </Student>
      <Student>
            <id>101</id>
            <firstname>Satoshi</firstname>
            <lastname>Nakamoto</lastname>
            <score_refid>al2</score_refid>
            <Score>
                  <id>al2</id>
                  <course>Mathematics</course>
                  <score>40</score>
                  <year>2018</year>
                  <passed>false</passed>
            </Score>
      </Student>
</StudentCollection>
```

Figure 4.62 Enriched Message Using the Content Enricher's Enrich Algorithm

Notice how the resulting message of using the **Enrich** algorithm (see Figure 4.62) is different from the one using the **Combine** algorithm (refer to Figure 4.60). This closes our discussion on using the **Content Enricher** step.

In this section, we showed you how to configure the connection to an external OData-based service provider, how to benefit from the Query Editor to construct the sometimes complex string for the resource path to actually retrieve the data you're interested in, and how to add a **Request-Reply** (or **Content Enricher**) step to your message processing pipeline. In the next section, we'll explain how to actually format the message to a target format of your choice by using mappings.

4.4 Working with Mappings

Typically, integration projects require mapping functionality due to the many different message formats in the systems that need to be connected. Hence, integration solutions such as SAP Cloud Platform Integration must provide capabilities to solve this problem elegantly. In this section, you'll learn how to apply mappings in your integration flows. We'll explain the configuration of the mapping step in detail. In addition, we'll show you how SAP Cloud Platform Integration message processing differs from message processing within SAP Process Integration, and what consequences this has on the mapping's configuration.

In every integration scenario, mapping between different data formats of the participating systems is a hot topic. In fact, it may be one of the most important tasks you have to complete for every integration project, and it always requires a certain amount of effort to implement. Supporting the modeler with a convenient mapping environment and a performance mapping engine is of the highest importance for every integration framework.

SAP gained some experience in building a mapping engine through its SAP Process Integration product. From the beginning, SAP Process Integration included a Java-based mapping engine. Consequently, it became an obvious choice to include the same mapping engine in SAP Cloud Platform Integration, as well. It's a stable and reliable engine that has been in productive use for many years. In addition, because of this reuse, you can also reuse your SAP Process Integration mappings in SAP Cloud Platform Integration, which saves your investment in developed mapping logic.

This section, however, isn't about the mapping engine itself, the functionality it provides, or how to solve certain mapping challenges because a plethora of material is already publicly available, either in SAP's online documentation for SAP Process Integration, or in SAP Community. Instead, we'll address the question of how to apply the mapping engine within SAP Cloud Platform Integration so that you know how to use a mapping step in your message processing chain correctly.

This is of particular importance because SAP Cloud Platform Integration is based on the Apache Camel integration framework, which can handle almost any message format—it's a payload-agnostic routing and mediation engine. Apache Camel doesn't follow the interface concept from SAP Process Integration, where you have to precisely define XML-based inbound and outbound interfaces in the Enterprise Services Repository (ESR) before you can actually start modeling an integration scenario.

The overhead of defining interfaces prior to modeling the integration isn't necessary for SAP Cloud Platform Integration. You can push anything to SAP Cloud Platform Integration, and, as long as you don't need access to the actual payload (e.g., for routing purposes), SAP Cloud Platform Integration forwards the message to the receivers as-is. However, the mapping engine has the same history as SAP Process Integration with its XML background. Therefore, it works on XML transformations only, which requires a conversion to XML before invoking the mapping engine in SAP Cloud Platform Integration. As such, you must provide the XML schema of the source and the target message by uploading respective XSD or WSDL files to SAP Cloud Platform Integration. Let's see what this looks like in a concrete example.

4.4.1 The Scenario

For this section, we continue from where we left off in Section 4.3. In that section, you learned how to invoke an OData service to retrieve order details for a given order number. The scenario is shown in Figure 4.53.

As part of the configuration of the OData connection to the receiver, the Query Editor was used to model the access to the OData source. The editor allows you, for example, to define the entities for which a query should search, the individual fields of the entity you're interested in, the filter criteria of the query, and the `order by` condition for sorting the retrieved entities accordingly.

One important part of configuring the connectivity to the OData service provider by the Query Editor is the automatic generation of an XSD file representing the return message of the service in XML format. (See the confirmation message in SAP Cloud Platform Integration's graphical modeling environment after finishing the configuration of the connection's properties with the Query Editor in Figure 4.50.)

This occurs even though an OData service typically returns its results in either JavaScript Object Notation (JSON) or Atom format. Obviously, the **Request-Reply** step of Figure 4.53 implicitly invokes a mapping from JSON/Atom to XML so that the message processing chain can continue working on XML in the forthcoming steps. But what if the current format within the route isn't in XML? In these cases, you have to explicitly call a transformation step. Currently, SAP Cloud Platform Integration supports steps for converting comma-separated values (CSV) and JSON to XML, and vice versa. SAP Cloud Platform, Enterprise Edition, is additionally equipped with an Electronic Data Interchange (EDI)-to-XML converter. In the web-based modeling environment of SAP Cloud Platform Integration, you find the respective converter beneath the **Message Transformers** icon (Figure 4.63).

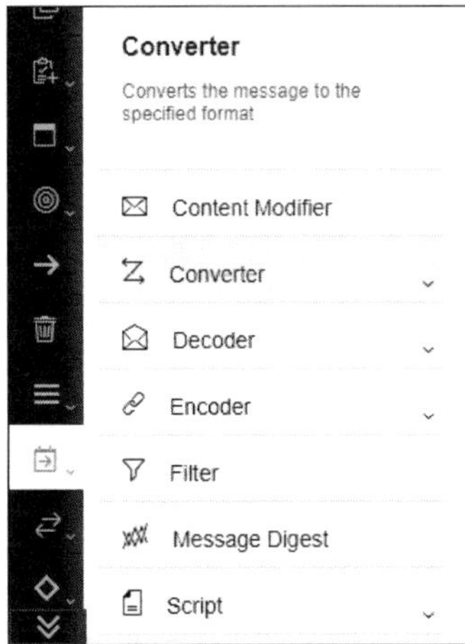

Figure 4.63 Pick a Converter Step from the Palette

Our goal for our example scenario is to map the returned entity into an XML format of our choice. The business scenario behind this assumption is that, quite frequently, data needs to be returned to a consumer in a specific XML format. You have to convert the automatically generated XML format of the **Request-Reply** step in your route to the target format the consumer expects.

Typically, the required target format is defined either by an XSD or a WSDL file. If you have an SAP Process Integration background, you can also easily define those files using the Enterprise Services Builder—the tool SAP Process Integration provides for designing interfaces in the ESR. Any other XML tool works as well. For our example, we've created such an XML file, called *GetOrderShipDetails_Sync.wsdl*, which we used for our first exercise in Section 4.1. For your convenience, you'll find an example message following the WSDL's description in Figure 4.64.

```
<soapenv:Envelope xmlns:soapenv="http://s
   <soapenv:Header/>
   <soapenv:Body>
      <demo:OrderNumber_MT>
         <orderNumber>10249</orderNumber>
      </demo:OrderNumber_MT>
   </soapenv:Body>
</soapenv:Envelope>
```

Figure 4.64 Example Message

To summarize, the source message for the mapping step is the structure defined in the automatically generated XSD file *OrdersEntityGETO.xsd* (refer to Figure 4.50), and the target message is the response part of the synchronous service interface described in *GetOrderShipDetails_Sync.wsdl.*

Before diving deeper into the mapping topic, let's first import the *GetOrderShipDetails_Sync.wsdl* WSDL file into our integration flow via the **Resources** view in the next section.

4.4.2 Adding and Using Resources via the Resources View

A typical integration scenario uses a variety of resources, such as mappings, archives, scripts, and schemas, in its steps. Any external file or artifact that can be imported or referred to for the purpose of being used in the integration flow can be considered as a resource. Let's first start by exploring the features of the integration flow. Later in the section, we'll discuss how to extend our example integration flow by adding a WSDL file using the **Resources** view.

The resources are typically grouped under the different categories listed in Table 4.3.

Category	Type	Supported Extensions	Source
Archives	Archive	*.jar*	Can be added from the file system
Mappings	Operation mapping	*.opmap*	Can be added from the ESR
	Message mapping	*.mmap*	
	XSLT mapping	*.xslt* *.xsl*	Can be added from the file system or another integration flow
Schemas	WSDL	*.wsdl*	Can be added from the file system or another integration flow
	XSD	*.xsd*	
	EDMX	*.edmx*	
Scripts	Groovy script	*.gsh* *.gy* *.groovy*	Can be added from the file system or another integration flow
	JavaScript	*.js*	

Table 4.3 Types of Files That the Resources View Supports

The columns used in Table 4.3 are explained here:

- **Category**
  A grouping under which the different resources can be classified.
- **Type**
  The types of resource files that can be added for each category.
- **Supported Extensions**
  The supported file extensions for each resource type.
- **Source**
  The source from where the resources can be added. Some resources can be uploaded from your local file system. It's also possible to add some resources from another existing integration flow. This reuse of resources from another integration flow prevents the duplication of resources.

The **Resources** view is a location from which all of the artifacts listed in Table 4.3 can be centrally managed. From this view, resources can be opened in their respective editors, downloaded, and deleted. After opening an integration flow, click on the area outside the integration flow model for the **Resources** view to appear at the bottom tabs, as shown in Figure 4.65.

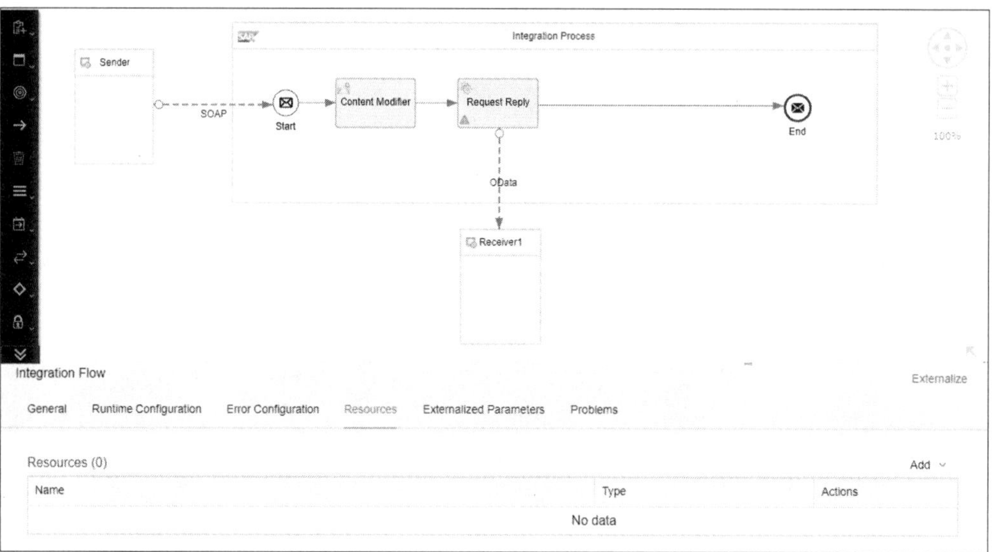

Figure 4.65 The Resources View Tab

Looking at the scenario we've been implementing in Section 4.1.4, the integration flow needs to be enriched by adding the WSDL resource that will be used to perform some mapping later in Section 4.4.3. In Section 4.1.4, we downloaded the WSDL file named *GetOrderShipDetails_Sync.wsdl*. You can now import it by following these steps:

1. Click Edit, and then click the area outside the integration flow model.
2. Select the **Resources** tab at the bottom section of the integration flow (refer to Figure 4.65).
3. Click the **Add** button. A menu appears from which you need to choose **Schema** and then **WSDL**, as shown in Figure 4.66.

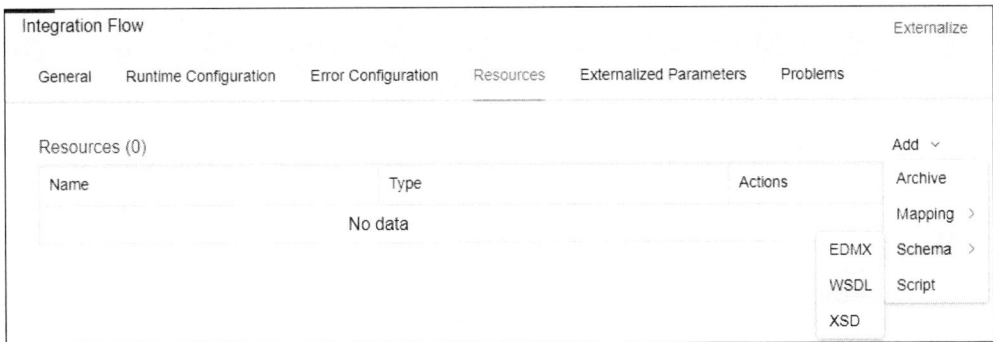

Figure 4.66 Adding an Object in the Resources View

4. You're redirected to a page from which you can browse to the WSDL on your local file system and upload it. As a result, the WSDL file is now added to the **Resources** tab, as shown in Figure 4.67.

Figure 4.67 Resource View after Adding a WSDL

Note

Because the WSDL can be categorized as a schema (as discussed in Table 4.3), note that it's placed under the **Schemas** node element in Figure 4.67.

You can also hover over the name of a resource shown in the **Resources** View to view its access path, or you can click on it to view the resource details via its editor.

A number of actions can be performed on the uploaded resources, including the following:

- **Delete**
  As shown in Figure 4.67, the delete icon can be used to delete the resource from the **Resources** tab.
- **Download**
  As shown in Figure 4.67, the download icon can be used to download the resource from the **Resources** tab.

By clicking on the name of the WSDL file resource in Figure 4.67, the WSDL file is loaded in the special view, as shown in Figure 4.68.

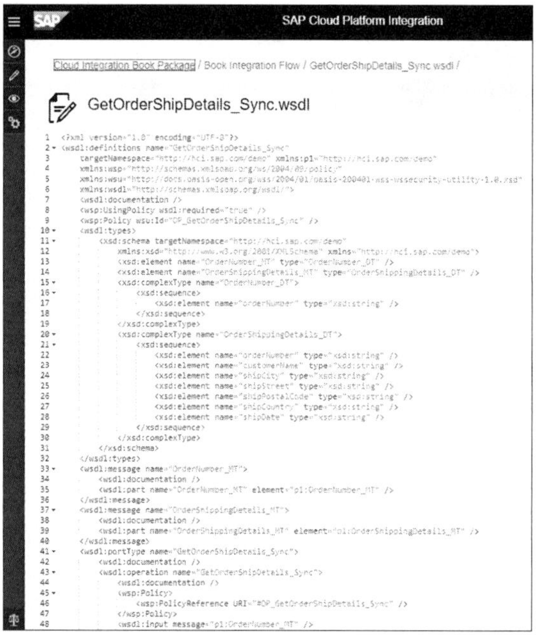

Figure 4.68 Viewing the Contents of the WSDL File

Now that you've successfully imported the WSDL file using the **Resources** view, let's see how this WSDL file can be useful to your integration flow by using it in the sender channel. You'll need to select the sender channel, which displays its details at the bottom of the screen (see Figure 4.69).

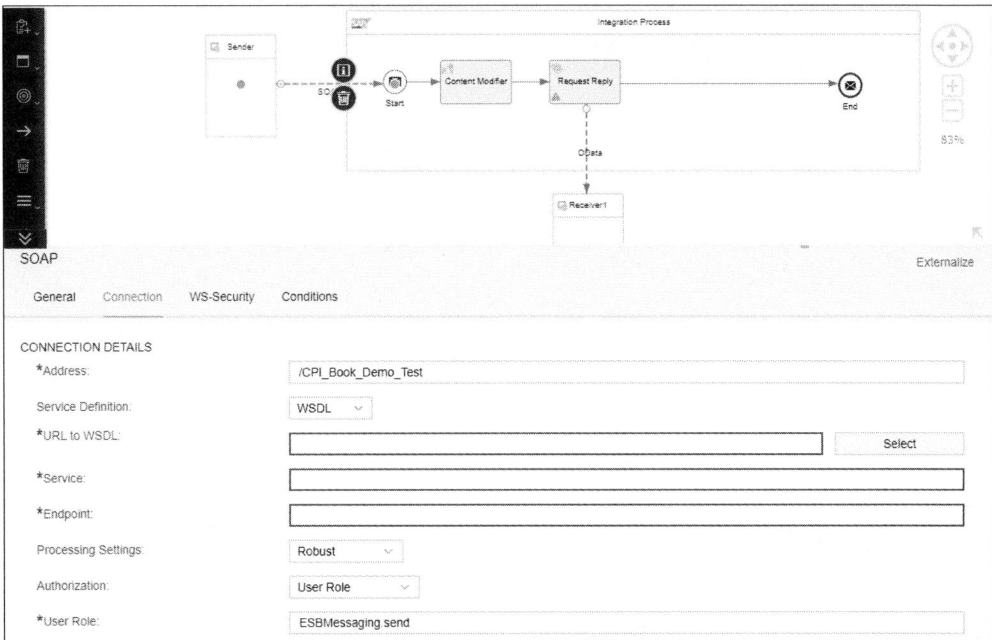

Figure 4.69 Adding a WSDL File to the Sender Channel

Then click on the **Select** button (Figure 4.69) to be presented with a new screen giving you the possibility to select a WSLD file (see Figure 4.70). Then select the **GetOrder-ShipDetails_Sync** row.

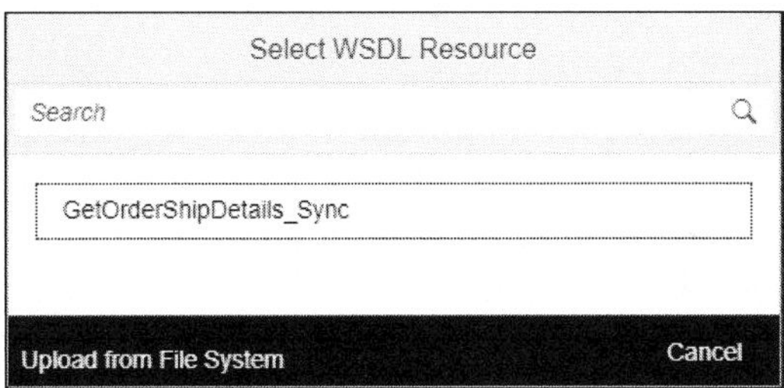

Figure 4.70 Selecting the WSDL File to Be Used in the Sender Channel

The screen is now populated with details of the WSDL file (see Figure 4.71).

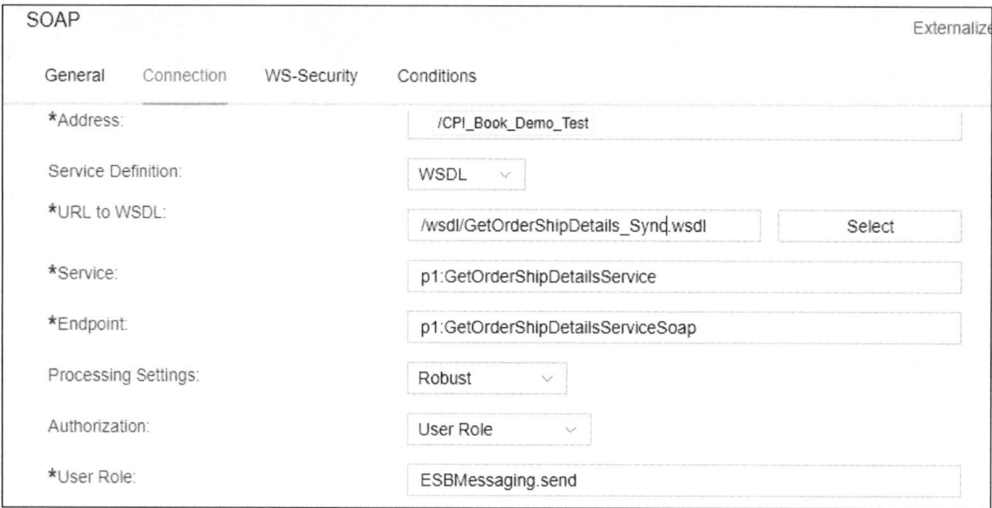

Figure 4.71 Sender Channel Populated with WSDL Details

You can now save and deploy your integration flow. We'll discuss the mapping step next.

4.4.3 Applying the Mapping Step in the Message Processing Chain

To use the mapping engine in the route, select the **Mapping** palette entry to open the submenu, as shown earlier in Figure 65. You first have to position the mapping step in the integration flow pool. In the palette, a dedicated mapping icon is available (Figure 4.72).

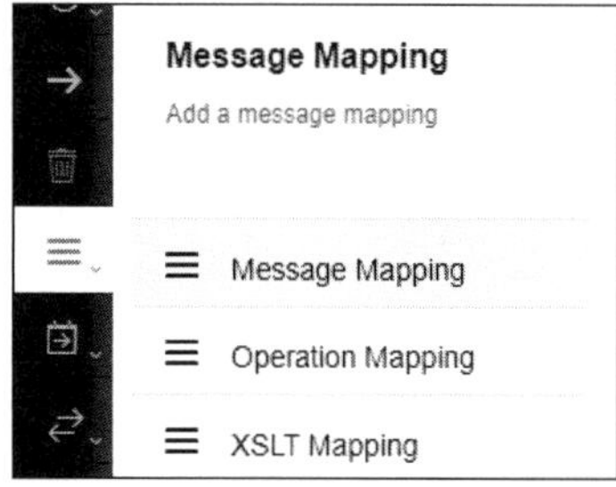

Figure 4.72 Select the Mapping Step from the Palette

Click the icon and then move the mouse pointer (which changed to three parallel horizontal bars) into the **Integration Process** pool (Figure 4.73). Then select the step from the integration flow and click on the ⊕ icon to create a message mapping (Figure 4.74). By doing this, you have to name the message mapping, as shown in Figure 4.75, and then click on the **Create** button.

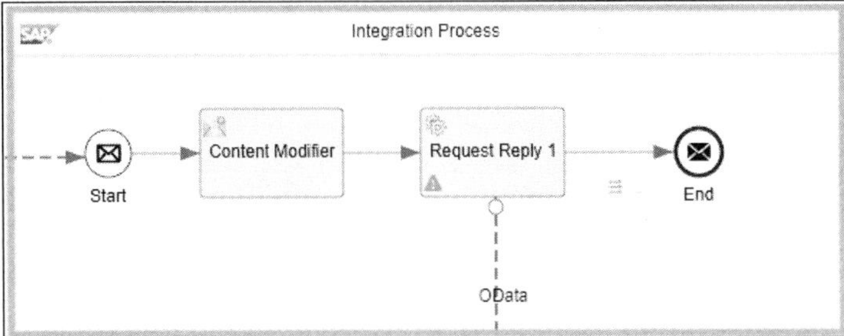

Figure 4.73 Positioning the Mapping Step in the Integration Flow (Mouse Pointer Changed to Three Horizontal Bars)

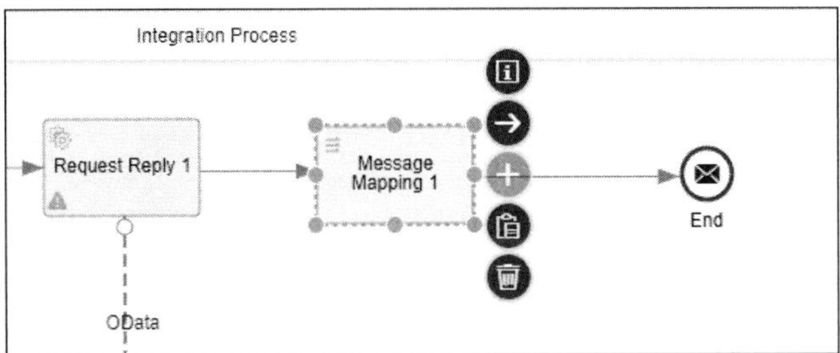

Figure 4.74 Creating a New Message Mapping

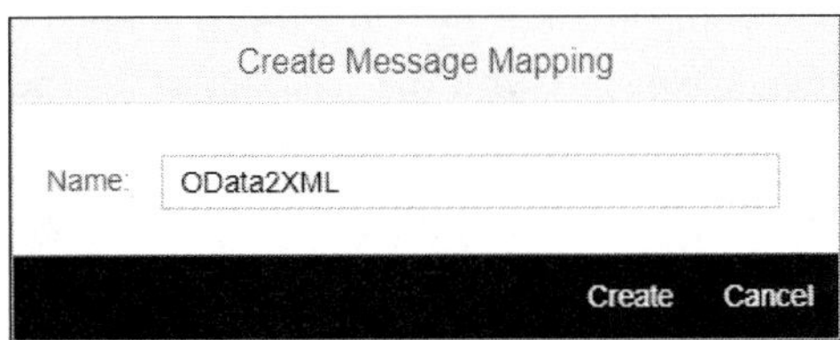

Figure 4.75 Naming the Message Mapping

After clicking on the **Save** button, the mapping editor opens immediately (Figure 4.76).

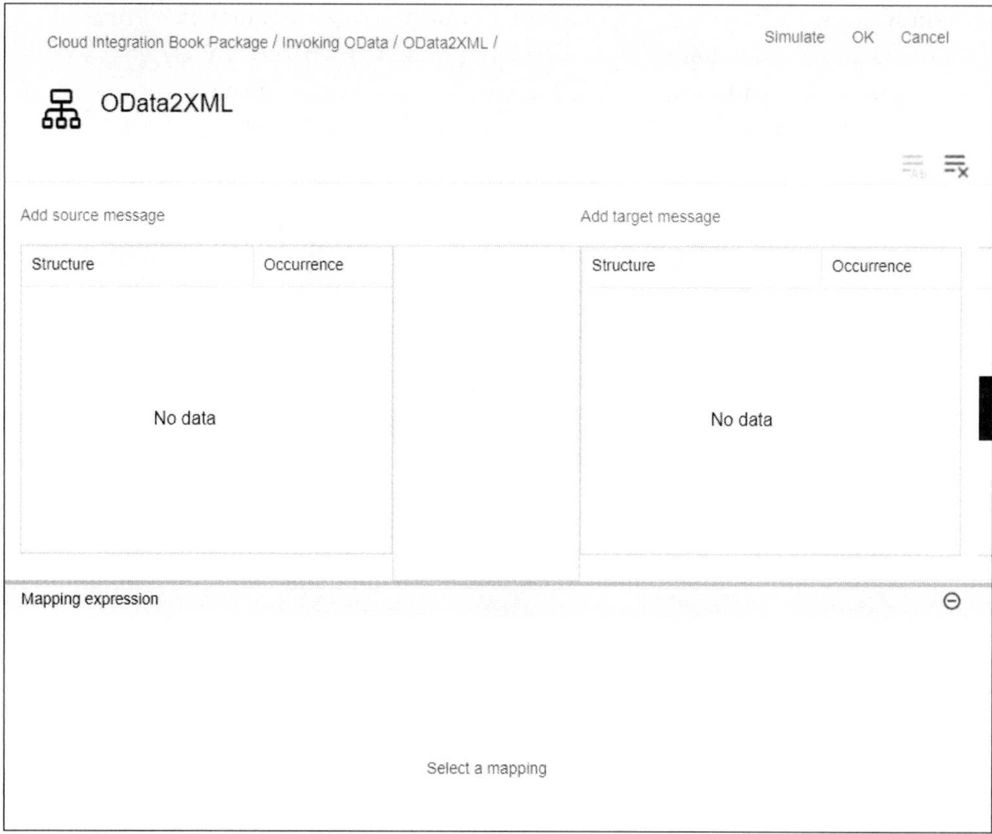

Figure 4.76 Mapping Editor Opens after Positioning the Mapping Task

As you can see, both the source and the target messages are missing. Next, we describe how to use either a pregenerated XSD file or a self-developed WSDL file for the definition of source and target messages. We'll start with the assignment of the source message. Click the **Add source message** link in Figure 4.76 to opens the **Select source message** dialog box shown in Figure 4.77.

The dialog box lists all the files that either have already been generated or have been uploaded from the file system. In our example, the file describing the OData service, as well as the file that has been automatically generated by the Query Editor, are listed. You know from the summary of the previous section that *OrdersEntity-GET0.xsd* is the file that describes the source message. Click it once. You'll immediately return to the mapping editor, which shows the **Structure** of the source message on the left side of the screen (Figure 4.78).

Select Source Message

GetOrderShipDetails_Sync.wsdl

OrdersEntityGET0.xsd

services_odata_org_Northwind_Northwind_svc.edmx

Upload from File System Cancel

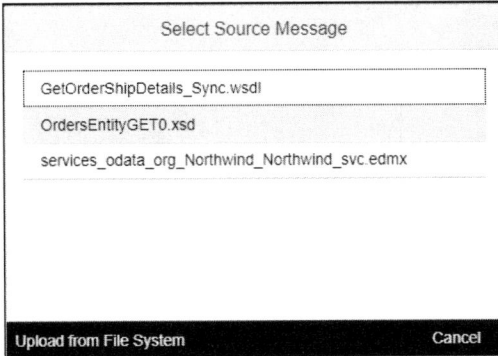

Figure 4.77 Dialog Box for Selecting the Target Message

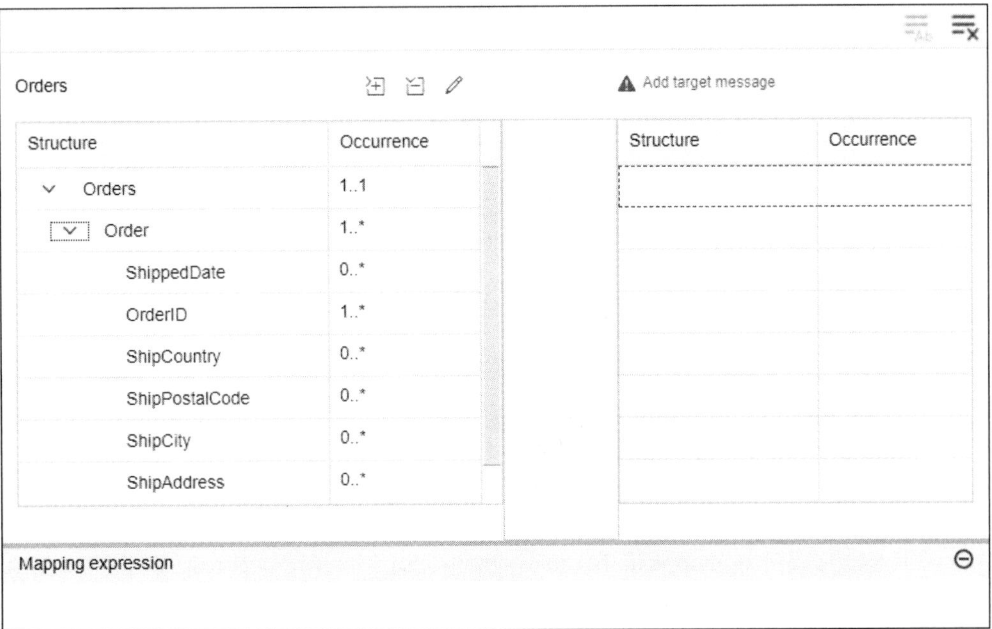

Figure 4.78 Mapping Editor Displaying the Structure of the Source Message after Assigning the XSD File

Next, assign the target message by clicking the **Add target message** link in the upper-right corner of the mapping editor. Again, the dialog box for assigning the appropriate file opens (Figure 4.79).

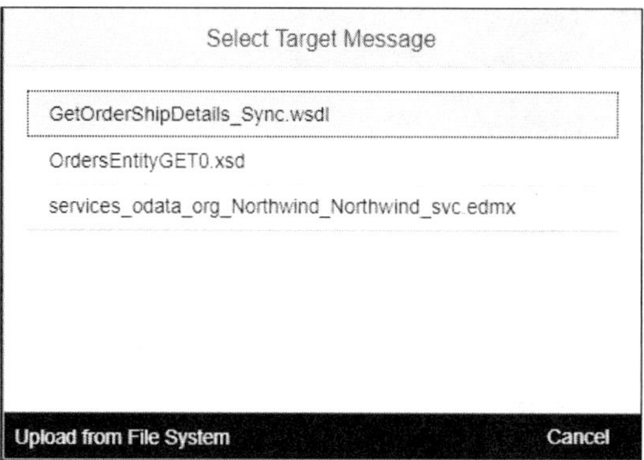

Figure 4.79 Selecting the Target Message's Structure

Note that the WSDL that we need is already available (*GetOrderShipDetails_Sync.wsdl*) because we already imported it via the **Resources** view in Section 4.4.2. As the WSDL file contains the description of a synchronous interface, another dialog box for selecting an element opens (Figure 4.80).

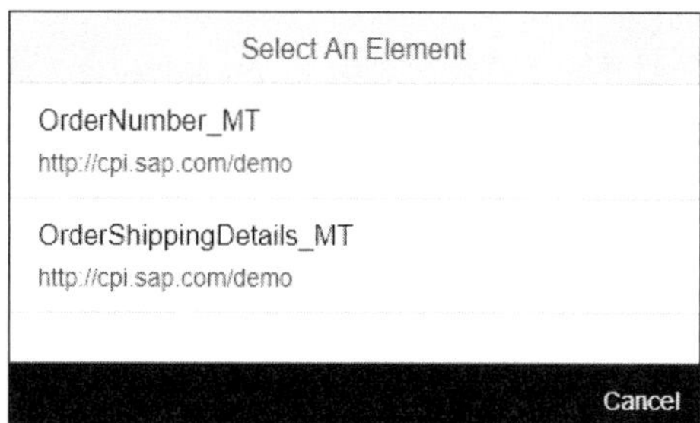

Figure 4.80 Selecting the Correct Target Structure from a Synchronous Interface

This second dialog appears because synchronous interfaces consist of two parts: a request and a response. Typically, these are two completely different structures.

Take our scenario as an example: We're retrieving details for an order based on an order number coming in via the request message, so the request message contains just one field, the order number. The response message, on the other hand, contains the details of the order. Hence, it comprises a number of fields. This is exactly what you see in Figure 4.80. The first entry, **OrderNumber_MT**, reflects the request message containing just the order number as the only field. The second entry, **OrderShippingDetails_MT**, stands for the response message and contains all details that make up the order.

Note

SAP Process Integration specialists will recognize the message type (MT) suffix (the string _MT after the data type's name) for both elements. It's a typical habit if you create message types in the ESR. And, yes, we've created the synchronous interface in the ESR. As such, the interoperability between SAP Process Integration and SAP Cloud Platform Integration on a data level is ensured.

You must pick the second entry from the list as your target message structure. Click it once, and the user interface (UI) immediately returns to the mapping editor. The mapping editor analyzes the structure of the response message and depicts it accordingly. Figure 4.81 shows the result on the right side of the screen.

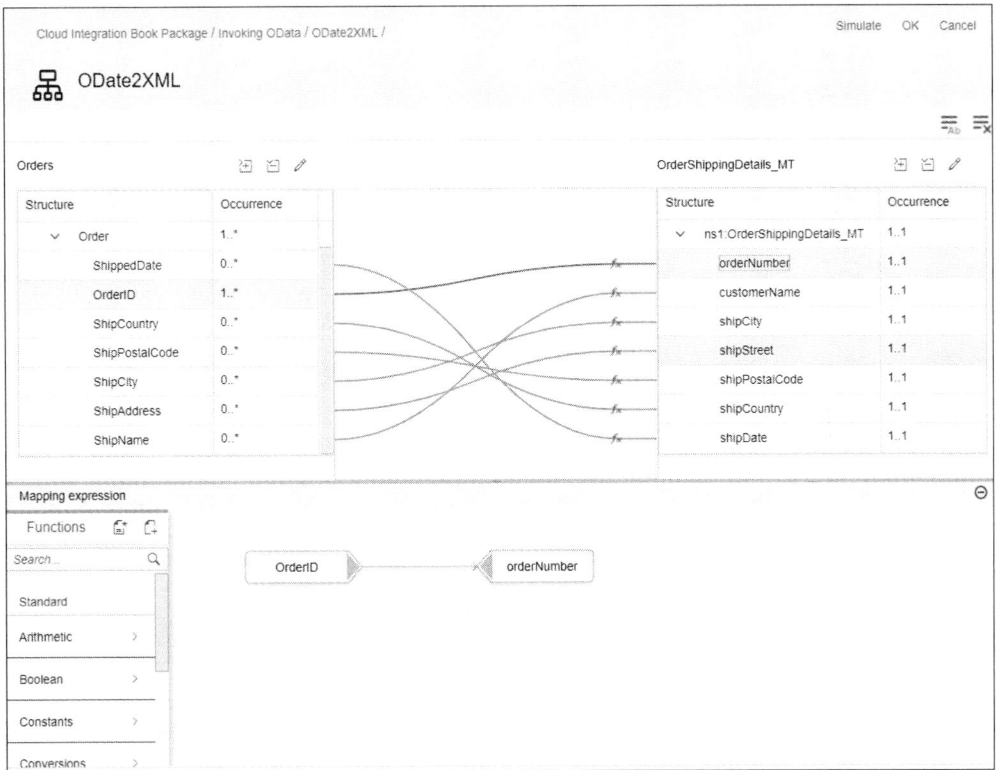

Figure 4.81 The Mapping Editor after Opening Both Structures and after Finishing the Mapping Exercise

The mapping editor itself should look familiar to those who have worked with SAP Process Integration before. You can now assign field mappings by simply dragging and dropping source fields from the left to the corresponding target fields on the right. We did this for our simple scenario, and the result is also depicted in Figure 4.81.

You can also benefit from several predefined functions that are shipped with the mapping editor and that are listed in the **Functions** area of Figure 4.81.

If you're dealing with a complex mapping, and the predefined functions don't have what you need, you also have the choice to build your own custom-built Java functions using user-defined functions (UDFs). UDFs are discussed in Chapter 9, Section 9.3. An alternative is to build an Extensible Stylesheet Language Transformation (XSLT) mapping.

As we've already explained, you'll find plenty of material in SAP Community and in the SAP Process Integration online help (*https://help.sap.com/viewer/product/SAP_NETWEAVER_PI/ALL/en-US*) when it comes to mappings that are more complex. You'll find the handling of the graphical mapper quite intuitive and convenient. It shouldn't be a problem to define the mapping between the two structures as it's shown in the figure.

Notice the **Simulate** button in the top-right corner of the mapping editor. You can immediately check your mapping for accuracy by uploading an example message to the mapping editor, which, in turn, runs your mapping and displays the result. This results in short turnaround cycles between development and test.

After you're done with your mappings, click the **Ok** button (also located in the top right corner of the mapping editor), and you're back in the UI for modeling your integration flow.

Finally, drag the mapping step on the arrow connecting the **Request-Reply** step with the **Message-End** event shown earlier in Figure 4.53 to position the mapping activity between the two. The result of your process model is shown in Figure 4.82.

That's it! You've finished the configuration of the mapping activity and can now save, deploy, and run your new integration flow. Use a SOAP tool of your choice (e.g., SoapUI), and invoke your solution. An appropriate request message might look like the one shown in Figure 4.83.

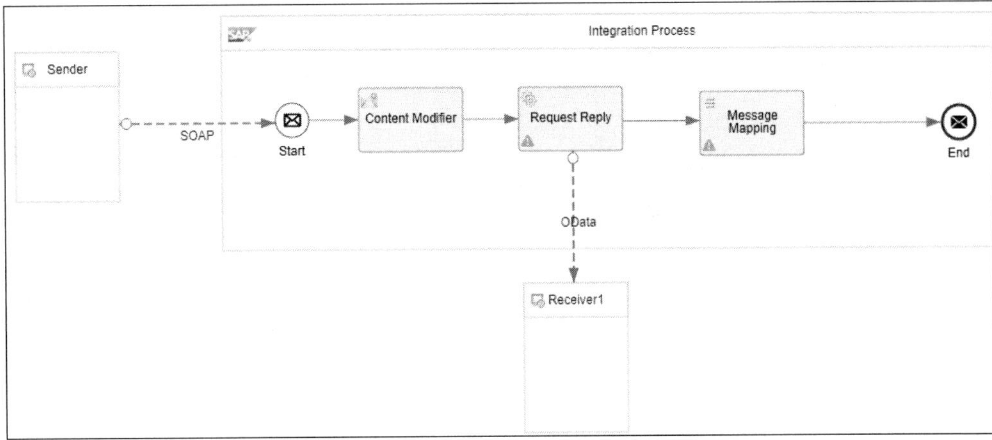

Figure 4.82 The Final Result of the Process Model after Positioning the Mapping Step before the End Event

```
<soapenv:Envelope xmlns:soapenv="http://schemas
   <soapenv:Header/>
   <soapenv:Body>
      <demo:OrderNumber_MT>
         <orderNumber>10249</orderNumber>
      </demo:OrderNumber_MT>
   </soapenv:Body>
</soapenv:Envelope>
```

Figure 4.83 Example Request Message

After passing through the integration flow, the result message should look similar to the one shown in Figure 4.84.

```
<soap:Envelope xmlns:soap="http://schemas.xmlsoap.org/soap/envelope/">
   <soap:Body>
      <ns1:OrderShippingDetails_MT xmlns:ns1="http://hci.sap.com/demo">
         <orderNumber>10249</orderNumber>
         <customerName>Toms Spezialitäten</customerName>
         <shipCity>Münster</shipCity>
         <shipStreet>Luisenstr. 48</shipStreet>
         <shipPostalCode>44087</shipPostalCode>
         <shipCountry>Germany</shipCountry>
         <shipDate>1996-07-10T00:00:00.000</shipDate>
      </ns1:OrderShippingDetails_MT>
   </soap:Body>
</soap:Envelope>
```

Figure 4.84 Reply Message after Successful Invocation of the Integration Flow, Including the Mapping Step

To summarize, mappings are an important aspect in every integration project. SAP Cloud Platform Integration benefits from a mapping engine originally developed for SAP Process Integration. You've learned how the mapping engine is integrated into SAP Cloud Platform Integration and how you can invoke it in your integration flows by applying the mapping activity. You've also seen how the message processing in SAP Cloud Platform Integration differs from SAP Process Integration (the payload-agnostic behavior in SAP Cloud Platform Integration) and that this difference requires the explicit definition of message structures by using either XSD or WSDL files to configure the mapping step. With this knowledge, you're now well equipped to tackle even more sophisticated integration challenges.

4.4.4 Using Value Mapping to Enhance Your Scenario

Value mappings are used to represent multiple values of an object. To better illustrate it, let's imagine that the consumer of the service who receives the response returned in Figure 4.84 doesn't accept country names in the `shipCountry` field but rather prefers to have a country ISO code. This means, for example, that instead of returning the value `Germany`, the consumer would rather receive the value `DE`. This is a common use case in integration scenarios and means that the object country can be represented in many ways (following our case here, it can be represented using a country name or an ISO code). It's in such cases where value mapping comes to the rescue.

Let's now try to extend the example of Figure 4.84 to return an ISO code in the field `shipCountry` instead of the country name. To achieve that, you'll need to create a **Value Mapping** artifact by following these steps:

1. Go to the **Design** section of SAP Cloud Platform Integration, and open your package in edit mode.
2. From your package, click on the **Add** button, and select **Value Mapping** from the resulting menu (Figure 4.85).
3. Provide a name for the value mapping, and click **Ok** (Figure 4.86).
4. Navigate to the right package, and open the value mapping that you just created in the previous step. You end up with a value mapping editor as shown in Figure 4.87.
5. Click on **Edit** to switch to an editable mode.

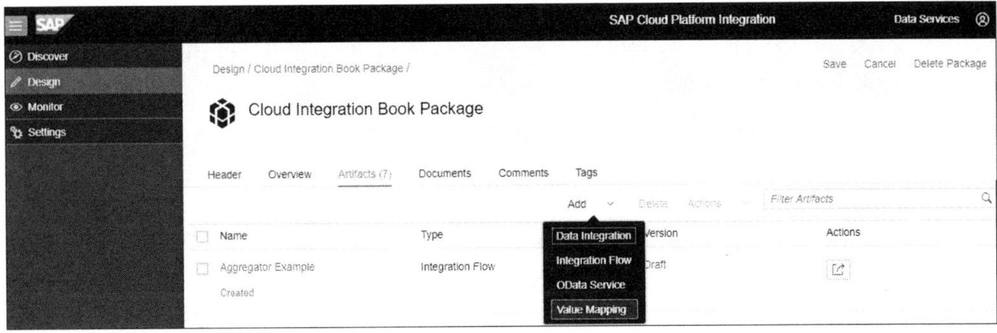

Figure 4.85 Creating a Value Mapping Artifact

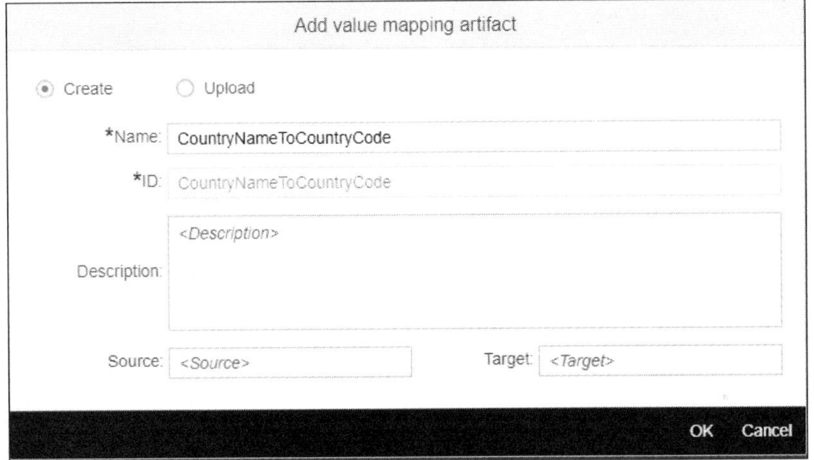

Figure 4.86 Naming the Value Mapping Artifact

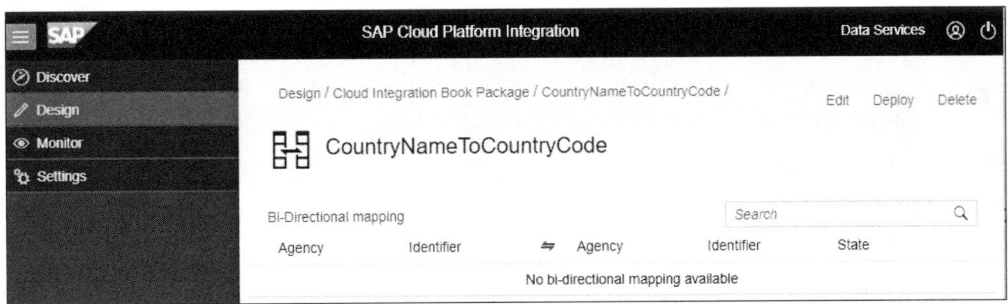

Figure 4.87 Value Mapping Editor

6. Click on the **Add** button in Figure 4.88. You're then presented with a list of fields that are explained in Table 4.4. For the sake of simplicity, fill in the columns as shown in Figure 4.88.

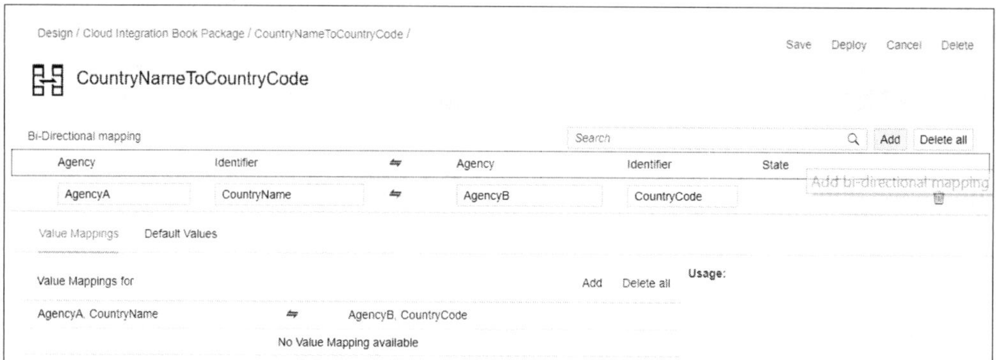

Figure 4.88 Adding Values to the Value Mapping

Column Name	Description
Agency	Represents the organization/scheme responsible for managing and issuing an identifier, for example, a company. Agency A is a country that is responsible for issuing the identifier "passport number" as a means to identify a person. At the same time, we have Agency B representing a company that identifies the same person using the identifier "employee number."
Identifier	A unique value issued by an agency, for example, a passport number.

Table 4.4 Columns of Value Mapping

7. It's now time to add a list of values for the source and target systems to provide a mapping of values between source and target. Click on the **Add** button at the bottom of the screen shown earlier in Figure 4.88.
8. You then get another screen similar to the one presented in Figure 4.89. After populating the value mapping with all required country names and country code values, click on the **Save** button to persist the changes.
9. Click on **Deploy** in the top -right corner of Figure 4.89.

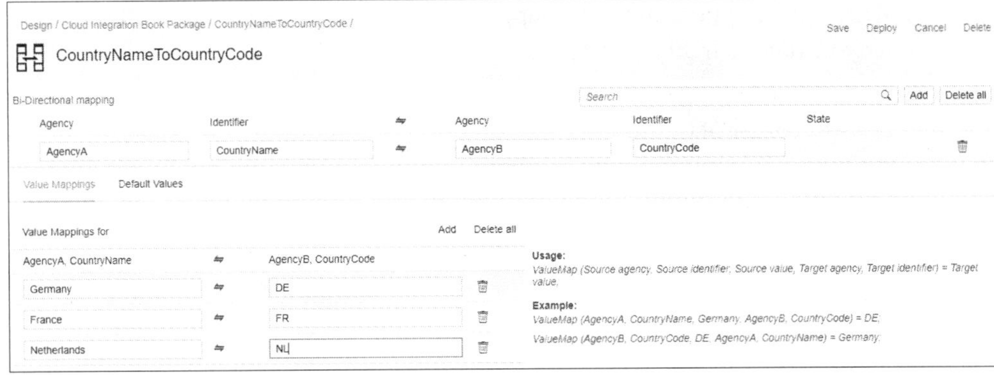

Figure 4.89 Populating the Value Mapping

After the value mapping is deployed, it's time to use it in our mapping. For that, we need to open the mapping that we developed in Figure 4.65 (refer to Figure 4.81).

To get back to that mapping, follow these steps:

1. Open the integration flow, click the **Edit** button, and select the **Mapping** step (Figure 4.90). The property of the mapping appears on the bottom section.
2. Select the **Processing** tab, and click on the mapping name (in our case **/ODate2-XML.mmap**) next to the resource field to navigate to the mapping editor.

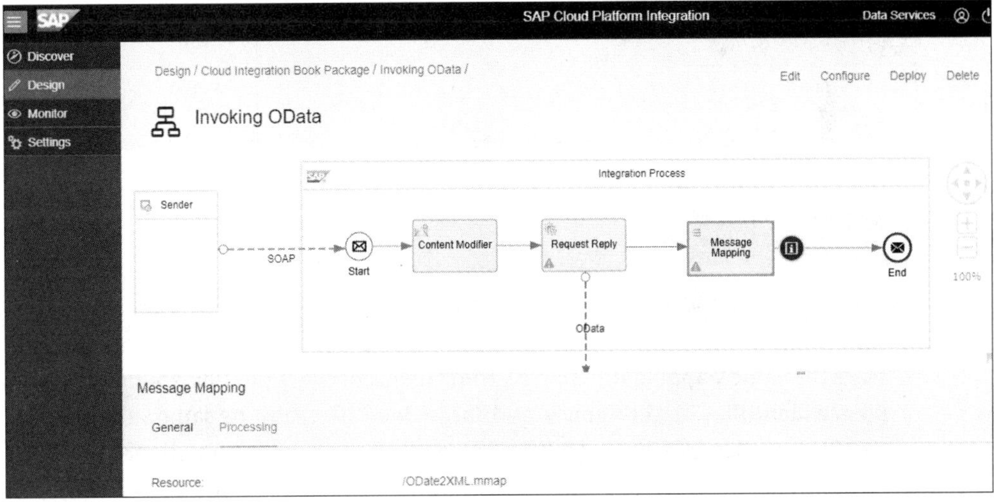

Figure 4.90 Overview of the Integration Flow

3. When you're redirected to the mapping editor, select the **shipCountry** field on the target structure (right side).
4. Select the **valueMapping** function under the **Conversions** function category (bottom-left corner of Figure 4.91).

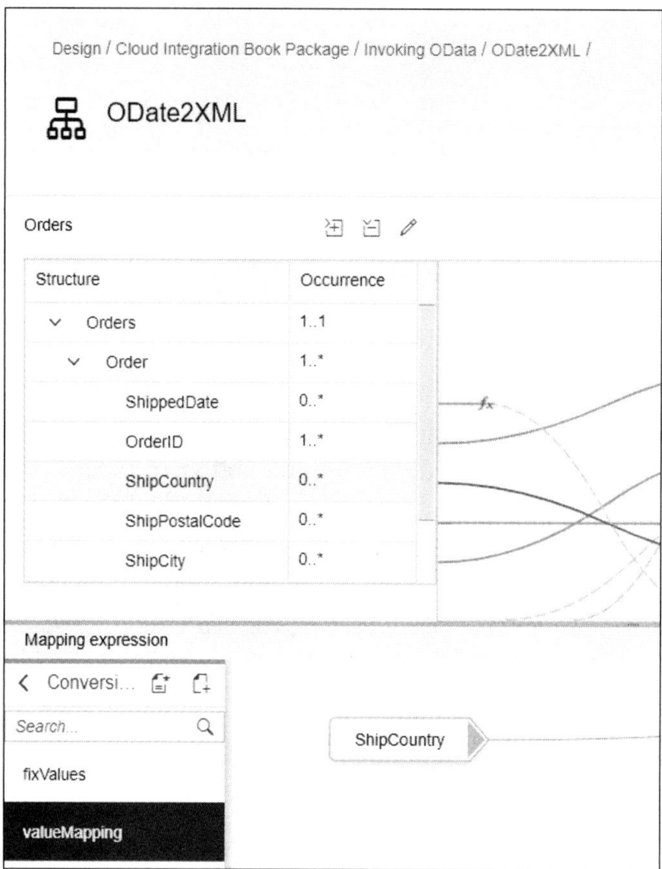

Figure 4.91 Adding a Value Mapping Function in the Mapping Logic

5. Place the **valueMapping** function on the screen. For the input fields **Source Agency**, **Source Identifier**, **Target Agency**, and **Target Identifier**, use the same values as you specified earlier in Figure 4.89. At the end, the configuration should look like Figure 4.92.

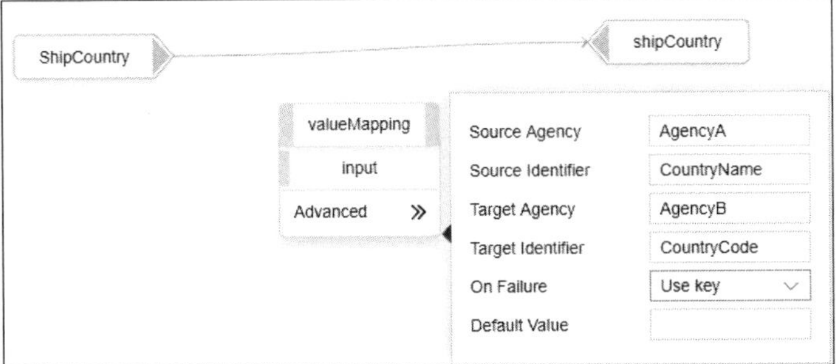

Figure 4.92 Configuring the Value Mapping Function

Note

By using the **Default Value** field in Figure 4.92, it's possible to specify a default value to be used if no matches are found for the incoming value. But for that to work, you'll need to set the **On Failure** dropdown option to **Use Default Value**.

Following is the full list of possible values for the **On Failure** dropdown:

- **Use Key**
  If there is no match, the incoming value will simply be passed to the target value without translation.
- **Throw exceptions**
  If there is no match, an exception will be thrown by the mapping framework.
- **Use Default Value**
  If there is no match, the default value (specified in the **Default Value** field) will be assigned to the target value.

6. After configuring the value mapping function, place it between the two **ShipCountry** fields to get to the final result, which is similar to Figure 4.93.

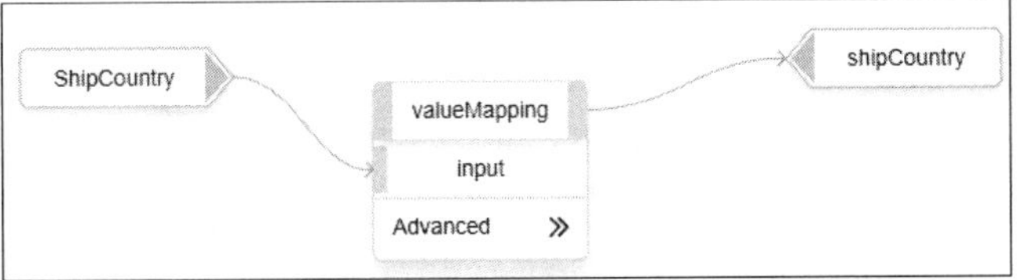

Figure 4.93 Performing a Value Mapping Translation

7. Save and deploy the integration flow.

Congratulations! You can now retest the service using SoapUI. The returned response is shown in Figure 4.94. Note that the value of `ShipCountry` is no longer `Germany`, but `DE`, as configured in our value mapping.


```
<soap:Envelope xmlns:soap="http://schemas.xmlsoap.org/soap/envelope/">
   <soap:Header/>
   <soap:Body>
      <ns1:OrderShippingDetails_MT xmlns:ns1="http://hci.sap.com/demo">
         <orderNumber>10249</orderNumber>
         <customerName>Toms Spezialitäten</customerName>
         <shipCity>Münster</shipCity>
         <shipStreet>Luisenstr. 48</shipStreet>
         <shipPostalCode>44087</shipPostalCode>
         <shipCountry>DE</shipCountry>
         <shipDate>1996-07-10T00:00:00.000</shipDate>
      </ns1:OrderShippingDetails_MT>
   </soap:Body>
</soap:Envelope>
```


Figure 4.94 Updated Response of the Service after Using Value Mapping

4.5 Defining and Providing an OData Service

In Section 4.3, we explored how to consume an external OData service from SAP Cloud Platform Integration. In this case, we used a receiver OData adapter to call the external OData service. There might also be cases where you, as an integration developer, are asked to provide an OData service in SAP Cloud Platform Integration. This will require using a sender OData adapter.

Next, let' explore how you can provide such an OData service from SAP Cloud Platform. Let's start by presenting the target scenario that will be used to explore the OData provisioning capabilities.

4.5.1 The Target Scenario

The integration flow in Figure 4.95 depicts the integration scenario we're going to build in the next section.

We're going to create an OData service that calls a SOAP web service. For simplicity, we'll use a publicly available SOAP web service provided by *http://webservices.oorsprong.org/websamples.countryinfo/CountryInfoService.wso*. This is just for illustration's sake, but you can use any web service of your choice.

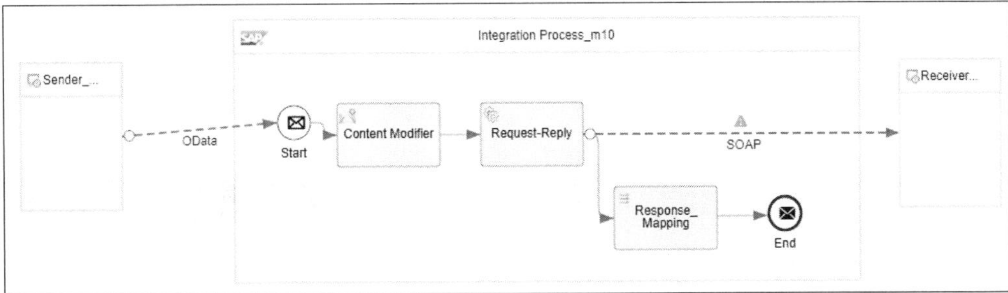

Figure 4.95 OData Integration Flow

One of the first steps is to download the suggested WSDL file available at *http://webservices.oorsprong.org/websamples.countryinfo/CountryInfoService.wso?WSDL* and save it to our local computer. Let's now dive into the details of how to provide such an OData service.

4.5.2 Providing an OData Service

SAP Cloud Platform facilitates the provision of an OData service with a powerful wizard that leads to an automatic generation of an integration flow in the background. While using the wizard, the following main steps are involved:

- **Import from Data Source**
  Helps in creating or updating an OData model by importing its definition from a SOAP, OData, or ODC data source.
- **Edit OData Model**
  Enables you to create or update an OData model using the OData Model Editor.
- **Bind to Data Source**
  Supports in binding entity sets and function imports to a data source such as SOAP, OData, or ODC endpoints.
- **Edit Integration Flow**
  Changes and customizes the generated integration flows with additional business logic.
- **Deploy OData Service**
  Deploys and starts using your OData service when it's ready.

Before exploring each one of the preceding steps in detail, let's first create the needed project by following these steps:

1. From the **Design** tab of your SAP Cloud Platform Integration tenant (left side of Figure 4.96), go to the respective package, and switch to the edit mode.
2. Select the **Add** button, and then click **OData Service** from the resulting menu (see Figure 4.96).

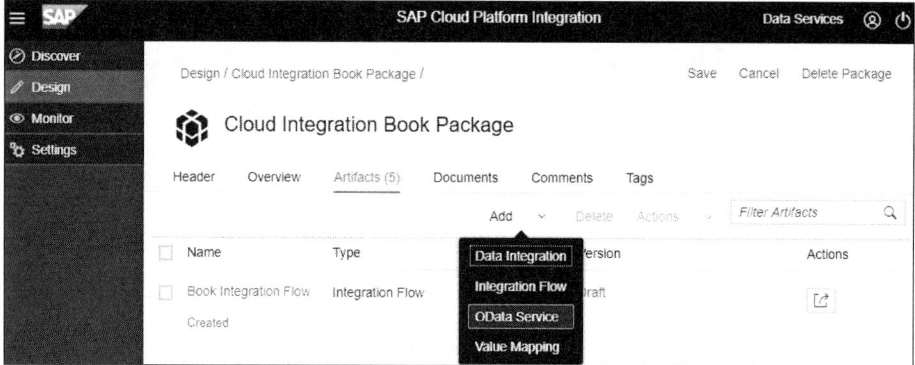

Figure 4.96 Creating an OData Service Artifact

3. Give the artifact a suitable name, such as "Country OData Service", and leave the other fields with their default values. Note that, by default, the namespace is set with the value **SAP** (see Figure 4.97). Then select the **OK** button.

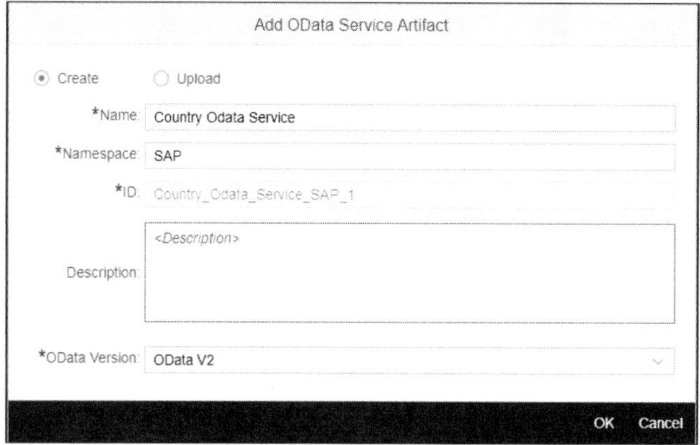

Figure 4.97 Details of the OData Service Artifact

You then get redirected to a page that looks like Figure 4.98 and Figure 4.99. This is the landing page and the main place to perform all tasks related to defining and provisioning an OData Service.

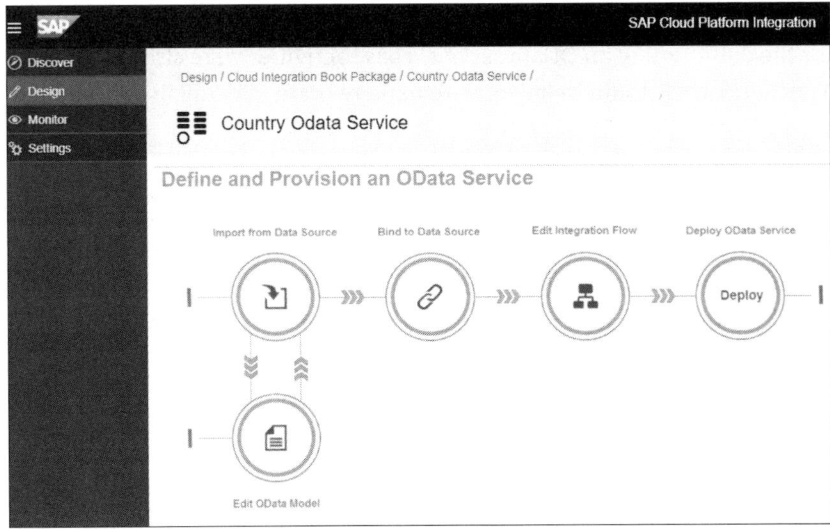

Figure 4.98 Main Landing Page to Define and Provision an OData Service A

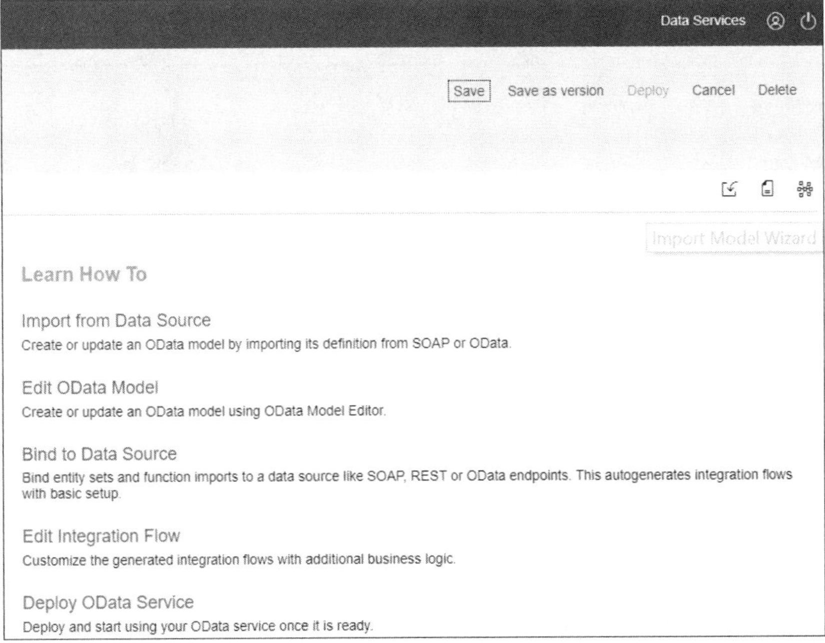

Figure 4.99 Main Landing Page to Define and Provision an OData Service B

As Figure 4.98 and Figure 4.99 show, this page lists the activities that need to be performed for the definition of an OData service. These activities were also listed in the beginning of Section 4.5.2, and we're going to explore them in detail in the next sections.

Import from Data Source

The first step is to import the definition of an existing service (data source) to be used as the basis for our OData model. When this book was written, you could import definitions from a SOAP, OData, or ODC (provided by SAP Gateway) data source. For simplicity, let's illustrate the provisioning of an OData service using the import of an existing SOAP web service—the WSDL that we downloaded in Section 4.5.1. Proceed as follows to import a WSDL data source:

1. Click the import model wizard button shown earlier on the right-top corner of Figure 4.99.
2. Select **SOAP** from the **Data Source Type** dropdown, and click on the **Browse** button to select the WSDL file that you downloaded in Section 4.5.1 (Figure 4.100).
3. Click on the **Step 2** button to proceed with the wizard.

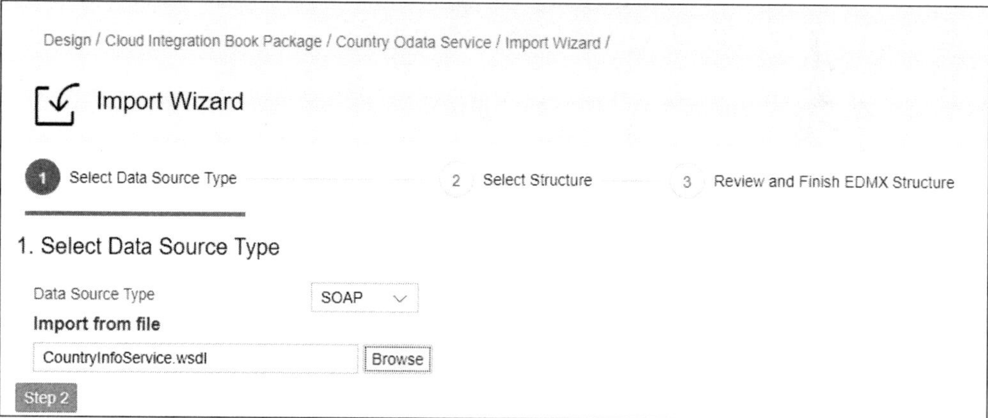

Figure 4.100 Importing a WSDL Data Source

4. Select the needed element from the data source. Note that we're going to use the `CountryISOCode` operation. Therefore, select its request and response structures (see Figure 4.101).
5. Click on the **Step 3** button.

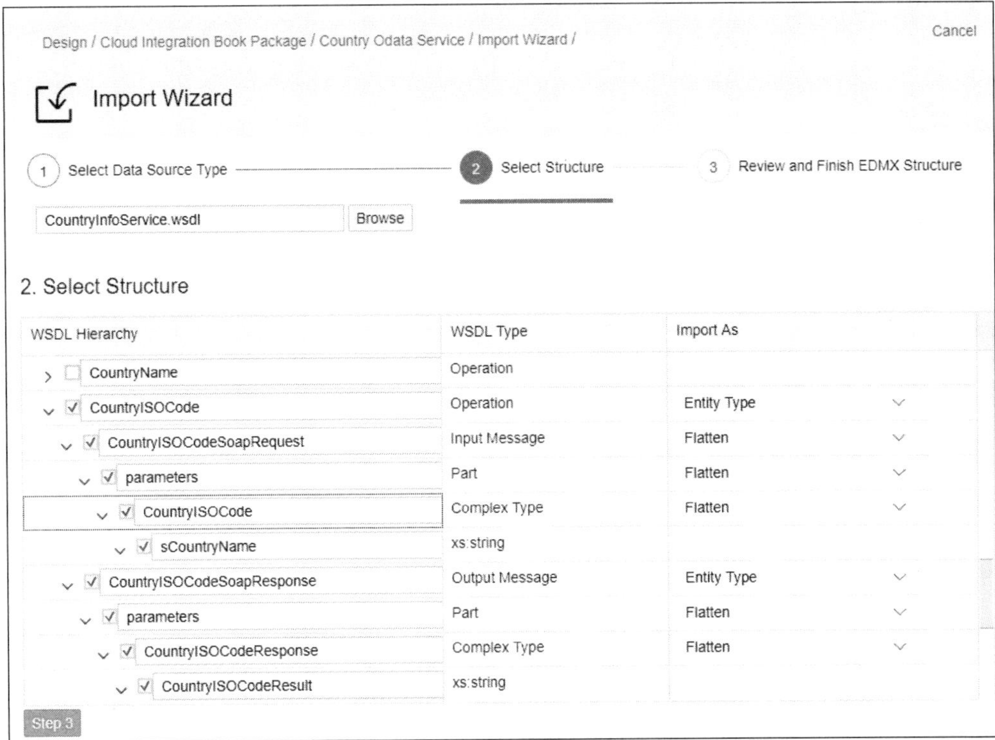

Figure 4.101 Selecting the Desired Request and Response Structures from the Data Source

6. You're redirected to the next page in the wizard where you can review the generated EDMX structure. You can change the names or EDM type of any element and add comments and descriptions for each element using the **Documentation** field (Figure 4.102). Be aware that it's mandatory to select one of the elements as the primary key. When done, click on the **Finish** button.

Note

In the step presented in Figure 4.102, it's mandatory to select a primary key that represents a unique identifier for the OData model. Without selecting a primary key, you're confronted with an error, and it's not possible to proceed to the next screen of the wizard.

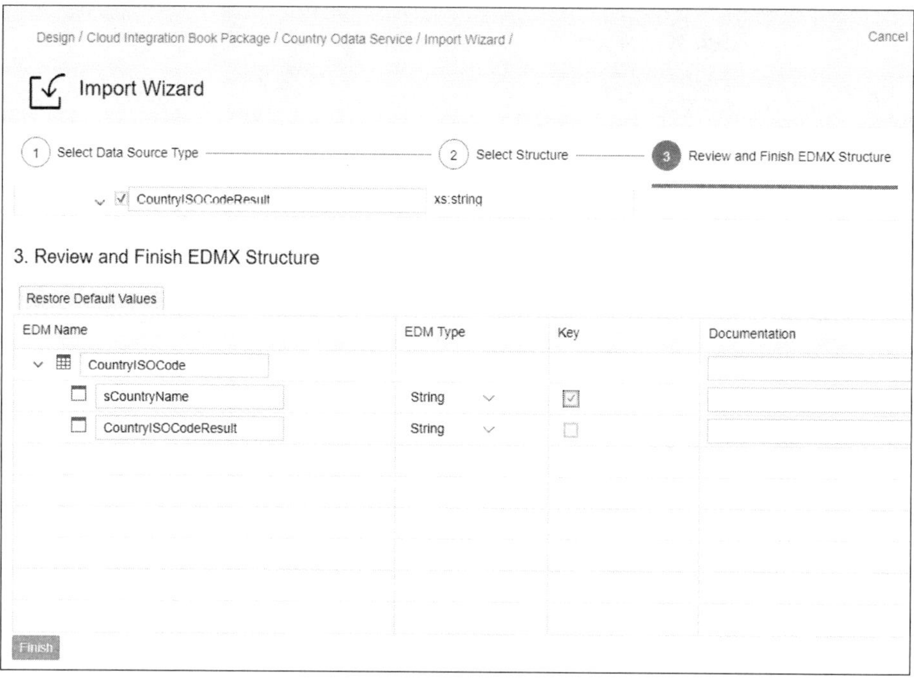

Figure 4.102 Reviewing the EDMX Structure

7. Now that you've imported the WSDL model, you're redirected to the **Define and Provision an OData Service** view (see Figure 4.103). This view presents the different operations possible in an OData Service, including **Query**, **Create**, **Read**, **Update**, and **Delete**, as shown in Figure 4.103.

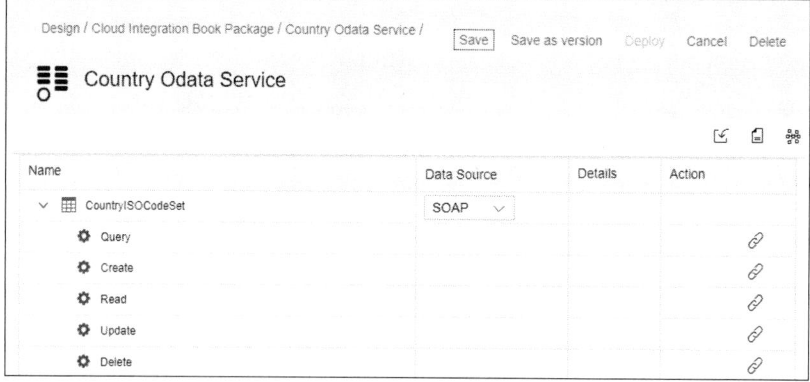

Figure 4.103 Define and Provision an OData Service View

Let's now explore how to edit the OData Model generated in the preceding steps.

Edit the OData Model

After importing a model based on a WSDL data source as discussed in the previous section, let's look at how to modify the generated OData model. This can be achieved by first returning to the **Define and Provision an OData Service** view (refer to Figure 4.103) and following these steps:

1. From the right corner of the screen shown previously in Figure 4.103, click on the OData Model Editor button . This opens the OData Model editor (see Figure 4.104).
2. If you're comfortable with OData models, you can edit and change the model to fit your requirements. The editor makes use of an auto-complete function to help you while editing the model. You need to press Ctrl + Spacebar to get a suggestion, as shown in Figure 4.104. Then save the final result using the **Ok** button.

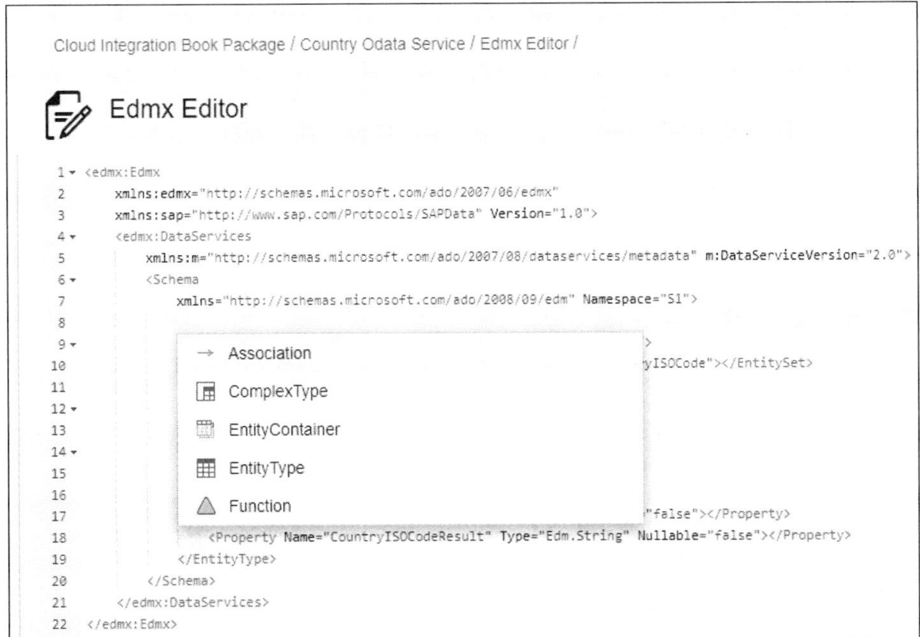

Figure 4.104 OData Model Editor

You can get back to the main page (refer to Figure 4.103) by clicking on the OData service name at the top of Figure 4.104. In our example, click on **Country OData Service**.

Note that it's also possible to see a graphical representation of the generated model. The graphical representation can be accessed using the button in the top-right corner of Figure 4.103. You then get something similar to Figure 4.105.

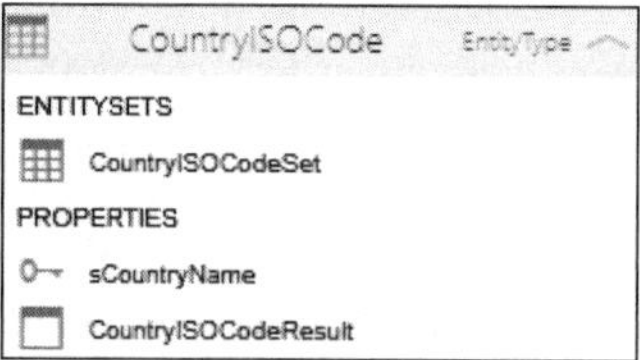

Figure 4.105 Graphical Model Viewer

Now that our model is ready, it's time to bind it to the SOAP web service.

Bind to the Data Source

Binding a model means that you need to link entity sets and function imports to a data source such as SOAP, REST, or OData endpoints. To perform the binding, first return to the **Define and Provision an OData Service** view. Then follow these steps:

1. Click on the bind button on the same row as the desired operation. For now, let's do that for the **Query** operation (refer to Figure 4.103). You're then redirected to a page similar to Figure 4.106.

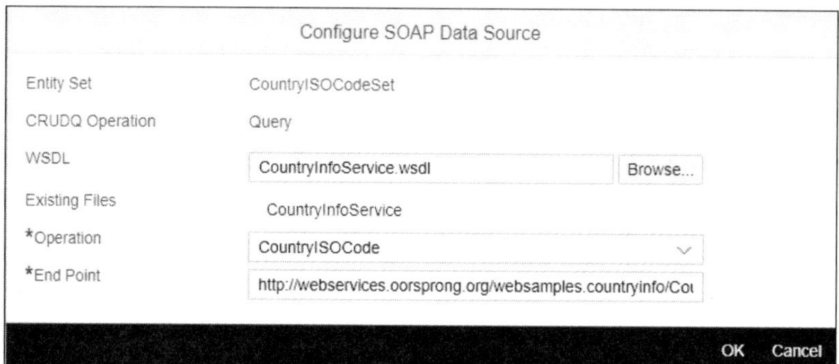

Figure 4.106 Binding an Operation to a Data Source

2. From this page, you can specify the operation to which the **Query** operation should be bound. As Figure 4.106 shows, choose **CountryISOCode** in the **Operation** dropdown of the SOAP service. Note that the **End Point** textbox is automatically filled in with the correct value.

3. Click on the **Ok** button to return to the **Define and Provision an OData Service** view (see Figure 4.107). Note that during this step, an integration flow is automatically generated in the background.

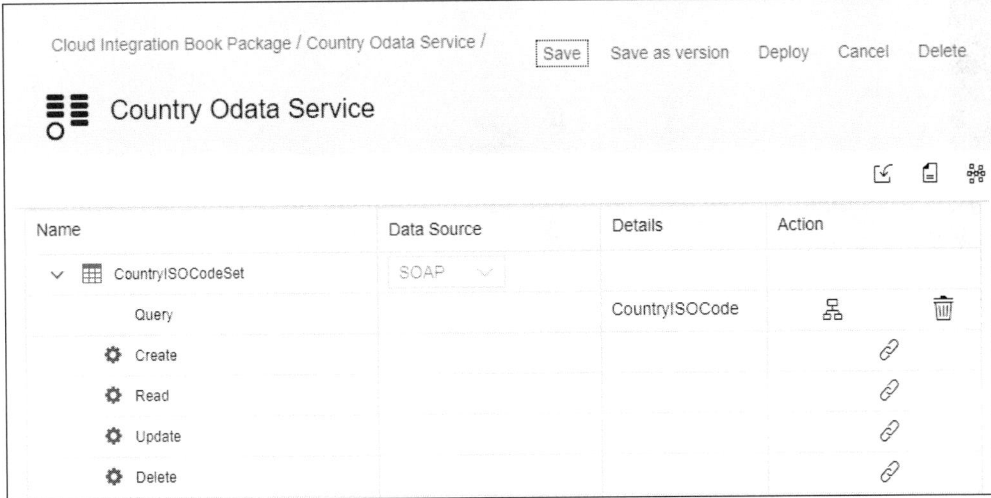

Figure 4.107 Define and Provision an OData Service View after Binding an Operation

4. Click on the **Save** button in Figure 4.107 to persist your changes.
5. Let's now navigate to the integration flow editor by clicking on the 品 button on the same row as the **Query** operation (see Figure 4.107).

We're redirected to the integration flow editor. Now we'll enhance and change the generated integration flow in the next section.

Edit the Integration Flow

As depicted in Figure 4.108, you're presented with the integration flow that was automatically generated based on the actions performed in the previous sections.

The generated integration flow has a basic setup with sender and receiver channels already configured automatically.

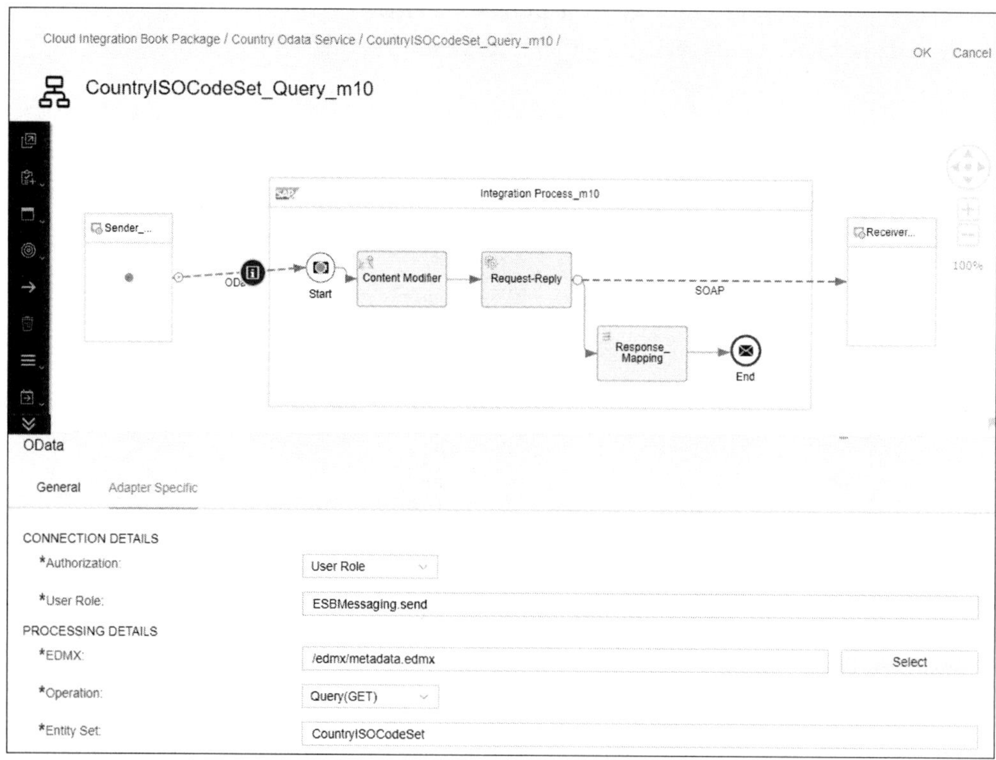

Figure 4.108 Generated Integration Flow for the OData Service

A look in the **Resources** view (Figure 4.109) shows that a number of artifacts are automatically included:

- **Resource_Mapping1**
  The message mapping artifact used in the **Message Mapping** step named **Response_Mapping** (refer to Figure 4.108).
- **CountryInfoService**
  WSDL of the Country Info SOAP service that we're consuming in our integration flow.
- **Error**
  XSD representing an error, which can be used to throw an exception.
- **Metadata**
  The EDM file that was automatically added by the OData service generation.

Integration Flow

General | Runtime Configuration | Resources | Problems

Resources (4)

Name	Type	Actions
Mappings (1)		
Response_Mapping1	Message Mapping	
Schemas (3)		
CountryInfoService	WSDL	
Error	XSD	
metadata	EDMX	

Figure 4.109 Overview of the Resources View

Let's now enhance the integration flow to suit our needs. A good start is to replace the **Content Modifier** with a **Message Mapping** step. We've already discussed how to use a **Message Mapping** step in Section 4.4. As a result, we're not going to repeat every step here in detail. Proceed as follows:

1. After opening the integration flow, click on the **Edit** button.
2. Remove the **Content Modifier** step, and replace it with a **Message Mapping** step (see Figure 4.110).

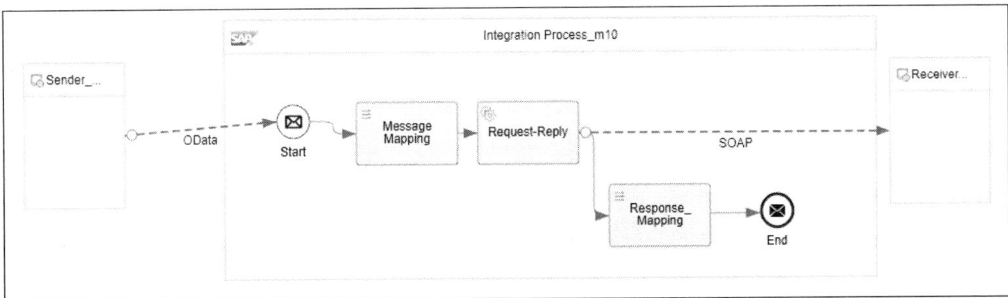

Figure 4.110 Integration Flow with Message Mapping Instead of Content Modifier

3. Create a message mapping, and assign the EDMX structure on the source message and the XSDL on the target message. In our case, the EDMX file is called *metadata.edmx*, and the WSDL file is called *CountryInfoService.wsdl*, as explained earlier and shown in Figure 4.109. The end result of the newly created message mapping

is shown in Figure 4.111. Note that in the target message, the `CountryISOCode` message structure needs to be selected.

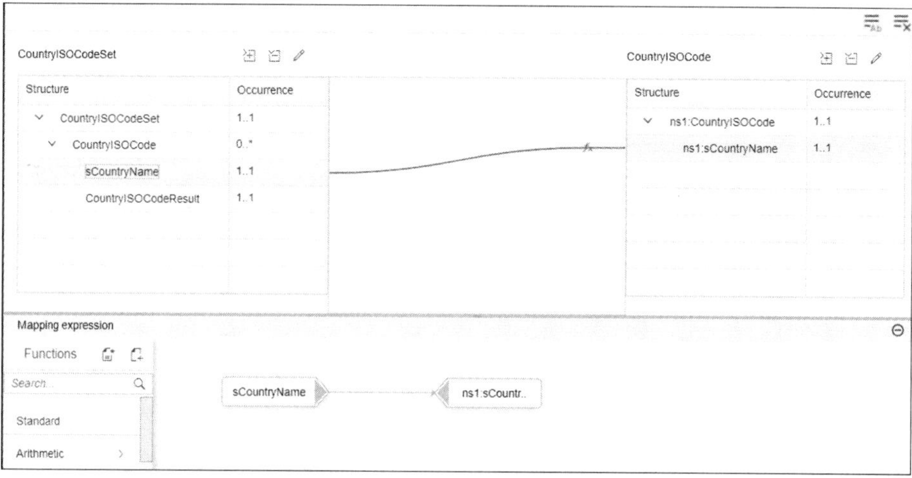

Figure 4.111 New Message Mapping

Finally, let's adjust the response mapping. As previously indicated, a response mapping called **Response_Mapping** (refer to Figure 4.108) was included in the **Resources** view. By default, there is no mapping logic defined in this message mapping.

Figure 4.112 depicts an example of the mapping logic.

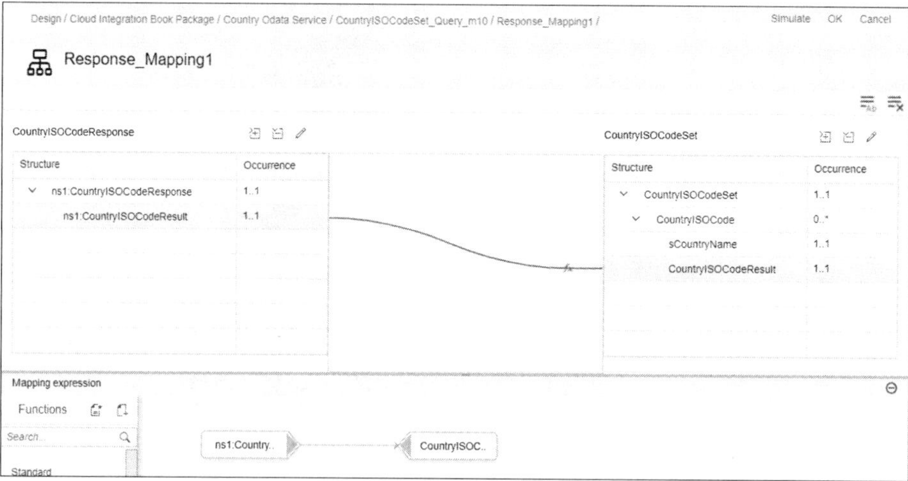

Figure 4.112 Defining the Response Mapping Logic

The integration flow is now enhanced and adjusted to suit our needs. Let's save it.

Note

At the time of authoring this book, the OData adapter only supports synchronous communication, which means that every request must have an associated response.

Deploy the OData Service

After the integration flow has been adjusted to your needs in the previous steps, the OData service can now be deployed. To do so, you'll first need to return to the **Define and Provision an OData Service** view (refer to Figure 4.107). Click on **Save** and then on **Deploy**. After a successful deployment, the OData Service should now be available in the **Manage Integration Content** section of the **Monitor** view, as shown in Figure 4.113.

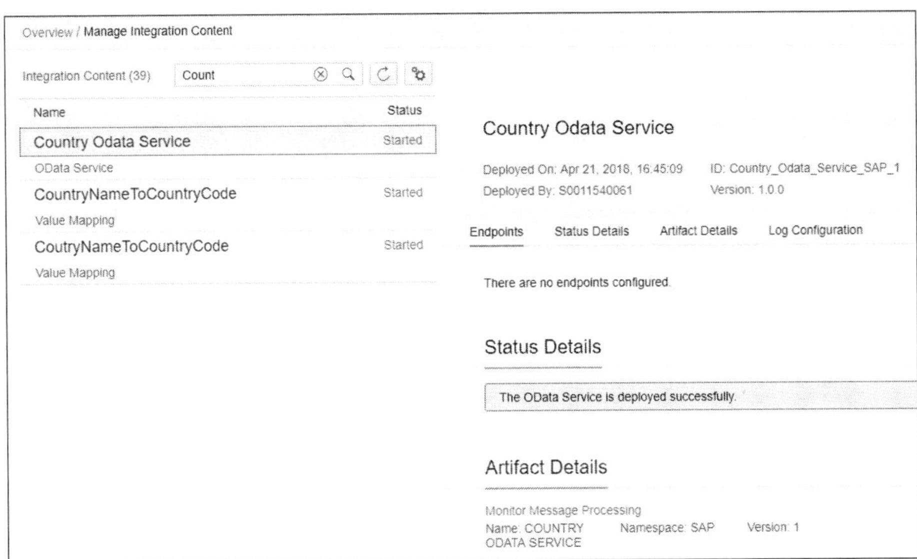

Figure 4.113 The Deployed OData Service from the Monitor

You can now call and test the newly provisioned OData service using the endpoint URL format:

https://<IFLMAP_URL>/gw/odata/<OData_Service_Namespace>/<OData_Service_Name>;V=<Version>

Note the following:

- *<IFLMAP_URL>* should be replaced with your runtime URL, for example, *https://<yourinstance>-iflmap.hci.eu1.hana.ondemand.com*.
- *<OData_Service_Namespace>* should be replaced by the value of the **Namespace** field found in the **Artifact Details** section shown in Figure 4.113.
- *<OData_Service_Name>* should be replaced by the value of the **Name** field found in the **Artifact Details** section shown in Figure 4.113.
- *<Version>* should be replaced by the value of the **Version** field found in the **Artifact Details** section shown in Figure 4.113.

Using our example, the resulting endpoint will be similar to the following:

https://<yourinstanc>-iflmap.hci.eu1.hana.ondemand.com/gw/odata/SAP/COUNTRY%20ODATA%20SERVICE;v=1

Note

The spaces included in the service name (*COUNTRY ODATA SERVICE*) are replaced by *%20*.

Well done, this was the last step in defining and provisioning an OData service.

4.6 Working with an Aggregator

According to the Enterprise Integration Patterns, an aggregator pattern answers the question of how to combine the results of individual but related messages so that they can be processed as a whole.

As Figure 4.114 depicts, imagine that you have a scenario involving system A, which needs to send an order message to system B. However, system A is capable of sending a message with a maximum of only 1 item at a time. This means that for system A to send an order with 10 items, it will need to send 10 different messages, each containing 1 item. For illustration's sake, let's assume that the incoming order item message looks like the one presented in Figure 4.115.

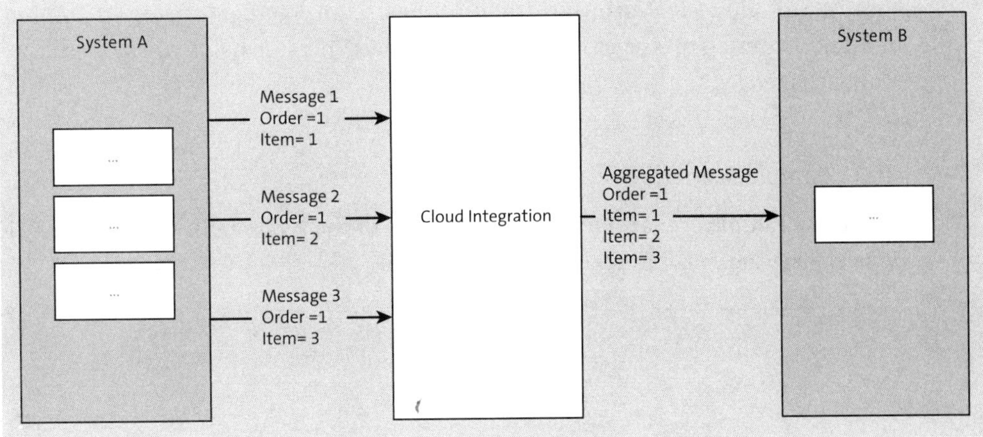

Figure 4.114 Sample Aggregator Situation

```
<OrderItem xmlns:demo="http://hci.sap.com/demo">
   <orderNumber>AA2345</orderNumber>
   <Item>
      <ItemNo>1</ItemNo>
      <Quantity>1</Quantity>
      <Unit>1</Unit>
      <LastStatus>false</LastStatus>
   </Item>
</OrderItem>
```

Figure 4.115 Sample Incoming Order Item Message

To solve this challenge, you'll need to use a stateful filter, also called an aggregator, to collect and store individual messages (each containing 1 item as shown in Figure 4.115) until a complete set of related messages has been received. Then, the aggregator sends a single message (with all 10 items) extracted from the individual messages.

When dealing with an aggregator, the following questions need to be addressed:

- How do we identify that an incoming message is related to another one?
- How do we identify that a complete set of messages has been received? In other words, how do we know that it's time to stop collecting incoming messages because we've received the last one?
- What do we do if the sender system never sends the last message?

Luckily, SAP Cloud Platform Integration provides an **Aggregator** step to combine multiple incoming messages into a single message. This step helps you solve the preceding challenges.

4.6.1 Sample Scenario

Let's use a sample scenario to illustrate the use of the **Aggregator** step. Figure 4.116 depicts what the final integration flow looks like.

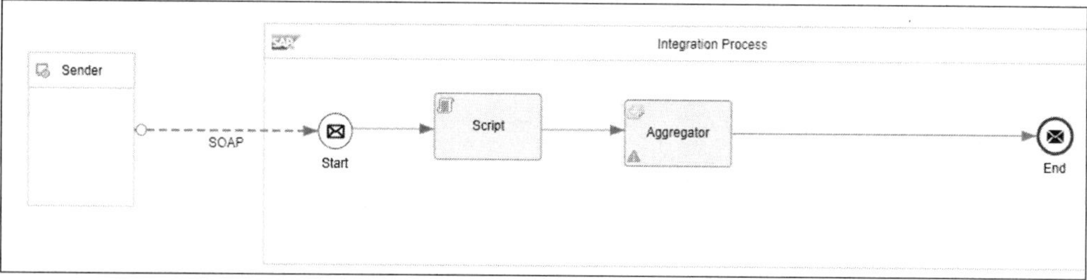

Figure 4.116 Sample Target Integration Flow

Note that in the sample integration flow presented in Figure 4.116, there are no receiver systems. This is purely for illustration purposes. In a real-life scenario, you'll generally want to send the aggregated message to a receiver system. Furthermore, the **Message Exchange Pattern** field of the SOAP adapter is set to **One-Way** for this example (Figure 4.117). This setting ensures that the message is asynchronous. We'll discuss about how to deal with asynchronous processing in Chapter 5.

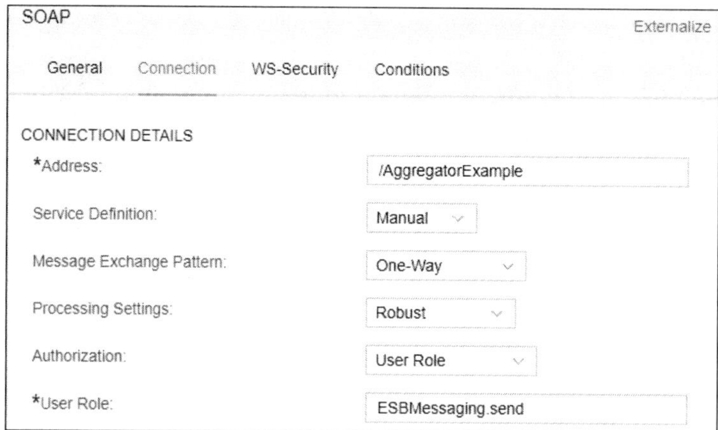

Figure 4.117 Settings of the Sender SOAP Channel

We won't spend time describing how to create the integration flow here because this has already been explained in the previous chapters. Instead, we'll mainly focus on the configuration of the aggregator step in SAP Cloud Platform Integration. Perform the following steps:

1. Navigate to the **Design** section of SAP Cloud Platform Integration, and select the **Aggregator** step from the palette, as shown in Figure 4.118.
2. Drag the step to your integration flow.

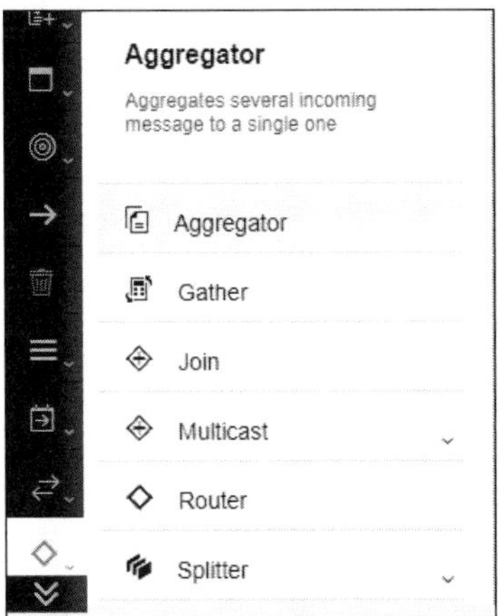

Figure 4.118 Aggregator Step in the Design Palette

3. Select the **Aggregator** step from the integration flow, and specify the different attribute properties (see Figure 4.119 and Figure 4.120). The description and meaning of the attributes of an **Aggregator** step are specified in Table 4.5.

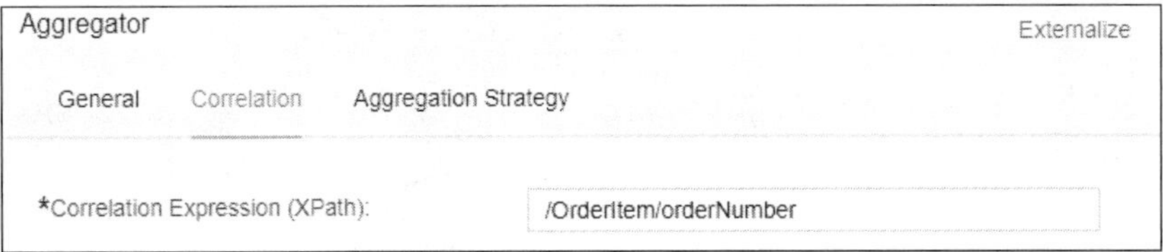

Figure 4.119 Aggregator Correlation Tab

Figure 4.120 Aggregation Strategy Tab

Name	Description
Correlation Expression (XPath)	An XPath expression that points to an element to be used to match all correlated incoming messages. This field provides a solution related to the question we've asked in the beginning of the section regarding how to identify that an incoming message is related to another one.
Incoming Format	Specifies the content type of the incoming message. At the time of publishing, , only **XML (Same Format)** can be selected.
Aggregation Algorithm	Specifies how the correlated messages will be aggregated. Possible aggregation methods include the following: ■ **Combine** All incoming and correlated messages are aggregated using a random order. ■ **Combine in Sequence** All incoming and correlated messages are aggregated according to a sequence order defined by the **Message Sequence Expression (XPath)** field.
Message Sequence Expression (XPath)	Specifies the sequencing order by which the messages need to be sorted during the aggregation. Note that this field is only present if the **Aggregation Algorithm** dropdown is set to **Combine in Sequence**.

Table 4.5 Attributes of the Aggregator Step

Name	Description
Last Message Condition (XPath)	An XPath value to specify how to identify the last message to be aggregated. This field provides a solution related to the question regarding how to identify that a complete set of messages has been received or how to know that it's time to stop collecting incoming messages because the last one has been received.
Completion Timeout (in min)	Specifies the maximum time between the processing of two messages before the aggregation is automatically stopped. The default value is set to 60 minutes. This field provides a solution related to the question about what to do if the sender system never sends the last message. Specifying a timeout ensures that the process doesn't wait forever for incoming messages. However, it goes without saying that the value to be used in this field needs to be agreed upon with the sender system. Messages arriving after the completion timeout has elapsed will start a new message processing.
Data Store Name	Specifies the name of the temporary data store to be used for storing the aggregated message. By default, SAP Cloud Platform Integration specifies a randomly generated name, but it can be changed to any other unique name. Note that it uses only local data stores. Global data stores currently aren't supported. See Chapter 5, Section 5.4.1, where the data store is explained.

Table 4.5 Attributes of the Aggregator Step (Cont.)

After you finish building the integration flow that includes the **Aggregator** step, save and deploy it.

4.6.2 Sending Messages via SoapUI

Let's now run the scenario by sending messages via SoapUI and observing how our integration flow behaves in the SAP Cloud Platform Integration monitor. The first message to be triggered is shown in Figure 4.121.

```
<soapenv:Envelope xmlns:soapenv="http://schemas.xmlsoap.org/soap/envelope/">
   <soapenv:Header/>
   <soapenv:Body>
      <OrderItem xmlns:demo="http://hci.sap.com/demo">
         <orderNumber>AA2345</orderNumber>
         <Item>
            <ItemNo>1</ItemNo>
            <Quantity>1</Quantity>
            <Unit>1</Unit>
            <LastStatus>false</LastStatus>
         </Item>
      </OrderItem>
   </soapenv:Body>
</soapenv:Envelope>
```

Figure 4.121 First Message for the Aggregation Scenario

Note that the example message in Figure 4.121 uses the correlation (`OrderNumber`) `AA2345` and sequence number (`ItemNo`) value `1`.

After triggering the message, look in the **Monitor Message Processing** section of SAP Cloud Platform Integration. As Figure 4.122 depicts, notice that two new log entries are added to the monitor.

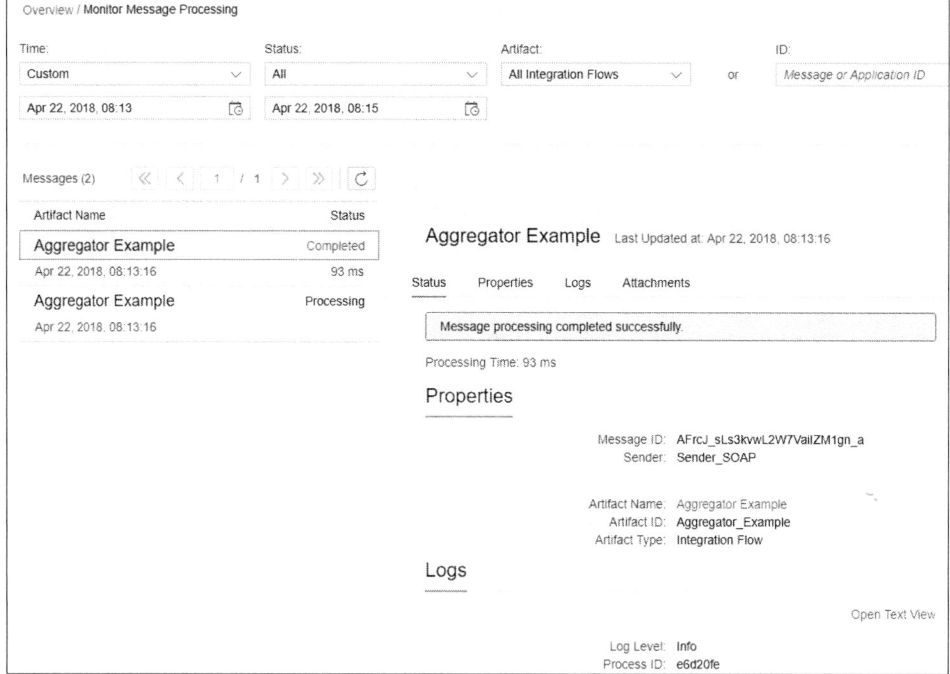

Figure 4.122 First Message Arriving in SAP Cloud Platform Integration

In an aggregation scenario, log entries are added in pairs:

- The first log entry represents the message received into the **Aggregator** step.
- The second log entry represents the confirmation that the message has been persisted into the data store. In our case, the data store is named `Aggregator-1`, as previously shown in Figure 4.120. Data stores are discussed in detail in Chapter 8, Section 8.4.

We can also observe from the **Manage Stores** monitor tiles that there are two entries in the **Data Stores** tile (Figure 4.123).

Figure 4.123 View of the Manage Stores Tiles

Click on the **Data Stores** tile to view its content. Note that the two entries include:

- **Data Store Aggregation Repository**
  In this repository, one entry is created for each new correlation ID (Figure 4.124).
- **Data Store**
  One entry is created for each correlated message (Figure 4.125).

Figure 4.124 View of the Data Store Aggregation Repository Entries after the First Message

Figure 4.125 View of the Data Store Entries after the First Message

Assuming three messages are sent to SAP Cloud Platform Integration with the same correlation ID; you can expect to have one entry in the **Data Store Aggregation Repository** and three entries in the **Data Store**.

Send the Second Message

Let's now send a second message (Figure 4.126) via SoapUI.

```
<soapenv:Envelope xmlns:soapenv="http://schemas.xmlsoap.org/soap/envelope/">
   <soapenv:Header/>
   <soapenv:Body>
      <OrderItem xmlns:demo="http://hci.sap.com/demo">
         <orderNumber>AA2345</orderNumber>
         <Item>
            <ItemNo>2</ItemNo>
            <Quantity>5</Quantity>
            <Unit>1</Unit>
            <LastStatus>false</LastStatus>
         </Item>
      </OrderItem>
   </soapenv:Body>
</soapenv:Envelope>
```

Figure 4.126 Second Message for the Aggregation Scenario

After sending the message in Figure 4.126, monitor the data store one more time (Figure 4.127). Notice that because the correlation ID of the second message is the same as the first message, no new entry is added to the **Data Store Aggregation Repository**. As a result, the second row of Figure 4.127 remains unchanged with one entry. However, a new entry has been added in the **Data Store**, as shown in the first row of Figure 4.127.

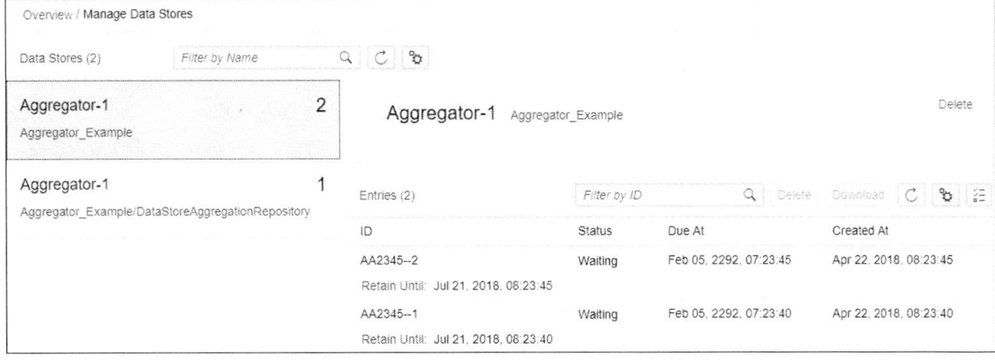

Figure 4.127 View of the Data Store Entries after the Second Message

Send the Third Message

Let's now send a third message (Figure 4.128) via SoapUI. Notice that this third message has the element LastStatus set to true. This wasn't the case for the other messages that we sent previously.

```
<soapenv:Envelope xmlns:soapenv="http://schemas.xmlsoap.org/soap/envelope/">
   <soapenv:Header/>
   <soapenv:Body>
      <OrderItem xmlns:demo="http://hci.sap.com/demo">
         <orderNumber>AA2345</orderNumber>
         <Item>
            <ItemNo>3</ItemNo>
            <Quantity>25</Quantity>
            <Unit>1</Unit>
            <LastStatus>true</LastStatus>
         </Item>
      </OrderItem>
   </soapenv:Body>
</soapenv:Envelope>
```

Figure 4.128 Third Message for the Aggregation Scenario

According to the configuration of the **Aggregator** step (as shown earlier in Figure 4.120), when a message is received with the element LastStatus set to true, this represents the last message. This completion condition can be seen via the **Last Message Condition (XPath)** field (refer to Figure 4.120). This condition has now been met with our last message of Figure 4.128.

As the left panel of the screen shown in Figure 4.129 demonstrates, there are four messages. The first three (from the bottom), represent the messages sent via SoapUI, whereas the last message (top) is automatically created after the last message is received or after the completion timeout condition has been met.

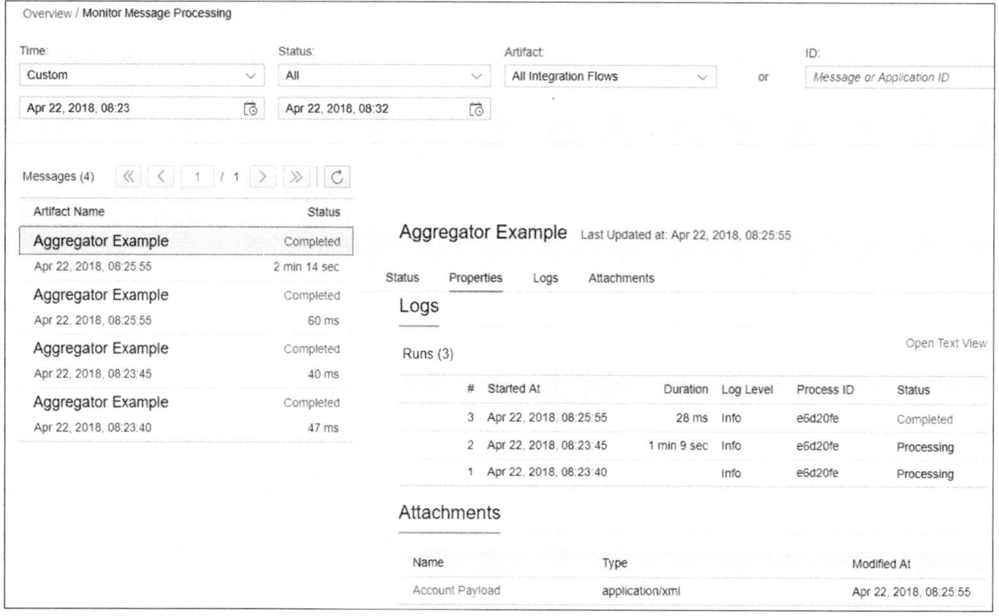

Figure 4.129 All Received Messages in the Monitor Message Processing

Also notice that the list of the correlated messages is mentioned under the **Logs** section (Figure 4.129). You can view more details by clicking on the **Open Text View** link (right side of Figure 4.129). The **Message Processing Log Attachment** opens where you can see the field `AggregateCompletedBy` (Figure 4.130). Possible values for this field include the following:

- **Predicate**: Indicates that the processing of the aggregate has been finished because the completion condition has been fulfilled.
- **Timeout**: Indicates that the processing of the aggregate is finished because the configured completion timeout has been reached.

Overview / Monitor Message Processing / Message Processing Log Attachments

Artifact Name: Aggregator Example Status: Completed Processing Time: 2 min 14 sec
Last Updated at: Apr 22, 2018, 08:25:55 Log Level: Info

Log Account Payload

```
Message Processing Log:
  StartTime             = Sun Apr 22 06:25:55.046 UTC 2018
  StopTime              = Sun Apr 22 06:25:55.074 UTC 2018
  OverallStatus         = COMPLETED
  MessageGuid           = AFrcKmwQO8ufZ2Kb-bEYO9eAF9g-
  AggregateCompletedBy= predicate
  AggregateCorrelationId= AA2345
  ChildCount            = 0
  ChildrenCounter       = 27
  ContextName           = Aggregator_Example
  CorrelationId         = AFrcKmyuIVoE2mVXbpv4oCLF3qyH
  IntermediateError     = false
  LastMessageNumber     = 3
  Node                  = vsa3953224
  ProcessId             = e6d20fef3a4137169155f19b0896c01f08575bed
  ReceivedSequenceNumbers= [1-3]


Message Processing Log:
  StartTime             = Sun Apr 22 06:23:45.835 UTC 2018
  StopTime              = Sun Apr 22 06:24:55.233 UTC 2018
  OverallStatus         = PROCESSING
  MessageGuid           = AFrcKmwQO8ufZ2Kb-bEYO9eAF9g-
  AggregateCorrelationId= AA2345
  ChildCount            = 0
  ChildrenCounter       = 1
  ContextName           = Aggregator_Example
  CorrelationId         = AFrcKmyuIVoE2mVXbpv4oCLF3qyH
  IntermediateError     = true
  LastError             = Messageprocessing has been blocked for more than 69s
  Node                  = vsa3953224
  ProcessId             = e6d20fef3a4137169155f19b0896c01f08575bed
  ReceivedSequenceNumbers= [1,2]


Message Processing Log:
  StartTime             = Sun Apr 22 06:23:40.213 UTC 2018
  StopTime              = Sun Apr 22 06:23:40.213 UTC 2018
  OverallStatus         = PROCESSING
  MessageGuid           = AFrcKmwQO8ufZ2Kb-bEYO9eAF9g-
  AggregateCorrelationId= AA2345
```

Figure 4.130 Message Processing Log Attachment

4.6.3 Viewing the Aggregated Message

To view the resulting aggregated message, click on the **Account Payload** tab (refer to Figure 4.130). You're then presented with a message that includes all received and correlated messages, as shown in Figure 4.131.

Artifact Name: Aggregator Example   Status: Completed   Processing Time: 2 min 14 sec
Last Updated at: Apr 22, 2018, 08:25:55   Log Level: Info

Log   Account Payload


```
<?xml version="1.0" encoding="UTF-8"?>
<multimap:Messages xmlns:multimap="http://sap.com/xi/XI/SplitAndMerge">
  <multimap:Message1>
    <OrderItem xmlns:demo="http://hci.sap.com/demo" xmlns:soapenv="http://schemas.xmlsoap.org/soap/envelope/">
      <orderNumber>AA2345</orderNumber>
      <Item>
        <ItemNo>1</ItemNo>
        <Quantity>1</Quantity>
        <Unit>1</Unit>
        <LastStatus>false</LastStatus>
      </Item>
    </OrderItem>
    <OrderItem xmlns:demo="http://hci.sap.com/demo" xmlns:soapenv="http://schemas.xmlsoap.org/soap/envelope/">
      <orderNumber>AA2345</orderNumber>
      <Item>
        <ItemNo>2</ItemNo>
        <Quantity>5</Quantity>
        <Unit>1</Unit>
        <LastStatus>false</LastStatus>
      </Item>
    </OrderItem>
    <OrderItem xmlns:demo="http://hci.sap.com/demo" xmlns:soapenv="http://schemas.xmlsoap.org/soap/envelope/">
      <orderNumber>AA2345</orderNumber>
      <Item>
        <ItemNo>3</ItemNo>
        <Quantity>25</Quantity>
        <Unit>1</Unit>
        <LastStatus>true</LastStatus>
      </Item>
    </OrderItem>
  </multimap:Message1>
</multimap:Messages>
```


Figure 4.131 Final Aggregated Order Item Message

Note

Using the **Aggregator** step in combination with a polling SFTP sender adapter can generate a high message volume and can consume a lot of resources. Use it cautiously.

4.7 Summary

Congratulations! You've now mastered the first basic integration scenarios using SAP Cloud Platform Integration. Look back and be proud of your achievements: you now know how to work with data within SAP Cloud Platform Integration, how to invoke external OData services, how to provision an OData service, how to map different data structures to each other, and finally how an **Aggregator** step works. You're now ready to tackle the next challenges: content-based message routing, the handling of messages containing lists of entries, and asynchronous message handling. These will all be covered in the next chapter.

Chapter 5
Advanced Integration Scenarios

So far, we've introduced the development environment, as well as the runtime, of SAP Cloud Platform Integration. The time has come to address more sophisticated, real-life integration scenarios. Here, more advanced patterns are supported for the integration developer.

In the previous chapter, we learned a lot about the inner workings of SAP Cloud Platform Integration. You've seen how to work with its data model, how to enrich messages with data retrieved from an external OData service, and how to solve mapping challenges using the built-in mapping engine. We'll continue our journey in this chapter with topics to help you address more advanced integration scenarios, such as the following:

- Message routing
- Working with lists
- Asynchronous message handling
- Sending messages to multiple receivers using multicast
- Asynchronous decoupling of inbound and outbound processing

Let's get started!

5.1 Message Routing

Cloud computing is currently one of the most talked-about topics in the IT industry. However, this trend of migrating toward cloud computing leads to an increased heterogeneity of a company's IT landscape, which itself brings increased need for integration. Messages need to be exchanged between on-premise and cloud applications. Fortunately, cloud-based integration solutions, such as SAP Cloud Platform Integration, can help companies solve this integration challenge.

If we take a closer look at how messages are treated within SAP Cloud Platform Integration, one question comes up repeatedly: How can we model different message handling execution paths (i.e., routes) in a single integration scenario? This question stands in the middle of what is known as content-based routing, the topic of this section. Content-based routing (CBR) takes care of forwarding messages to the right recipient depending on the contents of a message. As an example, let's look at an order. Depending on the type of item, an order might require different treatment within the processing chain or by dedicated backend systems. So, depending on the message's content, the order will need to be transferred to the respective system. That's what CBR is all about.

CBR is nothing new. It's one of the famous Enterprise Integration Patterns described in Hohpe and Woolf's *Enterprise Integration Patterns* (Addison Wesley, 2003). As we know from previous chapters, Apache Camel is the basic integration framework on which SAP Cloud Platform Integration is built. One major goal of the Apache Camel project was, from the beginning, the implementation of Enterprise Integration Patterns. Hence, we find the implementation of the CBR in SAP Cloud Platform Integration, as well. Let's see how you can apply the CBR pattern in your integration projects.

5.1.1 The Scenario

Let's start with a look at the scenario we want to build. An example integration flow using the CBR is shown in Figure 5.1.

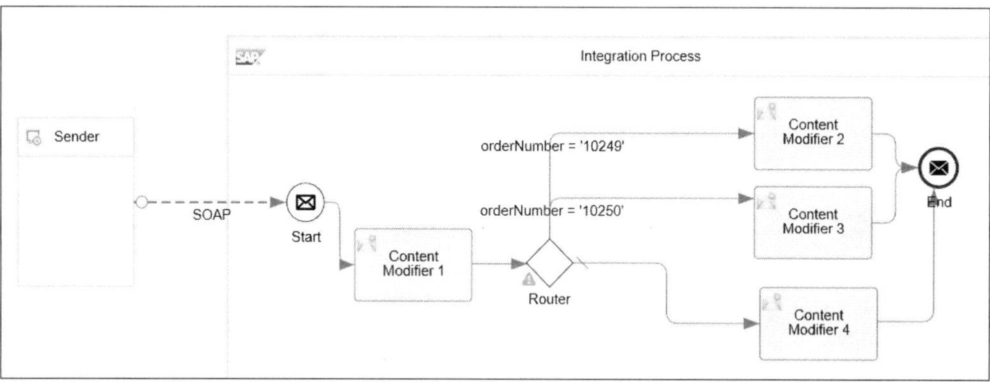

Figure 5.1 Example Integration Flow Using the Content-Based Router

The depicted integration flow shows different message handling execution paths after the diamond shape. The integration flow's semantical behavior can be described as follows: the sender on the left (represented by the **Sender** pool) sends a message via the **SOAP** channel to the integration flow. Again, we reuse the same input message as Chapter 4. Its structure is shown in Figure 5.2.

```
<soapenv:Envelope xmlns:soapenv="http://schemas
   <soapenv:Header/>
   <soapenv:Body>
      <demo:OrderNumber_MT>
         <orderNumber>10249</orderNumber>
      </demo:OrderNumber_MT>
   </soapenv:Body>
</soapenv:Envelope>
```

Figure 5.2 Example Message

The incoming message starts the integration flow on the SAP Cloud Platform Integration server. The first **Content Modifier** step, **Content Modifier 1**, takes the order number from the message and stores it in the message's header area. Figure 5.3 shows the **Content Modifier**'s configuration.

Content Modifier | Externalize

General | Message Header | Exchange Property | Message Body

Headers: | Add | Delete

	Action	Name	Type	Data Type	Value	Default
☐	Create	OrderNo	XPath	java.lang.String	//OrderNumber	

Figure 5.3 Writing Data into the Message's Header Area

The order number is stored in the newly created header variable, `OrderNo`. We can later access this value to define routing conditions. Next, the CBR comes into the picture (refer to Figure 5.1). It's modeled using a Business Process Model and Notation (BPMN)-exclusive gateway (the diamond shape). As you know from Chapter 4, the entire modeling environment of SAP Cloud Platform Integration is based on BPMN. In BPMN, the exclusive gateway is used to indicate the split of the sequence flow in several independent execution paths. Exactly one of the paths leaving the gateway (which is also known as a gate in BPMN nomenclature) will later be executed at runtime, depending on some conditions that are attached as labels to each of the outgoing sequence flows. However, if you take a close look at the gates, you'll recognize one exception: the sequence flow leaving the gateway vertically, which is decorated with the tick mark ✗, has no condition associated with it. This is a default gate, which is executed during runtime if none of the other conditions meet the Boolean value TRUE. Now, we can describe the behavior of the gateway as follows:

- If the incoming order number equals 10249, the upper path will be followed.
- If the incoming order number equals 10250, the gate in the middle will be taken.
- In all other cases, the default gate will be activated.

To verify the correct behavior of the gateway during runtime, we'll set the body of the message via the respective **Content Modifier** shapes, which are connected with each of the three sequence flows leaving the gateway. The **Content Modifier** steps write the following messages as reply into the message's body:

- orderNumber = 10249 for the upper sequence flow
- orderNumber = 10250 for the sequence flow in the middle
- orderNumber unknown for the default gate

Figure 5.4 shows an example configuration for the uppermost **Content Modifier**.

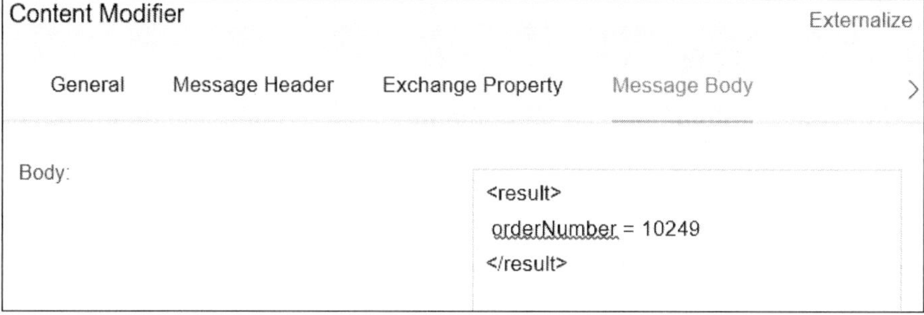

Figure 5.4 Configuration of the Content Modifier for the Uppermost Sequence Flow

5.1.2 Configuration of the Content-Based Router

Now we know how the CBR should behave during runtime. But how is this achieved during design time? Where can you find the gateway in the modeling palette of SAP Cloud Platform Integration's graphical editor? In the main menu of the palette shown in Figure 5.5, you'll find the **Message Routing** icon ◇.

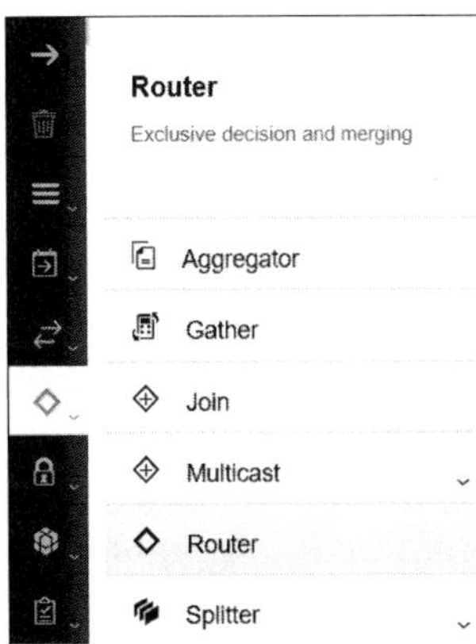

Figure 5.5 Router Shape in the Modeling Environment Palette

After you click on the **Message Routing** diamond, a submenu opens, revealing different routing options including the **Router** symbol (Figure 5.5). Click on it, move the mouse into the pool for the integration flow, and click again to position the shape. Then, model the three **Content Modifiers**, and connect them with sequence flows from the diamond shape to the respective **Content Modifier** activities. Note that you can only configure the gateway after you've connected it with the three previous steps; otherwise, you won't be able to configure the gates correctly because you won't have access to the sequence flow's properties to define the labels and evaluation conditions. So, let's configure each gate, one after another. We'll start with the uppermost one. Click on the sequence flow, leaving the gateway so that its color turns to orange (Figure 5.6).

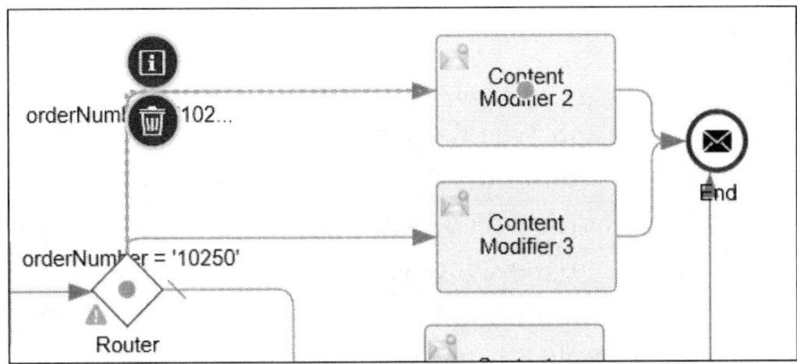

Figure 5.6 Selecting a Sequence Flow for Configuration

As always, you'll be able to configure the attributes of the selected shape in the **Properties** section, found beneath the process model. In our case, we want to tell the runtime engine that the execution of the model should be continued on the upper path of our model, if the order number equals 10249. You have two options for defining such a routing condition:

- Directly access the contents of the message (in the body area of Camel's message model), and retrieve the value that should be used for the decision from there.
- Use header variables that have been declared and set before.

Note

The first option is only possible for XML-based message content. If your incoming message isn't available in XML, you'll have to convert it first.

Let's begin with the first option. Here, you have to define an XML Path Language (XPath) expression to the field you want to access. In our case, it's the **orderNumber** field of the incoming message (refer to Figure 5.2). Hence, the configuration looks like the one depicted in Figure 5.7.

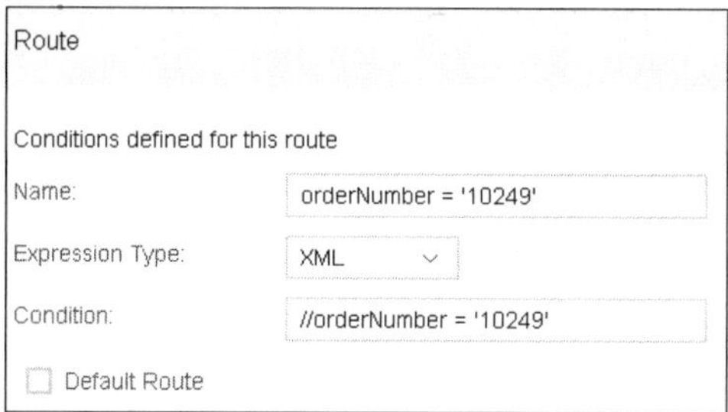

Figure 5.7 Defining the Condition for the Uppermost Sequence Flow

The **Name** field holds the string that shows up as a label attached to the sequence flow shown earlier in Figure 5.1. The **Expression Type** dropdown list shown in Figure 5.7, which contains the values **XML** and **Non-XML**, is of particular importance. The selected value influences how the **Condition** field is interpreted by the execution engine during runtime. If **XML** is chosen, the **Condition** is interpreted as an XPath expression. If **Non-XML** is chosen, it's interpreted as an expression using the Simple Expression Language. We'll see an example for the second case when we define the other gate. For now, though, stick with the XML case. The **Condition** is formulated using a classic XPath expression. You can also combine several expressions using the logical operators `and` and `or` (e.g., `//orderNumber = '10249' or //orderNumber = '10250'`) to formulate more sophisticated routing logic.

For the second gate, we'll make use of the header variable `OrderNo`, which we created by the invocation of the very first **Content Modifier** in Figure 5.1, in conjunction with the configuration shown in Figure 5.3. The condition can be formulated now, as indicated in Figure 5.8.

Route

Conditions defined for this route

Name:	orderNumber = '10250'
Expression Type:	Non-XML
Condition:	${header.OrderNo} = '10250'

☐ Default Route

Figure 5.8 Configuring the Gate's Condition Using the Content of a Header Variable

We can easily identify the typical Camel Simple Expression Language for accessing variables (e.g., `$` or `{}`). The string `header` in `${header.OrderNo}` indicates the area from which we want to load the value (the message's header area), and the `OrderNo` after the dot indicates the name under which we stored the value previously. Note that the **Expression Type** dropdown list has been changed to **Non-XML**. Because you use this dropdown list to define how the **Condition** string is interpreted, it should be clear that you can't mix XML-based variables with Camel-based variables. If you try to mix them, for example, `${header.OrderNo} = '10250' or //orderNumber = '10251'` you'll receive a validation error (see Figure 5.9).

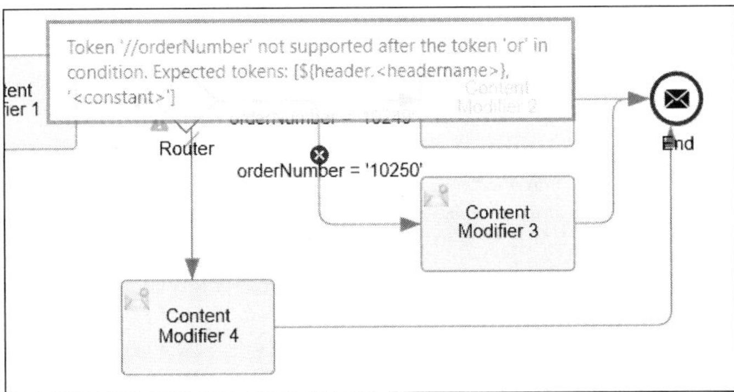

Figure 5.9 Validation Error if the Expression Contains a Mixed Expression of XML and Non-XML Parts

The definition of the last gate is probably the easiest part of the CBR's configuration. We simply have to set the **Default Route** checkbox (see Figure 5.10) to define the gate, which should be followed during runtime if none of the explicit conditions of the other gates evaluate to TRUE.

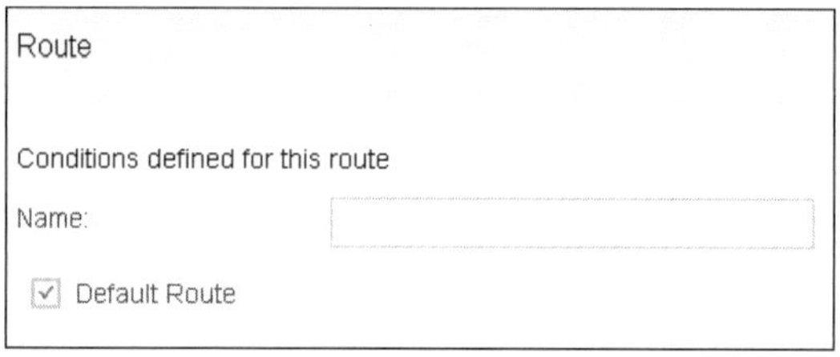

Route

Conditions defined for this route

Name:

☑ Default Route

Figure 5.10 Defining the Default Route

From what you've learned so far, you know how to formulate expressions for the XML setting of the **Expression Type** field shown earlier in Figure 5.7. You now need to apply the rules laid out in the XPath specification defined by the World Wide Web Consortium (W3C).

But what do you have to consider for the non-XML expressions, and which operators are allowed here? For your convenience, the table from the SAP Cloud Platform Integration help website has been reproduced (the original can be found at *https://help.sap.com/viewer/product/CLOUD_INTEGRATION/Cloud* and search for "Define Router") in Figure 5.11, which summarizes the operators allowed for formulating non-XML expressions.

Operator	Example
=	${header.SenderId} = '1'
!=	${header.SenderId} != '1'
>	${header.SenderId} > '1'
>=	${header.SenderId} >= '1'
<	${header.SenderId} < '1'
<=	${header.SenderId} <= '1'
and	${header.SenderId}= '1' and ${header.ReceiverId} = '2'
or	${header.SenderId}= '1' or ${header.ReceiverId}= '2'
contains	${header.SenderId} contains '1'
not contains	${header.SenderId} not contains '1'
in	${header.SenderId} in '1,2'
not in	${header.SenderId} not in '1,2'
regex	${header.SenderId} regex '1.*'
not regex	${header.SenderId} not regex '1.*'

Figure 5.11 Usage of Operators in Non-XML Expressions

5.1.3 Running the Content-Based Router Scenario

Now that our configurations are complete, we can finally run the scenario. Use a Simple Object Access Protocol (SOAP) tool of your choice (e.g., SoapUI), and invoke the solution. We'll use the input message shown earlier in Figure 5.2. Depending on the order number's value, you'll receive respective replies from the integration flow. If your order number is 10250, the reply should look similar to Figure 5.12.

If you provide a number for which no routing rule exists, you'll see the response shown in Figure 5.13 because the default route of the gateway was fired.

```
<soap:Envelope xmlns:soap="http://schemas.
   <soap:Body>
      <result>orderNumber = 10250</result>
   </soap:Body>
</soap:Envelope>
```

Figure 5.12 Reply Message if Order Number of Input Message Was Set to 10250

```
<soap:Envelope xmlns:soap="http://schemas.xml
   <soap:Body>
      <result>orderNumber unknown</result>
   </soap:Body>
</soap:Envelope>
```

Figure 5.13 Reply Message if an Order Number Was Provided for Which No Routing Rule Exists

At this point, we could stop with the description of the CBR. However, one interesting question hasn't yet been answered: What happens if the routing rules contain overlapping conditions? Mistakes are always possible, and especially for complex routing conditions, these mistakes may sometimes result in overlapping conditions, so that potentially two or more of the conditions could evaluate to `true` during runtime. Hence, more gates may be triggered. On the other hand, we know that the exclusive gateway will trigger one—and only one—gate. So, in the case of overlapping conditions, which of the gates will be triggered, and can we influence the sequence in which the expressions will be evaluated? Let's try a little experiment. We'll change the conditions in such a way so that they overlap. Let's change the condition of the gate labeled with **orderNumber = '10250'** to **${header.OrderNo} = '10249'**. This overlaps with the gate already labeled with **orderNumber = '10249'** and its condition **// orderNumber = '10249'**. Both are checking against order number 10249.

Now, save your changes, deploy them, and run the scenario again using 10249 as the input value for the order number. After we run the scenario in our own environment, we see the result shown earlier in Figure 5.12. Thus, the changed path was executed, although if you compare our design of the scenario shown earlier in Figure 5.1, you'll see it's positioned in the middle of the three gates. One might think the conditions are evaluated from top to bottom in the visual diagram, and so the model's visual appearance has something to do with execution sequence. Our experiment proves that this isn't the case. We also stress that *our* scenario works this way. It may be that *your* scenario is still working correctly!

What else influences the execution sequence, then? The answer is hidden behind the gateway shape itself. Select the diamond shape of the router and take a look at its properties. In our example, the gateway has the properties shown in Figure 5.14.

Router

Routing Condition

Order	Route Name	Condition Expression	Default Route
1	orderNumber = 10250	${header.OrderNo} = '10249'	☐
2	orderNumber = 10249	//orderNumber = '10249'	☐
3			☑

Figure 5.14 Configuration of the Exclusive Gateway

Take note of the **Order** column: it tells us the sequence in which the conditions will be evaluated. The route labeled with **orderNumber = 10250** will be evaluated first. Additionally, because the condition is true, we get the expected result. The second row will no longer be evaluated because the gateway has already found a valid gate, and no more gates are allowed to fire due to the exclusive behavior of the gateway.

This explains the gateway's behavior. But how can we influence the evaluation's sequence? The answer is rather straightforward: The order of the rows is determined by the connection's modeling sequence. Every connection you're modeling from the gateway to any task following the gateway adds a new row to this table. Note that every new row will be added at the bottom of the table. You can conclude from this description how we created the process model shown earlier in Figure 5.1. We first drew the connection to the **Content Modifier** in the middle (resulting in the first row in the table), then to the one at the top (second row in the table), and finally to the

Content Modifier at the bottom (third row in the table). If we want to change the execution sequence, what do we need to do? Take a look at Figure 5.14 again. We want the second row to be at the first position. So, in your process model, delete the connection responsible for the first table row: the connection labeled with **orderNumber = 10250**. The second row moves up to first place automatically, exactly like we want. Next, draw the connection that we just deleted again, add the label and the condition in its properties, and verify the condition's list at the gateway. It should now look like Figure 5.15.

Router

Routing Condition

Order	Route Name	Condition Expression	Default Route
1	orderNumber = 10249	//orderNumber = '10249'	☐
2			☑
3	orderNumber = 10250	${header.OrderNo} = '10249'	☐

Figure 5.15 Evaluation Sequence after Deleting and Redrawing the Connection with the Route Name orderNumber = 10250

Note the changed order sequence in comparison to the one shown earlier in Figure 5.14. If you invoke the route again with order number 10249, you'll see the expected (correct) result, as shown in Figure 5.16.

```
<soap:Envelope xmlns:soap="http://schemas.xml
   <soap:Body>
      <result>orderNumber = 10249</result>
   </soap:Body>
</soap:Envelope>
```

Figure 5.16 Returned Message after Correcting the Evaluation Sequence at the Gateway

To summarize, routing messages to different message handling paths is an important aspect in every integration project. SAP Cloud Platform Integration is based on Apache Camel, which implements typical Enterprise Integration Patterns. One of those patterns is the CBR, whose task is to split the sequence flow into different independent execution paths, which can then be activated based on certain conditions. Exactly one of those execution paths will be selected during runtime. You've learned how to model the CBR in SAP Cloud Platform Integration's graphical modeling environment and how to configure the conditions correctly. To define the expressions, you have two options at your disposal: XML and non-XML. You learned when to use which option, and how the condition's evaluation sequence can be influenced. Now it's your turn to work with the CBR in your own integration projects.

5.2 Working with Lists

So far, you've learned quite a bit about SAP Cloud Platform Integration's functionality, the basic concepts behind it, and the various modeling techniques for solving typical integration problems, such as message enrichment, message mapping, and message routing. However, in the examples so far, we focused on handling messages containing just one item, such as a single order. In this section, we'll dive into the details of coping with messages comprising a list of entries. Questions such as the following will be answered in the next sections:

- How do I split up such a message into individual pieces?
- How do I iterate over each list item?
- How do I handle the resulting single messages in a SAP Cloud Platform Integration message processing chain?
- How do I combine the results of each single message handling sequence back into one response message?

5.2.1 The Scenario

In real-life scenarios, integrators are quite frequently confronted with input messages consisting of several items of the same message structure, grouped in a list (e.g., order line items). The integrator wants to iterate over the list: individual list items have to be separated and individually managed by the integration flow. Finally, the result of each individual message handling procedure needs to be consolidated into one response message, sent to either the sender of the message (in the case of a synchronous scenario) or to the final recipient (in the case of an asynchronous scenario). To illustrate this functionality using SAP Cloud Platform Integration, we'll use the input message shown in Figure 5.17 throughout this section.

Figure 5.17 is based on a Web Services Description Language (WSDL) file, which was created using the Enterprise Services Builder of SAP Process Integration. You can, of course, use any XML tool supporting the WSDL standard. We've included our *SendOrderList_Async.wsdl* WSDL file with the book downloads at *www.sap-press.com/4650*. The message contains a list of order numbers; the other fields aren't yet relevant.

```
<soapenv:Envelope xmlns:soapenv="http://schemas
   <soapenv:Header/>
   <soapenv:Body>
      <demo:OrderList_MT>
         <!--Zero or more repetitions:-->
         <orders>
            <orderNumber>10248</orderNumber>
            <customerName>?</customerName>
            <orderAmount>?</orderAmount>
            <currency>?</currency>
            <taxAmount>?</taxAmount>
         </orders>
         <orders>
            <orderNumber>10249</orderNumber>
            <customerName>?</customerName>
            <orderAmount>?</orderAmount>
            <currency>?</currency>
            <taxAmount>?</taxAmount>
         </orders>
         <orders>
            <orderNumber>10250</orderNumber>
            <customerName>?</customerName>
            <orderAmount>?</orderAmount>
            <currency>?</currency>
            <taxAmount>?</taxAmount>
         </orders>
      </demo:OrderList_MT>
   </soapenv:Body>
</soapenv:Envelope>
```

Figure 5.17 Example Message Comprising a List of Order Numbers

Our goal is to split the message into individual order messages, enrich each individual order with order details (e.g., shipping date, shipping city, shipping address, etc.), and send back the enriched message as a reply to the sender in a synchronous scenario. We'll solve this problem in two steps. The first step is to understand splitting one input message into several individual messages (splitter pattern) and then joining back the pieces into one large message (gather/merge pattern). The second step explains how to enrich the individual messages with order details (enricher pattern) and then collect those results into one large message. You can see by this example how patterns help to build more complex integration solutions. We encourage you to recognize (and to implement) solutions based on patterns. After you understand the basic principle, you can apply this knowledge to even more complex scenarios.

The key to splitting large messages into individual pieces, iterating over them, and joining them back again into one large message is the use of two new steps from SAP Cloud Platform Integration's web-based graphical modeler and positioning them correctly in your message processing chain (i.e., route). The **Splitter** and **Gather** steps are used in the integration process model depicted in Figure 5.18. The figure shows the message processing chain for the first step of the implementation plan, as outlined previously.

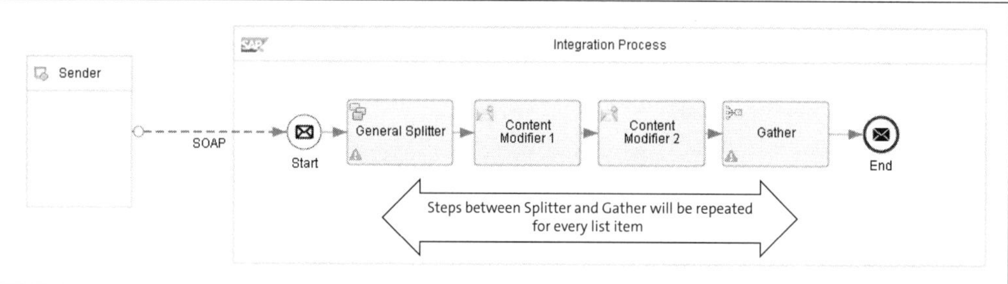

Figure 5.18 Splitting a Large Message into Single Pieces and Collecting them Back Using Gather

You can find the **Splitter** step at the beginning and the **Gather** step at the end of the processing chain. It's important for the overall understanding of the entire splitter-gather construct to recognize the following:

- The steps between a **Splitter** and a **Gather** step (the two **Content Modifier** steps in our case) are executed as many times as the **Splitter** creates individual messages.
- Each step within a **Splitter/Gather** pair will receive the separated individual messages that the **Splitter** has created as an input message, one after another.
- It's possible to model a splitter scenario without a **Gather** step. In those cases, all steps following the **Splitter** will be executed repeatedly until an **End** event is reached. So, the repeated execution of steps is dependent on the **Splitter** step, not on the **Gather** step.

5.2.2 Configuring the Integration Flow

Let's see what the configuration looks like for our scenario. As a reminder, we'll repeat the settings of the **Sender** pool and the message flow from the **Sender** pool to the **Start** message event.

When drawing the line for the message flow between the **Sender** pool and the **Start** message event, you select **SOAP** as **Adapter Type** and **SOAP 1.x** as **Message Protocol**. Figure 5.19 shows the **General** tab of the SOAP adapter's channel configuration, which opens in the **Properties** section after creation of the message flow.

SOAP
Externalize
General Connection WS-Security Conditions
Name: SOAP
CHANNEL DETAILS
Direction: Sender
System: Sender
Description:
ADAPTER DETAILS
Adapter Type: SOAP
Transport Protocol: HTTP
Message Protocol: SOAP 1.x

Figure 5.19 SOAP Channel: General Configuration

The connection details you can now configure in the **Connection** section of the SOAP adapter's configuration, as shown in Figure 5.20. The **Address** field is important here because the address entered will later be part of the URL used to call the flow.

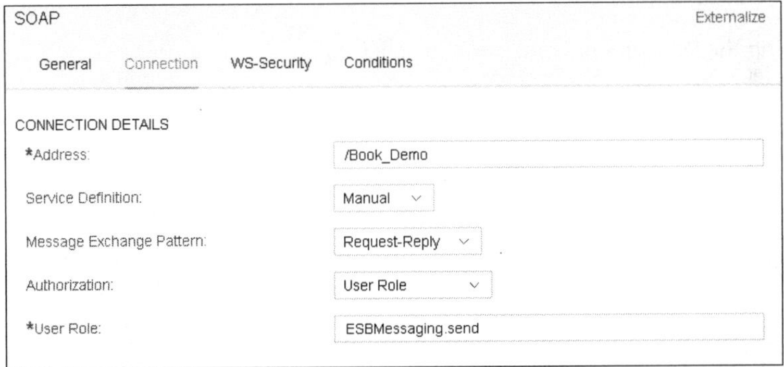

Figure 5.20 SOAP Channel: Connection Configuration

Because we want to get a response to our SOAP requests, we keep **Manual** as the **Service Definition** and **Request-Reply** as the **Message Exchange Pattern**. In Section 5.3.1, we'll go into more detail about message exchange patterns (MEPs). We'll try out different configuration options and see the different behaviors.

We set the **Authorization** dropdown field to **User Role** to allow the sender to call the integration flow with username and password credentials while invoking the integration flow. In the **User Role** field we keep the default value `ESBMessaging.send`. The different authorization options and available user roles were described already in Chapter 2.

Let's continue with the integration flow itself. The first step in the flow, after instantiating it, is the **Splitter** activity. As this step is new, we'll explain it in more detail. During development, you can find the activity in the palette on the left of the modeling environment following the path **Message Routing** ◇ • **Splitter** (Figure 5.21) • **General Splitter** (Figure 5.22).

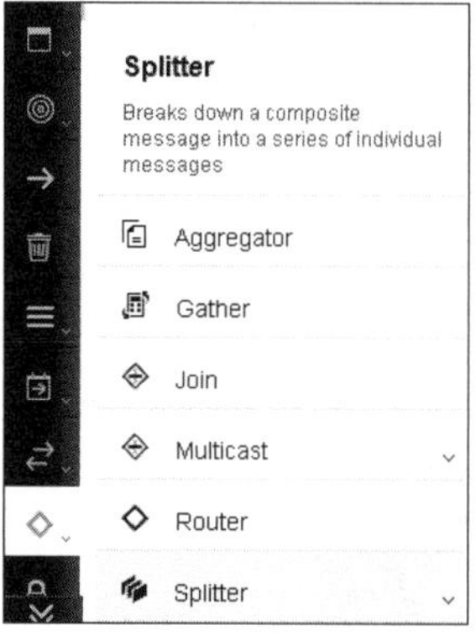

Figure 5.21 Opening the Splitter Submenu from the Palette

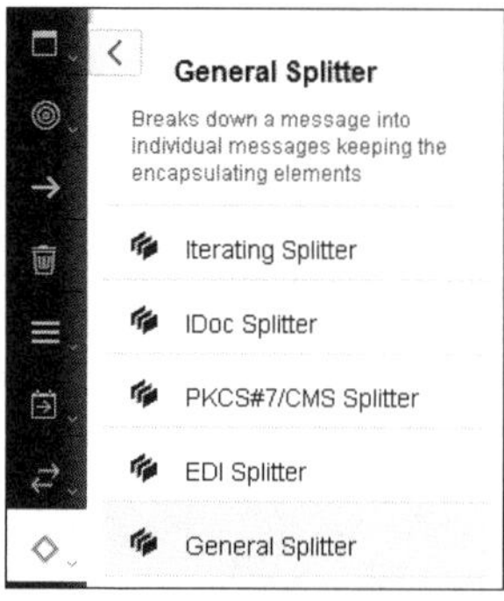

Figure 5.22 Selecting the General Splitter from the Splitter Submenu

SAP Cloud Platform Integration supports several different splitter types; however, in this section, we'll focus solely on the **General Splitter**.

5

Other Splitter Implementations in SAP Cloud Platform Integration

SAP Cloud Platform Integration provides several splitter implementations (see Figure 5.22). The **General Splitter** will described in more detail throughout this chapter, but the following splitters are also available:

- **Iterating Splitter**
  This splitter behaves most like the **General Splitter** as it also splits up a composite message into a series of individual messages; however, it doesn't copy the enveloping parts of a message to the single split messages. But what are enveloping elements, exactly? They are the message parts of the original incoming message above the nodes that are used for splitting. Figure 5.23 contains a visual depiction of the differences between the **General Splitter** and the **Iterating Splitter**.

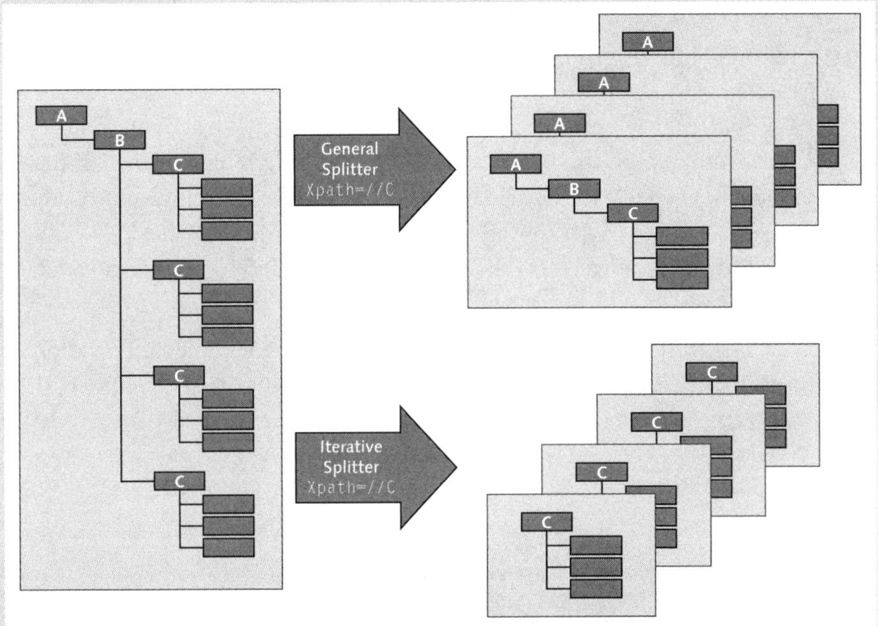

Figure 5.23 Differences between General Splitter and Iterating Splitter

The **Iterating Splitter** simply copies the parts beginning with the splitting tag (C, in the example shown in Figure 5.23) and the subnodes, whereas the **General Splitter** also copies the nodes above the splitting tag (A and B in the example). This is especially important if you want to navigate to elements in the tree structure using absolute XPath expressions.

- **IDoc Splitter**
  This dedicated splitter takes care of composite IDoc messages. By splitting the composite IDoc into a series of individual IDoc messages, including the enveloping elements of the composite IDoc message. There are no special configuration settings for this splitter.
- **PKCS#7/CMS Splitter**
  PKCS stands for Public-Key Cryptography Standard, which is used to sign and encrypt messages. This splitter is useful if a client sends a message that is PKCS# 7-signed and contains both a signature and content. This splitter type breaks down the signature and the content into separate files. For configuration, you can provide names for the files that should contain either the payload or the signature after the splitting step. You can also prescribe which file should be handled first after splitting (the signature or the content file), and you can decide whether the payload/signature should be Base64 encoded after splitting.
- **EDI Splitter**
  The **EDI Splitter** may not appear in your list, as it's available only with the SAP Cloud Platform, Enterprise Edition. It can be used to split composite Electronic Data Interchange (EDI) messages, and you can configure that inbound EDI messages are validated and acknowledged. The **EDI Splitter** will be described in more detail in Chapter 7, where we'll use it in a business-to-business (B2B) scenario.

After positioning the **General Splitter** shape in the main pool named **Integration Process** (refer to Figure 5.18), you can set its properties. We've configured it with the parameters shown in Figure 5.24.

Figure 5.24 Configuration of the Splitter Step

Let's walk through the parameters one by one:

- **Expression Type**
  In this dropdown, you select how the split points will be identified in the inbound message—either via **XPath** expression or **Line Break**. As our inbound message is an XML message, we can easily define the split points via XPath expression. The **Line Break** option is useful for non-XML messages that have multiple lines and need to be split into smaller messages. If your inbound message would, for example, be a .csv file containing several lines, the **Line Break** option can be used to split the message into smaller messages containing a defined number of lines or into messages containing only one line. Note that empty lines in the inbound message will be ignored; no empty messages will be created.
- **XPath Expression**
  This directs the integration engine during runtime to search for the given tag in the input message and take it as the split argument. In our example, we've used the relative path `//orders`. Relative paths are indicated by the double-slash at the beginning and are quite convenient for allowing the engine to search for the tag's occurrence in your input message. The alternative would have been to use absolute paths starting with a single forward slash. As a consequence, you would need to know the exact path, from the root to the tag that should be used for splitting. If you wanted to extend the message later, for example, by adding tags between the root tag and the splitting tag, the absolute path would no longer be valid, as it doesn't consider the new tag on the way from the root to the splitting tag. Hence, absolute paths are quite static and error-prone when it comes to changes on the message's structure. Conversely, this error would not happen with a relative path.

  Let's see how the definition of the XPath expression influences execution during runtime. Take a look at our example input message in Figure 5.17. We have three `<orders>` tags in our message. As such, the splitter will generate three individual messages. Each individual message forwarded to the two **Content Modifier** steps following the **Splitter** looks like Listing 5.1 (with different order number values):

```
<orders>
    <orderNumber>10248</orderNumber>
    <customerName>?</customerName>
    <orderAmount>?</orderAmount>
    <currency>?</currency>
    <taxAmount>?</taxAmount>
</orders>
```

Listing 5.1 Individual Message Containing Exactly One Order

Hence, the single messages will also contain the `<orders>` tags. Consider this while processing each of the individual messages. If you want to understand what the message produced by the splitter looks like in greater detail, read on to Section 5.2.3.

- **Grouping**
  With the grouping parameter, you define the number of items that should be grouped together into one message for individual processing. As we've chosen **1** as the value, *every* occurrence of `<orders>` results in a dedicated individual message for further processing. If we had selected **2** as our value, the splitter would group the first two items as a single message, the next two items in the second message, and so on. So, if the **Grouping** parameter was set to 2 and assuming an input message contains 10 items in total, the **Splitter** would generate 5 messages, each containing 2 items.
- **Streaming**
  The **Streaming** parameter is important with regards to memory consumption. Normally, the splitter works on messages by loading them completely into the main memory. However, messages can get quite large. Think about payments that are being sent to a bank once a day. They are collected over the course of the day and forwarded sometimes at night. These collected messages can become huge, and it doesn't make sense to load them entirely into main memory before processing them (sometimes it's even impossible to do so). Therefore, it's useful to let the **Splitter** start working on the incoming streamed data, even though it isn't yet entirely loaded. This is called *streaming*, as it allows you to read a chunk of data, work on it, read another chunk, and so forth, until the entire message is processed.
- **Parallel Processing**
  As the name indicates, this parameter allows you to run the individual message processing tasks in parallel, leveraging Java's concurrency features using thread pools. By parallelizing tasks, you can get more work done in less time. However, the execution sequence can't be guaranteed, as the threads run independent of each other.
- **Stop on Exception**
  If this checkbox is set, the route's processing will immediately stop if there is an error, and that error will be propagated back instantly. Otherwise, the splitter continues working on the individual messages and reports the error back at the end, after handling the complete input message.

Now that we have an understanding of how the **Splitter** handles the incoming message, we can continue with the first **Content Modifier**. Its behavior has been described several times already. As such, it's enough to just take a quick look at its configuration in Figure 5.25.

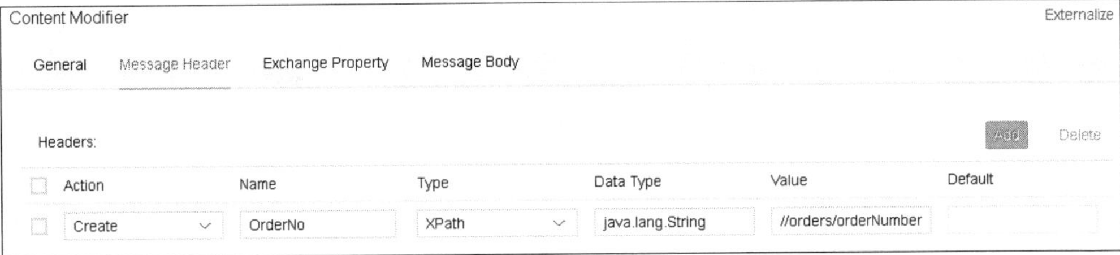

Figure 5.25 Configuration of the First Content Modifier in the Route

Note

Because this **Content Modifier** is placed after the **Splitter** step, it's invoked for each individual message created by the **Splitter** representing one order out of the original message's order list. This is crucial to understanding the entire route.

We're setting a variable named `OrderNo` in the message's header area and storing the current order number of the current item for later reference. We also could have chosen `//orderNumber` as an entry for the **Value** field as it's a relative path, and there is only one order number available in each individual message.

The recently stored header value will be retrieved by the second **Content Modifier** and copied into the result message as the configuration in Figure 5.26 shows.

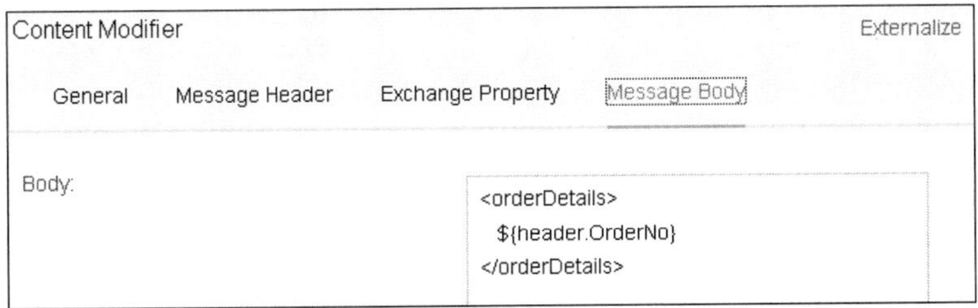

Figure 5.26 Configuration of the Second Content Modifier in the Route

Again, the second **Content Modifier** will also be invoked for each individual message. It's the **Gather** step that finally collects all the individual single messages created for each invocation of the **Splitter** into one bulk message. Figure 5.27 shows the **Gather** step's configuration.

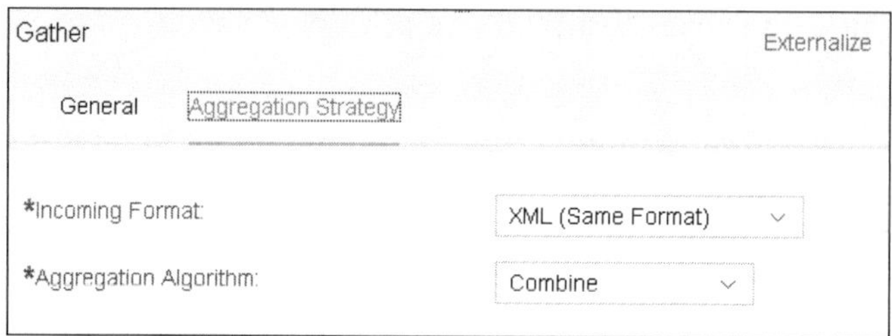

Figure 5.27 Configuration of the Gather Step

All of the resulting single messages are of the same format (hence, the **Incoming Format** dropdown field is set to **XML (Same Format)**), and the **Gather** step should simply put each of the individual pieces together into one result message. Consequently, the **Aggregation Algorithm** dropdown field is set to **Combine**.

The other configuration options provided by the **Gather** step actually depend all on the entry chosen from the **Incoming Format** dropdown list. The list provides three options:

- **Plain Text**
  For the **Aggregation Algorithm**, only **Concatenate** is allowed. All of the plain text messages generated by the single messages will simply be concatenated to one large string, one after another. This is the result being propagated back to the caller.
- **XML (Different Format)**
  For the **Aggregation Algorithm**, only **Combine** is allowed, which is similar to the behavior of the **Concatenate** option in the previous case. The individual XML fragments from the single messages will be brought together in one response message using a multimapping from SAP Process Integration's mapping engine.
- **XML (Same Format)**
  If you choose this option, you can influence the construction of the response message in two ways:
  - First, you can also apply the **Combine** option of the **Different Format** case. Its behavior is identical to the one just described.
  - Second, there is one more option that allows you to copy parts from the source message into a user-defined envelope consisting of XML tags. The XML node from which parts of the source message should be copied is formulated using

an XPath expression. The XML envelope is defined using an absolute path definition, such as /root or /level_1/level_2. The associated configuration screen is depicted in Figure 5.28. The behavior is actually pretty simple: the XPath expression of the **Combine from source (XPath)** field takes the source message (the single message created by the **Splitter**), navigates within that message to the node specified by the XPath expression, and copies the node, including all nested XML subnodes. It takes the copied XML-subtree snippet and pastes it after the tags that the user has defined as the envelope. The idea behind the envelope is that every valid XML document requires one root element, and this is exactly what you can define in the **Combine at target (XPath)** field: the root element (e.g., /root) or, if necessary, an absolute root path (e.g., /level_1/level_2). During runtime, the copied XML subtree will be pasted after the node(s) given in the **Combine at target (XPath)** field. In other words, the node in the **Combine at target (XPath)** field is the parent of the snippet that needs to be inserted. The corresponding closing tag(s) of the envelope will automatically be added, after the gathering has completed (e.g., </root> or </level_2></level_1>).

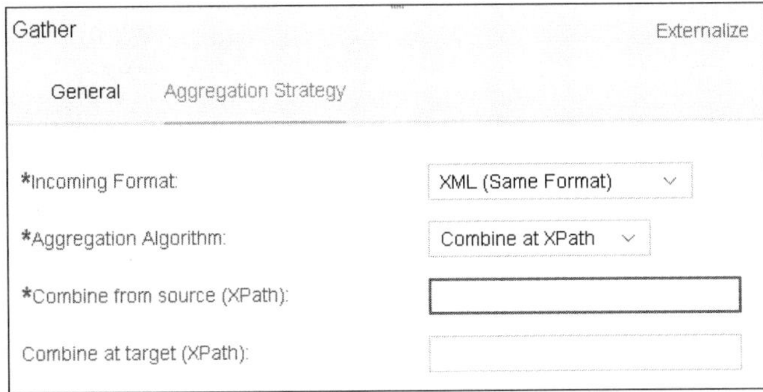

Figure 5.28 Configuration of the Gather Step When the Single Messages Should Be Combined Using XPath Expressions

Let's take a look at a concrete example. We'll assume the **Splitter** generates two messages, as shown in Listing 5.2 and Listing 5.3 (they will later be the source messages in the **Gather** step's configuration).

```
<payload>
    <route>
        <multicast>Parallel</multicast>
        <branch>A</branch>
```

```
    </route>
</payload>
```

Listing 5.2 First Generated Splitter Message

```
<payload>
    <route>
        <multicast>Parallel</multicast>
        <branch>B</branch>
    </route>
</payload>
```

Listing 5.3 Second Generated Splitter Message

Next, assume the following settings for the configuration of the **Gather** step:

- **Combine from source (XPath)** (only absolute XPath expressions are allowed for this field): `/payload/route`
- **Combine at target (XPath)**: `/xyz/abc`

The final resulting message looks like Listing 5.4.

```
<xyz>
    <abc>
        <route>
            <multicast>Parallel</multicast>
            <branch>A</branch>
        </route>
        <route>
            <multicast>Parallel</multicast>
            <branch>B</branch>
        </route>
    </abc>
</xyz>
```

Listing 5.4 Combined Message Generated by the Gather Step

You can now easily understand how this result message was created: the engine copied the parts from the source messages starting at the `/payload/route` node, including the `<route>` tag and all nested nodes, and pasted it into the target message, which starts with the `<xyz><abc>` nodes representing the opening part of the envelope. Remember: the pasting will be done for all messages resulting from the splitter.

Hence, we have two <route> tags in between the envelope. Finally, we add the closing tags of the envelope. They can be derived from the definition of the **Combine at target (XPath)** field. As the definition for that field was /xyz/abc, the closing tags must be in opposite sequence, resulting in </abc></xyz>.

Note

It isn't mandatory to provide an entry for the **Combine at target (XPath)** field. If you leave the field empty, the resulting message will have the same tags that are specified in the **Combine from source (XPath)** field. Referring to the preceding example, the resulting message would start with <payload><route>.

5.2.3 Running the Integration Flow

Now that we've configured the scenario completely, we can finally run it. Save your changes, and deploy your integration flow. Don't forget to retrieve the URL for invoking the integration scenario from SAP Cloud Platform Integration's **Monitor** (refer to Chapter 2, Section 2.3.7, for instructions on how to retrieve the URL). Provide the URL in the SOAP tool of your choice (e.g., SoapUI), and invoke the integration flow. The result should look like the one in Figure 5.29.

The flow successfully retrieved the order numbers from the incoming message containing the order list and created an appropriate response message, which is the exact result we hoped to achieve.

```
<soap:Envelope xmlns:soap="http://schemas.xmlsoap.org/soap/envelope/">
   <soap:Body>
      <multimap:Messages xmlns:multimap="http://sap.com/xi/XI/SplitAndMerge">
         <multimap:Message1>
            <orderDetails>10248</orderDetails>
            <orderDetails>10249</orderDetails>
            <orderDetails>10250</orderDetails>
         </multimap:Message1>
      </multimap:Messages>
   </soap:Body>
</soap:Envelope>
```

Figure 5.29 Final Response Message after Invoking the Integration Flow with a List of Order Numbers

What Is the Splitter Delivering to the Processing Chain?

In some situations, it might be useful to fully understand what the individual messages produced by the **Splitter** actually look like, and which ones reach the next step of the integration flow. Maybe you want to pick a concrete field by an absolute XPath expression instead of using a relative XPath due to a potential name conflict. In this case, you need to know exactly what the single message looks like; otherwise, your absolute path won't work. We'll take the process model shown earlier in Figure 5.18 as the basis for this task. Next, configure the first **Content Modifier**, as shown in Figure 5.30.

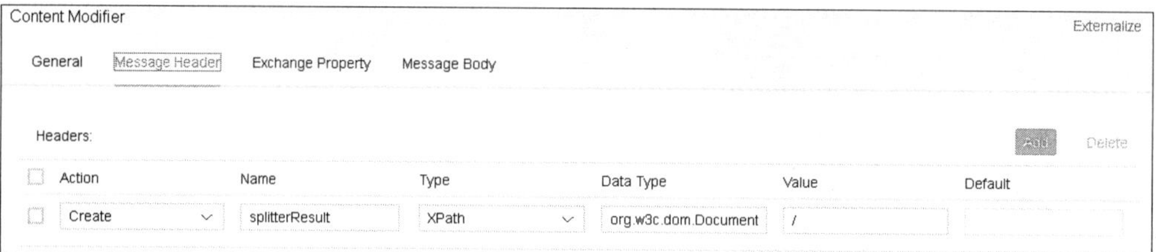

Figure 5.30 Adding the Complete Single Message into the Header Area

We're using an absolute XPath expression pointing to the root of the received single message. Hence, we really put the complete message into the header variable named `splitterResult`. In the second **Content Modifier**, we now simply pick the variable's content and place it into the body. The result of the second **Content Modifier**'s configuration is shown in Figure 5.31.

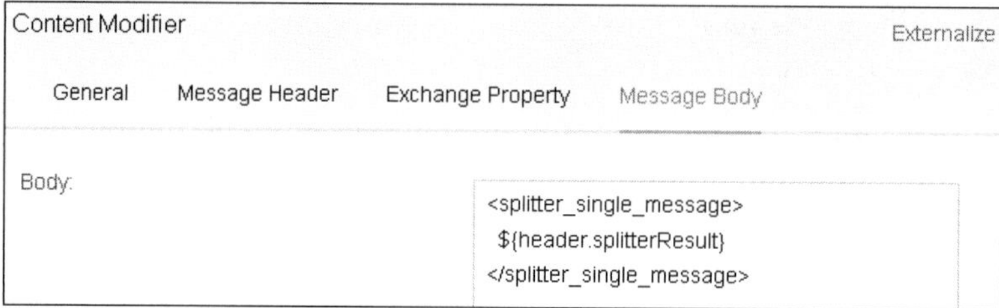

Figure 5.31 Copying the Splitter's Message into the Body

Running the scenario results in the output depicted in Figure 5.32.

```
<soap:Envelope xmlns:soap="http://schemas.xmlsoap.org/soap/envelope/">
   <soap:Header/>
   <soap:Body>
      <multimap:Messages xmlns:multimap="http://sap.com/xi/XI/SplitAndMerge">
         <multimap:Message1>
            <splitter_single_message>
               <demo:OrderList_MT xmlns:demo="http://cpi.sap.com/demo">
                  <orders>
                     <orderNumber>10248</orderNumber>
                     <customerName>?</customerName>
                     <orderAmount>?</orderAmount>
                     <currency>?</currency>
                     <taxAmount>?</taxAmount>
                  </orders>
               </demo:OrderList_MT>
            </splitter_single_message>
            <splitter_single_message>
               <demo:OrderList_MT xmlns:demo="http://cpi.sap.com/demo">
                  <orders>
                     <orderNumber>10249</orderNumber>
                     <customerName>?</customerName>
                     <orderAmount>?</orderAmount>
                     <currency>?</currency>
                     <taxAmount>?</taxAmount>
                  </orders>
               </demo:OrderList_MT>
            </splitter_single_message>
            <splitter_single_message>
               <demo:OrderList_MT xmlns:demo="http://cpi.sap.com/demo">
                  <orders>
                     <orderNumber>10250</orderNumber>
                     <customerName>?</customerName>
                     <orderAmount>?</orderAmount>
                     <currency>?</currency>
                     <taxAmount>?</taxAmount>
                  </orders>
               </demo:OrderList_MT>
            </splitter_single_message>
         </multimap:Message1>
      </multimap:Messages>
   </soap:Body>
</soap:Envelope>
```


Figure 5.32 Result Message after Invoking the Integration Flow

In between the `<splitter_single_message>` tags, you can now easily identify the fragment that was produced by the splitter. With this knowledge, you can formulate the absolute path within that single message to the `orderNumber` field: `/demo:OrderList_MT/orders/orderNumber`. Let's quickly verify this by adjusting the two **Content Modifier**'s configurations. You can find the updated properties in Figure 5.33 and Figure 5.34.

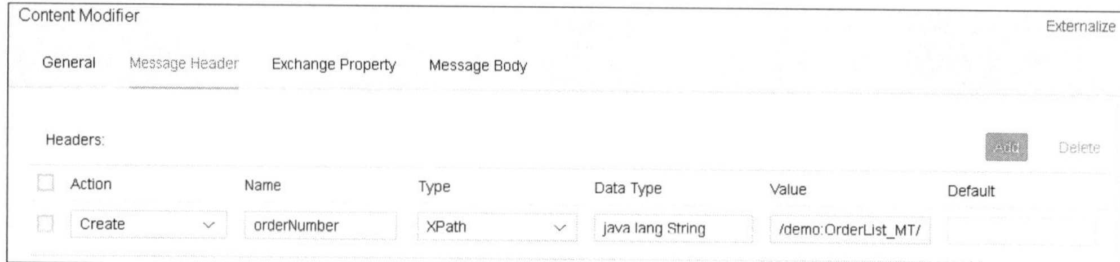

Figure 5.33 Accessing the orderNumber Field via an Absolute XPath Expression in the First Content Modifier

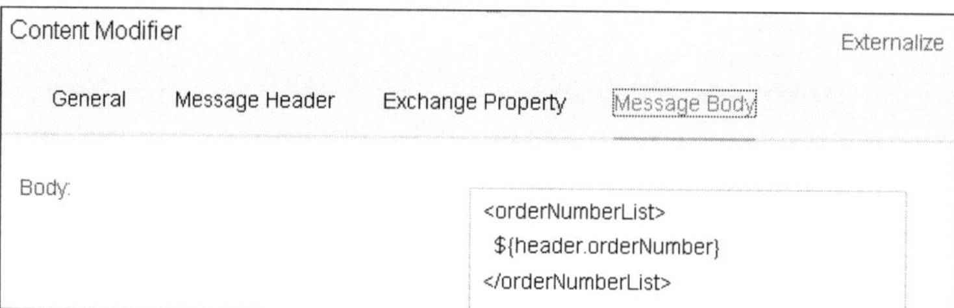

Figure 5.34 Pasting the Copied Order Numbers into the Result Message's Body in the Second Content Modifier

We can't run this scenario quite yet because we have to consider one small, but important, detail. Take a look at the **Value** column in Figure 5.33. The XPath expression begins with /demo:OrderList_MT, right? The important detail is the namespace demo:. The message handling route isn't aware of this namespace and what it means. Hence, we have to explicitly declare the namespace in the route's configuration. You can define some global settings for an integration flow by clicking somewhere outside of the pools to reach the route's properties beneath the process model. After you can see the properties of the integration flow, select the **Runtime Configuration** tab (see Figure 5.35).

The **Runtime Configuration** tab allows you to define the namespace mappings in a dedicated field. We've just copied the namespace definition from Figure 5.32. Remember to remove the quotation marks after pasting the string into the **Namespace Mapping** field! Now the route is aware of the namespace and can handle the XML fragment accordingly. Try out the changed integration flow. The result should look like Figure 5.36.

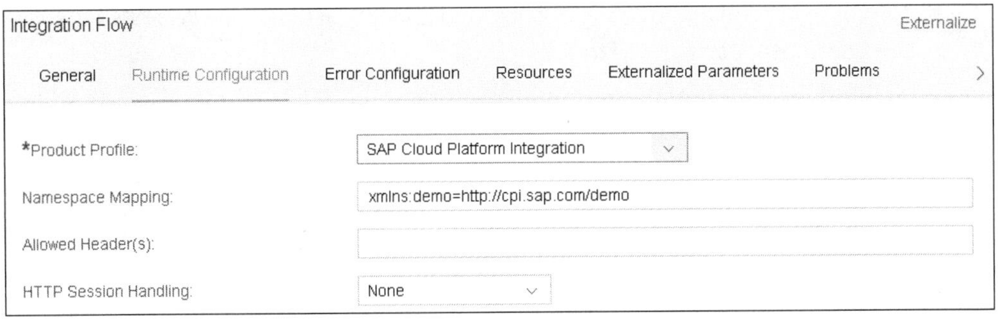

Integration Flow | Externalize

General | Runtime Configuration | Error Configuration | Resources | Externalized Parameters | Problems

*Product Profile:	SAP Cloud Platform Integration
Namespace Mapping:	xmlns:demo=http://cpi.sap.com/demo
Allowed Header(s):	
HTTP Session Handling:	None

Figure 5.35 Global Configuration Options for an Integration Flow

```
<soap:Envelope xmlns:soap="http://schemas.xmlsoap.org/soap/envelope/">
   <soap:Body>
      <multimap:Messages xmlns:multimap="http://sap.com/xi/XI/SplitAndMerge">
         <multimap:Message1>
            <orderNumberList>10248</orderNumberList>
            <orderNumberList>10249</orderNumberList>
            <orderNumberList>10250</orderNumberList>
         </multimap:Message1>
      </multimap:Messages>
   </soap:Body>
</soap:Envelope>
```

Figure 5.36 Result Message after Picking the Order Number via Absolute XPath Expression

5.2.4 Enriching Individual Messages with Additional Data

We began with a relatively simple example to concentrate on the behavior of the **Splitter** and **Gather**. However, we can now extend this example to something more useful by invoking an external OData data source and enriching our result message. This reflects a typical example where some basic data needs to be enriched by external sources. In our case, we want to retrieve order details for each of the order numbers that we've extracted. In Chapter 4, Section 4.3.3, we configured an OData connection to retrieve detailed data for order numbers. This is exactly what we'll do next: replace the second **Content Modifier** (which actually just sets the body of the single message artificially with the extracted order number) with a **Request-Reply** step invoking the OData service and providing useful data as response for each single message the **Splitter** created. After adding the **Request-Reply** step into the integration flow, the scenario finally looks like the one shown in Figure 5.37.

The configuration of the **Request-Reply** step is identical to the one described in Chapter 4, Section 4.3, and can be found there.

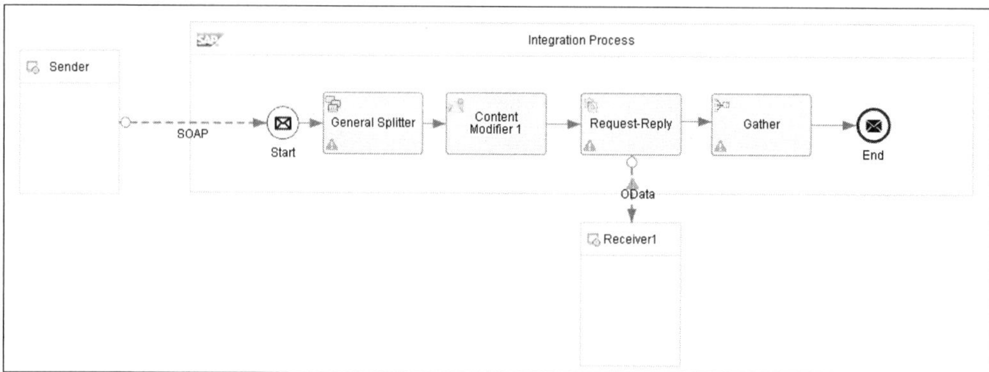

Figure 5.37 Integration Flow with Splitter, Gather, and the Invocation of an External OData Source

Note

The call of the **Request-Reply** step is executed for every order number of the original incoming message. We can't stress enough the importance of this specific behavior of an integration flow making use of the **Splitter** step. All activities following the **Splitter** are invoked for each single message generated by the **Splitter** until either the end of the flow or the **Gather** step is reached! The invocation of the integration flow finally results in the response message shown in Figure 5.38.

To summarize, SAP Cloud Platform Integration solutions frequently have to deal with handling messages containing lists of items. In this section, the **Splitter** step was used to split a message comprising several order numbers into individual single messages, each containing one order number. The individual messages can be treated separately by SAP Cloud Platform Integration. SAP Cloud Platform Integration can then combine the results of each individual message processing chain back into one integrated response message using the **Gather** activity. You've learned how to configure both the **Splitter** and the **Gather** steps correctly to benefit from the message handling behavior just described. In the next section, we'll take a close look at asynchronous message handling scenarios.

```
<soap:Envelope xmlns:soap="http://schemas.xmlsoap.org/soap/envelope/">
  <soap:Body>
    <multimap:Messages xmlns:multimap="http://sap.com/xi/XI/SplitAndMerge">
      <multimap:Message1>
        <Orders>
          <Order>
            <ShipPostalCode>51100</ShipPostalCode>
            <ShippedDate>1996-07-16T00:00:00.000</ShippedDate>
            <OrderID>10248</OrderID>
            <ShipCity>Reims</ShipCity>
            <ShipAddress>59 rue de l'Abbaye</ShipAddress>
            <ShipCountry>France</ShipCountry>
            <ShipName>Vins et alcools Chevalier</ShipName>
          </Order>
        </Orders>
        <Orders>
          <Order>
            <ShipPostalCode>44087</ShipPostalCode>
            <ShippedDate>1996-07-10T00:00:00.000</ShippedDate>
            <OrderID>10249</OrderID>
            <ShipCity>Münster</ShipCity>
            <ShipAddress>Luisenstr. 48</ShipAddress>
            <ShipCountry>Germany</ShipCountry>
            <ShipName>Toms Spezialitäten</ShipName>
          </Order>
        </Orders>
        <Orders>
          <Order>
            <ShipPostalCode>05454-876</ShipPostalCode>
            <ShippedDate>1996-07-12T00:00:00.000</ShippedDate>
            <OrderID>10250</OrderID>
            <ShipCity>Rio de Janeiro</ShipCity>
            <ShipAddress>Rua do Paço, 67</ShipAddress>
            <ShipCountry>Brazil</ShipCountry>
            <ShipName>Hanari Carnes</ShipName>
          </Order>
        </Orders>
      </multimap:Message1>
    </multimap:Messages>
  </soap:Body>
</soap:Envelope>
```


Figure 5.38 Result Message, Including Order Details Retrieved from the External OData Source

5.3 Asynchronous Message Handling

The core task of an integration solution is the routing of messages across a company's distributed IT landscape, including connectivity to partners and suppliers. Such integration scenarios can be synchronous or asynchronous in nature. *Synchronous* means, in this regard, the following procedure:

1. A sender opens a connection to SAP Cloud Platform Integration and sends a request message.
2. After sending the request message to SAP Cloud Platform Integration, the sender doesn't close the connection because a reply is expected.
3. SAP Cloud Platform Integration finds the receiver for the respective request message (e.g., by inspecting the message's content), opens a connection to the receiver, and routes the message to the receiver.
4. After sending the message to the receiver, SAP Cloud Platform Integration doesn't close the connection, either.
5. The receiver acts on the request message by creating a response message and returns it to SAP Cloud Platform Integration via the still opened connection.
6. After receiving the message, SAP Cloud Platform Integration will close the connection to the receiver and route the received message as a reply message to the original sender.
7. The sender can now close the connection to SAP Cloud Platform Integration after receiving the final reply message.

The connections from the sender to SAP Cloud Platform Integration, as well as the connection from SAP Cloud Platform Integration to the receiver, are still open, as long as message processing is ongoing. The communication involves a bidirectional message transfer in one session. This message handling procedure significantly differs from *asynchronous* message handling where the procedure looks like the following:

1. A sender opens a connection to SAP Cloud Platform Integration and sends a message.
2. After SAP Cloud Platform Integration receives the message correctly, it acknowledges its reception to the sender.
3. After receiving the acknowledgment from SAP Cloud Platform Integration, the sender closes the connection.
4. SAP Cloud Platform Integration opens a connection to the receiver of the message and forwards it accordingly.
5. After receiving the message completely, the receiver also acknowledges the message's reception to SAP Cloud Platform Integration.
6. After receiving the acknowledgment from the receiver, SAP Cloud Platform Integration closes the connection.

The connections are immediately closed as soon as the messages have been confirmed by the receiving parties. The overall communication only involves a message transfer in one direction. These are, in short, the main differences between synchronous and asynchronous communication. But how does this knowledge affect our discussion of SAP Cloud Platform Integration? First of all, SAP Cloud Platform Integration absolutely must support both communication styles because it is a general-purpose integration infrastructure that is prepared for all kinds of integration requirements. However, in the previous sections, all communications were synchronous. So far, this has been useful because we were able to see the immediate results of our integration flow invocations in the SOAP clients that we used to call the message handling chains. Now the time has come to take a closer look at asynchronous message handling as well, including how to influence the communication style.

5.3.1 Synchronous versus Asynchronous Communication from SAP Cloud Platform Integration's Perspective

Let's repeat some main aspects regarding the synchronous vs. asynchronous discussion from Chapter 4, Section 4.1.1. One of the key terms used in that chapter was *exchange* (Figure 5.39).

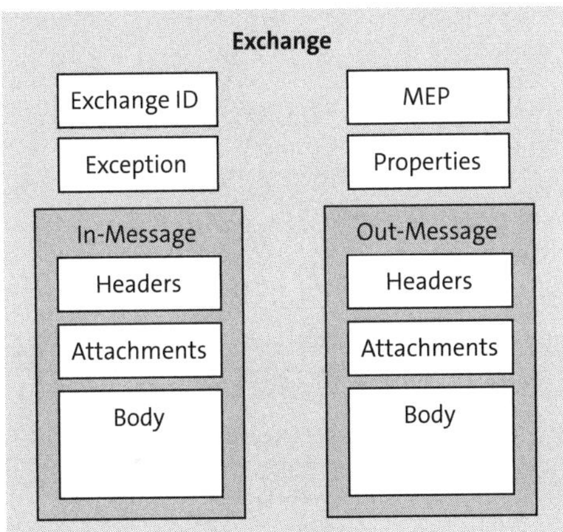

Figure 5.39 Structure of an Exchange

An exchange is a term from Apache Camel terminology that represents a container for a message while it's being processed inside the integration engine. We know so far that the exchange will be filled with an `In` message only if it's an asynchronous scenario, whereas the `Out` message within the exchange only plays a role for synchronous scenarios, as discussed in Chapter 4, Section 4.1.1. Additionally, the communication type (synchronous or asynchronous) is determined by the **Message Exchange Pattern** field (MEP) within the exchange. The MEP field can contain two potential values:

- **`InOnly`**
  The route handles a one-way message, and the sender doesn't expect a reply from the respective receiver. Hence, the exchange carries an In message only. `InOnly` represents the asynchronous use case.
- **`InOut`**
  The route handles a request-response message. The sender expects a reply from the route which will be stored as an Out message in the exchange. `InOut` represents the synchronous communication style.

The component that determines whether a message should be handled synchronously or asynchronously is, in fact, the channel! This might surprise you, but we'll show you how to influence synchronous and asynchronous message handling in SAP Cloud Platform Integration by using the SOAP adapter.

We're reusing the scenario we built in Section 5.2.4. For your convenience, we've added screenshots of the scenario in Figure 5.40 and the associated input message in Figure 5.41.

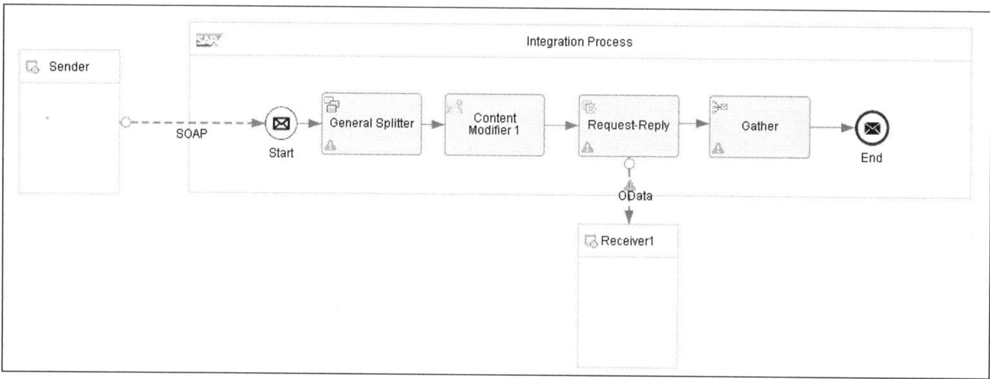

Figure 5.40 Demo Scenario for Splitting and Joining Messages

```
<soapenv:Envelope xmlns:soapenv="http://schemas
   <soapenv:Header/>
   <soapenv:Body>
      <demo:OrderList_MT>
         <!--Zero or more repetitions:-->
         <orders>
            <orderNumber>10248</orderNumber>
            <customerName>?</customerName>
            <orderAmount>?</orderAmount>
            <currency>?</currency>
            <taxAmount>?</taxAmount>
         </orders>
         <orders>
            <orderNumber>10249</orderNumber>
            <customerName>?</customerName>
            <orderAmount>?</orderAmount>
            <currency>?</currency>
            <taxAmount>?</taxAmount>
         </orders>
         <orders>
            <orderNumber>10250</orderNumber>
            <customerName>?</customerName>
            <orderAmount>?</orderAmount>
            <currency>?</currency>
            <taxAmount>?</taxAmount>
         </orders>
      </demo:OrderList_MT>
   </soapenv:Body>
</soapenv:Envelope>
```

Figure 5.41 Example Input Message for the Demo Scenario

The integration flow, in essence, splits the incoming message into three individual messages. Each of these three single messages contains exactly one order. The two **Content Modifier** steps are executed three times (for each of the single messages). The first **Content Modifier** extracts the order number from the single message and writes it into the message's header area, whereas the second **Content Modifier** retrieves the order number from the header area again and writes the number, embedded inside `orderDetails` tags, into the body area of the message. As this is done three times, the resulting message contains just the three order numbers, each one surrounded by `orderDetails` tags (Figure 5.42).

The screenshots for the input, as well as for the result message, are taken from a SoapUI test client. The scenario is currently a synchronous scenario; otherwise, we wouldn't have received a response back. Mysterious is the fact, that the incoming message was built using a WSDL file containing the description of an *asynchronous* interface. You can verify this by downloading the associated WSDL file called *SendOrderList_Async.wsdl* from *www.sap-press.com/4650*. You'll find the lines in the file shown in Figure 5.43.

```xml
<soap:Envelope xmlns:soap="http://schemas.xmlsoap.org/soap/envelope/">
   <soap:Body>
      <multimap:Messages xmlns:multimap="http://sap.com/xi/XI/SplitAndMerge">
         <multimap:Message1>
            <orderDetails>10248</orderDetails>
            <orderDetails>10249</orderDetails>
            <orderDetails>10250</orderDetails>
         </multimap:Message1>
      </multimap:Messages>
   </soap:Body>
</soap:Envelope>
```

Figure 5.42 Result Message after Invoking the Integration Flow

```xml
<wsdl:portType name="SendOrderList_Async">
   <wsdl:documentation/>
   <wsdl:operation name="SendOrderList_Async">
      <wsdl:documentation/>
      <wsp:Policy>
         <wsp:PolicyReference URI="#OP_SendOrderList_Async"/>
      </wsp:Policy><wsdl:input message="p1:OrderList_MT"/>
   </wsdl:operation>
</wsdl:portType>
```

Figure 5.43 Definition of the Service's Operation

The operation consists of an input message, but no output message, which would be needed for a synchronous interface. But why, then, is SAP Cloud Platform Integration interpreting it as a synchronous message exchange? Remember the setting for the **Message Exchange Pattern** we've made in the SOAP channel in Section 5.2.2? Let's take a closer look at the SOAP adapter's configuration (Figure 5.44).

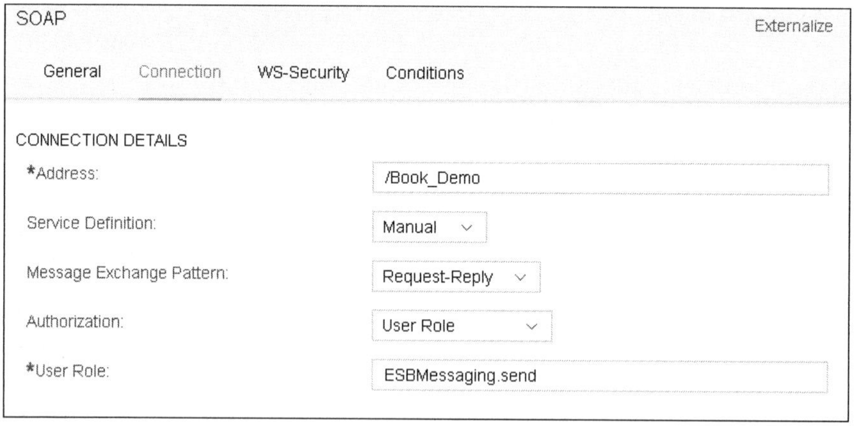

SOAP
Externalize
General | Connection | WS-Security | Conditions

CONNECTION DETAILS

*Address: /Book_Demo
Service Definition: Manual
Message Exchange Pattern: Request-Reply
Authorization: User Role
*User Role: ESBMessaging.send

Figure 5.44 Configuration of the SOAP Channel in the Demo Scenario

The **Address** field is set with a string used to create the URL for invoking the integration flow. In addition, we've chosen the default configuration for **Service Definition** and **Message Exchange Pattern**. This is exactly the place where the SAP Cloud Platform Integration's runtime finds the information about synchronous or asynchronous message handling.

When the channel receives a message from a client, it knows nothing about the data that arrives at its address, how the data it receives was constructed, or whether it's based on a synchronous or asynchronous WSDL file. It only knows whether the received message should be treated synchronously or asynchronously because of the configured **Message Exchange Pattern**.

Note

The WSDL file was just used in the SoapUI client to create a proper input message. However, the WSDL file was never used in any of the SAP Cloud Platform Integration configuration steps for that scenario. Hence, SAP Cloud Platform Integration knows nothing about the data it should process. This is the payload-agnostic behavior of Apache Camel we talked about in previous chapters. You can actually push anything to SAP Cloud Platform Integration: it would work as long as you don't have processing steps in your route that rely on a specific format.

We configured **Request-Reply** as **Message Exchange Pattern**; therefore, the SOAP channel sets the **MEP** field in the exchange to `InOut`. This explains the synchronous behavior of our scenario. So, the message walks through the steps of the integration flow, and we have a resulting message created at the end of the chain when we reach the **End** event (see Figure 5.40). Here, some magic happens: because there is no additional step to process, the last status of the message's body will be copied automatically into the body of the exchange's `Out` message. Remember, synchronous messages in an exchange have both an `In` and an `Out` message, and the reply needs to be in the `Out` message. The `Out` message (including body, headers, and attachments) is finally returned to the caller.

The next issue is how to make the route behave asynchronously. Actually, there are two options to do this: select **One-Way** for the **Message Exchange Pattern** or make the SOAP channel aware of the concrete message it receives.

Let's try out both options. We start with the easy one; we just change the value for the **Message Exchange Pattern** to **One-Way,** as shown in Figure 5.45.

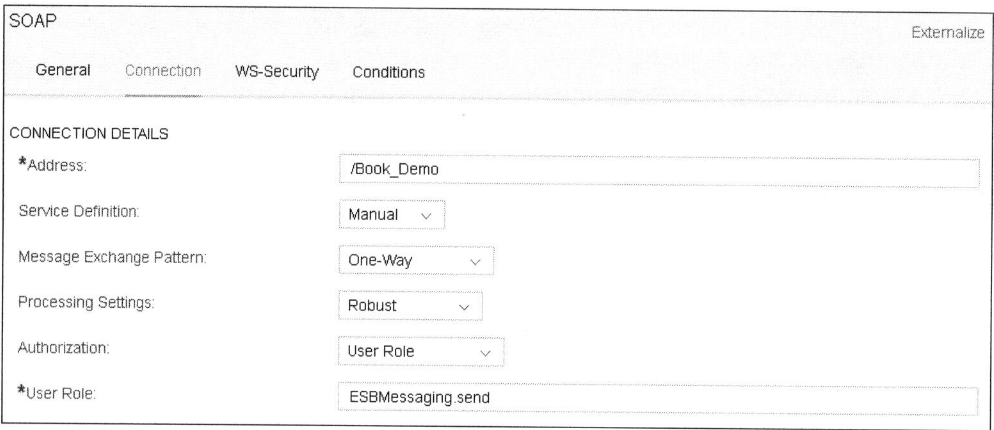

Figure 5.45 Configuration of the SOAP channel after Changing the Message Exchange Pattern Field to One-Way

As soon as we change the setting, a new **Processing Settings** dropdown appears. Two configuration options are available: **WS-Standard** and **Robust**, as described here:

- **WS-Standard**
  In the Web Service Standard, one-way processing is also known as the fire-and-forget method. This is useful if the sender of the message just wants to initiate a request but doesn't care if the request is really processed successfully. In SAP Cloud Platform Integration, this behavior can be configured with the **WS-Standard** option. SAP Cloud Platform will process the SOAP request received but won't report back any errors that may occur during processing of the message.
- **Robust**
  This is the default option available in SAP Cloud Platform Integration and is also known as Robust In-Only or Robust One-Way. With this configuration, the SOAP adapter synchronously reports back error information to the sender if there is an error during message processing in SAP Cloud Platform Integration or when calling the receiver. This is important for reliable one-way message exchanges, where the sender of a message needs guaranteed delivery by SAP Cloud Platform Integration. This is the option we select because we want to know if the message was processed in SAP Cloud Platform Integration or not.

After the changes are saved and deployed, you can invoke your integration flow again from your SOAP test client of choice. If you're using SoapUI, you'll get nothing back as a reply message. You'll only receive acknowledgment from SAP Cloud Platform Integration about the successful reception of the message as an HTTP response code 202 (Figure 5.46).

Header	Value
Strict-Transport-Security	max-age=31536000; includeSubDom...
Date	Thu, 19 Nov 2015 17:47:10 GMT
Content-Length	0
#status#	HTTP/1.1 202 Accepted
Set-Cookie	JSESSIONID=D8337A89C2EB478E51AE...
Set-Cookie	JTENANTSESSIONID_a29d0a049=IHQ...
Server	SAP

Headers (7) Attachments (0) SSL Info (3 certs) WSS (0) JMS (0)

Figure 5.46 Returned Header after Invoking an Asynchronous Route via SOAP Channel

Now, let's see if we correctly receive the error information back if there is an error in processing. For this, we need to change the integration flow in a way that an error is raised. This can, for example, be done by setting a wrong **Address** in the **OData** channel retrieving additional information for enriching the message. We set *http://test_error_situation* there, as shown in Figure 5.47, and then save and deploy the integration flow.

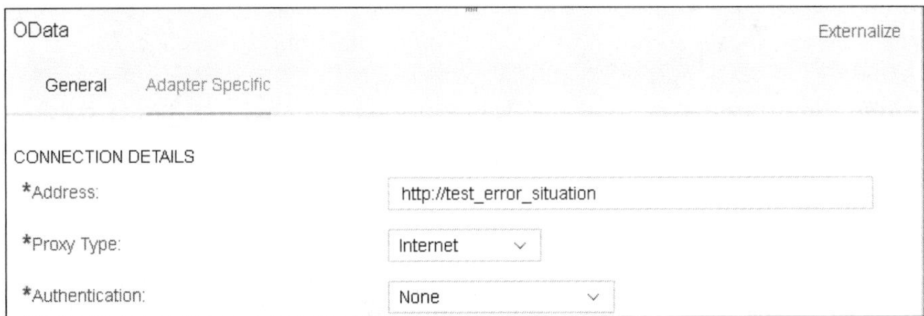

Figure 5.47 Configuration of the OData Channel after Changing the Address

When we now call the integration flow again from our SOAP test client, we receive a SOAP fault error (Figure 5.48). The SOAP fault contains `faultcode` and `faultstring`. Although the `faultcode` only tells us that an error occurred in the SOAP server, the error details can be found in `faultstring`.

```
<soap:Envelope xmlns:soap="http://schemas.xmlsoap.org/soap/envelope/">
   <soap:Header/>
   <soap:Body>
      <soap:Fault>
         <faultcode>soap:Server</faultcode>
         <faultstring>An internal error occurred. For error details check MPL ID ... in
         message monitoring or use the URL ... to directly access the error information.</faultstring>
      </soap:Fault>
   </soap:Body>
</soap:Envelope>
```

Figure 5.48 SOAP Fault Received in the SOAP Test Client

The real error, that the OData Call wasn't successful, isn't provided; only a generic error containing the message processing log (MPL) ID and the direct link to it in SAP Cloud Platform Integration's message monitoring are provided. We don't see the real error due to security guidelines; no internal details are to be provided externally to avoid attacks. So, we need to call the URL provided to access the MPL in SAP Cloud Platform Integration's message monitoring to investigate the real error (Figure 5.49). Calling the URL is secured by authentication in SAP Cloud Platform Integration so that only authorized users get access to the detailed error description.

```
com.sap.gateway.core.ip.component.odata.exception.OsciException: Host not found : 502 : HTTP/1.1
Request URI              :   GET http://test_error_situation/$metadata HTTP/1.1
Request Headers          :
  x-csrf-token             : fetch

HTTP Status Line         :   HTTP/1.1 502 Host not found
```

Figure 5.49 Error Details Shown in SAP Cloud Platform Integration's Message Monitor

We can now check what happens if **WS-Standard** is set for **Processing Settings** in the SOAP channel. Let's change the configuration (Figure 5.50), and then save and deploy the integration flow.

Invoke the integration flow from your SOAP test client. You now receive the same HTTP response code 202 as in the successful scenario execution (refer to Figure 5.46) because the message was successfully delivered to SAP Cloud Platform Integration, the error isn't given back to the sender—the fire-and-forget behavior explained before. You as sender aren't interested to know whether the message is processed successfully or not.

Figure 5.50 Configuration of the SOAP Channel with WS-Standard Processing

Now, let's try out the second option to configure asynchronous processing in the SOAP channel: we make the SOAP channel aware of the concrete message it receives. For this, the configuration of the SOAP channel provides an option to configure the service via WSDL. We switch the configuration for **Service Definition** to **WSDL**. Then, a dedicated field named **URL to WSDL** (see Figure 5.51) will appear below the **Service Definition** dropdown that allows us to point to our WSDL file.

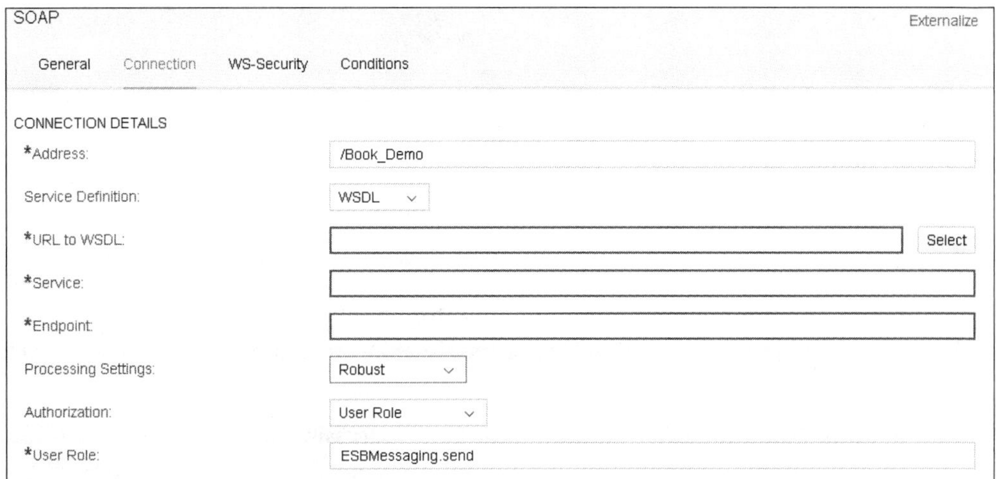

Figure 5.51 Configuration of SOAP Adapter Using Service Definition from WSDL

To assign the WSDL file, simply click on the **Select** button. In the **Select WSDL Resource** dialog box, click on the **Upload from File System** button (Figure 5.52).

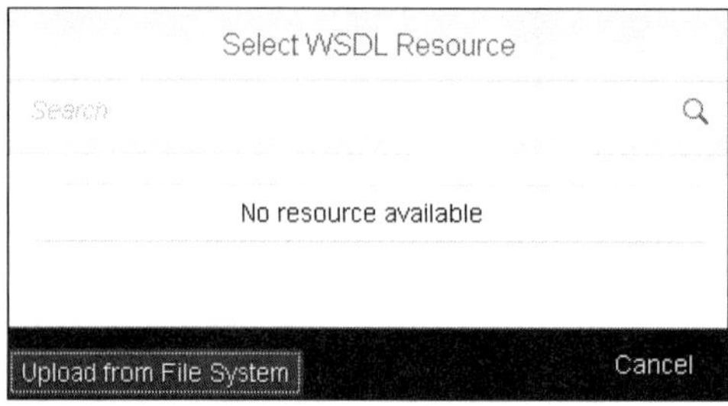

Figure 5.52 Adding a WSDL File to the SOAP Channel

The normal file picker dialog opens. Select the *SendOrderList_Async.wsdl* file from your file system. When uploading the WSDL into the integration flow, SAP Cloud Platform Integration is reading the services defined in the WSDL and automatically sets service and endpoint as defined in the WSDL. In our WSDL file, one service, `SendOrderList_Async`, is defined in the `service` tag, as depicted in Figure 5.53, with the endpoint `SendOrderList_AsyncBinding`.

```
<wsdl:service name="SendOrderList_Async">
    <wsdl:port name="SendOrderList_AsyncBinding" binding="p1:SendOrderList_AsyncBinding">
            <soap:address
        location="https://server:port/cxf/Book_Demo" />
    </wsdl:port>
</wsdl:service>
```

Figure 5.53 Service Definition in the WSDL

The service and endpoint are taken over into the SOAP adapter configuration, including the link to the WSDL file. The configuration should look like the one shown in Figure 5.54 now. Notice that the namespace `demo:` is added. The namespace definition `xmlns:demo=http://cpi.sap.com/demo` is automatically added into the integration flow's **Runtime Configuration** if not configured already. In our case, the namespace definition was already available because we've configured it earlier.

In addition to the WSDL-specific settings, the **Processing Settings** dropdown is also available for configuration via WSDL. Here, the same options, **Robust** and **WS-Standard**, are available as already described for the configuration without WSDL. We select **Robust** to receive error information back if the message processing in SAP Cloud Platform Integration isn't successful.

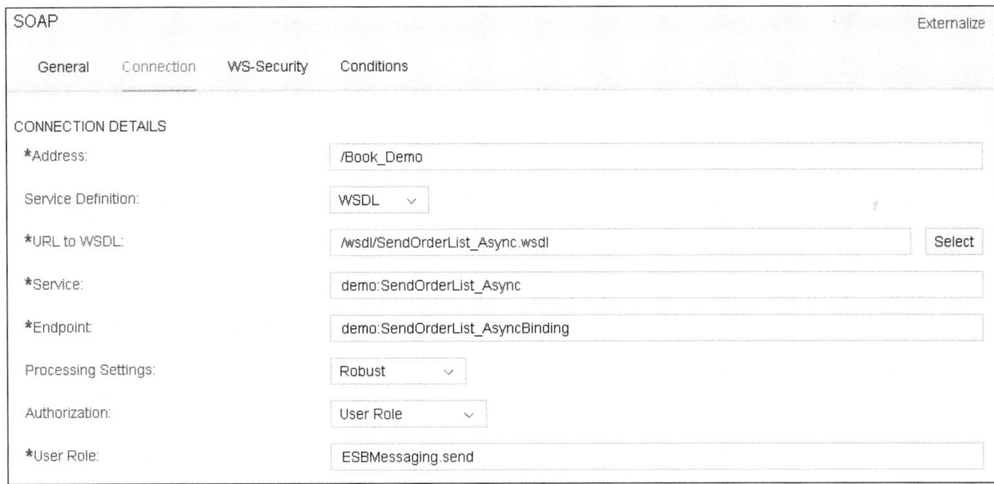

Figure 5.54 Configuration of SOAP Adapter after Assigning the WSDL File

Save and deploy your changes. By adding the WSDL file to the SOAP channel's configuration, correct asynchronous message handling can be ensured. The channel now knows that it receives an asynchronous XML message, compliant to the WSDL, and will set the **MEP** field of the exchange to `InOnly`. However, a validation of the incoming message against the WSDL isn't done for the incoming data. SAP Cloud Platform Integration provides a dedicated processing step for that purpose: the XML validator, which requires the assignment of a WSDL file in its configuration.

Once deployed, you can invoke your integration flow again from your SOAP test client of choice. You'll receive the same HTTP response codes as for the configuration without WSDL. If you still have the wrong address configuration set in the OData channel, you'll get a SOAP fault error because the **Processing Settings** are configured for robust processing (refer to Figure 5.48). Correct the OData address, and then save and deploy the integration flow. Now you should get the HTTP response code 202 (refer to Figure 5.46), which means the message processing was successful in SAP Cloud Platform Integration.

But what happened to our message inside SAP Cloud Platform Integration, and where can we track this, now that we don't have SoapUI showing the result? For this, simply navigate to SAP Cloud Platform Integration's monitoring dashboard by clicking on the three horizontal bars in the upper-left corner ☰ and choosing **Monitor** from the dropdown menu (Figure 5.55).

Figure 5.55 Switching to SAP Cloud Platform Integration's Monitoring Environment

The monitoring dashboard opens. Click on the tile for the successfully completed integration flows in the **Monitor Message Processing** area of the screen (Figure 5.56).

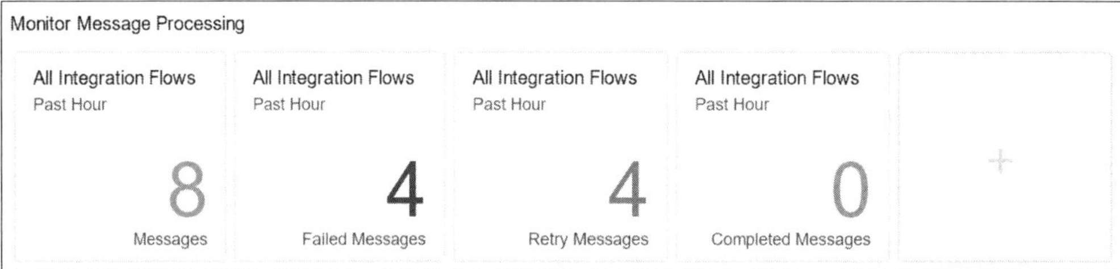

Figure 5.56 Tiles for the Monitors of Completed and Failed Messages

After you've clicked on the tile for completed messages, you'll receive an appropriate list of the successfully completed messages sorted by date and time (see Figure 5.57, left half of the screen). In the right half of the screen, you see the status, logs, and artifact details of the message's processing for the selected message.

If there are errors, you can open the **Failed Messages** tile in Figure 5.56 to see a list of the failed messages. Become familiar with the message processing monitor to use it for root cause analysis in erroneous situations. You'll find additional information about the message monitoring in Chapter 8.

Note

The SOAP channel supports both communication styles: synchronous and asynchronous. You've now seen how to influence its behavior. This isn't the case for all adapters, however. The Secure Shell File Transfer Protocol (SFTP) adapter, for example, supports asynchronous message handling only. Hence, it will merely support `InOnly` as entry in the **MEP** field. Consequently, communication styles are highly adapter dependent and differ from adapter to adapter.

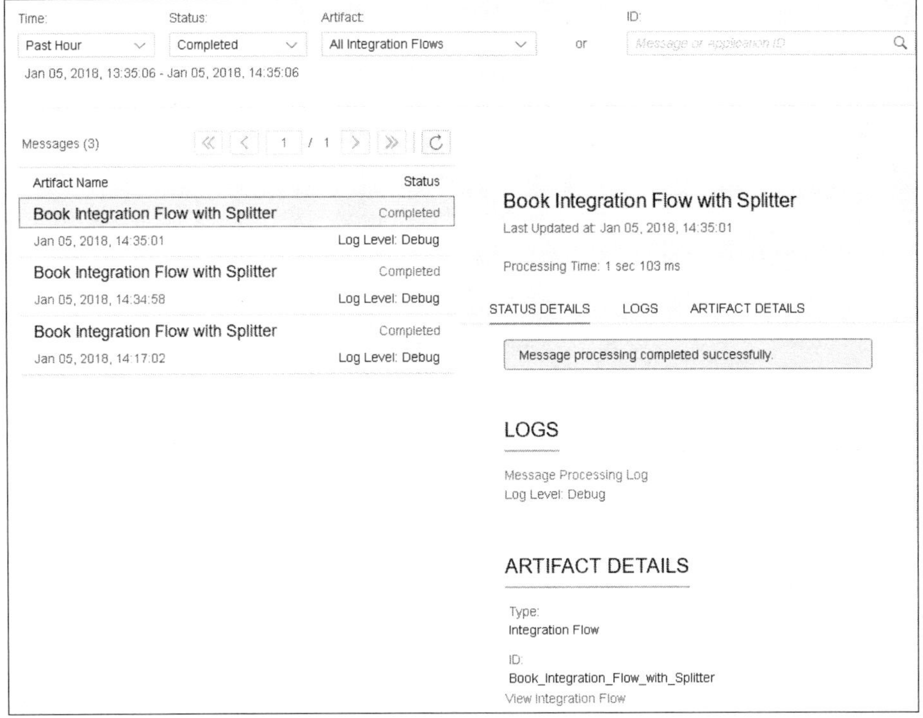

Figure 5.57 Details of a Successfully Completed Message

5.3.2 Adding an Asynchronous Receiver

Now that we know how to make a SOAP invocation asynchronous, we probably also want to deliver the message to an asynchronous receiver to really verify the correct content of the received message. To keep administration effort to a minimum, we'll make use of an email receiver. Because the email receiver was already introduced in Chapter 2, won't go into detail here, but we'll show the email adapter's configuration for your reference.

Here are the modeling steps you have to complete to run the scenario with an email receiver:

1. Add a **Receiver** to the model on the right side of the integration flow. You find the receiver besides the participant's node in the palette (Figure 5.58).
2. Position the **Receiver** on the right side of the **Integration Process**, close to the message **End** event (Figure 5.59).

Figure 5.58 Selecting a Receiver from the Palette

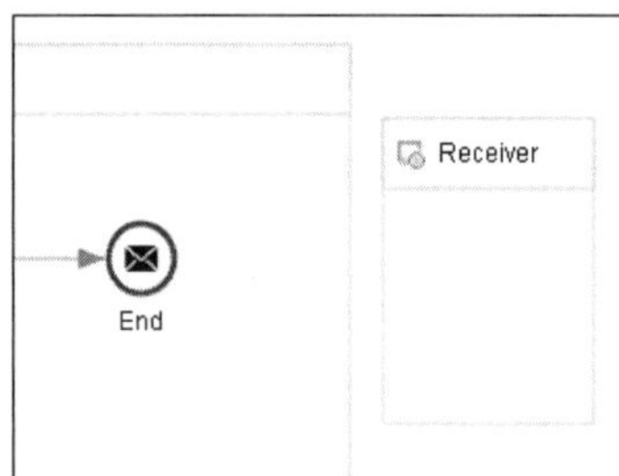

Figure 5.59 Positioning of the Receiver Pool Close to the End Event

3. Connect the **End** event with the **Receiver** pool (Figure 5.60).

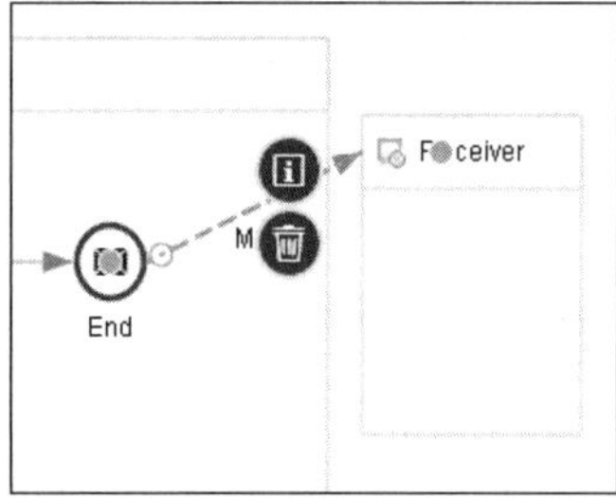

Figure 5.60 Connecting the End Event with the Receiver Pool

4. In the upcoming **Adapter Type** dialog, select the **Mail** entry. Configure the adapter according to your email account. The values shown in the screenshots (Figure 5.61) fit a Google email account.

> **Note**
>
> For details on configuration of the fields and creation of the user credentials, refer to Chapter 2.

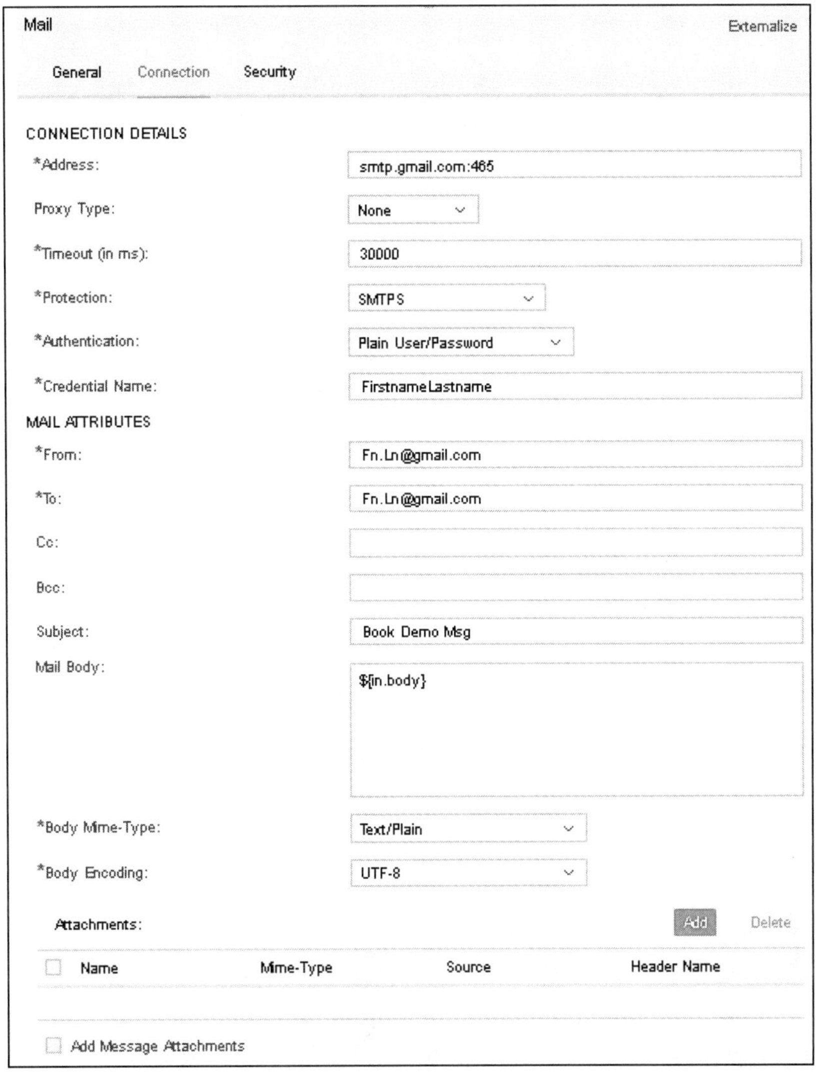

Figure 5.61 Configuring the Mail Adapter

The final scenario should look similar to the one depicted in Figure 5.62. You can easily identify the sender on the left, the message processing steps in the middle, and the final receiver on the right. That's the advantage of a graphical environment: it clearly and intuitively describes how the message arrives at the server, how it's handled within the SAP Cloud Platform Integration server, and to which systems using which channels it's forwarded.

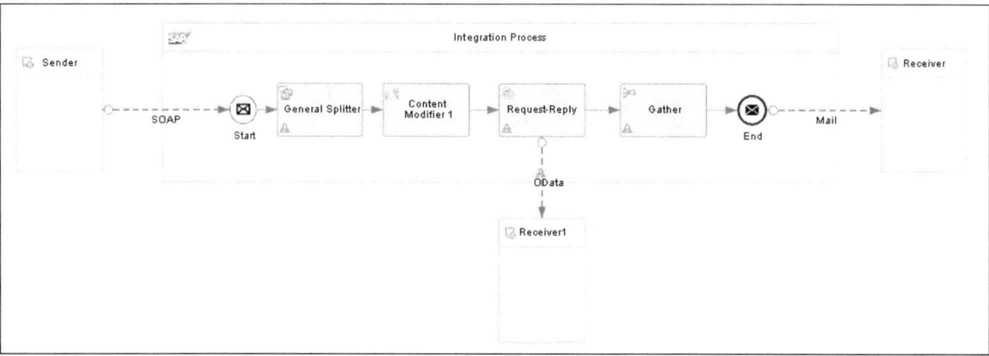

Figure 5.62 Asynchronous Integration Flow with Email Receiver

After you've finished your configurations, you can run the scenario again. This time, the message will be delivered to your email account. You should receive an email containing the three order numbers. A screenshot of the email's content is shown in Figure 5.63.

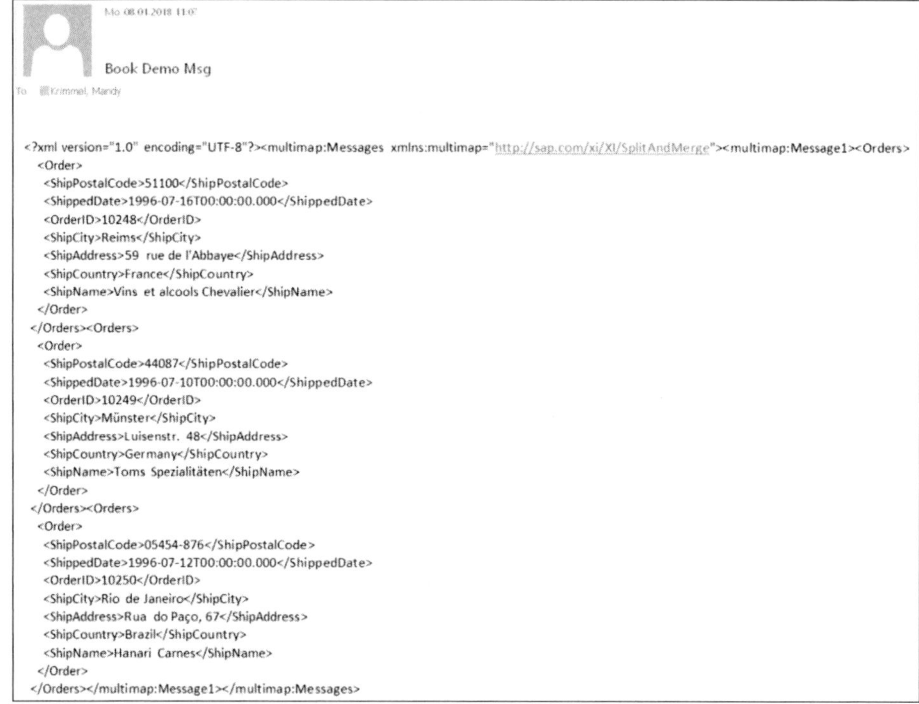


```
<?xml version="1.0" encoding="UTF-8"?><multimap:Messages xmlns:multimap="http://sap.com/xi/XI/SplitAndMerge"><multimap:Message1><Orders>
  <Order>
    <ShipPostalCode>51100</ShipPostalCode>
    <ShippedDate>1996-07-16T00:00:00.000</ShippedDate>
    <OrderID>10248</OrderID>
    <ShipCity>Reims</ShipCity>
    <ShipAddress>59 rue de l'Abbaye</ShipAddress>
    <ShipCountry>France</ShipCountry>
    <ShipName>Vins et alcools Chevalier</ShipName>
  </Order>
</Orders><Orders>
  <Order>
    <ShipPostalCode>44087</ShipPostalCode>
    <ShippedDate>1996-07-10T00:00:00.000</ShippedDate>
    <OrderID>10249</OrderID>
    <ShipCity>Münster</ShipCity>
    <ShipAddress>Luisenstr. 48</ShipAddress>
    <ShipCountry>Germany</ShipCountry>
    <ShipName>Toms Spezialitäten</ShipName>
  </Order>
</Orders><Orders>
  <Order>
    <ShipPostalCode>05454-876</ShipPostalCode>
    <ShippedDate>1996-07-12T00:00:00.000</ShippedDate>
    <OrderID>10250</OrderID>
    <ShipCity>Rio de Janeiro</ShipCity>
    <ShipAddress>Rua do Paço, 67</ShipAddress>
    <ShipCountry>Brazil</ShipCountry>
    <ShipName>Hanari Carnes</ShipName>
  </Order>
</Orders></multimap:Message1></multimap:Messages>
```


Figure 5.63 Content of Received Email

Note

For analyzing issues connecting to the email server, refer to the troubleshooting information in Chapter 2, Section 2.3.7.

5.3.3 Routing a Message to Multiple Receivers Using the Multicast Pattern

You've now successfully sent the message to one receiver, but some scenarios may require sending the same message to multiple receivers—either in the same or different format—or maybe even only parts of the message. This is also possible in SAP Cloud Platform Integration, so let's configure it now.

We'll use the scenario we set up in the preceding section and add another email receiver, which will just receive an email containing the information that the message was processed successfully.

In Section 5.1.2, we used the **Router** to configure routing messages to multiple receivers. However, we learned that the message will go only to the first receiver, the one for which the routing condition is met, because the **Router** is based on the BPMN-exclusive gateway. Therefore, it doesn't meet the requirements for our use case of sending the message to multiple receivers. To send the message to multiple receivers, we need a flow step based on the BPMN-parallel gateway. For such use cases, SAP Cloud Platform Integration offers the multicast pattern.

Two options are available for the multicast pattern:

- **Parallel Multicast**
  In this option, the message is routed to the different branches in parallel. This is the option we want to start with.
- **Sequential Multicast**
  In this option, an order of execution can be specified. This is especially important if the second branch won't be executed if the first branch wasn't successful. We'll go into more detail about this option later.

Let's start modeling. To add the **Multicast** option, from the main menu of the palette, select the **Message Routing** ◇ shape. A submenu opens, revealing different routing options, including **Multicast** (Figure 5.64).

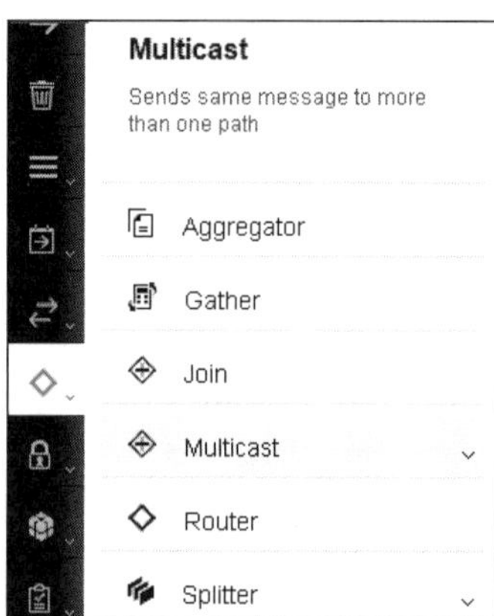

Figure 5.64 Multicast Shape in the Modeling Environment Palette

When you select **Multicast**, another submenu opens providing the two options of **Sequential Multicast** and **Parallel Multicast** (Figure 5.65). Select the **Parallel Multicast** option for now, and place it between **Gather** and the **End** event, as depicted in Figure 5.66.

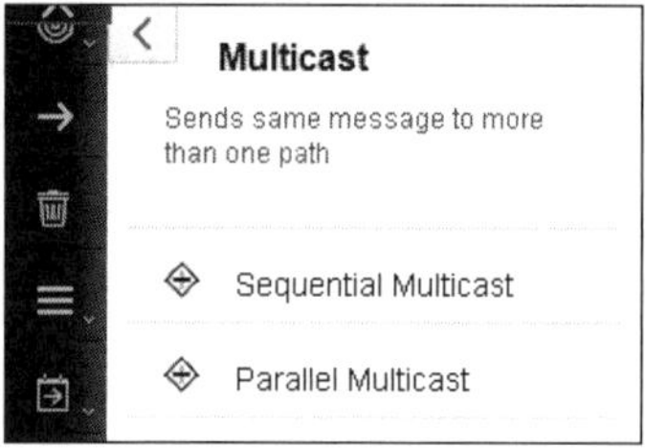

Figure 5.65 Multicast Options in the Modeling Environment Palette

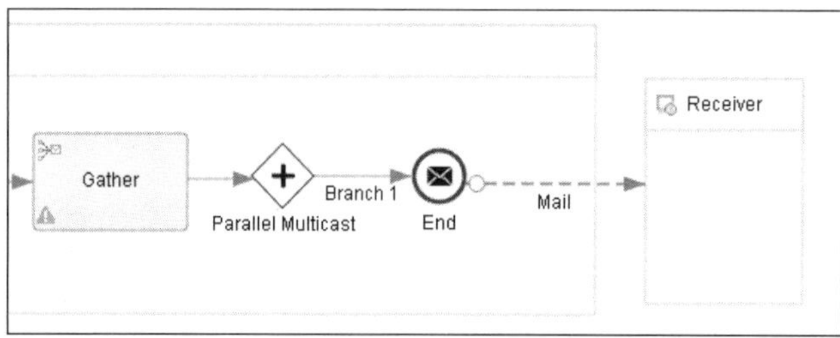

Figure 5.66 Placing a Parallel Multicast between Gather and the End Event

To send the message to a second receiver, we need to add another **End Message** event and one more **Receiver**. To add another branch for the multicast processing, draw a line between **Parallel Multicast** and the **End** event. Then, connect the **End** event with the new **Receiver**, select the **Mail** adapter, and configure it (as shown in Figure 5.67). We enter "Status of Message Processing" as the **Subject** and add a short status text in the **Mail Body** entry field. Notice, that we add the SAP header for the MPL ID, `SAP_MessageProcessingLogID`, into the email's body. This value will help later when searching for the message in the SAP Cloud Platform Integration's message monitoring.

Subject:	Status of Message Processing
Mail Body:	Message Processing for MPL ID ${header.SAP_MessageProcessingLogID} was successful.

Figure 5.67 Configuring the Mail Adapter for the Second Receiver

The scenario should now look similar to the one depicted in Figure 5.68. Two branches leave from the **Parallel Multicast** shape: **Branch 1** to the first mail receiver and **Branch 2** to the newly added mail receiver.

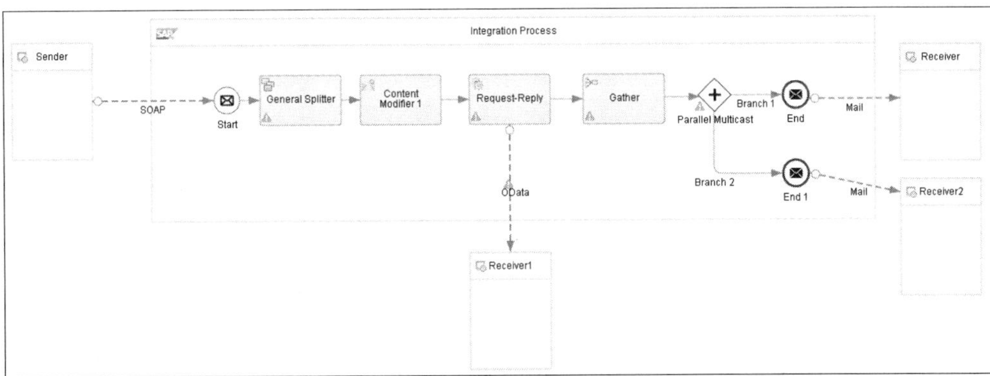

Figure 5.68 Integration Flow with Parallel Multicast and Two Receivers

Note

In each of the branches leaving the multicast shape, you can configure additional flow steps, for example, mappings or converters. With this, you can send different messages or different parts of the inbound message to specific receivers.

After you've finished your configurations, saved, and deployed the integration flow, run the scenario again. From the SOAP test client, the request will be sent successfully to SAP Cloud Platform Integration, and this time the message will be delivered twice to your email account: once with the message created by the **Gather** step (Figure 5.63) and the second time with the status mail text configured in the second **Mail** adapter channel. The received email's content of the status is shown in Figure 5.69.

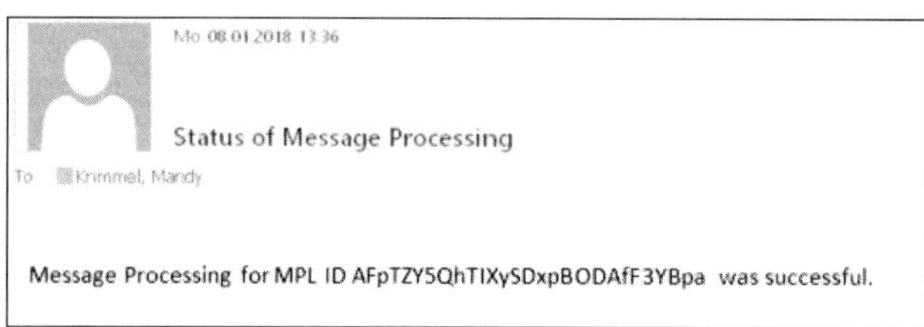

Figure 5.69 Content of Received Email Containing the Message Processing Status

In the email containing the processing status, we get the **MPL ID** for the message's processing in SAP Cloud Platform. With this information, we can easily check the processing and status in the message monitor by searching for the MPL ID, if required. To do that, open the **Monitoring** page as described in the previous section, and select the **All Messages** tile. In the search criteria, paste the MPL ID from your email into the **ID** field, as shown in Figure 5.70. Press Enter, or click the magnifier icon next to the added MPL ID to start the search. The search opens the **Message Processing** details of your message.

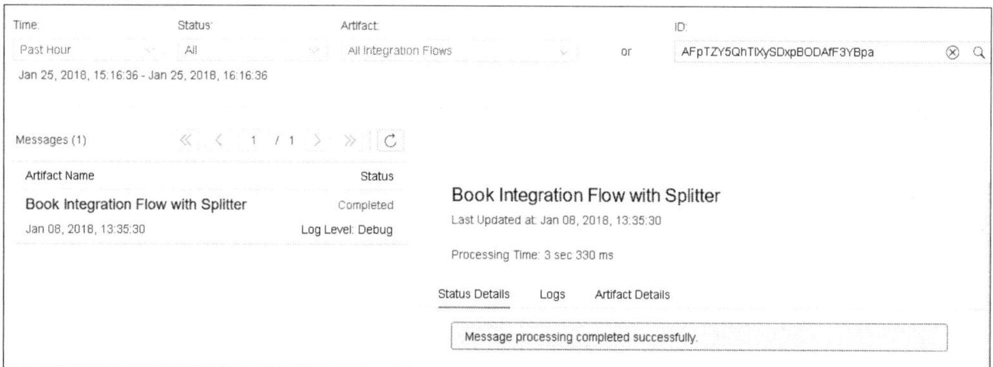

Figure 5.70 Searching for a Specific MPL ID in the Message Monitor

But what happens if Branch 1 could not be completed because of an error? Let's try it out. To produce an error in Branch 1, we change the **Address** field in the first **Mail** adapter channel to some configuration that doesn't work, for example, to smtp.gmail.com:444. Save and deploy the integration flow, and run the scenario again.

Now we get an HTTP 500 error in the SOAP test client because the message could not be processed successfully in SAP Cloud Platform Integration. This is what you probably expected, but we still get the email that the message processing was successful. Let's take a detailed look at the message processing of this message in SAP Cloud Platform Integration. We use the MPL ID received in the email as a search criteria in the **ID** field in message monitor, as shown in Figure 5.71.

We see that the message processing of the message has the status Failed, and we also see the reason: connection to smtp.gmail.com:444 wasn't possible. But why do we still get the status email, if the message processing is failing?

We need to understand the processing of a message in the multicast pattern in SAP Cloud Platform Integration. We already discussed the inbound processing in the SOAP adapter, in which the message is processed by each of the configured flow steps one after the other. But as soon as the message reaches the **Multicast** step, it's multiplied as many times as outbound branches leave the **Multicast**. Each of these messages is processed independently in its own branch until it reaches an **End** event or a **Join** step.

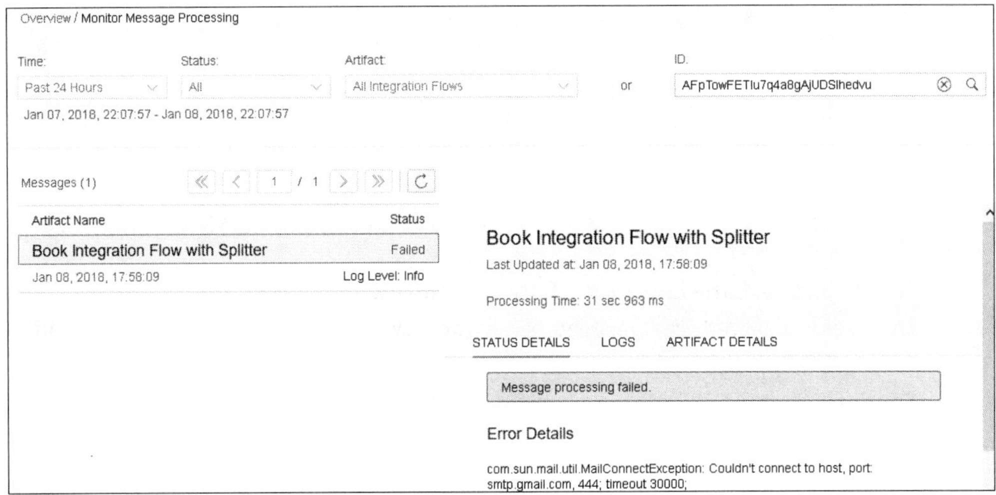

Figure 5.71 Searching for the MPL ID of the Failed Message in the Message Monitor

For our scenario, this tells us that our two branches leaving the parallel multicast are executed in parallel and are completely independent of each other. So, **Branch 2** is executed even if **Branch 1** fails. But this isn't what we want to have in our scenario; instead, we want to get the successful status email only when the first call was successful. We need to make sure the branches are executed one after the other and ensure that the second branch is executed after the first branch. In SAP Cloud Platform Integration, we can use the second multicast option for this: the **Sequential Multicast**.

Combination of Multicast with Join and Gather

In this chapter, we use the **Multicast** pattern to send messages to multiple receivers. However, in SAP Cloud Platform Integration, there is another use case for it; that is, in combination with **Join** and **Gather,** the **Multicast** step can be used to process the message in different branches; later bring the branches together using the **Join,** and combine the messages into a single message using **Gather.** This would look similar to the processing depicted in Figure 5.72. For more details about the detailed configuration, refer to the documentation for SAP Cloud Platform Integration (found at *https://help.sap.com/viewer/product/CLOUD_INTEGRATION/Cloud*) and search for "Defining Join and Gather."

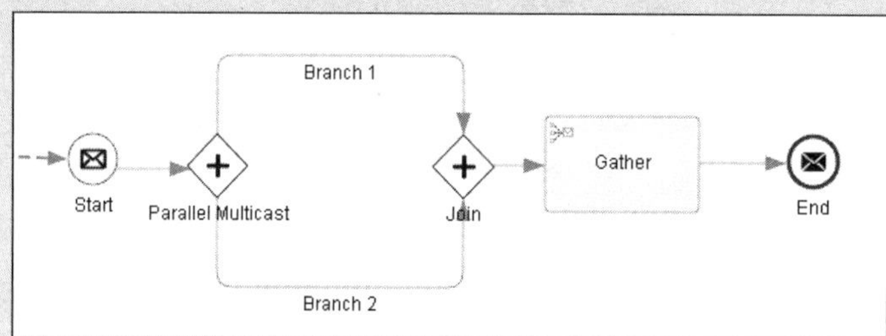

Figure 5.72 Using Multicast with Join and Gather

Now let's change the integration flow by removing the **Parallel Multicast** and adding the **Sequential Multicast** instead. Afterwards, we connect **Gather** with **Sequential Multicast** and **Sequential Multicast** with the two **End** events connected to the two **Receivers** (Figure 5.73).

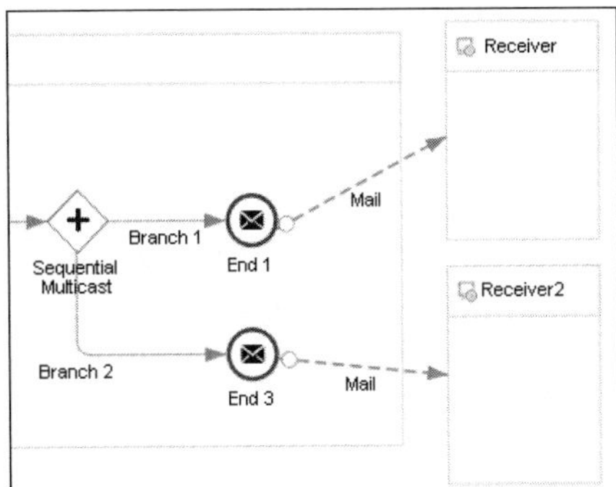

Figure 5.73 Sequential Multicast Connected with two Receivers

We need to make sure that the two branches, **Branch 1** and **Branch 2**, are executed in the correct order. First, **Branch 1** will be processed by sending out the message produced by the **Gather** step, and, if this is executed successfully, **Branch 2** will be processed. To check and, if necessary, change the order, we select the **Sequential Multicast** step to get its details in the **Properties** section. In the **Routing Sequence** tab, a table with the configured branches is shown (Figure 5.74). Make sure the branch to the first **Receiver** (in our integration flow, it's **Branch 1**) is at the top of the table to get executed first. If this isn't the case, the order can be changed with the **Move Up** and **Move Down** buttons.

If the configuration is done, save and deploy the integration flow. Trigger the scenario again from your SOAP test client. You'll still get the HTTP 500 error, but you won't receive the status email anymore.

Sequential Multicast Externalize

General Routing Sequence

Specify the sequence of execution of branches: Move Up Move Down

Sequence Order	Sequence Name
1	Branch 1
2	Branch 2

Figure 5.74 Configure Order in Sequential Multicast

To check the successful execution, correct the **Address** in the first **Mail** adapter channel, save, and deploy the change. The execution now correctly sends the message produced by **Gather** and the status email to your email account.

Now we know two different configuration options for the parallel gateway processing in SAP Cloud Platform Integration. But there is even a third, very special option to configure this specific multicast scenario. If, like in our case, no additional configuration step is to be executed in the first multicast branch, we can use the **Send** step instead.

Let's configure the scenario with a **Send** step by adding the **Send** step from the palette in your integration flow after the **Gather** step. You find the **Send** step under the **Call** ⇄ shape. Select the shape, and a submenu with the two options, **External CALL** and **Local Call**, opens (Figure 5.75). Select the **External Call** to see three options for doing external calls from SAP Cloud Platform Integration: **Request-Reply**, **Send**, and **Content Enricher** (Figure 5.76). **Request-Reply** and **Content Enricher** were already explained in some detail, so we focus now only on the **Send** step.

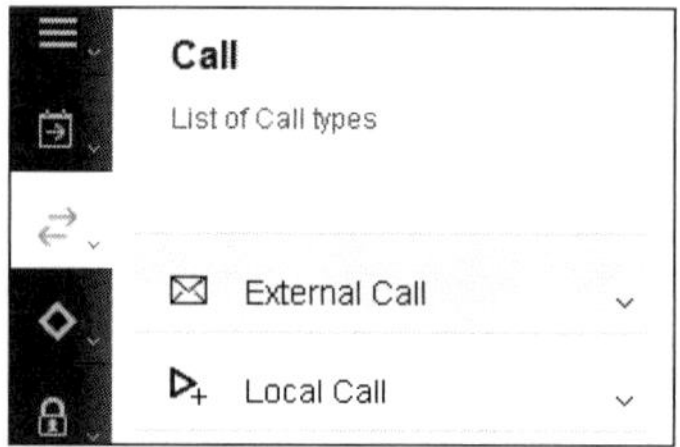

Figure 5.75 Call Shape in the Modeling Environment Palette

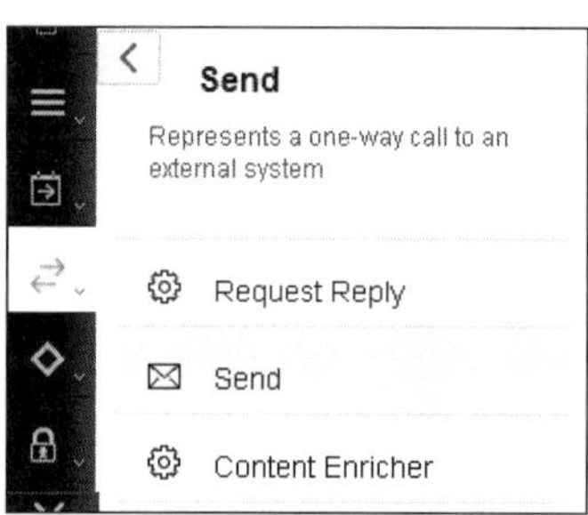

Figure 5.76 External Call Shape in the Modeling Environment Palette

Connect the **Gather** step with the **Send** step, and draw a line from the **Send** step to the first **Receiver**, which is expecting the message coming from **Gather**. Select the **Mail** adapter, and reconfigure the **Mail** channel like it was configured in the integration flow using **Multicast** (refer to Figure 5.61). Connect the **Send** step with the **End** event. Your integration flow should now look similar to Figure 5.77.

Save the configurations, and deploy the integration flow. Triggering the flow from your SOAP test client will produce the same result as when calling the integration flow with **Sequential Multicast**: the message will be sent successfully, and the two emails, one created by the **Gather** step and the status email, will be received in your mailbox.

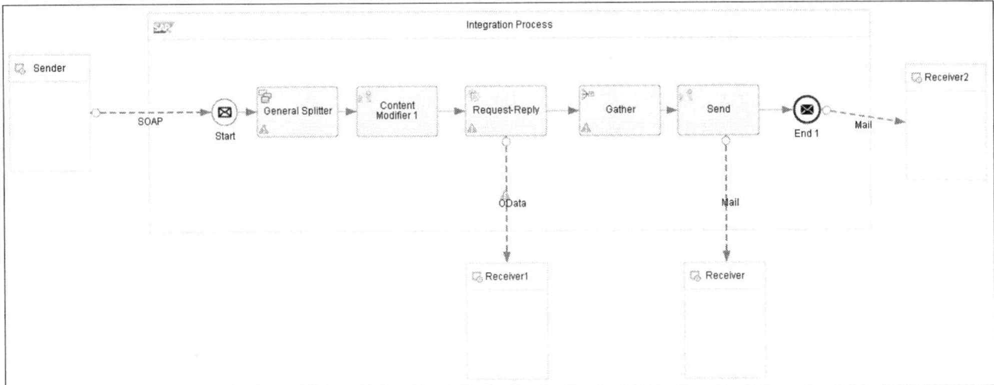

Figure 5.77 Integration Flow with Send Step and Additional Receiver

If during runtime, the sending of the email via the **Send** step fails, the processing will stop, and the status email won't be sent. Therefore, in the runtime, the **Send** step behaves like the **Sequential Multicast**. In fact, the **Send** step is a sequential multicast with exactly two branches: the first branch goes to the connected **Receiver**, and the second branch goes to the next processing step.

Synchronous and asynchronous message handling procedures are at the core of every integration solution, and SAP Cloud Platform Integration is no exception from this rule. In this section, you learned more about the internal message processing details of SAP Cloud Platform Integration. You've seen how synchronous and asynchronous message handling can be controlled for the SOAP channel and how multiple asynchronous receivers can be added to your scenario using the multicast pattern. The message monitor was finally used to help you track the message processing within SAP Cloud Platform Integration. In the next section, we'll go one step further and decouple inbound and outbound processing of the integration flow to make the scenario more robust for potential errors during message processing.

5.4 Reliable Messaging Using the JMS Adapter

In the previous section, you learned how asynchronous messaging can be configured in SAP Cloud Platform Integration, the basic concept behind it, and the different modeling techniques to send the message to multiple receivers. You've used robust one-way communication to make the asynchronous scenario reliable to ensure the message delivery is guaranteed and the sender is notified about errors to be able to resend the erroneous messages.

Following are the characteristics of such robust one-way scenarios using SAP Cloud Platform Integration:

- This pattern relies on a retry mechanism in the sender system. If there is an error during processing in SAP Cloud Platform Integration, for example, if one of the receivers isn't available temporarily, the error will be reported back to the sender, and the whole message processing needs to start from the beginning. Meaning it needs to be triggered by the sender system.
- If the parallel multicast is used, temporary connection issues associated with one of the receiver systems trigger retries from the sender system and may lead to duplicate messages in the other receiver systems.
- The overall execution time of an asynchronous reliable messaging scenario includes the whole message's processing in SAP Cloud Platform Integration until the message finally reaches the receiver. If there is a complex integration flow, the execution time may become undesirably long.

This isn't the desired behavior in many scenarios; often the sender wants to deliver the message and expects an asynchronous response later—and doesn't want to wait or care about retries. The sender usually wants to send the message and expects the middleware to handle temporary connection problems to receiver systems using built-in retry mechanisms. In this section, we'll extend the scenario developed in the preceding section in such a way that a retry is triggered from SAP Cloud Platform Integration automatically if there are execution errors.

5.4.1 Asynchronous Decoupling of Inbound Communication

To trigger the retries from SAP Cloud Platform Integration if there is an error during message processing, we need to decouple the inbound message processing in SAP Cloud Platform Integration from outbound processing, and we need to temporarily persist the message in SAP Cloud Platform Integration to be able to restart the message from SAP Cloud Platform Integration's persistency if an error happens during processing.

The next section discusses which SAP Cloud Platform Integration options exist to temporarily persist messages, how to configure such scenarios, and what monitoring options we can use.

Data Store and Java Message Service Queues

SAP Cloud Platform Integration provides two options—data store and JMS queues—to temporarily store messages during message processing:

- **Data store**
  Based on the database SAP Cloud Platform Integration is running on, data store is used to store messages using the **Write** step and subsequently read from data store using the **Select** or **Get** step. Because the data store isn't designed to execute high-performance messaging, it isn't the optimal solution for our scenario. The main use cases for the data store are as follows:
  - You need to temporarily store a message during message processing because the original payload is required later in the processing of the message. With the **Write** step, the initial message is saved in the data store. Afterwards, changes to the payload are made, for example, using mappings, converters, or scripts. Later in the processing, the initial message is fetched using the **Get** step.
  - The data store is often used in the push-pull pattern. The sender is sending messages to SAP Cloud Platform Integration, where the messages are temporarily stored in the data store. In a synchronous call, the receiver actively polls the messages from the data store using the **Select** step and acknowledges the receipt of each message. Afterwards, these acknowledged messages are deleted from the data store using the **Delete** step. We don't go into a detailed description of the push-pull pattern here, but a small sample integration flow is shown for your reference in Figure 5.78.

- **JMS queues**
  JMS queues are the second option to temporarily store messages in SAP Cloud Platform Integration. Messages are stored in JMS queues using the **JMS Receiver** adapter and read from JMS queues using the **JMS sender** adapter. Because JMS supports high-speed messaging with high throughput, it offers the optimal solution for reliable messaging using asynchronous decoupling. So, that is the option we go for in our scenario.

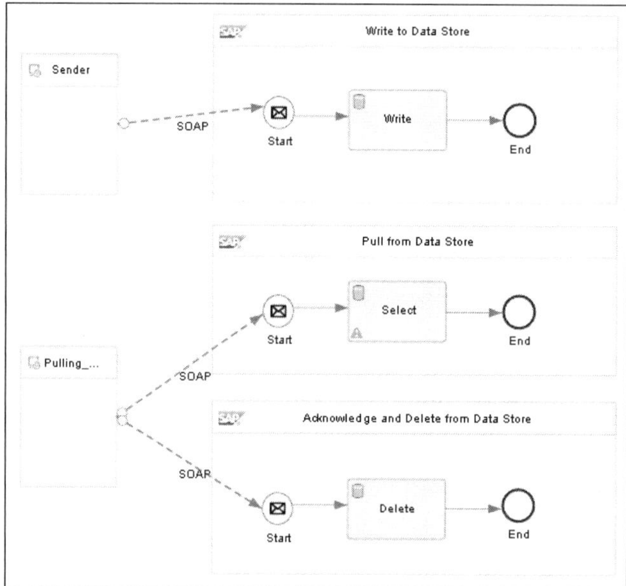

Figure 5.78 Sample Integration Flow for the Push-Pull Pattern

JMS

JMS is a Java-based standard application programming interface (API) for sending and receiving messages. It allows a reliable asynchronous communication between different components based on a JMS Message Broker. The JMS Message Broker is a separate runtime component that ensures the handling of the messages in JMS queues in the JMS Message Broker. The JMS adapter available in SAP Cloud Platform Integration is used to store messages in the JMS queue and to consume messages from the JMS queue in the JMS Message Broker.

The processing sequence used by the JMS adapter is first-in, first-out (FIFO), which means messages stored in the JMS queue latest are also consumed latest. But be aware that this doesn't mean that the messages are processed in a guaranteed order. This is because SAP Cloud Platform Integration uses several runtime nodes consuming messages from the JMS queue in parallel. Furthermore, messages that cause errors are taken out of the processing and are retried later according to the retry interval defined in the JMS channel.

To decouple the inbound processing of the integration scenario from the outbound processing, we need to split the scenario into two processes: one for receiving the message and storing it in a JMS queue and a second process for consuming the message from the JMS queue and further processing the message and sending it to the receiver.

Prerequisites for Using the JMS Adapter

JMS messaging is available only with the SAP Cloud Platform Integration, Enterprise Edition, or if a JMS messaging license is purchased separately. If your SAP Cloud Platform Integration system isn't running with the Enterprise license and no JMS messaging license is purchased, the JMS adapter doesn't appear in the list of available adapters.

Furthermore, you need to get a JMS Message Broker provisioned for your SAP Cloud Platform Integration tenant. The provisioning is triggered using a self-service in the account cockpit. Details about the provisioning of a JMS Message Broker can be found in the documentation for SAP Cloud Platform Integration (*https://help.sap.com/viewer/product/CLOUD_INTEGRATION/Cloud*) and in the "Provision Message Broker" blog in the SAP Community (*www.sap.com/community.html*).

Extending the Integration Scenario

Let's start extending the scenario we configured in the previous section. As a first step, to decouple the inbound processing from all the other processing steps, we create and configure a new integration process for the inbound processing by making the following changes to the integration flow:

1. Add a new **Integration Process** below the existing integration process by selecting it from the modeling palette under the **Process** shape. In the submenu, the **Integration Process** is one of the process elements available (Figure 5.79).

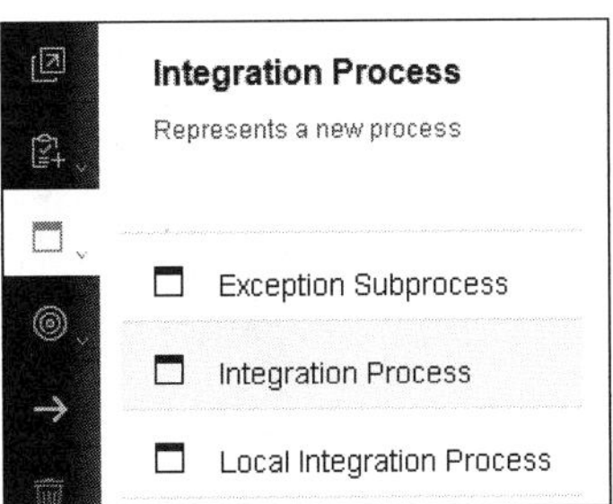

Figure 5.79 Process Shape in the Modeling Environment Palette

2. In the new integration process, add a **Start Message** event and an **End Message** event from the **Events** shape (Figure 5.80). Connect the **Start Message** event with the **End Message** event.

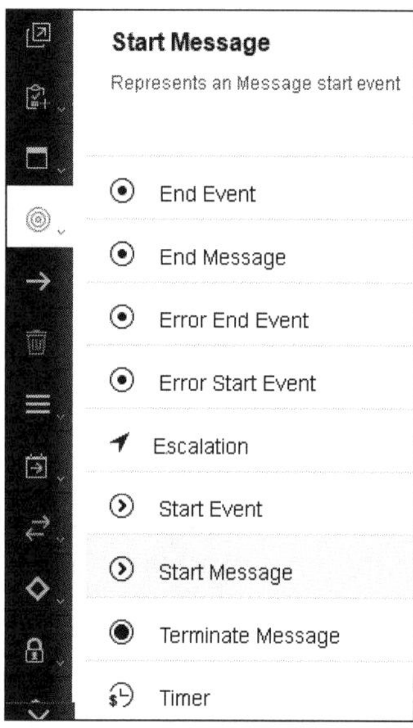

Figure 5.80 Events Shape in the Modeling Environment Palette

3. Select the dotted line representing the message flow from the **Sender** to the first integration process's **Start** event. The line gets orange with small blue dots at the start and the end of the line. Select the blue dot appearing at the **Start** event in the first **Integration Process**, and move it to the **Start** event in the new **Integration Process** (Figure 5.81). Now the existing **SOAP** channel points to the new integration process; you don't have to remodel the channel.
4. Add a **Receiver** to the model on the right side of new the integration process. Remember, you find the **Receiver** under the **Participant** shape in the palette.
5. Connect the **End** event of the new **Integration Process** to the new **Receiver**. In the adapter selection screen choose the **JMS** adapter. (Note that the JMS adapter entry will only appear in the list if you're using SAP Cloud Platform Integration, Enterprise Edition.)

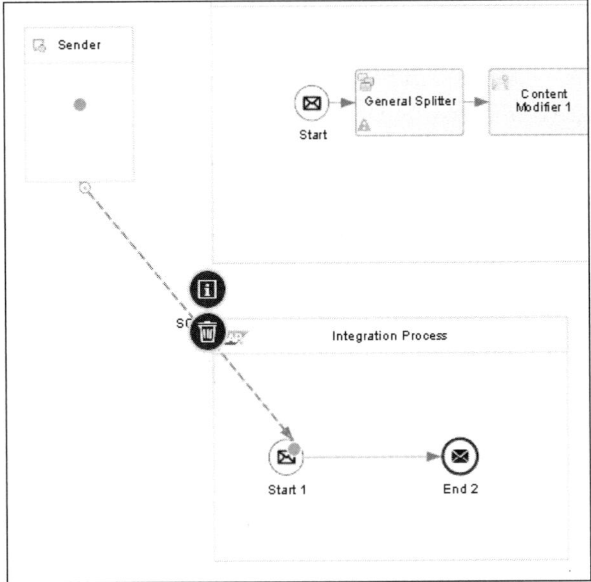

Figure 5.81 Connecting the SOAP Sender Channel to the New Integration Process

6. In the **JMS** channel's **Processing** tab, configure the following properties, as shown in Figure 5.82:
   - **Queue Name**: As the most important configuration setting, we specify a unique name for the JMS queue to be used for this scenario, that is, Inbound_Queue. The JMS queue is used by the **JMS** receiver adapter to store the message in and by the **JMS** sender adapter to consume the messages from. You'll see this when we configure the **JMS** sender later.
   - **Retention Threshold for Alerting**: You set the number of days the message should be picked up from the JMS queue and further processed. If the message stays in the JMS queue for a longer time than configured, the message appears as **Overdue** in the Monitor to indicate that there is some problem during processing: maybe the consuming integration flow doesn't run anymore.
   - **Expiration Period**: There are only limited resources available on the JMS instance configured for a SAP Cloud Platform Integration system. Therefore, JMS queues are only allowed for temporary storage. In the **Expiration Period** field, you define after how many days the message is automatically deleted from the JMS queue. The default value is 90 days, and the maximum value allowed is 180 days, but keep in mind that there is a maximum capacity allowed

in the JMS instance for all messages in all JMS queues in your SAP Cloud Platform Integration system. This maximum capacity is based on the number of messaging licenses purchased. The available and the used capacity are shown in the queue monitor. We'll see this later, when we run the scenario.

- **Encrypt Stored Message**: This checkbox should be enabled for security reasons to encrypt the messages in the JMS queue. For a scenario processing messages that aren't security relevant, the checkbox can be disabled to improve performance.
- **Transfer Exchange Properties**: Exchange properties are usually not transferred using JMS queues. If, for any scenario-specific reason, transferring them is required, the **Transfer Exchange Properties** checkbox can be enabled. But take into consideration that there is a hard limit of 4 MB for storing headers and properties in JMS queues. If the limit is hit during runtime, the message will go into **Failed** status with an error stating that the limit for headers and properties is reached.

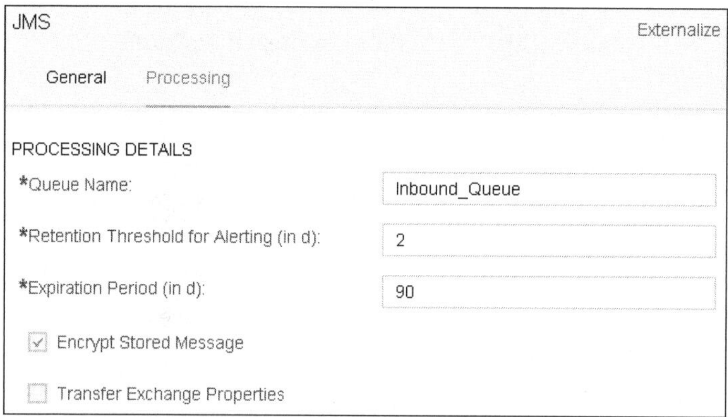

Figure 5.82 JMS Receiver Channel Configuration

Limits for JMS Resources

There are limited resources available on the JMS instance connected to the SAP Cloud Platform Integration tenant. The JMS resources available depend on the licenses purchased.

One hard limit is the overall size of 4 MB for storing headers and properties in a JMS queue. This limit can neither be configured nor increased, not even by purchasing additional licenses for JMS messaging. Our recommendation is to not transfer properties via JMS queues and to restrict the usage of headers.

More details about the JMS resources can be found in the "JMS Resource and Size Limits in CPI Enterprise Edition" blog in the SAP Community (*www.sap.com/community.html*).

Now the new integration process looks similar to the one in Figure 5.83.

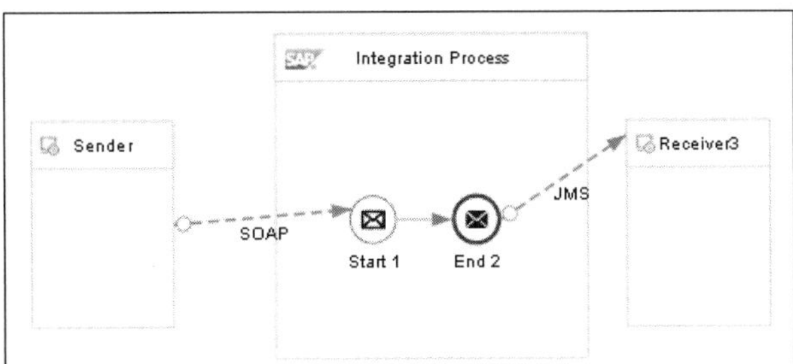

Figure 5.83 Integration Process with JMS Receiver

We've now changed the inbound processing in a way that the message isn't processed by SAP Cloud Platform Integration and sent to the receiver. Instead of this, after being received, the message is directly stored in a JMS queue. Let's run the scenario before we configure the main integration process that will consume the messages from the JMS queue.

Save and deploy the integration flow. Now trigger the integration flow from the SOAP test client. You'll notice that the HTTP response code 202 notifying you about successful execution is shown faster than in the executions triggered in the previous section. This is because with the change made in the integration flow, the message is just stored in the JMS queue, and no further processing is executed in SAP Cloud Platform Integration

The message is now stored in the JMS queue waiting for consumption and further processing. You can monitor the JMS queues in the SAP Cloud Platform Integration's monitoring dashboard to locate it. Open the dashboard, in the **Manage Stores** area of the screen, you find the **Message Queues** monitor (Figure 5.84).

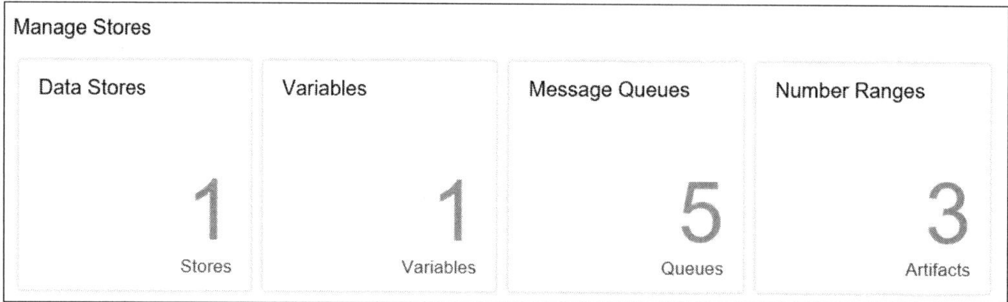

Figure 5.84 Manage Stores Section in the Monitoring Dashboard

Queue Creation during Deployment

The JMS queues are created automatically in the JMS messaging instance during deployment of the first integration flow using a new JMS queue name. Be aware of the following two aspects:

- If the same **Queue Name** is used in multiple integrations flows or integration processes, the same JMS queue is used in runtime. This means multiple processes may write to the same JMS queue, or even multiple JMS senders may consume from the same JMS queue. The integration developer may want this to happen if the same queue will be reused by different scenarios, but it may also happen by accident.
- JMS queues aren't deleted automatically during undeployment of the integration flow because there may still be messages in the JMS queue, and deleting the queue would delete them as well, which would lead to data loss. Only the owner of the scenario knows if the JMS queue can be deleted with all its content or if it's still required. A JMS queue can be deleted in the **Manage Message Queues** monitor using the **Delete** action.

Select the **Message Queues** monitor to get the list of JMS queues created in the JMS messaging instance of your SAP Cloud Platform Integration system. Search for the JMS queue with the name **Inbound_Queue**, which was the queue name we defined in the JMS receiver channel. Select the queue to get the messages in this specific queue displayed (Figure 5.85).

You notice that the message sent to SAP Cloud Platform Integration is displayed with the status **Waiting**. This status indicates that the message is waiting to be consumed by another process.

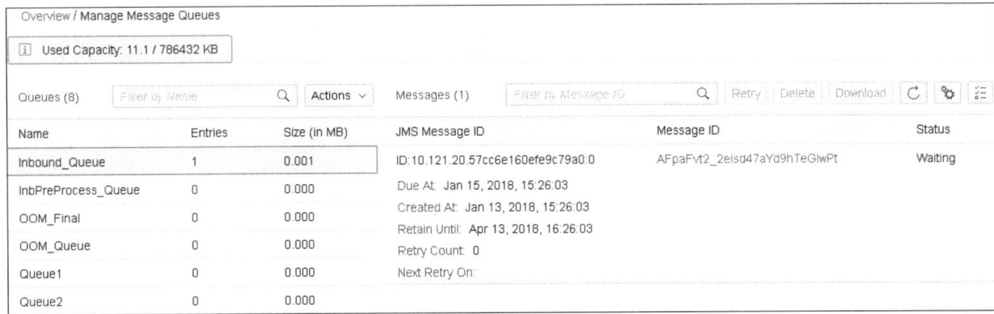

Figure 5.85 Message in Waiting Status in the Manage Message Queues Monitor

Configure the Integration Process

Now, let's configure the integration process, which consumes and finally sends the message to the receiver:

1. Add a **Sender** to the model on the left side of the integration process configuring the main processing. Remember, you find the **Sender** under the **Participant** shape in the palette.
2. Connect the **Sender** to the **Start** event of the integration process. In the adapter selection screen, choose the **JMS** adapter.
3. In the **JMS** channel's **Processing** tab, configure the properties as shown in Figure 5.86:
   - **Queue Name**: Define the same value as specified in the JMS receiver (**Inbound_Queue**) to consume the messages from the JMS queue that the inbound processing stores the messages in.
   - **Number of Concurrent Processes**: Messages from the JMS queue can be consumed in parallel if required for high message throughput. In the **Number of Concurrent Processes** field, you specify the number of parallel processes consuming messages from the JMS queue.
   - **RETRY DETAILS**: The retry configuration is specified in this section, as follows:
     - **Retry Interval (in min)**: Define after how many minutes the first retry is executed.
     - **Exponential Backoff**: Set this checkbox to avoid lots of retries in a short time. When **Exponential Backoff** is set the retry interval is doubled after each unsuccessful retry. For example, if a receiver system isn't available because of maintenance, it doesn't make sense to retry the message every second.

- **Maximum Retry Interval (in min)**: Define the maximum interval between two tries to avoid an endless increase of the retry interval if **Exponential Backoff** is used.
- **Dead-Letter Queue**: Take those messages out of processing that cause outages of the runtime node, for example, by an out-of-memory error. Messages where processing stopped unexpectedly are retried only twice when the **Dead-Letter Queue** checkbox is enabled. Further details about this feature, its usage, and its monitoring can be found in the "Configure Dead Letter Handling in JMS Adapter" blog in the SAP Community (*www.sap.com/community.html*).

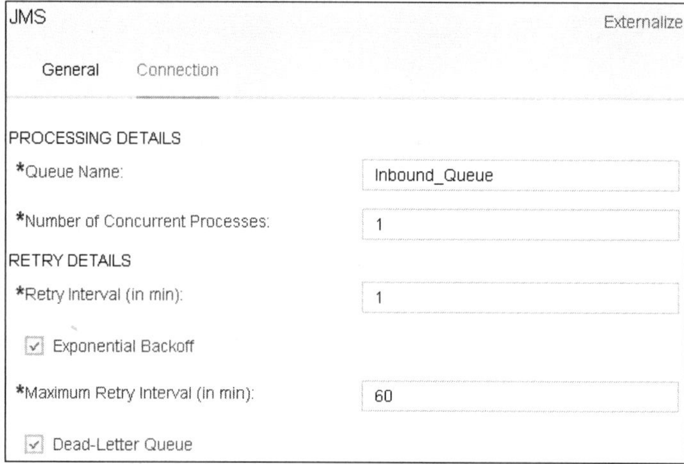

Figure 5.86 JMS Sender Channel Configuration

The integration flow with the two integration processes now looks similar to Figure 5.87.

Retry from JMS Queue

Messages in JMS queues are retried as long as the messages aren't successfully processed or the expiration period is reached. As soon as the message goes to **Completed** status, the message is removed from the JMS queue. The message can either get **Completed** after successful execution of the scenario or if the message processing error is caught in an **Exception Subprocess**. The second option will be discussed later in this chapter.

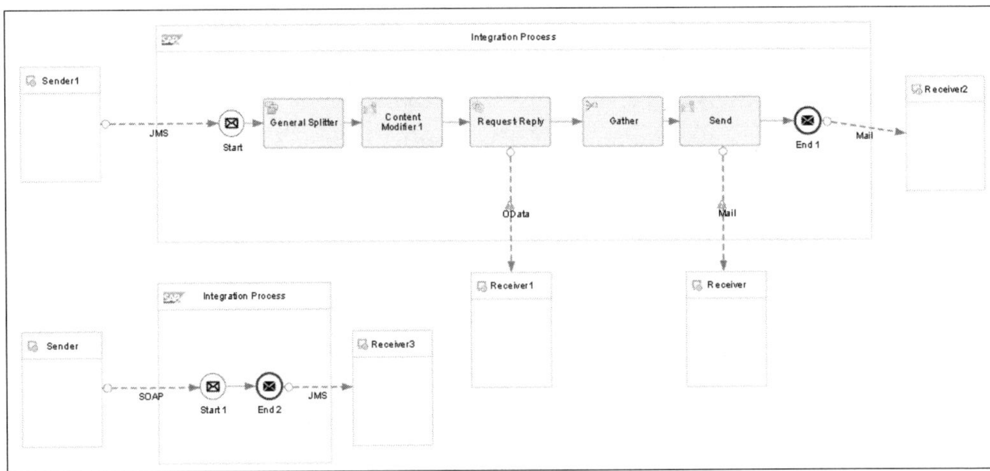

Figure 5.87 Integration Flow with JMS Sender and JMS Receiver Adapter

Save your changes and deploy the integration flow. The JMS sender channel now consumes the message from the JMS queue, and you get the missing emails. Triggering the integration flow again from your SOAP test client, you'll receive the emails directly because storing the message to the JMS queue and consuming it from there doesn't require much time in SAP Cloud Platform Integration.

You've seen now that for successfully delivered messages, not much changes from an end-to-end perspective. But how does SAP Cloud Platform Integration handle the retry if errors occur in SAP Cloud Platform Integration's runtime? Let's try it out. We change the **Address** field in the **Mail** channel connected to the **Receiver** from the **Send** step to an address to some configuration that doesn't work, for example, to `smtp.gmail.com:444`. Save and deploy the integration flow, and run the scenario again.

In the SOAP test client, we get an HTTP response code 202 because the message was successfully delivered to SAP Cloud Platform Integration, but we don't get an email. We've expected this, because of the wrong **Address** configuration in the **Mail** channel. But what happens in SAP Cloud Platform Integration? How is the retry executed, and where do we find the processing details for the message? Let's have a look in the SAP Cloud Platform Integration's monitoring.

Open the monitoring dashboard, and select the **Message Queues** monitor. Select the JMS queue **Inbound_Queue** that is used in the scenario. As shown in Figure 5.88 and Figure 5.89, the message in the JMS queue has the status **Failed**, and the retry count indicates the number of retries that were already executed. In addition, the time of the next retry is displayed.

Overview / Manage Message Queues

Used Capacity: 11.7 / 786432 KB

Queues (8) Filter by Name Actions

Name	Entries	Size (in MB)
Inbound_Queue	1	0.002
InbPreProcess_Queue	0	0.000
OOM_Final	0	0.000
OOM_Queue	0	0.000
Queue1	0	0.000
Queue2	0	0.000

Figure 5.88 Message in Failed Status in Manage Message Queues Monitor A

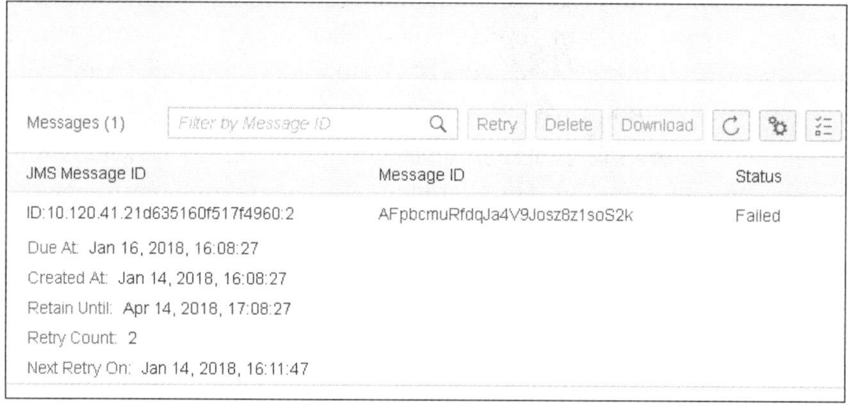

Figure 5.89 Message in Failed Status in Manage Message Queues Monitor B

Message Processing Details

To get more details for the processing of this message and the error, we need to check the message in the message processing monitor. We can do this either by searching for the message ID shown in the message processing monitor or directly selecting the link for the **Message ID** that opens the **Message Processing** monitor for this specific message (Figure 5.90). There we find the details of the message processing and the error information. Notice, that the status of the message in message processing monitor is **Retry**, indicating that this isn't a final status. In the **Status Details** for the message, the error details of the last retry are shown.

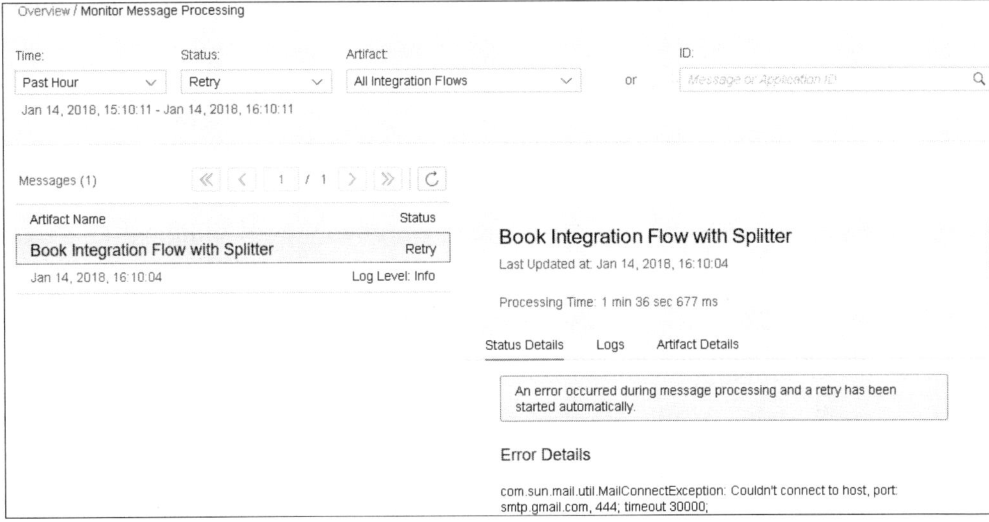

Figure 5.90 Message Processing Details for a Message in Retry Status

Correct the wrong address configuration in the mail channel, save, and deploy the integration flow. The next retry will consume the message and process it with the new configuration resulting in a successful execution. The emails finally arrive in your email account.

Trigger a Retry in Manage Message Queues Monitor

If you don't want to wait for the time of the next retry, you can initiate the retry in the **Manage Message Queues** monitor by selecting the **Retry** action for this message. Then the next retry is executed immediately, and the message gets processed.

Now you're able to configure reliable messaging scenarios with decoupled inbound processing in SAP Cloud Platform Integration, ensuring that retries of the message are executed in SAP Cloud Platform Integration if there are errors during message processing. With this, you've speeded up the processing time for the sender and ensured reliable messaging by using the retry functionality based on JMS queues offered by SAP Cloud Platform Integration.

5.4.2 Configure Retry for Multiple Receivers

For the scenario configured in the previous section, the retry initiated directly after the inbound processing is sufficient because the message isn't sent to multiple receivers in parallel. But for a parallel multicast scenario, where the message is to be delivered to multiple receivers in parallel, we still have the problem that some receivers get duplicate messages if there is a temporary communication error sending the message to one of the receivers. To address this, we use separate outbound queues for each of the receivers to execute the retry only for the message going to the receiver that is temporarily not available.

To showcase this, we change the scenario slightly by simply sending the same message out to two receivers using the mail adapter. For the ease of testing, we send both to the same email account using different subjects. Follow these steps:

1. Add another **End Message** event to the integration process configuring the main processing.
2. Select the dotted line representing the message flow from the **Send** step to the **Receiver**. The line gets orange with small blue dots at the start and the end of the line. Select the blue dot appearing at the **Send** step, and move it to the new **End** event. Now the existing **Mail** channel is connected from the **End** event.
3. Reconfigure the **Mail** channel going to **Receiver2** to send the message payload instead of the status email: in the **Subject** field, set **Message to Receiver2**, and as **Mail Body**, include the message's payload (Figure 5.91).

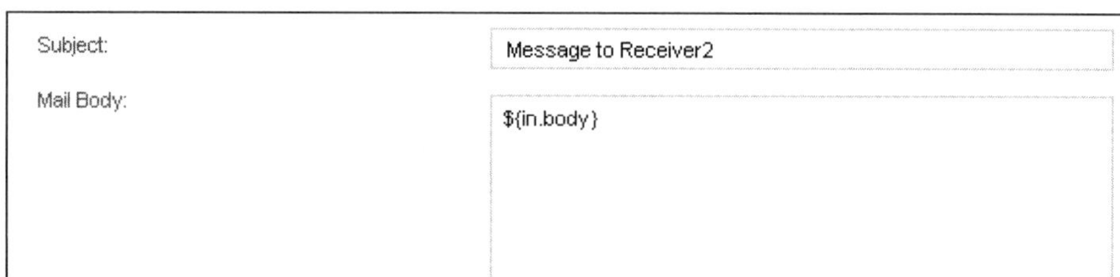

Figure 5.91 Configuring Subject and Mail Body in the Mail Adapter for Receiver2

4. Remove the **Send** step and add a **Parallel Multicast** instead. Draw a second line from the **Parallel Multicast** step to the new **End** event to configure the second multicast branch.

The changed part of the integration flow now looks similar to Figure 5.92.

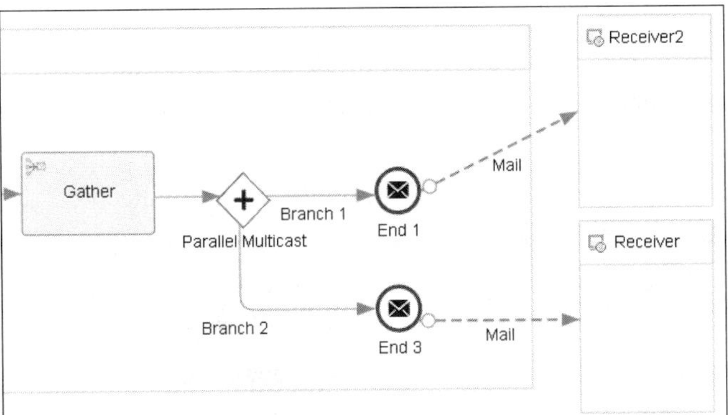

Figure 5.92 Configuration of a Parallel Multicast to Two Receivers

Save the changes, and deploy the integration flow. When triggering the integration flow from your SOAP test client, two emails are sent to your email account—each one representing the message flow in one of the multicast branches and both containing the same message in the email's body.

To test the retry behavior triggered from the inbound JMS queue for the parallel multicast scenario, we change the **Address** for one of the **Mail** channels to a configuration that doesn't work, for example, `smtp.gmail.com:444`. Save and deploy the integration flow. Call the integration flow from the SOAP test client. You now get the same email again and again, one for each retry triggered from the inbound JMS queue. Because the second **Mail** receiver can't be reached, the overall processing status of the message is **Retry**, so the message stays in the JMS queue and is retried according to the **Retry Details** configured in the **JMS** sender adapter.

The behavior to send the message again and again in error situations may cause problems in the receiver system if the receiver can't handle duplicates. To make sure the receiver doesn't get the same message multiple times, we'll now change the scenario in a way that separate outbound queues are used for each of the receivers:

1. Add a new **Integration Process** below the existing integration process. Remember, you find the **Integration Process** in the modeling palette under the **Process** shape.
2. In the new **Integration Process**, add a **Start Message** event and an **End Message** event from the **Events** shape. Connect the **Start** event with the **End** event.
3. Select the dotted line representing the message flow from the **End** event to **Receiver2** in the integration process doing the main processing. The line turns orange

with small blue dots at the start and the end of the line. Select the blue dot appearing at the **End** event, and move it to the **End** event in the new integration process. Now the existing **Mail** channel is connected from the **End** event of the new integration process.

4. Add a **Receiver** from the **Participant** shape to the model on the right side of the integration process doing the main processing.
5. Connect the **End** event of the integration process doing the main processing to the new **Receiver**. In the adapter selection screen, choose the **JMS** adapter.
6. In the **JMS** channel's **Processing** tab, configure **Outbound_Queue2** as **Queue Name**, and keep the defaults for the other configuration settings (Figure 5.93).

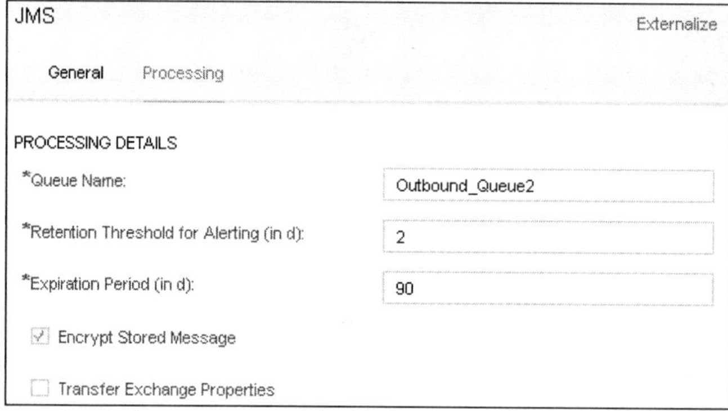

Figure 5.93 Configuration of the JMS Receiver Channel for Outbound Queue

7. Add a **Sender** from the **Participant** shape to the model on the left side of the new integration process.
8. Connect the **Sender** to the **Start** event of the new integration process. In the adapter selection screen, choose the **JMS** adapter.
9. In the **JMS** channel's **Processing** tab, in the **Queue Name** field, configure the same value as in the **JMS** receiver channel; **Outbound_Queue2**. With the JMS outbound queue configured for the first receiver, the extended parts of the integration flow now look similar to Figure 5.94.
10. Create another **Integration Process** configuring a JMS outbound queue for **Receiver**. Execute the same configuration steps, move the existing **Mail** channel to the new integration process, and use **Outbound_Queue1** as the **Queue Name** in the **JMS** adapter. The configuration of the JMS outbound queues now looks similar to Figure 5.95.

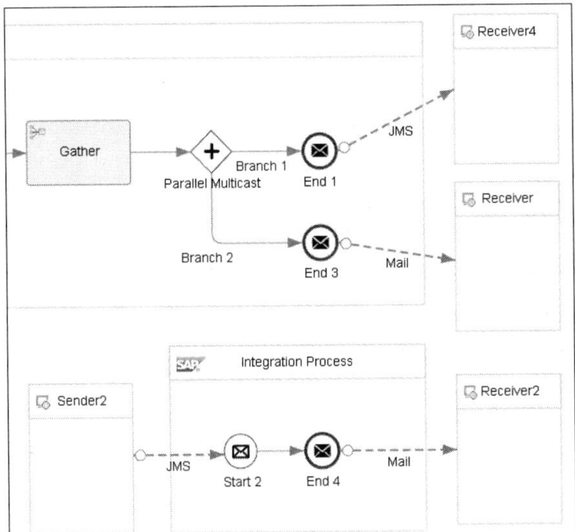

Figure 5.94 Configuration of JMS Outbound Queue for Receiver2

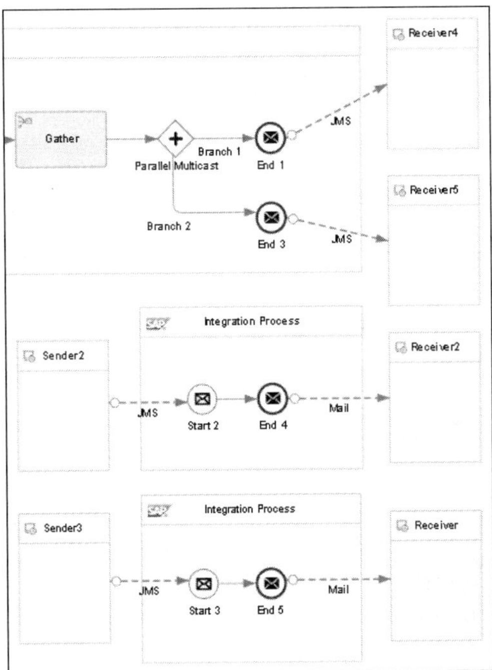

Figure 5.95 Configuration of JMS Outbound Queues for Both Receivers

11. Because we're using two **JMS** receiver channels in the same integration process, we need to configure a JMS transaction handler. The transaction handler makes sure the message is either stored in both JMS queues consistently or in none of them; if there is an error, the whole transaction is rolled back. Select the integration process configuring the parallel multicast, and the properties for the integration process are shown in the **Properties** section. In the **Processing** tab, the configuration options for transaction management are available. In the **Transaction Handling** dropdown, you configure the transaction handler for the integration process (Figure 5.96) with three available options:
    - **Required for JDBC**: Choose this option if Java Database Connectivity (JDBC) transacted resources such as **Data Store** steps are used in the scenario and it's necessary to ensure end-to-end transactional processing in all steps accessing the database.
    - **Required for JMS**: Choose this option if, like in our scenario, JMS transacted resources are used, and end-to-end transactional processing is required. This is the setting we configure for our integration process (Figure 5.96).
    - **Not Required**: Choose this option for most of the scenarios that don't use transaction resources and therefore don't require a transaction handler.

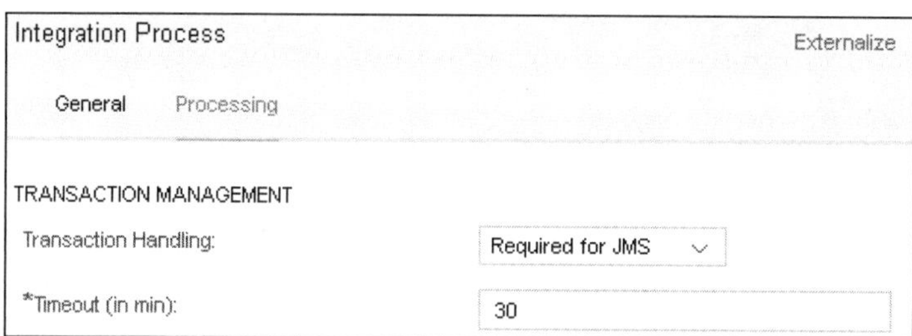

Figure 5.96 Configuration of Transaction Handling

If a transaction handler, JMS or JDBC, is configured, a **Timeout** needs to be defined. Because transactions are limited resources in the database and in the JMS instance, this setting is required to make sure the transaction is stopped after some time and doesn't run forever. You have to configure a timeout sufficient for your scenario but not too high, keeping the limited transactions in mind. If the available numbers of transactions are reached in runtime, no new messages can be processed.

Configuration of Transaction Handling

In integration scenarios, it's usually required to ensure consistent end-to-end processing and to roll back all actions in the database or in JMS queues consistently. This is ensured by a transaction handler. SAP Cloud Platform Integration offers two transaction handlers: one for JMS transactions and one for JDBC transactions. Distributed transactions between JMS and JDBC aren't supported in SAP Cloud Platform Integration. Recommendations and limitations using transaction handlers, including several sample scenarios, are explained in detail in the "How to Configure Transaction Handling in Integration Flow" blog in the SAP Community (*www.sap.com/community.html*).

Save the changes made in the integration flow to trigger the check's execution for the integration flow. We notice that a check error is now shown for the main integration process; the error tells us that the JMS transaction handling isn't allowed for parallel multicast (Figure 5.97).

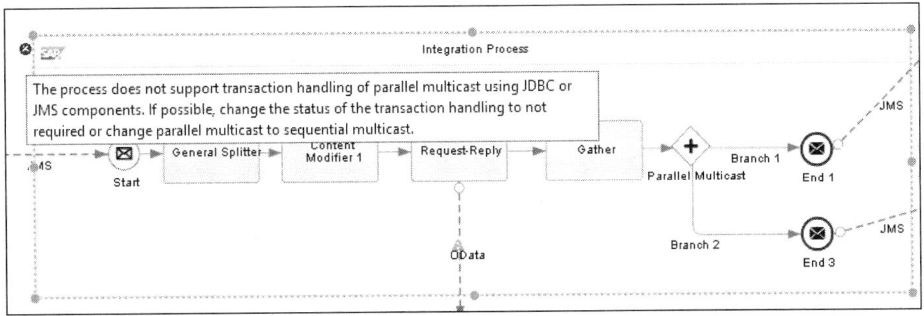

Figure 5.97 Error When Using JMS Transactions with Parallel Multicast

What is the background of this error, and what do we need to do? We already learned that the message is copied in the SAP Cloud Platform Integration's runtime in the parallel multicast pattern, and the different messages are processed independently in all branches leaving the multicast. The problem is that such independent requests can't be rolled back consistently. For our scenario, we need to use sequential multicast and store the messages in the different JMS outbound queues one after the other. If an error happens, the whole process is rolled back, no messages are stored in the JMS outbound queues, and the processing starts again from the JMS inbound queue or the sender system if no JMS inbound queues are used. After successfully storing the messages to all the JMS outbound queues, the consumption of the messages from the JMS outbound queues is executed in parallel for each of the receivers.

Make the necessary changes by following these steps:

1. Remove the **Parallel Multicast** step, and add a **Sequential Multicast** step instead.
2. Reconnect the **Gather** to the **Parallel Multicast** and the **Parallel Multicast** to the two **End** events.

The final integration flow now looks similar to Figure 5.98.

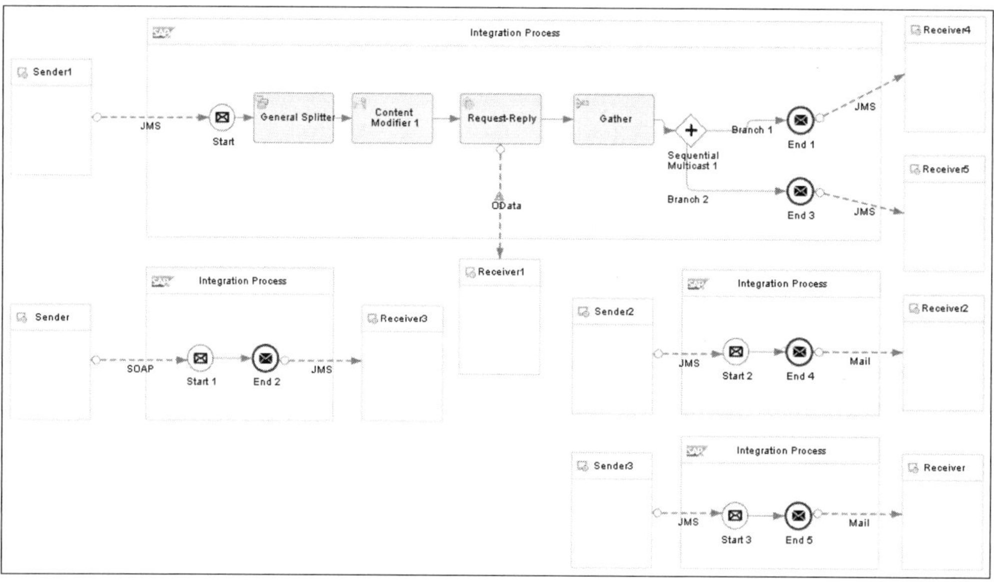

Figure 5.98 Integration Flow with Sequential Multicast and JMS Outbound Queues

Save and deploy the integration flow, and trigger the integration process from your SOAP test client. Now you get only one email, the one processed by the mail adapter that is configured correctly. The message for the second receiver, the one with the wrong configuration, is now available in the JMS outbound queue for this receiver (Figure 5.99 and Figure 5.100) and is retried from this queue. If the message in **Failed** status from the last scenario execution is still available in the JMS inbound queue, it will be retried at the next retry time, or you can trigger an immediate retry in the **Manage Message Queues** monitor.

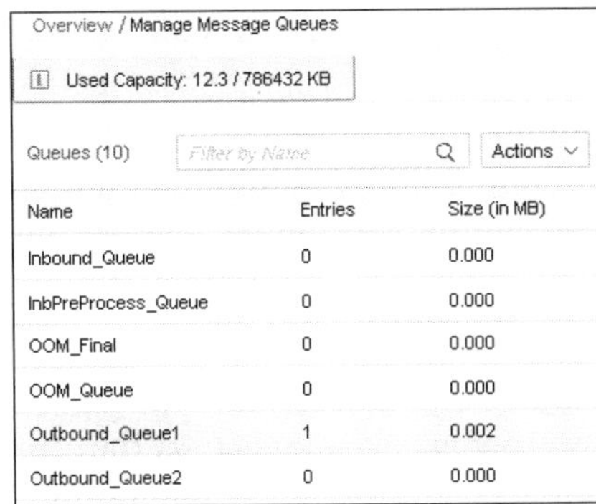

Figure 5.99 Message in JMS Outbound Queue in Failed Status in the Manage Message Queues Monitor A

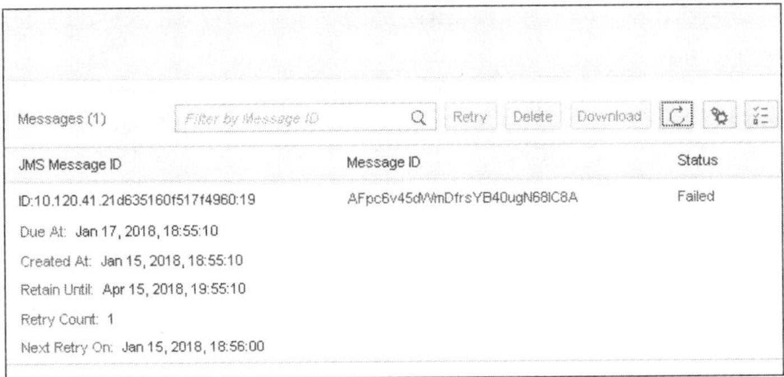

Figure 5.100 Message in JMS Outbound Queue in Failed Status in the Manage Message Queues Monitor B

Configuration Option: Use Separate Integration Flows

We configured the different integration processes for storing the messages in a JMS queue and consuming from the JMS queue in one single integration flow, but they can also be configured in different integration flows instead. When separate integration flows are used, you're more flexible when changes and redeployments of the integration flow are necessary.

You've now successfully set up a reliable messaging scenario using JMS inbound and JMS outbound queues, the inbound processing of your scenario is decoupled from further processing of the message in SAP Cloud Platform Integration, and the sending to multiple receivers is executed asynchronously using a separate JMS outbound queue for each receiver. You've significantly shortened the processing time for the sender and ensured reliable messaging to multiple receivers using the retry capabilities based on JMS queues offered by SAP Cloud Platform Integration.

5.4.3 Configure Explicit Retry with Alternative Processing

Depending on the scenario or on the receiver system, you may want to retry the message only a couple of times and then do an alternative processing of the message. This isn't possible with the default retry configuration offered in the JMS sender channel: the JMS sender adapter retries the message forever. But SAP Cloud Platform Integration offers the option to configure explicit retry handling by using the exception subprocess. In this section, we'll extend the scenario and configure explicit retry handling in the process, sending the message to one of the receivers.

To extend the integration flow to support explicit retry configuration, we need to create a local integration process that contains the configuration for the retry. More details about using local integration processes will be shared in Chapter 6. Execute the following steps to extend the integration flow:

1. Add a **Local Integration Process** below the existing integration processes by choosing it in the modeling palette under the **Process** ▭ shape. In the **General** tab, enter the name "Retry Configuration" to give the local process a meaningful name.
2. In the new **Local Integration Process**, add a **Router** from the **Message Routing** ◇ shape between the **Start** and **End** events. Add an **Error End** event from the **Events** ◎ shape below the newly added **Router** step. Connect the **Router** step to the **Error End** event, as depicted in Figure 5.101.

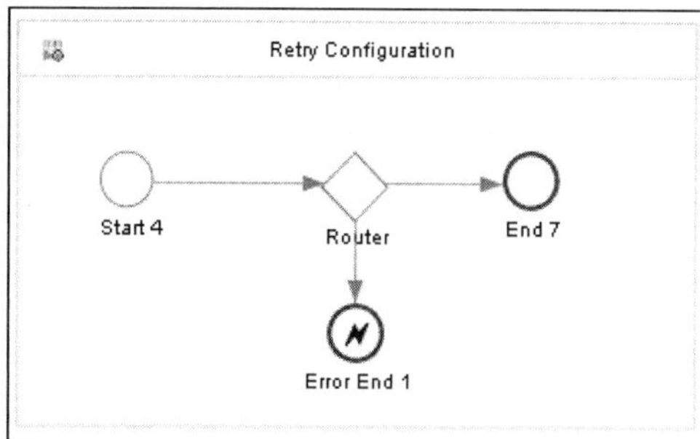

Figure 5.101 Configuration of a Local Integration Process

3. The JMS sender adapter sets the header `SAPJMSRetries` at runtime. This header allows you to configure a specific retry behavior: it contains the number of retries that already are executed. Based on the value of this header, we can configure whether the message processing continues or ends. If we configure it to end, we can also configure that the message is processed in an alternative way. This is done in the **Router** step. As a simple example, we want to configure that after five retries, the message is sent via email to an administrator, and no further retries are executed from the JMS queue. We configure the two routes leaving the **Router** step per Figure 5.102:
   - In the route going to the **End** event, we define a **Non-XML** condition based on the `SAPJMSRetries` header: `${header.SAPJMSRetries} > '5'`. With this configuration, the route to the **End** event is executed as soon as the value of the `SAPJMSRetries` header is larger than 5. This means that with the sixth retry (`SAPJMSRetries = 6`) the message is routed to the **End** event, which ends the processing. The message goes to the status **Completed** and is removed from the JMS queue.
   - The route to the **Error End** event we define as the default route so that during runtime, the message is routed to the **Error End** event as long as the value of `SAPJMSRetries` is smaller than 6. The **Error End** event raises an error and makes sure the message stays in the JMS queue, and the message gets the status **Retry**.

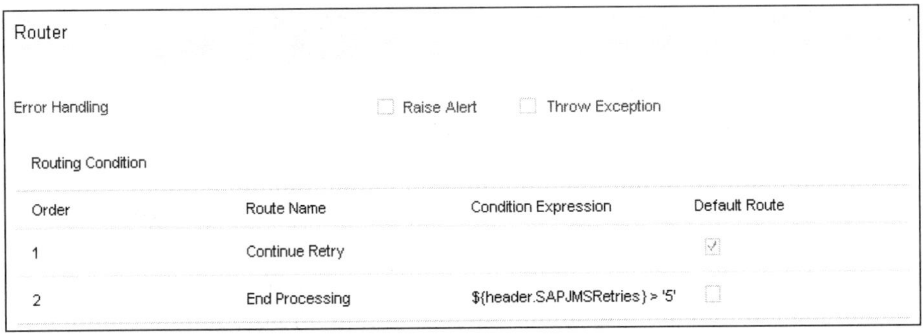

Router

Error Handling ☐ Raise Alert ☐ Throw Exception

Routing Condition

Order	Route Name	Condition Expression	Default Route
1	Continue Retry		☑
2	End Processing	${header.SAPJMSRetries} > '5'	☐

Figure 5.102 Configuration of Router Step in Local Integration Subprocess

4. Add an **Exception Subprocess** from the **Process** shape to the outbound integration process connected to the **Receiver** for which we want to configure the alternative processing. This **Exception Subprocess** is supposed to catch the error in the outbound processing.

5. Add a **Process Call** (from the **Call** shape, submenu **Local Call**), and place it between the **Error Start** event and the **End** event of the newly added **Exception Subprocess**. In the properties area for the **Process Call**, select the local integration process **Retry Configuration** created before (Figure 5.103).

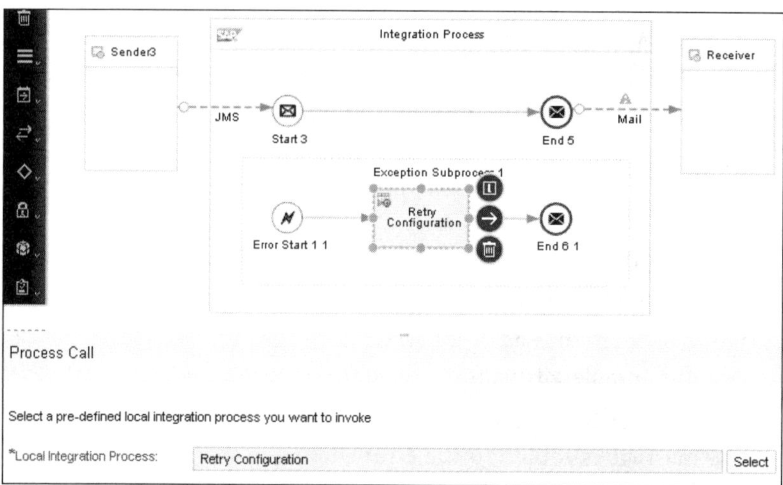

Figure 5.103 Configuration of the Process Call in the Exception Subprocess

6. Add a **Receiver** from the **Participant** shape, and place it on the right side of the integration process that contains the **Exception Subprocess**. In the properties for the **Receiver**, define **Administrator** as the **Name**. Draw a line from the **End** event of the **Exception Subprocess** to the newly added **Receiver**, and select the **Mail** adapter in the adapter selection screen.
7. In the **Connection** tab of the **Mail** adapter, configure the **Connection Details** according to your email account and the **Mail Attributes**, as shown in Figure 5.104. For the ease of testing, you can use the same email account to send the email created for the administrator too, but use a different **Subject** to identify that this email is meant for the administrator.

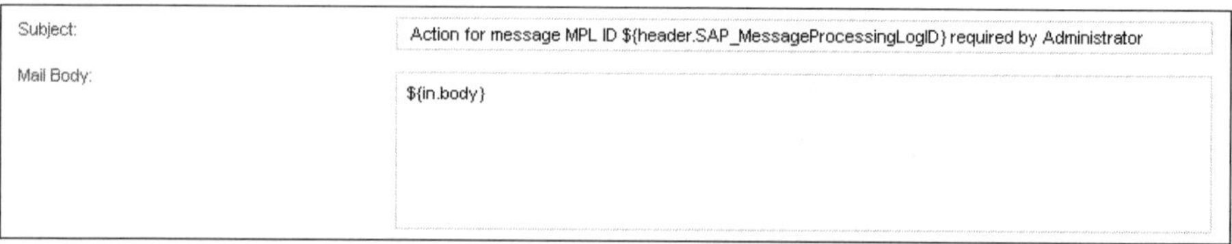

Figure 5.104 Configuring the Mail Adapter for the Administrator

The integration flow containing all of its integration processes, the local process, and the exception process now looks similar to Figure 5.105.

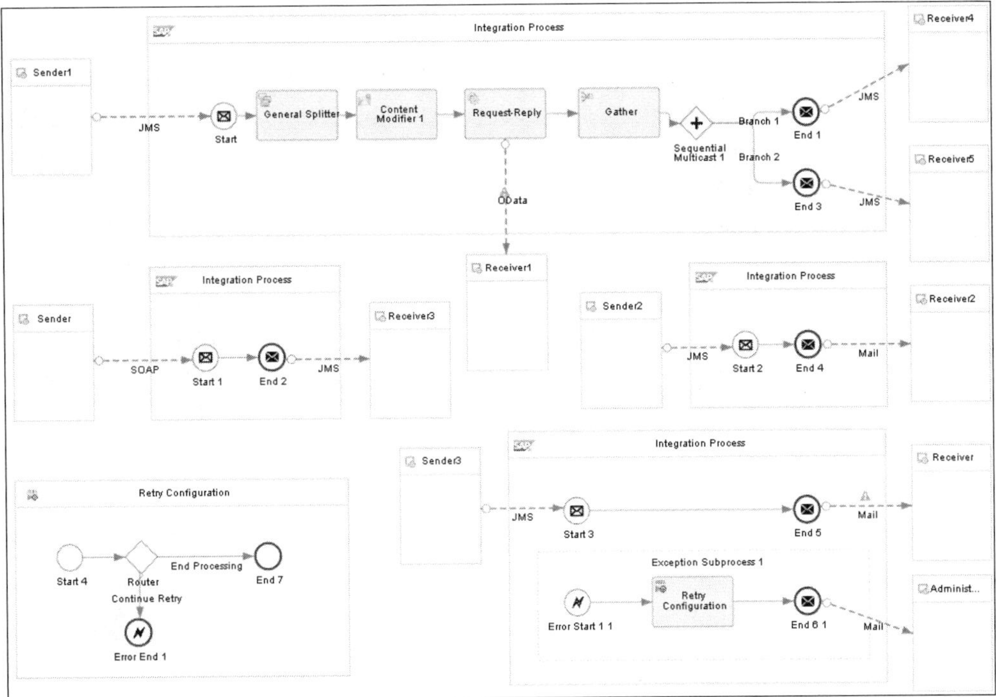

Figure 5.105 Integration Flow with Explicit Retry Configuration in Exception Subprocess

Save and deploy the integration flow. Now we use the integration flow to test the runtime and the retry behavior by triggering the processing from the SOAP test client. We adjust the **Address** in the different **Mail** adapter channels to raise an error during runtime to trigger the retries configured.

Successful End-to-End Processing

First, we need to test the successful scenario execution. Make sure the **Address** field is correct in both **Mail** adapter channels, save and deploy the integration flow, and trigger the integration flow from your SOAP test client.

The messages are sent successfully to both receivers, and you receive two emails after a short time, both containing the same message in the email's body. However, they have different subjects: **Book Demo Msg** (for **Receiver**) and **Message to Receiver2** (for

Receiver2) as configured in the **Mail** adapter channels for the two receivers. This indicates that the end-to-end processing of the message was executed without errors, and the messages were sent asynchronously to both receivers.

Let's have a look at the SAP Cloud Platform Integration's monitoring dashboard to understand what happens during runtime. Open the **Message Processing** monitor. As shown in Figure 5.106, four entries appear for this single scenario execution. This may be surprising, but it can be understood if you consider the end-to-end scenario configuration and the fact that SAP Cloud Platform Integration writes a separate message processing log for each integration process. The scenario consists of four integration processes: one integration process for inbound processing and storing the message in the JMS inbound queue, one integration process for the main processing and storing the message in the two JMS outbound queues for the two receivers, and one integration process for each of the two receivers. For each of these processes, a separate log entry is created in message monitoring.

To make the end-to-end monitoring easier the four MPLs are correlated by a **Correlation ID.** The **Correlation ID** is shown below the **Message ID** in the **Properties** of each MPL. As depicted in Figure 5.106, it's possible to search for all MPLs having the same correlation ID using the **ID** field in the search criteria.

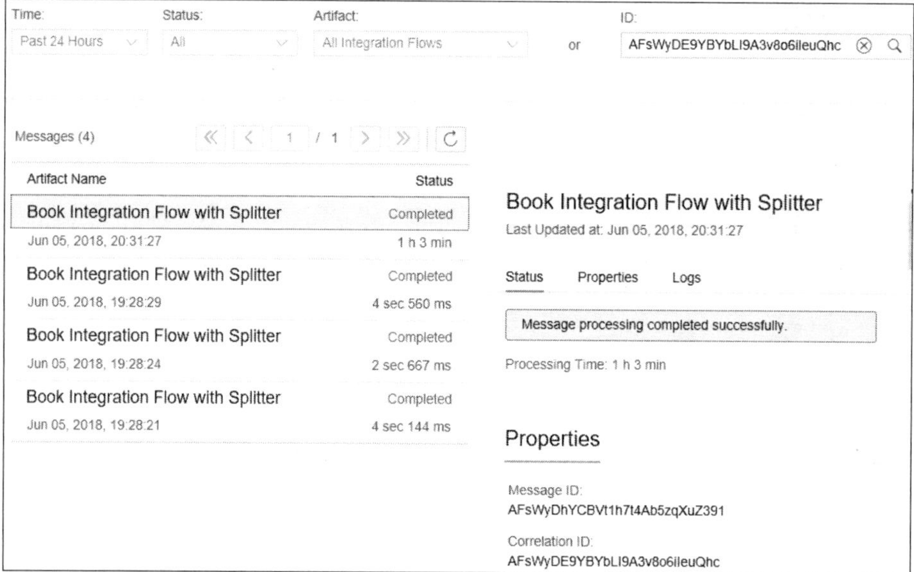

Figure 5.106 Message Processing Monitor for Successful Execution

All four MPLs have the status **Completed**, indicating that the message was executed successfully in all four integration processes.

In the **Manage Message Queues** monitor, there will be no message in any of the involved JMS queues because the messages were consumed and successfully processed.

Error Sending Message to Receiver2

We now change the **Address** field in the **Mail** adapter channel connected to the **Receiver** with name **Receiver2** to simulate that the processing to **Receiver2** is broken. Save and deploy the integration flow, and trigger the integration flow from your SOAP test client.

Because the message is successfully sent to **Receiver**, you get one email with the subject **Book Demo Msg**. The other message which is expected to be sent to **Receiver2** remains in the JMS outbound queue **Outbound_Queue2** configured for **Receiver2** and is retried according to the retry configuration in the JMS sender channel.

In the SAP Cloud Platform Integration's monitoring for this execution, we again find four entries in the **Message Processing** monitor, one for each process execution. The first three MPLs have the status **Completed**, but the most recent entry has the status **Retry** (Figure 5.107). This is what we expect because the message to **Receiver2** is being retried from the JMS queue.

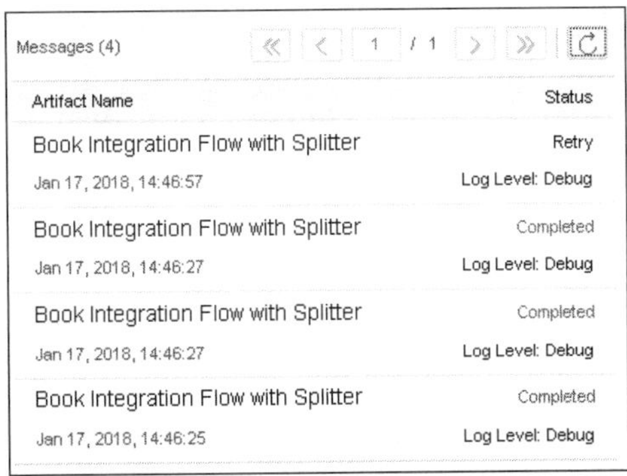

Figure 5.107 Message Processing Monitor for Erroneous Execution

As depicted in Figure 5.108, the message can be found in the **Manage Message Queues** monitor in the queue **Outbound_Queue2** with the status **Failed**, providing information about the retries already executed and the time of the next retry.

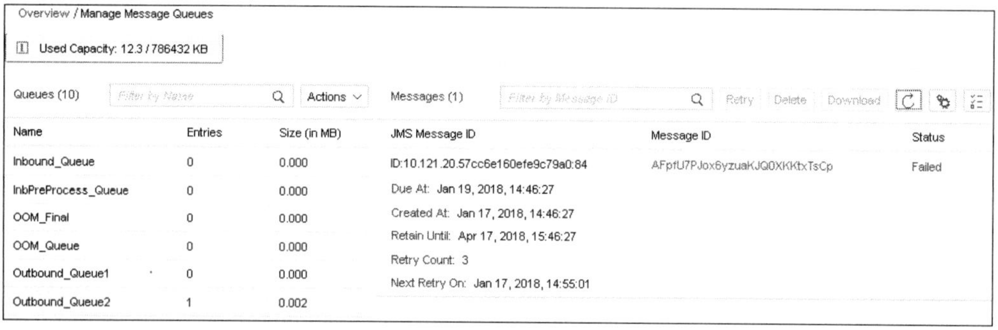

Figure 5.108 Message in Error in Outbound_Queue2 in Manage Message Queues Monitor

To clean up the **Manage Message Queues** monitor in preparation for the next test, you can either correct the **Mail** adapter's **Address** configuration, redeploy the integration flow, and retry the message by using the **Retry** action in the **Manage Message Queues** monitor, or you can delete the message from the JMS queue using the **Delete** action in the **Manage Message Queues** monitor. Otherwise, the message is retried again and again until it's finally deleted after it exceeds the **Retention Threshold** defined in the JMS receiver channel.

Error Sending Message to Receiver

In the next test, we change the **Address** field in the **Mail** adapter channel connected to the **Receiver** with name **Receiver** to a configuration that doesn't work. With this configuration, we simulate that the processing to **Receiver** is broken. If not already done, correct the address in the **Mail** adapter channel for **Receiver2** to make sure the message to this receiver can be sent successfully. Save and deploy the integration flow, and trigger the integration flow from your SOAP test client.

Because the message is successfully sent to **Receiver2**, you get one email with the subject **Message to Receiver2**. About one hour later (because of the configured six retries with **Exponential Backoff**), you get the email with the subject indicating that it's to be processed by the administrator.

If we check the **Message Processing** monitor directly after scenario execution, we see exactly the same message processing status as in the last test: three entries with the status **Completed** and the most recent entry with the status **Retry** (Figure 5.107). This time, the message that is being retried is the message to **Receiver**. In the **Manage Message Queues** monitor, you find the message in the **Outbound_Queue1** with the status **Failed** (Figure 5.109).

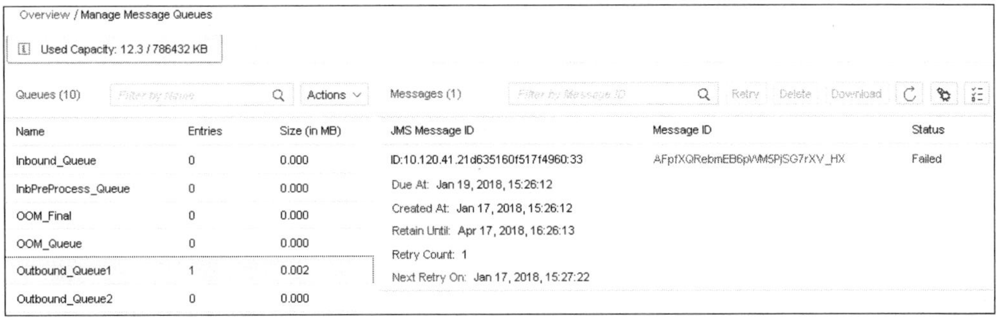

Overview / Manage Message Queues

Used Capacity: 12.3 / 786432 KB

Queues (10) | Actions | Messages (1) | Retry | Delete | Download

Name	Entries	Size (in MB)
Inbound_Queue	0	0.000
InbPreProcess_Queue	0	0.000
OOM_Final	0	0.000
OOM_Queue	0	0.000
Outbound_Queue1	1	0.002
Outbound_Queue2	0	0.000

JMS Message ID	Message ID	Status
ID:10.120.41.21d6351601517f4960:33	AFpfXQRebmEB6pVWM5PjSG7rXV_HX	Failed

Due At: Jan 19, 2018, 15:26:12
Created At: Jan 17, 2018, 15:26:12
Retain Until: Apr 17, 2018, 16:26:13
Retry Count: 1
Next Retry On: Jan 17, 2018, 15:27:22

Figure 5.109 Message in Error in Outbound_Queue1 in Manage Message Queues Monitor

If you check the **Message Processing** monitor again after you received the second email that is targeted for the administrator, you notice that all four entries in the monitor have the status **Completed** now. This is because all retries are executed in the same MPL entry; no new log is created to make the monitoring easier. The sixth retry, still running in an error, triggered the alternative route and completed the message.

Error Sending to the OData Receiver

In a scenario, not only can the final connection to the receivers be broken, but errors can happen during the other message processing steps as well. In our scenario, for example, the request-reply call to the OData receiver could fail. To see how the integration flow copes with this, we change the **Address** field in the **OData** adapter channel to a configuration that doesn't work. Save and deploy the integration flow and trigger the integration flow from your SOAP test client.

For this execution, you don't get any email because the message processing in SAP Cloud Platform Integration didn't even get to the outbound processing. This time, the main processing and the enrichment of the message with the additional data from the OData service could not be executed.

In the **Message Processing** monitor, we find only two entries this time (Figure 5.110), one with status **Completed** for the integration process storing the message in the JMS inbound queue, and one with status **Retry** for the integration process doing the main processing. So, the message in the **Manage Message Queues** monitor in the **Inbound_Queue** has the status **Failed** (Figure 5.111), and the retries are triggered from this JMS queue.

Figure 5.110 Message Processing Monitor for Errors in OData Connection

Overview / Manage Message Queues

Used Capacity: 11.7 / 786432 KB

Queues (10) Actions

Name	Entries	Size (in MB)
Inbound_Queue	1	0.002
InbPreProcess_Queue	0	0.000
OOM_Final	0	0.000
OOM_Queue	0	0.000
Outbound_Queue1	0	0.000
Outbound_Queue2	0	0.000

Messages (1) Retry Delete Download

JMS Message ID	Message ID	Status
ID:10.121.20.57cc6e160efe9c79a0:95	AFpfiOrtD8wqLe33ANVE2vN9ykCR	Failed

Due At: Jan 19, 2018, 18:33:30
Created At: Jan 17, 2018, 18:33:30
Retain Until: Apr 17, 2018, 19:33:29
Retry Count: 3
Next Retry On: Jan 17, 2018, 18:39:54

Figure 5.111 Message in Error in Inbound_Queue in Manage Message Queues Monitor

Delete the message from the JMS queue to stop the retries; otherwise, the message is retried again and again until it's finally deleted after exceeding the **Retention Threshold** defined in the JMS receiver channel.

Now you've successfully set up a reliable messaging scenario using JMS inbound and JMS outbound queues. You've also understood the different options for configuring the retries from JMS queues: either define the retry configuration in the JMS sender channel or model explicit retry configuration in an exception subprocess.

5.5 Summary

Congratulations! You've mastered another important chapter on your journey through the world of integration using SAP Cloud Platform Integration. We implemented more sophisticated integration scenarios, comprising steps for content-based message routing and managing messages containing lists of entries. You applied the splitter pattern to create individual messages out of the list and used the gather pattern to aggregate the individual messages back into one reply message.

You also learned how to influence synchronous and asynchronous message handling for the SOAP adapter and how to add asynchronous receivers to your integration flow. You used the multicast pattern to distribute the message to multiple receivers. At the end of the chapter, you used the JMS adapter to decouple inbound and outbound processing and to ensure retries of the message processing in SAP Cloud Platform Integration. This knowledge allows you to play around with SAP Cloud Platform Integration's more advanced features. However, our journey continues: the next chapter will reveal even more secrets about the timer-based start of integration flows, the structuring of large flows using modularization, and, finally, developing new adapters for SAP Cloud Platform Integration.

Chapter 6
Special Topics in Integration Development

In the previous chapters, you learned the basic concepts of integration development with SAP Cloud Platform Integration, but our discussion wouldn't be complete without covering a few special topics. This chapter discusses timer-based message handling processes, structuring large integration scenarios, using dynamic parameters, integration flow component versioning, transporting integration packages, and developing custom adapters, which may be required to connect to some external systems.

This chapter addresses typical integration scenarios that will require special attention from you. This chapter will provide answers if you have questions about the time-based triggering of integration flows, including the invocation of a Simple Object Access Protocol (SOAP) data source, the dynamic configuration of integration flows; the slicing and dicing of complex integration logic; the intrinsic versioning of integration flows and how to handle it. Furthermore, you'll learn how to transport integration packages from one tenant to another and how to develop your own adapters that can be integrated into the SAP Cloud Platform infrastructure. After you finish this chapter, you'll be well equipped to handle a variety of integration challenges.

6.1 Timer-Based Message Transfer

In previous chapters, we used SAP Cloud Platform Integration as the cloud-based solution for reliable message transfer between on-premise and on-demand enterprise applications. So far, the integration logic executed on SAP Cloud Platform Integration was mainly triggered by incoming messages, such as an order request originating from a sender customer relationship management (CRM) system, which needed to be routed to various backend enterprise resource planning (ERP) systems, depending on the message's content. However, not all integration scenarios require an incoming message to trigger their execution. Sometimes, you want to check for existing data on a regular basis, for example, retrieving the status of a machine or related machine data in the Internet of Things and forwarding the information to a business intelligence system for further analysis. Scenarios like this require a timely initiation of a message transfer. This section of the book will dive into the details on how this can be achieved using SAP Cloud Platform Integration.

6.1.1 The Scenario

To show how to design a timer-base integration flow, we'll modify the scenario from Chapter 4, Section 4.3 (Figure 4.44). You remember that in this scenario, we invoked an external OData service by sending a SOAP message with a dedicated order number. The SOAP service retrieved details for that specific order.

Let's assume now that you're interested in getting regular updates about all orders placed for a specific shipping country, for example, France. We can design a timer-based integration flow in such a way that we get a list of all such orders into your email account in regular intervals. With just a few steps, we can now modify the scenario without introducing any new steps except for the **Start Timer** event. Figure 6.1 shows the target scenario.

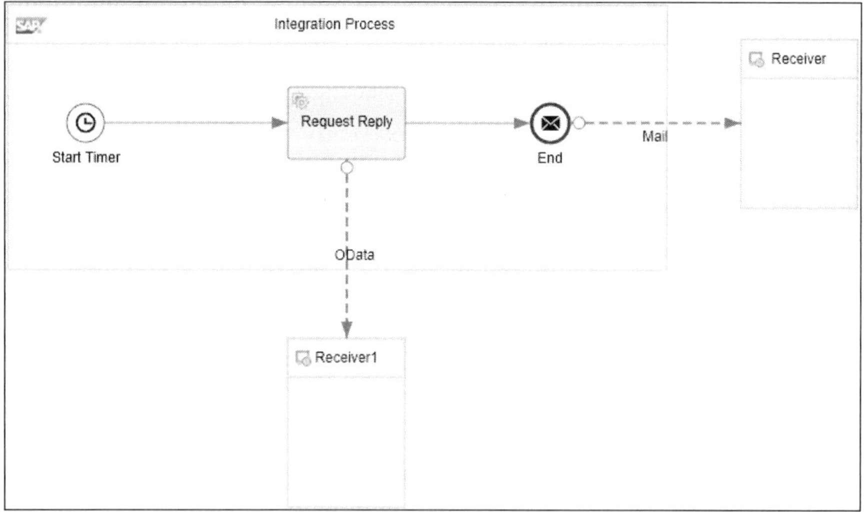

Figure 6.1 Timer-Based Invocation of an OData Service

At the start of the flow on the left side of the figure, you'll see the first difference compared to the other integration flows we've discussed so far. This integration flow begins with a new event called **Start Timer**, indicated by the clock ◷. We'll take a closer look at its configuration in a moment. The **Start Timer** event is followed by a **Request-Reply** step and connected via OData to the external service (the same service we've used in Chapter 4, Section 4.3). After we receive the result from the service, it's sent to the receiver via a **Mail** adapter. It shouldn't be a problem for you to model the scenario based on the knowledge you've acquired so far. The only new shape in this integration flow is the **Start Timer** event. You'll find it in the palette beneath the event's main entry ◎ (see Figure 6.2).

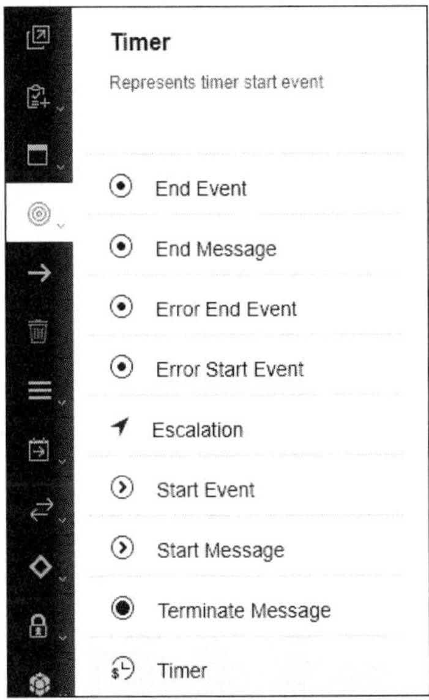

Figure 6.2 The Timer Start Event in the Modeling Palette

6.1.2 Configuring a Timer-Based Integration Flow

We'll begin by configuring the most important shape of the flow: the **Start Timer** event. This event is responsible for initiating the flow's execution without requiring a dedicated start message. The configuration options are depicted in Figure 6.3 and Figure 6.4.

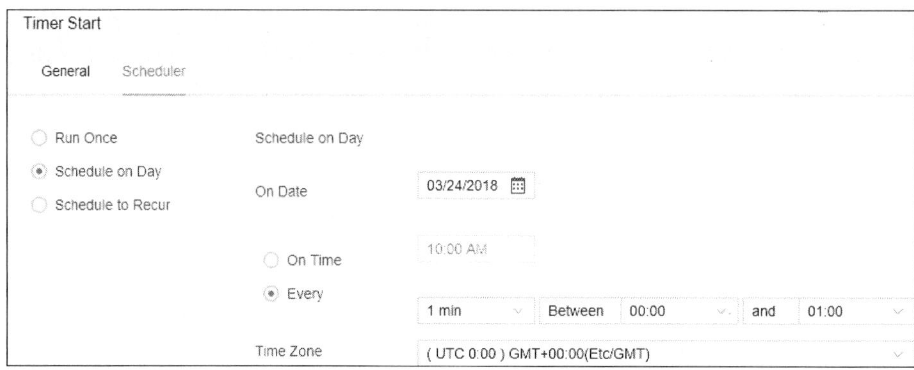

Figure 6.3 Configuration of the Start Timer Event for a Scheduled Start on a Certain Day

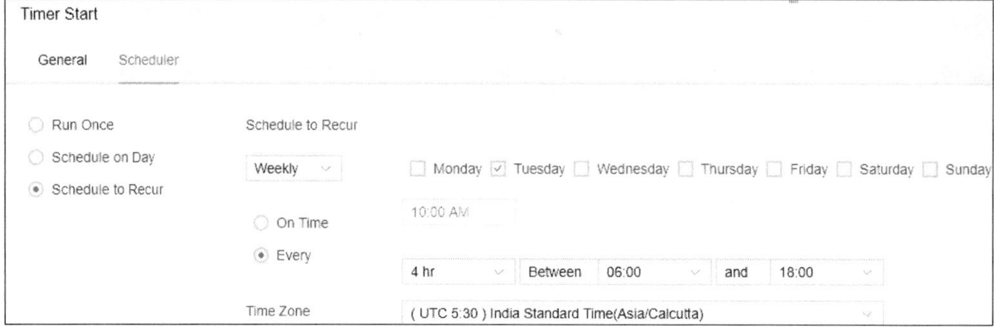

Figure 6.4 Configuration of the Start Timer Event for a Weekly Recurring Schedule

You have three options at your disposal for starting the integration flow:

- **Run Once**
  Run only once immediately after deployment of the flow.
- **Schedule on Day**
  Scheduled execution on a concrete day at a well-defined time (or well-defined times).
- **Schedule to Recur**
  Recurring schedule on a daily, weekly, or monthly basis at a well-defined time (or well-defined times).

The **Run Once** option allows you to trigger the flow's execution immediately after a successful deployment. It can also be used for testing purposes, if you want to try out certain integration functionalities without sending incoming messages all the time, just to get the flow started. Obviously, you don't have to configure additional settings for this option, as the exact point of time is given by the finalization of the flow's deployment.

The **Schedule on Day** option (shown in Figure 6.3) defines a concrete day on which the integration flow should run. In the **On Date** field, you enter the respective execution date. However, you can also specify either the one-time execution or a recurring execution on that particular date. If you want to run the flow only once, you have to set the **On Time** checkbox, accompanied by a concrete time. For a recurring invocation of the flow's logic, select the **Every** radio button. In addition, you have to define two intervals:

- **The interval during which the flow should be activated**
  Every minute? Every hour? There are even other intervals possible: every second minute, every four hours, and so on. You select the respective interval from the dropdown list to the right of the **Every** radio button.
- **Between which times of the day the flow should run**
  For this, you can define the start and end time. The respective dropdown lists are positioned to the right of the **Between** label in Figure 6.3, the first representing the start time, and the second representing the end time.

The settings in Figure 6.3 represent a recurring invocation of the integration flow on March 24, 2018. The flow will be called every minute in the time between midnight and 1:00 a.m. (Greenwich Mean Time zone).

With these options, you can quite flexibly schedule the flow's execution for a certain day. And even for that particular day, you can define a recurring execution. However, the repetition of the invocation is limited to one day. To overcome this limitation, you want to make use of the third option, which allows you to define a more flexible period for the flow's repetition. For this purpose, select the **Schedule to Recur** radio button (Figure 6.4). The dropdown list beneath the **Schedule to Recur** label allows you to select the period: currently **Daily**, **Weekly**, and **Monthly** repetitions are supported. Depending on your choice, you can define additional attributes:

- **Daily**
  Define whether the flow should run only once on that day or on a recurring basis. You have exactly the same options described for the **Schedule on Day** selection.
- **Weekly**
  Define the days per week on which the flow should be invoked. The chosen days

will activate the flow every week. You can even pick several days, such as Monday, Wednesday, and Friday.

- **Monthly**
  Specify the date on which the integration flow should run every month. If a chosen date isn't applicable for a certain month (e.g., 31 isn't a valid date for February, April, June, September, and November), the flow isn't executed. Only one day can be selected.

With the configuration shown in Figure 6.4, the integration flow will be activated every week on Tuesday. The flow runs on this day every four hours, between 6:00 a.m. and 6:00 p.m. The time zone has been set to India Standard Time.

Of course, many configuration options are available to schedule the execution of your integration flows. The **Start Timer** event is the element of choice for start, end, and recurring times, periods, and time spans. Returning to our initial goal of receiving order information in regular intervals, we assume that we want to get this information into our inbox every morning at 7:00 a.m.

Therefore, a reasonable configuration is the selection of the **Schedule to Recur** radio button with the identically named dropdown list set to **Daily**. In addition, select the **On Time** radio button, and set the according time to **7:00 AM** (Figure 6.5).

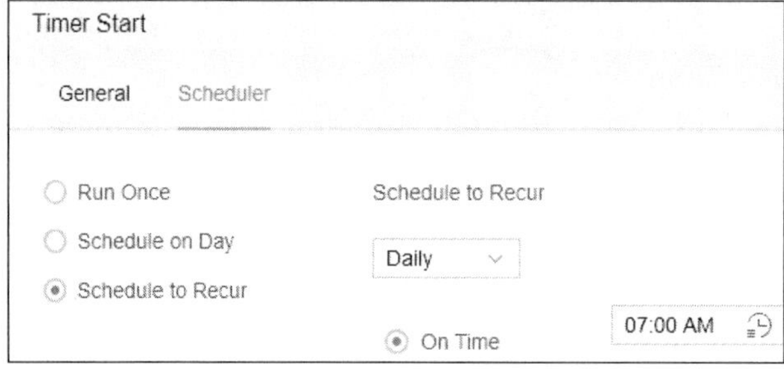

Figure 6.5 Setting the Recurrence to Every Day at 7:00 a.m.

However, there is an alternative approach possible, especially if you want to retrieve the information only for workdays. In this case, choose the **Weekly** entry from the **Schedule to Recur** dropdown list, and set the checkboxes for the required workdays (Monday to Friday in our example; see Figure 6.6).

It's quite impressive what can be configured for the **Start Timer** event. Use the many configuration options available to define your own schedule.

Timer Start

General Scheduler

Run Once | Schedule on Day | Schedule to Recur

Schedule to Recur: Weekly — Monday, Tuesday, Wednesday, Thursday, Friday (checked); Saturday, Sunday (unchecked)

On Time: 07:00 AM

Figure 6.6 Setting the Recurrence to Workdays Only

To continue, we'll now configure the OData connection. To find out how to configure an OData connection in general, refer to Chapter 4, Section 4.3. We just modify the OData adapter by configuring the following settings (Figure 6.7).

OData

General Adapter Specific

CONNECTION DETAILS

*Address:	http://services.odata.org/Northwind/Northwind.svc
*Proxy Type:	Internet
*Authentication:	None

PROCESSING DETAILS

*Operation Details:	Query(GET)
*Resource Path:	Orders
Query Options:	$select=CustomerID,OrderDate,ShipAddress,ShipCity,ShipCountry,ShipName&$filter=ShipCountry eq 'France'
Custom Query Options:	
Page Size:	200
Process in Pages	☐
*Timeout (in min):	1

Figure 6.7 OData Adapter Settings to Retrieve All French Orders

Note that in the **Query Options** field, we've entered the expression `$filter=ShipCountry eq 'France'` at the end of the string, which makes sure that we retrieve French orders as expected.

Before we can test the integration flow, we must define the connection to the email server. This has already been explained in the previous chapter about asynchronous message handling. Refer to Chapter 5, Section 5.3.2, and Figure 6.1 in this chapter to configure the connection to the email server correctly.

6.1.3 Running the Integration Flow

Now that our integration flow has been configured, it's time to try it out. It's recommended to set the **Start Timer** event to **Run Once** for the very first time, just to avoid waiting for the timer to expire on the next day at 7:00 a.m. With the timer set to **Run Once**, the integration flow will begin automatically after deployment, which is exactly what we need for test purposes. Once deployed, connect to your email provider to check the email.

When the integration flow executes successfully, you should find an email with a list of orders (and details as configured in the OData adapter), as shown in Figure 6.8.


```
<Orders>
  <Order>
    <OrderDate>1996-07-04T00:00:00.000</OrderDate>
    <ShipCity>Reims</ShipCity>
    <CustomerID>VINET</CustomerID>
    <ShipAddress>59 rue de l'Abbaye</ShipAddress>
    <ShipCountry>France</ShipCountry>
    <ShipName>Vins et alcools Chevalier</ShipName>
  </Order>
  <Order>
    <OrderDate>1996-07-08T00:00:00.000</OrderDate>
    <ShipCity>Lyon</ShipCity>
    <CustomerID>VICTE</CustomerID>
    <ShipAddress>2, rue du Commerce</ShipAddress>
    <ShipCountry>France</ShipCountry>
    <ShipName>Victuailles en stock</ShipName>
  </Order>
  <Order>
    <OrderDate>1996-07-25T00:00:00.000</OrderDate>
    <ShipCity>Strasbourg</ShipCity>
    <CustomerID>BLONP</CustomerID>
    <ShipAddress>24, place Kléber</ShipAddress>
    <ShipCountry>France</ShipCountry>
    <ShipName>Blondel père et fils</ShipName>
  </Order>
  <Order>
    <OrderDate>1996-08-06T00:00:00.000</OrderDate>
    <ShipCity>Reims</ShipCity>
    <CustomerID>VINET</CustomerID>
    <ShipAddress>59 rue de l'Abbaye</ShipAddress>
```


Figure 6.8 Excerpt from the Received Email

To summarize, regularly fetching data and forwarding messages to systems are typical requirements for integration solutions such as SAP Cloud Platform Integration. In this part of the book, we've shown you how to prepare integration flows for this purpose. You've seen how to apply the **Start Timer** event for triggering the integration flow's execution on a regular basis. It doesn't matter whether you want to run the flow only once or in a recurring fashion: the **Start Timer** event is prepared for all kinds of invocation scenarios.

6.2 Using Dynamic Configuration via Headers or Properties

All integration flows you've learned about so far in this book have been designed under the tacit assumption that when modeling the integration flow (during design time), you already know the values of all adapter and integration flow step attributes. However, you can easily think of scenarios where this assumption doesn't apply and where certain attribute values are only known during runtime—when the integration flow is being executed.

You might, for example, like to configure an integration flow with a mail receiver adapter, and the **Subject** field of the outbound email isn't known yet during design time. It should, instead of this, depend on the content of the inbound message (to anticipate an example, we'll show you how to configure this in a minute).

SAP Cloud Platform Integration also has a solution for use cases like this: various integration flow step and adapter attributes that can be configured *dynamically*. To understand how this works, think again about Camel's data model as introduced in Chapter 4. There, you learned that SAP Cloud Platform Integration provides the option to pass along certain information during the processing of a message, namely, first in the message header and, secondly, in the exchange (as an exchange property). During message processing, this data can be used in various ways. For example, with the content modifier integration flow step, you can write data into the message header or (as a property) into the exchange container in a well-defined way so that it can be accessed at a later step during the message processing (e.g., in a routing condition). We've shown how to use the content modifier several times within this book.

Dynamic configuration of an attribute now means that instead of a concrete value, you enter a reference to a certain header or property for this attribute. At runtime, SAP Cloud Platform Integration resolves this reference by looking up the actual value of this header or property in the incoming message. The term *incoming message* in this case relates to the actual instance of the message that exists when message processing reaches the adapter or step that contains the dynamically configured attribute. Figure 6.9 shows the general principle.

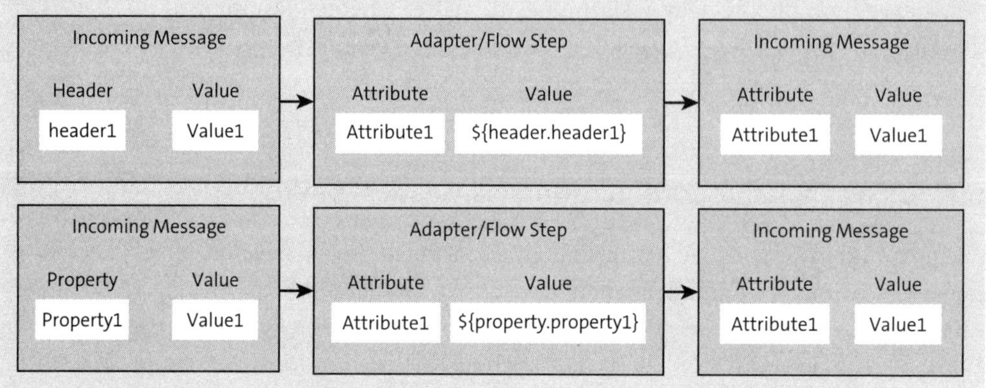

Figure 6.9 How Dynamically Configured Attributes Are Processed during Runtime

The upper part shows how a dynamically configured attribute is handled when a message header is used, and the lower part of the figure shows the same for when a property is used. To refer to a message header or property, you need to apply a certain syntax, which you already have seen in this book:

- The expression `${header.header1}` points to the field `header1` in the incoming message.
- The expression `${property.property1}` points to the property `property1` in the message exchange container.

You remember that expressions such as `${header.header1}` are expressions from Camel Simple Expression Language (described at *http://camel.apache.org/simple.html*), as has been already introduced in Chapter 4, Section 4.1.4.

You've seen already specific usage of dynamically configured attributes in the following sections:

- In Chapter 4, Section 4.3.4, in the context of the OData adapter, we showed you how to dynamically configure a filter condition for an OData request by referring to a specific header.
- In Chapter 5, Section 5.1.2, a specific header was used in a routing condition to allow you to configure a content-based routing (CBR) scenario.
- Furthermore, in Chapter 5, Section 5.4.3, we showed you how to use a specific header (`SAPJMSRetries`) to access the number of already executed retries in a scenario when Java Message Service (JMS) queues are used.

Therefore, the topic of dynamic configuration isn't completely new. In this section, we show you some more simple examples of how to use dynamic parameters, and we provide more background information.

Before going into the details, we would like to mention that many, but not all, integration flow attributes support dynamic configuration. To get a list of integration flow attributes that support dynamic configuration, check out the documentation for SAP Cloud Platform Integration (*https://help.sap.com/viewer/product/CLOUD_INTEGRATION/Cloud*) and search for the topic **Dynamic Parameters**.

6.2.1 An Integration Flow with a Dynamically Configured Attribute

To show how to use dynamic attributes step by step, we provide a simple example. We won't create a new demo example from scratch, but we'll show you how to extend an already introduced integration flow (from Chapter 4, Section 4.3).

This is how the integration scenario works: your integration flow invokes an OData service to retrieve information about a certain order and sends this information (using the mail receiver adapter) to an email account. The first part of the scenario (invoking the OData service) is identical to the scenario we've explained already in Chapter 4, Section 4.3. In this example, you'll configure the **Subject** field of the outbound email dynamically to contain the name of the country associated with the order. Figure 6.10 illustrates how the dynamically configured **Subject** field is handled during runtime.

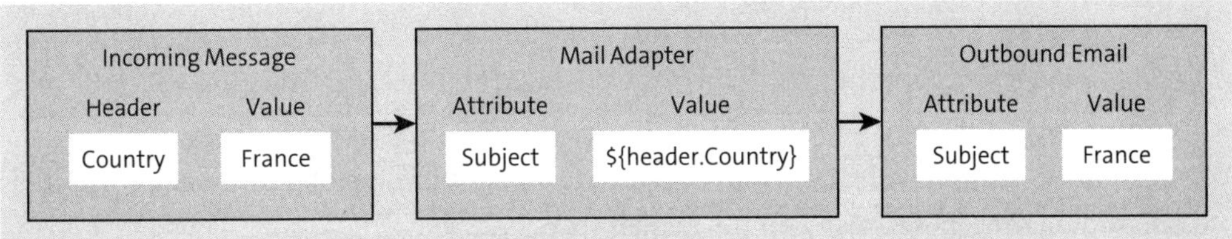

Figure 6.10 Dynamically Configuring the Subject Field of the Receiver Mail Adapter

Figure 6.11 shows the integration flow.

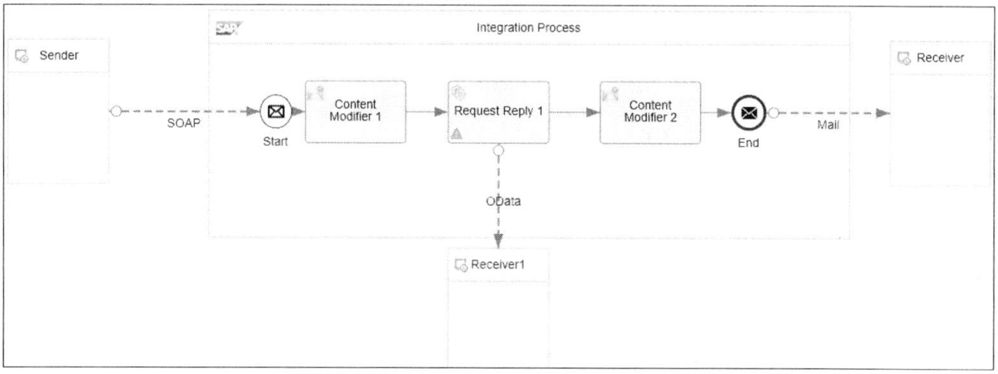

Figure 6.11 Target Integration Flow

This is how the integration scenario is supposed to work at runtime:

1. With a SOAP client (implemented by the SoapUI), you send a SOAP message containing an order number (e.g., `10249`).
2. Using the first content modifier, the order number is retrieved from the incoming message and stored in the message's header field for later reference.
3. The **Request-Reply** step invokes an external OData service through the OData channel to retrieve the details of that particular order. In essence, the scenario implements a request-reply pattern scenario. The OData adapter is configured in such a way that certain details of the order are retrieved, among them also the country related to the order, which is contained in the `ShipCountry` field of the order.
4. The second content modifier writes the value of the `ShipCountry` field into the message header field `Country`.
5. The mail receiver adapter is configured so that the value of the **Subject** attribute is dynamically set based on the header `Country`.
6. The outbound email contains the **Subject** with the actual name of the country for the specified order number (e.g., **Germany** for order number `10249`).

How to configure the first part of this integration flow was already shown in Chapter 4, Section 4.3. Therefore, we refer to this section for the details. We'll now explain each step for configuring the rest of the integration flow, starting with the second content modifier step.

Let's assume you've already configured the integration flow as shown in Chapter 4, Section 4.3. For your convenience, we again show the attributes of the OData adapter in Figure 6.12.

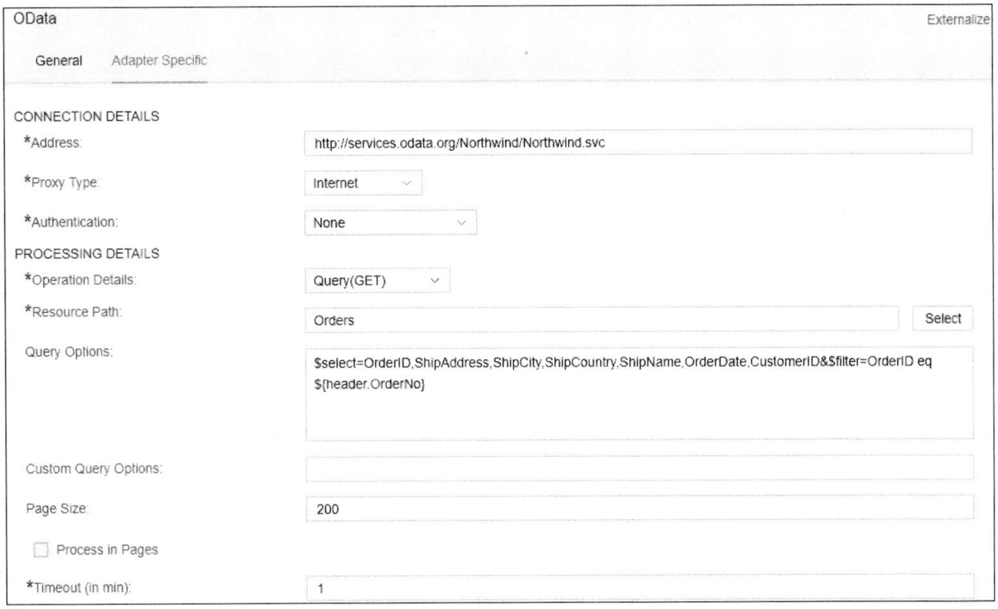

Figure 6.12 OData Adapter Configuration (Example)

Note

Consider the following regarding the configuration of the OData adapter:

- You can, of course, configure the OData adapter differently than explained in Chapter 4, Section 4.3. However, make sure that you also specify the field `ShipCountry` (to be retrieved during the OData request), as shown in Figure 6.12.
- The expression **${header.OrderNo}** in the field **Query Options** makes sure that the order number from the header of the incoming message is retrieved at runtime (and the OData request gets the order for exactly this order number). As mentioned, this expression indicates that we've already intrinsically used a dynamic parameter at this step.

To enhance the integration flow from Chapter 4, Section 4.3, proceed as follows:

1. Edit the integration flow and add a second **Content Modifier** between the **Request-Reply** step and the **Message End** event (as shown in earlier Figure 6.11).
2. Configure the second **Content Modifier** so that the value of the `ShipCountry` field of the OData message is written into the newly defined message header `Country` (Figure 6.13).

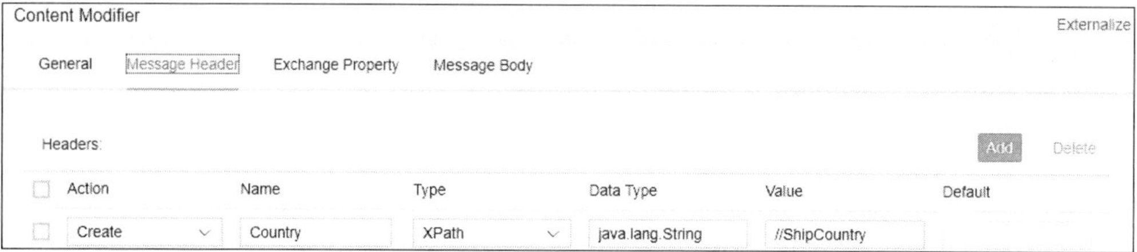

Figure 6.13 Setting the Header in the Second Content Modifier

3. Connect the **Content Modifier** with the message **End** event.
4. Add a second **Receiver** (refer to Figure 6.11).
5. Connect the message **End** event with the second **Receiver**, and specify **Mail** as the adapter type.
6. Configure the mail adapter as shown in Chapter 2, Section 2.3.4. Figure 6.14 shows the **Connection** settings of the adapter.

   You can use the same mail adapter configuration as shown in Chapter 2, Section 2.3.4, except you should enter "${header.Country}" for the **Subject**.
7. Save and deploy the integration flow.
8. Run the integration flow (specifying a certain order number, e.g., `10249`).
9. Check in your mail Inbox for the received message. It should look similar to that shown in Figure 6.15.

   Notice that the email contains the subject **Germany** (as order number `10249` identifies a German order).

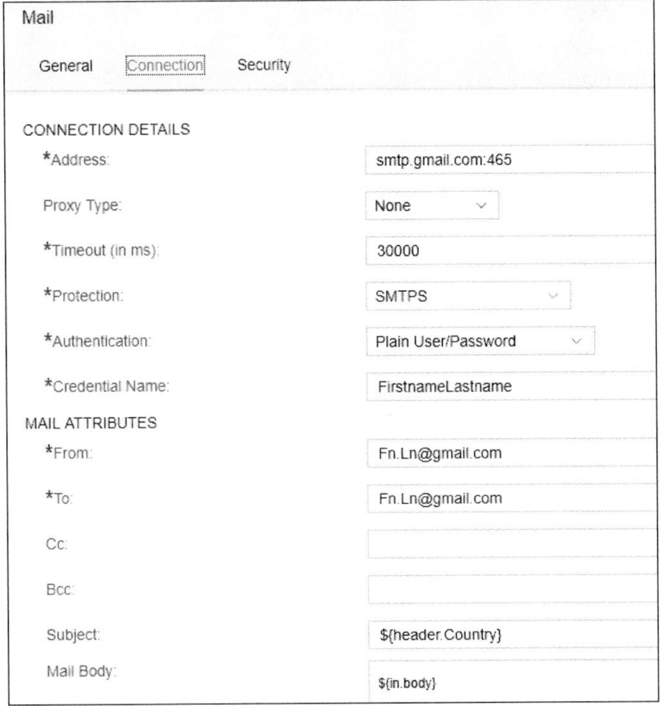

Figure 6.14 Mail Adapter with Dynamically Configured Subject Attribute

Figure 6.15 Email with Subject Germany

10. Run the integration flow again, this time entering order number "10250".
11. You should receive an email that looks similar to the one shown in Figure 6.16, this time with the Subject **Brazil** (as the order number 10250 identifies a Brazilian order).

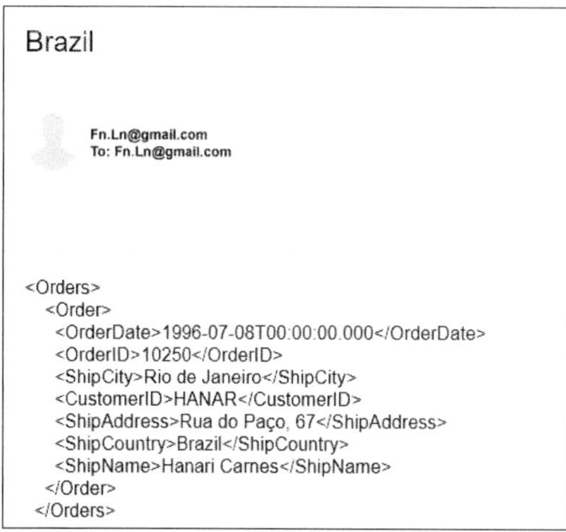

Brazil
Fn.Ln@gmail.com
To: Fn.Ln@gmail.com
<Orders>
<Order>
<OrderDate>1996-07-08T00:00:00.000</OrderDate>
<OrderID>10250</OrderID>
<ShipCity>Rio de Janeiro</ShipCity>
<CustomerID>HANAR</CustomerID>
<ShipAddress>Rua do Paço, 67</ShipAddress>
<ShipCountry>Brazil</ShipCountry>
<ShipName>Hanari Carnes</ShipName>
</Order>
</Orders>

Figure 6.16 Email with Subject Brazil

This shows that you've correctly configured your dynamic parameter for the mail **Subject**.

Note that the mail adapter isn't the only part of the integration flow where a value is dynamically retrieved at runtime. As already mentioned, the OData adapter uses the expression `${header.OrderNo}` in the filter condition (refer to Figure 6.12), which has the effect that the OData request retrieves the order for exactly that order number value provided in the incoming message. Strictly speaking, the integration flow developed in this section contains two dynamically configured attributes.

6.2.2 Monitoring Dynamically Configured Attributes at Runtime

Next we'll show how you can monitor what happens with dynamically configured attributes during message processing. For this purpose, you need to look into the message content during message processing. As we'll show in detail in Chapter 8, Section 8.2.2, the monitoring application provides the option to configure different log levels to specify in which detail processing-related information is to be displayed during monitoring. For the following exercise, it's required that you set the log level

Trace that makes sure payloads and headers are logged after each processing step. This log level is only activated for a short period.

In addition, you need to make sure that your user has the right permissions to display the message content (as provided by this log level). In particular, the authorization group `AuthGroup.BusinessExpert` (or the role `esbmessagestorage.read`) has to be assigned to your user. How authorization groups or roles are assigned to a user is shown in detail in Chapter 10, Section 10.3.

For the following steps, we assume that you've activated the log level **Trace** for your tenant (see Chapter 8, Section 8.2.2. Proceed as follows:

1. Go to the monitoring application of the Web UI, and under **Manage Integration Content**, select your integration flow.
2. As **Log Level**, select **Trace**. Note that after this activity, this log level setting is effective only for 10 minutes to save resources.
3. Run the integration flow again, and choose a tile under **Monitor Message Processing**.
4. Select your message flow, and click the **Trace** link in the **Logs** section.

   An overview of the message processing steps and the integration flow model appears below the list of steps (Figure 6.17).

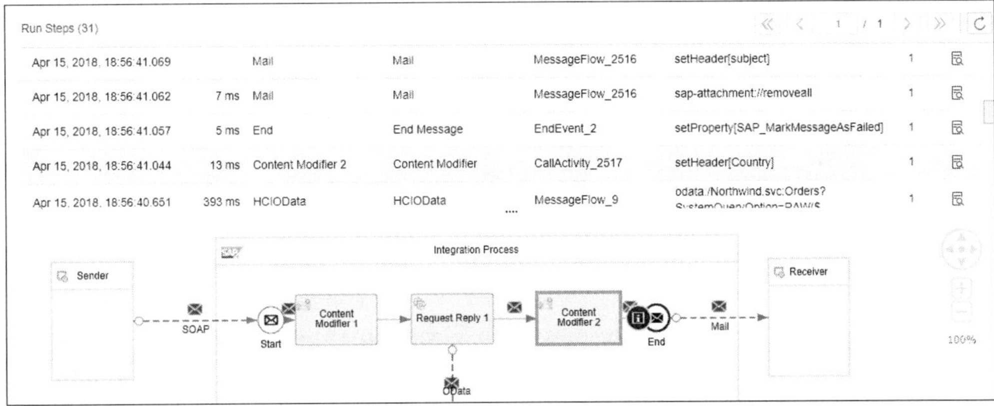

Figure 6.17 The Monitoring Application Shows the Individual Steps during Message Processing

5. Click on the entry for the second **Content Modifier**. The corresponding shape is highlighted in the integration flow model, as shown in Figure 6.17.

6. Click the **View Step Details** icon under **Actions** at the right end of the table row.
7. Select **Message Content** (the **Message Content** tab is shown only when you've specified a log level **Trace**,).

The message header fields (on top) and the message payload (at the bottom) are shown. Figure 6.18 shows the section with the message header for the selected step shown in Figure 6.17.

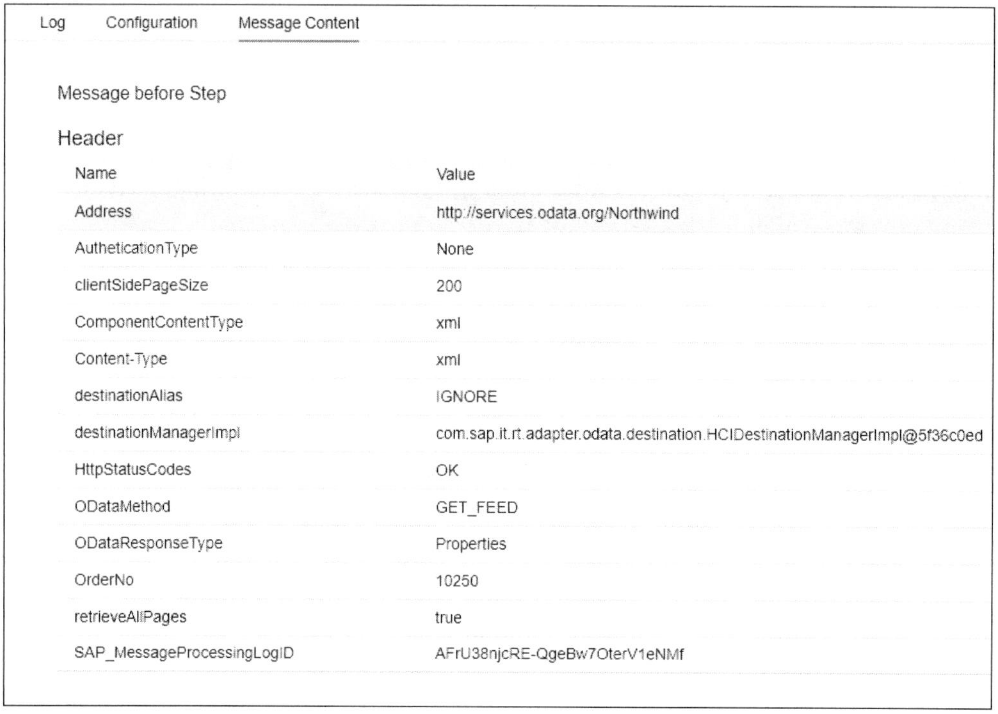

Log Configuration Message Content

Message before Step

Header

Name	Value
Address	http://services.odata.org/Northwind
AutheticationType	None
clientSidePageSize	200
ComponentContentType	xml
Content-Type	xml
destinationAlias	IGNORE
destinationManagerImpl	com.sap.it.rt.adapter.odata.destination.HCIDestinationManagerImpl@5f36c0ed
HttpStatusCodes	OK
ODataMethod	GET_FEED
ODataResponseType	Properties
OrderNo	10250
retrieveAllPages	true
SAP_MessageProcessingLogID	AFrU38njcRE-QgeBw7OterV1eNMf

Figure 6.18 Actual Message Header at the Second Content Modifier

Below the header, you find the message payload with the data of the actual order (not shown in Figure 6.18), but we'll keep our focus on the header. It contains several fields related to the OData request, such as the address of the OData source, the request method, and other fields we won't elaborate on. But what is important for the actual discussion is that at this processing step, the header **Country** isn't shown yet, which is as expected if you remember that this header has just been created by the second **Content Modifier** step.

Now, let's see how the message has changed with the following processing step:

1. Navigate back from the step details to the message processing overview. To do that, click the **Message Processing Run** link in the breadcrumb link at the top of the screen.

   Notice the overview with the integration flow model shown earlier in Figure 6.17.
2. Select the **End Message** step (one row on top of the second **Content Modifier** in Figure 6.18).
3. Click the **View Step Details** icon under **Actions** at the right end of the table row.

The **Header** section again shows various header fields. Notice that now the header **Country** has been added (Figure 6.19) as you would also expect from how the integration flow has been designed.

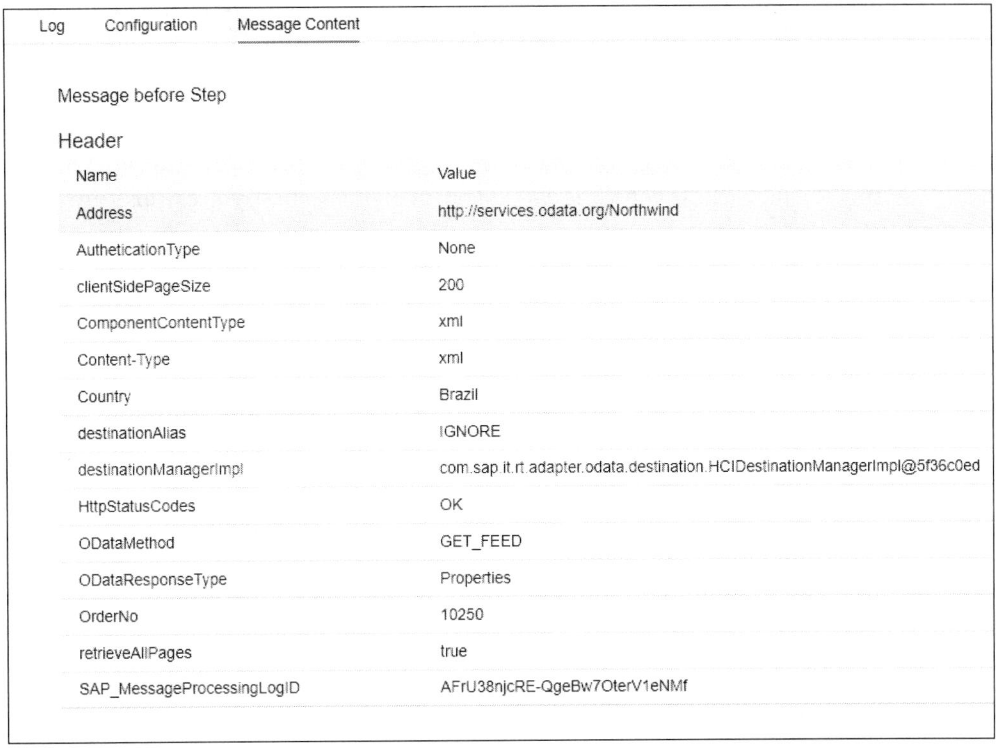

Log Configuration Message Content

Message before Step

Header

Name	Value
Address	http://services.odata.org/Northwind
AutheticationType	None
clientSidePageSize	200
ComponentContentType	xml
Content-Type	xml
Country	Brazil
destinationAlias	IGNORE
destinationManagerImpl	com.sap.it.rt.adapter.odata.destination.HCIDestinationManagerImpl@5f36c0ed
HttpStatusCodes	OK
ODataMethod	GET_FEED
ODataResponseType	Properties
OrderNo	10250
retrieveAllPages	true
SAP_MessageProcessingLogID	AFrU38njcRE-QgeBw7OterV1eNMf

Figure 6.19 Message Headers during Message Processing before the Message End Event

Note

In addition, for the actual message flow, the header **Country** has been set now and has the value **Brazil**. This value is given over to the mail adapter.

We've shown you with a simple example how you can easily dynamically configure a certain integration flow attribute (by referring to a certain header) and how you can monitor the usage of this header during message processing.

At runtime, the actual value for this header is retrieved from the incoming message and used to (dynamically) set an attribute of a subsequent step (for our example, of the mail adapter). Note that in this example, we explicitly had to create the header during message processing (with the second **Content Modifier** step) just to create a data container for the data to be used to dynamically set the mail adapter attribute.

There's more to tell about dynamic parameters. In addition to using a specially created header to dynamically configure a certain integration flow attribute, you can use a number of *predefined* headers and exchange properties that are provided by the SAP Cloud Platform Integration framework to retrieve specific data during the processing of a message. In the same way as shown in this section, you can also use these special headers and properties to dynamically configure integration flow attributes.

6.2.3 Using Predefined Headers and Properties to Retrieve Specific Data Provided by the Integration Framework

In Chapter 5, Section 5.4.3, you already came across an example for a header predefined by the integration framework when using the JMS adapter. The header field `SAPJMSRetries` is automatically created by the integration framework when you use JMS queues. It records the number of retries of a JMS message that are already executed. In Chapter 5, Section 5.4.3, we showed you how to use the content of this header to dynamically define a routing condition (by entering the expression `${header.SAPJMSRetries}`).

This header is only set when using the JMS adapter. Similarly, other adapters and integration flow steps set other, specific headers and properties to store data that is specific to this adapter or integration flow step.

To get an overview of the predefined headers and properties provided by the SAP Cloud Platform Integration framework, check out the documentation for SAP Cloud Platform Integration at *https://help.sap.com/viewer/product/CLOUD_INTEGRATION/*

Cloud, and search for the topic **Headers and Exchange Properties Provided by the Integration Framework**.

To round out this topic, we'll show you how to use another header. As you can see from the documentation of SAP Cloud Platform Integration, the splitter step also creates the exchange property `CamelSplitSize`, which provides the total number of split items of an exchange. To show how to use this property to dynamically configure a certain integration flow attribute, refer to the integration flow explained in Chapter 5, Section 5.2 (see Figure 5.18).

To briefly recap, the integration flow splits a single message that contains multiple order items (as depicted in Chapter 5 in Figure 5.17) into individual messages with one order item per message (by applying the **General Splitter**). Each split message is enriched by additional details (by an OData request to an external source, as depicted in Chapter 5, Figure 5.37). Finally, the split messages are joined to a single one (with multiple items) by the **Gather** step. However, we'll skip the message enrichment and only use the very simple, first variant of the integration flow as the basis for our integration scenario, as depicted in Chapter 5, Figure 5.18.

We'll now modify the integration scenario shown in Chapter 5, Figure 5.18, in the following way: After having split the larger message into individual messages and joining it back into a single one (as depicted in Chapter 5, Figure 5.29), we introduce a **Routing** step that sends the final message to a dedicated email receiver (with a specific email **Subject**) in case the message contains exactly three items. In all other cases (when the joined message contains a different number of items than three), the message is forwarded to another email receiver (to keep it simple, we in fact use the same email account for both receivers, but we only specify another email **Subject** in the other mail adapter). The integration flow is shown in Figure 6.20.

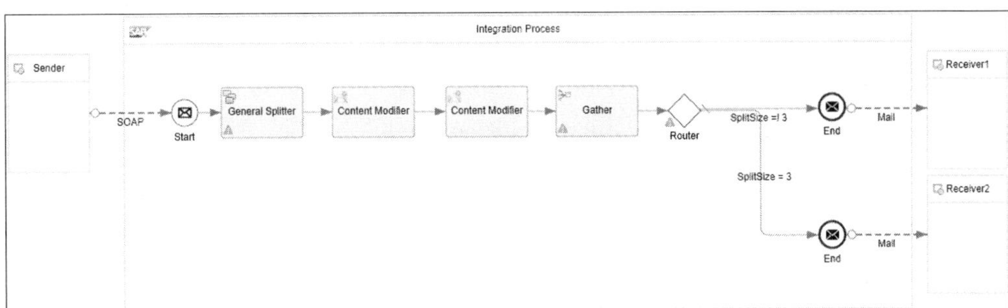

Figure 6.20 Message Split Integration Flow with an Additional Routing Step and Two Email Receivers

We won't explain in detail how to modify the various integration flow steps, as you're already an expert in these topics. We'll just make you aware of the following aspects:

- In the **General Splitter** dialog box, deselect the **Streaming** checkbox (Figure 6.21).

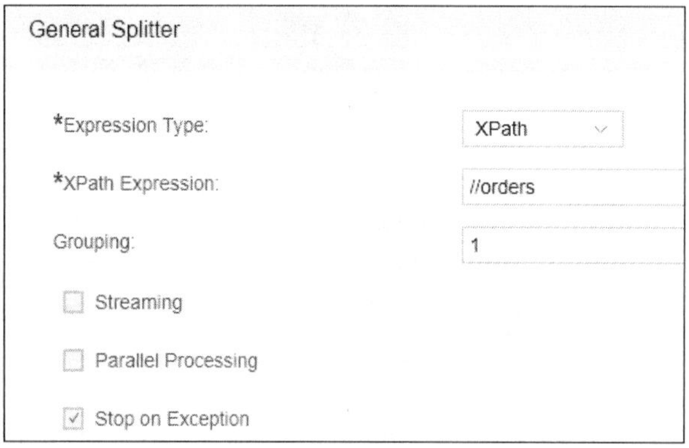

General Splitter

*Expression Type:	XPath
*XPath Expression:	//orders
Grouping:	1

☐ Streaming

☐ Parallel Processing

☑ Stop on Exception

Figure 6.21 Deselecting the Streaming Checkbox in the General Splitter Dialog Box

In Chapter 5, Section 5.2.1 (Figure 5.24), we kept this option selected. However, when using the property `CamelSplitSize`, we propose to disable the **Streaming** option because the property `CamelSplitSize` is only applied on the complete exchange if **Streaming** is enabled.

- You can use the same mail adapter settings as already shown at various times within this book (e.g. Chapter 2, in Figure 2.31 and Figure 2.32). Note, however, that you specify two different email subjects in the two different mail adapters:
  - In the upper mail adapter to which messages with the condition `SplitSize =! 3` (refer to Figure 6.20) are routed, enter, for example, "No of items =! 3" as the **Subject**.
  - In the lower mail adapter to which messages with the condition `SplitSize = 3` are routed, enter, for example, "No of items = 3" as the **Subject**.
- We also explicitly show how the routing conditions should be defined in Figure 6.22.

Notice that for the lower route, we enter the routing condition "${property.Camel-SplitSize} = '3'". The property `CamelSplitSize` wasn't defined at any previous step in the integration flow (e.g., in a **Content Modifier**). When running the scenario, this property is set automatically and provides the specific information related to the processed message (in this case, the total number of split items).

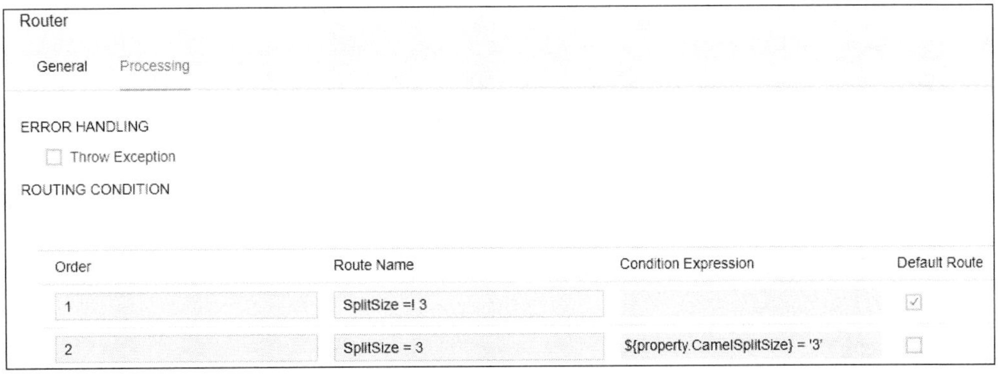

Router

General Processing

ERROR HANDLING

Throw Exception

ROUTING CONDITION

Order	Route Name	Condition Expression	Default Route
1	SplitSize =! 3		☑
2	SplitSize = 3	${property.CamelSplitSize} = '3'	☐

Figure 6.22 Routing Conditions

Now, run the scenario with the following input message (to be edited in SoapUI), as shown in Figure 6.23.

```
<soapenv:Envelope xmlns:soapenv="http://schemas.xmlsoap.org
   <soapenv:Header/>
   <soapenv:Body>
      <demo:OrderList_MT>
          <orders>
            <orderNumber>10251</orderNumber>
            <customerName>?</customerName>
            <orderAmount>?</orderAmount>
            <currency>?</currency>
            <taxAmount>?</taxAmount>
         </orders>
         <orders>
            <orderNumber>10252</orderNumber>
            <customerName>?</customerName>
            <orderAmount>?</orderAmount>
            <currency>?</currency>
            <taxAmount>?</taxAmount>
         </orders>
      </demo:OrderList_MT>demo:OrderList_MT>
   </soapenv:Body>
</soapenv:Envelope>
```

Figure 6.23 Input Message with Two Items

The input message contains two items. The result (as received in your email account) should look like Figure 6.24.

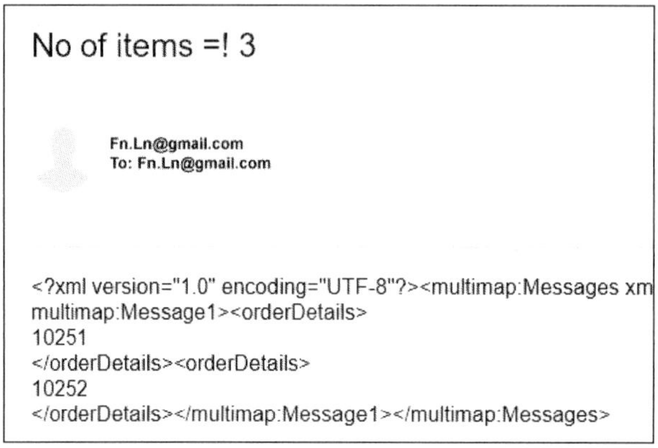

No of items =! 3

Fn.Ln@gmail.com
To: Fn.Ln@gmail.com

```
<?xml version="1.0" encoding="UTF-8"?><multimap:Messages xm
multimap:Message1><orderDetails>
10251
</orderDetails><orderDetails>
10252
</orderDetails></multimap:Message1></multimap:Messages>
```

Figure 6.24 Email with Two Split Items and Subject "No of Items =! 3"

The email subject is **No of items =! 3**, which proves that the message has taken the upper route in Figure 6.20, shown previously.

Repeat the same with the input message shown in Figure 6.25.

```
<soapenv:Envelope xmlns:soapenv="http://schemas.xmlsoap.org
   <soapenv:Header/>
   <soapenv:Body>
      <demo:OrderList_MT>
          <orders>
            <orderNumber>10250</orderNumber>
            <customerName>?</customerName>
            <orderAmount>?</orderAmount>
            <currency>?</currency>
            <taxAmount>?</taxAmount>
         </orders>
          <orders>
            <orderNumber>10251</orderNumber>
            <customerName>?</customerName>
            <orderAmount>?</orderAmount>
            <currency>?</currency>
            <taxAmount>?</taxAmount>
         </orders>
         <orders>
            <orderNumber>10252</orderNumber>
            <customerName>?</customerName>
            <orderAmount>?</orderAmount>
            <currency>?</currency>
            <taxAmount>?</taxAmount>
         </orders>
      </demo:OrderList_MT>demo:OrderList_MT>
   </soapenv:Body>
</soapenv:Envelope>
```

Figure 6.25 Input Message with Three Items

As the input message now has three items (processed by the **General Splitter**), the result (as received in your email account) should look like Figure 6.26.

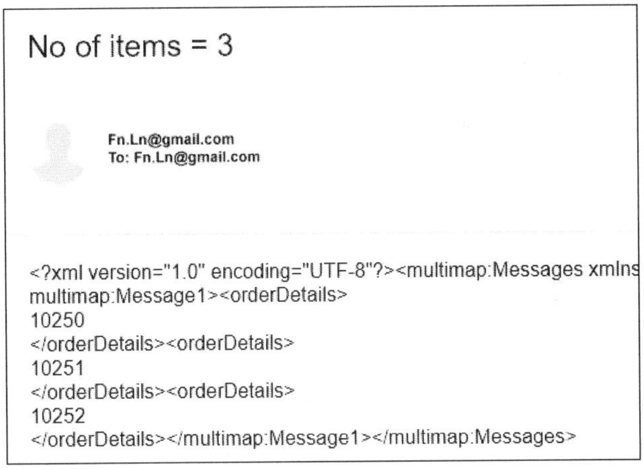

No of items = 3

Fn.Ln@gmail.com
To: Fn.Ln@gmail.com

<?xml version="1.0" encoding="UTF-8"?><multimap:Messages xmlns
multimap:Message1><orderDetails>
10250
</orderDetails><orderDetails>
10251
</orderDetails><orderDetails>
10252
</orderDetails></multimap:Message1></multimap:Messages>

Figure 6.26 Email with Three Split Items and Subject "No of Items = 3"

The email subject is **No of items = 3**, which proves that the message has taken the lower route in Figure 6.20, shown earlier.

That's it! You've now seen how to dynamically configure an integration flow attribute by using data provided by the integration framework by one of the various predefined headers.

You're now well equipped with knowledge to design more sophisticated scenarios. The more creative you are with modeling even more complicated message flows, the higher the risk is that you'll easily lose the overview of the overall integration flow. In the subsequent sections, we show you some options to manage complexity by modularizing your integration logics into smaller chunks by using subprocesses. Thereafter, we introduce the ProcessDirect adapter as an option to implement direct communication between different integration flows (on the same tenant), which also can be a good approach to modularizing a comprehensive integration scenario into smaller pieces.

6.3 Structuring Large Integration Flows Using Local Processes

With SAP Cloud Platform Integration, you can model fairly large integration scenarios. Due to the flexible pipeline of the underlying Apache Camel integration engine, you could potentially add as many processing steps to your route as are necessary to fulfill your integration needs. However, as we're using a graphical modeler, those large models can easily become confusing, and with that, you lose all the benefits of a graphical notation. In this section of the book, which is about modeling and running integration flows on SAP Platform Cloud Integration, you'll learn how to structure large process models using subprocesses.

6.3.1 Taking Hold of Complexity by Modularization

It's never a good idea to put too much logic in one module. This holds true for classical programming languages, such as Java, as well as for graphical environments, such as the Web UI being used in SAP Cloud Platform Integration. In your informatics classes, you've certainly learned how to slice large programs into manageable logical units and treat them separately (*separation of concerns*). The same can be applied to graphically modeled integration flows. To achieve this in SAP Cloud Platform Integration, we need to use subprocesses, or *local processes,* as they are called in SAP Cloud Platform Integration. (The terms subprocess and local process (integration) will be used interchangeably throughout this book.)

As you'll see, it isn't that difficult to work with subprocesses. We encourage you to make use of them, simply to keep your individual processes and subprocesses at a reasonable size. As a rule of thumb, process models shouldn't contain more than 10 to 15 elements. If your models become larger, it's recommended to refactor them and reduce their size by moving parts of your model into newly created subprocesses. To apply this rule, you need to know how subprocesses can be modeled and how parameters are exchanged between parent and child processes. As an example, we'll use the process model shown in Figure 6.27.

Let's see how this process works. We'll take a look at the execution sequence first, before diving into the detailed configuration of each step. The main process, modeled at the top of the diagram, is triggered by an incoming SOAP message. A **Content Modifier** step will set some header and exchange properties, as we've done several times before in this book. The exchange is the central container carrying all necessary data, including the message's payload and header information from step to step inside of the integration flow.

Returning to our model of Figure 6.27, the main process invokes the subprocess entitled **Execute Business Logic**. Within the subprocess, a **Content Modifier** step is used to work with the variables being set in the parent process, simply to highlight the availability of those variables in the child process, although they have been set in the parent process. Additionally, the first **Content Modifier** step in the local process will add a new header variable to the exchange. The goal is to demonstrate how variables created in a child process will also be available in the parent process after the subprocess has finished. To add some more logic, a gateway (the diamond shape in the **Execute Business Logic** subprocess of Figure 6.27) representing a CBR is used to distinguish between different order number ranges (see the respective labels at the two gates).

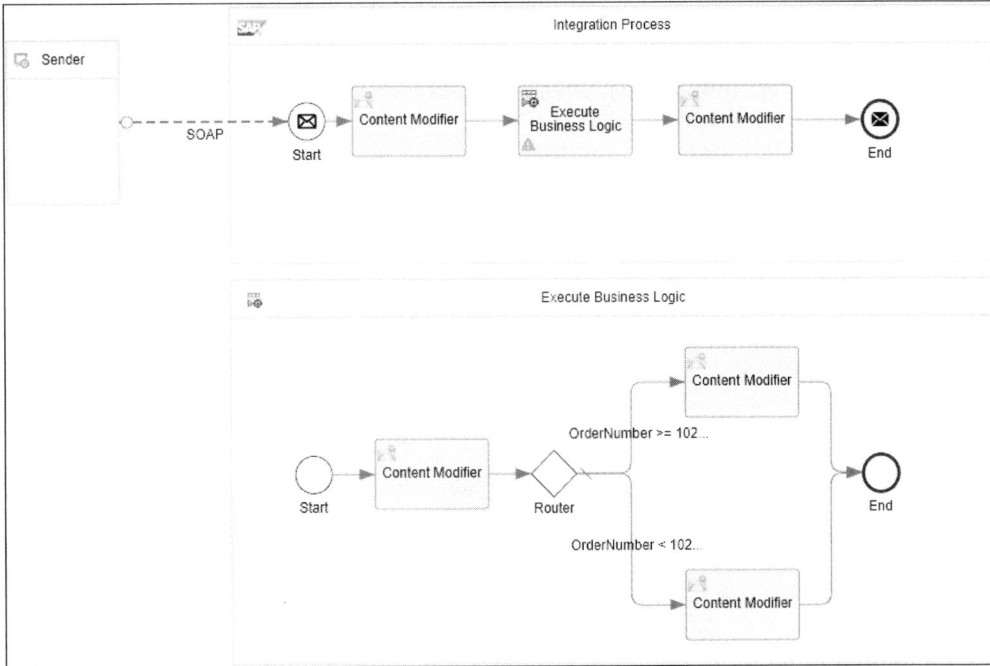

Figure 6.27 Process Model Calling the "Execute Business Logic" Local Process

The two **Content Modifier** steps following the gateway set the content of the reply message. Once executed, the subprocess is finished, and the process execution continues in the main process by calling the last **Content Modifier** step. Here we'll access the variable set in the local process. It verifies its availability although the subprocess has already been finished.

We take the well-known structure we've used in several scenarios before, which is shown again in Figure 6.28 for your convenience, as the input message.

```
<soapenv:Envelope xmlns:soapenv="http://s
   <soapenv:Header/>
   <soapenv:Body>
      <demo:OrderNumber_MT>
         <orderNumber>10249</orderNumber>
      </demo:OrderNumber_MT>
   </soapenv:Body>
</soapenv:Envelope>
```

Figure 6.28 Input Message

We're really focusing on the cooperation between parent and child processes, as well as how the parameter transfer between the two works. Let's see how to configure the individual steps to make the collaboration executable.

6.3.2 Configuring the Collaboration between Parent and Child Processes

We begin with the configuration of the first **Content Modifier** step in the main process. The settings are shown in Figure 6.29 and Figure 6.30.

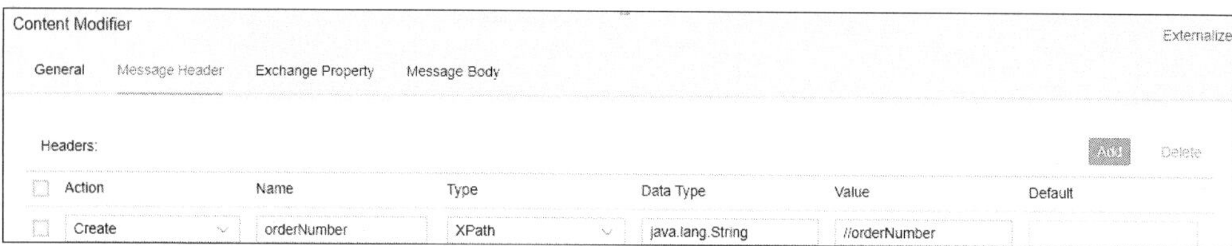

Figure 6.29 Setting a Message Header

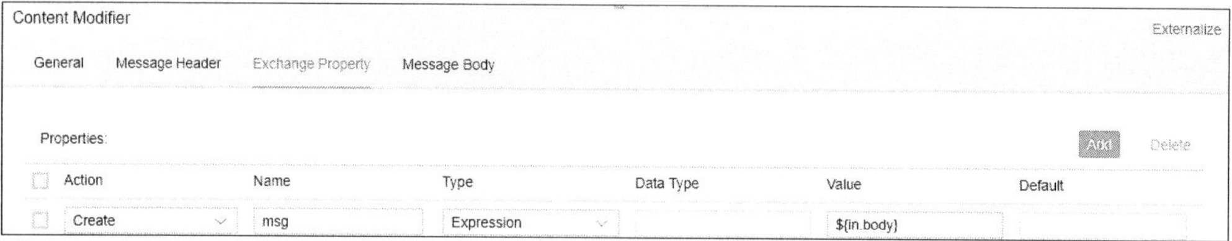

Figure 6.30 Setting an Exchange Property

Two variables are being set here: one with the name **orderNumber** in the **Name** field of the **Message Header** area (Figure 6.29), and the other with the **msg** in the **Name** field of the **Exchange Property** area (Figure 6.30). This should remind you of the very first scenario that we built back in Chapter 4, where we did exactly the same thing. As a result, our exchange will contain the two variables in their respective locations. Now comes the interesting part: the integration flow invokes the subprocess. So, how do you model the subprocess and its invocation? We need to begin with the subprocess first. This is important because the parent process will have to reference the subprocess later. Hence, the subprocess must be in place or such a reference can't be established. Follow these steps:

1. Model the subprocess alongside the main process by picking the **Local Integration Process** entry from the palette, which can be found beneath the **Process** main menu entry (Figure 6.31).

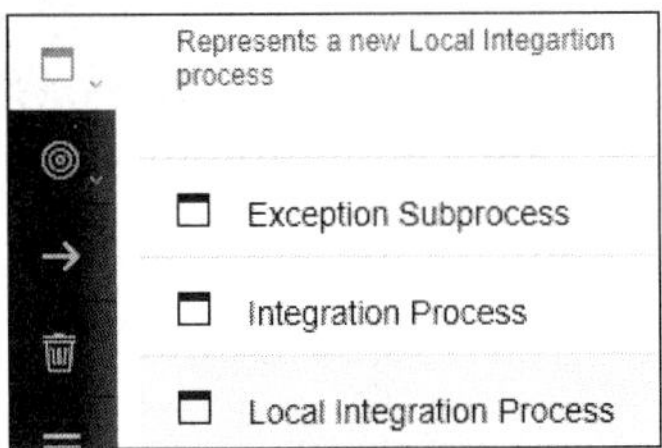

Figure 6.31 Modeling a Local Integration Process

2. After you've positioned the subprocess beneath the main process, you'll get a new pool containing an empty flow (Figure 6.32).

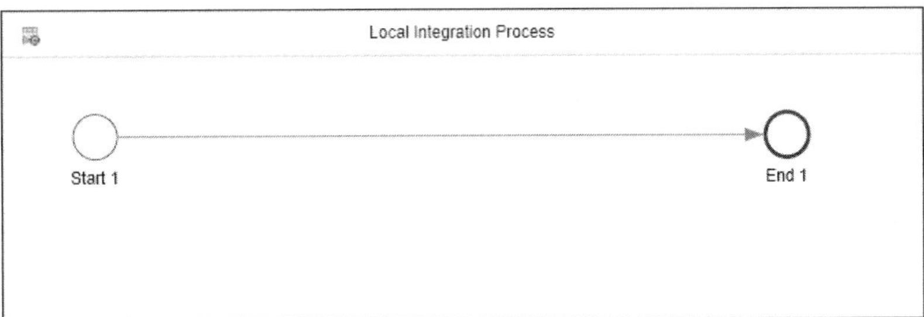

Figure 6.32 Newly Positioned Local Integration Flow

Note the new icon in the upper-left corner of the local process, signifying it as a subprocess, which can't be started by an incoming message or by a **Timer Start** event. It can only be invoked from a parent process by a respective **Process Call** shape, which we'll explain soon. Because of this invocation relationship to a parent process, the subprocess needs to start with an empty **Start** event. The only attribute you can change when selecting the subprocess is its name. You should adjust it and give it a self-explanatory name. Within the subprocess, you can model any integration logic, as you would for the main process.

Limitations of Local Integration Processes

Note that there are some limitations when using local integration processes. You can't use the following integration flow components within a local integration process:

- Aggregator
- Process call
- End message event

Furthermore, using the **Splitter** step in a local integration process also requires some specific considerations because it behaves differently compared to when it's used in the main process. For more information, see the "Cloud Integration – Usage of Splitter Flow Steps in Local Process" blog in the SAP Community (*www.sap.com/community.html*).

Next, we need to model the invocation of the local integration process from the main process—the referencing of the child process from the parent process we were talking about previously. This is done in the following way:

1. In the palette, click the **Call** icon to open the **Call** submenu (Figure 6.33).

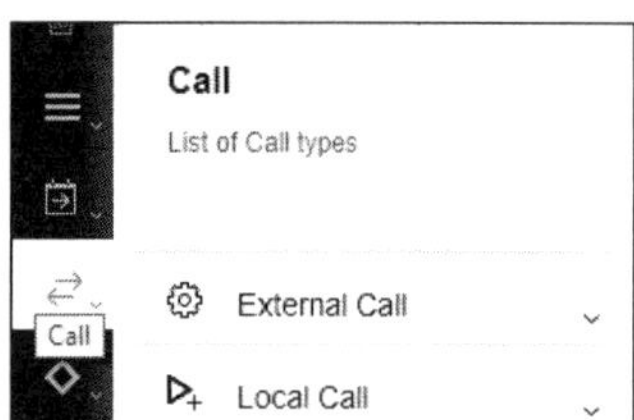

Figure 6.33 The Call Submenu from the Palette

2. Click **Local Call** to open another submenu (Figure 6.34).

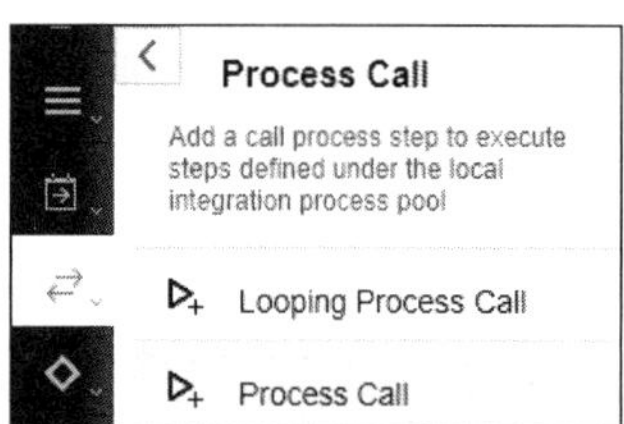

Figure 6.34 The Process Call Shape Located Under Local Call

3. Position the **Process Call** shape shown in Figure 6.34 inside the main process.

The last step is to connect the newly positioned **Process Call** shape with the subprocess itself. This is done by selecting the **Process Call** rounded rectangle in the main process and adjusting the **Local Integration Process** field in the associated properties area beneath the process model in the **Processing** tab. Click on the **Select** button to open another dialog box listing all modeled local integration processes. Pick the one you want to invoke (as we've modeled only one local process, there should only be one entry). The dialog box closes automatically after you've chosen one entry from the list (Figure 6.35).

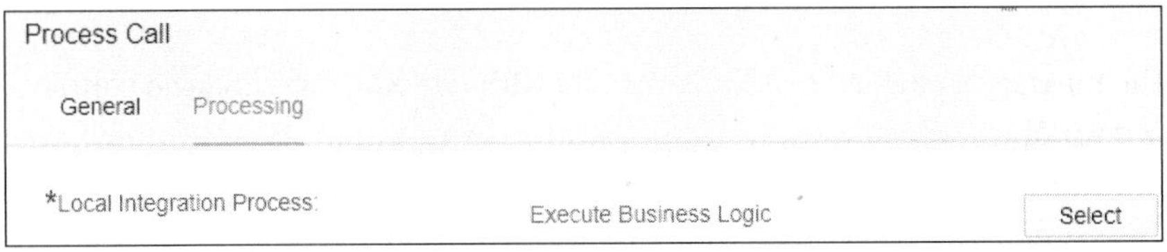

Process Call		
General Processing		
*Local Integration Process:	Execute Business Logic	Select

Figure 6.35 Connecting the Process Call Step with the Subprocess

That's all you need to do to model a subprocess invocation from the main process. However, you may wonder whether there is a need to define an interface for your subprocess that describes which data the subprocess expects from its parent process and which data it will return after it finishes its execution. The answer is that you don't have to define such an interface because the called subprocess also relies on the same exchange the main process is working on, which is automatically handed over from step to step within the main process as well as within the subprocess. This again stresses the importance of the exchange as *the* central data container within integration flows while working with SAP Cloud Platform Integration and its underlying Camel framework.

It should be clear now how data transfer between parent and child processes works. There is no need for local or global variables, as you might typically find in programming languages. The only container carrying variables and their values is the exchange, which is being transferred back and forth between parent and child.

We continue with the configuration of the first **Content Modifier** inside of the local integration flow **Execute Business Logic** (refer to Figure 6.27). Its configuration is shown in Figure 6.36.

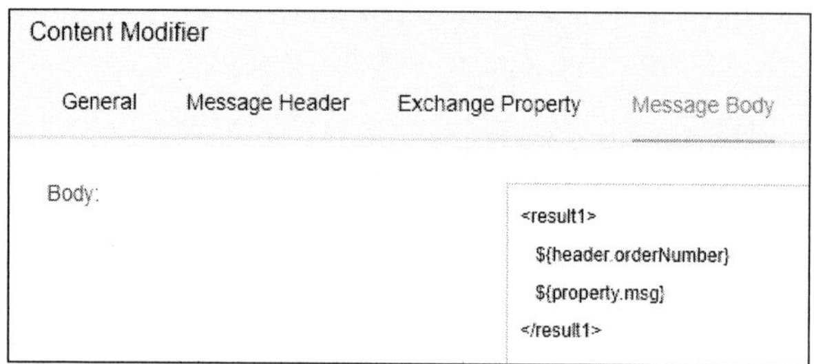

Figure 6.36 Setting the Message's Payload in the Subprocess

We set the message's payload by filling its body with two XML tags and the contents of the two variables, which were set previously in the parent process. By doing this, we demonstrate the availability of data in the child process, which has been set before by the parent process. To display the data transfer in the reverse direction (from child to parent process), we create a new variable named **VarFromSubprocess** within the same **Content Modifier** (Figure 6.37 and Figure 6.38).

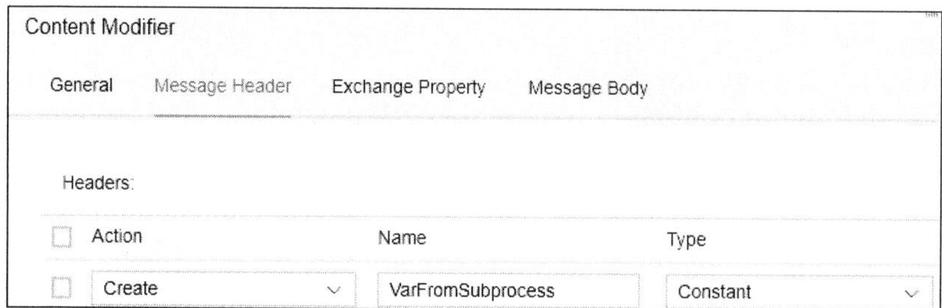

Figure 6.37 Subprocess Setting a Variable in the Message Header Area of the Exchange A

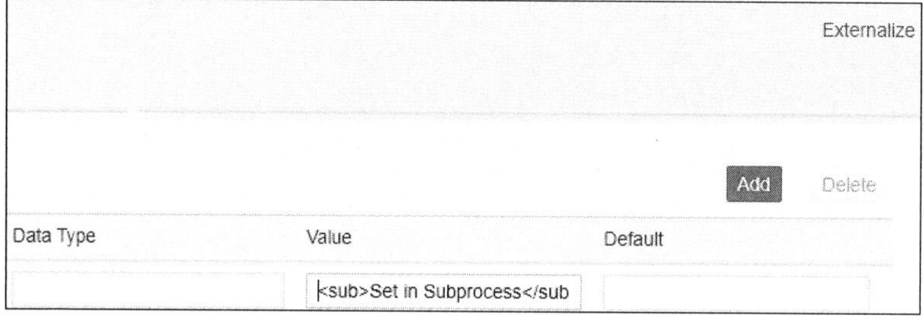

Figure 6.38 Subprocess Setting a Variable in the Message Header Area of the Exchange B

The new variable just contains a `String` constant, which will later be added to the response message by the parent process.

Following the first **Content Modifier** in the subprocess, a CBR, represented by the diamond-shaped **Exclusive Gateway**, takes care of adding more information to the response message. The gateway's configuration is depicted in Figure 6.39.

Router

Error Handling ☐ Raise Alert ☐ Throw Exception

Routing Condition

Order	Route Name	Condition Expression	Default Route
1	OrderNumber < 10250		☑
2	OrderNumber >= 10250	${header.orderNumber} >= '10250'	☐

Figure 6.39 Configuration of the Gateway

Note the **Condition Expression** column in the second row of the **Routing Condition** table: for the decision of which route to follow, the condition again relies on the header variable set by the parent process.

We continue with the two **Content Modifier** steps following the gateway. They just add some static text to the already existing payload. The configuration of the upper **Content Modifier** is shown in Figure 6.40.

Content Modifier

General | Message Header | Exchange Property | Message Body

Body:

```
<result2>
 OrderNumber greater equal 10250
 ${in.body}
</result2>
```

Figure 6.40 Setting the Body's Content Using the Content Modifier

Note the two new surrounding XML tags labeled `result2`. They wrap the current payload referenced by the Camel variable `${in.body}`. In addition, the constant text will later reveal whether the right path was chosen. The lower **Content Modifier** is similarly configured. The text has just been changed to `OrderNumber lower 10250`.

This concludes the explanation of the subprocess. We can continue with the last **Content Modifier** in the main process following the step, which caused the subprocess's invocation. Its settings are straightforward and are shown in Figure 6.41.

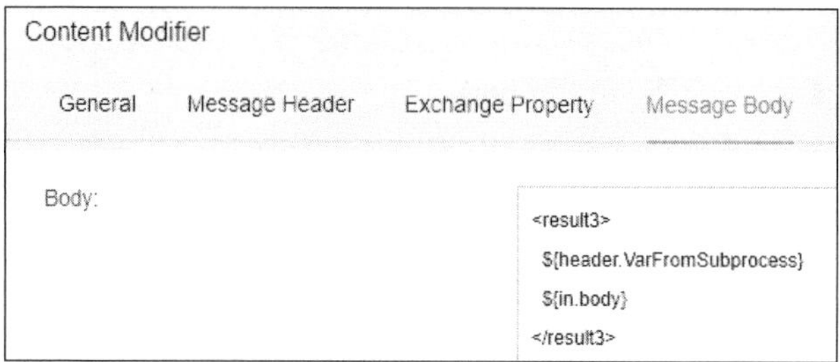

Figure 6.41 Configuration of the Last Content Modifier in the Main Process

What is missing now is proof that the variables being set in the subprocess can be accessed by the parent process. That's why you find the expression `${header.VarFromSubprocess}` inside the **Message Body**'s definition. It accesses the variable, which we set before in the called local integration process (refer to Figure 6.37). Note also the new XML tags labeled with `result3`, which again wrap the current payload plus the contents of the variable `VarFromSubprocess`. If everything works correctly, we should see three nested tags labeled `result3`, `result2`, and `result1`, respectively. So, let's see that integration flow in action. After invoking our demo process, you'll see the reply depicted in Figure 6.42.

```
<soap:Envelope xmlns:soap="http://schemas.xmlsoap.org/soap/envelope/">
   <soap:Header/>
   <soap:Body>
      <result3>

         <sub>Set in Subprocess</sub>

         <result2>
              OrderNumber greater equal 10250

            <result1>
                 10250

               <demo:OrderNumber_MT xmlns:demo="http://cpi.sap.com/demo" xmlns:soap
                  <orderNumber>10250</orderNumber>
               </demo:OrderNumber_MT>
            </result1>
         </result2>
      </result3>
   </soap:Body>
</soap:Envelope>
```

Figure 6.42 Response Message Produced by the Integration Flow

Everything worked as expected. The `result` tags are nested, and depending on the entered order number, you'll get the respective text message whether the number was lower than 10250.

To summarize, real-life integration scenarios can grow quite large. That's why a means to structure large process models is urgently required. SAP Cloud Platform Integration supports structuring large process models by using local integration processes to keep each individual process model at a reasonable size. The parameter transfer between parent and child processes is solved by the exchange, the standard container for managing data within an integration flow. As we've seen in the previous exercise, the exchange isn't only handed over from step to step, on one process level. It's also the vehicle for moving data around from parent to child processes and vice versa. This makes the definition of global or local variables superfluous. You're now able to model, run, and monitor really complex scenarios. If you follow the recommendations given in this section, you'll also ensure manageable process sizes, making it fun to work with.

6.3.3 Using Exception Subprocesses

The exception is a special kind of subprocess you can use to handle error situations that occur during message processing. We use a very simple integration flow that contains nothing more than a **SOAP Sender** and a **Mail Receiver** adapter as shown in Figure 6.43 (similar to the first integration flow shown in Chapter 2).

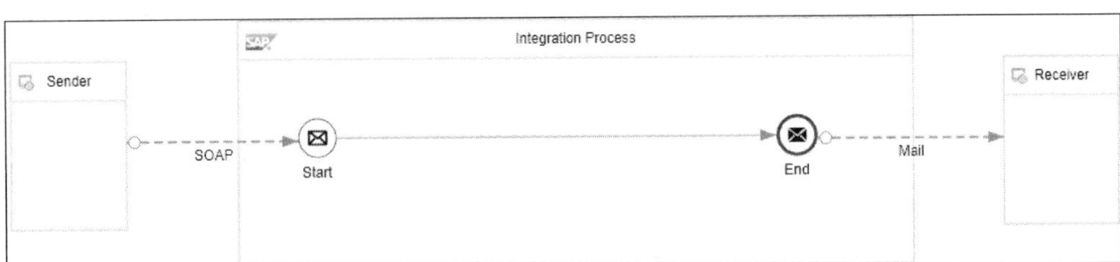

Figure 6.43 Simple Integration Flow with SOAP Sender and Mail Receiver

For the configuration of the mail adapter, we assume that a **User Credentials** artifact has been deployed that contains the credentials to access the email account. Follow these steps to modify the integration flow:

1. Add an exception subprocess to the integration flow by selecting **Exception Subprocess** under the **Process** root node (Figure 6.44).

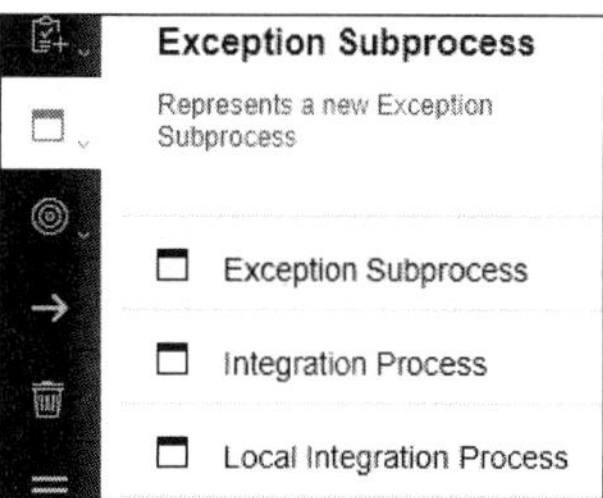

Figure 6.44 Selecting an Exception Subprocess in the Palette

2. You can only place the **Exception Subprocess** in the **Integration Process** shape, which results in the change shown in Figure 6.45.

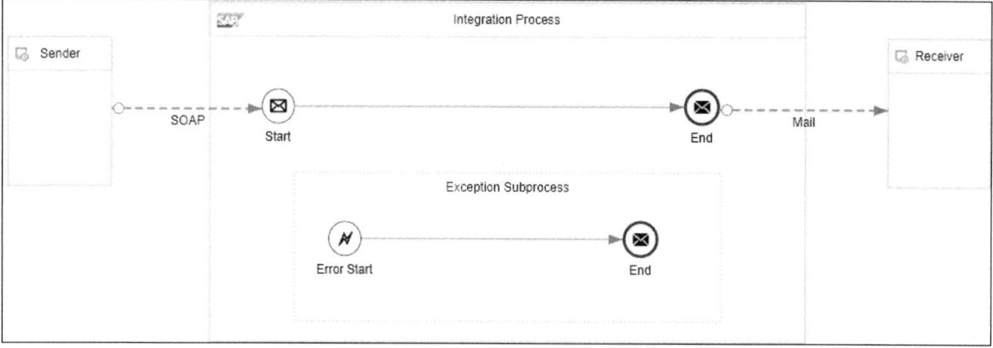

Figure 6.45 Exception Subprocess Placed within the Integration Process Shape

3. Add a **Content Modifier** to the **Exception Subprocess** between the **Error Start** and **End** events.
4. In this step, we define how to handle error situations. To do that, in the **Message Body** tab, specify the setting shown in Figure 6.46.

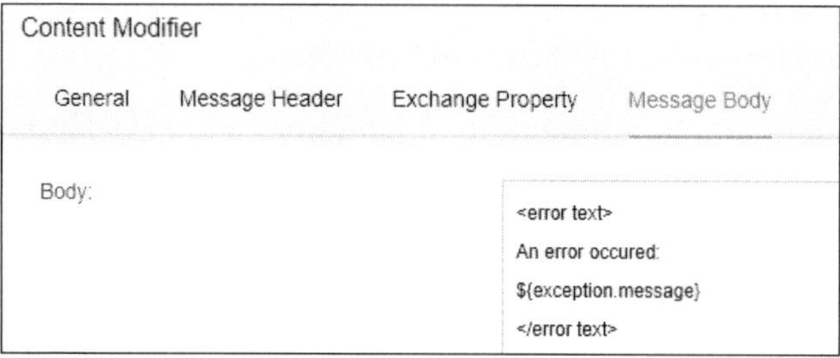

Figure 6.46 Error Message Configured in the Content Modifier in the Exception Subprocess

The expression `exception.message` is a variable provided within Camel's Simple Expression Language that allows you to access information on error situations stored in the exchange (see *http://camel.apache.org/simple.html*).

5. Connect the message **End** event of the **Exception Subprocess** with a second **Receiver**, and select the **Mail** adapter as the connectivity option. You can use the same **Mail** adapter settings as for the first receiver connected to the main **Integration Process** (Figure 6.47).

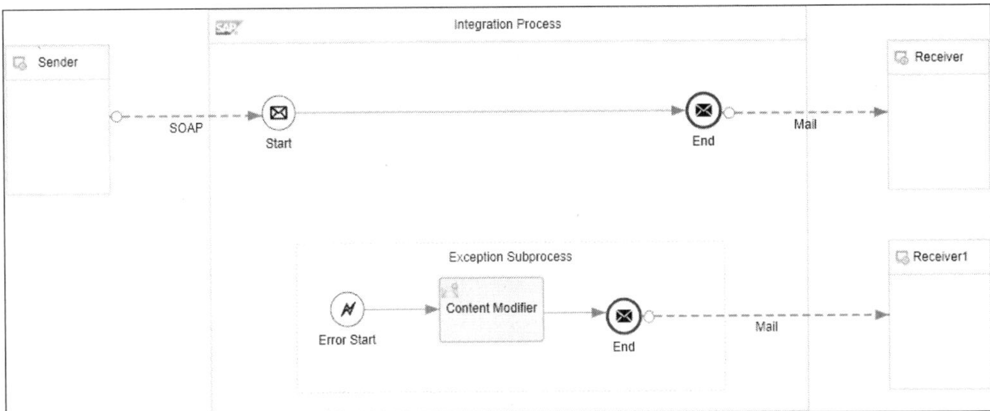

Figure 6.47 Final Integration Flow

Make sure, however, to refer to another **User Credentials** artifact for the **Mail** lower connection in Figure 6.47. The idea is to enforce an exception by editing the **User Credentials** artifact (referenced in the upper **Mail** connection between the **End** message event of the main process and the upper **Receiver**), and enter a wrong password there. Therefore, to make sure the error details are received in your mail account, in the lower **Mail** adapter (connecting the **End** message event of the **Exception Subprocess** with the email server), use another **User Credentials** artifact with the correct credentials. Note that for simplicity, we'll use one and the same email account for the different email receivers like we did in the integration flows before.

To summarize:

- The **Mail** adapter connected to the upper receiver (**Receiver**) refers to a **User Credentials** artifact with wrong credentials.
- The **Mail** adapter connected to the lower receiver (**Receiver1**) refers to a **User Credentials** artifact with correct credentials.

Running the integration flow should result in an error message received in your mail account, as shown in Figure 6.48.

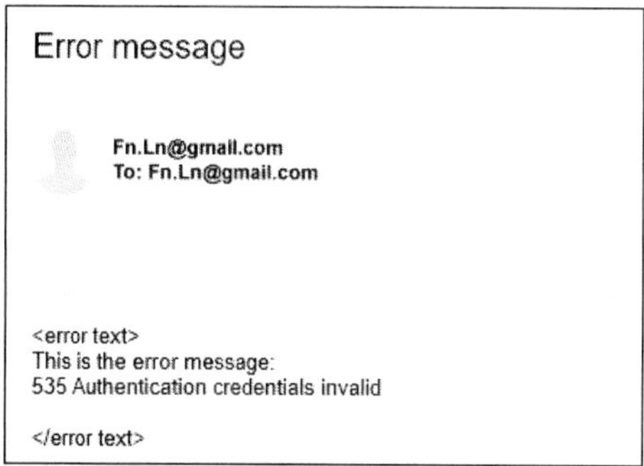

Error message
Fn.Ln@gmail.com
To: Fn.Ln@gmail.com
<error text>
This is the error message:
535 Authentication credentials invalid
</error text>

Figure 6.48 Email Containing the Error Message Configured in the Content Modifier of the Exception Subprocess

There's another use case where an exception subprocess comes into play. In Chapter 5, Section 5.4.3, we showed you how to use an exception subprocess for the explicit retry configuration in a scenario with the JMS adapter.

You've now learned how you can modularize integration scenarios by using subprocesses and how to handle error situations by using the exception subprocess.

Next, we'll show you another option for modularizing integration content: the ProcessDirect adapter.

6.4 Connecting Integration Flows Using the ProcessDirect Adapter

In Section 6.3, we showed how you can use subprocesses to modularize larger integration flows. This capability supports you in situations where you need to manage bigger integration projects with comprehensive integration scenarios and distributed responsibilities.

Another option to overcome such complex situations is obvious: designing different parts of the integration logics of a complex scenario in individual, "smaller" integration flows and connecting them with each other. SAP Cloud Platform Integration comes with a variety of different adapters, so you might already have had the idea to use certain adapters to connect different integration flows with each other to build a larger scenario. Obviously, the HTTP-based adapters might be the option of choice. So why not put parts of the integration logics into n different integration flows and connect them with each other; for example, integration flow 1 calls integration flow 2, integration flow 2 calls another one, and so forth. But wait—you also know that each such HTTP connection (which is, to mention one example path, an outbound connection from the perspective of integration flow 1 and an inbound connection from the perspective of integration flow 2) is routed through the load balancer. Check out Chapter 2, Section 2.1, to remind you of that (in particular, see Figure 2.3). This means that another component is involved in each such communication, and this brings about a higher network load so that you can expect the performance of your integration scenario in total to suffer from these extra intra integration flow connections—even if you connect integration flows deployed on the same tenant.

To overcome this issue, the SAP Cloud Platform Integration team has developed a dedicated adapter, the *ProcessDirect* adapter, which allows you to directly connect two integration flows without the load balancer being interconnected. Figure 6.49 illustrates a sending (at left) **Integration Flow** and a receiving (at right) **Integration Flow** that are both connected over the **ProcessDirect** adapter.

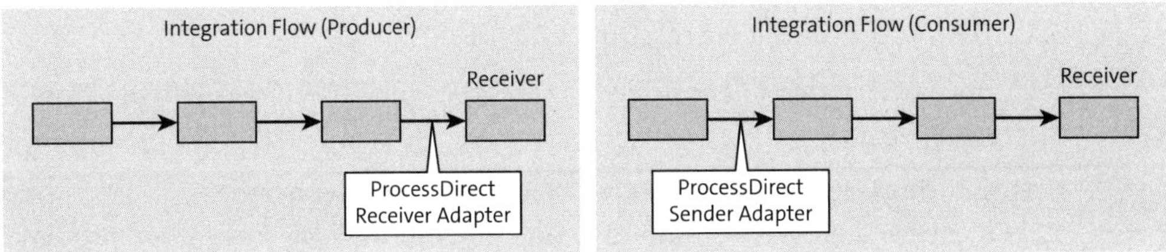

Figure 6.49 Producer and Consumer Integration Flow Communication over ProcessDirect Adapters

To simplify the following discussion, when we're talking about two integration flows connected over the ProcessDirect adapter, we distinguish between a *producer integration flow* and a *consumer integration flow* in the following sense:

- The producer integration flow sends the message to another integration flow over the **ProcessDirect** adapter.

  In the producer integration flow, you need to configure a **ProcessDirect** receiver adapter (to send the message to the target integration flow).

- The consumer integration flow receives a message from another integration flow over the **ProcessDirect** adapter.

  In the consumer integration flow, you need to configure a **ProcessDirect** sender adapter (to receive the message from the producer integration flow).

Limitations

Note the following limitations for the usage of the **ProcessDirect** adapter:

- Producer and consumer integration flows must be deployed on the same tenant.
- The cardinality of producers to consumers is restricted so that you can send messages from N producers to 1 consumer but not vice versa (cardinality rule reads `producer:consumer = N:1`).

However, you can use **ProcessDirect** adapters to connect integration flows from different integration packages (as long as they reside on the same tenant).

The **ProcessDirect** adapter is quite simple; it has exactly one attribute, which is the **Address** of the integration flow to connect to (defining the endpoint). We'll discuss how to use this adapter in just a minute, but let's briefly summarize the use cases for this adapter first.

6.4.1 Use Cases for the ProcessDirect Adapter

Following is an overview of possible use cases that you can address with the ProcessDirect adapter:

- **Structuring large integration flows and separation of concerns**
  As mentioned previously, similar to how you can use local integration processes to structure larger integration flows (refer to Section 6.3), you can use separate ("smaller") integration flows and connect them through ProcessDirect adapters. Note that using separate integration flows (also, if required, within different integration packages), enables you to clearly manage different responsibilities within an integration project (separation of concerns) in the following way: different integration developers can work independently on that part of the integration logic they are responsible for by decomposing the overall scenario into several "smaller" integration flows with different owners.
- **Reuse integration logic**
  You can "source out" generic functions and parts of the integration logic that are used at many places into dedicated integration flows. Such (consumer) integration flows can be called from multiple (producer) integration flows independently. As an example of such generic integration logics, think about error-handling strategies. If you need to do changes to the generic part, this doesn't impact the producer integration flows, as long as you don't change the address of the consumer.

In the example of error-handling strategies, N producers can send messages to 1 consumer that contains the error-handling logic.

- **Dynamic endpoint configuration**
  As we'll show later, you can dynamically configure the **Address** of the **ProcessDirect** adapter. This leaves room to define sophisticated integration scenarios where it can be dynamically "decided" during runtime which consumer integration flow is called by the producer.
- **Creating multiple message processing logs (MPLs)**
  As the overall integration scenario is split into several independent integration flows, during the operations of the scenario, MPLs are generated. This might also make it easier to analyze errors and to also distribute the operations tasks among different people.

6.4.2 A Simple Example

We first show how to use the ProcessDirect adapter by modifying the integration scenario that we've used in Section 6.3 to illustrate the usage of local integration processes. We change the design in a way that the overall integration logic is split into two individual integration flows.

Figure 6.50 shows the producer integration flow:

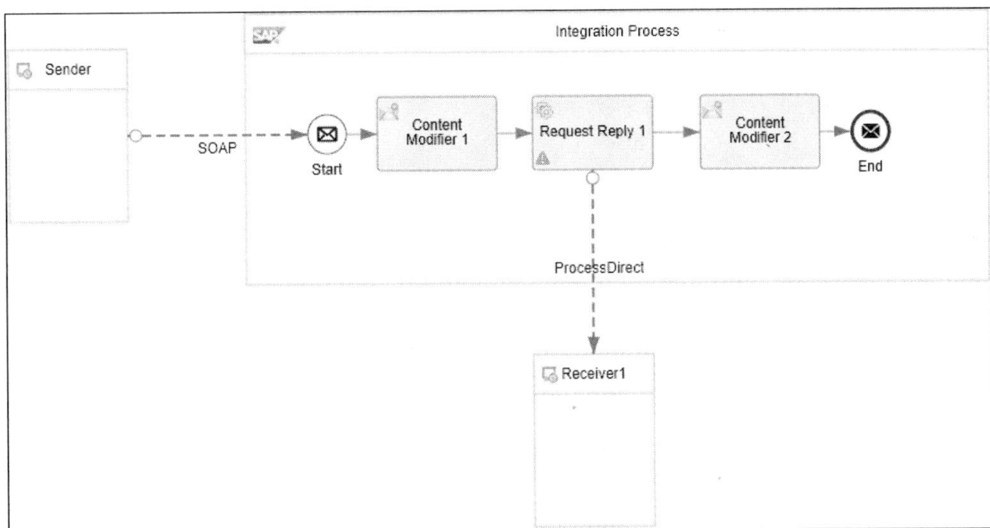

Figure 6.50 Producer Integration Flow

To configure the two **Content Modifier** steps, use the exact settings shown in Section 6.3. However, add a receiver (**Receiver1**) and replace the **Process Call** with a **Request-Reply** step that calls **Receiver1** through the **ProcessDirect** adapter. Due to the **Request-Reply** step, the message that is produced by the second (consumer) integration flow is sent back as a response.

As **Address** in the **ProcessDirect** adapter, use **/pd2router** (Figure 6.51).

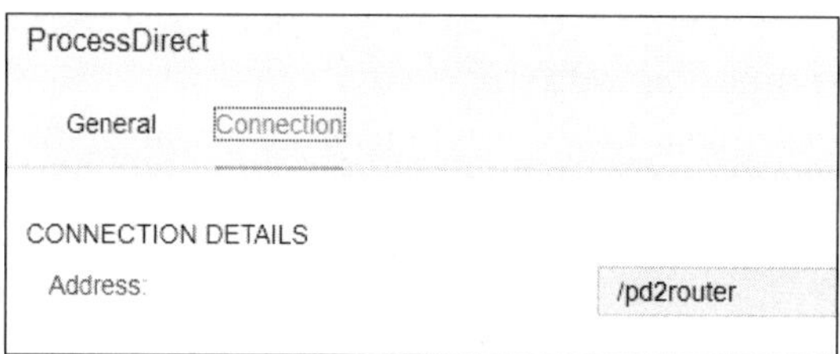

Figure 6.51 Address Configured in the ProcessDirect Adapter of the Producer Integration Flow

The consumer integration flow contains the integration logic that was sourced out into the local integration process in the previous section (Figure 6.52).

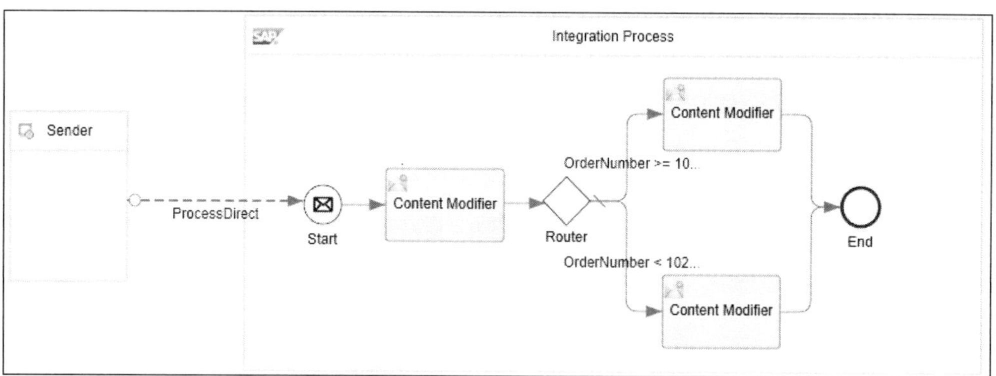

Figure 6.52 Consumer Integration Flow

Compared to the local integration process discussed in Section 6.3, replace the **Start** event with a **Start Message** event, and add a **Sender** pool that connects to the **Start Message** event through the **ProcessDirect** adapter. In the **ProcessDirect** adapter, enter the same address as in the producer integration flow. Deploy both integration flows, and run the scenario by invoking the producer integration flow with SoapUI.

The result should be the same as in Section 6.3 (with the local integration process) with one exception: in the **Monitoring** application of the Web UI, you'll notice that the two integration flows have been processed individually and that, consequently, two MPLs have been generated.

6.4.3 Dynamic Endpoint Configuration with the ProcessDirect Adapter

We'll wrap up the discussion of the ProcessDirect adapter capabilities with a simple example where we combine this feature with dynamic configuration (as explained in Section 6.2).

To keep it simple, we slightly modified the scenario explained in Section 6.2. As you remember, in this scenario, an external OData resource is accessed by SAP Cloud Platform Integration. Depending on an order number provided with the initial SOAP request, we get different orders related to different values for the `ShipCountry` field. The integration flow further sends out an email with the details of the order. We showed in Section 6.2 that we can dynamically configure the **Subject** attribute of the **Mail** adapter so that, depending on the value of the `ShipCountry` field, another email subject was written into the outbound email (**France** or **Brazil**, depending on whether it was a French or a Brazilian order).

Now we want to modify this scenario slightly: we'll use the same inbound processing (defined in a producer integration flow), but we'll define the outbound processing (defined in consumer integration flows) depending on the shipment country of the looked-up order.

Accordingly, we split this integration scenario in the following way:

- The producer integration flow contains the part of the original integration flow from Section 6.2 (refer to Figure 6.11) that receives the SOAP request, modifies the inbound message, sends a request to the OData source, and then creates the `Country` header (which contains the value of the `ShipCountry` field of the order).

  We dynamically configure the **Address** field of the **ProcessDirect** adapter. In the producer integration flow, we use the expression `${header.Country}` to specify the **Address**, which means that it will depend on the value of the header `Country` of the message as to which consumer integration flow will be called.

- We then create two consumer integration flows (each one for a different country) that do nothing but send the incoming message to the email account with different mail subjects. We define the **ProcessDirect** adapter **Address** field in the consumer integration flow by entering the name of a country. For the consumer integration flow that handles French orders, we enter "France", and for the consumer integration flow that handles Brazilian orders, we enter "Brazil". Consequently, when the header **Country** (in the message coming from the producer integration flow) has the value **France**, the "French" consumer integration flow is called, and when this header has the value **Brazil**, the "Brazilian" consumer integration flow is called.

We could, of course, define different consumer integration flows for all existing countries. To keep it simple, we define only two different consumers and will show how to handle all other countries (besides France and Brazil) at the end of the section.

We don't go any further into the details here, but you can easily imagine extending such an integration scenario by defining completely different further processing steps, depending on the shipment country. To keep it simple, we only configure different email subjects depending on the country.

Let's get started.

First, define the producer integration flow shown in Figure 6.53, and use the same settings for the **Content Modifiers** and the **OData** adapter as shown in Section 6.2 (refer to Figure 6.12).

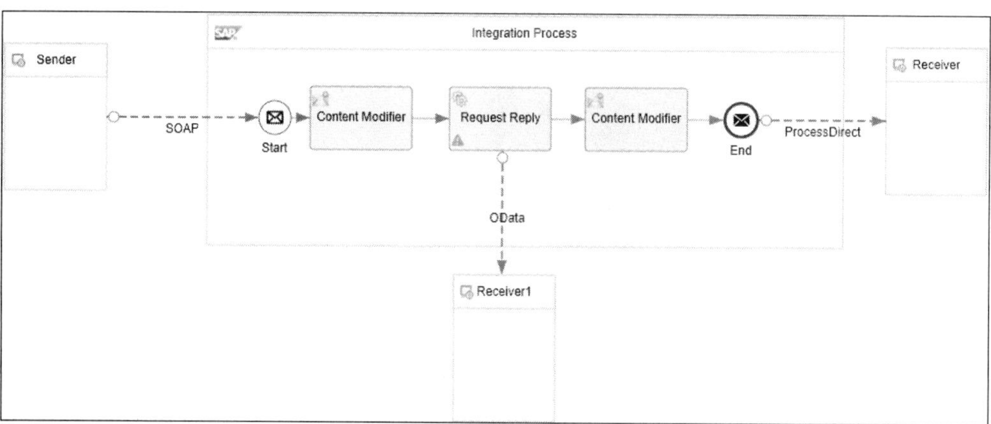

Figure 6.53 Producer Integration Flow

For the **ProcessDirect** adapter, specify the following **Address** attribute: "${header.Country}" (Figure 6.54).

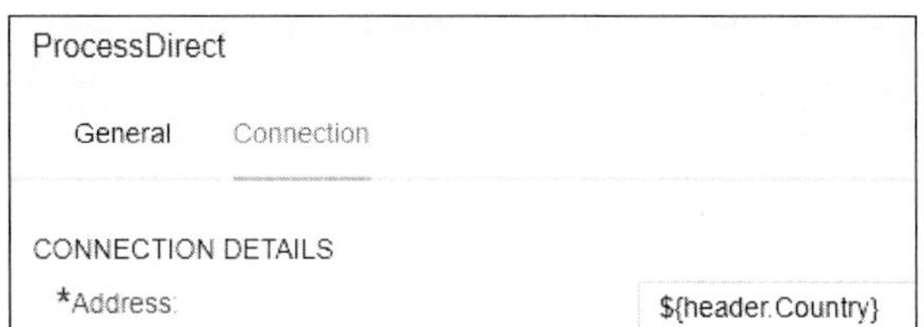

Figure 6.54 Dynamically Configured Address in the ProcessDirect Adapter of the Producer Integration Flow

Now design the consumer integration flow (e.g., to handle French orders) shown in Figure 6.55.

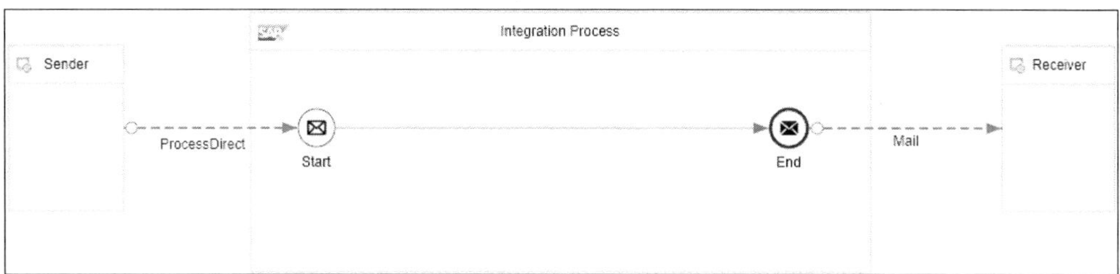

Figure 6.55 Consumer Integration Flow

In the **ProcessDirect** adapter, specify **France** as the **Address** (Figure 6.56).

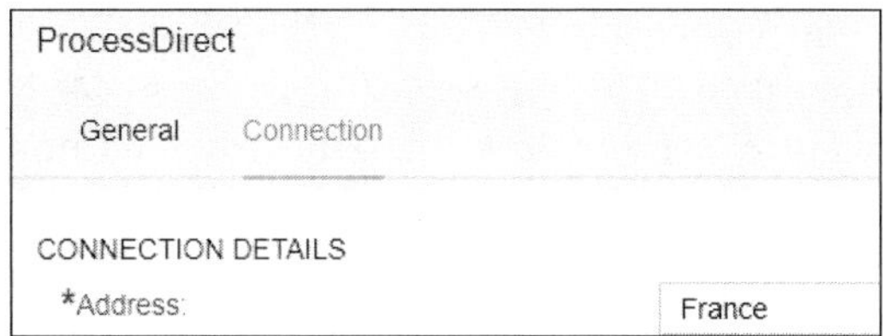

Figure 6.56 ProcessDirect Adapter for the "French" Consumer Integration Flow

In the **mail** adapter, enter the settings you've used already in the previous scenarios, except for the **Subject** attribute. For the **Subject**, enter "Bonjour!".

Design a second consumer integration flow with the following different settings:

- In the **ProcessDirect** adapter, specify the **Address** as **Brazil**.
- For the **Subject** for the **Mail** adapter, enter "Boa tarde!".

Deploy all integration flows and, first, run the producer integration flow by providing orderNumber 10250 with the SOAP request. You get an email in your inbox that looks like in Figure 6.57.

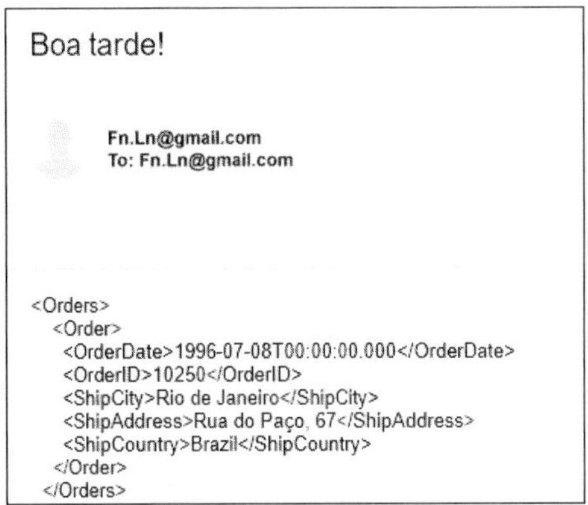
Boa tarde!
Fn.Ln@gmail.com
To: Fn.Ln@gmail.com
<Orders>
<Order>
<OrderDate>1996-07-08T00:00:00.000</OrderDate>
<OrderID>10250</OrderID>
<ShipCity>Rio de Janeiro</ShipCity>
<ShipAddress>Rua do Paço, 67</ShipAddress>
<ShipCountry>Brazil</ShipCountry>
</Order>
</Orders>

Figure 6.57 Received Email for an Order with Shipment Country Brazil

As expected, you get the details of a Brazilian order and the email subject is **Boa tarde!**. If you run the scenario with `orderNumber` `10251`, you get an email with a French order and subject **Bonjour!**.

The differently configured **Mail** adapter **Subject** attribute should illustrate in a simple way that in the different consumer integration flows, you can define whatever outbound processing for your message that you like. Depending on the country, you might have additional processing steps to apply to the message, or you might want to enrich the outbound message with country-specific data. We skip such additional steps here for the sake of simplicity.

In addition, as mentioned, we've only designed consumer flows for two example countries; therefore, if you provide the SOAP request an `orderNumber` that doesn't match either of the two countries, the integration flow will run into an error. In a real-world situation, you need to invest in a strategy for how to handle such situations. One option to solve this could be that in the producer integration flow, you define a routing step after the second content modifier that makes sure another receiver is addressed for all orders with shipment countries other than France or Brazil. For example, you can enhance the producer integration as shown in Figure 6.58.

In this integration flow, you only have added a **Router** step and a second email receiver. The upper path contains the default route.

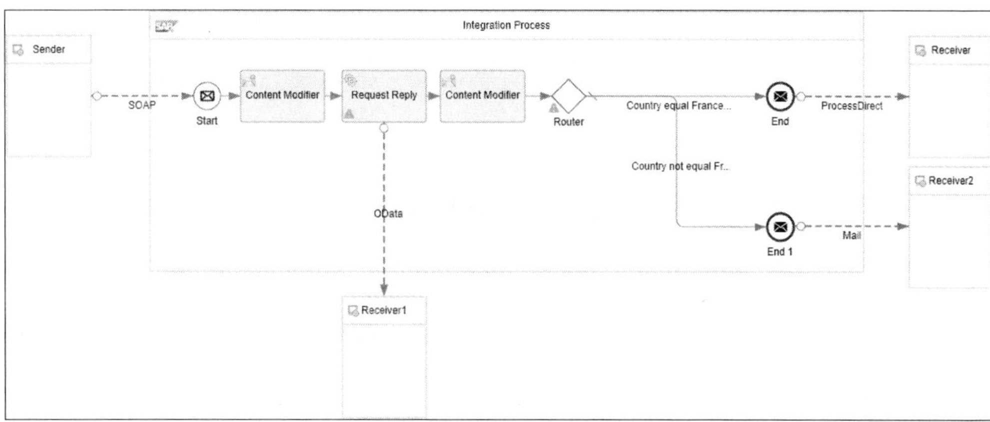

Figure 6.58 Producer Integration Flow Handles All Other Countries by Routing the Message to a Second Receiver

For the lower path, in the **Condition** field, you can enter the following (see Figure 6.59): "${header.Country} != 'France' and ${header.Country} != 'Brazil'".

Route

Conditions defined for this route

Name:	Country not equal France or Brazil
Expression Type:	Non-XML
Condition:	${header.Country} != 'France' and ${header.Country} != 'Brazil'

☐ Default Route

Figure 6.59 Lower Route Forwarding All Messages Related to Shipment Countries Other Than France or Brazil to Another Receiver

The email receiver configured through the lower **Mail** adapter (connecting to **Receiver2**) will then receive all messages related to orders associated with any other country besides France or Brazil.

When you now run the scenario by providing **orderNumber** 10252 (which is associated with a Belgian order), you'll receive an email in the email account configured in the lower **Mail** adapter (**Receiver2**).

If you provide `orderNumber 10251`, you'll (like above) receive an email with subject **Bonjour!** and the French order in the email account configured in the upper **Mail** adapter (**Receiver**).

6.5 Versioning and Migration of Integration Flows

SAP Cloud Platform Integration is an on-demand software product, for which SAP provides monthly updates. SAP Cloud Platform Integration customers work and run their scenarios on a platform that is enhanced constantly, which makes it a critical requirement that the software lifecycle doesn't impact any productive scenarios. SAP also needs to ensure that integration developers can seamlessly enhance integration content and use new features while minimizing change efforts with regards to existing integration flows.

SAP Cloud Platform Integration offers also a hybrid SAP Cloud Platform Integration content approach in which integration content designed with the Web UI can also be used on the on-premise integration bus of SAP Process Orchestration (assuming that you have a license for that product). This makes high demands on the versioning concept behind the SAP Cloud Platform Integration software. In this section, we provide an overview of the versioning concept and the integration content migration capabilities, including how to migrate integration flow components to a higher version. Finally, we show how to "downgrade" integration flow components, which is required when using integration content on the SAP Process Orchestration integration bus.

6.5.1 Integration Flow Component Versions

With a monthly release of the SAP Cloud Platform Integration tools, integration flow components updated with new features (e.g., new adapter or flow step attributes) are released as components with a new version (also referred to as *component version*). (*Component*, refers in the following either to an adapter or an integration flow step.)

To find out more, open an integration flow. To check out the version of a SOAP adapter (as one example for an integration flow component), click on the **SOAP** channel in the model, and then click on the **Information** icon (Figure 6.60).

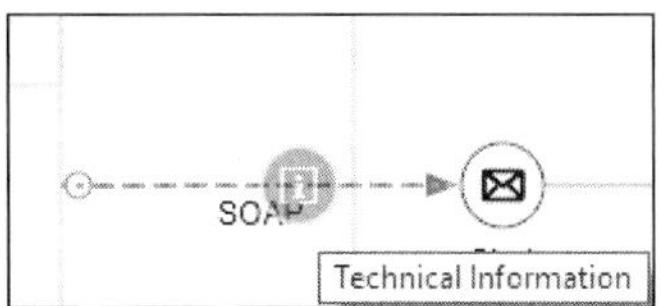

Figure 6.60 Selecting the Information Button for an Adapter

The **Technical Information** screen in this case indicates that the component version is 1.6 (Figure 6.61).

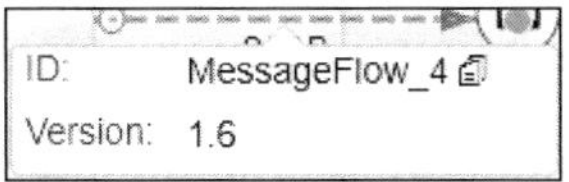

Figure 6.61 Technical Information for an Adapter

The general nomenclature of a component version is **<major version>.<minor version>**, where the parts of the version indicator have the following meaning:

- **Major version**
  The major version is usually not changed to ensure backward compatibility of the component.
- **Minor version**
  The minor version is incremented when new features have been added to the component (e.g., when a new adapter attribute has been added).

Playing in the background and not indicated for the user is a third, additional version counter for the micro version, which is related to smaller improvements such as changes of UI labels. We won't elaborate further on this concept.

To summarize, Figure 6.62 shows how SAP Cloud Platform Integration software versions are related to component versions when the software is being updated.

Figure 6.62 illustrates the situation for the monthly software release in April 2018 (to mention an example). Components A, B, and C stand for three different integration flow components that belong to the SAP Cloud Platform Integration design tooling. Imagine that A, B, and C can represent adapter or integration flow step types. In a real-life picture, we would need to sketch many more components. We only show three of them (each one with just a few features) for simplicity.

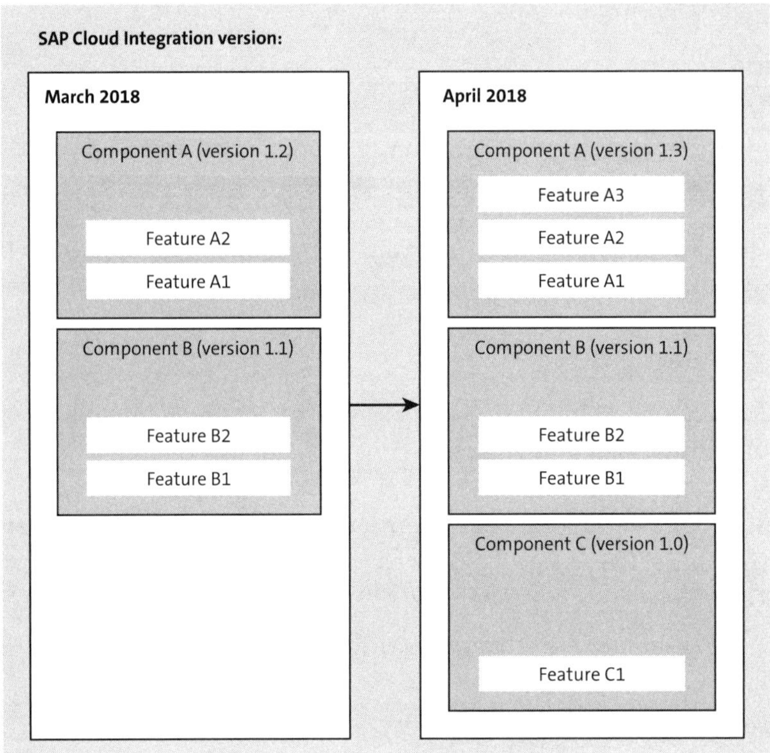

Figure 6.62 How Software Versions and Component Versions Are Related to Each Other

In the shown example, the software version from March 2018 already contains the two components A and B. With software updates to the April 2018 version, component A is enhanced by a new feature (A3), and, accordingly, the component version for A is changed from 1.2 to 1.3. Component B isn't changed during this update, so the feature scope remains the same. Consequently, the component version for B isn't changed, so it stays on 1.1. However, component C is added as a new component during this update. For C, you can imagine that SAP has added, for example, a new adapter type with a software update in April 2018. The new component gets the initial component version 1.0.

You'll understand the implications and importance of this versioning concept as soon as we introduce the concept of migrating an integration flow component. We first explain how *upgrading* an integration flow component works, which means migrating a component to a newer version.

6.5.2 Upgrading an Integration Flow Component

Consider the situation that you've created, deployed, and put into operation an integration flow at a certain point in time, for example, shortly before you left for a longer break or vacation. However, the SAP Cloud Platform Integration development team never rests and provides a software update every month. When you come back from vacation a few weeks later, a new feature for a component used in your integration flow is available. It goes without saying that your concrete integration flow that you deployed weeks ago doesn't reflect this new feature yet. However, reading the release notes of SAP Cloud Platform Integration, you become aware of the new feature and want to update your specific integration flow to also support the new feature in this certain component.

The best option is to migrate the integration flow component. This enables you to update your integration flow component to support the newest features made available by SAP without the need to re-create the component from scratch.

Save the Integration Flow as a Version First

After you've migrated a component to a new version, you can't undo this action to revert back to the old version. Therefore, it's recommended that before migrating a component, you save your integration flow as a version. When you've opened an integration flow, the **Save as version** option can be found next to the **Save** option on top of the integration flow model (see Chapter 3, Figure 3.13). Using this option, you create a copy of the integration flow, and you can move back to the older version of your integration flow if the migration results in any issues.

To migrate a component, for example, an **Integration Process** component, proceed as follows:

1. Open the integration flow, and click **Edit**.
2. Click on the component you want to migrate (in this case, on the **Integration Process** shape).
3. To check the current version of the component, click on the **Information** icon. The information screen shows that the version is 1.0 (Figure 6.63).

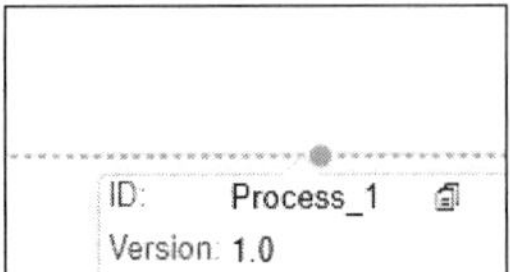

Figure 6.63 Version of the Selected Integration Process Prior to Migration

4. Click **Migrate** (Figure 6.64).

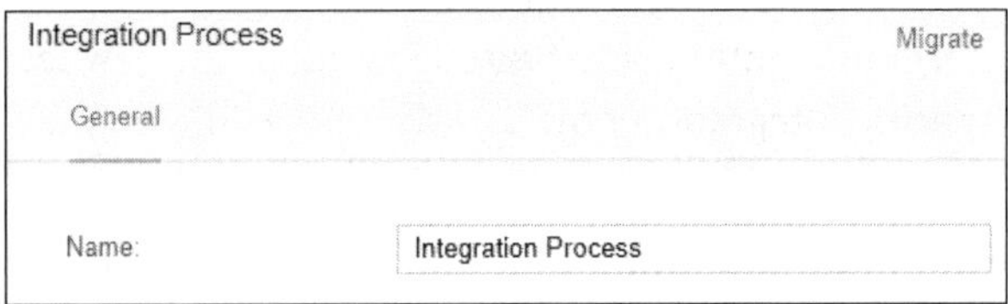

Figure 6.64 Migrating an Integration Process

   At the time this book went to press, only a few integration flow components could be migrated (see the information box later in this section).

5. When you've clicked **Migrate**, a confirmation dialog shows the source and target version (Figure 6.65).

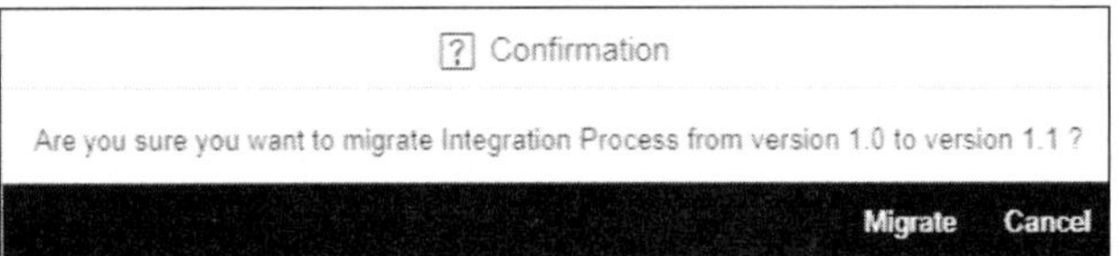

Figure 6.65 Confirmation Message

6. Choose **Migrate** to confirm your selection. The component will be migrated to the latest available version.
7. To check this, again click the **Information** icon to display the technical information. It will now show the new version 1.1 (Figure 6.66).

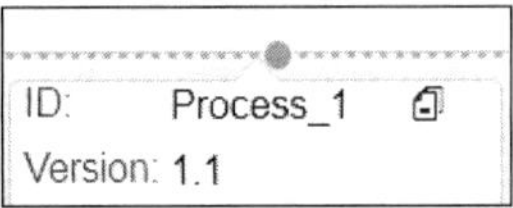

Figure 6.66 Version of Selected Component Increased to 1.1 after Migration

8. After migration, the new features can be consumed.

Component version 1.1 of the **Integration Process** element has a new feature called **Transaction Management**, as shown in Figure 6.67 (compare with Figure 6.64, which shows the **Integration Process** component prior to migration). For more information about this feature, see Chapter 5, Section 5.4.2.

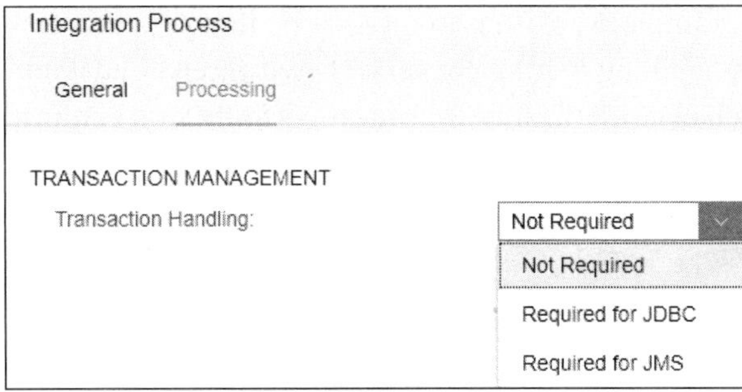

Figure 6.67 New Feature Transaction Management in Upgraded Process

9. Save the integration flow.

If there are incompatibilities with versions of other components within the integration flow, these are indicated in the integration flow model as errors (on explicit save of the integration flow).

Alternatively, you can delete the component and re-create it. This action should also bring up the up-to-date set of features for that component.

When Is Migration Supported

Migrating an integration flow component is only supported when there is a newer version of the component available (and your integration flow contains still an older one). When no migration option is available, no newer version is available for that component (and also no **Migrate** option is shown for the component).

Furthermore, note that migration of integration flow components is only available for editable integration flows. That means, for configure-only content (see Chapter 3), you can't use this feature.

As of this book's publishing, SAP supports migration of the following components:

- Integration flow
- Integration process
- Local integration process

It's on the SAP Cloud Platform Integration product roadmap that migration of further components, such as adapters or integration flow steps, will be supported in the future. Check out the product documentation regularly to find out more.

We would like to give another example: Migrating an integration flow supports consuming a newer HTTP session-handling feature for HTTP-based receiver adapters. This feature has been made available with the July 2017 release of SAP Cloud Platform Integration.

When you edit an "old" integration flow (created prior to that release date) and click on the area outside the **Integration Process** shape in the integration flow modeler, you find these features in the **Runtime Configuration** tab (Figure 6.68).

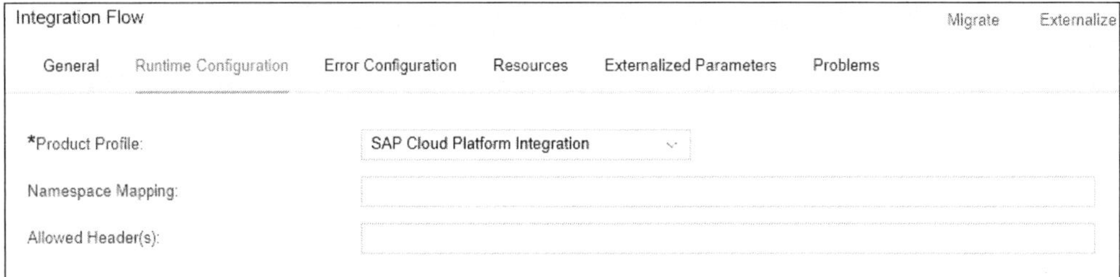

Figure 6.68 Runtime Configuration Features Prior to Migration

You also notice the **Migrate** option on the top-right corner of the screen, indicating that this component (the integration flow) can be migrated.

Now migrate this component as described previously. After migration, you'll notice that the **Runtime Configuration** tab now shows an additional feature, **HTTP Session Handling** (Figure 6.69).

Note

For more information on the session-handling feature, see the "Cloud Integration – How to Configure Session Handling in Integration Flow" blog in the SAP Community (*www.sap.com/community.html*).

So far, we've discussed how you can migrate *upward* to a newer version (in case you like to keep pace with the monthly updates of the SAP Cloud Platform Integration software and adapt your integration flow to the newest available features).

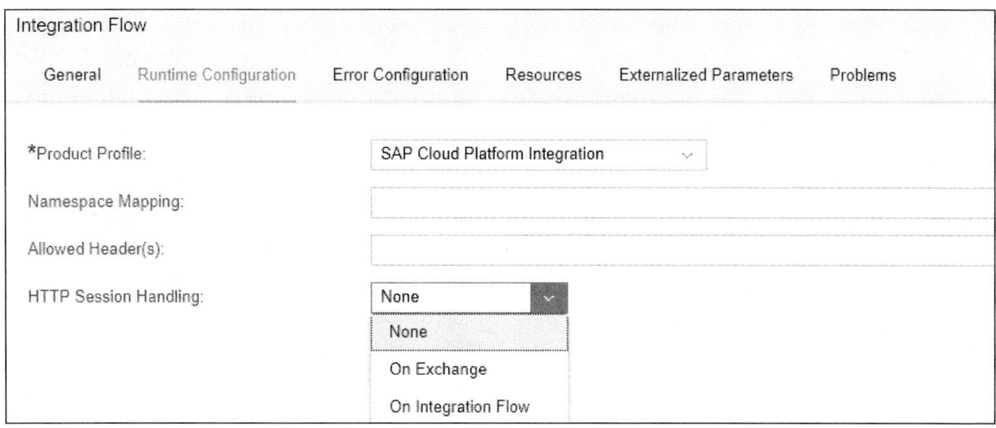

Figure 6.69 Runtime Configuration Features after Migration

To complete the story, we'll show you how SAP Cloud Platform Integration also supports *downward* migration to an older feature set. Check out the next section to learn more.

6.5.3 Downgrading Integration Content for SAP Process Orchestration

Why would it make sense to migrate integration flow components the other way around? Let's briefly set the context.

Throughout this book, we've focused on cases where you deploy and run integration flows on your SAP Cloud Platform Integration tenant. In other words, all integration flows we've developed throughout the chapters of this book have been executed on a runtime node of SAP Cloud Platform. SAP provides updates for both the capabilities of the integration runtime and of the integration design environment (the Web UI) on a monthly basis in the same development cycles. The development of new integration flow features and of the corresponding runtime capabilities is synchronized. That means, for each new capability released for the integration flow designer (e.g., for a new flow step offered in the palette), you can always be sure that this feature is also supported by the actual integration runtime on SAP Cloud Platform.

Product Profiles

If you're solely working with SAP Cloud Platform Integration, that is fine, and you're happy with the migration capability we explained in the previous section. However, SAP also provides another powerful integration solution that has been already been in place for many years and has been used by many SAP customers: SAP Process Orchestration. For a comprehensive introduction of this product, check out *SAP Process Orchestration: The Comprehensive Guide* by Bilay and Blanco (SAP PRESS, 2017, *www.sap-press.com/4431*).

As explained already in Chapter 1, many customers use a hybrid system and process landscape where parts of the scenario run in the cloud and other parts are handled by components installed on the premises of the customer. In addition, many customers use both integration platforms in combination: the cloud-based SAP Cloud Platform Integration and SAP Process Orchestration on premise. So why not use the Web UI centrally to design both integration flows that are able to run on SAP Cloud Platform Integration and integration flows that are able to run on SAP Process Orchestration? When you have a license for SAP Cloud Platform Integration *and* for SAP Process Orchestration, you can go for this hybrid approach. To support this use case, SAP has introduced product profiles in the Web UI (we've already briefly touched on this in Chapter 2, Section 2.2.1, Table 2.3).

What are product profiles good for? To understand this, note that SAP Process Orchestration and SAP Cloud Platform Integration are developed and updated in different cycles (as we'll illustrate in more detail later). However, it's important that the features you can use in the integration content design tool (Web UI) correspond to the capabilities of the target runtime (integration bus) where you intend to deploy the integration flow. Because the release cycles of the integration platforms—SAP Process Orchestration and SAP Cloud Platform Integration—also might differ slightly, SAP has introduced product profiles. Choosing the right product profile makes sure that the integration developer gets exactly those design and modeling features in the Web UI that are also supported by the target integration runtime corresponding to the product profile—and no more. You can choose among SAP Cloud Platform Integration and the recent versions of SAP Process Orchestration product profiles.

Product Profile

A product profile defines the capabilities of the Web UI design environment that are supported for a chosen target integration runtime. If you've only purchased an SAP Cloud Platform Integration license, you only need the product profile **SAP Cloud Platform Integration**. If you've purchased an SAP Process Orchestration license as well, you can get the option to choose between the following product profiles:

- **SAP Cloud Platform Integration**
- **SAP PO <Support Package>**

The latest available support packages of SAP Process Orchestration 7.5 are offered. Earlier releases of SAP Process Orchestration (prior to release 7.5) aren't supported: only the runtime components for that latest SAP Process Orchestration release are enhanced with regard to the runtime features of SAP Cloud Platform Integration.

To go into more detail and to understand how product profiles are related to the topic of downgrades, let's look at the different development cycles of both integration runtimes.

Updates for SAP Cloud Platform Integration (both the integration runtime components and the Web UI as the central, cloud-based design tool) are released monthly. On the other hand, updates for SAP Process Orchestration are released in "slower" cycles together with SAP NetWeaver (roughly in quarterly shipments). Therefore, the capabilities of SAP Process Orchestration (as one target integration runtime for your integration flows) lag behind the capabilities of the integration flow design tool (Web UI). When selecting a certain SAP Process Orchestration product profile, the scope of capabilities of the Web UI is adapted so that you can only choose among those features that are also supported by the respective SAP Process Orchestration runtime. Because SAP Process Orchestration is an on-premise solution, and the features of a dedicated release aren't enhanced further, there is always a maximum version of all components for a dedicated SAP Process Orchestration product profile, whereas for the SAP Cloud Platform Integration product profile, the set of features is enhanced constantly each month. Only when a new release of SAP Process Orchestration is made available can you also select a new product profile offering the exact updated set of design features that are then also supported by the new SAP Process Orchestration release (Figure 6.70).

In the example, in **SAP Process Orchestration 7.5 SP x**, the SAP Process Orchestration runtime can provide maximum support for those integration features that are developed in the Web UI prior to (and including) version n. That means, the Web UI product profile **SAP Process Orchestration 7.5 SP x** has to "filter out" all newer integration capabilities that are developed after version n. For the product profile **SAP Process Orchestration 7.5 SP x+1**, newer features can then be taken into account.

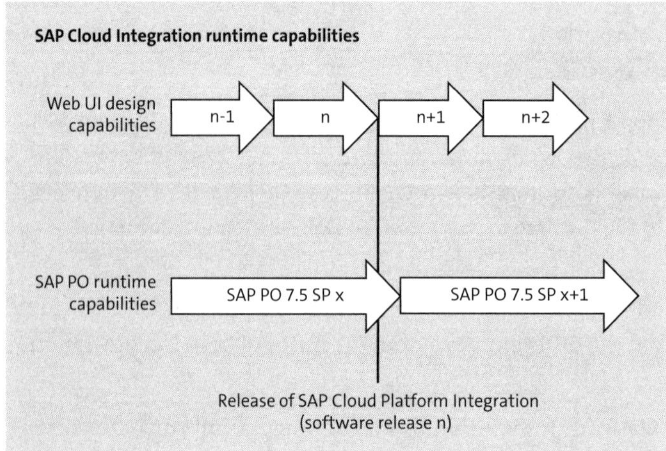

Figure 6.70 Release Cycles of SAP Cloud Platform Integration (with Web UI) Compared to SAP Process Orchestration

Versioning of an individual integration flow component looks like Figure 6.71 (to give an example).

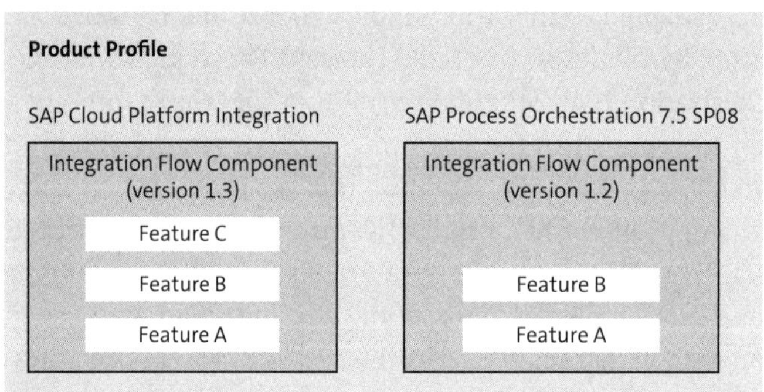

Figure 6.71 Integration Flow Components Showing Different Feature Sets Depending on the Chosen Product Profile

Working with Product Profiles

When you have both an SAP Process Orchestration and an SAP Cloud Platform Integration license, you can choose among different product profiles in the Web UI **Settings** section (Figure 6.72).

Note that you need to have assigned the authorization group `AuthGroup.Administrator` (tenant administrator) to be authorized to access the tenant settings.

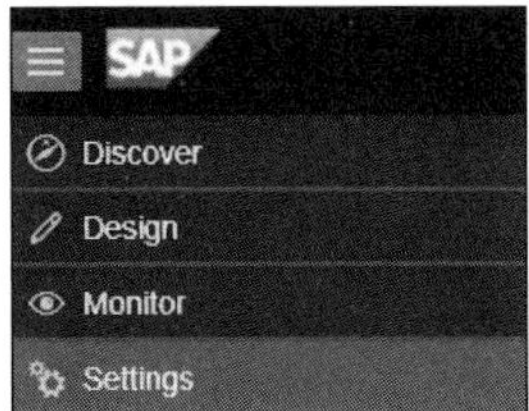

Figure 6.72 Choosing the Tenant Settings Section on the Web UI

Notice that for this tenant, the product profile **SAP Cloud Platform Integration** and those for the recent releases of **SAP Process Orchestration** are available (Figure 6.73).

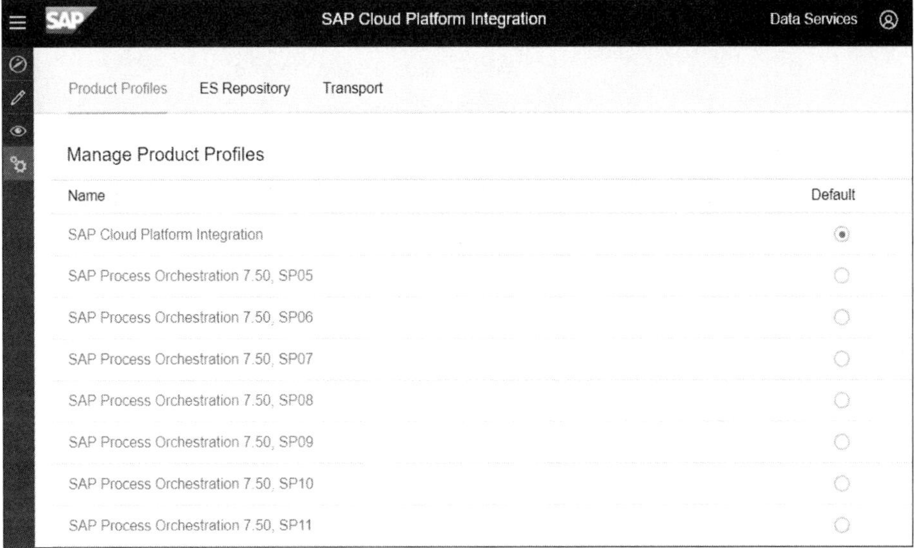

Figure 6.73 Tenant Settings Showing the Available Product Profiles

If you see only the **SAP Cloud Platform Integration** product profile, but you want to work with the other product profiles also, create a ticket for your SAP Cloud Operations team (that provided you with the tenant). Note that when clicking on one of the product profiles, you'll get a list of component versions supported by the selected product profile.

By editing the settings, you can define a default product profile. When creating a new integration flow, the default setting will be used for this integration flow. You can also set product profiles not only globally for the tenant (as shown for the **Settings** section) but also on an integration flow level. To see this, open an integration flow, click on the area outside the **Integration Process** shape, and open the **Runtime Configuration** tab (Figure 6.74).

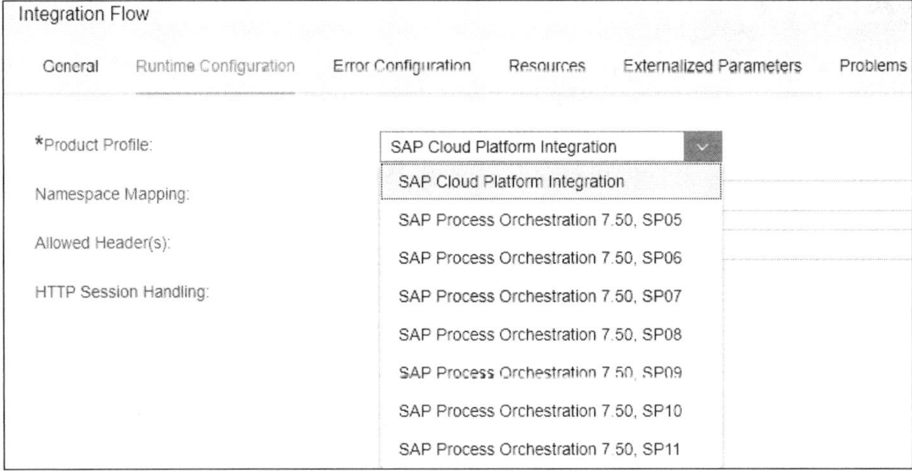

Figure 6.74 Setting a Product Profile for an Integration Flow

Select product profile **SAP Cloud Platform Integration**, and add a new **Receiver** communication channel to your integration flow. Notice that you have a large variation of receiver adapters among which you can select, as shown in Figure 6.75.

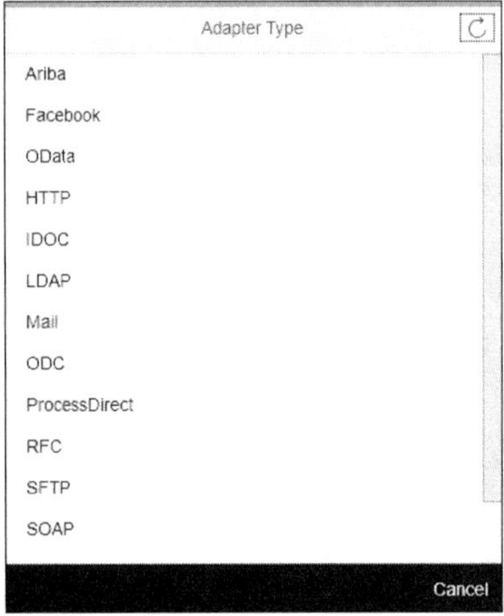

Figure 6.75 Offered Receiver Adapter Types for the SAP Cloud Platform Integration Product Profile

Cancel this activity, go back to the **Runtime Configuration** tab, and choose the product profile **SAP Process Orchestration 7.50, SP09**. Again, add a new **Receiver** channel, and you'll get the following selection of receiver adapters (Figure 6.76).

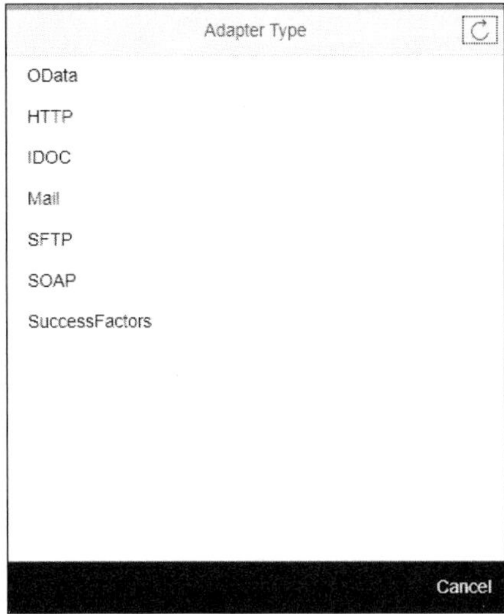

Figure 6.76 Offered Receiver Adapter Types for SAP Process Orchestration 7.50, SP 09 Product Profile

Some adapters are missing, for example, the Facebook and Twitter adapter, because the selected SAP Process Orchestration runtime (for the chosen release 7.50 SP 09) doesn't support the connectivity with these platforms. Future releases of SAP Process Orchestration might support such a connectivity, however. If that is the case, product profiles corresponding to such future SAP Process Orchestration releases available with future releases of the Web UI might offer these additional adapter types.

To show another example, edit an integration flow, specify product profile **SAP Cloud Platform Integration**, and go to the palette. Click the **Security Elements** icon, and then select **Encryptor**. You'll notice that only the **PKCS7 Encryptor** is available (Figure 6.77).

If you select product profile **SAP Cloud Platform Integration** and repeat these steps, you notice (as expected) that the **PGP Encryptor** is also available (Figure 6.78).

Figure 6.77 Offered Encryption Step for Product Profile SAP Process Orchestration 7.50, SP 09

Figure 6.78 Offered Encryption Steps for Product Profile SAP Cloud Platform Integration

Web UI capabilities might also differ on the detail level of each individual integration flow component so that certain features of an adapter or flow step are missing when an SAP Process Orchestration product profile is selected (as shown earlier in Figure 6.71). But we won't go into more detail here.

Migrating within an SAP Process Orchestration Product Profile

To conclude this section, note that migration of integration flow components, as described in Section 6.5.2, is also supported within an SAP Process Orchestration product profile. However, upgrading is then only possible to the maximum component version supported for the chosen SAP Process Orchestration product profile. If you want to use features of the component that are released later, you need to check out if a newer SAP Process Orchestration product profile (and, correspondingly, a newer SAP Process Orchestration release) is available.

For more information on the topic of migration, check out the "Versioning & Migration of Components of an Integration Flow in SAP Cloud Platform Integration's Web Application" blog in the SAP Community (*www.sap.com/community.html*). If you want to learn more about using integration content together with SAP Process

Orchestration, check out the "Best Practices Cloud Integration Content in SAP Process Orchestration – Overview" blog.

6.6 Transporting Integration Packages to Another Tenant

In this section, we provide an overview of the options that are available to transport integration content across tenants. Here, a typical use case is that you first design and run your integration scenarios in a development landscape and, after development is finished, you transfer your scenarios into a test landscape.

SAP provides the following options to transport integration content:

- Manual transport
- Using enhanced Change and Transport System (CTS+)
- Using the Transport Management Service

We describe these options in the following sections.

6.6.1 Manually Transporting Integration Packages

To manually transport integration packages, you don't need to do any prerequisite steps to set up this scenario. In the Web UI **Settings** in the **Transport** tab, you can keep the default **Transport Mode** setting of **None**.

In your source tenant, you then have to open the Web UI, go to the **Design** section, and open the integration package that you want to transport. You can use the **Export** option in the upper-right corner of the screen (Figure 6.79) to store the integration package as a *.zip* file on your computer.

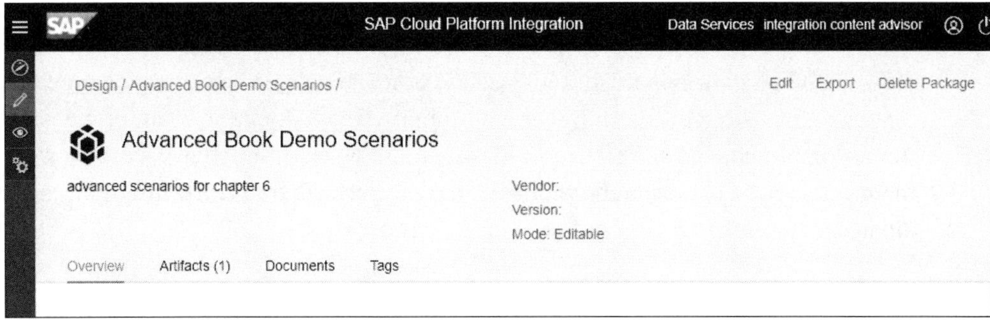

Figure 6.79 Export Function for an Integration Package (on Source Tenant)

Subsequently, you open the Web UI for your target tenant, go to the **Design** section, and click **Import** (Figure 6.80).

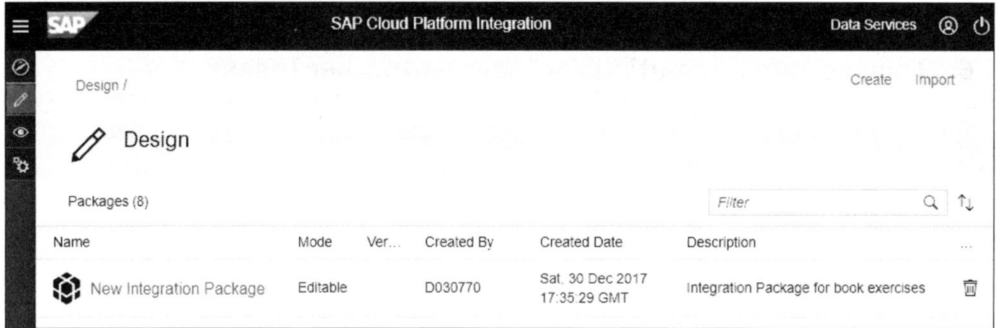

Figure 6.80 Import Function in Web UI Design Section (of Target Tenant)

You can now browse for and double-click the *.zip* file on your computer. As a consequence, the integration package is added to the target tenant (Figure 6.81).

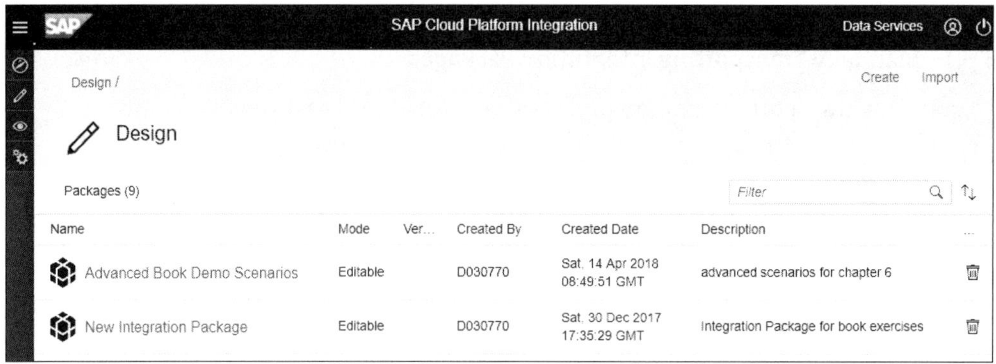

Figure 6.81 The Imported Integration Package Added to the Target Tenant

This is quite straightforward and may be the best way to go when transporting content as an occasional task. However, you might want to look for a comprehensive framework for change and transport management when productively working with many integration packages and when you have to perform transports in a more coordinated way. Check out the next sections for the options.

6.6.2 Transporting Integration Packages Using CTS+

This option might be interesting for you if you already use SAP's enhanced Change and Transport System (CTS+). CTS+ is SAP's enhanced on-premise transport management system that comes with SAP NetWeaver. Note that using CTS+ as transport management system requires a system landscape where your source tenant is connected to a CTS+ system through SAP Cloud Platform Connectivity service.

In this book, we won't elaborate further on this option. Instead, we refer you to a blog series in SAP Community that provides a detailed step-by-step description of how to set up this transport scenario and how to use it. At *www.sap.com/community.html*, search for "Content Transport Using CTS - Cloud Integration – Part 1" and "Content Transport Using CTS - Cloud Integration – Part 2."

6.6.3 Transporting Integration Packages Using the Cloud-Based Transport Management Service

You can transport integration content across tenants with a few clicks through the cloud-based Transport Management Service. At the time this book is written, this feature is in beta phase.

To use this feature, you need to contact SAP first. For more information, check out the "Transport Integration Content across Tenants Using the Transport Management Service Released in Beta" blog in SAP Community (at *www.sap.com/community.html*), which provides good help to get started with the topic of adapter development.

For the setup, we assume that you'll use the Transport Management Service to transport integration content from a development tenant to a test tenant.

Figure 6.82 shows the landscape for our transport scenario.

Figure 6.82 indicates that SAP Cloud Platform Integration tenants run in the SAP Cloud Platform Neo environment, whereas the Transport Management Service runs in the Cloud Foundry environment. This fact is important for the setup of the transport scenario as described in detail in a separate blog (see further below). For more information on the different SAP Cloud Platform environments, go to the online documentation at *https://help.sap.com/viewer/p/CP*, and search for "Environments".

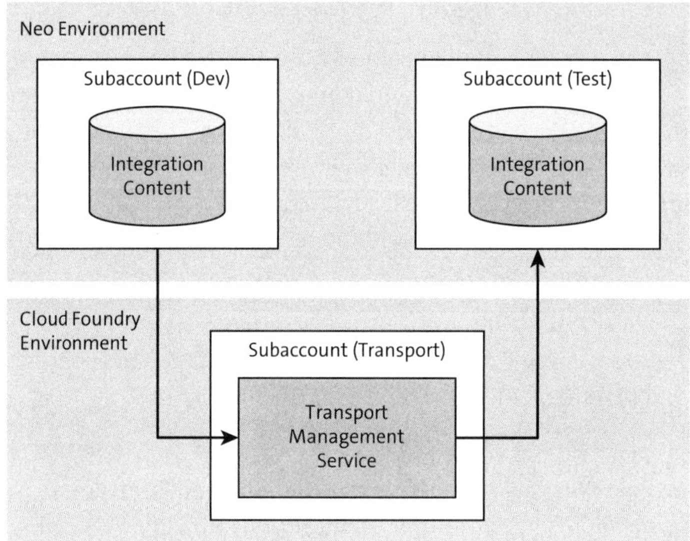

Figure 6.82 Transport Scenario

To enable the Transport Management Service and configure a transport landscape, the following steps are required:

1. Get access to a Transport Management Service account.
2. In the Cloud Foundry environment, create a subaccount of your global account, and subscribe to Transport Management Service.
3. Enable API access to Transport Management Service.
4. Create the required destinations.
   - In the Neo dev subaccount: Create two destinations to a Cloud Foundry subaccount (Transport Management Service).
   - In the Neo dev subaccount: Create one destination used by the Solution Lifecycle Management Service in the Neo dev account to point to the SAP Cloud Platform Integration dev tenant (same Neo subaccount).
   - In the Cloud Foundry subaccount (Transport Management Service): Create one destination to point to each target subaccount (Neo) of your transport landscape. In our example (transport from Neo dev tenant to Neo test tenant), create one destination that points to the test subaccount.
5. In Transport Management Service, create source and target nodes and a transport route to connect both.

All these tasks are described in detail and step by step in the "Cloud Integration – Using Transport Management Service (Beta) for a Simple Transport Landscape" SAP Community blog.

In the following parts of this section, we focus on the content transport itself and describe how to transport content from a dev to a test tenant.

In the mentioned blog, exactly the same transport landscape as depicted in Figure 6.82 is used, so that you easily can tie up the following description to the steps described in the blog.

As we assume that all these steps have been performed successfully, you can now start transporting content. As the first task, go to your source tenant (dev), and specify the transport mode. Then, you can transport an integration package to the target (test) tenant.

Configuring the Transport Mode in the SAP Cloud Platform Integration Web UI

In the Cloud Integration Web UI, you need to specify the desired option how to transport integration content (also referred to as transport mode). As described in the beginning of Section 6.6, there are different options such like using CTS+ or the Transport Management Service (beta).

1. Open the Web UI for the dev tenant, choose **Settings**, and select the **Transport** tile.
2. Click **Edit**.
3. As **Transport Mode**, select **Transport Management Service (Beta)** (Figure 6.83).

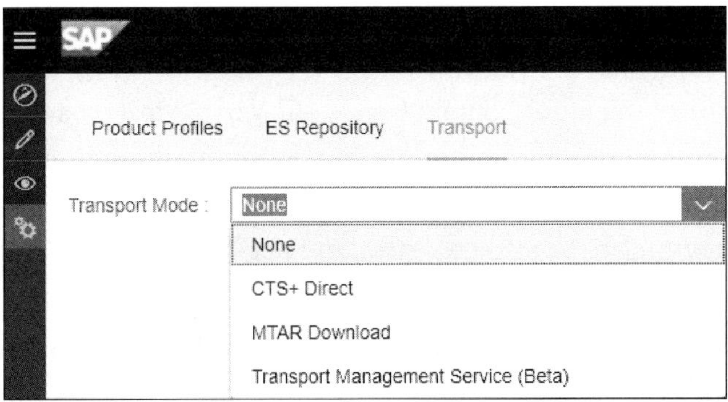

Figure 6.83 Transport Modes in the Web UI Settings Section

4. Click **Save**.

For the sake of completeness, Table 6.1 summarizes the supported transport modes.

Transport Mode	Description
None	Manually export an integration package from the source tenant to your computer, and import it to the target tenant from there.
CTS+ Direct	Transport an integration package directly (with one click) from a source tenant (e.g., a dev tenant) to a target tenant (e.g., a test tenant) through CTS+. *Directly* means that the integration package will be attached to your open transport request in CTS+. With this option, the integration content to transport is transferred directly as a Multi-Target Application (MTA) Archives file (MTAR file with extension *.mtar*) to an open transport request in the configured CTS+ system. The MTA defines a file format to package a heterogeneous set of software pieces that can be created with different technologies but that all share a common lifecycle.
MTAR Download	Download an MTAR file from the tenant you want to export integration content from, and manually upload the MTAR file to a CTS+ system (or to Transport Management Service, depending on your setup).
Transport Management Service (Beta)	Transport integration content across tenants with a few clicks through the cloud-based Transport Management Service of SAP Cloud Platform. This feature currently is in beta phase.

Table 6.1 Transport Modes Available for Integration Content Development

You can now start transporting integration content from the dev to the test tenant.

Transporting Integration Content Using the Transport Management Service

You have now prepared everything to be ready to transport integration content. The following steps show how to transport integration content across two tenants:

1. Open the Web UI for the dev tenant (from where you want to transport the integration content).
2. Select the integration package you want to transport (let's assume it's the package **Advanced Demo Scenarios**).
3. Choose **Transport**.

This option is only shown when you've enabled Transport Management Service as shown earlier.

4. Enter a transport comment, and choose **Transport** (Figure 6.84).

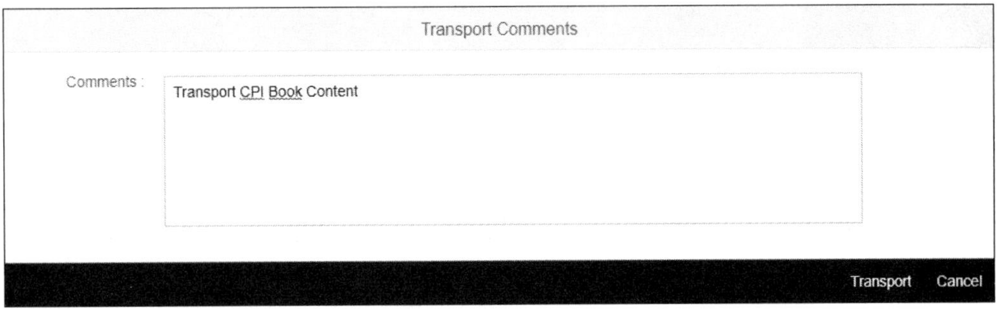

Transport Comments

Comments : Transport CPI Book Content

Transport Cancel

Figure 6.84 Transport Comments Dialog in Web UI

You get an **Information** screen stating that the transport request has been created (Figure 6.85).

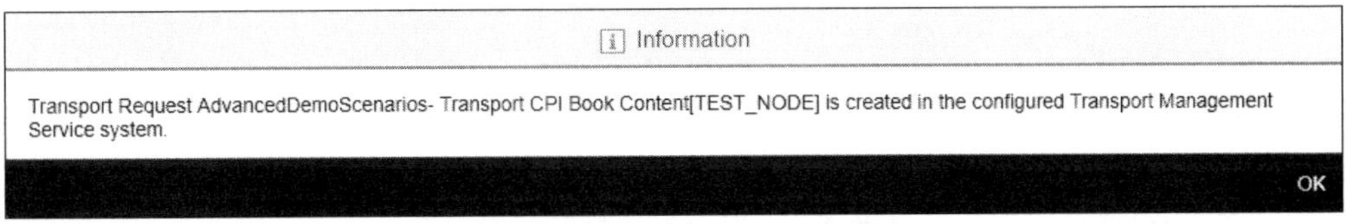

Information

Transport Request AdvancedDemoScenarios- Transport CPI Book Content[TEST_NODE] is created in the configured Transport Management Service system.

OK

Figure 6.85 Transport Information Screen

Notice the name of the target transport node (TEST_NODE) configured in Transport Management Service for the target tenant (which is the test tenant) is part of the transport landscape defined in the Transport Management Service. In the blog mentioned earlier, we show how to create this node and how it's related to the other required configuration settings in all involved accounts.

5. Check the transport import queue by opening the Transport Management Service and choosing **Transport Nodes** (see the blog referred to earlier to find more details on how to access the Transport Management Service).
6. Select the transport node for your target account (**TEST_NODE** in our example). You should find the transport in the **IMPORT QUEUE** tab (Figure 6.86).
7. Select the queue, and choose **Import** (Figure 6.87).

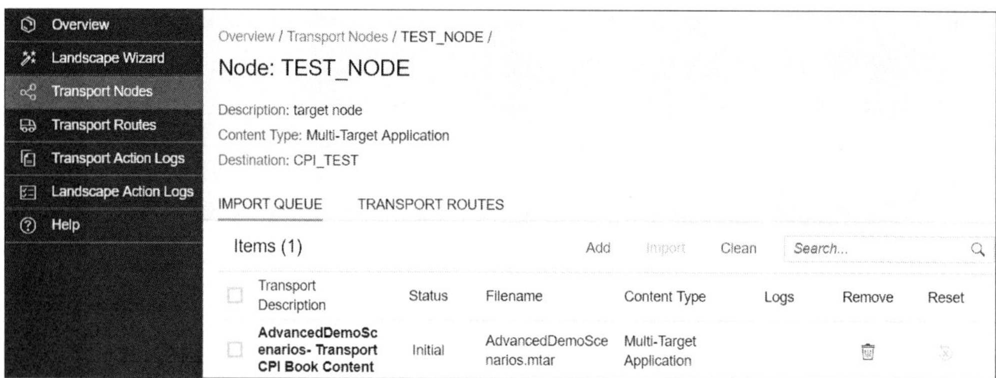

Figure 6.86 Import Queue for Selected Transport Node

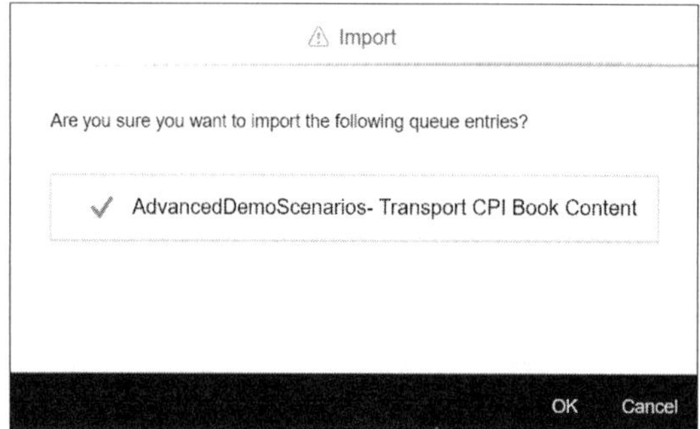

Figure 6.87 Confirmation of Import

8. On the confirmation screen, choose **OK**.
9. Go to the test tenant (the target tenant of your transport), and check whether the package arrived there (Figure 6.88).

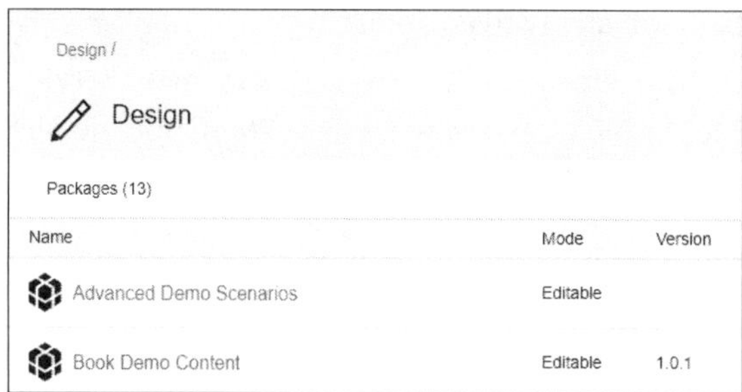

Figure 6.88 Target Tenant Now Showing the Imported Package

The transported package (**Advanced Demo Scenarios**) has been imported. That's it! You've successfully used the Transport Management Service to transport an integration package from a source to a target tenant.

6.7 Using the Adapter Development Kit

SAP Cloud Platform Integration is able to connect to a multitude of systems (in the cloud and on premise). It already comes with an impressive number of adapters that allow communication with other systems on different levels, considering different technologies, security standards, and application-specific requirements. Typical examples are adapters connecting to Twitter, SAP Ariba, and SAP SuccessFactors applications, or adapters connecting via protocols, such as HTTP, SOAP, IDoc, OData, or Secure Shell File Transfer Protocol (SFTP). However, SAP will never be able to cover the huge variety and combinations of applications, protocols, security standards, and versions solely on its own. This gives customers and partners the unique opportunity to fill those gaps by providing their own adapters. Note that SAP Partners have already developed various adapters and published them in the Integration Content Catalog. You can find this information by choosing the **Discover** section of the Web UI and filtering for "adapter."

In this section, we provide you a brief introduction into the Adapter Development Kit (ADK), which enables you to develop your own adapters for SAP Cloud Platform Integration.

6.7.1 The Adapter Development Kit (ADK)

In previous chapters, we frequently referred to the Apache Camel engine as the central integration framework working under the hood of SAP Cloud Platform Integration. As such, when it comes to the development of adapters for SAP Cloud Platform Integration, it essentially means developing adapters for Camel. The official term in Apache Camel's nomenclature for adapters is *components*. As Camel is an open-source framework, many articles have been published explaining how to implement components to increase Camel's connectivity options. See Camel's official documentation web page for component development at *http://camel.apache.org/writing-components.html*, where you can find more information about a component's implementation. It's also recommended that you take a closer look at the book *Camel in Action* (Manning Publications, 2010). Finally, to get to know the Camel components that are already available, we recommend checking out *http://camel.apache.org/components.html*. You'll be surprised at how many Camel components simplify your life! In any case, there's no need to dive into those details here again.

However, to make those components enterprise-ready, provide a configuration UI for the adapters in the SAP Cloud Platform Integration Web UI, and provide the integration of components within the SAP Cloud Platform Integration monitoring infrastructure, there is more to be done than merely writing a simple Camel component. This is why SAP released the ADK for SAP Cloud Platform Integration. Here's the trick: after you've developed a component following the Apache Camel guidelines, as described in the various resources mentioned previously, the ADK allows you to wrap that component with additional code to make it compliant with the SAP Cloud Platform Integration infrastructure.

In this section, we show how you can develop a new adapter. For that purpose, we show you how to work with the ADK and how you can add a new sample adapter to your portfolio of adapters. For more detailed guidelines for adapter development, we also refer you to a number of blogs.

6.7.2 Installing the Adapter Development Kit

The development process for an adapter differs significantly from modeling and running integration flows, as we've discussed so far in this book. It can't be done using a web-based graphical modeling tool. It requires a full-blown development environment, such as Eclipse. That's why the ADK comes as an Eclipse installation.

Note that to successfully execute the steps described in this section, you need to make sure that you've installed Apache Maven and that you point to a Java Development Kit (JDK) in your Eclipse rather than a Java Runtime Environment (JRE) installed on your computer. For more details on these steps, refer to the documentation of SAP Cloud Platform Integration at *https://help.sap.com/viewer/product/CLOUD_INTEGRATION/Cloud*, and search for "Adapter Development Process."

The current ADK was tested with Eclipse Oxygen (equivalent to Eclipse version 4.7). Download the respective release for your operating system from the Eclipse web page at *www.eclipse.org/oxygen/*. Once downloaded, extract the ZIP file into a folder of your choice. The folder will contain another folder named *Eclipse*. The *eclipse.exe* file inside the *Eclipse* folder can be started by double-clicking on it. You'll be asked for an appropriate folder where Eclipse can store the project files during development.

This special area is called an Eclipse workspace. To separate several Eclipse workspaces, it's recommended to have a dedicated folder for your new installation. We've chosen the *C:\EclipseWorkspaces\Oxygen* folder for this purpose.

Click on **OK** to continue. After the Eclipse environment is up and running, we can install the ADK by selecting **Install New Software** from Eclipse's **Help** main menu (Figure 6.89).

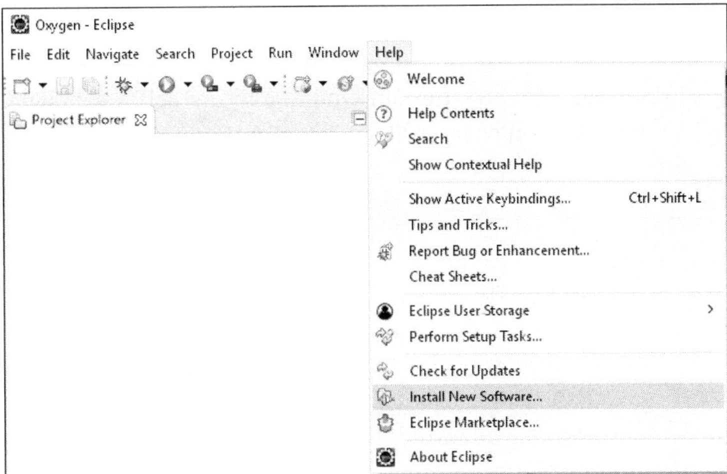

Figure 6.89 Starting the Wizard for Installing Additional Software

The installation wizard opens. The wizard asks you to provide the location on the Internet from where the new software can be downloaded. Click on the **Add** button next to the **Work with** dropdown list (Figure 6.90).

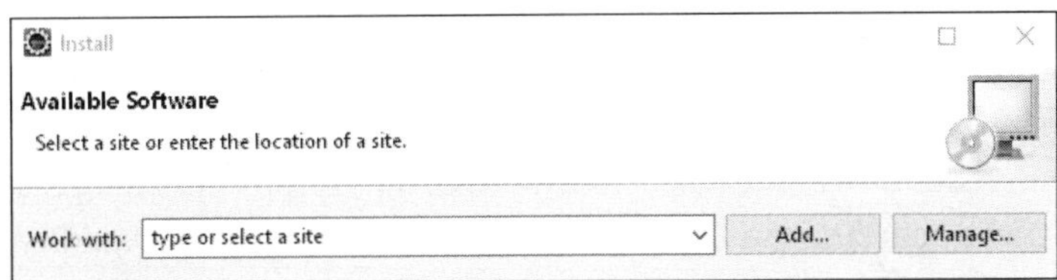

Figure 6.90 Assigning the Download Location for New Software

The **Add Repository** dialog opens (Figure 6.91).

Give your download location an appropriate name (e.g., "SAP Development Tools for Eclipse Oxygen"), and assign it to the location URL *https://tools.hana.ondemand.com/oxygen*. Click on **OK** to proceed.

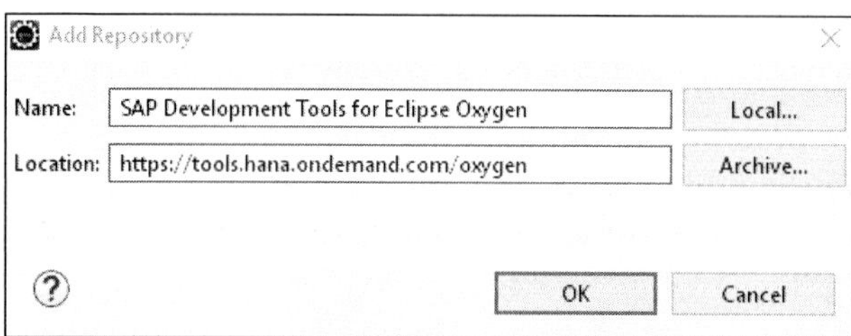

Figure 6.91 Adding the URL for Downloading the SAP Cloud Platform Integration Tools

On the next screen, a list of available software components appears. Select the **Cloud Platform Integration Tools** package. It's recommended to select the complete package, as shown in Figure 6.92.

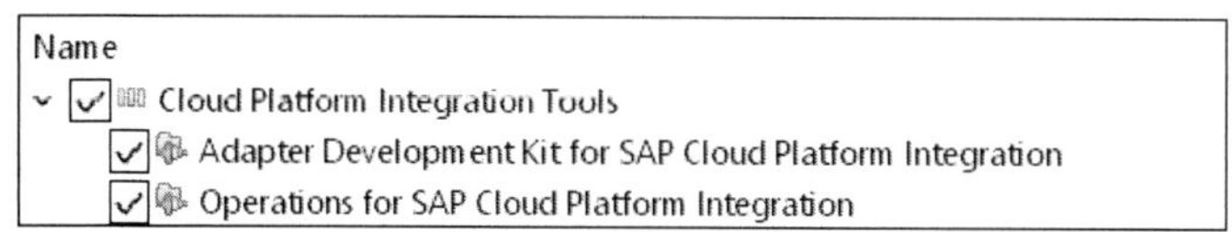

Figure 6.92 Selecting the SAP Cloud Platform Integration Tools for Installation

Click **Next**, confirm this selection, and all forthcoming steps without modifications. At the end of the wizard, accept the license agreement, and then click on **Finish**. The tools will be installed, and a restart of Eclipse is necessary to complete the installation. After restarting, we have to connect the Eclipse environment with your SAP Cloud Platform Integration tenant, on which we'll deploy our newly developed adapter. Open the **Preferences** dialog by selecting **Window • Preferences** from the Eclipse main menu. The **Preferences** dialog opens (Figure 6.93).

Expand the **SAP Cloud Platform Integration** node on the left of the **Preferences** dialog, select the **Operations Server** node beneath, and enter the **URL** to your tenant. This URL has been sent to you by your SAP Cloud Operations team, including username and password. Add the credentials in the respective fields of the **Preferences** dialog, as well. Test the connection by clicking the **Test Connection** button to verify the validity of your entries. Once done, close the dialog by clicking the **Apply and Close** button. We're now ready to develop the adapter.

There are some additional prerequisites you have to meet with regard to your Eclipse installation. Make sure that you've implemented Maven (download from *https://maven.apache.org/download.cgi*).

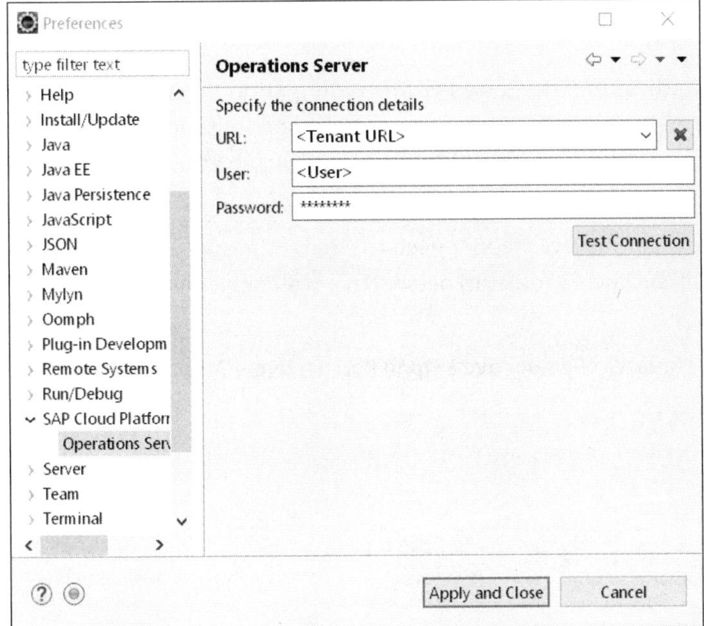

Figure 6.93 Preferences Dialog for Specifying the Connection to the SAP Cloud Platform Integration Tenant

Furthermore, make sure that your Eclipse installation uses and points to a JDK instead of a JRE. You can specify the location of your JDK in Eclipse under **Windows • Preferences • Java • Installed JREs**.

In the next section, we show how you can start developing a sample adapter with just a few clicks.

6.7.3 Developing a Sample Adapter

With the following steps, you can develop and deploy a simple sample adapter project that has been predefined by the SAP Cloud Platform Integration team.

People familiar with software development, and in particular, with Apache Camel and OSGi, can easily enhance such a project to define their own custom adapter. In this section, we won't go into the details of adapter development. Instead, at the end of the section, we refer to the online documentation and a number of blogs that will help you get into the topic of adapter development. In this section, however, we'll show you how to start developing an adapter project by simply using the predefined sample adapter and how you can immediately use the sample adapter in an integration flow.

The sample adapter built in to SAP Cloud Platform Integration does nothing more than either reading a greetings message from a sender or sending such a message to a receiver. We focus on the sender part and leave it to you to enhance the project as required.

To start creating an adapter project, we first need to choose the appropriate perspective in Eclipse. Check if the Java EE (default) perspective is already opened. If not, perform the following steps:

1. In Eclipse, choose **Window • Perspective • Open Perspective • Other** (Figure 6.94).

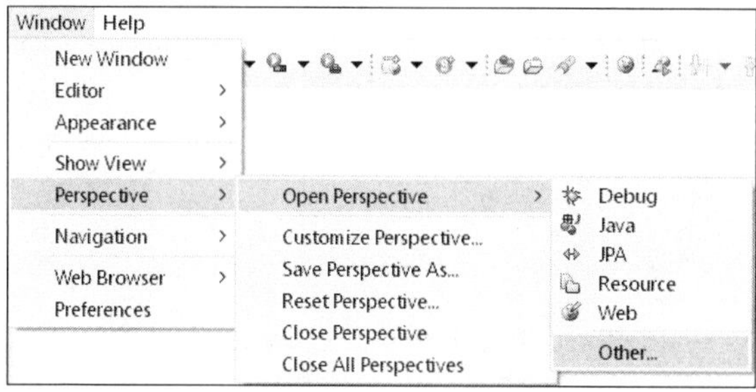

Figure 6.94 Opening a New Eclipse Perspective

2. Select **Java EE (default)** (Figure 6.95).

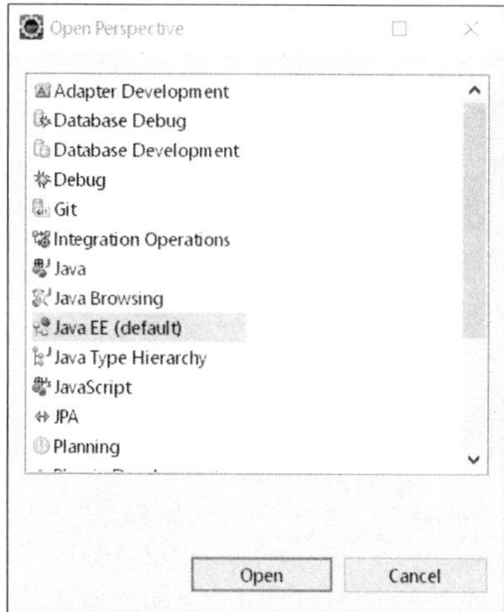

Figure 6.95 Selecting the Integration Designer Perspective

3. Choose **Open**.

We'll now create an adapter project. Here, we define the basic data for the new adapter type (for example, its name). Based on our entries, the system generates a Java project structure which contains all components required to implement the adapters' runtime and its configuration user interface. Perform the following steps:

1. Choose **File • New • Other** (Figure 6.96).

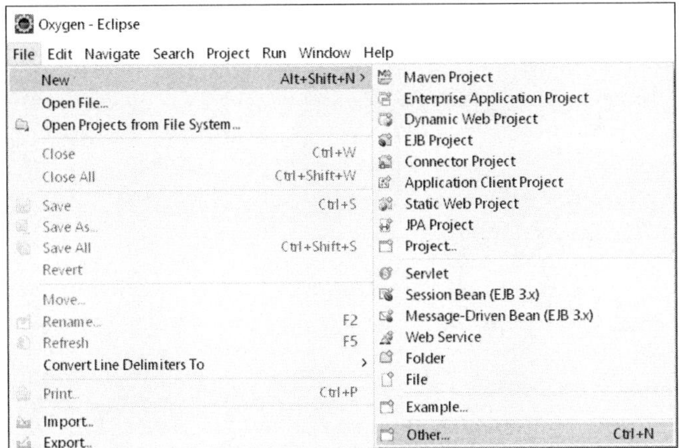

Figure 6.96 Creating a New Project in Eclipse

2. On the next screen, expand the **SAP Cloud Platform Integration** node, and select **Adapter Project** (Figure 6.97).

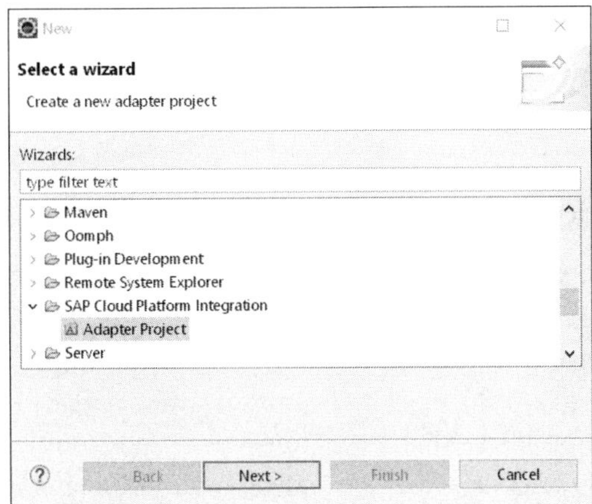

Figure 6.97 Selecting a Wizard for an Adapter Project

3. Choose **Next**.
4. Enter meaningful basic data for the project (Figure 6.98). The next screenshot shows some proposals (note that the sample adapter does nothing but send a greetings message, unless we further change it).

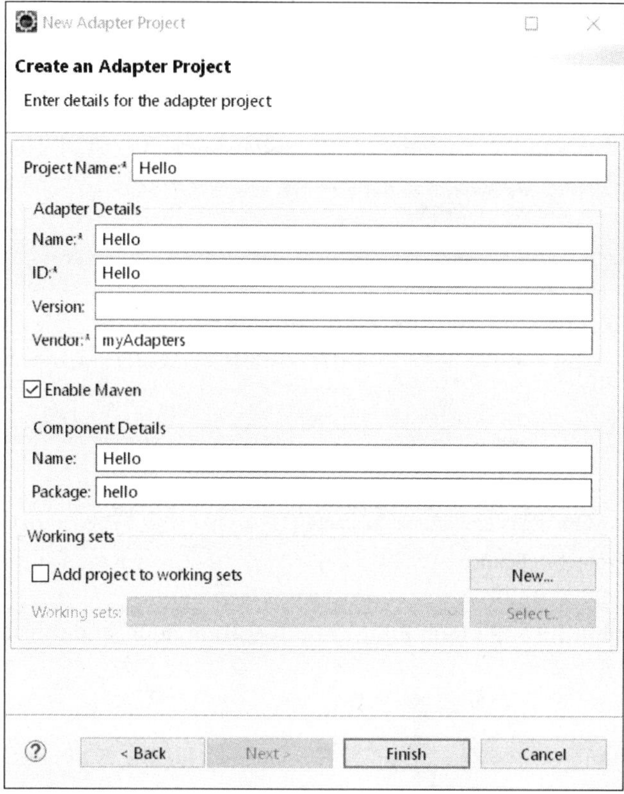

Figure 6.98 Project Details

5. Keep the **Enable Maven** checkbox selected, which is the default setting.

Maven Support for Adapter Development

Adapter development for SAP Cloud Platform Integration also integrates Maven support. Maven is a build management tool from the Apache software foundation. Selecting the **Enable Maven** checkbox makes sure that development of a Camel component is integrated into your adapter project and that dependencies are automatically resolved. This option is selected by default. If you keep this setting, you can create a sample adapter with a few clicks and modify it later. Maven support also has the advantage that all components required for an adapter can be maintained at one place: the runtime components that control how the adapter processes messages at runtime, as well as the user interface (UI)-related components that determine the adapter UI in the integration flow.

If you want to reuse an existing Camel component (as you can find, for example, under *http://camel.apache.org/components.html*), we recommend deselecting **Enable Maven**. In that case, however, you need to maintain all dependencies of your software packages manually, which can sometimes imply tedious effort.

6. Click **Finish**. The project is added to the **Project Explorer** view (Figure 6.99).

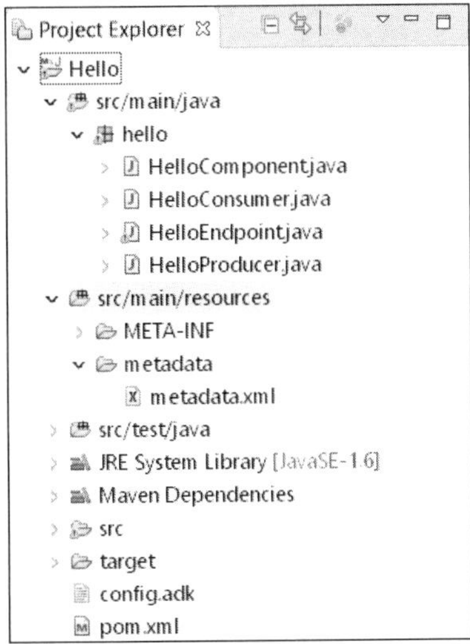

Figure 6.99 New Adapter Project Added to the Project Explorer View

In this figure we've expand some of its nodes and briefly explain what they are for in the following list:

- *HelloConsumer.java*: Implements the sender adapter, which polls messages according to a certain schedule. It generates a greetings message with the current timestamp.
- *HelloProducer.java*: Implements the receiver adapter.
- *HelloEndpoint.java*: Implements the endpoint and contains the string variable `greetingsMessage` for the message to be polled or sent when keeping the sample

adapter as it is. Furthermore, this component provides a logger to log data during the processing of the adapter.

- *metadata.xml*: Contains the metadata for the adapter UI.

7. You can open the file *metadata.xml* by double-clicking on it.

Figure 6.100 shows an excerpt of the file. Note the selection of the **Source** tab at the bottom of the screen. The configurable attributes of the adapter are assembled in attribute groups. You'll find identically named XML tags throughout the metadata file.

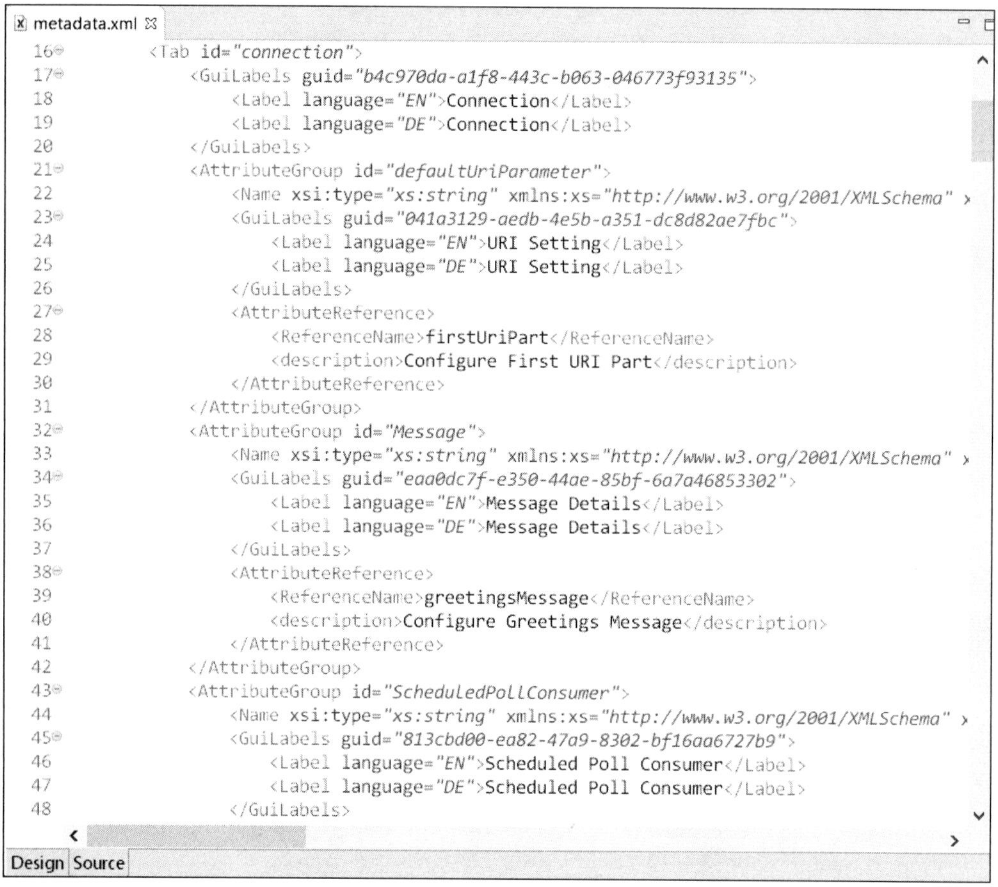

metadata.xml

```
        <Tab id="connection">
            <GuiLabels guid="b4c970da-a1f8-443c-b063-046773f93135">
                <Label language="EN">Connection</Label>
                <Label language="DE">Connection</Label>
            </GuiLabels>
            <AttributeGroup id="defaultUriParameter">
                <Name xsi:type="xs:string" xmlns:xs="http://www.w3.org/2001/XMLSchema"
                <GuiLabels guid="041a3129-aedb-4e5b-a351-dc8d82ae7fbc">
                    <Label language="EN">URI Setting</Label>
                    <Label language="DE">URI Setting</Label>
                </GuiLabels>
                <AttributeReference>
                    <ReferenceName>firstUriPart</ReferenceName>
                    <description>Configure First URI Part</description>
                </AttributeReference>
            </AttributeGroup>
            <AttributeGroup id="Message">
                <Name xsi:type="xs:string" xmlns:xs="http://www.w3.org/2001/XMLSchema"
                <GuiLabels guid="eaa0dc7f-e350-44ae-85bf-6a7a46853302">
                    <Label language="EN">Message Details</Label>
                    <Label language="DE">Message Details</Label>
                </GuiLabels>
                <AttributeReference>
                    <ReferenceName>greetingsMessage</ReferenceName>
                    <description>Configure Greetings Message</description>
                </AttributeReference>
            </AttributeGroup>
            <AttributeGroup id="ScheduledPollConsumer">
                <Name xsi:type="xs:string" xmlns:xs="http://www.w3.org/2001/XMLSchema"
                <GuiLabels guid="813cbd00-ea82-47a9-8302-bf16aa6727b9">
                    <Label language="EN">Scheduled Poll Consumer</Label>
                    <Label language="DE">Scheduled Poll Consumer</Label>
                </GuiLabels>
```

Design Source

Figure 6.100 Excerpt from the Metadata.xml File

We leave everything as it is.

As the next step, we build the adapter project by following these steps:

1. Right-click the adapter project **Hello,** and choose **Run As • 3 Maven build** in the context menu (Figure 6.101).

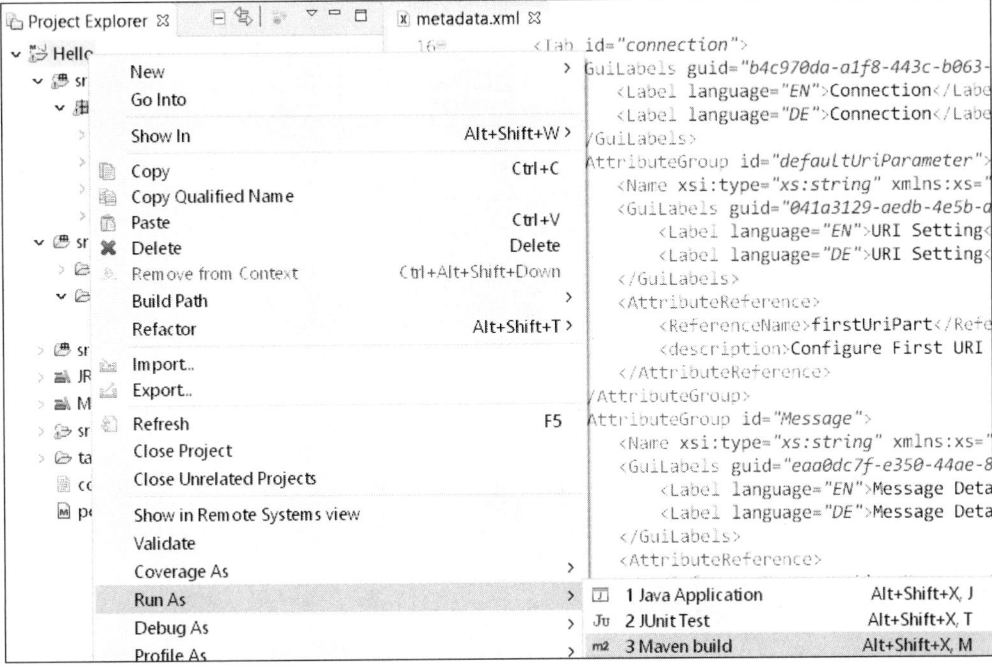

Figure 6.101 Build Adapter Project

After a successful build of the project, you should find additional artifacts in the project tree under **target**.

2. After the success message appears, select again the root node of the project, and choose **Deploy Adapter Project** in the context menu (see Figure 6.102).
3. The **Deploy Adapter Project** dialog box appears (Figure 6.103) where the tenant is displayed (it should be the tenant to which you're connected with Eclipse; if there are doubts, check the settings under **Window • Preferences • SAP Cloud Platform Integration • Operations Server**).

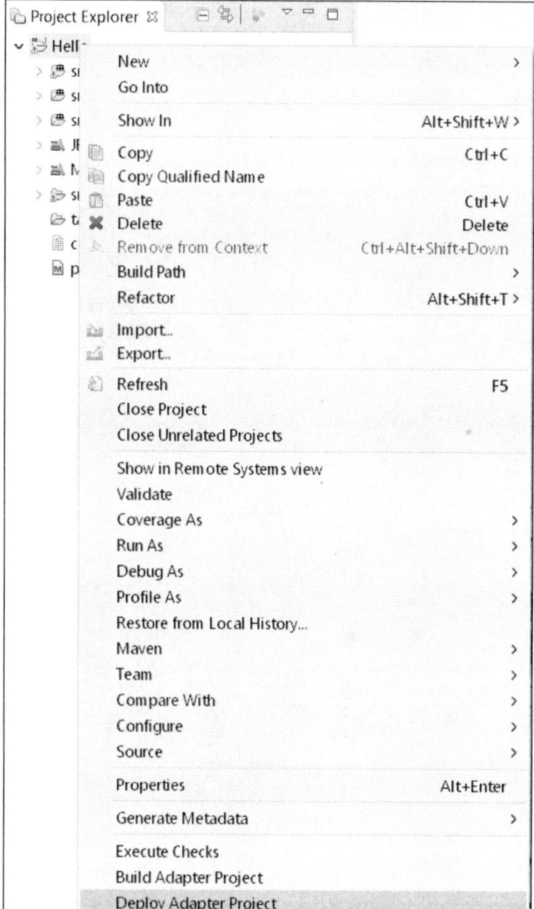

Figure 6.102 Deploy Adapter Project

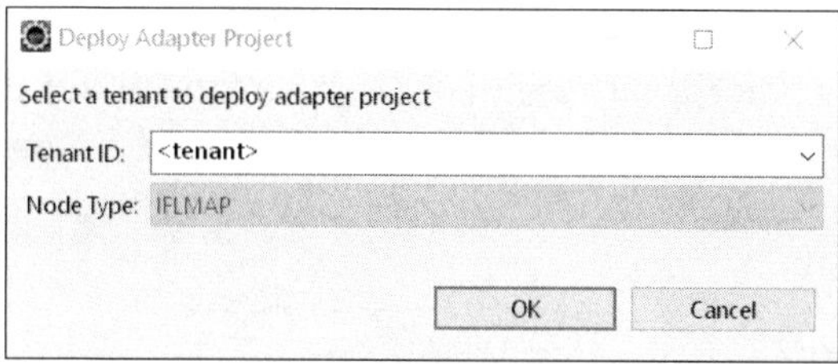

Figure 6.103 Confirming the Tenant to Which the Adapter Project Will Be Deployed

4. Choose **OK**.

Now you can check for the deploy state of your project by following these steps:

1. Open the **Integration Operations** perspective in Eclipse. Choose **Window • Perspective • Open Perspective • Other**, and select the **Integration Operations** perspective (Figure 6.104).

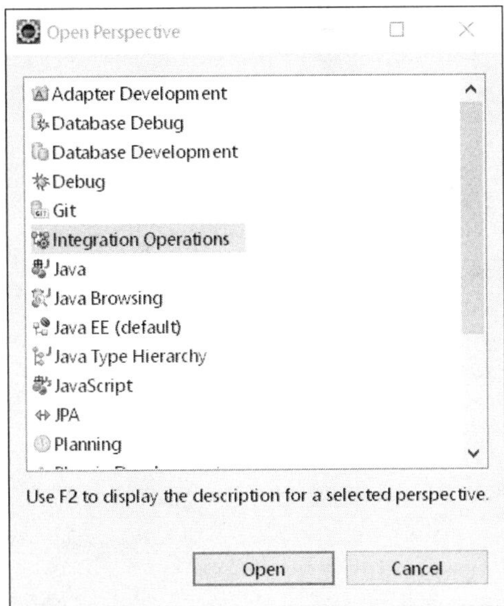

Figure 6.104 Selecting the Integration Operations Perspective in Eclipse

2. Double-click the tenant in the **Node Explorer** view, and select the **Deployed Artifacts** editor (Figure 6.105).

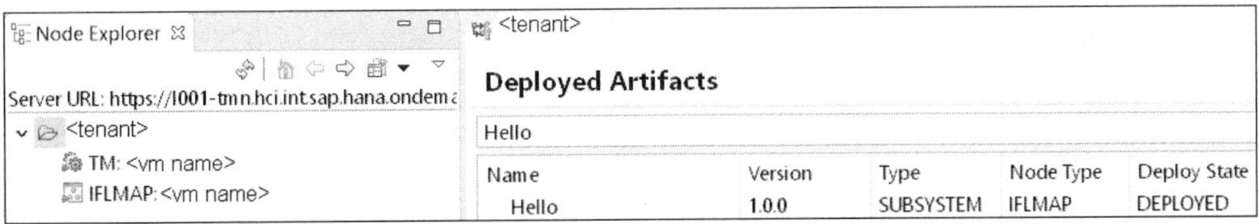

Figure 6.105 Deployed Artifacts Editor for the Tenant Selected in the Node Explorer

Notice that the adapter project is shown as a deployed artifact (with the project name, in our example: **Hello**). When everything goes correctly, the **Deploy State** is **DEPLOYED**.

Now we're ready to test the sample adapter. To keep it simple, we propose using an integration flow with an email receiver (as configured several times within the course of this book). Now let's test the new **Hello** sender adapter by following these steps:

1. Open the Web UI for the tenant, and go to the **Design** section.
2. Either create a new integration flow or reuse an existing one. We propose that you start with this integration flow model (Figure 6.106).

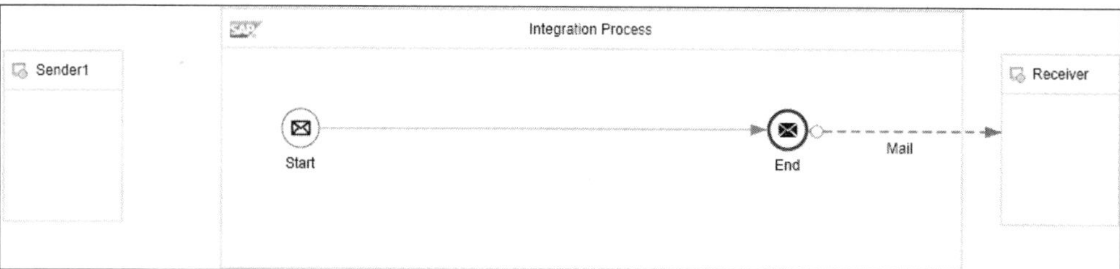

Figure 6.106 Simple Integration Flow to Start With

3. Add a new **Sender** channel between the **Sender** pool and the message **Start** event. You'll notice the new adapter type **Hello** in the **Adapter Type** list (Figure 6.107).

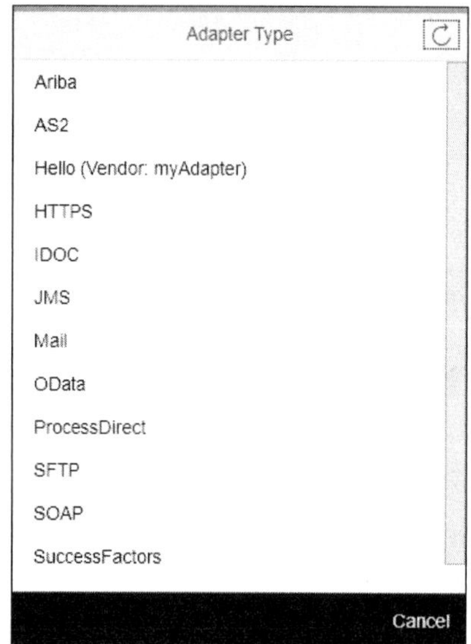

Figure 6.107 New Adapter Offered When Creating a Channel

Also notice that the vendor specified in the project is indicated to show that this adapter is a custom adapter that isn't part of the SAP Cloud Platform Integration portfolio provided by SAP (refer to Figure 6.98).

4. Select the **Hello** adapter type, and go to the **Connection** section of the adapter (Figure 6.108).

   Use these settings. Notice that the adapter sends hello messages to your email account. Choose some larger intervals for the scheduling options not to spam your email account.

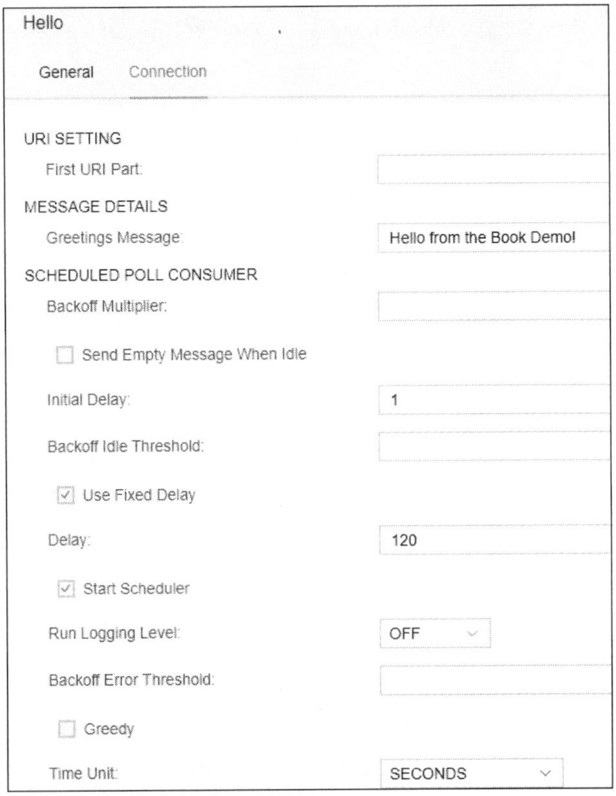

Figure 6.108 Example Settings for the Sender Hello Adapter

Predefined Settings of the Sample Adapter

The sample adapter implements the Camel polling consumer integration pattern. Similar to the mail sender adapter (described in Chapter 2, Section 2.3.8), SAP Cloud

Platform Integration polls (reads) a message from a sender before actually processing it. The settings predefined for the sample adapter are given by the scheduler component of Apache Camel. For example, with a combination of the settings **Backoff Multiplier** and **Backoff Error Threshold**, you can control how the adapter should behave if there are erroneous polls. With the attribute **Backoff Error Threshold**, you can specify the number of subsequent erroneous polls before the attribute **Backoff Multiplier** becomes effective. With the latter one, you can then specify the number of skipped polling attempts before polling occurs again. For example, if you enter the value "2" for **Backoff Error Threshold** and the value "3" for **Backoff Multiplier**, then after two erroneous polling attempts, the adapter waits for another three attempts before becoming active again.

For more information about all predefined attributes, check out the documentation of the Camel scheduler component at *http://camel.apache.org/scheduler.html*.

5. Deploy the integration flow.
6. Check the email account (specified in the mail receiver adapter).

The email will contain a message similar to the following (with the actual timestamp when the message has been processed):

Hello from the Book Demo! Now it is Tue May 01 14:15:19 UTC 2018

According to the settings in Figure 6.108, the adapter will send an email every two minutes. Finally, don't forget to undeploy the adapter after you do this test. Otherwise, SAP Cloud Platform Integration will continue to send messages to your email account.

We won't go any further into the details. If you're interested in developing your own adapters with more meaningful features than those shown for the sample adapter, refer to the following blogs in the SAP Community (*www.sap.com/community.html*), which provide help getting started with the topic of adapter development:

- "SAP CPI Adapter Development – Consuming an External JAR into an Adapter"
- "Extension of Runtime Capabilities Using Blueprint Metadata in Cloud Platform Integration SDK"

You should also check the online documentation of SAP Cloud Platform Integration at regular intervals to find out news about adapter development. Go to *https://help.sap.com/viewer/product/CLOUD_INTEGRATION/Cloud*, and search for the topic "Adapter Development Process."

For more information on available Camel components, refer to the documentation at *http://camel.apache.org*.

Now that the previous chapter and this chapter have given you a good and detailed overview of integration development, let's round up this chapter with a summary of integration design best practices.

6.8 Best Practices for Integration Flow Development

Each integration flow processes data that is transferred from sender systems to the SAP Cloud Platform Integration platform. These practices will make sure that your integration flows are optimized with regard to performance of the scenario and memory consumption:

- Limit the size of inbound messages. Certain sender adapters—SOAP (SOAP 1.x), SOAP (SAP Reliable Messaging), and IDoc—allow you to restrict the incoming message size (**Maximum Message Size** parameter). You can restrict the size of the body and of the attachments independently. The smallest value for a size limit is 1 MB in that case. The default setting for these adapters are maximum body size = 40 MB and maximum attachments size = 100 MB.
- Don't store payloads in the MPL. This recommendation holds in particular for productive integration flows. Using a script step, you can store the message payload in the MPL, which is a convenient measure to analyze the message body in the monitoring. However, doing this can cause issues with memory consumption and even with the failure of the integration scenario because memory and CPU available on your tenant are shared by tasks such as message processing (which should never fail) and message monitoring. Therefore, use this option with care. If, nevertheless, you need to write the message payload into the MPL, you can do so in error cases only.

  Use integration flow tracing by setting the **Trace** log level instead of this.

  For more information, read the "How to Avoid Excessive Storage Load Caused by Using MPL Attachments for Message Logging" blog in SAP Community (*www.sap.com/community.html*).

Note

Use the **Trace** log level only in test environments. Intentionally, the **Trace** log level is only active for 10 minutes.

- Consider certain best practices when using JavaScript and Groovy Script (with the script step). There are certain risks with regard to memory consumption and overall performance of your scenario if you don't use this option with care. The following blogs in SAP Community can help you avoid some of these risks: "Avoid Binding Variables in Groovy Scripts" and "Stream the XMLSlurper Input in Groovy Scripts."
- When using the JMS adapter (as explained in Chapter 5, Section 5.4), keep in mind certain resource limits for JMS queues. To find out the actual limitations, check out the online documentation or read the "Cloud Integration – JMS Resource and Size Limits" blog in SAP Community (*www.sap.com/community.html*).
- Configure transaction handling in an appropriate way. There are different adapter and integration flow step types that store data (either in the database or in a JMS queue). If there is an erroneous processing of the integration flow, any actions that relate to persistence (storing or deleting data) must be rolled back in a consistent way (so that no data inconsistencies are generated). Transaction handling is the way to go here. In Chapter 5, Section 5.4, we discussed transaction handling in the context of the JMS adapter.

  Recommendations and limitations with regard to transaction handling are explained in detail (also together with example scenarios) in the "How to Configure Transaction Handling in Integration Flow" blog in the SAP Community. However, note the following recommendation with regard to an optimized resource consumption: Use as short as possible transactions by "sourcing out" transactional processing to subprocesses. As every transaction consumes resources in a considerable amount, make sure that you avoid keeping a transaction open until the whole integration process is finished.
- If you enable streaming (if this is supported), a document is processed in parts or segments. Use streaming whenever this is applicable. For example, the splitter step allows you to enable the **Streaming** option. If you deactivate this option, in the splitter case, the message is transferred fully to the memory before it's split and processed further. Activating **Streaming**, on the other hand, can help you to avoid such a behavior. Another example for a step where streaming is supported is the XML-to-JSON Converter.
- Use HTTP session handling. Various HTTP-based adapters (e.g., the SOAP and IDoc adapters, but many more) support HTTP session handling (to be configured under **Runtime Configuration** after clicking outside the **Integration Process** shape; refer

to Figure 6.69). One advantage of session handling is that the client is only authenticated once with the first call, which will result in better performance. However, there are also certain restrictions that you should consider when using session handling. For more information about HTTP session handling and its restrictions, as well as to find example scenarios, check out the following SAP Community blog: "Cloud Integration – How to Configure Session Handling in Integration Flow."

- Avoid writing large message parts or even complete messages into headers or properties. Writing much data into headers can cause issues when sending out the message because headers are transferred along with the message to the receiver. Writing much data into properties might cause memory issues.
- When modifying a message, use properties instead of headers because properties aren't passed along with the message by the receiver adapter.
- Delete headers and properties explicitly (in particular, the large ones) if not required anymore. This helps to save memory. You can use the content modifier to do that.
- Avoid memory-intensive steps such as mapping or accessing elements with XPath expressions when processing large messages. Such operations will blow up the message in memory.

As a tip, check out the *SAP Cloud Platform Integration Community* in regular intervals at *www.sap.com/germany/community/topic/cloud-integration.html*.

6.9 Summary

We've reached the end of our journey through the more development-oriented topics of the book. In this chapter, you learned how to trigger integration processes on time-based criteria, how to modularize complex real-life scenarios using subprocesses, and, finally, how to extend SAP Cloud Platform Integration's capabilities by developing your own adapters, allowing you to connect to a wide variety of external systems and technologies. Now your task is to play around with SAP Cloud Platform Integration's modeling environment to further stabilize your knowledge. You can then continue with the next chapter, which deals with a more specific topic: business-to-business integration and how SAP Cloud Platform Integration can help you master use cases related to this. Thereafter, you'll learn more about typical operational tasks you'll need to take care of to run SAP Cloud Platform Integration and the deployed artifacts.

Chapter 7
B2B Integration with SAP Cloud Platform Integration

The end-to-end flow of a business-to-business (B2B) integration project includes defining and implementing interfaces for different partners, creating mappings between those interfaces, and, finally, setting up the integration scenarios. With the B2B capabilities provided with the SAP Cloud Platform Integration, Enterprise Edition, SAP supports you throughout your entire B2B integration project. In this chapter, you'll get to know the B2B features provided in SAP Cloud Platform Integration and learn how to use them in your B2B integration project.

In the previous chapters, you learned how to implement simple as well as more complex integration scenarios using SAP Cloud Platform Integration. But SAP Cloud Platform Integration can also support you in simplifying, streamlining, and configuring complex business-to-business (B2B) integration processes.

Integration between different businesses, for example, between a manufacturer and a wholesaler, is known as B2B integration. B2B integration typically relies on a variety of industry standards for electronic business document exchange, including Accredited Standards Committee X12 (ASC X12), United Nations Electronic Data Interchange for Administration, Commerce and Transport (UN/EDIFACT), and SAP Intermediate Document (IDoc).

B2B integration projects are known to be long-running and complex projects that imply tedious and time-consuming tasks. Throughout such a project, the following tasks need to be fulfilled:

- Defining interfaces for the involved partners
- Creating mappings between the interfaces
- Maintaining partner-specific configuration data
- Creating integration content

- Deploying and testing the integration content
- Monitoring the integration scenario

This chapter will describe the B2B capabilities available with the SAP Cloud Platform Integration, Enterprise Edition, that can help you execute those integration tasks.

7.1 B2B Capabilities in SAP Cloud Platform Integration: Overview

To support you in your B2B integration projects SAP Cloud Platform Integration provides a set of B2B-specific capabilities, such as a web-based application to define interfaces and mappings, B2B-specific adapters and flow steps, and a persistency to store configuration data for different business partners.

Table 7.1 gives you a complete overview of the available B2B capabilities in SAP Cloud Platform Integration. Note that this list reflects the set of capabilities available at the time of publishing the book. More B2B-specific adapters and flow steps are on the roadmap and will be provided in future releases. For the most recent list of B2B-specific features, check out the online documentation for SAP Cloud Platform Integration at *https://help.sap.com/viewer/product/CLOUD_INTEGRATION/Cloud.*

Capability	Description
Integration Content Advisor (ICA)	Web-based application that facilitates the definition of interfaces based on industry standards and the configuration of mappings between those interfaces. You can export documentation and generated runtime artifacts from this tool. The generated runtime artifacts can be used in integration flows.
Library of type systems	A collection of Electronic Data Interchange (EDI) standard interfaces provided by agencies that maintain the B2B standards. You can access these libraries from the ICA. Each of the type systems is developed and maintained by the agency that owns it. For example, the SAP IDoc type system is developed and maintained by SAP. The external libraries need to be purchased separately.
Partner Directory	Repository to store configuration data for different business partners. Application Programming Interfaces (APIs) are available to maintain the data in the Partner Directory. The configuration data from the Partner Directory can be used in integration flow configuration.

Table 7.1 B2B Capabilities in SAP Cloud Platform Integration

Capability	Description
Number range objects (NROs)	Artifact to define unique interchange numbers for each EDI document. NROs can be used in scripts and in the EDI splitter in integration flow configuration.
AS2 Sender and Receiver Adapter	Adapter in integration flow designer to exchange business documents with your partner using the AS2 (Applicability Statement 2) protocol. Can be used to encrypt, decrypt, sign, and verify documents.
AS4 Receiver Adapter	Adapter in the integration flow designer to exchange business documents with your partner using the AS4 (Applicability Statement 4) protocol.
EDI splitter	Variant of the splitter step in the integration flow designer that splits, validates, and acknowledges inbound bulk EDI messages.
EDI to XML Converter	Converter step in the integration flow designer that transforms a message from EDI format to XML format. You can convert EDIFACT and ASC X12 formats.
XML to EDI Converter	Converter step in the integration flow designer that transforms a message from XML format to EDI format. You can convert to EDIFACT and ASC X12 formats.

Table 7.1 B2B Capabilities in SAP Cloud Platform Integration (Cont.)

B2B Capabilities Only Available in SAP Cloud Platform Integration, Enterprise Edition

Some of the B2B capabilities are only available in your tenant if you've purchased the SAP Cloud Platform Integration, Enterprise Edition. Otherwise, you can't use the ICA or the B2B-specific flow steps and adapters when designing integration flows.

What can we do with those capabilities, and how do they help us in our tasks throughout the B2B integration project? We give answers to these questions in the following sections. We'll explain the B2B capabilities in detail and show how to use most of them throughout one sample B2B scenario.

In the sample B2B scenario, the sender posts EDI messages to SAP Cloud Platform Integration using the AS2 protocol. SAP Cloud Platform Integration receives and acknowledges receipt of the message, transforms it into an IDoc message, and sends it to the receiver using the IDoc adapter. At the end of the chapter, we'll make the integration flow dynamic so that the configuration data is read from the Partner Directory, where the partner-specific configuration data is stored. See Figure 7.1 for an overview of the different configuration steps necessary to set up the sample scenario.

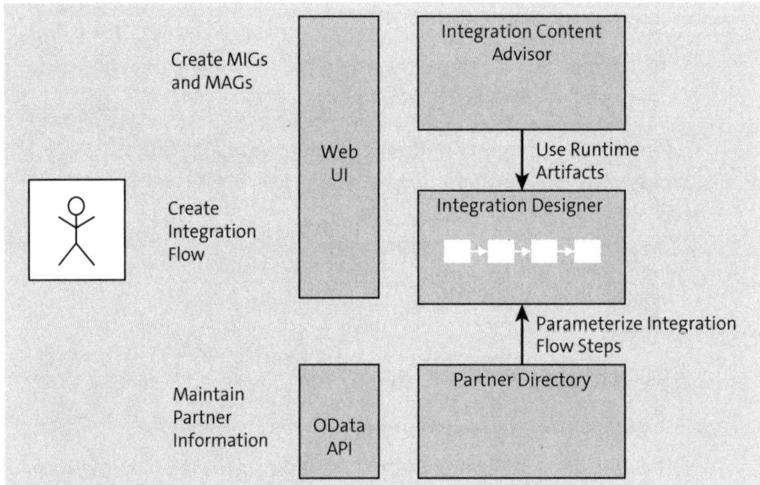

Figure 7.1 Schema of Involved Components in Configuring the B2B Scenario

Let's get started with creating the interfaces and mappings in the ICA.

7.2 Defining Interfaces and Mappings in the Integration Content Advisor

The starting point to set up a new B2B integration scenario is to define the interfaces required by the business partners and to create mappings between those interfaces. Until now, this is one of the biggest challenges for B2B integration projects because it means connecting and managing a potentially large number of business partners with a wide variety of different business requirements. Defining and implementing these interfaces based on the standards for electronic business document exchange usually requires tedious manual effort.

To overcome those efforts, SAP offers the Integration Content Advisor (ICA), a cloud-based design-time solution that accelerates the implementation of B2B scenarios. The ICA unifies all the required tasks for creating integration content based on a comprehensive knowledge base.

The ICA's design time is based on the following main pillars:

- **Library of type systems**
  The ICA includes a set of B2B industry standard libraries containing a collection of messages/message interfaces, associated complex and simple types, and code lists used in the messages. Such a collection is referred to as type system.
- **Message implementation guidelines (MIGs)**
  One main focus of the ICA is assisting in the writing of interface specifications. The specifications provide instructions and constraints for implementing a certain message interface using a B2B standard message provided by the type system in a certain business context. These specifications determine the behavior and the use of each B2B standard message, including limitations or customizations. They contain the definitions of mandatory elements and occurrences, property definitions for each element, permitted code lists and code values, and, finally, the definition of validation constraints and business rules.
- **Mapping guidelines (MAGs)**
  A mapping guideline is the detailed specification of a mapping from a source MIG to a target MIG in a given business context. The focus is on the description of each mapping entity across the corresponding elements, so that business domain experts understand the reason and meaning of the mappings. All technical aspects are implicitly calculated and derived into the technical artifacts, which is the fourth pillar.
- **Automatically generated runtime artifacts**
  The runtime artifacts generated by the ICA are required for preprocessing and postprocessing, conversion, detailed validation, or even the transformation (mapping) from source to target message. The ICA generates a number of artifacts based on XML Schema Definition (XSD) Version 1.0 and Extensible Stylesheet Language Transformation (XSLT) Version 2.0, which can be directly used in a prepared integration flow in the designer of SAP Cloud Platform Integration.

Now that you understand the main parts of the ICA, let's check how interfaces and mappings are created in the ICA.

7.2.1 Create Message Implementation Guidelines

The first task when using the ICA is to create the message interfaces that the involved partners require for the scenario. A message interface is usually defined based on a B2B standard interface.

B2B integration relies on a variety of industry standards, also known as B2B standards, for electronic business document exchange. At the time of publishing this book, the ICA supports the following standards in its type systems:

- **ASC X12 (*www.x12.org*)**
  This standard, maintained by the American National Standards Institute Accredited Standards Committee X12 (ANSI ASC X12), is one of the commonly used EDI standards for electronic data exchange, mainly in the United States. The ICA offers several hundred messages with the corresponding complex types, simple types, and code lists in many versions.
- **UN/EDIFACT (*www.unece.org/cefact/edifact/welcome.html*)**
  This standard is maintained and further developed through the United Nations Centre for Trade Facilitation and Electronic Business (UN/CEFACT). It's widely used in Europe. The ICA offers around 200 messages with the corresponding complex types, simple types, and code lists in many versions (in syntax version S3).
- **UN/CEFACT**
  Additional code lists are offered separately in ICA and are maintained by UN/CEFACT (*www.unece.org/cefact.html*). Eight additional code lists are available in multiple versions.
- **ISO (International Organization for Standardization) (*www.iso.org*)**
  ISO develops and maintains international standardized code lists and identifier schemas. The ICA offers five code lists in versions 2004, 2012, and 2017.
- **SAP IDoc**
  This is the SAP-owned document format for business transaction data transfers. The ICA offers the IDoc versions of the SAP S/4HANA 1709 release. The most commonly used IDoc messages with the corresponding complex types, simple types, and code lists are offered.

Prerequisites for Using the Integration Content Advisor

To use the ICA, you need to get an ICA application provisioned for your SAP Cloud Platform Integration tenant, and you must assign certain user roles to the users who want to access the application.

The provisioning is done via self-service from the SAP Cloud Platform cockpit as described in the documentation for SAP Cloud Platform Integration (*https://help.sap.com/viewer/product/CLOUD_INTEGRATION/Cloud*) in the topic "Subscribing to Integration Content Advisor From SAP Cloud Platform Cockpit." After the provisioning, you'll find the URL to the ICA application in the **Details** section of the SAP Cloud Platform cockpit.

To call the ICA application URL, you need to assign the user roles `Guidelines.ReadWrite` and `TypeSystem.Read` to the users who want to access the ICA application. This is described in detail in the documentation for SAP Cloud Platform Integration (*https://help.sap.com/viewer/product/CLOUD_INTEGRATION/Cloud*) in the topic "Assigning Users for Integration Content Advisor for SAP Cloud Platform Integration."

To use the non-SAP type systems, such as UN/EDIFACT, you need to purchase additional licenses. As long as the license isn't purchased for a specific type system, it's shown as **Unlicensed** in the ICA.

In our sample scenario, we're going to use the 850 Purchase Order message from the ASC X12 type system as the inbound message and the ORDERS.ORDERS05 IDoc from SAP IDoc type system as the outbound message. We'll take a look at those messages in the ICA and get to know how MIGs and MAGs can be created based on it.

Note

We won't explain step by step how to create the MIGs and the MAGs for the sample scenario as this would fill a book on its own. We'll describe the overall process and the features the ICA offers to create MIGs and MAGs. We'll also explore how to export the runtime artifacts, which are then used in the integration flow configuration. The generated runtime artifacts from ICA needed for the B2B sample scenario are provided with the book downloads at *www.sap-press.com/4650.*

Because the sample scenario uses the 850 Purchase Order message from ASC X12 type system as the inbound message and the ORDERS.ORDERS05 IDoc from SAP IDoc type system as the outbound message, we need the B2B standard message templates from those two type systems as the starting point for creating our own MIG. Afterwards, we tailor the MIG to suit the scenario-specific requirements.

Search for Standard Messages in Type Systems

To create MIGs, you first need to explore the messages provided by the ICA and select the ones you require for the scenario. To do this, execute the following steps:

1. Launch the ICA application from the URL provided in the SAP Cloud Platform cockpit. The ICA entry page opens. As depicted in Figure 7.2, it's divided into different

sections: in the upper **General** section, you have the option to navigate to the **Library of Type Systems**, and in the lower **Own** section, you can check your **Profile** and create your own MIGs and MAGs.

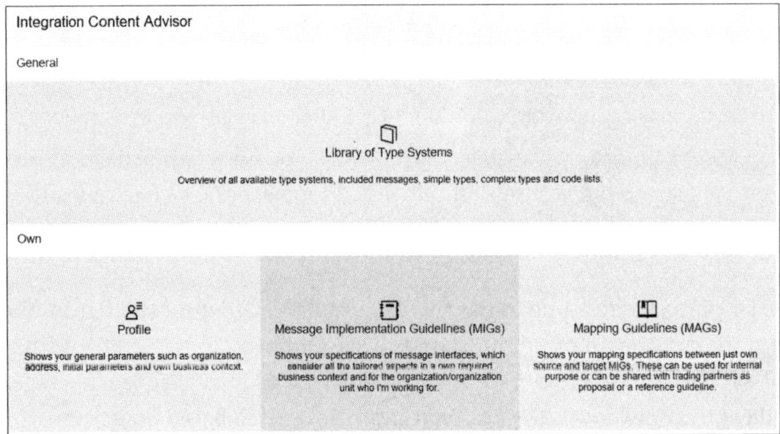

Figure 7.2 ICA Entry Page

2. Select the **Library of Type Systems** link to get the overview of the type systems available in your ICA (Figure 7.3). By default, only the **SAP IDoc** and the **UN/CEFACT** type systems are shown as **Licensed**. All the other non-SAP type systems are available as well but are shown as **Unlicensed** if you haven't purchased them. You'll get an error message when trying to access the details of the unlicensed type systems.

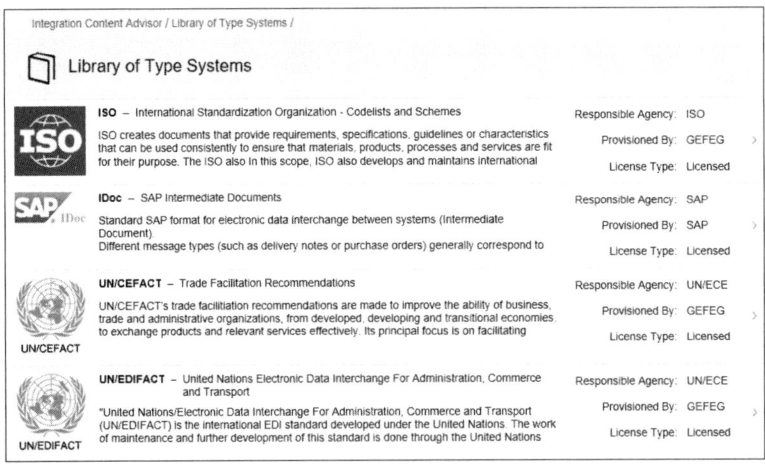

Figure 7.3 Type Systems in ICA

3. Let's first explore the SAP IDoc type system, as our outbound interface will be based on it. Select the **SAP IDoc** type system. A new window opens providing the details, as depicted in Figure 7.4. The **OVERVIEW** tab shows **General Information**, such as the **Responsible Agency** and the **Status**, as well as further **Documentation** about the type system. In addition, creation and modification information is shown in the **Administrative Data** area.

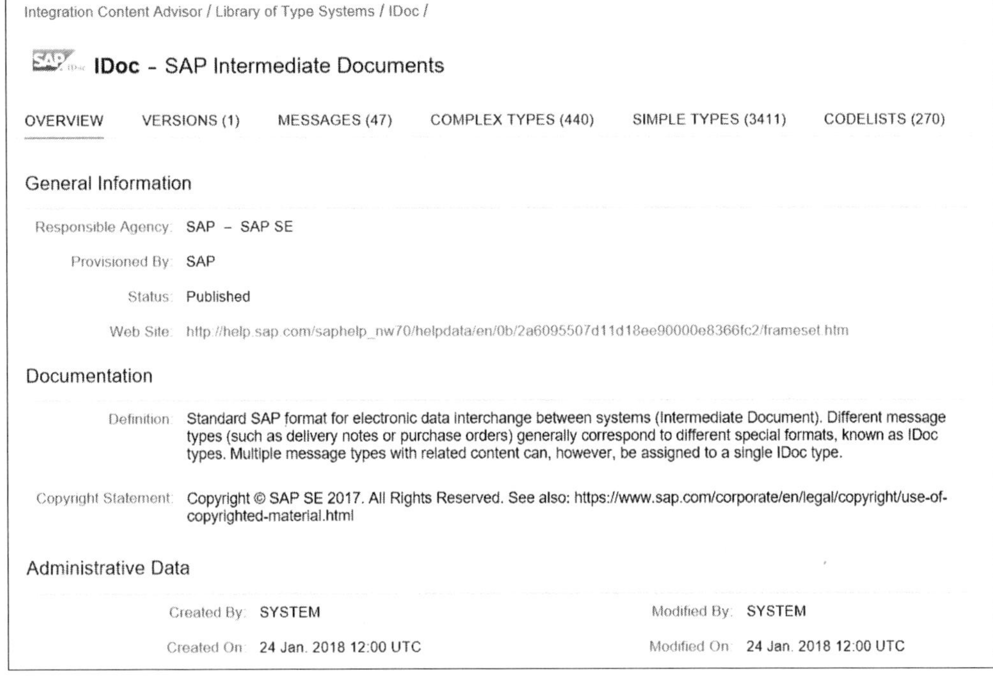

Integration Content Advisor / Library of Type Systems / IDoc /
IDoc - SAP Intermediate Documents
OVERVIEW
VERSIONS (1)
MESSAGES (47)
COMPLEX TYPES (440)
SIMPLE TYPES (3411)
CODELISTS (270)
General Information
Responsible Agency: SAP - SAP SE
Provisioned By: SAP
Status: Published
Web Site: http://help.sap.com/saphelp_nw70/helpdata/en/0b/2a6095507d11d18ee90000e8366fc2/frameset.htm
Documentation
Definition: Standard SAP format for electronic data interchange between systems (Intermediate Document). Different message types (such as delivery notes or purchase orders) generally correspond to different special formats, known as IDoc types. Multiple message types with related content can, however, be assigned to a single IDoc type.
Copyright Statement: Copyright © SAP SE 2017. All Rights Reserved. See also: https://www.sap.com/corporate/en/legal/copyright/use-of-copyrighted-material.html
Administrative Data
Created By: SYSTEM
Modified By: SYSTEM
Created On: 24 Jan. 2018 12:00 UTC
Modified On: 24 Jan. 2018 12:00 UTC

Figure 7.4 SAP IDoc Type System: Overview

4. In the **VERSIONS** tab, all available versions in the SAP IDoc type system are shown (Figure 7.5). As mentioned already, the only version in the SAP IDoc type system available at the time of publishing this book is **S/4HANA Release 1709**.

5. The **MESSAGES** tab lists all available messages provided by this type system in a tree structure. As depicted in Figure 7.6, the **SAP IDoc** type system contains the most commonly used IDoc messages. Opening one of them in the tree structure shows the versions available for this message. As only one version is available in the SAP IDoc type system, only one version is shown for the selected message. In other type systems, several versions appear for one message.

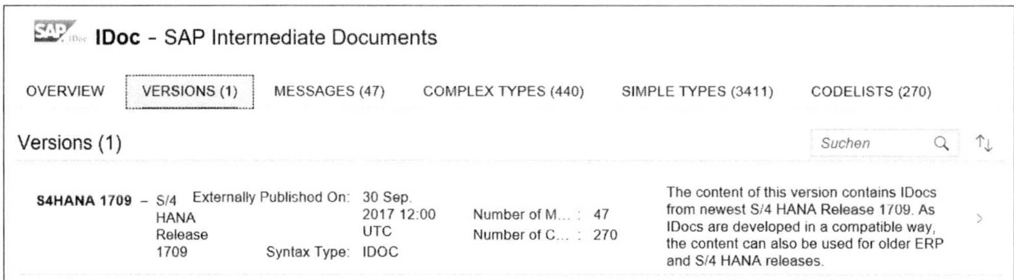

Figure 7.5 Versions for the SAP IDoc Type System

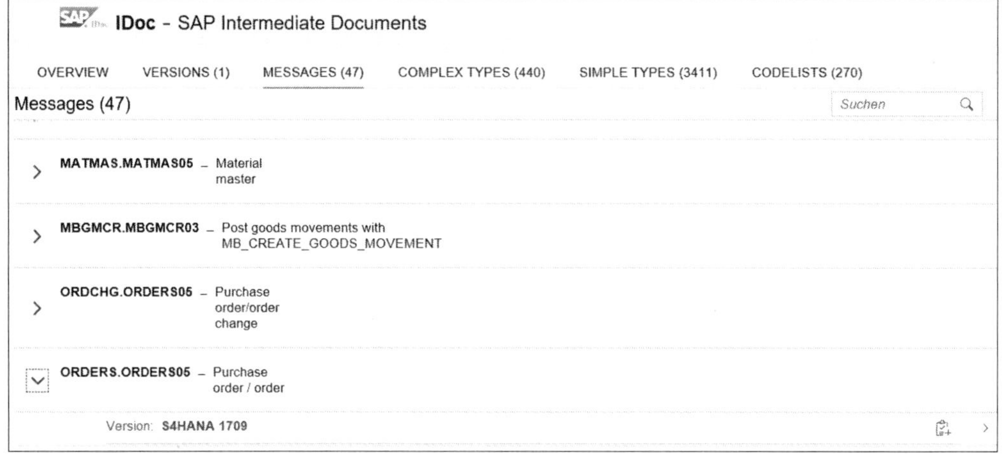

Figure 7.6 Message Interfaces in SAP IDoc Type System

6. When you click the row containing the **Version** information for the selected message, the detailed structure of the message is shown in a new window. In Figure 7.7, you find the structure of the **ORDERS.ORDERS05** message we're going to use in the scenario we want to set up. You can use this view to explore the message's structure.
7. You can drill down into single fields by opening the tree structure. Selecting dedicated fields opens the **Properties** view for the selected field below the tree structure. In Figure 7.8, for example, the details of the field **CURCY** are shown. The **DETAILS** tab provides information such as the **Tag**, **Name**, **Cardinality,** and **Documentation** for the field.

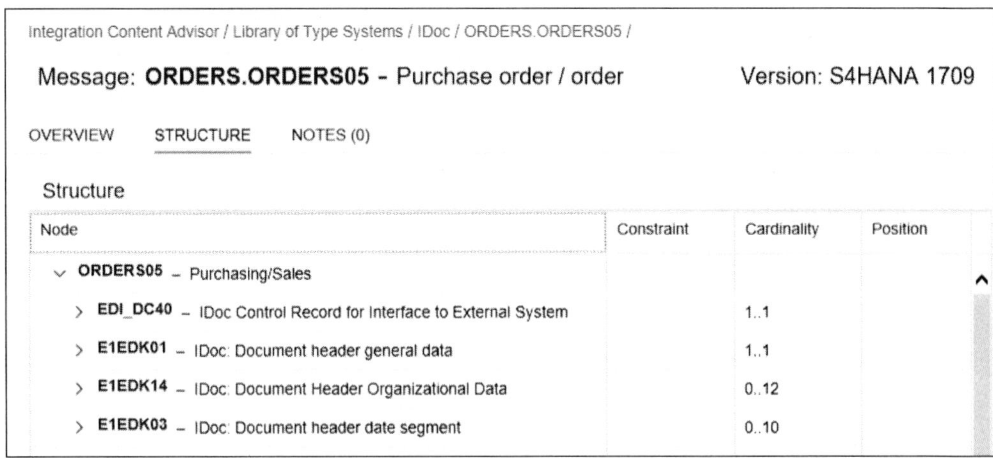

Figure 7.7 Structure of Message ORDERS.ORDERS05

Integration Content Advisor / Library of Type Systems / IDoc / ORDERS.ORDERS05 /

Message: **ORDERS.ORDERS05** - Purchase order / order Version: S4HANA 1709

OVERVIEW STRUCTURE NOTES (0)

Structure

Node	Constraint	Cardinality	Position	Primitive...	Syntax D...	Length	Codelist
> **EDI_DC40** – IDoc Control Record fo		1..1					
˅ **E1EDK01** – IDoc: Document header		1..1					
ACTION – Action code for the wh		0..1	001	String	CHAR	0..3	☑
KZABS – Flag: order acknowledg		0..1	002	String	CHAR	0..1	☑
CURCY – Currency		0..1	003	String	CHAR	0..3	☑

DETAILS NOTES (0) CODELIST: ISO_4217

Properties

Tag: CURCY

Name: Currency

Cardinality: min : 0 max: 1

Documentation

EDI6345_A General ISO code for the currency (e.g. DEM for German Marks (deutschmark)).

Figure 7.8 Properties of the Field CURCY

8. The **CODELIST** tab is very important because it shows the values of the linked code list. You notice already from the name of the tab that the code list **ISO_4217** is linked, which means that the values from this code list apply for this field. Note

that you can navigate to the **CODELIST** tab for this field only if the ISO type system is licensed because the linked code list is an ISO code list (name: ISO_xxx). If a code list from the SAP IDoc type system is linked, or the ISO type system was purchased, you can navigate to the **CODELIST** tab where you find the allowed values in a table (Figure 7.9).

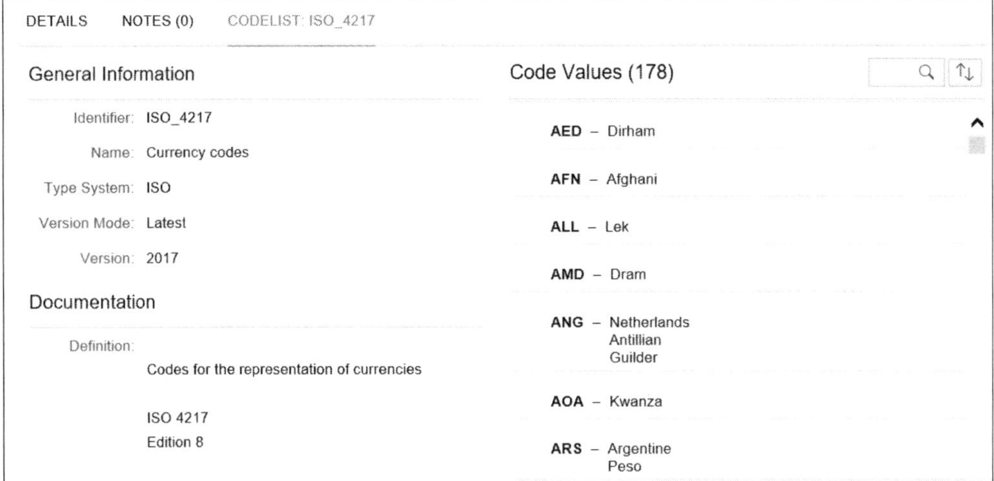

Figure 7.9 Code List Values for Field CURCY

9. In the **COMPLEX TYPES** and **SIMPLE TYPES** tabs, you can navigate to all data types used in the messages in this type system. Note that this is the same information shown when you inspect the properties of a selected field in the tree structure of a specific message. The same holds true for the **CODELISTS** tab: you can navigate to the available code lists either from the type system or when checking the properties of dedicated fields.
10. Get familiar with the type system browser, and navigate to the message **850 - Purchase Order** in version **004010** in the ASC X12 type system. This is the message interface we're going to use for our inbound message.

No License for ASC X12 Messages?

If you don't have a license for the ASC X12 type system to explore its messages but you want to set up the B2B sample scenario, you can download the runtime content—the mappings and XSDs—that the ICA would generate from the book downloads at *www.sap-press.com/4650*. Using this content, you can continue with the integration flow creation in Section 7.3 and further explore the runtime features SAP Cloud Platform Integration offers for B2B integration.

You're now familiar with browsing messages in the available type systems and know how to explore the structure of single messages. Let's now create the MIGs for the messages.

Create Message Implementation Guidelines

To create MIGs, execute the following steps:

1. To create a MIG based on the ORDERS.ORDERS05 message, open the **MESSAGES** tab in the **SAP IDoc** type system, and expand the message **ORDERS.ORDERS05**. In the line containing the version information select the **Create a New MIG** icon to create a new MIG for this message (Figure 7.10).

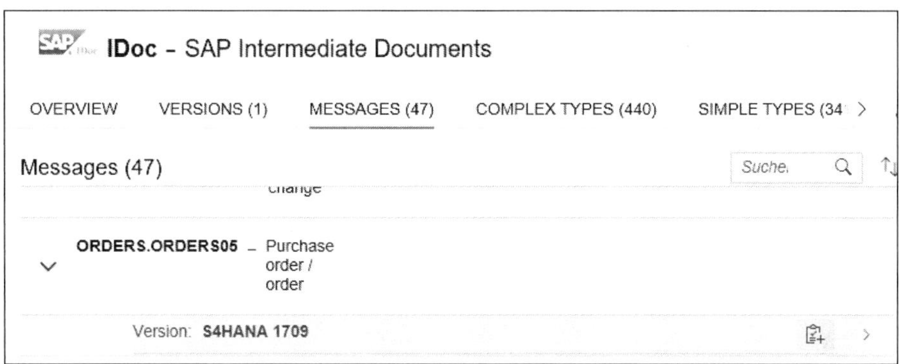

Figure 7.10 Creating a New MIG for ORDERS.ORDERS05

2. On the MIG creation screen, enter a **Name** for your MIG, select the **Direction**, and specify the **Business Context**, as depicted in Figure 7.11 and described here:
   - The **Direction** dropdown list offers three values: **In**, **Out**, and **Both**. You can choose whether the interface is used in inbound or outbound direction or if it can be used in both directions in the context of a B2B transaction. Setting the correct direction will make the proposal service more precise. We choose **Out** as the **Direction** for our MIG because we want to use this message interface as the target interface.
   - During creation of a new MIG, the **Version** is set to **1.0** with the **Status** as **Draft**.

- The fields **Message Type**, **Type System**, and **Type System Version** are prefilled based on the selected template message and can't be changed.
- You can use the **Documentation** field to add a description for the MIG. This text is visible as short text in the MIG overview list.
- In the **Business Context** field, you specify the business context in which the interface will be used. Use the + icon to add a business context. Note that you can define multiple entries. Based on the business context, you'll be provided with further options in the dropdown list. For example, add the business context **Business Process** with the value **Create Order**. The defined business context is used by the proposal service to provide optimal proposals.

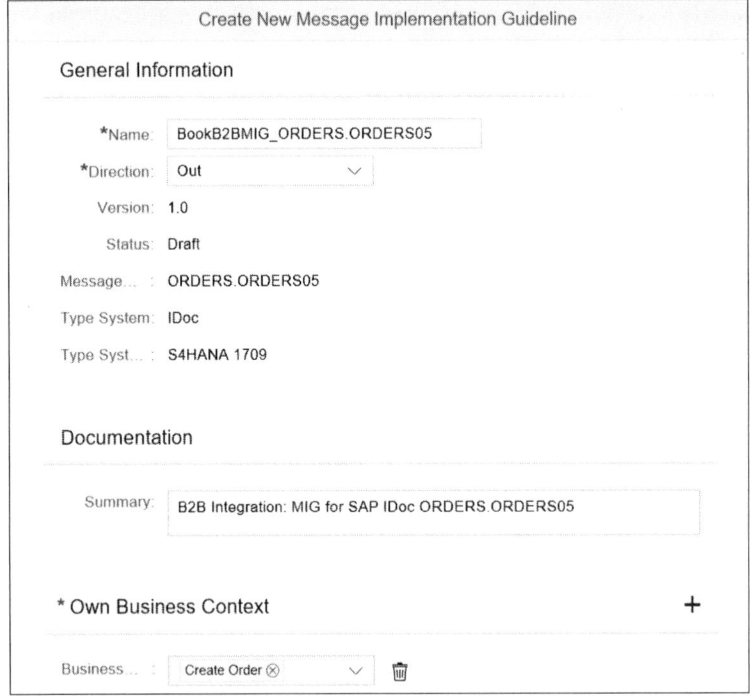

Create New Message Implementation Guideline
General Information
*Name: BookB2BMIG_ORDERS.ORDERS05
*Direction: Out
Version: 1.0
Status: Draft
Message... : ORDERS.ORDERS05
Type System: IDoc
Type Syst... : S4HANA 1709
Documentation
Summary: B2B Integration: MIG for SAP IDoc ORDERS.ORDERS05
* Own Business Context
Business... : Create Order

Figure 7.11 Creating the MIG for ORDERS.ORDERS05

3. Click **Create,** and then the MIG editor opens.
4. Choose **Edit** in the upper-right corner to switch to edit mode. In the **STRUCTURE** tab, the whole message structure of the used template message is shown (Figure 7.12). In this view, you select the fields you need for your scenario. By default, all

mandatory fields are preselected. In addition to the preselected fields, you can select additional fields required for your scenario.

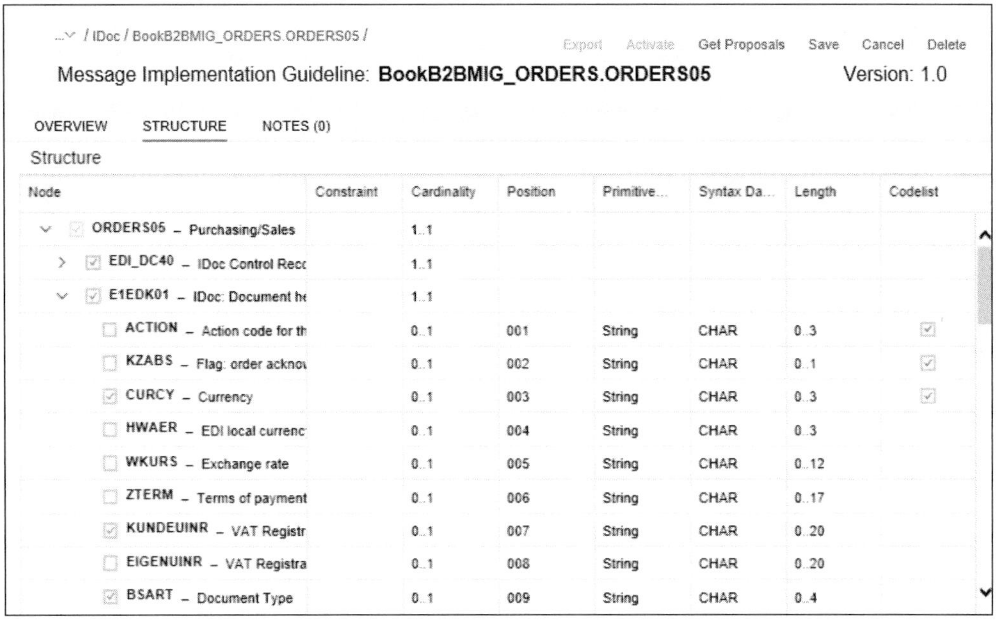

.../ IDoc / BookB2BMIG_ORDERS.ORDERS05 /

Export Activate Get Proposals Save Cancel Delete

Message Implementation Guideline: **BookB2BMIG_ORDERS.ORDERS05** Version: 1.0

OVERVIEW STRUCTURE NOTES (0)

Structure

Node	Constraint	Cardinality	Position	Primitive...	Syntax Da...	Length	Codelist
ORDERS05 – Purchasing/Sales		1..1					
EDI_DC40 – IDoc Control Recc		1..1					
E1EDK01 – IDoc: Document he		1..1					
ACTION – Action code for th		0..1	001	String	CHAR	0..3	☑
KZABS – Flag: order acknov		0..1	002	String	CHAR	0..1	☑
CURCY – Currency		0..1	003	String	CHAR	0..3	☑
HWAER – EDI local currenc		0..1	004	String	CHAR	0..3	
WKURS – Exchange rate		0..1	005	String	CHAR	0..12	
ZTERM – Terms of payment		0..1	006	String	CHAR	0..17	
KUNDEUINR – VAT Registr		0..1	007	String	CHAR	0..20	
EIGENUINR – VAT Registra		0..1	008	String	CHAR	0..20	
BSART – Document Type		0..1	009	String	CHAR	0..4	

Figure 7.12 Structure of the MIG for ORDERS.ORDERS05

5. Using the **Get Proposals** button on the top-right corner of the screen, you activate a proposal indicator that displays which fields might be most relevant for you. This is calculated based on the other available MIGs. Note that this is just a proposal that can help you define the MIG more quickly, but you don't have to accept the fields proposed.
6. Using the context menu option **Qualify Node**, you can qualify a node by specifying a qualifier marker and qualifier value. The qualifier is then shown in the structure as an arrow with the defined qualifier value (see Figure 7.13). Using qualifiers helps to simplify the MAG creation in the next step.
7. For fields that have fixed values in your scenario, you can a define **Fixed Value** in the **Properties** section (Figure 7.14). Those values will be mapped automatically later in the MAG configuration.

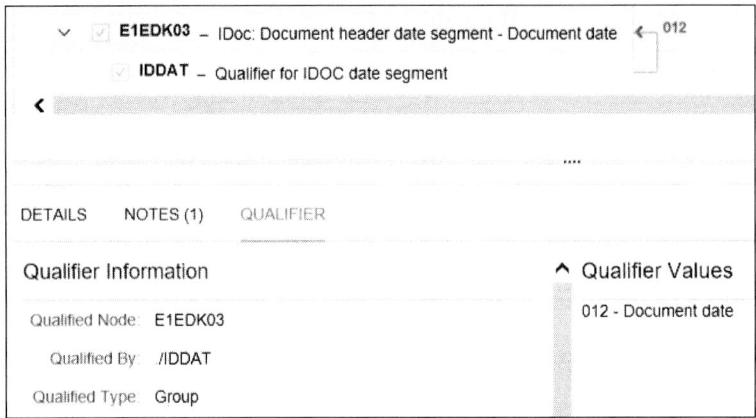

Figure 7.13 Qualified Field in the MIG

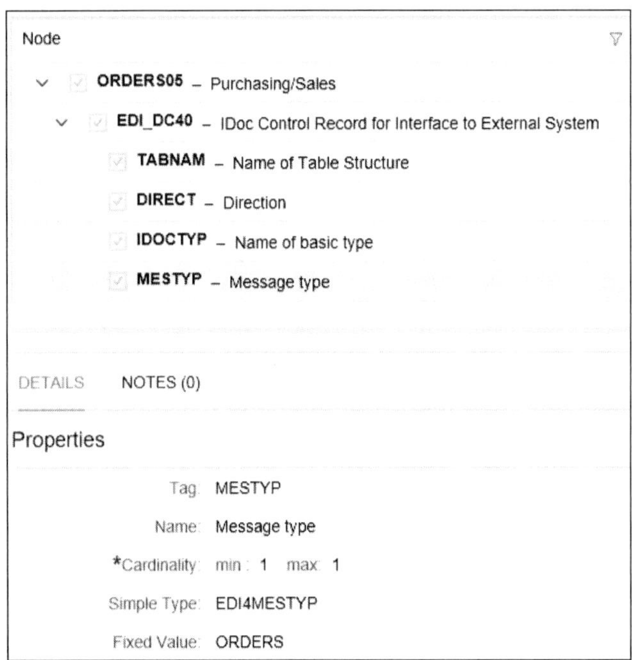

Figure 7.14 Defining a Fixed Value for the Message Type

8. In the **Properties** section, you can also change further field properties (e.g., the cardinality and the length of fields), define example values, and select code values from the linked code lists.

9. After you've selected the required fields, save the MIG using the **Save** button in the upper-right corner of the screen. Note that the activation of the MIG using the **Activate** button should be done only after creating and testing the MAG because this will save the MIG as the main version. Then no more changes are allowed to this version to protect it against unwanted changes; a new version would have to be created instead.
10. After creating a MIG, you can export the runtime artifacts using the **Export** button in the upper-right corner of the screen. A **.zip* file is created in your local download folder containing the **.xsd* and **.xsl* descriptions for the MIG. Those files can be imported into integration flows for the sake of performing validations and transformations.
11. Following the same procedure, you can create a MIG for the inbound interface based on the message 850 - Purchase Order with version 004010 from the ASC X12 type system. Select direction **In** when creating the MIG, and choose the same business context used for the ORDERS.ORDERS05 message: **Business Process** with the value *Create Order*. Note that it isn't mandatory to define the MIG to continue with the sample scenario because the generated runtime artifacts are provided in the book downloads as mentioned before.
12. Keep the mandatory fields and also define additional fields you require for the scenario. Use the proposal service as described before, and define qualifiers and constants as required.
13. You can save the MIG and export the runtime artifacts as described before.

Now that the MIGs are created, you can create a MAG based on them.

7.2.2 Configure Mapping Guidelines

After defining the MIGs for the source and target message interface, a mapping between the fields of those interfaces needs to be created. This step is executed in the MAG editor.

To create the MAG for the scenario, execute the following steps:

1. Start the MAG editor from the ICA entry screen (Figure 7.2). Select the **Mapping Guidelines** section in the lower section on the right side of the screen. A table containing all existing MAGs opens. In your case, the table may still be empty because no MAGs are created yet.

2. At the top of the table, select the **Create a New MAG** icon to create a new MAG. The MAG creation wizard opens.
3. In the first screen of the wizard, select the source MIG (Figure 7.15). Choose the MIG created for the **850 Purchase Order** message, and select **Next** at the bottom of the screen.

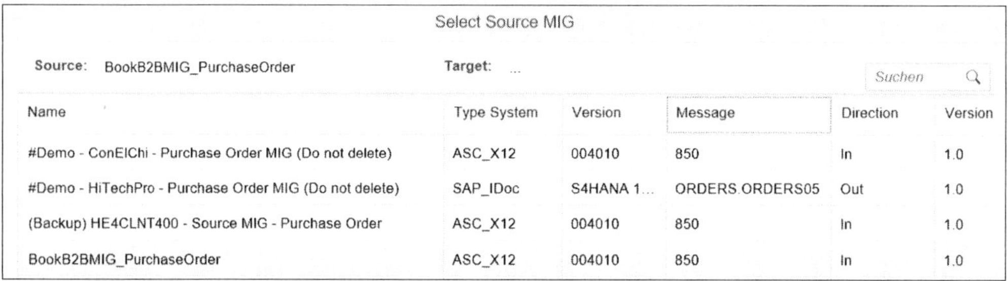

Select Source MIG

Source: BookB2BMIG_PurchaseOrder Target: ... Suchen

Name	Type System	Version	Message	Direction	Version
#Demo - ConElChi - Purchase Order MIG (Do not delete)	ASC_X12	004010	850	In	1.0
#Demo - HiTechPro - Purchase Order MIG (Do not delete)	SAP_IDoc	S4HANA 1...	ORDERS.ORDERS05	Out	1.0
(Backup) HE4CLNT400 - Source MIG - Purchase Order	ASC_X12	004010	850	In	1.0
BookB2BMIG_PurchaseOrder	ASC_X12	004010	850	In	1.0

Figure 7.15 Selecting the Source MIG

4. In the **Select Target MIG** screen, select the MIG you created based on **ORDERS.ORDERS05** (Figure 7.16), and click **Create**.

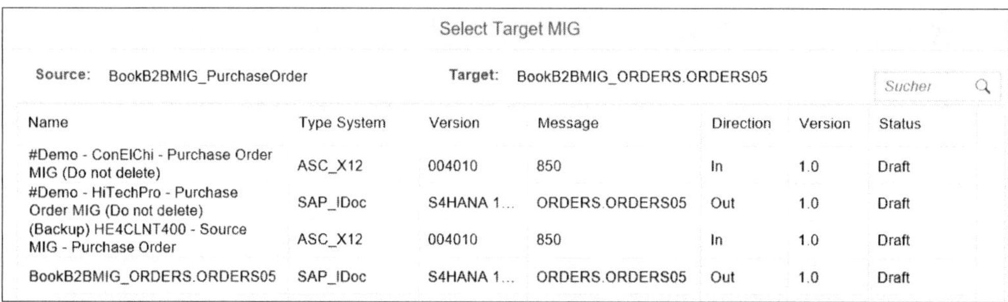

Select Target MIG

Source: BookB2BMIG_PurchaseOrder Target: BookB2BMIG_ORDERS.ORDERS05 Suchen

Name	Type System	Version	Message	Direction	Version	Status
#Demo - ConElChi - Purchase Order MIG (Do not delete)	ASC_X12	004010	850	In	1.0	Draft
#Demo - HiTechPro - Purchase Order MIG (Do not delete)	SAP_IDoc	S4HANA 1...	ORDERS.ORDERS05	Out	1.0	Draft
(Backup) HE4CLNT400 - Source MIG - Purchase Order	ASC_X12	004010	850	In	1.0	Draft
BookB2BMIG_ORDERS.ORDERS05	SAP_IDoc	S4HANA 1...	ORDERS.ORDERS05	Out	1.0	Draft

Figure 7.16 Selecting the Target MIG

5. The MAG editor opens. As depicted in Figure 7.17, the **OVERVIEW** tab contains information about the MAG and the selected source and target MIGs.

Figure 7.17 Overview Tab for Mapping Guidelines

6. Select the **MAPPING** tab to open the mapping editor. In this view, you map the fields from the source MIG to the target MIG. As depicted in Figure 7.18, draw a line from **Source** field to **Target** field to create the mapping between the fields. In the **FUNCTION** tab, you can define functions for the mapping of specific fields, and the defined code snippets are then generated into the XSLT mapping. You can also use the proposal service by selecting **Get Proposal** to get some mappings proposed in the table. We won't describe how to map all fields step by step because this would fill pages. Instead, we point you to the downloadable XSL transformation file provided with the book downloads (*www.sap-press.com/4650*).

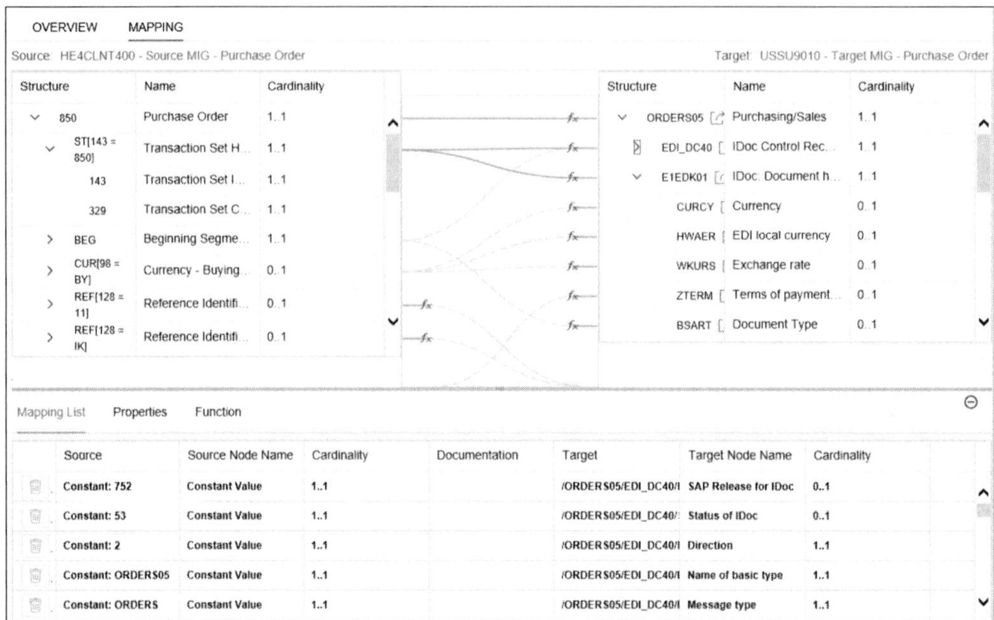

Figure 7.18 Creating Mapping between Source and Target MIGs

7. After finishing the mapping, save the MAG. Activate it after successful testing to protect it against unwanted changes.

> **Most Recent Features in Integration Content Advisor**
>
> To find the newest features in ICA, check the blogs in the SAP Community (*www.sap.com/community.html*), including "Integration Content Advisor: Discover B2B/A2A Standard libraries."

After defining the desired interfaces and mappings in the ICA, you can generate the runtime artifacts. You can use these runtime artifacts in the integration content, for example, in a mapping step of an integration flow.

7.2.3 Generate the Runtime Content

To use the mapping and the message interface definitions at runtime, you need to export the runtime artifacts from ICA.

To export the runtime artifacts, use the **Export** button in the upper-right corner of the MAG editor screen. A **.zip* file is created in your local download folder containing the **.xsd* and **.xsl* descriptions of the source and target MIG and an **.xsl* file containing the mapping between the source and target MIG.

Those artifacts are required in the integration flow configuration. Note that the runtime artifacts to be used in the sample scenario are provided with the book downloads at *www.sap-press.com/4650*. Download the runtime artifacts from the book download page, and continue with creating the integration flow based on a template.

7.3 Configure a B2B Scenario with AS2 Sender and IDoc Receiver Adapters

After defining the message interfaces for a B2B scenario and creating the mappings, the usual task for a content developer is to create the integration flow that handles the processing of the messages for this scenario.

In this section, we'll create the integration flow and use the generated message definitions and mappings within its processing steps. We create a sample scenario with the following processing steps:

1. An ASC X12 Purchase Orders message is received by the AS2 sender adapter.
2. The message content is validated.
3. A 997 acknowledgement is sent back to the sender.
4. After successful validation, the message is transformed into a SAP IDoc ORDERS.ORDERS05 message.
5. At the end of the processing, the IDoc message is send via the IDoc adapter to a receiver backend.

Let's get started.

7.3.1 Create an Integration Flow Using a Template

At first, we need to create the integration flow. To enable easy configuration, SAP provides predefined templates for the different B2B integration patterns. Those templates are offered in the Integration Content Catalog in the EDI Integration Templates for Integration Content Advisor package. In this package, you find all the predefined templates published by SAP for setting up B2B scenarios.

Integration Templates

At the time of publishing this book, not all the integration templates are final yet, and changes to the templates are still expected. Because of this we provide the template *EDI_IDoc_Template.zip* used for the sample scenario in the book downloads at *www.sap-press.com/4650*. Please download this template to set up the sample scenario.

Create a new integration flow in the integration designer perspective. In the creation wizard, select **Upload**, select the template *EDI_IDoc_Template.zip* file you downloaded from the book downloads, and enter a **Name**, as shown in Figure 7.19. Select **OK** to create the integration flow.

Figure 7.19 Creating an Integration Flow from a Template

The created integration flow looks like the one in Figure 7.20. There are lots of flow steps configured, and several of them have error markers because the flow isn't configured yet; we haven't yet added the generated runtime content from ICA.

In the next sections, we'll explore all of these steps and how to configure them to get the scenario running. Let's start from left to right as this is also the message processing order.

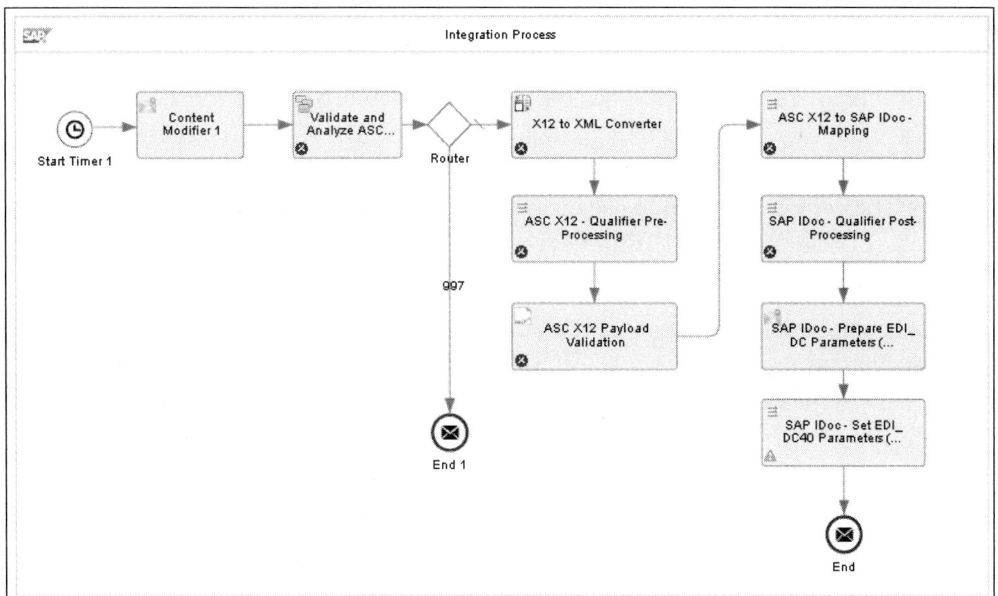

Figure 7.20 Created Integration Flow Based on a Template

Trigger Message Using Timer Start Event

In the imported template, the first two steps are a **Start Timer** event configured to run once at deployment of the integration flow and a **Content Modifier** that sets an inbound payload. Those steps were explicitly added to the original SAP template for the sample scenario to make the scenario configuration easier for you. Usually, the SAP template starts with a Message Start event without a sender adapter because the payload could be received by different adapters, such as SOAP or AS2, and continues directly with the EDI splitter.

With the **Start Timer** event, it's easy to trigger the first test message without having to configure a sender. Later, in Section 7.3.2, we'll change this configuration when we configure the AS2 sender adapter to receive messages for this scenario.

In the **Content Modifier** step, a sample payload is set in the **Message Body** tab. This is the same sample payload as provided in the *850 - Purchase Order.txt* file provided in the book downloads at *www.sap-press.com/4650*.

Validate EDI Messages Using EDI Splitter

In the next step of the processing, **Validate and Analyze ASC X12 Interchange**, the incoming EDI message is validated. We need to define based on which XSD a technical validation of the inbound message will be done. The EDI splitter is used for this as it can split and validate UN/EDIFACT and ASC X12 EDI messages based on configured XSD schemas. You need to use the generated XSD schema from ICA for the X12 Purchase Order definition. Use the generated content provided in the book downloads at *www.sap-press.com/4650*.

As our inbound message is an X12 message, open the **X12** tab in the flow step and configure it as depicted in Figure 7.21. Select **ISO-8859-1** as **Source Encoding**, and define that a **Standard Validation** of the message will be executed. Click on the **Add** button to add the schema `ASC-X12_850_004010.xsd` to do the technical validation based on the XSD for the standard X12 EDI message. Use the **Upload from File System** option in the selection dialog to add the XSD to the integration flow.

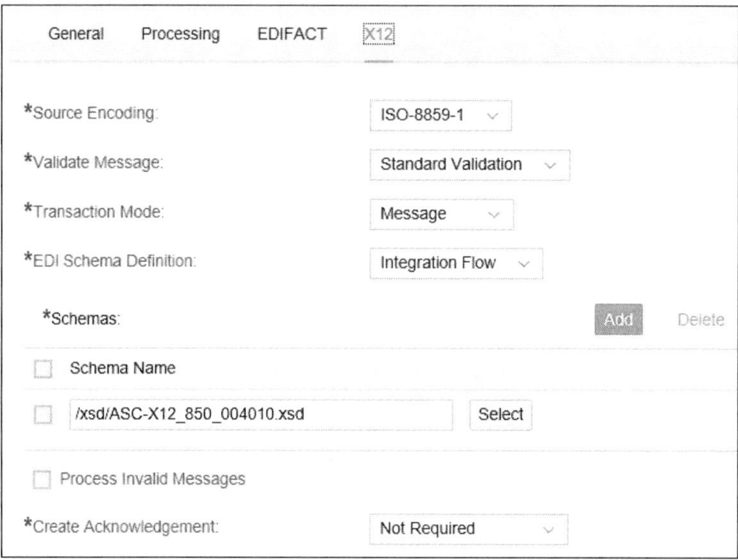

Figure 7.21 Configuring the EDI Splitter

Note that for now, we set **Create Acknowledgement** to **Not Required**. The acknowledgement handling will be configured in Section 7.3.4.

We leave the **Router** and **End Message** event after the EDI splitter as they are for now; they are used when we configure acknowledgement handling in Section 7.3.4.

Detailed Documentation of the Used Integration Flow Steps

For the sake of simplicity, we won't explain all configuration options of the integration flow steps in detail. Refer to the "Define EDI Splitter," "Define EDI to XML Converter," "Validating Message Payload against XML Schema," and "Create XSLT Mapping" sections in the documentation for SAP Cloud Platform Integration at *https://help.sap.com/viewer/product/CLOUD_INTEGRATION/Cloud.*

Convert EDI Messages to XML Format Using the EDI to XML Converter

In the **X12 to XML converter** step in the template, the conversion of the EDI message to XML is executed using the EDI to XML converter, which can convert UN/EDIFACT and ASC X12 EDI messages. As our inbound message is an X12 message, open the **X12** tab, and configure it as shown earlier in Figure 7.22.

Define **ISO-8859-1** as **Source Encoding**, and add the schema `ASC-X12_850_004010.xsd` to do the conversion to XML based on the MIG created for the ASC X12 source message. Use the XSD already uploaded in the last step.

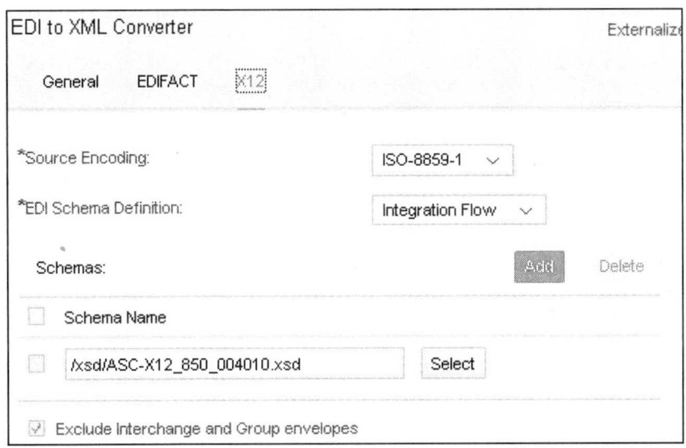

Figure 7.22 Configuring the EDI to XML Converter

After this step, the EDI message is available as an XML representation in the runtime, so that additional conversions, validations, and mapping to the target structure can be done.

Configure ASC X12 Qualifier Preprocessing

In the **ASC X12 Qualifier Pre-processing** step, qualifier suffixes are added to the XML based on the MIG definition from ICA in order to perform a content validation of the message in the next step. The preprocessing is executed via the XSLT mapping generated by the ICA.

In the **PROCESSING** tab, select the mapping `ASC-X12_004010_850_preproc.xsl` generated from ICA and provided in the book downloads (Figure 7.23). Use the **Upload from File System** option in the selection dialog to add the mapping to the integration flow.

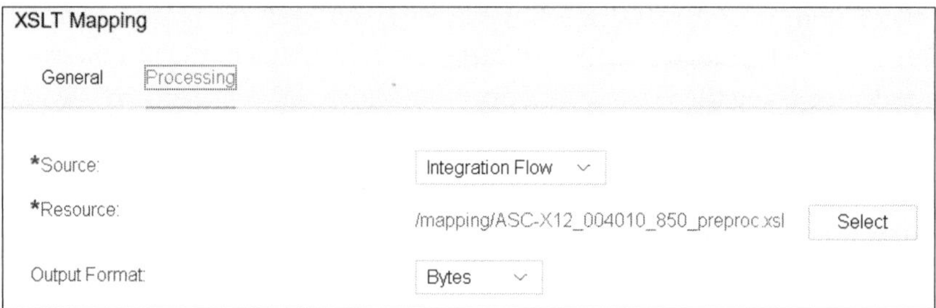

Figure 7.23 Configuring X12 Preprocessing

After this step, the real payload validation can be executed based on the defined qualifiers and qualifier values.

Configure XML Validator

In the **ASC X12 Payload Validation** step, the payload validation of the inbound message is done using the XML validator. The validation is done against the "Russian doll" (RD) XSD generated from ICA for the source MIG. (RD style means that the XSD schema structure mirrors the XML document structure.) For the content validation, this XSD is required because it contains the constraints defined in the MIG and provides a high-precision validation of each segment of the payload supporting qualifiers and code lists.

In the **Validation** tab of the XML validator step, select the `ASC-X12_850_004010_RD.xsd` representing the schema of the ASC X12 850 Purchase Order in RD format, as depicted in Figure 7.24. Use the **Upload from File System** option in the selection dialog to add the XSD to the integration flow.

If the validation isn't successful during runtime, an error is raised. If the validation passes successfully, the XML is transformed to the IDoc XML format in the next step.

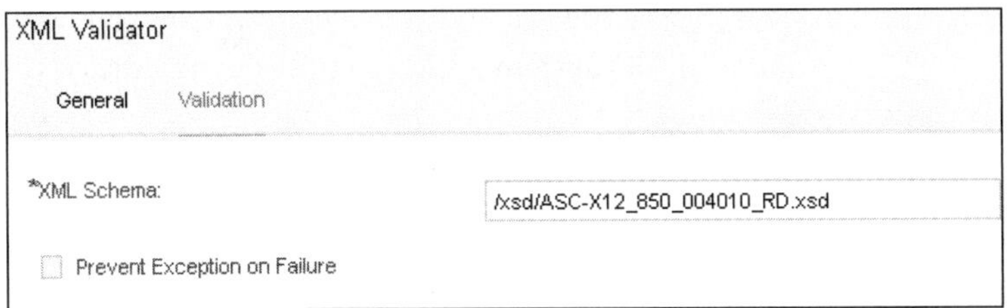

Figure 7.24 Configuring the XML Validator

Configure Mapping from EDI to IDoc Format

The **ASC X12 to SAP IDoc – Mapping** step converts the X12 message into SAP IDoc format using the XSLT mapping generated by the ICA.

To configure this, in the **Processing** tab of the XSLT mapping step (Figure 7.25), select the `ASC_X12_to_SAP_IDoc_Purchase_Order_Mapping.xsl` file generated by the ICA and provided in the book downloads. Use the **Upload from File System** option in the selection dialog to add the mapping to the integration flow.

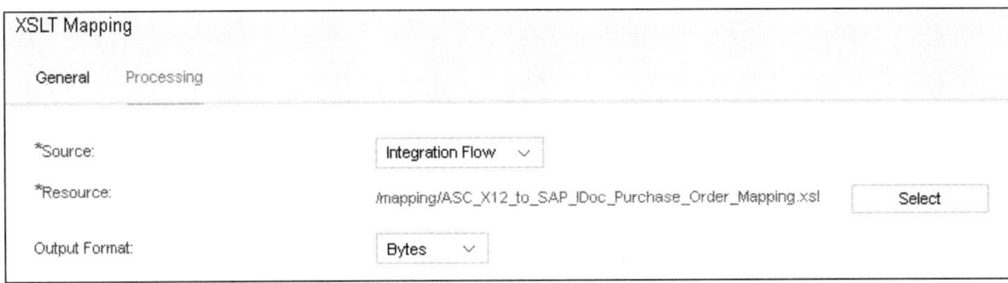

Figure 7.25 Configuring XSLT Mapping

After the transformation to the IDoc XML format, the postprocessing steps for the IDoc format have to be executed.

Configure IDoc Postprocessing

For the IDoc postprocessing, first the qualifier suffixes are removed because they aren't required in the final IDoc payload. Then, the IDoc control record EDI_DC40 needs to be defined.

To configure the IDoc qualifier postprocessing in the **SAP IDoc – Qualifier Post-Processing** step, in the **Processing** tab, select the XSLT mapping `SAP_IDoc_ORDERS05_`

S4HANA 1709_PostProc.xsl file generated by the ICA and provided in the book downloads (Figure 7.26). Use the **Upload from File System** option in the selection dialog to add the mapping to the integration flow.

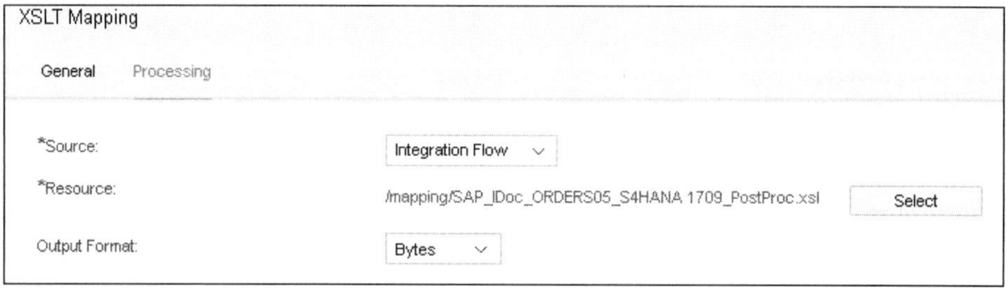

XSLT Mapping

General Processing

*Source: Integration Flow

*Resource: /mapping/SAP_IDoc_ORDERS05_S4HANA 1709_PostProc.xsl Select

Output Format: Bytes

Figure 7.26 Configuring the IDoc Postprocessing

To configure the IDoc control record, a set of properties is defined in the **Content Modifier** step named **SAP IDoc - Prepare EDI_DC Parameters**. In the **Properties** tab, you can define the values that will be generated into the EDI_DC IDoc control record. Those values are required for the IDoc configuration in the receiver system (see also Section 7.3.3). Most of the properties are filled automatically from the source payload using an XPath expression; some are set to constants, and some are filled from headers. For the sample scenario, you may keep the default values or adjust them, if required. The following values are of special interest because they define the processing in the receiver system:

- **SAP_IDoc_EDIDC_SNDPOR**
  Port of the sender; if you don't change it, the value **SAPABC** is used.
- **SAP_IDoc_EDIDC_SNDPRT**
  Partner type of the sender; if you don't change it, the value **LS** is used.
- **SAP_IDoc_EDIDC_SNDPRN**
  Partner number of the sender; if you don't change it, the value **myAS2ID** from the inbound request is used.
- **SAP_IDoc_EDIDC_RCVPOR**
  Port of the receiver; if you don't change it, the value **SAPABC** is used.
- **SAP_IDoc_EDIDC_RCVPRT**
  Partner type of the receiver; if you don't change it, the value **LI** is used.
- **SAP_IDoc_EDIDC_RCVPRN**
  Partner number of the receiver; if you don't change it, the value **USSU9010** from the inbound request is used.

After defining the values for the IDoc control record, those values have to be taken over into the EDI_DC control record. This is done in the XSLT mapping named **SAP IDoc - Set EDI_DC40 Parameters**, which is using a predefined XSLT mapping to insert the defined properties into the IDoc payload.

With this last processing step in the integration flow, you've completed the configuration of the validations and mappings of the EDI message. Now we can configure the receiver of the message.

Send the Message Using Mail Receiver Adapter

In the template, no receiver channel is configured because the message could be sent out using different adapters. The usual one for an IDoc message is the IDoc adapter, but for our first sample execution, let's use the **Mail** adapter. With this, you can easily send the first test message to your mail account to check how the validations and mappings are executed. Configure the **Mail** adapter as described in Chapter 5, Section 5.3.2. Configure the message body as attachment, so that the IDoc message is sent as an attachment in the email (Figure 7.27).

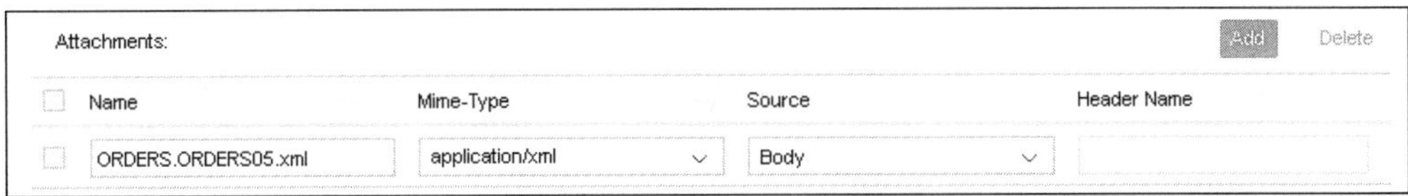

Figure 7.27 Mail Receiver Adapter's Attachment Configuration

With this configuration, you'll receive the mapped IDoc ORDERS.ORDERS05 message as email attachment in your mail account.

Test the Integration Flow

After you've configured all the steps and adapters, save the integration flow, and deploy it on the SAP Cloud Platform Integration tenant. In monitoring, check that the integration flow started and the message was processed successfully. In your mail account, you should have received an email with the mapped IDoc message.

Now that you've successfully executed the scenario with all its validation and mapping steps, you can configure a real sender adapter, enabling the ASC X12 850 Purchase Order message to be sent to the integration flow from a sender system.

7.3.2 Configure AS2 Sender Channel to Receive EDI Messages

As in a real-life B2B scenario, messages are sent from a sender system to the SAP Cloud Platform Integration tenant, so we now need to replace the timer start event with a real sender configuration. In our sample scenario, we'll use the **AS2** sender adapter to receive the 850 Purchase Order messages via the AS2 protocol.

Open the integration flow in edit mode, and delete the timer **Start** event and the **Content Modifier** that defined the sample payload. Add a **Start** message event and a **Sender** participant from the palette. Connect the **Start** message event with the first flow step in the integration flow and the **Sender** participant with the **Start** message event (Figure 7.28). In the adapter selection screen, select the **AS2** adapter with message protocol **AS2**.

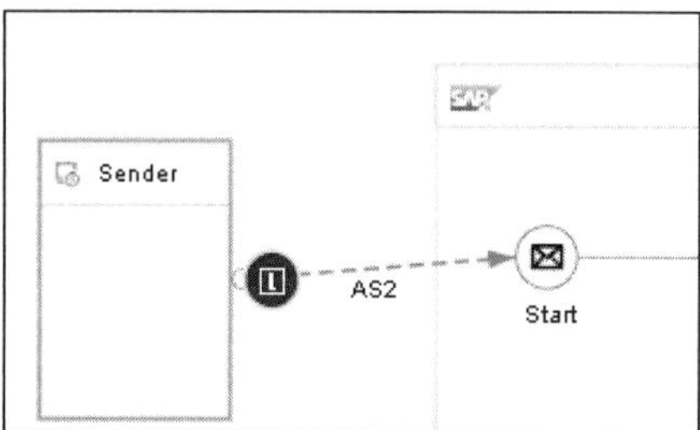

Figure 7.28 Integration Flow with AS2 Adapter

Configure the **AS2** sender adapter's **Processing** tab, as shown in Figure 7.29.

> **Detailed Documentation of the AS2 Sender Adapter**
>
> Note, that for the sake of simplicity, we won't describe all possible configuration options in the **AS2** sender adapter in detail in the book. You can refer to the "Configure Communication Channel with AS2 Adapter" section in the documentation for SAP Cloud Platform Integration at *https://help.sap.com/viewer/product/CLOUD_INTEGRATION/Cloud*.

The most important settings are the configurations for the **Expected Messages: Message ID Left Part, Message ID Right Part, PARTNER AS2 ID, Own AS2 ID**, and **Message Subject** because those parameters define the expected inbound message. The combination of the parameters must be unique across all the integration flows deployed on the tenant. You'll need the defined settings when setting up the sender simulation tool in the next section.

AS2

General Processing Security MDN Retry

EXPECTED MESSAGES

Message ID Left Part:	.*
Message ID Right Part:	.*
Partner AS2 ID:	myCompanyAS2ID
Own AS2 ID:	ABCCompanyID
Message Subject:	AS2 message
Number of Concurrent Processes:	1
Authorization:	User Role
User Role:	ESBMessaging.send

MESSAGE SETTINGS

- [ ] Mandatory File Name
- [ ] Duplicate Message ID
- [ ] Duplicate File Name

Figure 7.29 AS2 Sender Adapter Configuration

AS2 Sender Adapter Uses JMS Queues for Storage

Because the **AS2** sender adapter is using JMS queues to temporarily store messages for retry in error cases, you need to get a JMS Message Broker provisioned to successfully use it in an integration flow. If no broker is provisioned, the integration flow using the **AS2** sender adapter won't start, and an error stating that no broker is available will appear in the **Manage Integration Content** monitor.

Check the "Provision Message Broker" blog in the SAP Community (*www.sap.com/community.html*) about the provisioning of a JMS Message broker for your tenant.

The configurations in the **Security**, **MDN**, and **Retry** tabs can be left with the default settings. For our simple sample scenario, we don't use signing, encryption, or asynchronous message disposition notification (MDN). A synchronous MDN is sent back to the receiver as a receipt to acknowledge that the message was successfully received. A retry will be executed every minute if there is an error. Check out the documentation for SAP Cloud Platform Integration to get more details about the configuration options for those features.

Sample Scenario with Signing, Encryption, and Asynchronous MDN

If you want to extend the simple sample scenario by using signing, encryption, and asynchronous MDN, refer to the detailed "B2B Capabilities in SAP Cloud Platform Integration – Part 2" blog in the SAP Community (*www.sap.com/community.html*).

Save and deploy the integration flow. The integration flow is now ready to be called from the sender system.

Get the Endpoint URL

To call this integration flow, the sender needs to know the URL where to send the message to. The endpoint URL can be retrieved the same way as we've explained in several places in the book for the SOAP adapter. Open the **Manage Integration Content** monitor, and select the deployed integration flow. The endpoint URL is shown in the **Endpoints** section in the details screen on the right (Figure 7.30 and Figure 7.31) and has the structure *https://<runtime node>/as2/as2*.

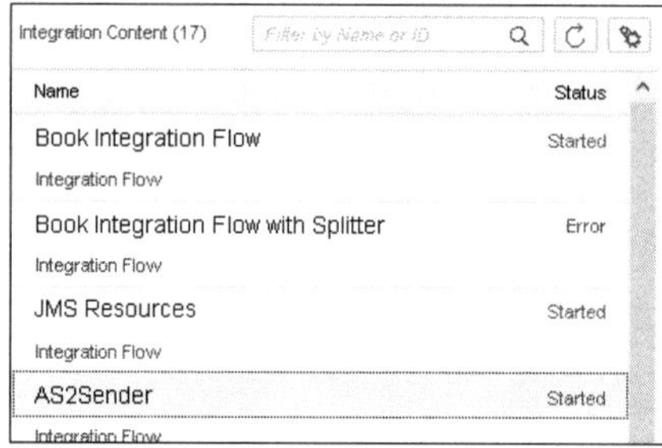

Figure 7.30 Endpoint of the AS2 Sender Adapter A

Figure 7.31 Endpoint of the AS2 Sender Adapter B

With this change, the sender needs to trigger the scenario execution by sending a message to the endpoint. For that, you need to configure a sender backend or application to send a message via the AS2 protocol to the **AS2** sender adapter.

Configure the Mendelson Tool to Send AS2 Test Messages

In our sample scenario, we'll send the test message from the open-source Mendelson AS2 tool (*http://as2.mendelson-e-c.com*). Mendelson AS2 can be used to simulate AS2 partners sending test messages via AS2 to the SAP Cloud Platform Integration tenant.

Install and configure Mendelson AS2 as described in the "B2B Capabilities in SAP Cloud Platform Integration – Part 1" blog in the SAP Community (*www.sap.com/community.html*). Make sure the following configured values are matching (fields are case-sensitive):

- The defined **AS2 id** for the local Mendelson AS2 partner configuration (Figure 7.32) needs to match with the **Partner AS2 ID** in the **AS2** sender channel (refer to Figure 7.29).

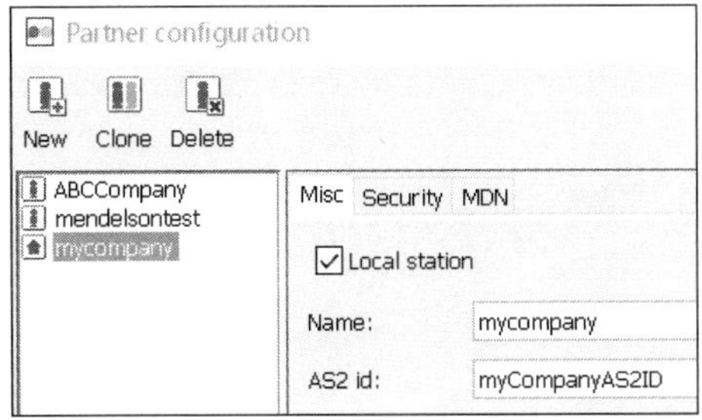

Figure 7.32 Own Partner Configuration in Mendelson

- The defined **AS2 id** for the AS2 partner created for the SAP Cloud Platform Integration tenant (Figure 7.33) needs to match the **Own AS2 ID** in the **AS2** sender channel (refer to Figure 7.29).
- In the **Send** tab of the configured AS2 partner, enter the endpoint URL retrieved from the **Endpoints** section in the **Manage Integration Content** monitor (Figure 7.34).
- The defined **Payload Subject** in the **Send** tab of the configured AS2 partner that was created for the SAP Cloud Platform Integration tenant (Figure 7.34) needs to match the **Message Subject** configured in the **AS2** sender channel (refer to Figure 7.29).
- In the **MDN** tab, select **Request sync MDN**, as shown in Figure 7.35.

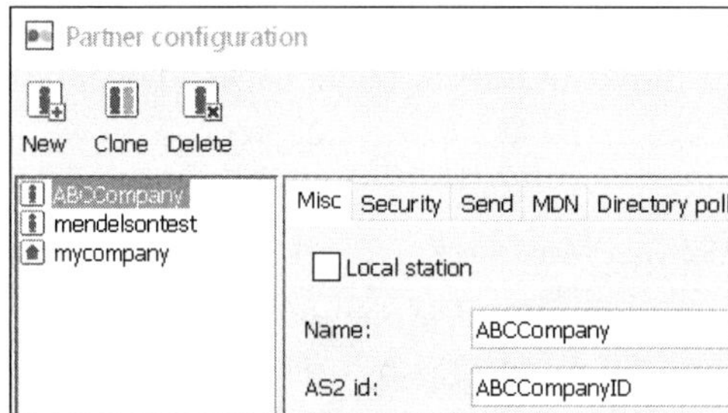

Figure 7.33 Partner Configuration for the SAP Cloud Platform Integration Tenant in Mendelson

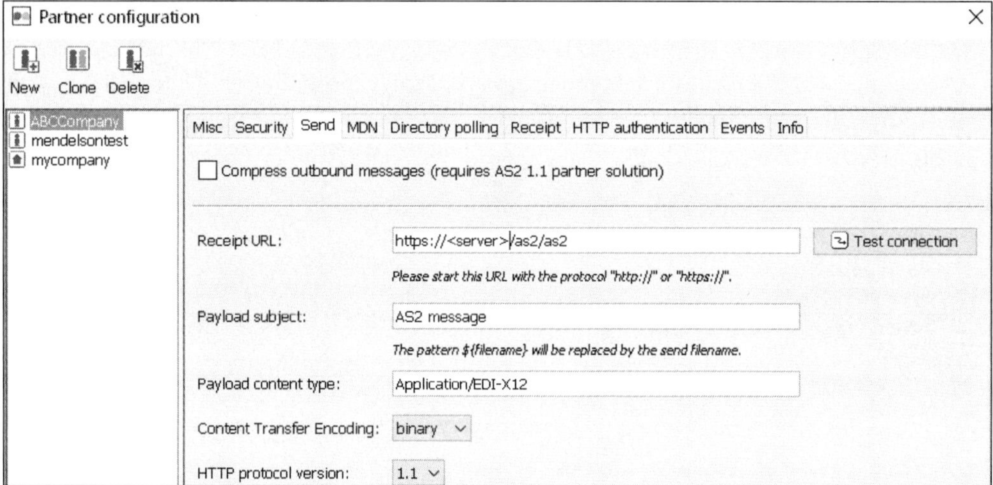

Figure 7.34 Configuring Endpoint and Payload Subject in Mendelson

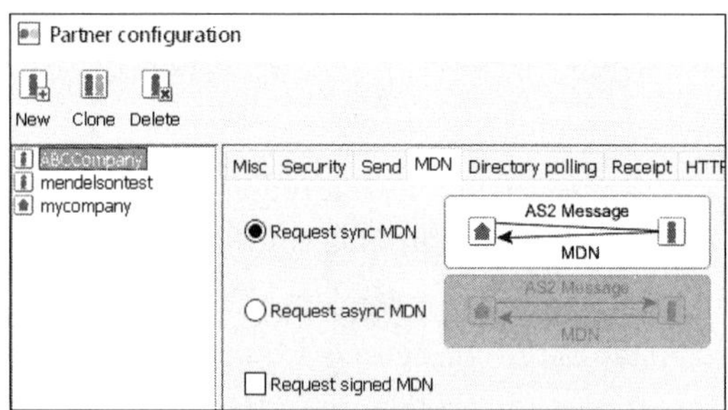

Figure 7.35 MDN Configuration in Mendelson

- In the **HTTP Authentication** tab, select **Use HTTP Authentication to Send AS2 Messages**. Furthermore, enter the **Username** and **Password** of the SAP Cloud Platform Integration user you want to use to log in to the SAP Cloud Platform Integration tenant.
- Import the SSL certificate from SAP Cloud Platform Integration tenant's keystore monitor as described in the blog *B2B Capabilities in SAP Cloud Platform Integration – Part 1* in the SAP Community (*https://www.sap.com/community.html*) to establish the HTTPS connection.

Now that you've set up and configured the AS2 partner, you can use the **Test Connection** option in the **Send** tab to test the connection to the SAP Cloud Platform Integration tenant. The test should pass successfully, and then you can continue with sending a real message to the integration flow.

Trigger a Test Message

To trigger a message from the Mendelson AS2 tool use the sample message *850 - Purchase Order.txt* provided in the book downloads at *www.sap-press.com/4650*. Download the message, and save it to your local workstation.

Trigger sending the message in Mendelson AS2 by choosing **File • Send File to Partner**. Use the configured AS2 partner, and select the downloaded sample message, as shown in Figure 7.36.

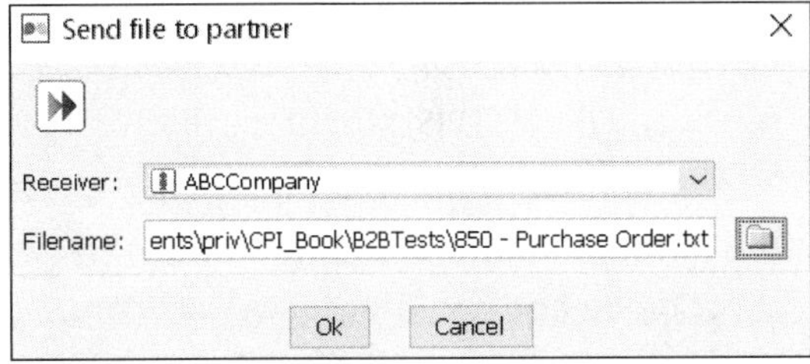

Figure 7.36 Sending a Test Message in Mendelson

Select **OK** to send the message. Then, check in the SAP Cloud Platform Integration's message monitoring to verify that the request was successfully received and processed. Check in your mail account to see that you received the mapped ORDERS.ORDERS05 IDoc message.

Now you've successfully set up a real AS2 sender to your integration flow, so you're able to send messages to the **AS2** sender adapter in your integration flow. The next step in the scenario setup is to send the message to a real IDoc receiver.

7.3.3 Add an IDoc Receiver

To configure the receiver of your scenario as an IDoc receiver, you need to set up an IDoc receiver adapter, which sends the ORDERS.ORDERS05 IDoc to the receiver backend, and you have to configure the receiver backend for IDoc inbound processing.

No IDoc Receiver Backend Available?

If you have no receiver backend available or don't want to set up the SAP Cloud Platform Connectivity service to connect to the on-premise backend, you may skip this section and keep the mail receiver channel. You'll still be able to continue with the sample scenario creating the acknowledgement in the next section.

For configuring the connection to the IDoc receiver, open the integration flow in edit mode, and delete the **Mail** receiver channel. Draw a new line between the **End** message event and the **Receiver.** Then select the **IDoc** adapter in the adapter selection screen.

Configure the IDoc adapter channel as depicted in Figure 7.37. In the **Address** field of the **Connection** tab, set the URL to call the IDoc processing of the receiver system. The URL is constructed as follows: *http://<server>:<port>/sap/bc/srt/idoc?sap-client=<client>*, where *server* and *port* are the server and the HTTP(S) port of the receiver system, respectively, and the *client* is the ABAP client in the system you want to post the IDoc to.

As **Proxy Type**, you probably have to select **On-Premise** because you want to connect to an on-premise system, which is usually not accessible from the Internet. To configure this connection, you have to set up and configure SAP Cloud Platform Connectivity, which will be described in the next section. If your on-premise system can be called from the Internet, you choose **Internet** as the **Proxy Type**, and then you don't have to set up SAP Cloud Platform Connectivity and can skip the next section.

As the **IDoc Content Type**, select **Text/XML** to send out the IDOC in XML format.

IDOC

Externalize

General Connection

CONNECTION DETAILS

*Address:	http://<server>:<port>/sap/bc/srt/idoc?sap-client=<client>
*Proxy Type:	On-Premise
Location ID:	
IDoc Content Type:	Text/XML
Authentication:	Basic
*Credential Name:	<credential_alias>

Figure 7.37 Configuring the IDoc Channel

Only HTTP Allowed If the Proxy Type On-Premise Is Used

Note that you need to define the address in the IDoc channel starting with *http://* if the connection is configured via SAP Cloud Platform Connectivity. However, the port you define can be either an HTTP or an HTTPS port as configured in the SAP Cloud Platform Connectivity configuration in the next section. This is because the connection to SAP Cloud Platform Connectivity is always done using a secure HTTP tunnel. The connection to the backend itself is then established via HTTPS or HTTP as configured in the system mapping in the SAP Cloud Platform Connectivity configuration. Further details can be found in the "Using SAP Cloud Platform Cloud Connector with SAP Cloud Platform Integration" blog in the SAP Community (*www.sap.com/community.html*).

If you want to use basic authentication to connect to the receiver backend, deploy the user credentials in the **Security Artifacts** monitor as already described in several scenarios in the book. You then use this security artifact and configure it in the **Credential Name** field of the IDoc channel.

Configure SAP Cloud Platform Connectivity

As already mentioned, you need to set up and configure SAP Cloud Platform Connectivity to set up a secure connection to an on-premise system. The detailed installation and configuration procedure is described in the online documentation for SAP Cloud Platform at *https://help.sap.com/viewer/p/CP* in the **Cloud Connector** section and in the "Using SAP Cloud Platform Cloud Connector with SAP Cloud Platform Integration" blog in the SAP Community (*www.sap.com/community.html*). After you've done the installation and initial configuration of SAP Cloud Platform Connectivity, you can connect SAP Cloud Platform Connectivity to your SAP Cloud Platform Integration account. Create and configure the subaccount in the subaccount dashboard of the SAP Cloud Platform Connectivity configuration per the description in the online documentation.

Now that your SAP Cloud Platform Integration tenant is connected to SAP Cloud Platform Connectivity, you can create the cloud to on-premise system mapping for your IDoc backend in the SAP Cloud Platform Connectivity configuration for your subaccount. In the **Cloud To On-Premise** section (Figure 7.38), add a new system mapping using the + icon at the top of the upper table.

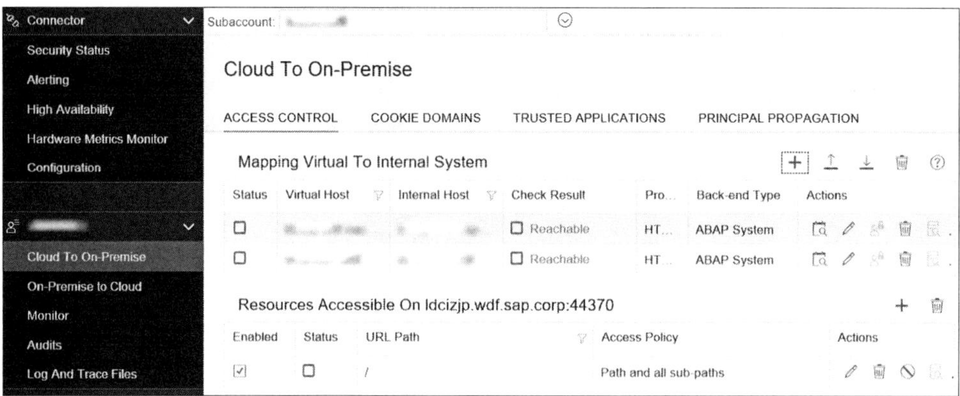

Figure 7.38 Adding System Mapping in SAP Cloud Platform Connectivity

In the **Add System Mapping** wizard, configure the connection to your ABAP receiver system via HTTP or HTTPS, and enter the hostname and the HTTP or HTTPS port of your IDoc receiver system. As principal type, select **None** if you want to forward the credentials entered in the IDoc channel.

After defining the system mapping to your receiver system, execute the availability check using the icon. Your system should then appear as **Reachable** in the **Check Result** column (see Figure 7.38).

For this newly created system mapping, you then need to define the accessible resource using the + icon at the top of the lower table. In the **Add Resource** dialog, either enter "/" as the **URL Path** and allow access to all subpaths (see Figure 7.39) or define the specific **URL Path** as "/sap/bc/srt/idoc" as configured in the IDoc channel.

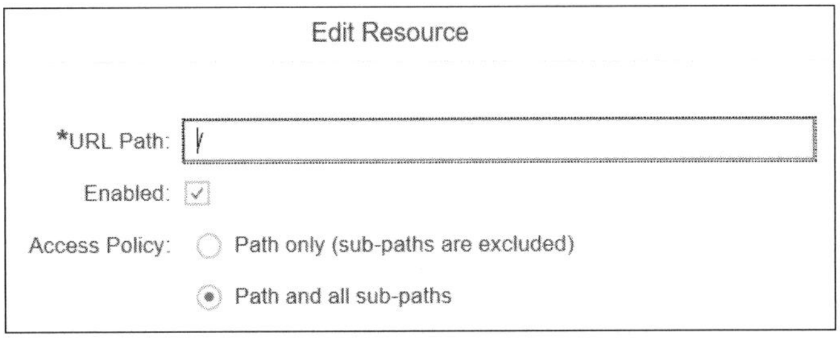

Figure 7.39 Edit Resource Dialog

Client Certificate-Based Authentication Using SAP Cloud Platform Connectivity

If you want to use client certificate-based authentication to the receiver system, you need to set up the client certificate in SAP Cloud Platform Connectivity as described in the "HCI: Integrate On-Premise ERP with HCI IDoc Adapter Using HANA Cloud Connector & Client Authentication" blog in the SAP Community (*www.sap.com/community.html*).

After you've set up SAP Cloud Platform Connectivity to connect your SAP Cloud Platform Integration tenant to your receiver system, you need to configure the IDoc processing in the receiver system.

Configure IDoc Processing in the Receiver System

To receive and process the IDoc in an SAP system based on an Application Server ABAP (AS ABAP), multiple configuration steps are required: you have to define logical system settings, set up ports, and configure partner profiles. As these are basic IDoc configuration steps, we won't explain them in detail here in this book. You can refer to the detailed documentation in Transaction SALE in your receiver backend.

Note that for the sample scenario, it isn't urgently required to configure all the IDoc configurations if you don't want to get the order processed in the application. It's sufficient to activate the HTTP service to receive IDocs via HTTP, and then you can monitor the IDoc in the system's IDoc runtime. The IDoc will be in error state, but from the connectivity point of view, the IDoc is received by the receiving system.

To receive IDoc documents via HTTP, you need to register the IDoc service in the SOAP runtime using Transaction SRTIDOC. Run the transaction, and select **Execute** to activate the HTTP-based IDoc service (Figure 7.40).

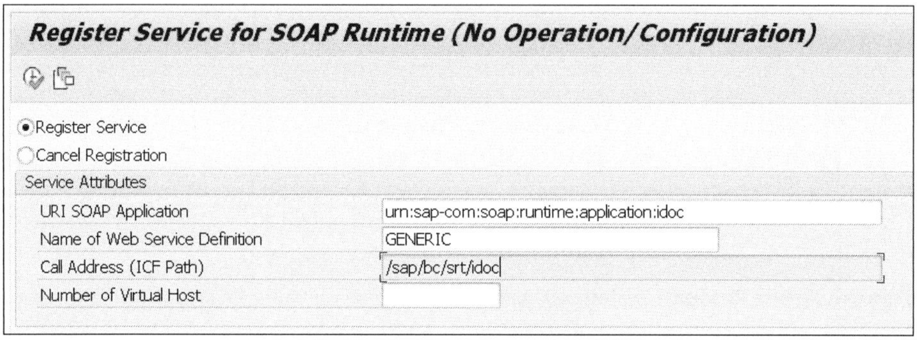

Register Service for SOAP Runtime (No Operation/Configuration)

(•) Register Service
( ) Cancel Registration

Service Attributes

URI SOAP Application	urn:sap-com:soap:runtime:application:idoc
Name of Web Service Definition	GENERIC
Call Address (ICF Path)	/sap/bc/srt/idoc
Number of Virtual Host	

Figure 7.40 Registering the HTTP Service for IDoc Processing

Now your receiver system can receive IDoc documents via HTTP from the SAP Cloud Platform Integration tenant.

Let's try it out.

Trigger Scenario Execution

To start the processing, trigger a message from the Mendelson AS2 test tool. Then, check in the SAP Cloud Platform Integration's message monitoring that the message was processed successfully.

To check if the IDoc was received by the receiver backend, search for the ORDERS05 IDoc in the IDoc monitoring. Call Transaction WE05, and search for IDoc documents with basic type ORDERS05. If you haven't executed all the IDoc-specific configurations, the ORDERS IDoc should appear in error status, as shown in Figure 7.41. The error **56 EDI: Partner profile not available** indicates that the partner profile isn't available for further processing of the IDoc. This shows that the IDoc is successfully received in the receiver system with the settings we've defined, but the IDoc-specific configuration is missing. If you want, you can configure the partner profile in Transaction WE20 and continue with configuring the IDoc inbound processing so that the order is processed in the system and finally an invoice is sent back.

Because the IDoc-specific settings aren't in scope of this B2B sample scenario, we skip the configuration of the IDoc processing and continue with the configuration of acknowledgement handling in SAP Cloud Platform Integration.

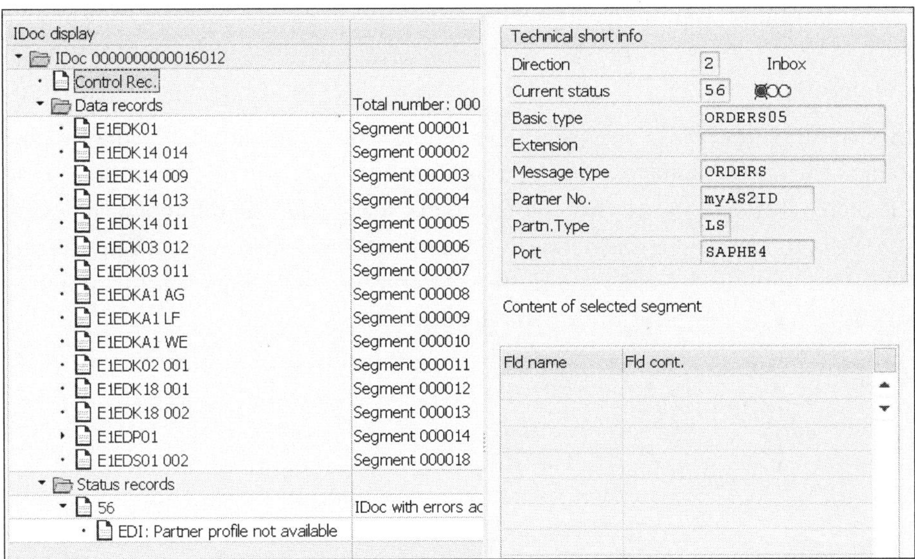

Figure 7.41 IDoc Monitoring in the Receiver System

7.3.4 Configure Acknowledgement Handling

When sending an EDI message, the sender usually expects a functional acknowledgement, also known as a 997 acknowledgement. The acknowledgement is used to notify that the message was received and validated and so can be further processed.

To address this requirement, SAP Cloud Platform Integration offers the option to validate the incoming EDI message and generate an acknowledgement in the **EDI Splitter** flow step.

This section will describe how to configure the acknowledgement in the integration flow. We'll extend the integration flow so that after the functional validation, an acknowledgement will be generated and sent via the **AS2** receiver adapter back to the original sender of the EDI message.

Let's get started.

Define a Number Range Object

Let's first configure a number range object (NRO) that will be required in the next configuration step to define the unique interchange number. Using number ranges, the runtime generates unique IDs for a specific NRO. Those unique IDs can be used in steps, such as the **EDI Splitter** step, or in scripts. For a brief introduction of NRO, refer to Table 7.1.

In the SAP Cloud Platform Integration's monitoring dashboard, select the **Number Ranges** tile in the **Manage Stores** section (for more details of the monitor, refer to Chapter 8, Section 8.4.4). At the top of the table, select **Add** to define a new NRO. Give the NRO a unique **Name**, and define the **Minimum Value** and **Maximum Value** (Figure 7.42). Furthermore, select **Rotate** so that the numbers will start with the minimum value again when the maximum is reached.

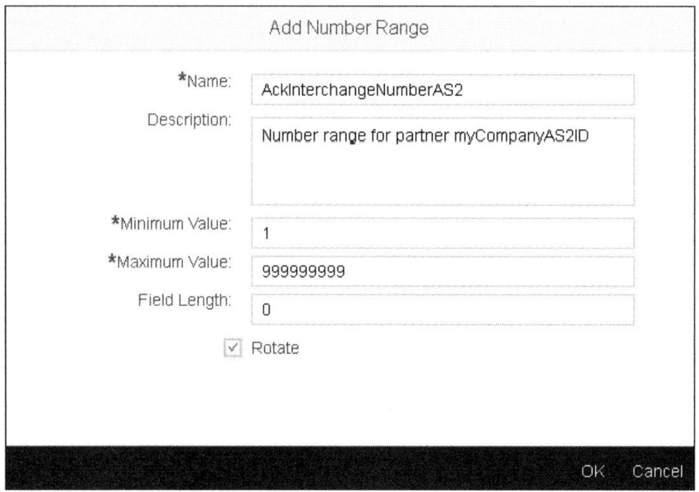

Figure 7.42 Defining the NRO

Configure Acknowledgement Handling in the Integration Flow

After the NRO is created, we can configure the acknowledgement handling in the EDI splitter and define the outbound processing for the acknowledgement.

As already indicated, the EDI splitter splits the incoming EDI bulk messages into single EDI messages. However, it can also validate them and generate an acknowledgement for the whole interchange containing the validation result.

To activate the acknowledgement creation, open the **EDI Splitter** step in the integration flow, and select **Required** in the **Create Acknowledgement** dropdown in the **X12** tab (Figure 7.43). One additional configuration option appears in which you need to define whether the **Interchange Number** for the acknowledgement is taken from the inbound EDI message (**Use From EDI Message** option) or whether it's generated using an NRO (**Number Range** option). Usually, the interchange number is taken from the inbound message, but to demo the NRO feature in SAP Cloud Platform Integration, select the **Number Range** option for our sample scenario. After selecting this option, an input field for the **Number Range** is shown where you enter the name of the number range you created in the last step.

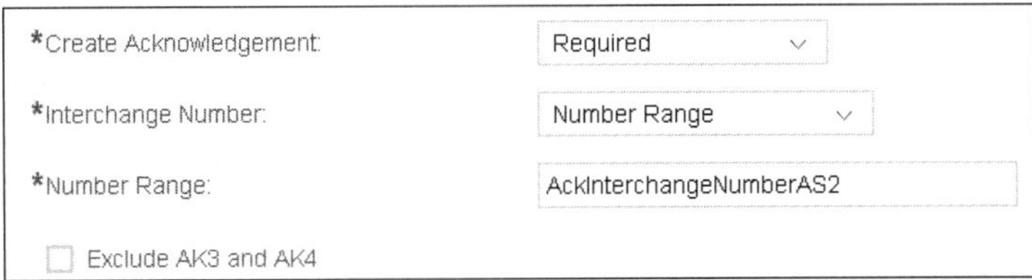

Figure 7.43 Configuring Acknowledgement Handling in EDI Splitter

The **Exclude AK3 and AK4** checkbox defines whether you want to get the detailed error information in the acknowledgement in the segments AK3 and AK4 in case of an error during validation. We don't select this flag, so that we get the detailed validation error later in our test.

Now that we've configured that an acknowledgement will be sent, we have to configure its receiver.

Configure the AS2 Receiver Adapter

As we received the inbound message in our scenario via the **AS2** adapter, we'll also send the acknowledgement back to the sender using the AS2 protocol. For this, we also use the **AS2** receiver adapter.

To configure the receiver of the acknowledgement, add another **Receiver** participant to the integration flow, and connect the **End** message event coming from the router to the new receiver, as depicted in Figure 7.44. Select the **AS2** adapter in the adapter selection dialog.

Configure the **AS2** receiver adapter as depicted in Figure 7.45. In the **Connection** tab, in the **Recipient URL** field, enter the URL of the local HTTP receiver from the AS2 Mendelson client. To get this URL, check in the **MDN URL** field in the **MDN** tab of your local AS2 partner configured in the AS2 Mendelson client (Figure 7.46). Make sure the correct IP address of your local system is entered there.

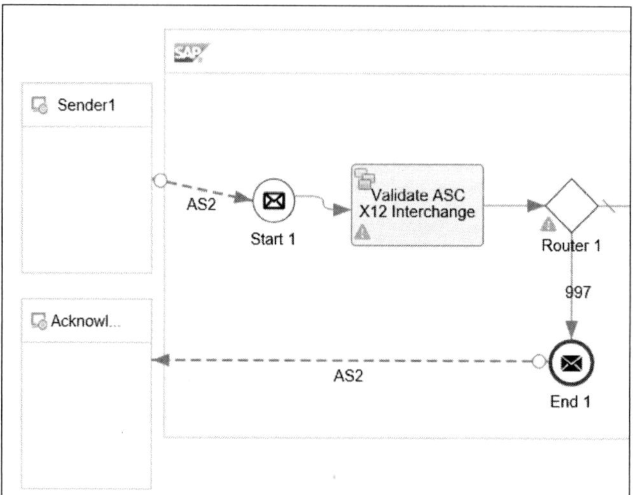

Figure 7.44 Adding the Receiver of the Acknowledgement

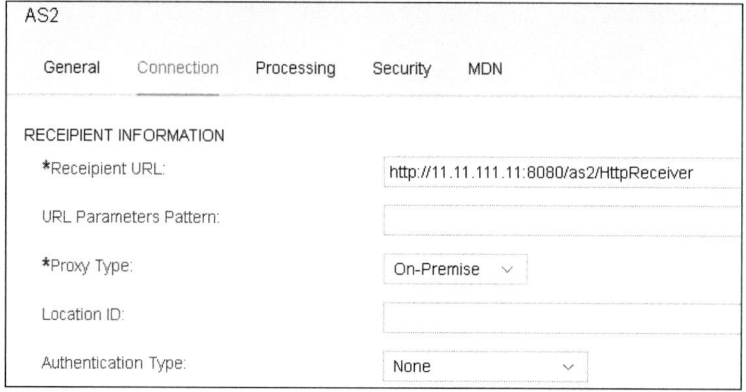

Figure 7.45 Configuring the Connection Tab in AS2 Receiver Channel

Figure 7.46 Getting the URL of the Mendelson Receiver

As **Proxy Type**, you most likely have to configure **On-Premise** because the system where the AS2 Mendelson client is installed isn't reachable from the Internet. Because of this, you need to set up the connection using SAP Cloud Platform Connectivity whose configuration is done in the next section.

No SAP Cloud Platform Connectivity Configured?

To set up that an acknowledgement is sent back via **AS2** receiver adapter, you need to configure SAP Cloud Platform Connectivity to connect to the local Mendelson AS2 tool. If you don't want to set up SAP Cloud Platform Connectivity for this scenario, you could also use a **Mail** receiver adapter and send the acknowledgement to your mailbox for test purposes.

In addition to the connection details, you configure the specific AS2 processing settings in the **Processing** tab. As depicted in Figure 7.47, configure the AS2-specific settings. For the sample scenario, you enter the following mandatory settings:

- **Own AS2 ID**
  Specify the same ID as used in the **AS2** sender channel. This is the AS2 ID identifying the SAP Cloud Platform Integration system.
- **Partner AS2 ID**
  Specify the ID of the partner receiving the acknowledgement. It should also match the ID used in the **AS2** sender channel.
- **Message Subject**
  Define **997** to indicate that this is a 997 acknowledgement.
- **E-Mail Address**
  Enter an email address. Note that this address is required per the AS2 protocol but not used at runtime.
- **Content-type**
  Define the content type of your acknowledgement. We set **application/edi-x12** because it's an ASC X12 message.

For a detailed explanation of the configuration fields in the **AS2** receiver channel, refer to the "Configure Communication Channel with AS2 Adapter" section in the documentation for SAP Cloud Platform Integration at *https://help.sap.com/viewer/product/CLOUD_INTEGRATION/Cloud*.

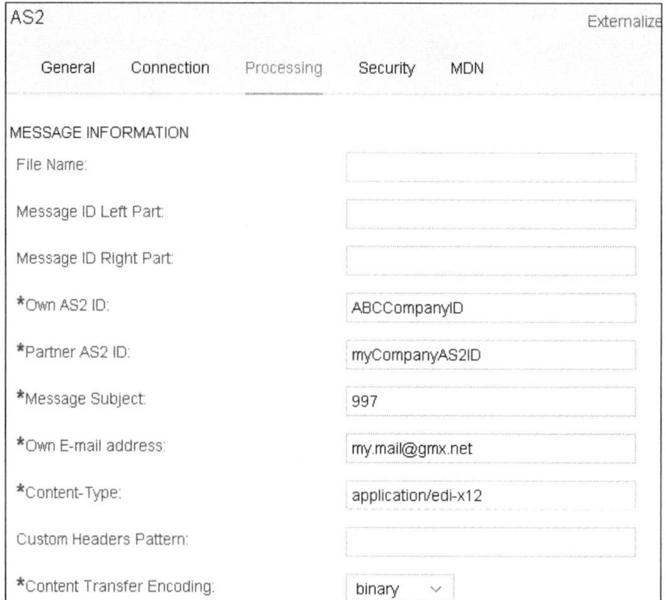

Figure 7.47 Configuring the Processing Tab in the AS2 Receiver Channel

You can leave the default values in the configuration options in the **Security** and **MDN** tabs because we don't want to use signature and encryption in the sample scenario. We also don't request an MDN for the acknowledgement. If you want to extend the sample scenario, refer to the "B2B Capabilities in SAP Cloud Platform Integration – Part 2" blog in the SAP Community (*www.sap.com/community.html*).

Save and deploy the integration flow.

Configure SAP Cloud Platform Connectivity

As already indicated, the connection to the HTTP URL of the AS2 Mendelson tool will probably have to be established using SAP Cloud Platform Connectivity because the system AS2 Mendelson is running on can't be reached from the Internet.

In Section 7.3.3, you've already seen how to set up SAP Cloud Platform Connectivity and how to connect it to your SAP Cloud Platform Integration tenant. There we showed you how to configure the connection to an SAP system based on AS ABAP to send the IDoc messages to. Now you have to configure a connection to your local system, where the AS2 Mendelson tool is running.

Log on to SAP Cloud Platform Connectivity. In the **Cloud To On-Premise** section (Figure 7.48), add a new system mapping using the + icon at the top of the upper table. In the **Add System Mapping** wizard, configure the connection to a **Non-SAP System** via HTTP, and enter the IP address and the HTTP port of your local system. As **Principal Type**, select **None**.

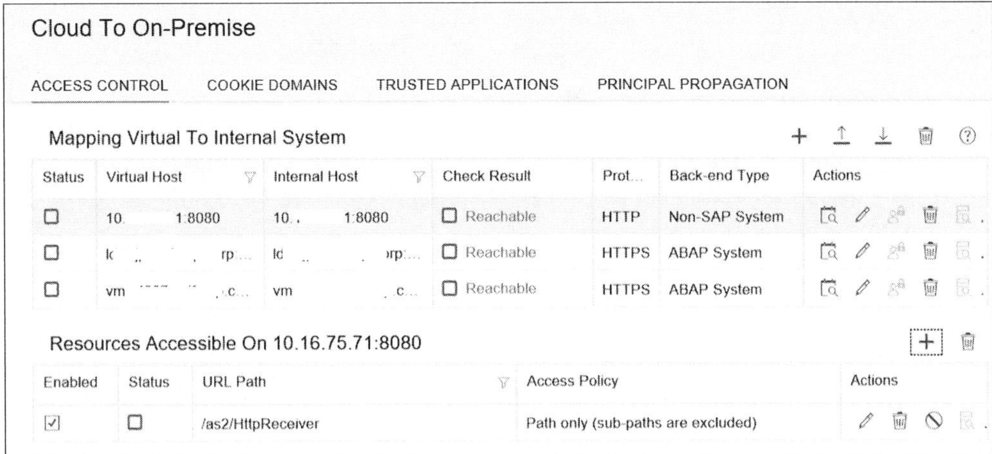

Figure 7.48 Adding Mapping to the Local System in SAP Cloud Platform Connectivity

After defining the system mapping to your receiver system, execute the availability check using the icon. Your system should then appear as **Reachable** in the **Check Result** column.

For this newly created system mapping, you then need to define the accessible resource using the + icon at the top of the lower table. In the **Add Resource** dialog, either enter "/" as the **URL Path** and allow access to all subpaths, or define the specific **URL Path** as "/as2/HttpReceiver", as configured in the AS2 channel.

Now the configuration of the acknowledgement handling is completed. You're ready to run your scenario.

Run the E2E Scenario

Trigger the scenario from your AS2 Mendelson tool as described before. Use the sample message `850 - Purchase Order.txt` as EDI test message. In the SAP Cloud Platform Integration's monitoring, you should see one message with **Completed** status. The receiver system should still receive the ORDERS IDoc. So far, there's no difference. But now, the AS2 Mendelson tool should indicate that it got back an acknowledgement message as a response to the request (Figure 7.49).

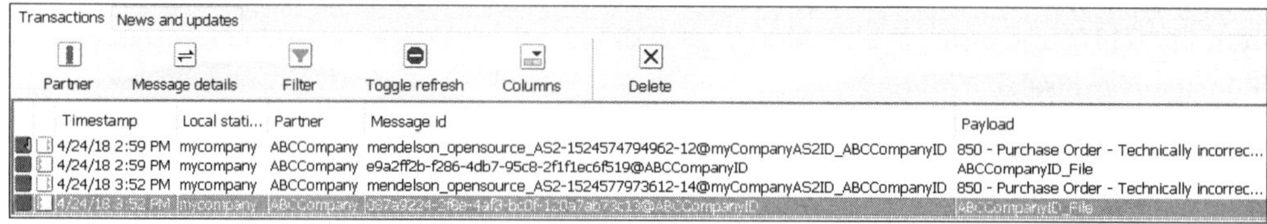

Figure 7.49 Transactions in AS2 Mendelson

On double-clicking the acknowledgement entry, the **Message Details** screen opens. Select the **Transferred Payload** tab to see the received acknowledgement. As the payload is an X12 EDI message, you need to have some knowledge about the structure of a 997 acknowledgement to understand its content. We won't describe this in detail here as this can be found online at several places, but we point you to the segments that indicate whether the message was accepted.

Let's have a look at the 997 acknowledgement we received in Figure 7.50. The first segments provide the header details of the interchange, and the important segment to identify if the message was accepted is AK5. AK5 in this sample acknowledgement shows that the whole transaction sent in the interchange was accepted; this is indicated by the A in the AK5 segment.

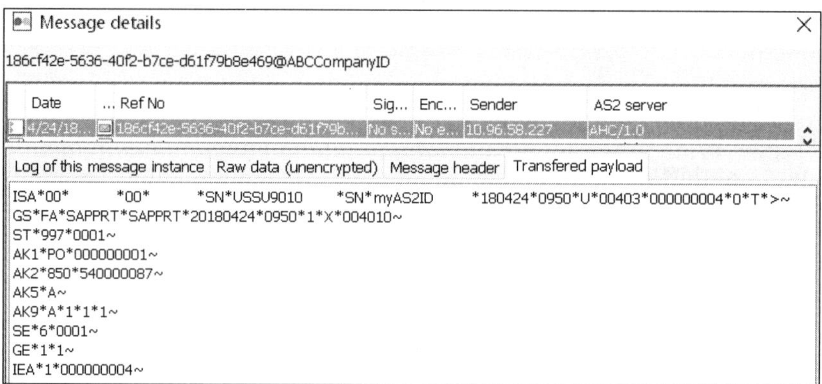

Figure 7.50 997 Acknowledgement for an Accepted EDI Message

Now let's execute the scenario with a message that won't pass the validation. In the AS2 Mendelson tool, select the sample message 850 - Purchase Order - Technically `incorrect.txt` (the file is also available with the book downloads) as the EDI test message and send it. In the SAP Cloud Platform Integration's message monitoring, you should still see one message with **Completed** status, but the receiver system should not receive the ORDERS IDoc.

Why is the message completed, and where does the error appear? The logic is that the validation of the EDI inbound message is executed, and if there is an error, the sender is notified via the 997 acknowledgement that the message wasn't accepted. With this, the processing is completed from SAP Cloud Platform Integration's perspective, and the sender needs to correct the message and send it again.

Open the message monitoring, and search for your message. As shown in Figure 7.51, in the **Attachments** tab, you can find an attachment with the name **Splitter Validation Error Document**. This file contains the error information of the validation. The details of the validation error are given back in the 997 acknowledgement in case of a validation error.

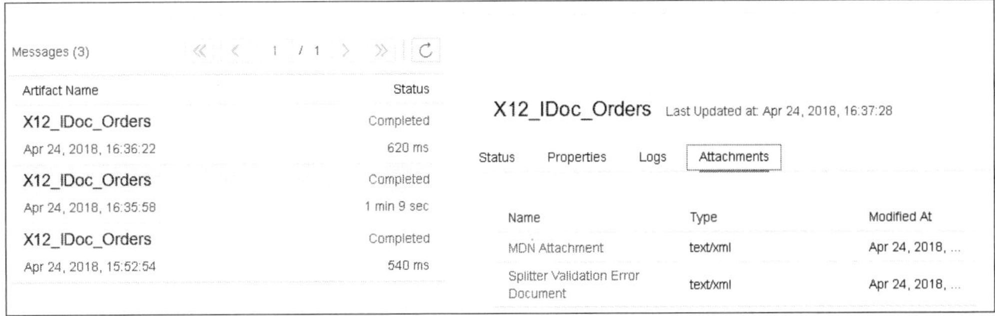

Figure 7.51 Message with Validation Error Attachment

Select the **Splitter Validation Error Document** to get the details as depicted in Figure 7.52. You see that there was a segment error with error code `5`, which means that the data element on position `1` in segment `2` was too long.

Now let's have a look at the 997 acknowledgement in the AS2 Mendelson tool to see if we can find the same details there. Open the received 997 acknowledgement message. It should look like the one shown in Figure 7.53. In segment `AK5`, we see that the message was rejected indicated by the `R`. We also see the error code `5 - One or more segments in error`.

Artifact Name: X12_IDoc_Orders Status: Completed Processing Time: 2 min 39 sec
Last Updated at: Apr 24, 2018, 16:37:28 Log Level: Debug

Log MDN Attachment Splitter Validation Error Document


```
<Interchange>
  <DocumentStandard>ASC-X12</DocumentStandard>
  <InterchangeSender>
    <Identification>myAS2ID        </Identification>
    <Qualifier>SN</Qualifier>
  </InterchangeSender>
  <InterchangeReceiver>
    <Identification>USSU9010       </Identification>
    <Qualifier>SN</Qualifier>
  </InterchangeReceiver>
  <InterchangeControlNumber>000000001</InterchangeControlNumber>
  <FunctionalGroup>
    <GroupControlNumber>000000001</GroupControlNumber>
    <GroupSender>
      <Identification>SAPPRT</Identification>
    </GroupSender>
    <GroupReceiver>
      <Identification>SAPPRT</Identification>
    </GroupReceiver>
    <MessageError type="850">
      <MessageControlNumber>540000087</MessageControlNumber>
      <SegmentError>
        <Error>
          <ElementType>DataElement</ElementType>
          <XPath>/Interchange/S_GS/M_850/S_BEG/D_353</XPath>
          <ErrorCode>5</ErrorCode>
          <ErrorText>Data element is too long</ErrorText>
          <SegmentPosition>2</SegmentPosition>
          <DataElementPosition>1</DataElementPosition>
        </Error>
      </SegmentError>
    </MessageError>
  </FunctionalGroup>
</Interchange>
```


Figure 7.52 Splitter Validation Error Document

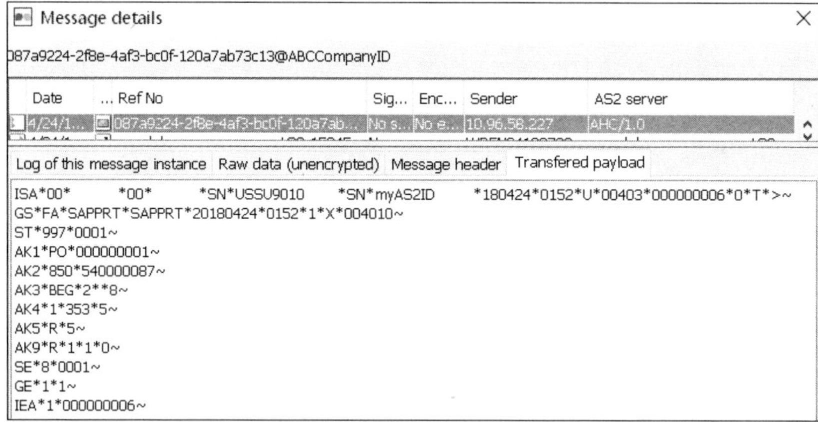

Figure 7.53 997 Acknowledgement for a Rejected EDI Message

But where is the detailed error information? For this, you have to check the segments AK3 and AK4. In segment AK3, you find the information regarding which segment of the inbound message caused the validation error (BEG), the count of the segment in error (2), and the error code (8 - Segment has data element errors). To know which data element in the indicated segment caused the error, you need to check segment AK4 of the 997 acknowledgement. The first data element (1) with the X12 data element number 353 caused the error 5 - Data element is too long.

You can now easily relate to the sample message. Open the file 850 - Purchase Order - Technically incorrect.txt in a text editor. Search for the segment BEG on position 2 in the group segment (GS), and check the first data element there (Listing 7.1). The data element reads 022.

```
GS*PO*SAPPRT*SAPPRT*20080404*091606*000000001*X*004010~
ST*850*540000087~
BEG*022*KN*5400000087**20180328~
```

Listing 7.1 Segments in the EDI Message

To check how long this field needs to be, you can easily use the ICA and check the structure of the inbound MIG. There you see that the data element 353 in segment BEG is expected to be exactly two characters long. Furthermore, in the code list, you see that only value 02 is allowed (Figure 7.54). This explains the error because the value in the sample message has three characters.

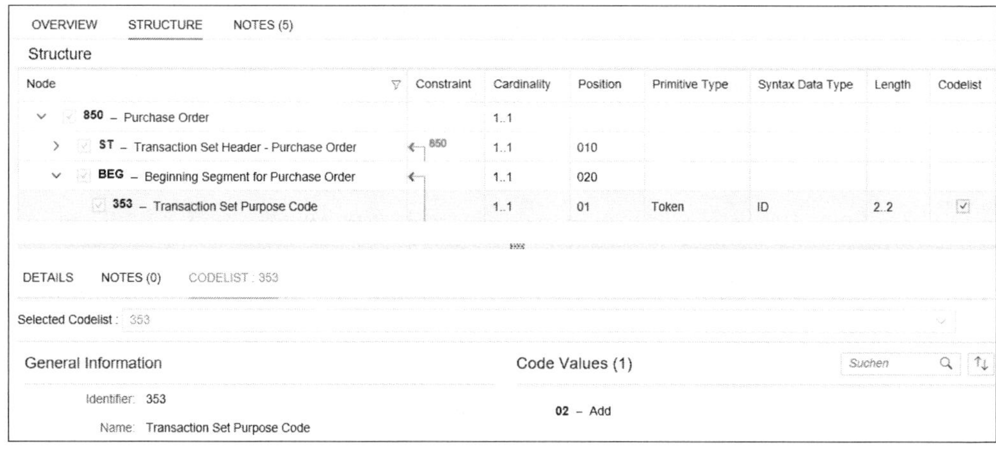

Figure 7.54 Data Element 353 in MIG in ICA

You may correct the payload and set 02 instead of 022 and resend the message. Then it should pass the validation, and the IDoc should be sent successfully to the receiver system.

Now that you've configured the complete B2B scenario, you may wonder how to make the integration flow more dynamic, so that different partner-specific configuration settings can be used within the same integration flow. This will be explained in the next section.

7.4 Using the Partner Directory for Partner-Specific Configuration Data

When establishing a communication network between many communication partners, the tenant Partner Directory helps you to simplify the configuration and maintenance of the integration flows. In such scenarios where many communication partners are involved, you don't need to set up specific integration flows for every partner, but you can build a single one or a few integration flows that are then parametrized by partner-specific information stored in the Partner Directory. With this approach, you reduce the numbers of integration flows, which also results in lower maintenance costs of the overall scenario.

7.4.1 Concept of Partner Directory

The design of the Partner Directory is shown in Figure 7.55. The Partner Directory is a tenant-specific database-based component used to store partner-specific configuration data relevant for the scenario execution, such as endpoints, alternative partner IDs, XSLT mappings, XSD definitions, or certificates. This configuration data is used dynamically at runtime when an integration flow is executed.

To allow you to store those parameters in the Partner Directory, SAP Cloud Platform Integration provides a set of OData APIs. At the time of publishing this book, no UI is delivered from SAP Cloud Platform Integration to maintain the configuration data in the Partner Directory. Using the OData APIs, the owner of the tenant, who is the host of the whole B2B scenario, builds an application where the partners involved in the scenario can maintain their specific configuration data.

The different flow steps and adapters in the integration flow configured for the B2B scenario have to be parametrized to read the partner-specific information from the Partner Directory during the runtime of the integration flow.

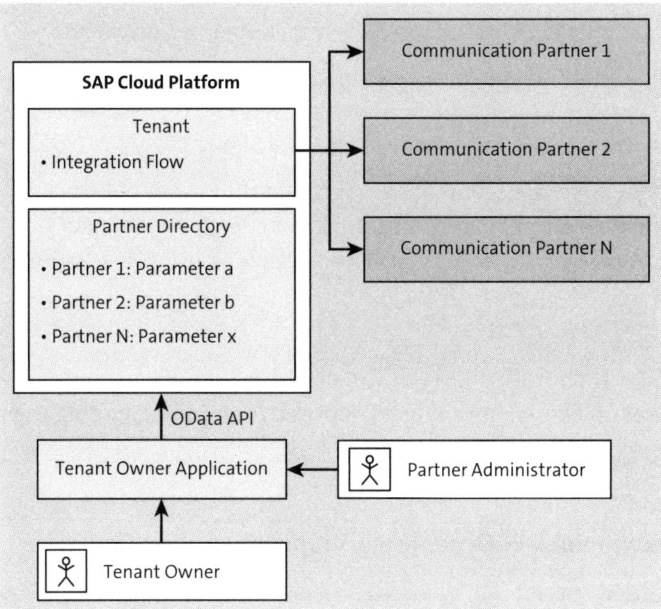

Figure 7.55 Usage of Partner Directory

It's important to understand that because the parameters in the Partner Directory are partner-specific, they have to be read at runtime based on partner-specific values from the incoming request or payload so that the correct configuration is used. The partners, sender and receiver, are usually identified by specific values from the payload.

With the Partner Directory, you can add new communication partners without downtime and without changing or redeploying the integration flows. You can enter attributes of a new partner via the OData API without interrupting the message processing.

Further Details and Sample Scenarios Using the Partner Directory

The Partner Directory offers additional advanced features beside storing simple configuration data:

- XSLT mappings and XSD schemas can be stored.
- Alternative partner IDs can be defined for specific partners.

- Authorized users can be created and used for advanced authorization checks.
- User credential aliases and certificates can be stored and used for authentication and authorization.

Although we don't explain these options in detail here, refer to the "Cloud Integration – Partner Directory – Step-by-Step Example" blog and the referenced blogs in the SAP Community (*www.sap.com/community.html*) to understand the details of those configuration options and to set up advanced scenarios using the Partner Directory.

Now that you understand the idea behind the Partner Directory, let's enhance the sample scenario we've set up by making some attributes dynamic and reading them from the Partner Directory.

7.4.2 Use a Receiver Endpoint URL Dynamically in the Integration Flow

In this section, we'll extend the sample scenario so that specific configuration settings are read from the Partner Directory instead of being defined as fixed values in the integration flow.

To keep the scenario simple, we'll just parameterize the endpoint URL and the corresponding credential alias in the IDoc receiver channel. You could also parametrize XSLT mappings and XSD definitions and make all the partner-specific configurations in the integration flow dynamic, but this is beyond the scope of this chapter. Refer to the SAP Cloud Platform Integration documentation and the referenced blogs.

You Didn't Set Up the IDoc Receiver?

If you kept the mail receiver in your sample scenario and didn't set up the IDoc receiver adapter but want to extend the scenario using dynamic configuration from the Partner Directory, you may parameterize the mail address in the mail receiver channel instead. With this, you're able to continue with the sample scenario using the Partner Directory; just store the mail address in the Partner Directory instead of the IDoc receiver URL.

To use partner-specific attributes from the Partner Directory, we need to extend the integration flow in a way that it first reads that attribute from the Partner Directory and then uses it in a specific integration flow step or adapter. In our sample scenario, we read the endpoint URL and the credential alias for the EDI receiver partner from the Partner Directory and use it in the IDoc adapter.

Read Configuration Data from the Partner Directory Using the Script Step

To read a specific attribute from the Partner Directory, we need to know the partner ID for which the configuration data is defined and the parameter name that is used in the Partner Directory to store the configuration. For the sample scenario, we use the EDI receiver partner ID `USSU9010` defined in the sample payload, and we'll create two parameters, `Endpoint` and `CredentialAlias`, for this partner in the Partner Directory containing the address and the credential alias, respectively, of the receiver system for the IDoc message.

At runtime, you have to retrieve the receiver partner ID from the incoming message to use it for reading parameters for this partner from the Partner Directory. In the sample scenario, the EDI splitter already does this for us; it reads the EDI receiver partner ID from the incoming EDI message and sets it as header `SAP_EDI_Receiver_ID`. We use this header to retrieve the specific endpoint URL for this receiver partner.

You can easily read parameters from the Partner Directory using a script step, using the Java APIs exposed for the Partner Directory. We won't explain the APIs in detail, but point you to the online documentation (*https://help.sap.com/viewer/product/CLOUD_INTEGRATION/Cloud)* chapter *Accessing Partner Directory Content with the Script Flow Step*.

To extend the sample integration flow, open it in edit mode, and add a **Groovy Script** step from the **Message Transformers** group before the message **End** event, as depicted in Figure 7.56.

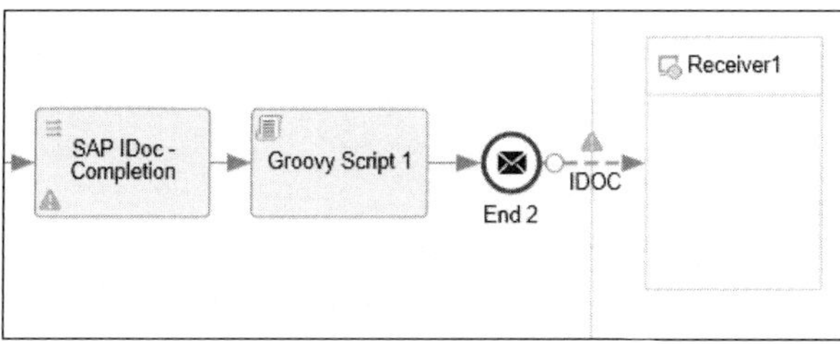

Figure 7.56 Adding a Groovy Script

Create a new groovy script using the **create** ⊕ action on the right side of the flow step. Copy the coding (Listing 7.2) from the prepared script file *GroovyScript.txt* provided in the book downloads at *www.sap-press.com/4650* into the **Groovy Script**. Select **OK** to get back to the integration flow configuration.

```
import com.sap.gateway.ip.core.customdev.util.Message;
import java.util.HashMap;
import com.sap.it.api.pd.PartnerDirectoryService;
import com.sap.it.api.ITApiFactory;
def Message processData(Message message) {
       def service = ITApiFactory.getApi(PartnerDirectoryService.class, null);
       if (service == null){
          throw new IllegalStateException("Partner Directory Service not
found");
       }
       def map = message.getHeaders();
       def receiverId = map.get("SAP_EDI_Receiver_ID");
       if (receiverId == null){
          throw new IllegalStateException("Receiver ID is not set in the
header 'SAP_EDI_Receiver_ID'")
       }

     def parameterValue = service.getParameter("Endpoint", receiverId ,
String.class);
     if (parameterValue == null){
        throw new IllegalStateException("Endpoint parameter not found in the
Partner Directory for the partner ID "+receiverId);
     }
     def parameterValueCredential = service.getParameter("CredentialAlias",
receiverId , String.class);
     if (parameterValueCredential == null){
        throw new IllegalStateException("CredentialAlias parameter not found
in the Partner Directory for the partner ID "+receiverId);
     }
      message.setProperty("RECEIVER_Endpoint", parameterValue );
      message.setProperty("RECEIVER_CredentialAlias", parameterValueCredential
);
       return message;
}
```

Listing 7.2 Groovy Script Code for Accessing the Partner Directory

At runtime, the script reads the header SAP_EDI_Receiver_ID, which represents the EDI receiver partner, and searches in the Partner Directory for the parameters Endpoint and CredentialAlias for this partner. The values of those parameters are then set as properties RECEIVER_Endpoint and RECEIVER_CredentialAlias.

Now that we've read the parameters from the Partner Directory, we can use it in the IDoc receiver channel in the next step.

Dynamic Configuration in the IDoc Receiver Channel

In the sample scenario, we've currently configured the **Address** field in the **IDoc** receiver channel with the URL to the **IDoc** endpoint in the **Receiver** system, and we configured a fixed credential **Alias**. As we want to set these parameters dynamically from the properties defined in the **Groovy Script**, we have to change this configuration.

To change the configuration, open the **IDoc** receiver channel. First copy the URL currently defined in **Address** field and the **Credential Name** into a notepad because we'll need them later when we define the parameters in the Partner Directory. Change the settings to ${property.RECEIVER_Endpoint} and ${property.RECEIVER_CredentialAlias} }, as shown in Figure 7.57, to read the address and the credential alias dynamically from the properties defined in the script (you can refer to Chapter 6, Section 6.2, for dynamic configuration).

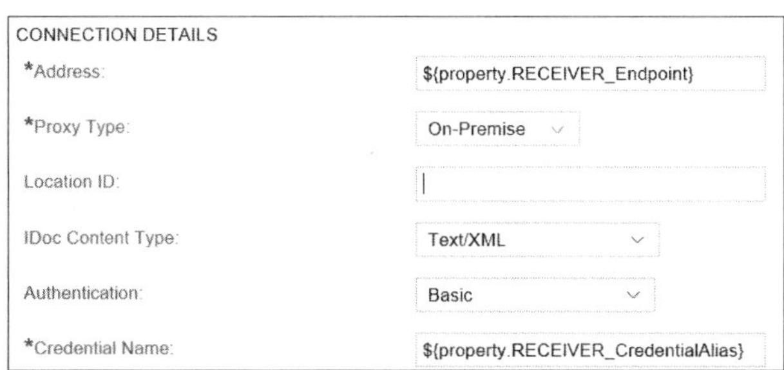

Figure 7.57 Configure Address and Credential Name in IDoc Receiver via Property

Save and deploy the integration flow. Now the endpoint address and the credential alias will be dynamically determined during runtime. If you were to send a message to your integration flow using the AS2 Mendelson tool, the message would end with the error Endpoint parameter not found in the Partner Directory for the partner ID USSU9010 in the script step. The reason is that we haven't yet defined the endpoint in the Partner Directory. We'll do the necessary configuration in the next step.

7.4.3 Store the Partner-Specific Endpoint URL in Partner Directory

Now, to get the scenario running successfully, we have to add the `Endpoint` and `CredentialAlias` parameters for the partner `USSU9010` to the Partner Directory. As already mentioned, usually the partner would enter this configuration parameter using the application the tenant owner offers. But for our sample scenario, we'll create the entry directly via the OData API. The OData API can be called by the tenant administrator (`AuthGroup.Administrator`) or by a user with the role `AuthGroup.PartnerDirectoryConfigurator`.

Because the Partner Directory OData API is protected against cross-site request forgery (CSRF) attacks, you first have to fetch an X-CSRF Token before you can make create, change, or delete requests to entries in the Partner Directory. Refer to documentation for SAP Cloud Platform Integration (found at *https://help.sap.com/viewer/product/CLOUD_INTEGRATION/Cloud*) in the OData API topic for detailed information. In addition, refer to Chapter 9 for details on API availability and usage.

Fetch X-CSRF Token

The easiest way of calling OData APIs in the SAP Cloud Platform Integration tenant is using Postman (*www.getpostman.com*). Download, install, and start it, and you're ready to trigger your first request.

Use a **Get** request to the OData API root URL *https://<TMN-host>/api/v1* on the tenant management node (TMN). Select **Basic Auth**, and enter your credentials in the **Authorization** tab, as shown in Figure 7.58. In the **Headers** tab, create a new key `X-CSRF-Token` with the value `Fetch` to request for an X-CSRF Token (Figure 7.59).

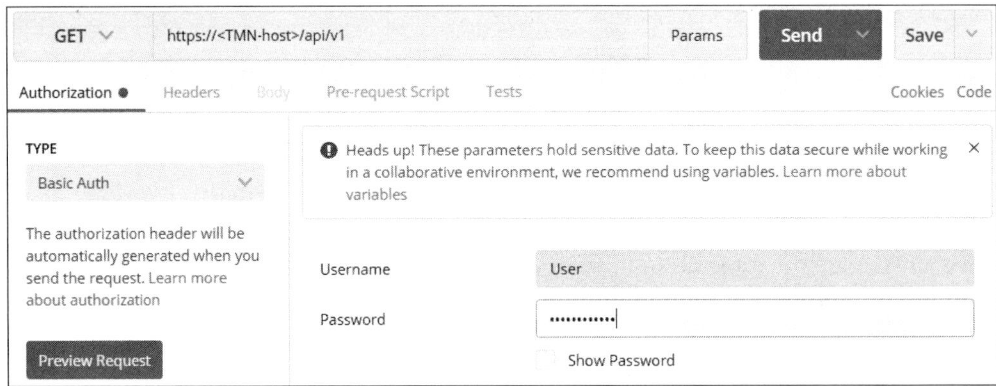

Figure 7.58 Configuring Authorization in Postman

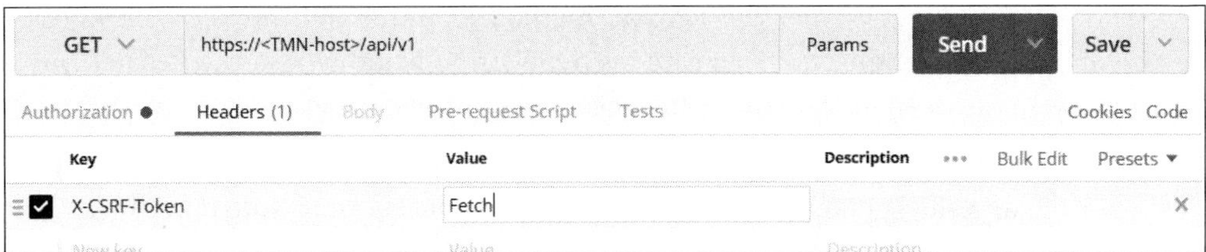

Figure 7.59 GET Request for an X-CSRF Token in Postman

Select **Send** to trigger the request. In the response, you receive a list of all available APIs in the **Body** tab. But more important for us is the very last header `X-CSRF-Token` in the **Headers** tab (Figure 7.60). This is the header we have to provide in our subsequent **PUT** request. Copy the value to use it in the next request.

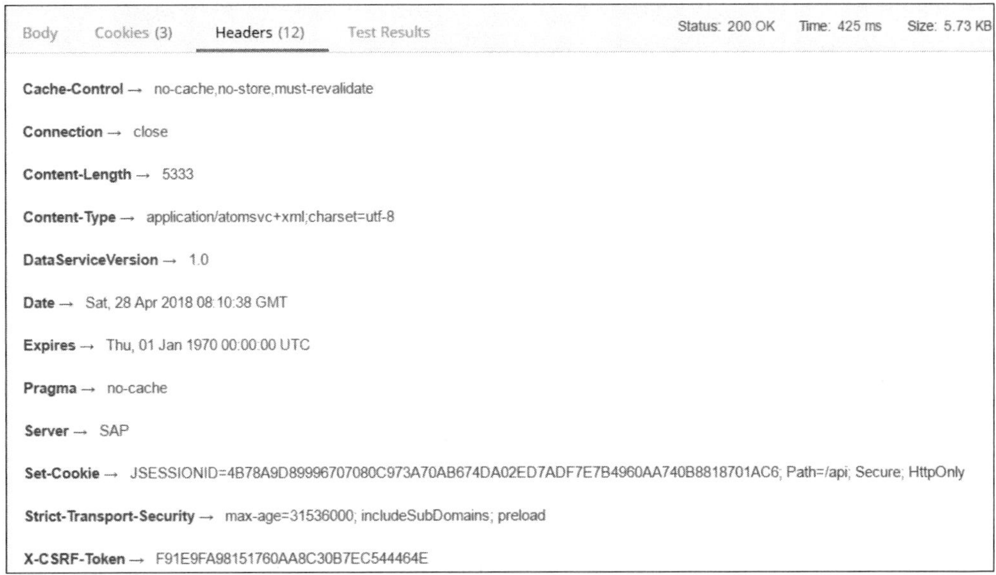

Figure 7.60 Received X-CSRF Token in the Headers Tab

Store the Endpoint URL and Credential Alias in the Partner Directory

Now that you've retrieved the X-CSRF Token, you can use it to trigger a POST request to store the endpoint URL of the IDoc receiver and the credential alias to the Partner Directory.

Create a new request and select **Post** as method. Enter the URL "https://<TMN-host>/api/v1/StringParameters" to create a simple string parameter in the Partner Directory. In the **Headers** tab, create three headers, as shown in Figure 7.61:

- `X-CSRF-Token`
  As the **Value**, enter the token you received in the last step. Note that the token is only valid for 30 minutes; afterwards, you need to retrieve a new token as described in the last step.
- `Accept`
  As the **Value**, select `application/json`.
- `Content-Type`
  As the **Value**, select `application/json`.

Figure 7.61 Required Headers in a POST Request to Create Parameters in the Partner Directory

In the **Body** tab, you need to provide the details for the POST request. Select **Raw** and **JSON(application/json)** to post the request in JSON format. In the entry field, enter the details of the partner and the parameter you want to create. For the endpoint URL, you enter the following JSON request: `{"Pid":"USSU9010","Id":"Endpoint", "Value":"http://<host>:<port>/sap/bc/srt/idoc?sap-client=<client>"}`, as depicted in Figure 7.62. As the **URL**, enter the real URL to your IDoc receiver system, which you copied from the IDoc channel into the notepad in the previous section.

Select **Send** to post the request. With this request, a new parameter `Endpoint` is created in the Partner Directory for the partner `USSU9010` with the URL *http://<host>:<port>/sap/bc/srt/idoc?sap-client=<client>*. If the call was successful, you receive the details of the created entry in the response (Figure 7.63).

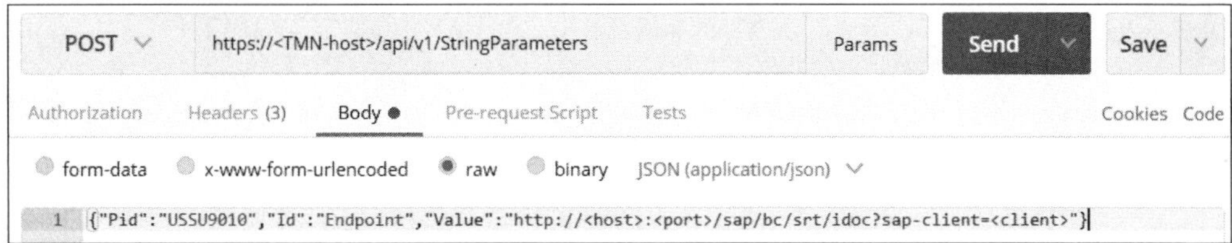

Figure 7.62 Body in the POST Request to Create the Endpoint Parameter

Body | Cookies (3) | Headers (10) | Test Results | Status: 201 Created | Time: 611 ms | Size: 973 B

Pretty | Raw | Preview | JSON


```
{
    "d": {
        "__metadata": {
            "id": "https://d                    lemand.com:443/api/v1/StringParameters(Pid='USSU9010'
                ,Id='Endpoint')",
            "uri": "https://d0                   lemand.com:443/api/v1/StringParameters(Pid
                ='USSU9010',Id='Endpoint')",
            "type": "com.sap.hci.api.StringParameter"
        },
        "Pid": "USSU9010",
        "Id": "Endpoint",
        "LastModifiedBy": "[      9",
        "LastModifiedTime": "/Date(1524905240181)/",
        "CreatedBy": "[      9",
        "CreatedTime": "/Date(1524905240181)/",
        "Value": "http://              70/sap/bc/srt/idoc?sap-client=300"
    }
}
```

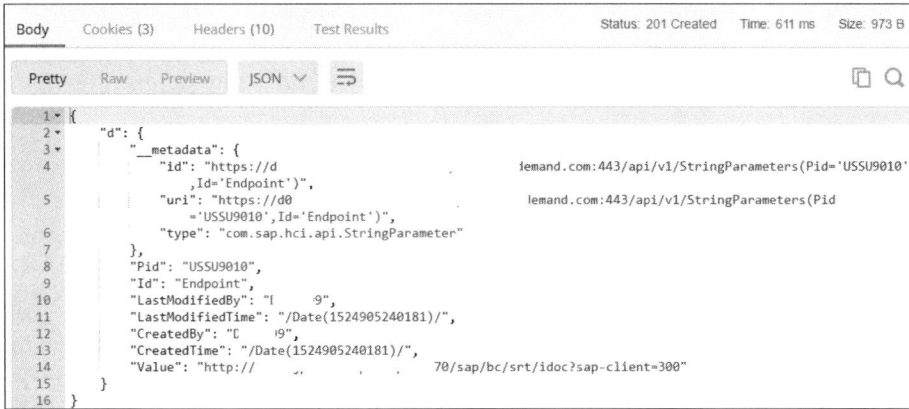

Figure 7.63 Response for a Successful POST Request

Execute another POST request for the parameter `CredentialAlias`. In the **Body** field, use the following JSON request: `{"Pid":"USSU9010","Id":"CredentialAlias", "Value":"<credential alias>"}`. As the **Credential** alias, enter the alias of the credentials as deployed for this receiver.

With this last step, you finished the configuration of the scenario so that the endpoint address and the credential alias are retrieved dynamically from the Partner Directory during runtime. Let's test to see if it works.

Run Scenario

From your AS2 Mendelson test client, trigger a new message to the integration flow. The message should be sent successfully, and an acknowledgement should be received.

In the SAP Cloud Platform Integration's message monitoring, the message should be in status **Completed**, and the IDoc should be successfully received by the receiver backend.

Error Sending Acknowledgement?

If your message is in status **Retry** in the message monitor, you have to check the error message. If the error message is `Remote server returned response code 502 and error message Bad Gateway`, most probably the acknowledgement can't be sent because the IP address of your AS2 Mendelson HTTP server to receive the acknowledgement changed. This happens because local machines usually get new IP addresses dynamically when they connect to a network. To fix this problem, get your new IP address, and enter it in the SAP Cloud Platform Connectivity's configuration in the **Internal Host** field. Keep the **Virtual Host** as is because SAP Cloud Platform Connectivity maps the virtual host (used in the **AS2** receiver channel) to the internal host (refer to Section 7.3.4 for how to configure SAP Cloud Platform Connectivity).

Now you've successfully extended your sample scenario to fetch the endpoint address and the corresponding credential alias dynamically. Now you can easily add a second receiver partner to the same scenario by just adding another partner with its endpoint URL and the credential alias to the Partner Directory. In addition, you would have to deploy the credentials for the new receiver backend. If a message for this partner is received, it would automatically be routed to the new receiver using the newly deployed credentials.

7.5 Summary

You're now able to configure MIGs and MAGs in the ICA and can configure B2B scenarios based on available B2B templates with the adapters and flow steps available in SAP Cloud Platform Integration. You understand the B2B acknowledgement handling and are able to interpret 997 acknowledgements. You also learned to define partner-specific attributes in the Partner Directory and how to use them in the integration flow. With this knowledge, you're now well equipped to configure your own B2B scenarios.

With this chapter we complete the design and configuration of integration scenarios in the web designer of SAP Cloud Platform Integration and come to another important part in the lifecycle of integration content, the monitoring. In the next chapter we will work you through the monitoring capabilities of SAP Cloud Platform Integration.

Chapter 8
SAP Cloud Platform Integration Operations

As an expert service provider, SAP ensures the support and maintenance of the hardware and software needed to keep SAP Cloud Platform Integration running optimally. However, there are a few operational tasks that need to be understood and performed by consumers themselves. This chapter explains the operational tasks to be performed by the customer to optimize running integration scenarios.

In Chapter 4, Chapter 5, and Chapter 6, you learned how to implement simple and complex integration scenarios using SAP Cloud Platform Integration. When you've successfully developed, configured, and deployed integration flows in SAP Cloud Platform Integration, your business will be ready to use and trigger them during runtime.

As integration scenarios are being used at runtime, the customer needs to keep maintaining them to ensure that the organization continues to reap the benefits that these integration scenarios provide. For you as a customer, maintenance is an ongoing job that includes regularly monitoring integration flows and temporary data as well as managing users and security artifacts.

To gain access to the details of integration flow instances during runtime, you need to use SAP Cloud Platform Integration's monitoring capabilities. The monitoring features give customers insight into running integration flows to ensure they are correctly performing the job they were built for and are helping the business achieve its goals.

This chapter will focus on what is required to properly manage, track, and detect issues in running integration scenarios in your SAP Cloud Platform Integration tenant. Additionally, the features and tools to support the ongoing maintenance and operation jobs are explored. Let's start by giving you the big picture on the operational activities needed for your SAP Cloud Platform Integration tenant.

8.1 Operations: Overview

In traditional on-premise platforms, the customer is responsible for the entire maintenance and operation of the platform. For instance, this is the case for customers running an SAP Process Orchestration installation. SAP Process Orchestration is SAP Cloud Platform Integration's sister on-premise integration platform. The customer is solely responsible for maintaining the hardware and software, and monitoring the integration scenarios that are built on top of it.

SAP Cloud Platform Integration, as a cloud-based platform, brings a number of benefits to the customer when it comes to maintenance and operational aspects. As a service provider, SAP eliminates most of the headaches that come from the day-to-day support and maintenance of the SAP Cloud Platform Integration platform. Customers can thus use their energy on the core business at hand: developing, running, and monitoring integration scenarios.

Although most people are aware of the operational benefits of using a cloud-based platform such as SAP Cloud Platform Integration, not everyone has a clear view of the demarcation line between what operational activities are taken care of by SAP as a service provider and which ones still need to be covered by the customer. Table 8.1 provides an overview of tasks to consider as part of SAP Cloud Platform Integration's day-to-day operations. The table also provides a responsibility matrix covering the tasks both performed at SAP and by a SAP Cloud Platform Integration customer.

Task	Responsibility	Description
Manage users and roles	Customer	Maintain users and assign roles to them to clearly define what actions they can perform on the SAP Cloud Platform Integration tenant.
Hardware and infrastructure maintenance	SAP Team	SAP is responsible for ensuring that SAP Cloud Platform Integration runs properly. This includes performing "health checks" in areas covering the operating system, memory, CPU, and so forth.

Table 8.1 Responsibility Matrix of Operational Tasks

Task	Responsibility	Description
Software updates and maintenance	SAP Team	Software updates are performed on a regular basis by SAP while ensuring near-zero downtime. The customer's tenant is upgraded automatically, and the newly installed features can immediately be used by all customers. The SAP team ensures that the updates performed don't negatively affect running integration scenarios.
SAP content update	SAP Team	Updates to the prepackaged content in the content catalog are regularly performed by SAP.
Update of consumed SAP content	Customer	Updates to the content packages in the content catalog need to be consumed by the customer, either manually or automated. Refer to Chapter 3 for more details.
Monitoring of runtime messages and bug fixes	Customer	Customers are responsible for monitoring, fixing, and maintaining their own integration scenarios and content.
Manage SAP keys	SAP Team	SAP-owned keys are updated by SAP before they expire. We'll look at this later in this chapter.
Manage security material	Customer	Customers deploy and maintain security artifacts needed for their integration flows. Certificates are a good example of such artifacts.

Table 8.1 Responsibility Matrix of Operational Tasks (Cont.)

SAP Cloud Platform Integration is constantly being developed and maintained; SAP releases updates for the platform about once a month. This short update cycle ensures that you continually receive new features and improvements to your SAP Cloud Platform Integration platform. During these updates, there is no downtime for customers. Table 8.1 contains a number of activities that are performed by SAP. However, this chapter mainly focuses on those activities listed that fall under the responsibility of the customer.

Now that you're aware of the activities required to maintain your SAP Cloud Platform Integration tenant, this section will take you through each of the tools and features that are available to perform operational tasks. We'll cover the following aspects:

- Monitoring integration components and message processing
- Security material management
- Monitoring message stores, such as data stores and Java Message Service (JMS) queues
- Monitoring locks created during message processing
- Checking log files

Let's start with how to monitor your SAP Cloud Platform Integration tenant.

8.2 Monitoring Integration Content and Message Processing

After an integration flow has been deployed to the SAP Cloud Platform Integration tenant, it's time to monitor all running integration artifacts to make sure that they are correctly doing the job for which they were built. This section will focus on looking at what is required to properly manage, track, and detect issues on running integration flows. The monitoring of deployed artifacts is part of the ongoing job of maintaining and improving your organization's IT environment. Besides monitoring the runtime artifacts deployed on your tenant, this section also focuses on monitoring the message processing in the cluster's runtime.

Open the Web UI's homepage at *http://<server>:<port>/itspaces*. The monitoring screens can be accessed via the **Monitor** menu item on the left menu, as indicated in Figure 8.1.

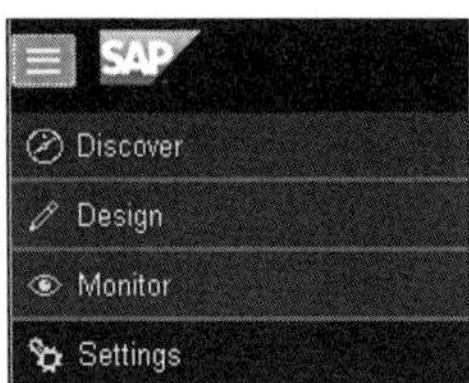

Figure 8.1 Accessing SAP Cloud Platform Integration's Monitoring Features

After clicking the **Monitor** tab, you're taken to a screen with a number of tiles displaying various statistics, numbers and statuses pertaining to the messages that have been processed by the runtime engine of SAP Cloud Platform Integration. Figure 8.2 presents an overview of the main monitor screen. From this screen, also known as the monitoring dashboard, you can access the different monitors available for integration content and message monitoring.

A tile is a block in a page that filters messages or artifacts corresponding to a particular status (e.g., completed messages). As shown in Figure 8.2, the screen contains six main tile groupings, namely:

- **Monitor Message Processing**
- **Manage Integration Content**
- **Manage Security**
- **Manage Stores**
- **Access Logs**
- **Manage Locks**

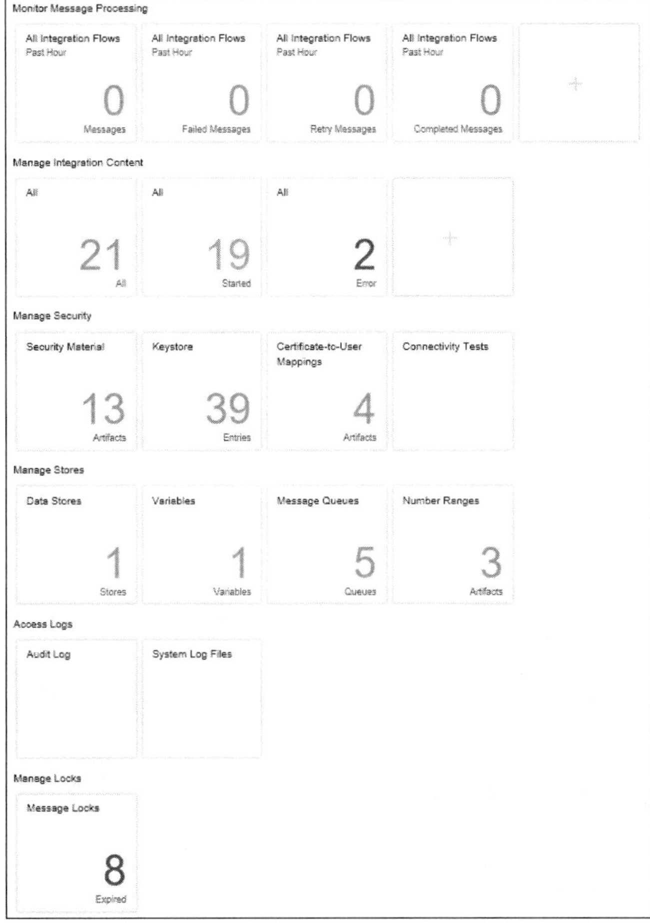

Figure 8.2 Overview of the Monitoring Dashboard

Let's first explore the **Manage Integration Content** section's set of tiles because we need to understand the monitoring options for the integration content to relate them to the monitoring of the message processing.

8.2.1 Manage Integration Content

The tiles in the **Manage Integration Content** section of the screen display the statuses of the different integration artifacts that have been deployed on the tenant. Deployed integration artifacts include, for instance, integration flows and OData services. Referring to the screen shown in Figure 8.2, you can see that a total of 21 integration artifacts have been deployed (first tile in the **Manage Integration Content** section). Out of those 21, it shows that 19 have successfully started (second tile), and 2 have failed (third tile). You can click on the second tile to view all integration artifacts that have been successfully deployed on your SAP Cloud Platform Integration tenant, as shown in Figure 8.3.

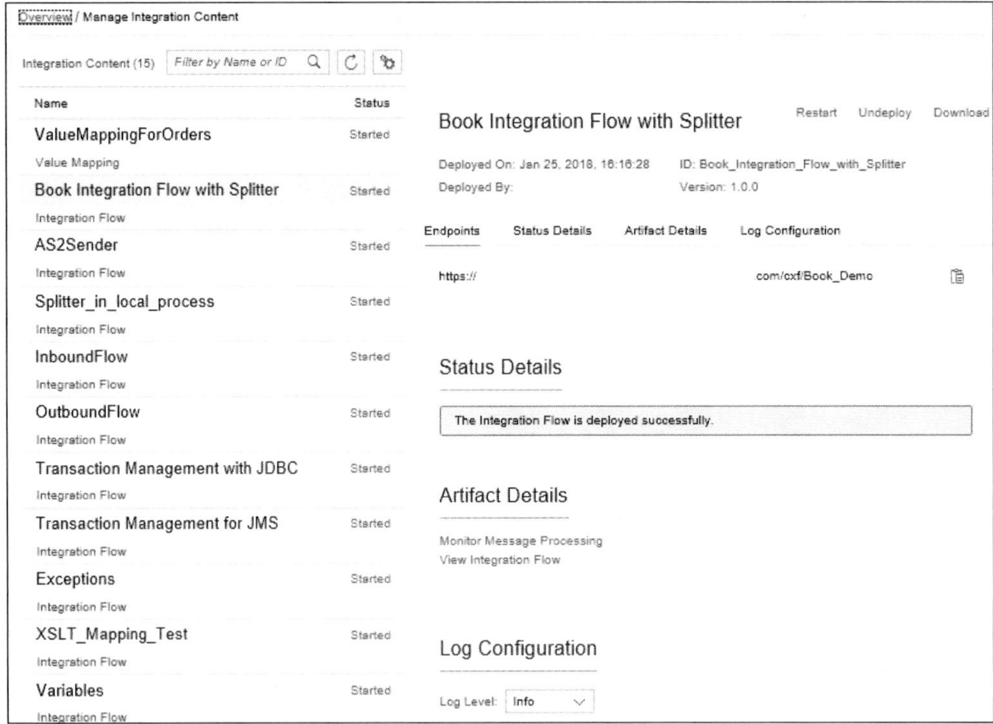

Figure 8.3 Manage Integration Content Monitor

As depicted in Figure 8.3, the monitor presents the deployed artifacts in a table on the left side of the monitor with status and artifact type. Table 8.2 contains a detailed description of those attributes and the possible values.

Attribute	Description
Name	The name of the integration artifact that has been deployed.
Type	The type of integration content, for example, **Value Mapping**, **Integration Flow**, or **OData service**.
Status	The deployment status of the integration artifact: ■ **Starting**: The integration artifact is starting, but it can't be executed yet. ■ **Started**: The integration artifact is ready to be used. ■ **Error**: The integration artifact is in error state; it needs manual action, for example, a change of the artifact and redeployment. ■ **Stopping**: The artifact is stopping, for example, after undeployment. It can't be executed anymore.

Table 8.2 Attributes of the Integration Artifact on the Left Side of the Monitor

The content of the table is sorted by the time of the last deployment, which means that the artifact deployed at the latest is shown on top. To customize the list of displayed artifacts, you can either search for specific artifacts by artifact name or ID, or you can filter the table content by attributes such as status or artifact type. To sort or filter the content of the table, select the **Table Settings** icon at the top of the table. On the subsequent screen, you can define how the table entries are to be sorted by specifying an attribute and whether the entries are to be sorted for that attribute in ascending or descending order. You can also filter the table entries for certain attributes.

On the right side of the monitor the details of the selected artifact are shown. At the top, the most important details about the deployed integration artifact are provided, such as ID, version, and who deployed it when. The description of those attributes is summarized in Table 8.3.

Attribute	Description
Deployed On	Specifies date and time at which the last deployment was performed.

Table 8.3 Attributes of the Integration Artifact on the Top of the Right Side of the Monitor

Attribute	Description
Deployed By	Specifies the user who deployed the artifact.
ID	The technical ID of the integration artifact. This ID is necessary, for example, when searching for errors in the log files.
Version	The version number of the deployed integration artifact.

Table 8.3 Attributes of the Integration Artifact on the Top of the Right Side of the Monitor (Cont.)

The following actions, among others, can be performed on each artifact:

- **Undeploy**
  Remove an artifact that was previously deployed in the tenant. To undeploy an integration artifact, select the artifact in the table on the left of the monitor, and choose **Undeploy**.
- **Restart**
  Restart if there was a problem with the integration artifact that was solved in the meantime, such as the credentials weren't deployed on the tenant. Such errors don't need a redeployment; they just need to restart the integration artifact. If changes in the integration artifact were required to solve the error, the integration artifact needs to be redeployed from design view, and restart isn't sufficient then. Note that the **Restart** action isn't always available; it depends on the status of the artifact and the type of error.
- **Download**
  Download the content of an integration artifact. The artifact is then stored on the local machine in form of a Java Archive (JAR) file. Downloading integration content can be useful as a backup method. The backed-up data can then, for instance, be reimported or transported into another SAP Cloud Platform Integration tenant. Note that read-only integration artifacts can't be downloaded.

The actions available on the top-right corner of the monitor depend on the status of the artifact and whether it's a read-only artifact.

Below the header information, the view is divided into different sections. You can navigate between them using the tabs, which are shown on top:

- **Endpoints**
  The HTTP-based sender adapters, such as SOAP or HTTP, expose endpoints, which

can be called to start the runtime processing of a specific artifact. In the **Endpoints** section, all accessible endpoints are listed, which are exposed by the selected artifact. We already used this option in some of the sample scenarios to retrieve the URL to be called to trigger the integration flows using a SOAP sender adapter.

- **Status Details**
  This section provides the overall status of the integration artifact. For started integration artifacts, you'll see the message that the integration artifact is deployed successfully (refer to Figure 8.3). But if the integration artifact is in error status, the error details are provided as depicted in Figure 8.4. You also have the option to download the log by clicking the **Download** icon ⤓, for example, to attach it to a support ticket.

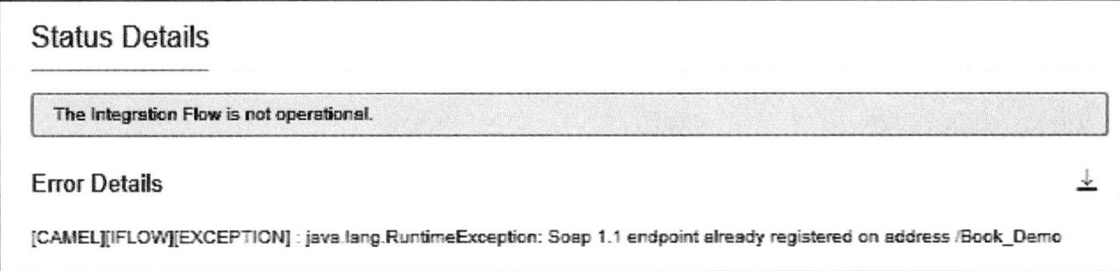

Status Details
The Integration Flow is not operational.
Error Details
[CAMEL][IFLOW][EXCEPTION] : java.lang.RuntimeException: Soap 1.1 endpoint already registered on address /Book_Demo

Figure 8.4 Error Details in the Manage Integration Content Monitor

- **Artifact Details**
  This section provides two important links. When selecting the **Monitor Message Processing** link, the message monitor opens and shows all messages processed for the selected artifact in the last hour. Note that this link isn't available for value mappings. The second link, **View Integration Flow**, opens the selected artifact in its modeler in read-only mode. You can, for example, use this view to explore the configured steps and adapters in an integration flow and check the properties defined. You can't change the configuration and redeploy the artifact from this view, however. The view is meant for monitoring only. If changes to the integration artifact are required, you need to change to the design view and adjust it there.
- **Log Configuration**
  You can configure different log levels for the integration flows and OData services deployed on the tenant in the **Log Configuration** section. This section isn't available for value mappings.

Let's take a more detailed look at the log levels available for integration flows and the consequences of changing them.

8.2.2 Log Configuration

To monitor the integration flows most efficiently in all phases of developing a new scenario, different log levels are available. With this configuration option, you can, for example, monitor integration flows during development and test phases with a high log level, which provides details about runtime execution in all steps and adapters, and observe payloads and headers after each step. Later, when the integration flow runs in a productive scenario, you won't need such detailed logs anymore.

As depicted in Figure 8.5, the following **Log Levels** are provided by SAP Cloud Platform Integration

- **None**
  No message processing log (MPL) is written.
- **Info**
  This is the default log level set when a new integration flow is deployed . With this log level, only the most important information about the runtime execution of a message is logged, such as start and stop time and the overall status. Nevertheless, if the message encounters an error during runtime execution, the last steps are logged in detail in order to analyze the error. This is the log level you should use for integration flows running in a productive scenario.
- **Debug**
  All flow steps and adapter calls are logged in detail, even on successful execution of a message. This log level is mostly used during development and testing of a new scenario. This log level should not be used in productive scenarios due to the negative impact on performance and data volume stored in the database.

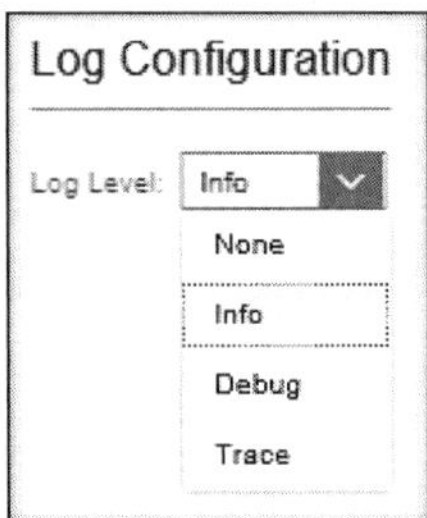

Figure 8.5 Log Levels for Log Configuration

- **Trace**
  This is the most detailed log level available. With this log level, payloads and headers are logged after each processing step. **Trace** is activated only for a short period to analyze issues in scenario execution in detail. The maximum time the log level **Trace** can be activated for is 10 minutes to avoid overloading the database with too much data. After this time, the log level is reset automatically to the log level that was configured before activating **Trace**.

During the first deployment of a new integration flow, the log level is set to **Info**. Then, you can configure the log level as desired in the **Manage Integration Content** monitor. Subsequent deployments of the same integration flow don't reset the log level; the setting is kept.

As soon as you change the log level in the **Log Configuration** dropdown, it's active; no additional save action and no restart of the integration flow is required. The next MPL of a message is written with the new log level.

Log and Trace Configuration: Additional Features

The logging and tracing feature will be extended by additional features, such as a dedicated log level adapter trace. The most recent features are documented in the "Troubleshooting Message Processing in the CPI Web Application" blog in the SAP Community (*www.sap.com/community.html*).

Now you know how to monitor your integration content and how to define the log level for deployed integration flows. With this information, we can dive into the details about monitoring the message processing in the SAP Cloud Platform Integration runtime.

8.2.3 Monitor Message Processing

As depicted earlier in Figure 8.2, within the monitoring dashboard, the top section of the screen includes a list of tiles that all relate to message processing. After clicking on any of the tiles in this section, you're taken to a new page, which looks like the one shown in Figure 8.6.

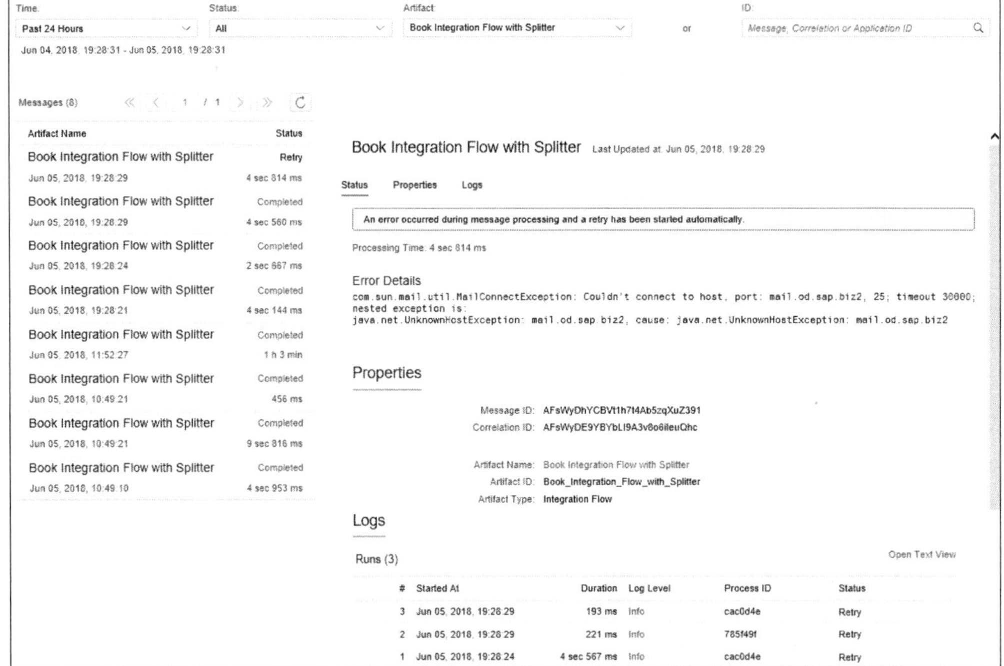

Figure 8.6 Monitor Message Processing

By default, the screen displays two views:

- A left view, with a list of messages matching the tile configuration. It's possible to select any of the listed messages to further view its log details in the right view.
- A right view, with the message details of the selected entry on the left side of the screen. **Status**, **Properties**, and **Logs** are provided and offer further navigation to the MPL, MPL attachments, and the integration flow.

As shown in Figure 8.6, it's also possible to further filter the messages by changing the filtering settings. Messages can be filtered based on **Time, Status**, **Artifact**, **Message**, **Correlation**, or **Application ID**. Table 8.4 provides a description of these filter attributes.

Filter Name	Description
Time	The date and time at which the message was triggered.

Table 8.4 List of Filter Attributes in the Monitor

Filter Name	Description
Status	The status of the MPL entry in the monitor. Possible values include the following: ▪ **All** ▪ **Failed** ▪ **Retry** ▪ **Completed** ▪ **Processing** ▪ **Escalated**
Artifact	The name of the integration flow or OData service as created in your design workspace.
Message ID	A unique identifier for a specific MPL across the tenant. This attribute is often used in a filter when troubleshooting a specific integration flow instance with a known message ID.
Correlation ID	A unique identifier for a specific group of messages that belong together. This attribute is relevant for scenarios where different MPLs belong to one end-to-end process, for example, in a JMS scenario where a message is stored in a JMS queue using one MPL and consumed in a second MPL.
Application ID	Only relevant when the `SAP_ApplicationID` header element has been specified using either the content modifier or script step.

Table 8.4 List of Filter Attributes in the Monitor (Cont.)

On the left side of the screen, you get the overall number of messages matching the selection criteria. Using the arrows at the top of the **Messages** table, you can navigate between the different pages of the monitor to check all the messages available (Figure 8.7).

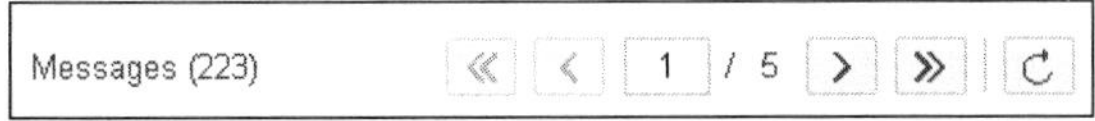

Figure 8.7 Navigation in the Message Monitor

For each message entry on the left view, the processing time, the status of the message, and the configured log level are displayed. Upon selection of any entry in the left view, further details in respect to the message are displayed on the right side of the screen:

- At the top, the time of the last update in the log for this message is shown.
- The **Status Details** section provides the overall status of the message processing, together with the overall processing time. If an error occurred during processing of the message, the error details are shown (Figure 8.8).

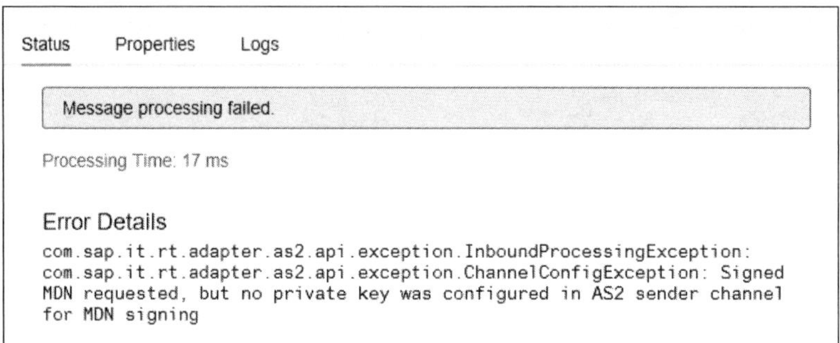

Status
Properties
Logs
Message processing failed.
Processing Time: 17 ms
Error Details
com.sap.it.rt.adapter.as2.api.exception.InboundProcessingException:
com.sap.it.rt.adapter.as2.api.exception.ChannelConfigException: Signed
MDN requested, but no private key was configured in AS2 sender channel
for MDN signing

Figure 8.8 Status Details for an Erroneous Message

- In the **Properties** section, the message ID, the correlation ID, and the details of the deployed integration artifact are displayed, including the name, the ID, and the type of the artifact, together with a link that opens the artifact in display mode.
- The **Logs** section contains information about the **Log Level** and the **Process ID** for the message processing. The **Process ID** indicates the ID of the runtime node the message was executed on; this information is important to find the related system log if an error needs to be analyzed in detail (Section 8.5.2). The **Log Level**, for example **Debug**, is shown as a link, and, if selected, it will open the detailed steps of the message processing in a new window. There the processing steps are shown in a table at the top, and the message traversal path is depicted in the model below. We'll discuss this in more detail later in this section. The textual representation of the **Message Processing Log** can be accessed using the **Open Text View** link.
- If MPL attachments are created during message processing, an additional tab, **Attachments**, is available. There the MPL attachments are listed in a table showing the name of the attachment, the type, and the time the attachment was modified last. MPL attachments can, for example, be created during message processing using the script step.

Let's check out the available sections in more detail.

Properties

In the **Properties** section, the message ID for this specific message processing and the properties of the deployed integration flow are listed. Table 8.5 describes each of these attributes.

Attribute	Description
Message ID	ID of the selected MPL that can be used as search criteria in message monitoring and in log files.
Correlation ID	ID of a group of MPLs that belong together and can be used as search criteria in message monitoring.
Artifact Name	Shows the name of the integration artifact.
Artifact ID	The technical artifact ID of the integration flow or the OData project.
Artifact Type	Can be either **Integration Flow** or **OData Project**.

Table 8.5 List of Attributes in the Properties Section

If the artifact for this message is still deployed on the tenant, the name of the artifact is shown as a link (refer back to Figure 8.6). Selecting the link opens the artifact in read-only mode (Figure 8.9). You can use this view to explore the configured steps and adapters in the integration flow and check the defined properties.

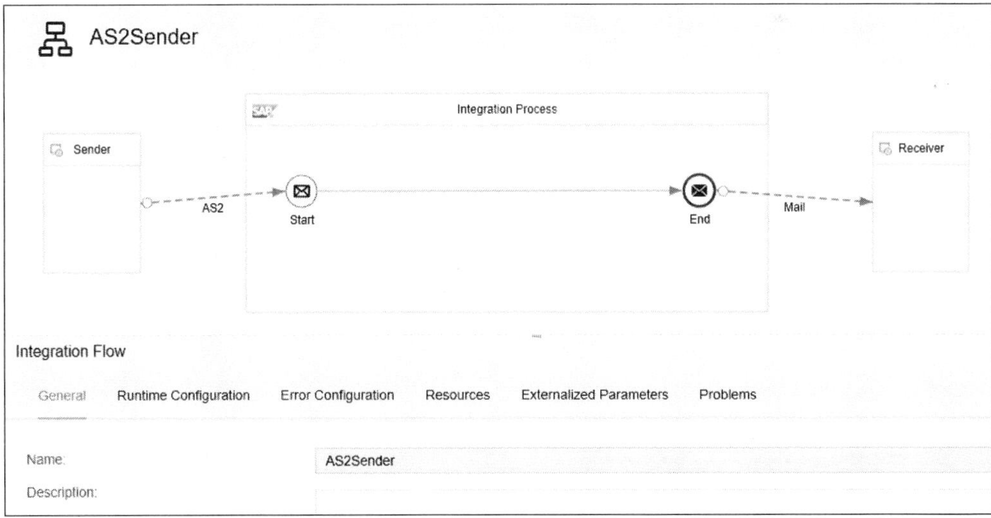

Figure 8.9 Integration Flow in Read-Only Mode

Note that it isn't possible to change the configuration and redeploy the integration flow in this view. The view is meant for monitoring only. If changes to the integration flow are required, you need to change to the design view and adjust the integration flow there.

Logs

Let's take a deeper look at the **Logs** section (refer to Figure 8.6). There the MPL can be explored in visual and in textual representation.

The **Logs** tab may contain a table listing several message processing runs, as shown previously in Figure 8.6. This is the case, for example, when JMS queues are used for temporary message storage, such as in the XI or AS2 adapter, or if the message is retried by the JMS sender adapter. Then, for each message processing run, one line appears in the table. However, in most of the scenarios, the **Logs** tab looks similar to Figure 8.10. Because only a single message processing run is executed, the data isn't provided in a table.

Figure 8.10 Logs Tab for a Single Message Processing Run

The log level is displayed that was used to write the MPL. Remember that we learned which log levels exist and how to set the log level in Section 8.2.1. The **Log Level** value is shown as a link in the **Logs** tab. As depicted in Figure 8.11, selecting the link opens a new window that provides a table with all the processing steps and the graphical model of the integration flow. Note that the details shown depend on the log level being used; we'll elaborate more on this in the next couple of pages.

As depicted in Figure 8.12, for erroneous messages, the error is highlighted in the table with an **Error** icon ⓘ, which shows the error details when clicked.

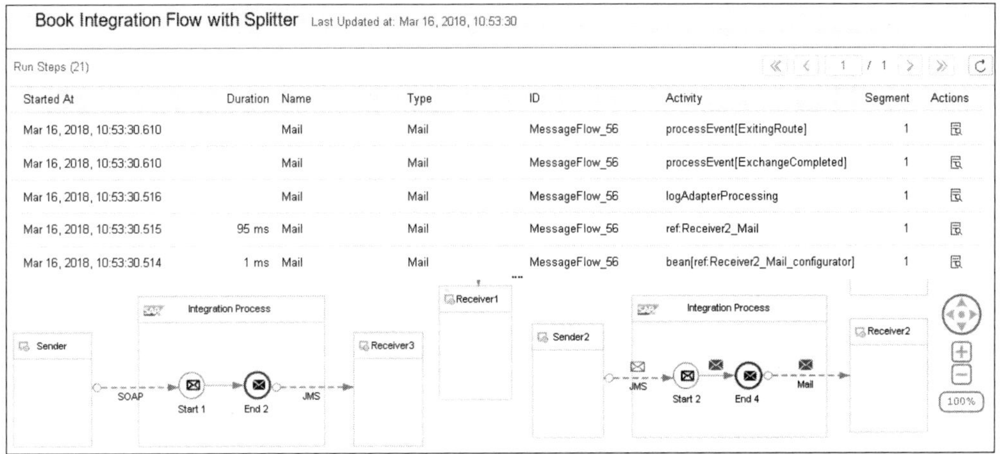

Figure 8.11 Visual Representation of the Message Processing Log

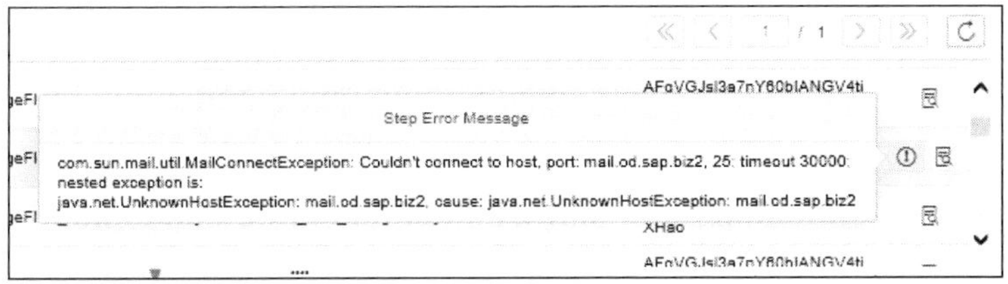

Figure 8.12 Visual Representation of the Message Processing Log for an Erroneous Message

The table at the top of the window contains all executed processing steps sorted by execution time, starting with the last step executed. The different columns of the table are described in detail in Table 8.6.

Attribute	Description
Started At	Time the step was started.
Duration	Overall time of the execution of the step.
Name	Name of the flow step or adapter channel.
Type	Type of the flow step or adapter, for example, **Mail**.
ID	ID of the flow step or adapter in the integration flow model. All steps with the same ID belong to the same flow step or adapter in the integration flow.

Table 8.6 Description of the Columns in the Message Processing Log

Attribute	Description
Activity	Detailed activity executed by the flow step or adapter. There are typically several activities executed by one flow step or adapter, which are grouped by the model step ID.
Segment	ID of the processing segment in the runtime. This value gets especially interesting if multiple branches are executed for one message processing because then multiple processing segments are available. This is the case, for example, if splitter or multicast patterns are used.
Actions	Actions for the single step. Currently you can show the step details using the **Show Step Details** icon.

Table 8.6 Description of the Columns in the Message Processing Log (Cont.)

At the bottom of the screen, the model of the integration flow is shown with the traversal path for the message processing. As depicted in Figure 8.11, envelope icons are shown in the model to indicate the path this specific message has taken during processing. For steps causing an error, the envelope is shown in red.

Icons for Path Traversal Depend on the Log Level

Note that the filled envelopes are shown only if log level **Trace** was used for the message processing, indicating that a full trace with payloads and headers is available in the details. If trace level **Info** or **Debug** was used, no payload data is available in the detailed log data. In this case, the envelopes indicating the traversal path aren't filled. Blue envelopes show the traversal path for successfully executed steps, and a red envelope points out that there was an error executing this step.

When you select the **Show Step Details** icon for one specific processing step in the table, a new window opens. As depicted in Figure 8.13, the screen shows multiple tabs for the selected processing step. The **Log** tab contains a table with key/value pairs written by this processing step.

In the **Configuration** tab, the defined settings in the flow step or adapter can be explored. The configuration tabs available for the flow step or adapter are shown in read-only mode. In Figure 8.14, the **Configuration** tabs for the **Mail** receiver adapter are **General**, **Connection**, and **Security**. You can navigate between the tabs and discover all configurations defined for this flow step or adapter.

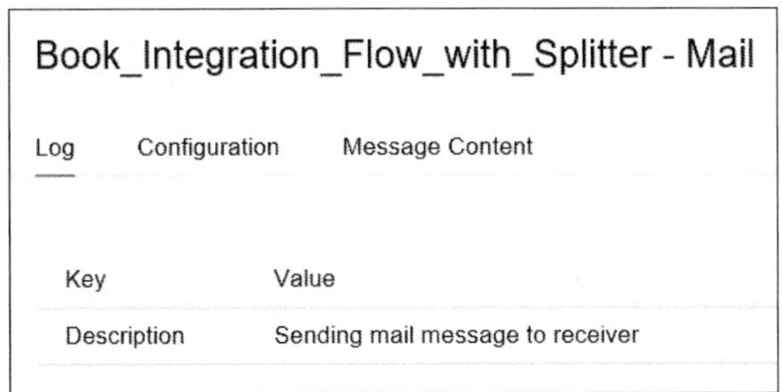

Figure 8.13 Log of a Single Processing Step

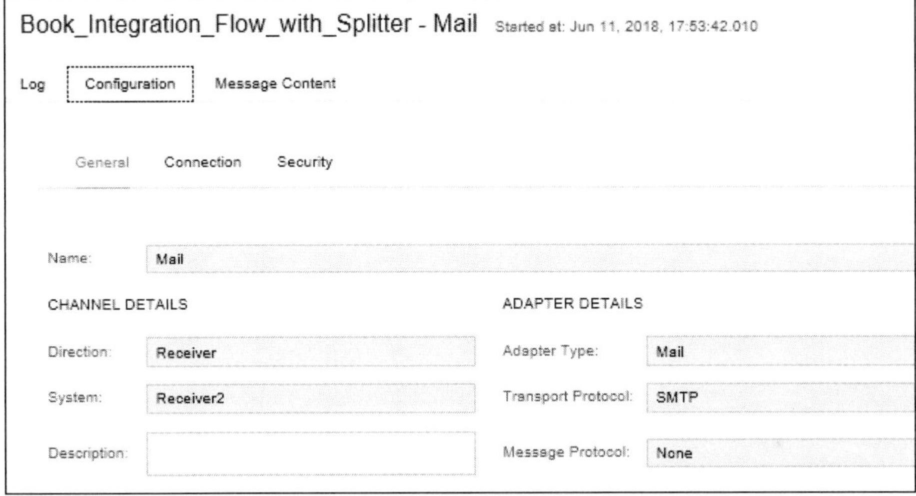

Figure 8.14 Configuration Details of a Single Processing Step

The **Message Content** tab, if available, provides the payload and header data written during execution of the flow step or adapter (Figure 8.15). The screen is divided into two sections, the **Header** section at the top and the **Payload** section at the bottom. In the **Header** section, all the headers available during execution of this step or adapter are shown. In Figure 8.15, for example, you see all the headers set by the mail receiver adapter. In the **Payload** section, the corresponding payload sent to the mail server is shown.

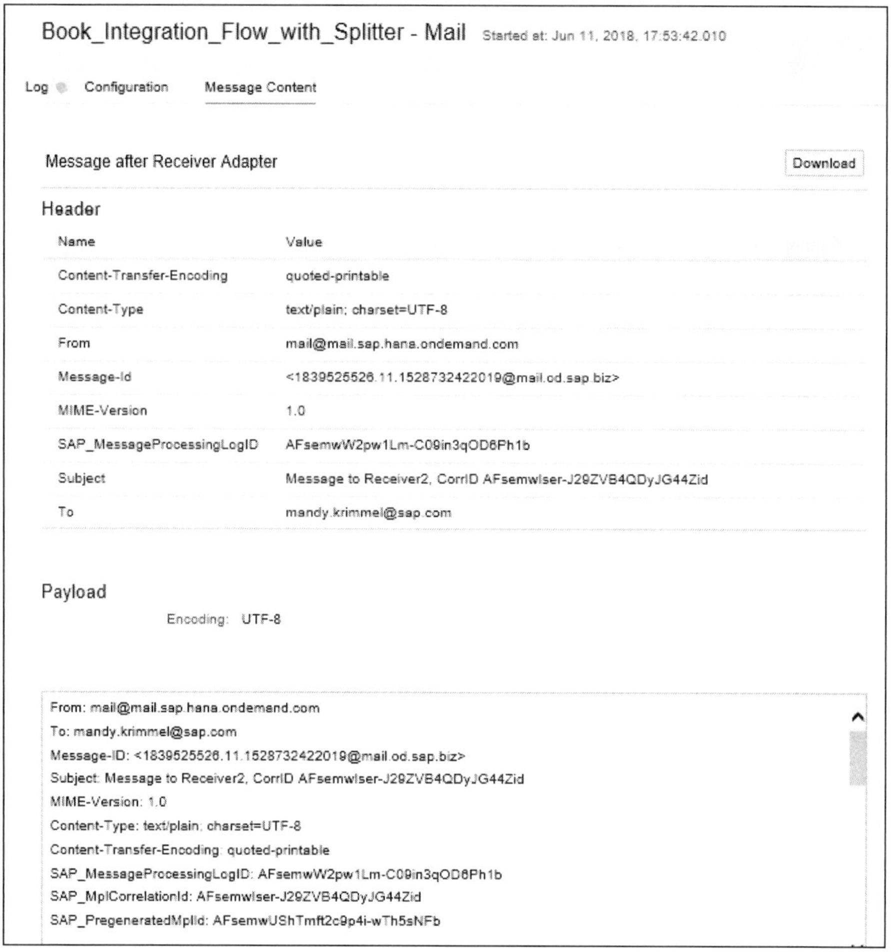

Book_Integration_Flow_with_Splitter - Mail Started at: Jun 11, 2018, 17:53:42.010

Log Configuration Message Content

Message after Receiver Adapter Download

Header

Name	Value
Content-Transfer-Encoding	quoted-printable
Content-Type	text/plain; charset=UTF-8
From	mail@mail.sap.hana.ondemand.com
Message-Id	<1839525526.11.1528732422019@mail.od.sap.biz>
MIME-Version	1.0
SAP_MessageProcessingLogID	AFsemwW2pw1Lm-C09in3qOD6Ph1b
Subject	Message to Receiver2, CorrID AFsemwlser-J29ZVB4QDyJG44Zid
To	mandy.krimmel@sap.com

Payload

Encoding: UTF-8

From: mail@mail.sap.hana.ondemand.com
To: mandy.krimmel@sap.com
Message-ID: <1839525526.11.1528732422019@mail.od.sap.biz>
Subject: Message to Receiver2, CorrID AFsemwlser-J29ZVB4QDyJG44Zid
MIME-Version: 1.0
Content-Type: text/plain; charset=UTF-8
Content-Transfer-Encoding: quoted-printable
SAP_MessageProcessingLogID: AFsemwW2pw1Lm-C09in3qOD6Ph1b
SAP_MplCorrelationId: AFsemwlser-J29ZVB4QDyJG44Zid
SAP_PregeneratedMplId: AFsemwUShTmft2c9p4i-wTh5sNFb

Figure 8.15 Message Content Sent by the Mail Receiver Adapter

With these details, it's possible to know exactly how the headers and payload changed during execution of this specific step. This can especially be useful if you need to understand a specific error situation in the scenario execution. Using the **Download** link, you have the option to download the payload and the headers.

Message Content Not Available?

Note that the message content for a specific step is only available if log level **Trace** was defined for this message processing.

Details Available Depend on the Defined Log Level

Depending on the log level set for the integration flow, different details are available in the MPL:

- **None**
  The MPL isn't available at all.
- **Info**
  Only the traversal path is available in the model combined with the **Configuration** tab. If the message processing ended with the status **Failed**, the last processing steps are listed, and the **Properties** and **Configuration** tabs are shown in the details of the processing steps with the respective data.
- **Debug**
  The traversal path is available in the model. In addition, all processing steps are listed, and the **Properties** and **Configuration** tabs are shown in the details of the processing steps with the respective data.
- **Trace**
  The traversal path is available in the model. In addition, all processing steps are listed, and the **Properties**, **Message Content**, and **Configuration** tabs are shown in the details of the processing steps with the respective data.

In addition to the graphical representation of the MPL, a textual representation is available that contains the details of all executed steps during processing of the message in one single file. You can select the **Open Text View** link in the message processing monitor (refer back to Figure 8.6) to open the textual log view.

As depicted in Figure 8.16, the main attributes of the message processing are shown, such as the start and stop time, overall status, and message guide. If log level **Info** was set for this message processing, no additional details are shown, and the single steps and adapters aren't logged.

If there was an error when processing the message, a more detailed log is available for the last steps before the error occurred (Figure 8.17), even for log level **Info**. This log provides integration developers enough information to easily spot problems or errors at hand. Aside from exploring the contents of the log, you can also download the log using the **Download** button at the top-right corner of the page.

Note that for log level **Debug**, all steps and adapters are always logged, independent of whether the message was processed successfully or ended with an error.

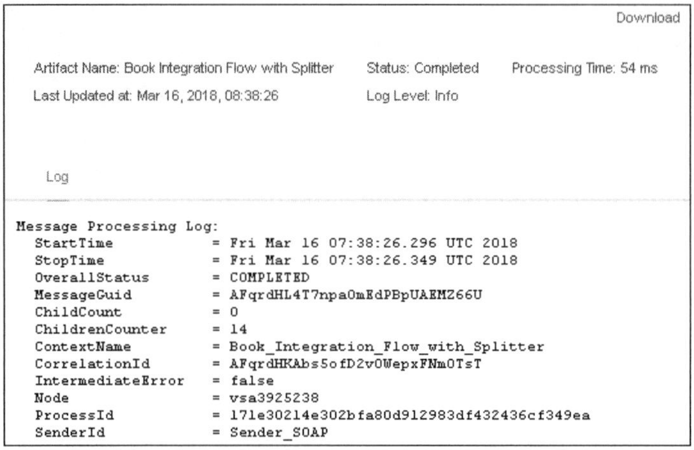

Download

Artifact Name: Book Integration Flow with Splitter | Status: Completed | Processing Time: 54 ms
Last Updated at: Mar 16, 2018, 08:38:26 | Log Level: Info

Log

```
Message Processing Log:
  StartTime             = Fri Mar 16 07:38:26.296 UTC 2018
  StopTime              = Fri Mar 16 07:38:26.349 UTC 2018
  OverallStatus         = COMPLETED
  MessageGuid           = AFqrdHL4T7npa0mEdPBpUAEMZ66U
  ChildCount            = 0
  ChildrenCounter       = 14
  ContextName           = Book_Integration_Flow_with_Splitter
  CorrelationId         = AFqrdHKAbs5ofD2v0WepxFNm0TsT
  IntermediateError     = false
  Node                  = vsa3925238
  ProcessId             = 171e30214e302bfa80d912983df432436cf349ea
  SenderId              = Sender_SOAP
```

Figure 8.16 Log of a Completed Message

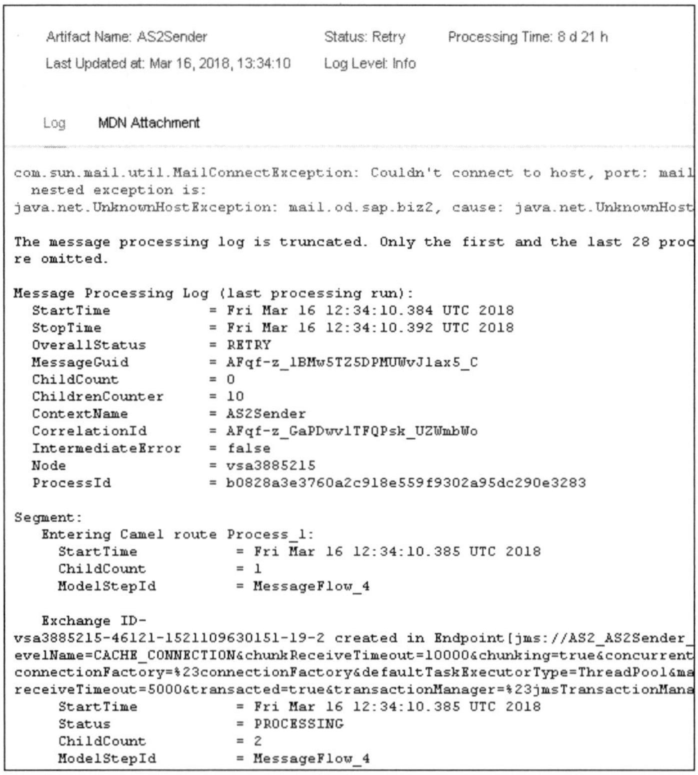

Artifact Name: AS2Sender | Status: Retry | Processing Time: 8 d 21 h
Last Updated at: Mar 16, 2018, 13:34:10 | Log Level: Info

Log MDN Attachment

```
com.sun.mail.util.MailConnectException: Couldn't connect to host, port: mail
  nested exception is:
java.net.UnknownHostException: mail.od.sap.biz2, cause: java.net.UnknownHost

The message processing log is truncated. Only the first and the last 28 proc
re omitted.

Message Processing Log (last processing run):
  StartTime             = Fri Mar 16 12:34:10.384 UTC 2018
  StopTime              = Fri Mar 16 12:34:10.392 UTC 2018
  OverallStatus         = RETRY
  MessageGuid           = AFqf-z_lBMw5TZ5DPMUWvJlax5_C
  ChildCount            = 0
  ChildrenCounter       = 10
  ContextName           = AS2Sender
  CorrelationId         = AFqf-z_GaPDwvlTFQPsk_UZWmbWo
  IntermediateError     = false
  Node                  = vsa3885215
  ProcessId             = b0828a3e3760a2c918e559f9302a95dc290e3283

Segment:
   Entering Camel route Process_1:
     StartTime            = Fri Mar 16 12:34:10.385 UTC 2018
     ChildCount           = 1
     ModelStepId          = MessageFlow_4

   Exchange ID-
vsa3885215-46121-1521109630151-19-2 created in Endpoint[jms://AS2_AS2Sender_
evelName=CACHE_CONNECTION&chunkReceiveTimeout=10000&chunking=true&concurrent
connectionFactory=%23connectionFactory&defaultTaskExecutorType=ThreadPool&ma
receiveTimeout=5000&transacted=true&transactionManager=%23jmsTransactionMana
     StartTime            = Fri Mar 16 12:34:10.385 UTC 2018
     Status               = PROCESSING
     ChildCount           = 2
     ModelStepId          = MessageFlow_4
```

Figure 8.17 Log of a Message in Error Status

As stated earlier, the log details are often referred to as the *MPL*. The textual MPL represents a well-structured tree of log information. The MPL structure consists of two main components: the top and bottom sections. The top section contains the properties and metadata of the message as a whole, similar to a header section. This is the section available with log level **Info**. The bottom section contains one or more branches with entries for each step of a particular integration flow. This section is only available with log level **Debug** or if an error occurred during processing of the message.

The MPL structure always includes a predetermined set of attributes, which are listed in Table 8.7 and Table 8.8. Becoming familiar with these attributes will enable you to better understand the logs and therefore improve your ability to troubleshoot issues. Note that not all properties listed in the tables are present in every MPL. Depending on the status of a message, only a few properties might be shown in the MPL. For instance, the **Error** attribute is only present if a message is in **Failed** status, as you can see in Figure 8.17.

Property	Description
`Error`	Specifies the error of a particular step in the integration flow. Note that this attribute is displayed at the top of the log in red color and is only available in the MPL of messages that are in a failed state.
`StartTime`	The time that message processing started.
`StopTime`	The time that message processing ended.
`OverallStatus`	The status of the message processing, as discussed earlier in the chapter (see Table 8.4).
`ChildCount`	The serial number of the current processing step. For the overall overview at the top of the MPL, this number is always 0.
`ChildrenCounter`	The total number of message processing steps executed.
`ContextName`	The name of the integration flow.

Table 8.7 Properties Contained in the MPL Header

Property	Description
CorrelationId	The ID that identifies correlated messages. Messages can be correlated, for example, when different integration flows on the same tenant communicate with each other, for example, using JMS queues. A correlation ID is a base64-encoded ID that is generated in this case by the first integration process and stored in the message header. As part of the message header, the CorrelationId is then propagated across all related integration flows.
CustomHeaderProperties	Shown if you specify your own headers via the script application programming interface (API) in the script step.
IntermediateError	If, during message processing, an error occurred, or message processing needed more than one minute, the value of this property is set to true.
LastErrorModelStepId	ID of the step that caused the error. Note that this attribute is only available in the MPL of messages that are in a failed state.
MessageGuid	A key that identifies the message uniquely in the database.
Node	The host name of the runtime node that processed the message.
Process ID	The ID of the runtime process that executed the message. This information is useful to identify the system log file, in which details to the message processing are logged.
ReceiverId	The name of the receiver as configured in the integration flow using the header SAP_Receiver, for example, in a content modifier or script step.
SenderId	Specifies the name of the sender as configured in the integration flow using the header SAP_Sender, for example, in a content modifier or script step.
Id	Displayed in the MPL header if the ID has been defined using the header SAP_ApplicationID in the integration flow, for example, in a content modifier or script step.
MessageType	Displayed in the MPL header if the message type has been defined using the header SAP_MessageType in the integration flow, for example, in a content modifier or script step.

Table 8.7 Properties Contained in the MPL Header (Cont.)

Property	Description
Segment	Indicates that the following steps have been processed in the same processing segment. If a split or multicast step is used, the steps belonging to one subroute are grouped together within one segment.
StartTime	The time that each step of the integration flow started.
StopTime	The time that each step of the integration flow stopped.
Status	The status of each step of the integration flow.
ChildCount	The serial number of the current processing step.
ModelStepId	The ID of a particular step in the integration flow. This ID is used to specify the relation between a modeled step (in the integration flow) and an MPL entry. The integration flow model steps are fragmented in the Camel runtime environment into several processing steps.
StepID	The ID of a particular step in the log.

Table 8.8 Properties Contained in the MPL for Each Step

Attachments

In addition to viewing the log, it's also possible to access MPL attachments written during message processing. As depicted earlier in Figure 8.6, in the **Attachments** tab, all MPL attachments are listed in a table showing the name of the MPL attachment, the type, and the time the attachment was modified last. The name of the attachment is shown as a link. When you select this link, the attachment opens in a new window. In Figure 8.18, for example, an MPL attachment with the name **MDN Attachment** is shown.

MPL attachments are written by some adapters, such as the AS2 adapter. But you can also create MPL attachments yourself with the help of a script step. Refer to Chapter 9, Section 9.4, for details about using Java APIs in scripts.

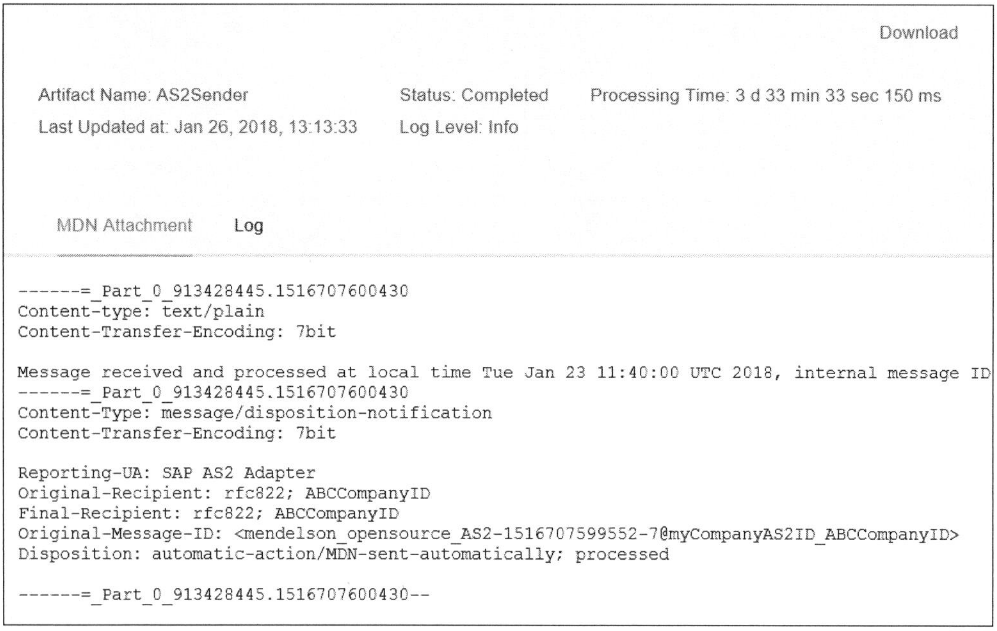

Download

Artifact Name: AS2Sender | Status: Completed | Processing Time: 3 d 33 min 33 sec 150 ms
Last Updated at: Jan 26, 2018, 13:13:33 | Log Level: Info

MDN Attachment   Log

```
------=_Part_0_913428445.1516707600430
Content-type: text/plain
Content-Transfer-Encoding: 7bit

Message received and processed at local time Tue Jan 23 11:40:00 UTC 2018, internal message ID
------=_Part_0_913428445.1516707600430
Content-Type: message/disposition-notification
Content-Transfer-Encoding: 7bit

Reporting-UA: SAP AS2 Adapter
Original-Recipient: rfc822; ABCCompanyID
Final-Recipient: rfc822; ABCCompanyID
Original-Message-ID: <mendelson_opensource_AS2-1516707599552-7@myCompanyAS2ID_ABCCompanyID>
Disposition: automatic-action/MDN-sent-automatically; processed

------=_Part_0_913428445.1516707600430--
```

Figure 8.18 Accessing the MPL Attachment

Using MPL Attachments

MPL attachments can be created in the script step using the `MessageLog` API. You should use this option with care and avoid writing the whole payload into the MPL attachment because this can cause out-of-memory errors in the worker node, which can lead to unavailability of the whole scenario.

Important recommendations for using MPL attachments can be found in the "Avoid Storing Payloads in the Message Processing Log" blog in the SAP Community (*www.sap.com/community.html*).

Now that you know how to monitor messages through SAP Cloud Platform Integration's monitors, let's explore how you can manage and customize the tiles on your monitoring dashboard.

8.2.4 Managing Tiles

As mentioned earlier, a tile in the monitor page is a block in a page that filters messages or artifacts corresponding to a particular status. Each one of these tiles can be clicked to display a list of messages or artifacts matching the status. The message and artifact tiles are presented and grouped by statuses. For messages, the following tiles are available by default:

- **All Messages**
- **Failed Messages**
- **Retry Messages**
- **Completed Messages**

> **Note**
>
> By default, all tiles in the **Monitor Message Processing** section use a one-hour period, which means, for instance, that the **Failed Messages** tile only shows failed messages of the last hour. However, this can be changed easily by choosing another value from the **Time** dropdown menu, as shown in Figure 8.19.

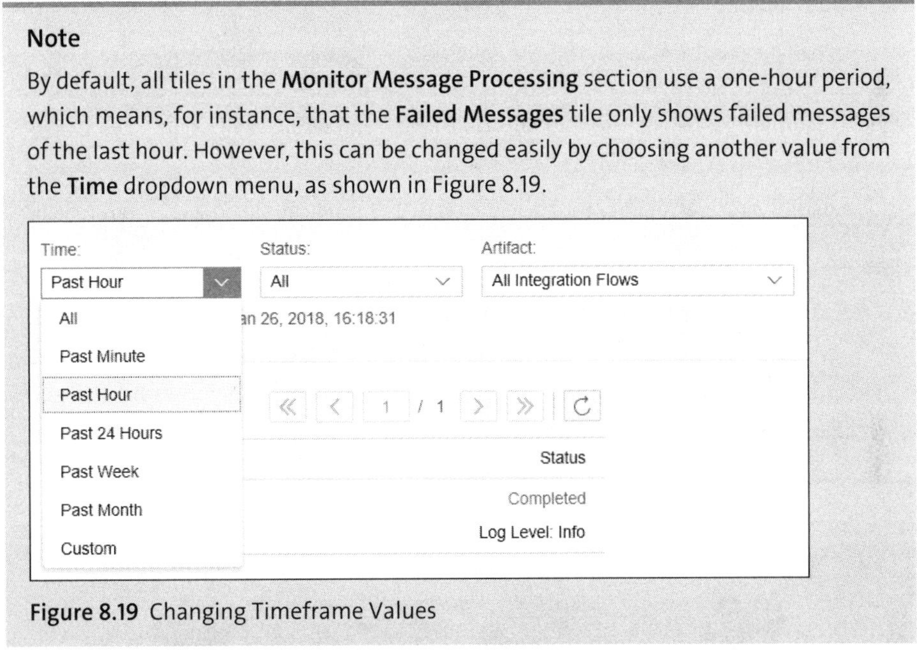

Figure 8.19 Changing Timeframe Values

You may think of these tiles as preconfigured message or artifact filters, or as shortcuts to access the messages or artifacts quickly that you're looking for. Furthermore, you can also remove or move the default tiles to suit your needs. To move the position of a tile, proceed as follows:

1. Mouse over the tile to be moved.
2. Drag and drop the tile to the desired location.

To completely delete or remove an existing tile, follow these steps:

1. Right-click on the concerned tile.
2. From the resulting context menu, select the **Delete** option, as shown in Figure 8.20.

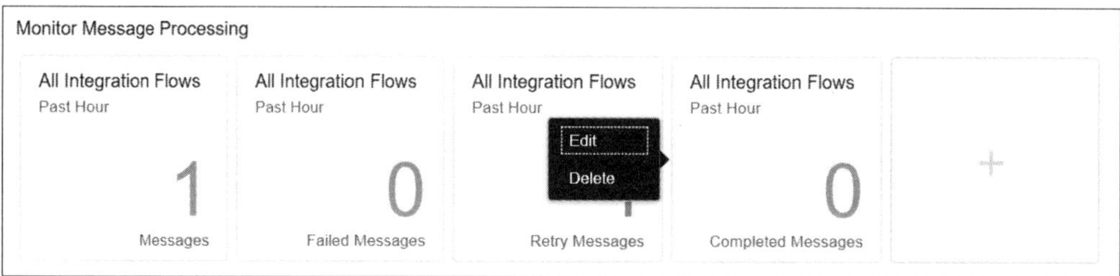

Figure 8.20 Editing and Managing Monitor Message Processing Tiles

If you often apply a particular filter to messages or artifacts, you can also create a new tile for it. For the sake of illustration, imagine that you want to create a tile to view all escalated messages. Follow these steps:

1. Click on the empty tile on the right side of the screen with the **+** sign.
2. A new **Tile Settings** popup screen appears, from which you can specify the filtering criteria to be applied on past runtime messages. Figure 8.21 shows how to select the **Escalated** option from the **Status** dropdown menu.

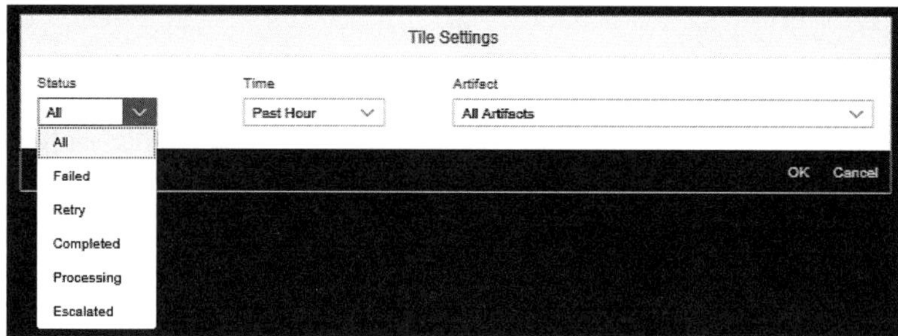

Figure 8.21 Creating a New Message Monitoring Tile

Note that in the **Tile Settings** popup screen for messages, the following filtering options are available:

- **Status**
  Different message statuses can be selected, such as **Failed**, **Retry**, **Completed**, and so on.
- **Time**
  Different filtering timeframes are available to be selected, including **Past Minute**, **Past Hour**, **Past 24 Hours**, **Past Week**, and so on.
- **Artifact**
  All available integration flows and OData services on the target runtime system and tenant are listed. By selecting a particular integration flow or OData service on your tile settings, you can further restrict the filtering of messages to entries of the selected integration flow or OData service, as depicted in Figure 8.22.

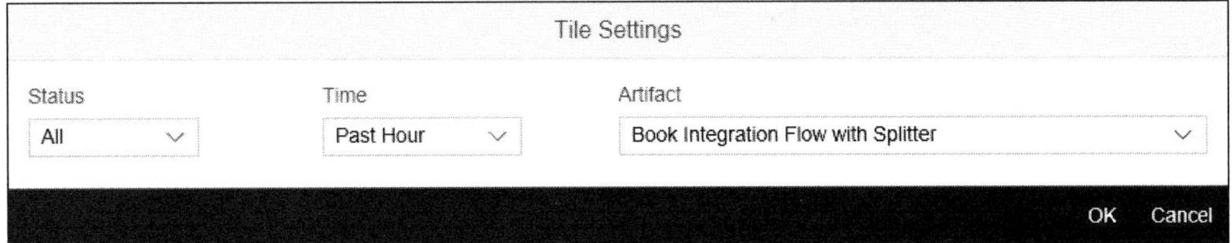

Figure 8.22 Selecting a Specific Integration Flow in the Tile Settings

As an administrator of your SAP Cloud Platform Integration tenant, it's important to gain a good understanding of what each message status in the monitor means. Currently, five statuses are available, as described in Table 8.9.

Status	Description
`Failed`	The message hasn't been delivered to the receiver, and message processing failed and ended in a dead end. Message processing has ultimately failed, and no more retries are possible.
`Escalated`	The message runs into an escalation end event as configured in the integration flow. There are several escalation categories available for configuration, for example `Receiver not reachable`, `Receiver not found`, `Not authorized to invoke the receiver`, and so on. An error is raised back to the sender.
`Retry`	The message processing went into **Error** status, and an automatic retry was triggered.

Table 8.9 Possible Message Statuses in the Message Monitor

Status	Description
`Processing`	The message is currently being processed.
`Completed`	The message has been successfully delivered to the receiver.

Table 8.9 Possible Message Statuses in the Message Monitor (Cont.)

Now that you understand how to monitor integration artifacts and messages processed by the artifacts we'll explore how to maintain the security artifacts for your integration content.

8.3 Manage Security

When dealing with integration scenarios, security is an important topic. To consume other services, you'll most likely need to use security objects such as certificates, user names, passwords, and so forth. The types of objects needed to secure your interfaces are recognized as *security artifacts*. Table 8.10 presents the complete list of security artifacts available in SAP Cloud Platform Integration.

> **Note**
>
> We mainly focus in this chapter on how to manage these artifacts. For more information on the security concepts behind the artifacts, see Chapter 10.

Type	Description
SSH Known Hosts	Contains the trusted hosts that need to be specified when the tenant is connected with a remote component using Secure Shell (SSH).
OAuth2 Credentials	Contains the client ID and client secret of the client you're connecting to using OAuth 2.0 authentication.
PGP Public Keyring	Contains the public keys required when the exchanged messages are digitally signed or encrypted using Open Pretty Good Privacy (Open PGP). See Chapter 10, Section 10.4.

Table 8.10 Integration Artifact Types Related to Secure Messaging

Type	Description
PGP Secret Keyring	Contains the private keys required when the exchanged messages are digitally signed or encrypted using Open PGP. See Chapter 10, Section 10.4.
Secure Parameter	Contains credentials to be used together with specific authentication options, such as OAuth. To find out how to use such an artifact when setting up a scenario with OAuth authentication, see Chapter 10, Section 10.4.5.
User Credentials	Contains username and password information for basic authentication. We introduced this artifact type already with the first scenario described in this book (Chapter 2, Section 2.3.4).
Keystore artifacts	In the keystore, the keys and certificates required to enable secure connection of the tenant with other components based on public key certificates (type X.509) are maintained. See also Chapter 10, Section 10.5 for more details.
Certificate-to-User Mapping	Client certificates mapped to users for role-based authorization. See Chapter 10, Section 10.4.4, to find out how to use such an artifact when setting up a secure connection.

Table 8.10 Integration Artifact Types Related to Secure Messaging (Cont.)

The security-related artifacts can be maintained in the monitoring dashboard in the **Manage Security** section. As depicted in Figure 8.23, three tiles are available in this section for the different security artifacts: one for the **Keystore** material, such as certificates and key pairs; one for the **Certificate-to-User Mappings;** and one for the additional **Security Material**, such as credentials, PGP keyrings, and secure parameters.

In addition to the security-related tiles, a tile for **Connectivity Tests** is available, in which you have the option to execute several outbound connectivity tests to test that the security material is maintained correctly and the connection can be executed successfully.

Let's explore the different tiles in more detail. We'll start with the **Security Material** tile.

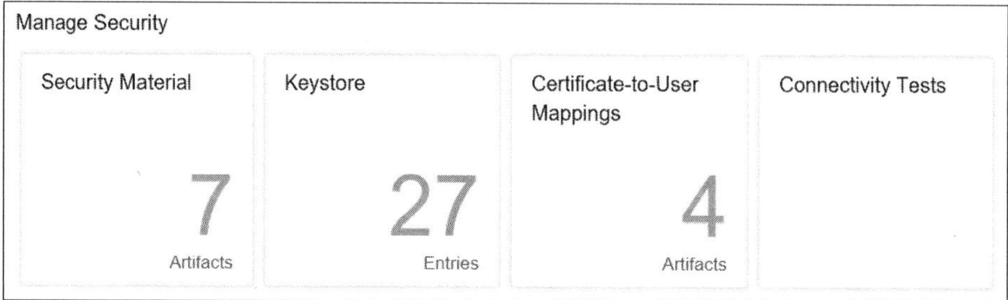

Figure 8.23 Manage Security Section in the Monitoring Dashboard

8.3.1 Maintain Security Material

SAP Cloud Platform Integration provides the security material tile to enable users to manage the tenant's security material. The tile can be accessed via the **Security Material** link, as shown previously in Figure 8.23.

After clicking on the link, you're redirected to a page similar to Figure 8.24. The table displays a list of the different security materials that have been deployed on the tenant and shows the details of the security artifacts in different columns. Table 8.11 provides descriptions of the columns.

Column Name	Description
Name	Contains the name of the security artifact.
Type	Specifies the type of the security artifact. The possible values for this field are as follows: ■ **Credentials**: Used for user credentials, OAuth2 credentials, and secure parameters. ■ **PGP public keyring:** Contains the public keys used for PGP encryption and signature verification. ■ **PGP secret keyring:** Contains the private and public keys used for PGP decryption and signing. ■ **SSH known hosts:** Contains the public keys of the connected SFTP servers. ■ **Keystore**: Used for certificates and private keys

Table 8.11 Attributes of a Security Material

Column Name	Description
Status	Specifies the states of the deployed artifact on the SAP Cloud Platform Integration server. Possible values include the following: ■ **Error**: Security artifact has an error. ■ **Deployed**: Security artifact is successfully deployed on the worker node. ■ **Deploying**: Security artifact is being deployed on the worker node. ■ **Stored**: Security artifact is stored on the tenant management node but not yet deployed on the worker node.
Deployed By	The name of the user who performed the deployment.
Deployed On	The date and time when the deployment was performed.

Table 8.11 Attributes of a Security Material (Cont.)

If you're not satisfied with the layout of the table shown in Figure 8.24, you can change and customize it using the **Table Settings** icon .

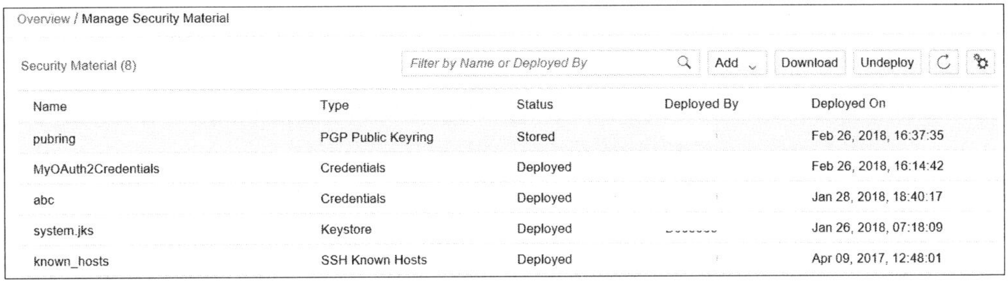

Overview / Manage Security Material

Security Material (8)				
Name	Type	Status	Deployed By	Deployed On
pubring	PGP Public Keyring	Stored		Feb 26, 2018, 16:37:35
MyOAuth2Credentials	Credentials	Deployed		Feb 26, 2018, 16:14:42
abc	Credentials	Deployed		Jan 28, 2018, 18:40:17
system.jks	Keystore	Deployed		Jan 26, 2018, 07:18:09
known_hosts	SSH Known Hosts	Deployed		Apr 09, 2017, 12:48:01

Figure 8.24 Manage Security Material

Let's now explore what is needed to add or deploy a new security artifact to your tenant. Proceed as follows:

1. At the top-right side of the screen, select the **Add** button, as shown in Figure 8.25.
2. Select the desired type of artifact (e.g., **User Credentials**), and fill in the requested details, as shown in Figure 8.26.
3. If the desired artifact is a credential to be used for an SAP SuccessFactors-related integration scenario, select the **SuccessFactors** checkbox, and fill in the **Company ID** field. The **Company ID** represents the client instance used to connect to the SAP SuccessFactors system. Refer to Figure 8.26 as an example.

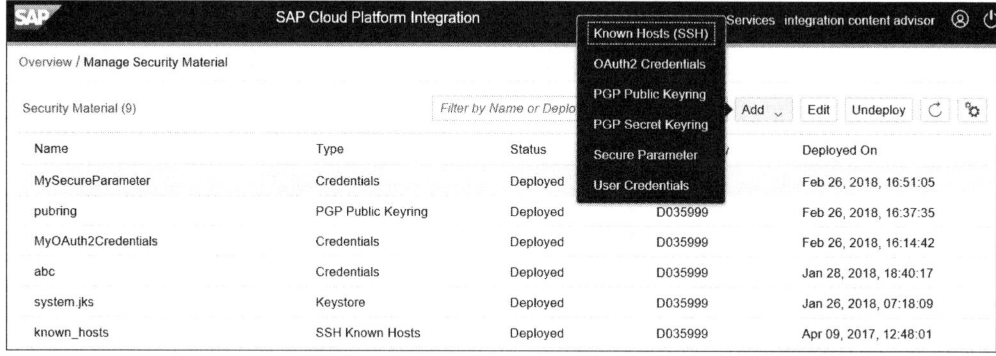

Figure 8.25 Adding a New Security Artifact

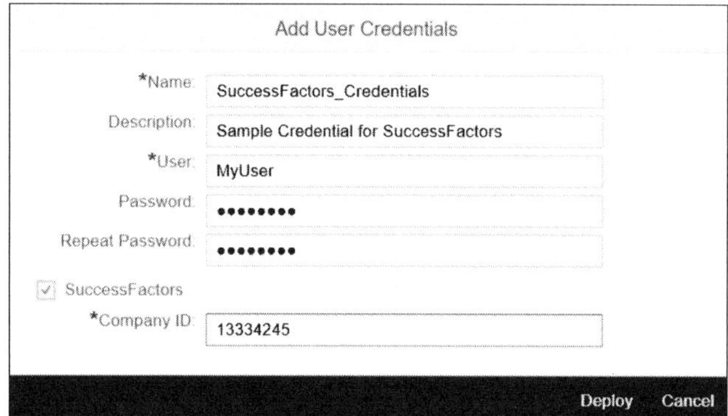

Figure 8.26 Sample Security Credentials for an SAP SuccessFactors Scenario

4. Select **Deploy** at the bottom of the **Add User Credentials** dialog. The new security artifact is deployed and added to the list.

Keystore Entry in the List of Security Material

You may have noticed that an entry for the keystore exists in the table of security artifacts, but you can't add a keystore using the **Add** action. This is because a dedicated monitor exists for managing the keystore entries, which can be accessed via the **Keystore** tile.

Credential artifacts can be changed and edited by performing the following steps:

1. Select a credential entry from the table of security artifacts. An **Edit** button then appears on the top-right corner (Figure 8.27).

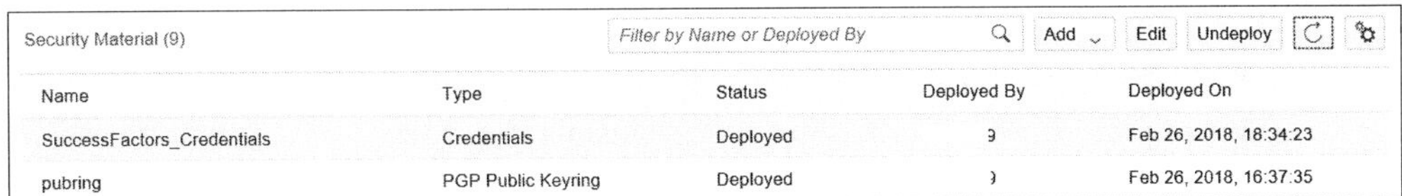

Figure 8.27 Selecting a Credential Artifact for Editing

2. Click **Edit** to change the properties of the credential artifact. Figure 8.28 shows an example of a user credential being edited.

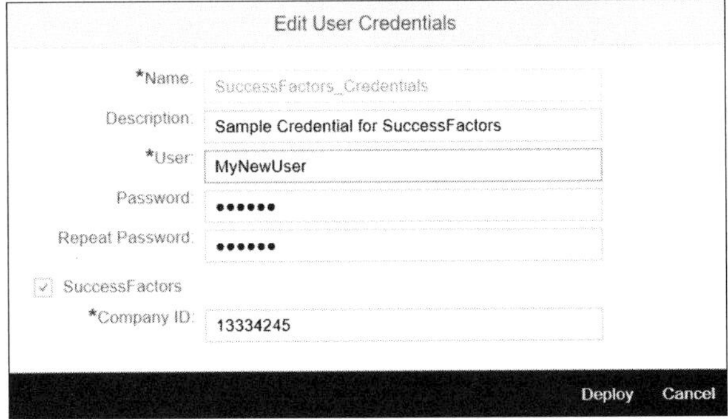

Figure 8.28 Updating Security Material of Type User Credential

PGP keyrings and SSH known hosts can be downloaded from the list by using the **Download** button, as shown in Figure 8.29. Furthermore, all artifact types (except the **Keystore**) can be removed from the tenant using the **Undeploy** button.

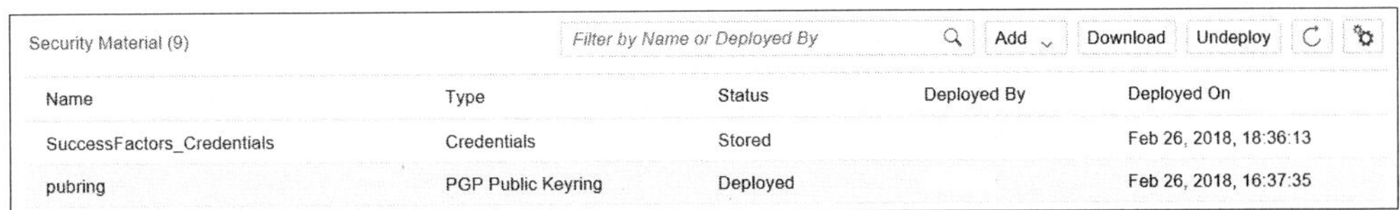

Figure 8.29 Selecting a PGP Keyring for Downloading

Let's now discuss how you can manage the certificates and key pairs in the keystore monitor.

8.3.2 Manage the Keystore

Using the second tile in the **Manage Security** section, the **Keystore** tile, you can maintain the certificates and private key pairs deployed on the tenant.

Preinstalled Artifacts in the Keystore

When provisioning a new tenant, SAP preinstalls the following artifacts in the keystore:

- One key pair with the alias `sap_cloudintegrationcertificate`
- Some SAP-owned root certificates, which enable communication with other SAP cloud systems, such as SAP Ariba and SAP Customer Relationship Management (SAP CRM)

Those certificates and key pairs can be used by customers to set up secure HTTP connections to backend systems using client certificates; for scenarios using message-level security; to sign or decrypt messages using PKCS7, XML, or simple signer; or in WS-Security.

More details about the different security features SAP Cloud Platform Integration offers are provided in Chapter 10.

To open the keystore monitor, select the **Keystore** tile. As depicted in Figure 8.30, four tabs are available, and the most important tab **Current** is opened when selecting the **Keystore** tile. It shows all certificates and key pairs currently deployed on the tenant in a table. The expired artifacts are highlighted in red to bring them to your attention because they usually need to be updated to guarantee successful scenario execution.

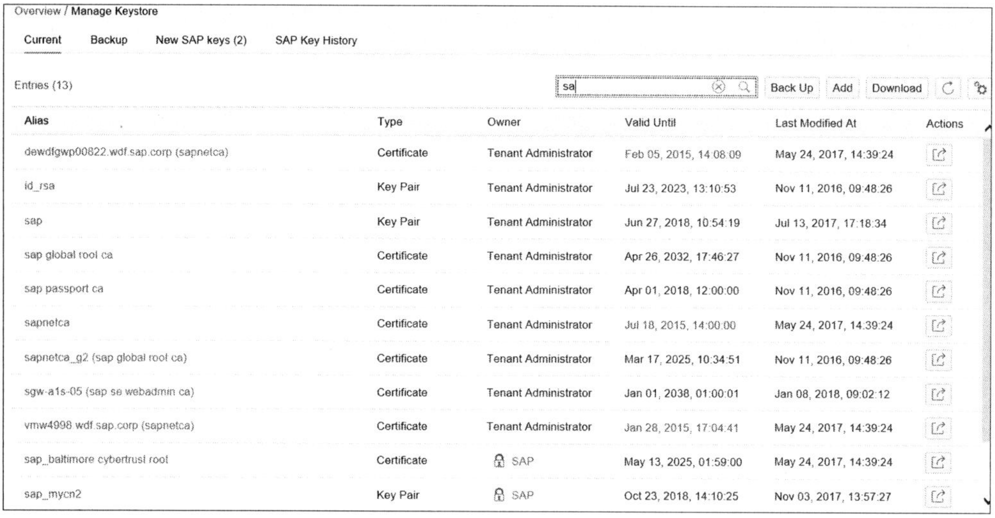

Overview / Manage Keystore

Current Backup New SAP keys (2) SAP Key History

Entries (13) sa Back Up Add Download

Alias	Type	Owner	Valid Until	Last Modified At	Actions
dewdfgwp00822.wdf.sap.corp (sapnetca)	Certificate	Tenant Administrator	Feb 05, 2015, 14:08:09	May 24, 2017, 14:39:24	
id_rsa	Key Pair	Tenant Administrator	Jul 23, 2023, 13:10:53	Nov 11, 2016, 09:48:26	
sap	Key Pair	Tenant Administrator	Jun 27, 2018, 10:54:19	Jul 13, 2017, 17:18:34	
sap global root ca	Certificate	Tenant Administrator	Apr 26, 2032, 17:46:27	Nov 11, 2016, 09:48:26	
sap passport ca	Certificate	Tenant Administrator	Apr 01, 2018, 12:00:00	Nov 11, 2016, 09:48:26	
sapnetca	Certificate	Tenant Administrator	Jul 18, 2015, 14:00:00	May 24, 2017, 14:39:24	
sapnetca_g2 (sap global root ca)	Certificate	Tenant Administrator	Mar 17, 2025, 10:34:51	Nov 11, 2016, 09:48:26	
sgw-a1s-05 (sap se webadmin ca)	Certificate	Tenant Administrator	Jan 01, 2038, 01:00:01	Jan 08, 2018, 09:02:12	
vmw4998.wdf.sap.corp (sapnetca)	Certificate	Tenant Administrator	Jan 28, 2015, 17:04:41	May 24, 2017, 14:39:24	
sap_baltimore cybertrust root	Certificate	SAP	May 13, 2025, 01:59:00	May 24, 2017, 14:39:24	
sap_mycn2	Key Pair	SAP	Oct 23, 2018, 14:10:25	Nov 03, 2017, 13:57:27	

Figure 8.30 Keystore Monitor

The table on the screen provides the header details of the certificates and key pairs in different columns. Table 8.12 describes the columns.

Column Name	Description
Alias	Contains the alias name of the certificate or key pair. The alias name is shown as a link, and selecting it opens the details of the certificate or key pair, as shown in Figure 8.31. Note that the prefix sap_ is reserved for SAP-owned key pairs and certificates.
Type	Specifies the type of the keystore artifact. The possible values for this field are as follows: ▪ **Certificate** ▪ **Key Pair** For more details, see Chapter 10, Section 10.5.2.
Owner	Identifies the owner of the keystore artifact. The possible values are as follows: ▪ **Tenant Administrator**: Those artifacts are maintained by the customer's tenant administrator. ▪ **SAP**: SAP-owned artifacts are maintained by SAP, and they can't be changed or deleted by the customer. This is also indicated by the **Lock** icon .
Valid Until	Validity of the certificate or key pair. As shown in Figure 8.30, if the artifact is already expired, the validity timestamp is shown in red.
Last Modified At	The date and time when the artifact was changed.
Actions	The actions available differ for the different artifacts and also depend on the owner of the artifacts: ▪ For **Certificates**: **Delete, Download, Rename, Update**. ▪ For **Key Pairs**: **Delete, Download Certificate, Download Certificate Chain, Rename, Update**. ▪ For **id_rsa/id_dsa** keys: **Delete, Download Certificate, Download Certificate Chain, Download Public OpenSSH Key, Rename, update**. ▪ For **SAP-owned certificates**: **Download**. ▪ For **SAP-owned Key Pairs**: **Download Certificate, Download Certificate Chain**. Detailed descriptions of the actions can be found in the "Keystore Monitor Now Available for Tenant Administrator" blog in the SAP Community (*www.sap.com/community.html*).

Table 8.12 Attributes of Keystore Artifacts

id_rsa/id_dsa Keys in the Keystore Monitor

The key pair aliases id_dsa and id_rsa are reserved for key pairs used in setting up secure SFTP connections. This is described in detail in the "How to Set Up a Secure Connection to an SFTP Server" blog in the SAP Community (*www.sap.com/community.html*).

On the top of the table, actions for the whole keystore are available. See Table 8.13 for details of those actions.

Action	Description
Filter	Filter for specific artifacts. The filter is executed for the alias name field.
Back Up	Back up all certificate and key pairs owned by the tenant administrator. Backups for SAP-owned artifacts are executed by SAP and aren't visible in the keystore monitor.
Add	Add entries from keystore files, single certificate, and key pairs. Note that you're not allowed to add artifacts with the prefix sap_ because this prefix is reserved for SAP-owned key pairs and certificates.
Download	Download the public content of the keystore. The downloaded keystore file is named *PublicContentKeystore.jks* and is saved without a password. It can be opened and maintained by any external keystore editor. Note that private key pairs aren't downloaded; for security reasons, private keys don't leave the tenant.
Reload	Reload the content of the page.
Settings	Define specific table settings such as sorting and filtering owner and artifact types.

Table 8.13 Actions for Keystore

As you saw in Figure 8.30, the alias name of the certificate or key pair is shown as a link. When you click the link, the details of the selected entry are provided in a new window. In Figure 8.31, for example, you see the details of a key pair. On the left side of the screen, the certificate chain, also known as the chain of trust, is shown as a tree with the key pair at the bottom and one or more certificates above. For a signed key pair, you usually have the key pair at the bottom, one or more intermediate certificates, and the root certificate at the top that identifies the root certificate authority

(CA). You can click all the entries in the tree to get the details of all the involved certificates.

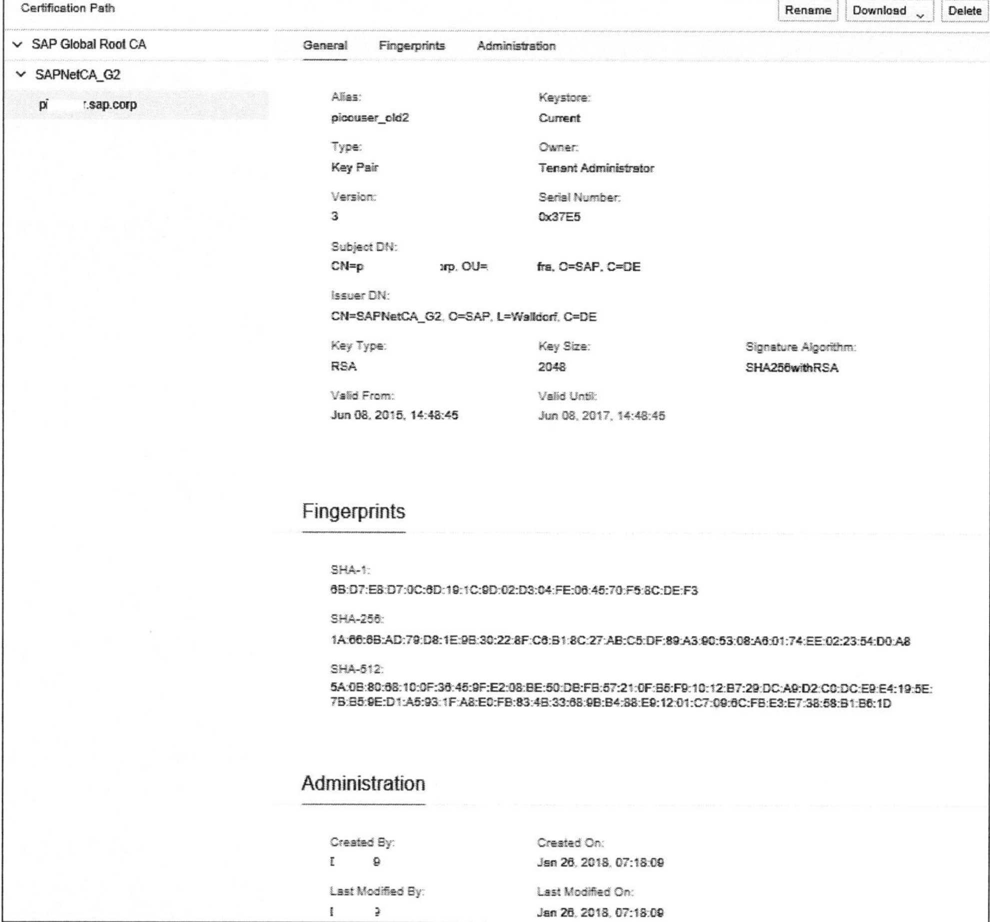

Figure 8.31 Details of a Keystore Artifact

On the right side of the screen, the details of the certificate or key pair are provided, such as **Subject DN**, **Issuer DN**, **Key Type**, **Signature Algorithm**, and **Valid From/Valid Until** (see also Chapter 10, Section 10.5.2). The unique fingerprint of the artifact, also known as a thumbprint, is provided in the **Fingerprints** tab. The fingerprint is shown in hexadecimal format and can be used to check that the key wasn't being injected by an attacker during key exchange.

The **Administration** tab shows the user who created and modified the artifact and the time of the creation and change.

Note

More details about the security and especially the keystore artifacts together with processes for how to handle security material are provided in Chapter 10.

On the right top of the screen, the same actions are offered as in the single line actions in the table containing all certificates and key pairs, such as **Delete**, **Rename**, and **Download**.

Keystore Monitor: Additional Features

The keystore monitor will be further extended in the future with additional features, such as creating private keys and handling certificate signing requests. The "Keystore Monitor Now Available for Tenant Administrator" blog in the SAP Community (*www.sap.com/community.html*) is regularly updated with the new features.

Backup

For secure system management, it's important to be able to restore certificates and key pairs if there are problems. To support you in performing this task, SAP Cloud Platform Integration offers the **Back Up** option in the keystore monitor. With this option, a backup can be created for all keystore artifacts owned by the tenant administrator.

No Backup for Single Certificates or Key Pairs

Note that when creating a backup, ALL certificates and key pairs from the keystore are backed up; there is no option to back up single artifacts of the keystore.

The backup can be explored in the **Backup** tab in the keystore monitor. As depicted in Figure 8.32, the table available in the **Backup** tab contains all certificates and key pairs backed up.

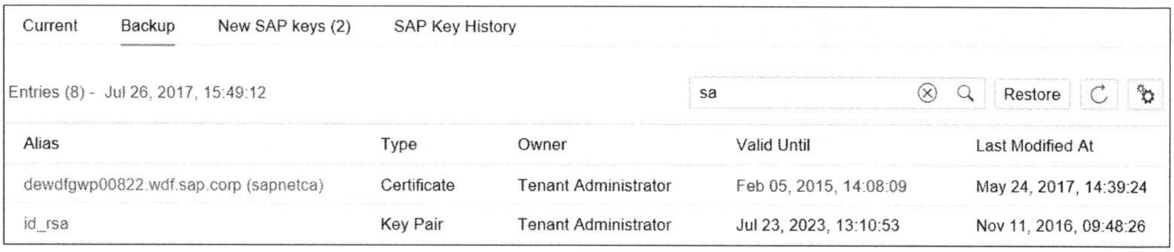

Current	Backup	New SAP keys (2)	SAP Key History	
Entries (8) - Jul 26, 2017, 15:49:12			sa	Restore
Alias	Type	Owner	Valid Until	Last Modified At
dewdfgwp00822.wdf.sap.corp (sapnetca)	Certificate	Tenant Administrator	Feb 05, 2015, 14:08:09	May 24, 2017, 14:39:24
id_rsa	Key Pair	Tenant Administrator	Jul 23, 2023, 13:10:53	Nov 11, 2016, 09:48:26

Figure 8.32 Backup Tab in Keystore Monitor

At the top of the table, the timestamp shows when the backup was performed. Note that there is always only one backup kept, which means the next backup will overwrite the backup created before.

The **Backup** tab provides the same artifact details for the artifacts in the backup as the **Current** tab for the currently active artifacts (see Table 8.12), except that the **Actions** column isn't available because artifacts from the backup can't be changed. As in the **Current** tab, the alias name is shown as a link, which allows you to access the details of the artifact in a new window. You can use this view to explore the content of the backup, but you can't modify the artifacts in the backup.

The only action available in the **Backup** view is **Restore**. Using **Restore**, the active keystore is overwritten by all the certificates and key pairs from the backup. This option helps you switch back to the old keystore, for example, if changes in the keystore caused communication errors in running integration scenarios.

Restore Overwrites Active Keystore with Backup

Note that when using **Restore**, the whole keystore is replaced, meaning newly created artifacts in the active keystore that don't exist in the backup are removed. Only the SAP-owned entries are kept; they aren't touched by the backup and restore operations.

It's recommended to always create a backup before making any changes to keystore artifacts, such as renaming aliases or overwriting key pairs and certificates. Using the backup, you then have the option to switch back to the last keystore version that worked correctly.

SAP Keys

As explained already you're not allowed to change SAP-owned key pairs and certificates, but you can use them in your integration scenarios. When such SAP-owned artifacts expire, SAP is responsible for renewing them. The renewal process differs depending on the artifact type:

- For SAP-owned root certificates, the process is easy: SAP adds the new root certificate to the keystore, and it's active immediately. There is no need for customers to react on the update.
- If the SAP-owned key pair expires, the process is more complex because SAP can't just update the key pair as this would lead to errors in existing scenarios. If the SAP Cloud Platform Integration tenant gets a new key pair, all backends connected using this key need to be updated as well.

To address the need to involve customers in updating associated keys in the involved backends, the keystore monitor offers the **New SAP keys** tab. As depicted in Figure 8.33, the table in the **New SAP keys** tab contains the new key pairs uploaded by SAP. Refer to Table 8.14 for a description of the columns in the table.

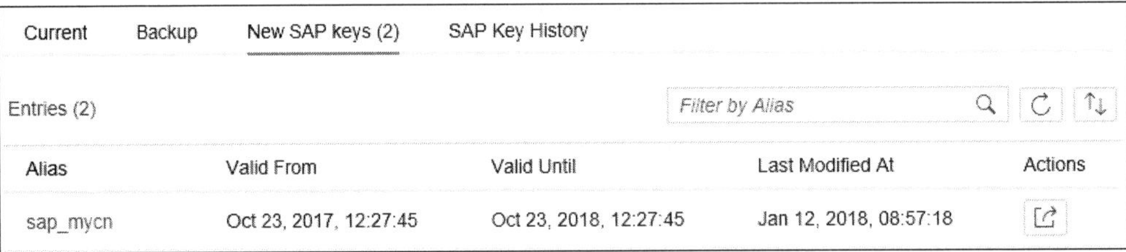

Figure 8.33 New SAP Keys Tab in the Keystore Monitor

Column Name	Description
Alias	Contains the alias name of the new SAP key pair. The alias name is shown as a link, and selecting it opens the details of the key pair.
Valid from	Start time the key pair is valid from.
Valid Until	Validity of the new key pair.
Last Modified At	The date and time when the new key pair was changed.
Actions	Actions available for the new SAP key pair: ■ **Activate** ■ **Download Certificate** ■ **Download Certificate Chain**

Table 8.14 Attributes of SAP Key Pairs in the New SAP Keys Tab

The new SAP key pair isn't active yet in the keystore, but it's available to trigger the update process from the customer's side. The tenant administrator needs to coordinate the overall renewal process as described in Chapter 10, Chapter 10.5.3, as well as in the "Activate SAP Keys in Keystore Monitor" blog in the SAP Community (*www.sap.com/community.html*).

During activation of the new SAP key pair, a backup of the old SAP key pair with the respective alias is stored in the **SAP Key History** tab to revert the change, if necessary. The **SAP key history** tab lists all SAP key pairs that were active in the tenant (Figure 8.34). See Table 8.15 for a description of the columns in the table.

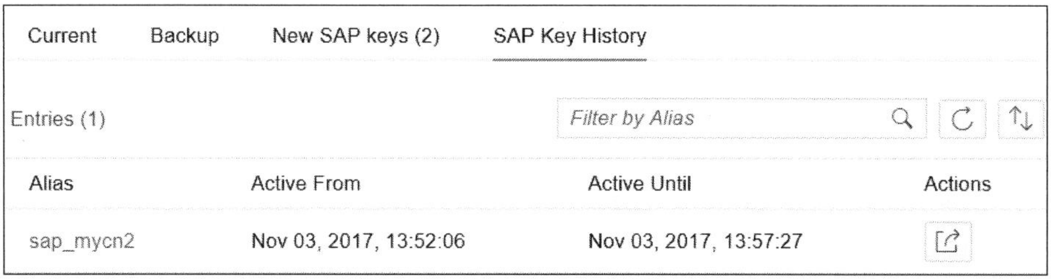

Figure 8.34 SAP Key History Tab in the Keystore Monitor

Column Name	Description
Alias	Contains the alias name of the backed up SAP key pair. The alias name is shown as a link, and selecting it opens the details of the key pair.
Active from	Time the key pair was active from.
Active Until	Time the key pair was active until.
Actions	Actions available for the backed up SAP key pair: ■ **Add to New SAP keys** ■ **Download Certificate** ■ **Download Certificate Chain**

Table 8.15 Attributes of SAP Key Pairs in the SAP Key History Tab

The most important action in the **SAP Key History** tab is the **Add to New SAP Keys** action. With this option, you can revert to the old SAP key pair. When you select this option, the SAP key pair is written back to **New SAP Keys**, and you can reactivate it from there. When reverting to the old SAP key pair, keep in mind that some backends may have already activated the new certificate. Therefore, use this option with care!

Automatic Activation of New SAP Key Pair

If the new SAP key pair wasn't activated by the tenant administrator before the key pair expired, a job activates the new SAP key automatically on behalf of the tenant administrator. This is done to ensure that the tenant has a valid key pair in the keystore.

For more information on the lifecycle management for keys, read Chapter 10, Section 10.5.3.

Now that you're aware of how to manage security material such as credentials, certificates, and key pairs, you need to understand the mapping of certificates to users to be able to use client certificates for inbound authorization.

8.3.3 Maintain Certificate-to-User Mappings

In a more commonly known on-premise corporate environment, systems live in the limited network of your organization. With a controlled network, it can be argued that there are relatively few threats, and that the user account/password model works well to secure your platforms. However, the Internet being a potentially hostile environment, cloud-based platforms are more prone to user account/password attacks. A certificate-to-user mapping provides a good alternative solution to the user/password model by using public-key (certificates) technology. Certificates are much more difficult to hack than password-based systems.

SAP Cloud Platform Integration uses certificate-to-user mappings to map a certificate that has been issued to a user's account. SAP Cloud Platform Integration can then use public-key technology to authenticate a user through his certificate. The result is the same as if a user had applied a username and password, but the approach is more secure. With this approach, a user presents a certificate to SAP Cloud Platform Integration, and the platform looks at the mapping to determine which user account should be logged on.

The usage and setup of certificate-to-user mappings in scenarios using this option for inbound authorization are described in detail in the "How to Set Up a Secure HTTP Inbound Connection with Client Certificates" blog in the SAP Community (*www.sap.com/community.html*).

Now that you understand the idea behind using certificate-to-user mappings, the question is how to create them. From within the **Manage Security** section of the monitoring dashboard (refer back to Figure 8.23), one of the included tiles is **Certificate-to-User Mappings.** This tile provides access to all certificate-to-user mappings defined and deployed in your tenant. After clicking on this tile, you're redirected to a page with a list of available certificate-to-user mappings, as shown in Figure 8.35.

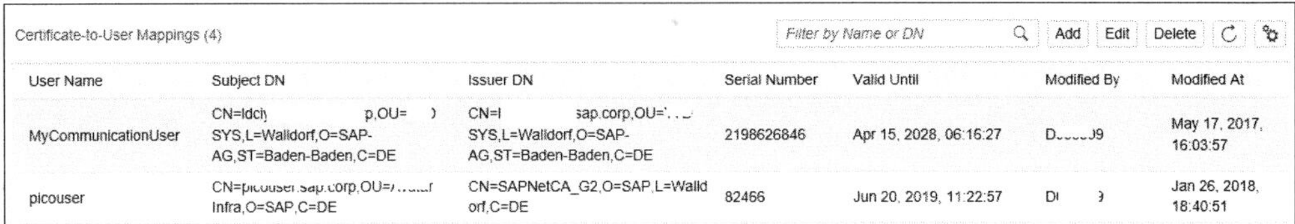

Certificate-to-User Mappings (4)
Filter by Name or DN
Add
Edit
Delete
User Name
Subject DN
Issuer DN
Serial Number
Valid Until
Modified By
Modified At
MyCommunicationUser
SYS,L=Walldorf,O=SAP-AG,ST=Baden-Baden,C=DE
SYS,L=Walldorf,O=SAP-AG,ST=Baden-Baden,C=DE
2198626846
Apr 15, 2028, 06:16:27
May 17, 2017, 16:03:57
picouser
Infra,O=SAP,C=DE
CN=SAPNetCA_G2,O=SAP,L=Walldorf,C=DE
82466
Jun 20, 2019, 11:22:57
Jan 26, 2018, 18:40:51

Figure 8.35 Listing Certificate-to-User Mappings

A certificate-to-user mapping comprises a number of attributes, which are listed in Table 8.16.

Attribute Name	Description
User Name	The unique identifier of the user to which the certificate needs to be mapped
Subject DN	The unique identifier for the object being secured with information about the object being certified, including common name, organization, organization unit, and country codes, among others
Issuer DN	The name of the party that signed the certificate
Serial Number	A number that uniquely identifies the certificate, which is issued by the CA
Valid Until	The date and time the certificate expires
Modified By	The user that last changed the certificate-to-user mapping artifact
Modified At	The date and time the certificate-to-user mapping artifact was most recently changed

Table 8.16 Attributes of a Certificate-to-User Mapping

On the page presented in Figure 8.35, you can edit mappings using the **Edit** button or delete them using the **Delete** button. Furthermore, you can add new certificate-to-user mappings to your tenant by following these steps:

1. Select the **Add** button at the top-right corner of the screen (refer to Figure 8.35).
2. Specify the **User Name** to which the certificate needs to be mapped (see Figure 8.36).

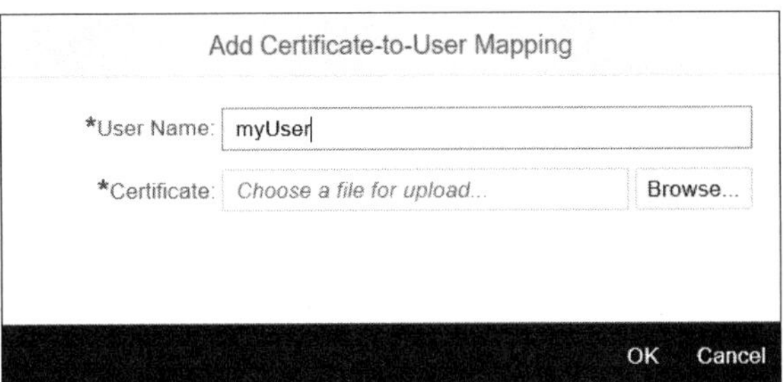

Figure 8.36 Adding a New Certificate-to-User Mapping

3. Click the **Browse** button, and search for the certificate file (you're looking for a `*.cer` file) on your local file system. The details of the certificate, as indicated in Table 8.16, are automatically populated based on the imported certificate.
4. Select **OK**.

> **Note**
> For more information on how to use a certificate-to-user mapping when setting up a secure connection, see Chapter 10, Chapter 10.3.5.

With the maintenance of the certificate-to-user mappings, we finish the section about managing security material. However, as you saw already in the monitoring dashboard (refer to Figure 8.23), there is one more tile in the **Manage Security** section: **Connectivity Tests**. Let's check out how this can help us test the security material.

8.3.4 Test Outbound Connectivity

Using the tests available in the **Connectivity Tests** tile, you can check that the security material deployed can be used successfully to establish secure connections to the connected backends, mail servers, and SFTP servers.

As depicted in Figure 8.37, when you select the **Connectivity Test** tile, a new window opens that has tabs for the different connection options:

- **TLS**
  This test tries to establish an HTTPS connection via Transport Layer Security (TLS) to a backend. HTTPS is used by several receiver adapters, such as SOAP, IDoc, and HTTP, to connect to the backends.
- **SSH**
  This test tries to establish a connection via SSH to an SFTP server. The SSH protocol is used by the SFTP sender and receiver adapters to communicate with the SFTP server.
- **SMTP**
  This test tries to establish a Simple Mail Transfer Protocol (SMTP) connection to a mail server. This is the protocol used by the mail receiver adapter to send messages to the mail server. You used this tool already when setting up the first integration flow covered in this book (Chapter 2, Section 2.3.6).
- **IMAP**
  This test tries to establish a connection via the Internet Message Access Protocol (IMAP) to a mail server. This is one of the protocols used by the mail sender adapter to poll messages from mail servers.
- **POP3**
  This test tries to establish a connection via Post Office Protocol version 3 (POP3) to a mail server. This is the second protocol that can be used by the mail sender adapter to poll messages from mail servers.

Figure 8.37 Connectivity Tests

Let's take a look at the different options.

Test HTTPS Connection

The **TLS** test tries to establish an HTTPS connection via TLS to the server specified. For the **TLS** test, the **Host** and **Port** fields of the server to connect to must be set. In Figure 8.38, a test is executed against **google.com**. You see that the response indicates an error during the Secure Sockets Layer (SSL) handshake because no valid certificate can be found in the keystore.

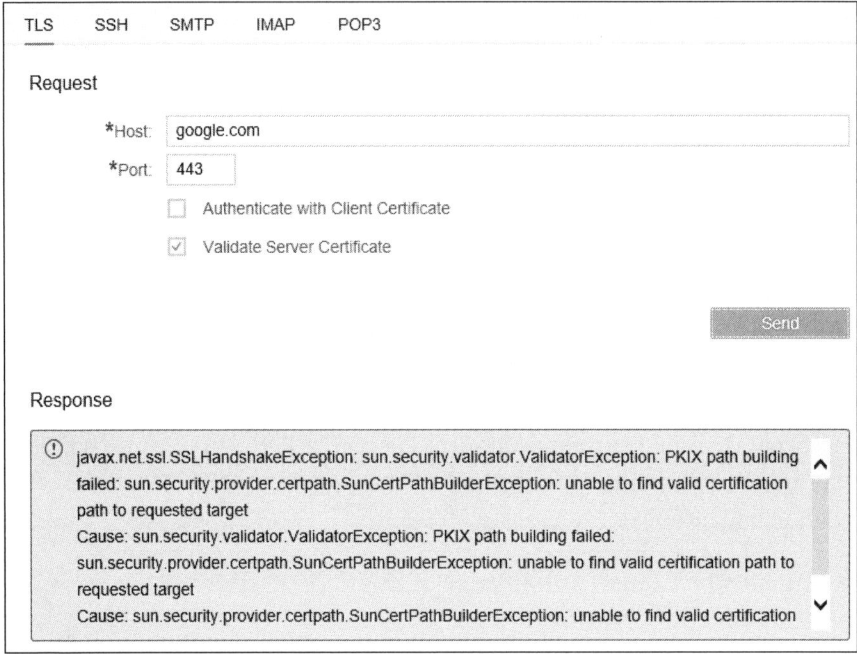

Figure 8.38 TLS Connection Test with SSL Handshake Error

You see that the default setting is to validate the server certificate, which is always the case when a TLS connection is established during runtime. But in the connection test, you have the option to deselect the **Validate Server Certificate** checkbox. By using the option to establish a connection without validation of the server certificate, you can check that the server can be reached at all, and the certificates are displayed that the server provides for validation. In Figure 8.39, you can see that the TLS test without validation check is executed successfully, and the certificates are displayed in the **Response** view.

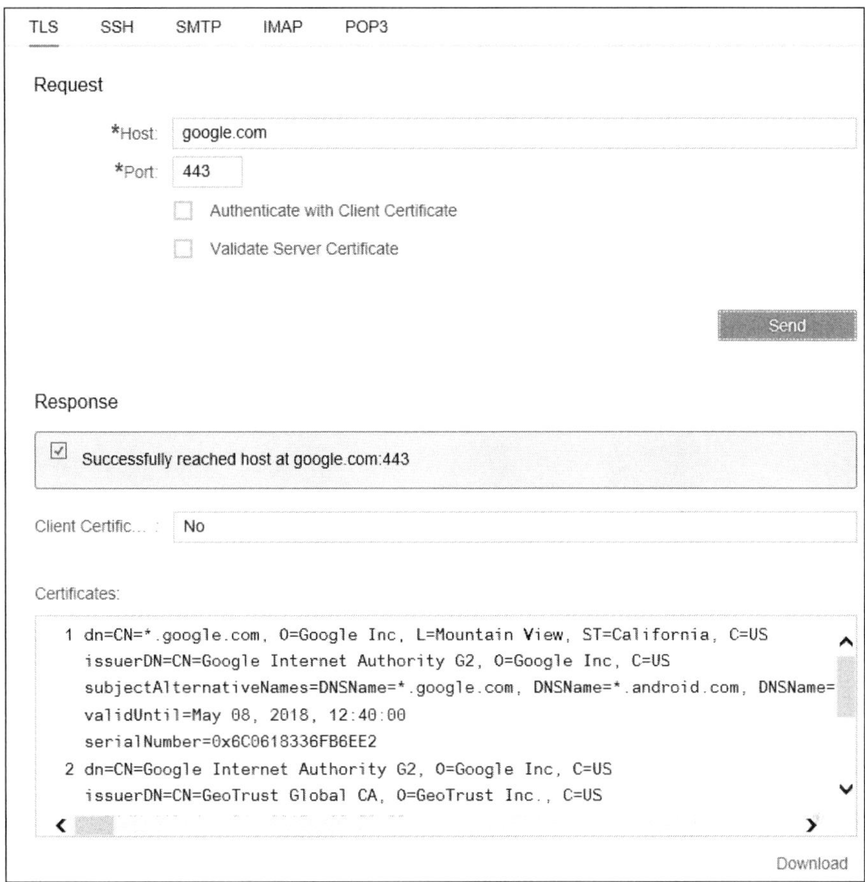

Figure 8.39 TLS Connection Test without Validating Server Certificate

You don't need much more to get the TLS connection established successfully: you can either get the trusted root certificate from the backend server or simply download the certificates shown in the TLS connection test via the **Download** button at the bottom of the screen. The **Download** action creates a *certificates.zip* file in the download folder of your local PC. The file contains all certificates from the connection test. Extract the `*.cer` file of the root CA, in this case, the GeoTrust Global CA, and add it to the keystore in the keystore monitor. Execute the test again with the **Validate Server Certificate** checkbox checked. The test should now pass successfully because the certificate can be validated by SAP Cloud Platform Integration.

The second checkbox, **Authenticate with Client Certificate**, can be used to test the client-certificate based authentication at the backend. As shown in Figure 8.40, when you select the checkbox, a new entry field **Alias** appears, where you can enter a keystore alias for the key pair you want to use for authentication. If the **Alias** field is left empty, the system tries to find a valid key pair in the keystore and uses it.

After execution of the test, the **Response** section indicates whether the client certificate-based authentication was used and shows the **Alias** that was used.

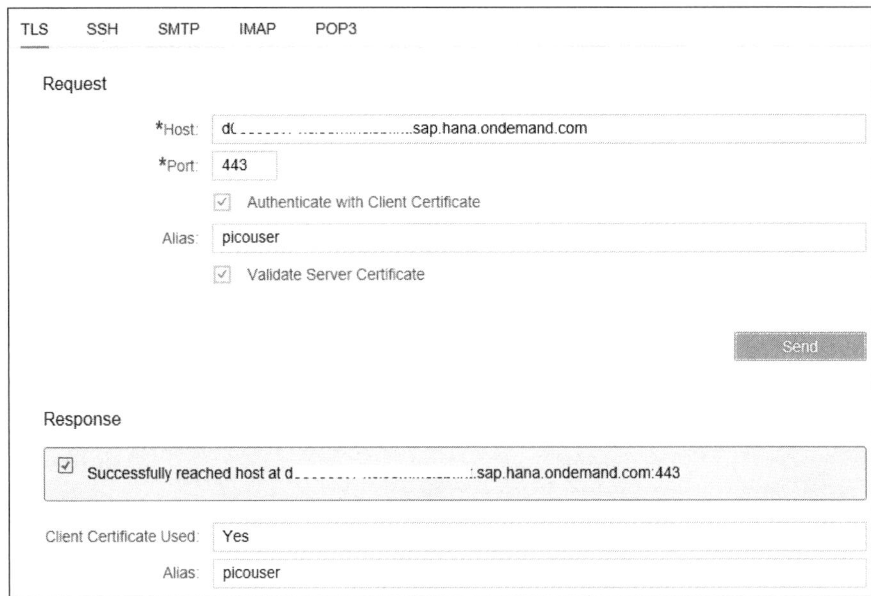

Figure 8.40 TLS Connection Test with Client Certificate Authentication

You've now learned that the TLS test can be used to test the transport layer security against backends connected via HTTPS. With this, you have to option to test the connection and authentication settings used in the integration flow channels of all adapters using HTTPS, such as SOAP, HTTP, IDoc, and XI.

Test the Connection to the SFTP Server

To test the connection to an SFTP server, the **SSH** test can be used. The **Host** and **Port** fields of the SFTP server need to be entered, together with the **Authentication** option to be used when connecting to the SFTP server (Figure 8.41).

Using **Authentication** option **None**, you can test that the SFTP server can be reached at all, and you can download the host key of the SFTP server using the **Copy Host Key** button at the bottom of the **Response** screen. This host key needs to be added to the known hosts file and deployed in the **Manage Security Material** tile to be able to successfully establish an SSH connection to the SFTP server. This is described in detail in the "How to Setup Secure Connection to sftp Server" blog in the SAP Community (*www.sap.com/community.html*).

Figure 8.41 SSH Connection Test without Authentication

Authentication: None

Note, that the **Authentication** option **None** is only available in the SSH test to be able to download the host key without authentication. This option isn't available in the SFTP adapter because either public key or user/password authentication is mandatory in runtime.

If either **Public Key** or **User Credentials** are used for **Authentication**, two new checkboxes appear (Figure 8.42):

- **Check Host Key**
  Selecting this checkbox causes the SSH test to check that the host key is deployed

in the known hosts file and that the SAP Cloud Platform Integration tenant trusts this SFTP server. In runtime, this is mandatory; otherwise, messages cannot be polled from the SFTP server nor sent to the SFTP server.

- **Check Directory Access**
  Using this checkbox, you can test whether the user connecting to the SFTP server has the authorization to access its directories. If you enter a specific directory in the **Directory** field, you get all files in this directory listed in the **Response** screen.

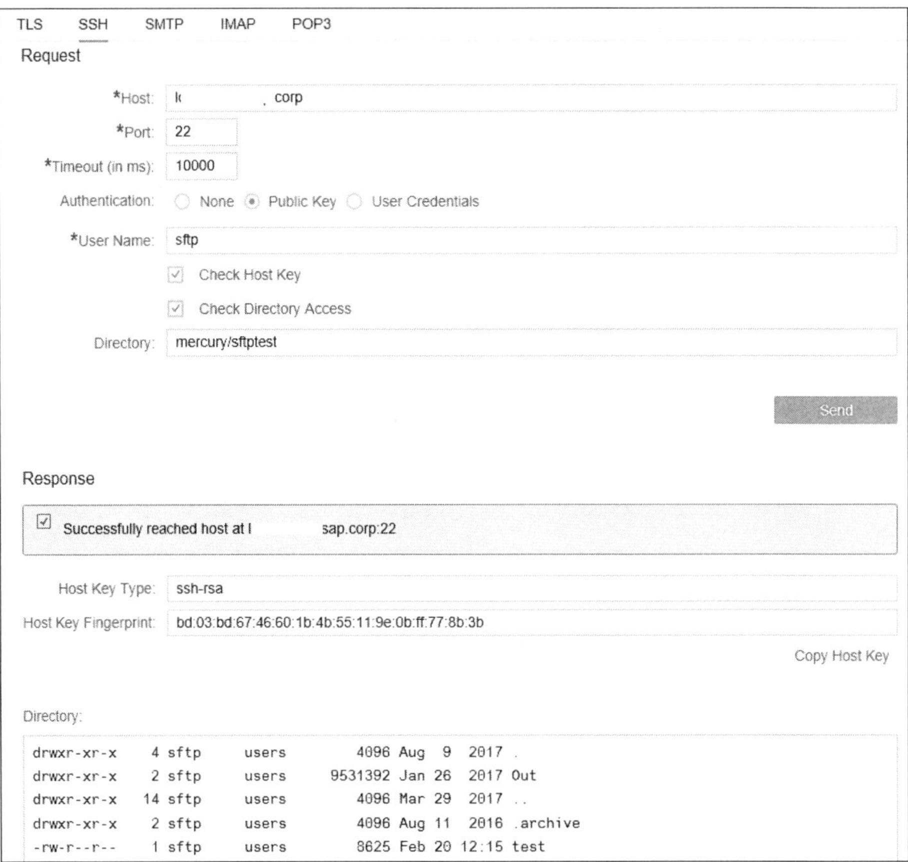

Figure 8.42 SSH Connection Test with Public Key Authentication

Now that you know how to test the connection to SFTP servers and how to download the host key, you can successfully set up and test scenarios using the SFTP sender or receiver adapter.

Test the Connection to the Mail Server

If you need to analyze issues connecting to a mail server, either for sending messages to the mail server or for polling messages from the mail server, there are three different tests to assist you. While the **SMTP** test checks the outbound connection to send messages to the mail server, the **IMAP** and **POP3** tests check whether messages can be polled from the mail server.

As depicted in Figure 8.43 for executing the **SMTP** test to the mail server, you specify the **Host** and **Port** of the mail server, and then you select the **Protection** mechanism the mail server supports. With the **Authentication** option set to **None**, you can test whether the mail server can be reached and the secure connection can be established.

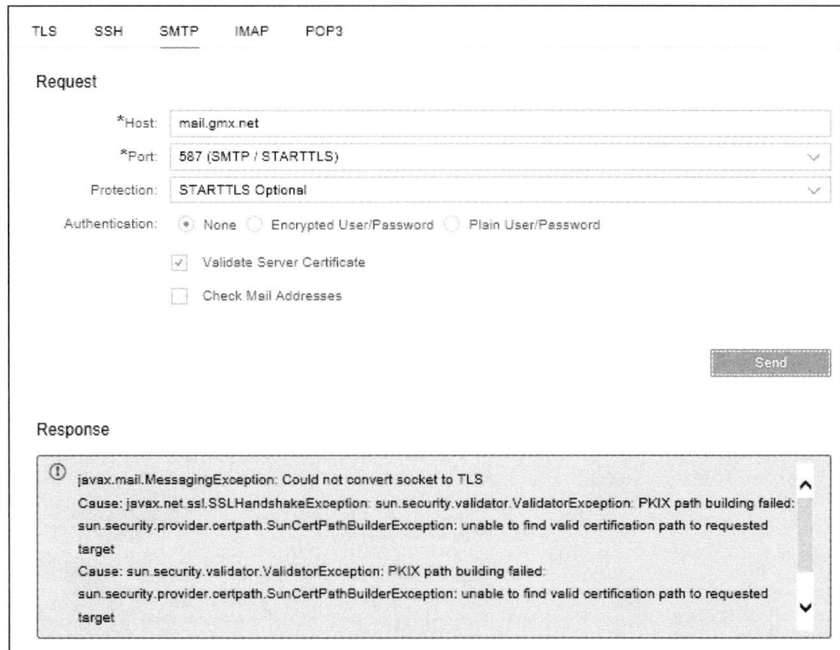

Figure 8.43 SMTP Connection Test with an Error

In Figure 8.43, you see that an error occurred during the SSL handshake when connecting to the mail server. As in the TLS test, you have the option to execute the **SMTP** test without validating the server certificate by deselecting the **Validate Server Certificate** checkbox. Then you use the **Download** option for the certificates and add the root CA to the keystore using the keystore monitor. Afterward, the **SMTP** test should pass successfully. The **Response** screen displays whether the server certificate is valid.

If **Authentication** with user and password is used, either **Plain User/Password** or **Encrypted User/Password**, a new entry field named **Credential Name** appears where the name of the deployed credential needs to be entered (Figure 8.44). The **Response** screen displays whether the authentication with the credentials was successful.

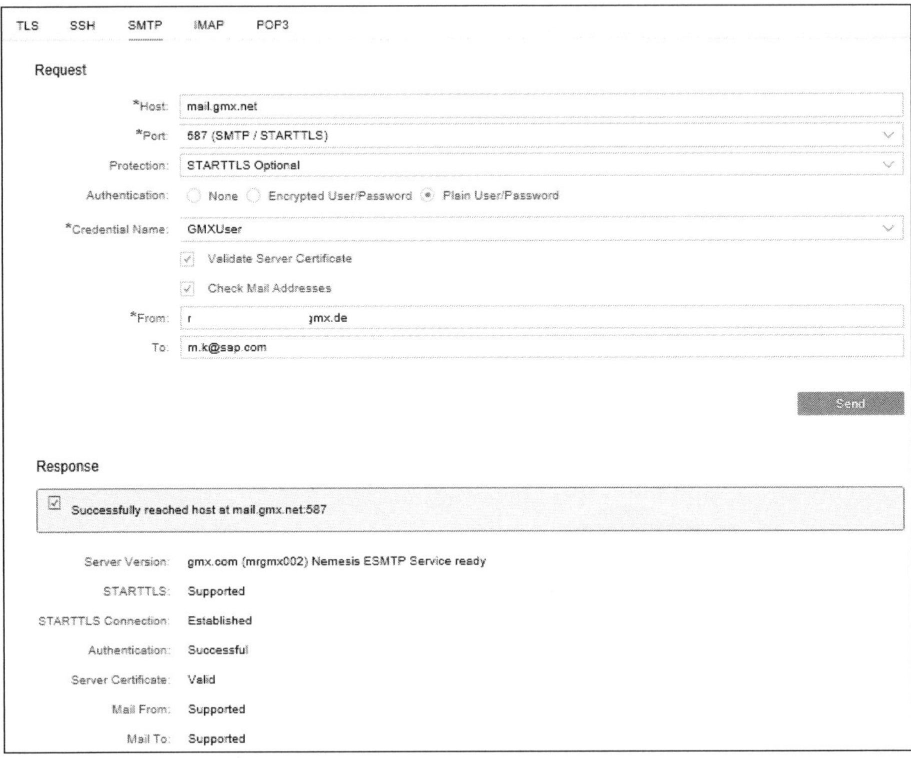

Figure 8.44 SMTP Connection Test with Checking of Mail Addresses

A useful option in the SMTP test is to check the mail addresses used in the mail receiver channel. When selecting the **Check Mail Addresses** checkbox, two new entry fields are displayed: **From** and **To**. There you enter the mail addresses used in your integration flow in the mail receiver channel. The **SMTP** test checks if the mail server supports those addresses and shows the check result in the **Response** screen (Figure 8.44).

The **IMAP** and **POP3** tests support similar features as the **SMTP** test, except the check for the mail addresses. This is simply because this option isn't relevant for the mail sender adapter where messages are polled from a mail server.

In Figure 8.45, the **IMAP** test to *gmx.net* is shown as a sample. You see that the **Host** and **Port** of the mail server need to be entered together with the **Protection** mechanism, **Authentication**, and **Credential Name**.

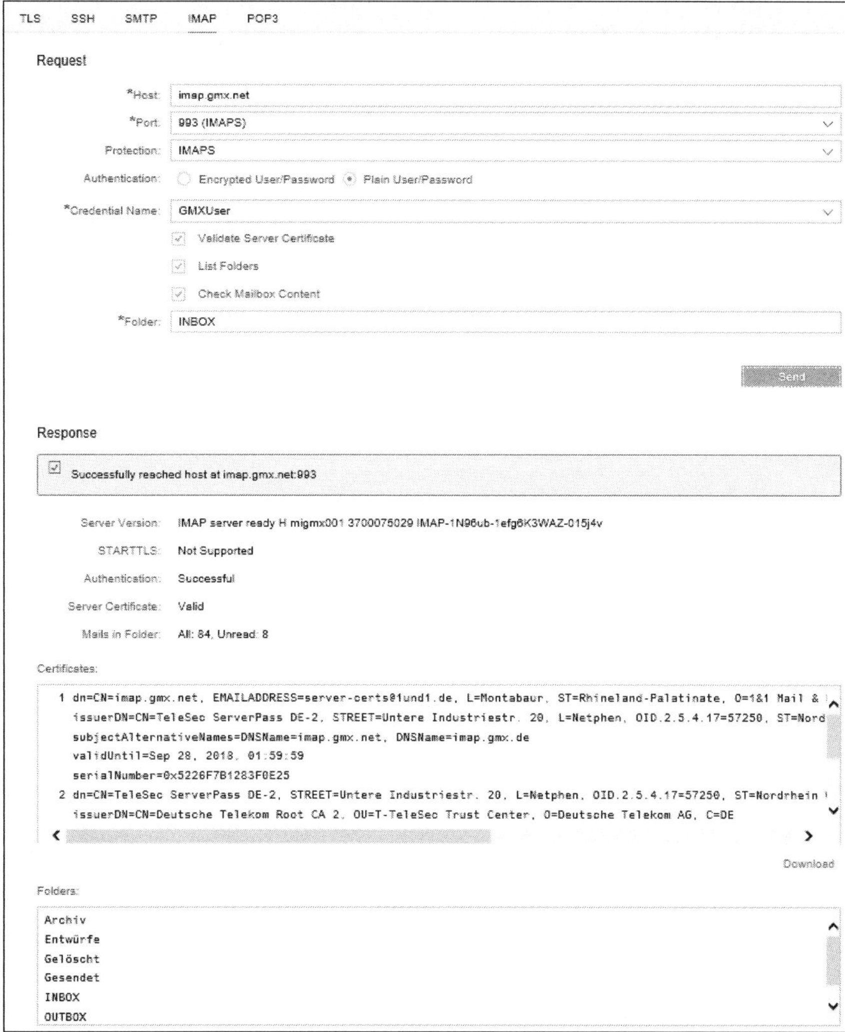

Figure 8.45 IMAP Connection Test with Folders

For the **IMAP** test, the following check features are available:

- **Validate Server Certificate**
  As in the **SMTP** test, deselecting this checkbox can test whether the mail server can

be reached at all. Furthermore, the provided mail server certificates can be downloaded and added to the keystore.

- **List Folders**
  If selected, the test lists all folders in the mail server for the user connected using the credentials. As depicted in Figure 8.45, the **Folders** are shown at the end of the **Response** screen.
- **Check Mailbox Content**
  If selected, a new entry field named **Folder** appears, where the folder in the mail server must be entered. The test checks how many mail messages are available in the specified folder and how many of them are **Unread**. The result of the check is shown in the **Response** screen.

The **POP3** test is very similar to the **IMAP** test. As depicted in Figure 8.46, the **Request** and **Response** details look almost identical to the **IMAP** test.

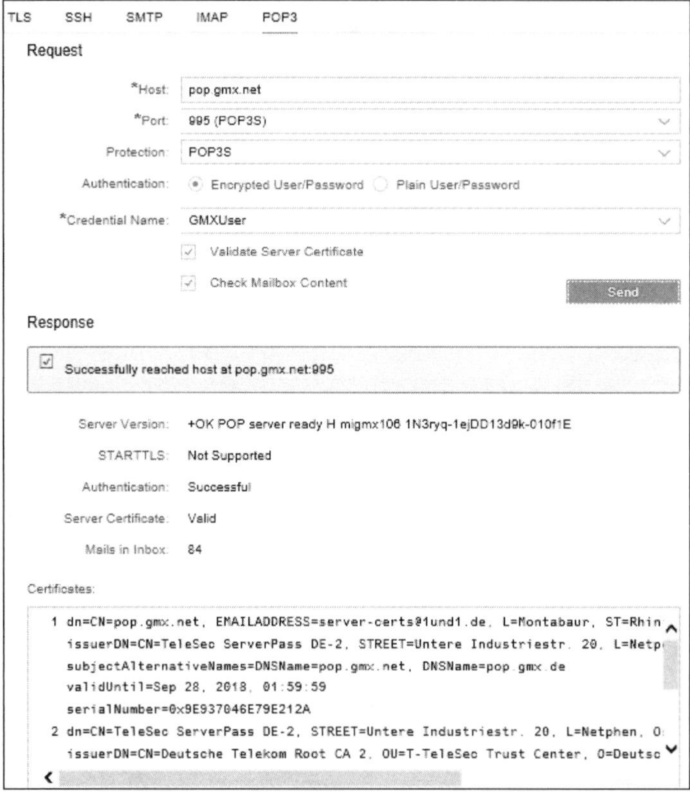

Figure 8.46 POP3 Connection Test

The following check features are available for the POP3 test:

- **Validate Server Certificate**
  As in the **SMTP** and **IMAP** tests, deselecting this checkbox can test whether the mail server can be reached at all. Furthermore, the provided mail server certificates can be downloaded and added to the keystore.
- **Check Mailbox Content**
  The test checks how many mail messages are available in the *Inbox* folder. The result of the check is shown in the **Response** screen.

8

Note

POP3 doesn't support different folders, so only the **Inbox** folder is relevant. Because of this, the check for mailbox content doesn't offer an option to specify a dedicated folder but provides the mail messages contained in the **Inbox** folder. In addition, POP3 doesn't distinguish between read and unread mail, so all mail messages in the **Inbox** folder are shown.

Now that you know how to manage the security-relevant artifacts in the SAP Cloud Platform Integration tenant and how to test connections using transport-level security, we'll discuss some monitors that are relevant only in specific scenarios. Let's first look into scenarios using temporary data, such as data stores and JMS queues.

8.4 Manage Temporary Data

In many scenarios, temporary data needs to be stored; this data can be either whole messages, parts of messages, error messages, or configuration data. The main storage options available in SAP Cloud Platform Integration are data stores and JMS queues.

In the **Manage Stores** section in the monitoring dashboard, you find the monitors to handle the temporary data (Figure 8.47).

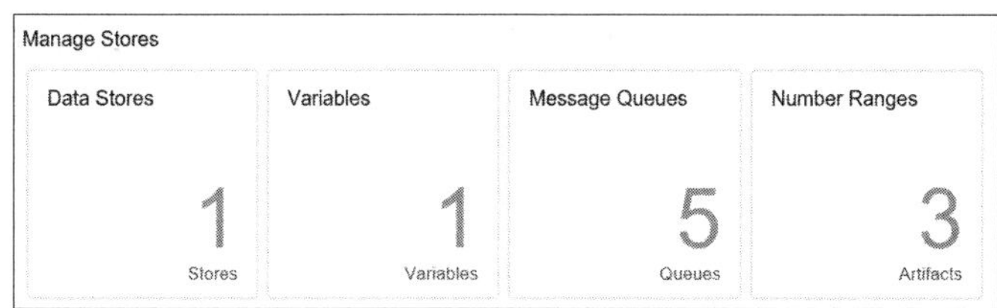

Figure 8.47 Manage Stores Section in the Monitoring Dashboard

8.4.1 Monitor Data Stores

The first tile in the **Manage Stores** section shows the **Data Stores** used in the deployed integration flows. Data stores are used by the following flow steps and adapters:

- **Data Store flow steps**
  The following four flow steps work on data contained in the data store: **Write**, **Get**, **Select**, and **Delete.** Refer to Chapter 5, Section 5.4.1, for more information about use cases for the data store.
- **XI adapter**
  The XI adapter temporarily stores messages for exactly-once (EO) scenarios, either in a data store or in a JMS queue. If storage in a data store is configured in the XI adapter, those messages appear in the **Manage Data Stores** monitor.

As depicted in Figure 8.48 and Figure 8.49, the data store monitor consists of two sections: the master table on the left and the details table on the right. The master table on the left shows all data stores on the SAP Cloud Platform Integration tenant that contain messages. Table 8.17 provides a detailed description of the attributes.

Data Stores without Messages Not Visible

Note that only data stores containing data are shown in the monitor because a data store is only created and kept in runtime as long as there are entries available in that specific data store. As soon as all data/messages are consumed from the data store, it's removed.

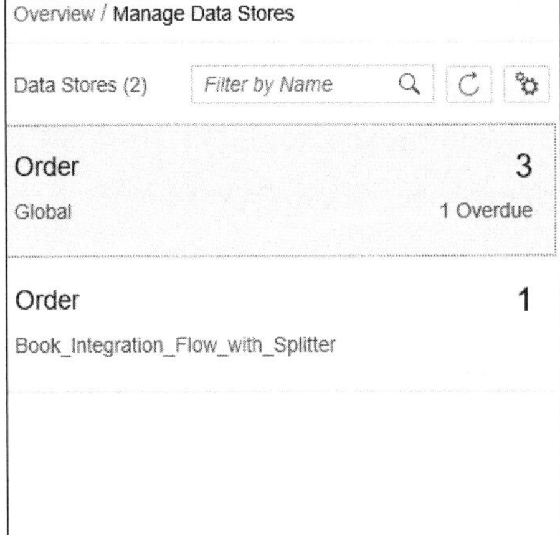

Figure 8.48 Manage Data Stores Monitor A

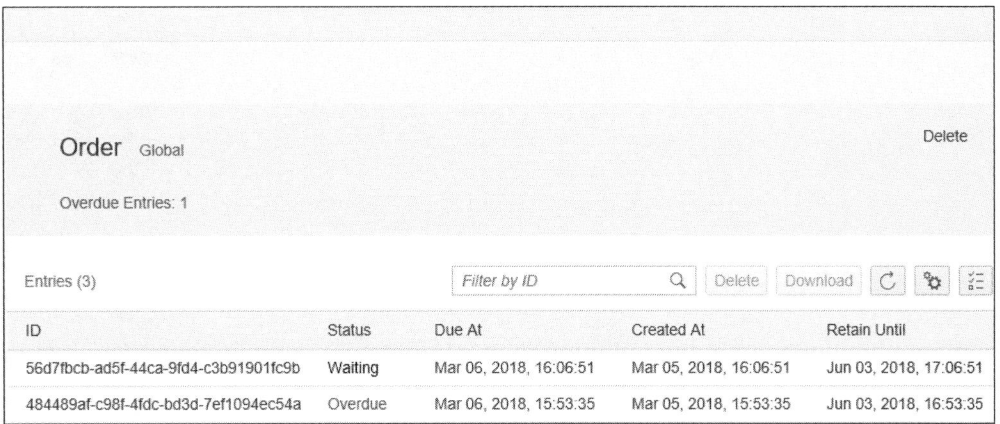

Figure 8.49 Manage Data Stores Monitor B

Attribute	Description
Name	The name of the data store as configured in the data store flow step. If the data store is used by an XI adapter, the data store name is generated per the following pattern: `<participant>_<channel name>`.
Visibility	The visibility of the data store as configured in the data store flow steps. The possible values are as follows: ■ **Global:** The data store can be used globally by all integration flows deployed on the tenant. ■ **Integration Flow Name:** The data store is used by the specified integration flow only. If the data store is used by an XI adapter, the integration flow name shown has the following pattern: `<integration flow>/XI`.
Number of Entries	The number of entries currently contained in the data store.
Number of Overdue Entries	The number of entries that already should have been processed but are still stored in the data store. This value is shown in red.

Table 8.17 Attributes of Data Stores on the Left Side of the Monitor

When you select a data store on the left side of the screen, all entries in this specific data store are shown on the right side in the details table. Table 8.18 describes the attributes of single data store entries and their possible values.

Column	Description
ID	The ID of the entry in the data store. The entry ID can be specified in one of the following ways: ▪ It can be specified in the data store **Write** step (e.g. by using a specific unique ID from the message payload). ▪ If it isn't specified in the data store **Write** step, a unique ID is generated by the runtime when the entry is written to the data store. ▪ The XI adapter generates a unique ID when the message is written to the data store.
Status	The status of the data store entry. The possible statuses are as follows: ▪ **Waiting**: This is the status after the entry was written to the data store. The message/data is waiting to be consumed by another process or integration flow. ▪ **Overdue**: If the message wasn't consumed in the due time specified in the data store **Write** step, the message get the status **Overdue**. For such entries, the tenant administrator should check why the data isn't consumed (e.g., maybe the consuming integration flow doesn't run anymore) and solve the problem.
Due At	The date and time the entry is expected to be consumed latest. This time is configured in the data store **Write** step in the configuration field **Retention Threshold for Alerting.** If the message is processed by the XI adapter, the due time is set to two days by the adapter.
Created At	The date and time the entry was created in the data store.
Retain Until	The date and time the entry will be deleted. This time is configured in the data store **Write** step in the configuration field **Expiration Period**, which is 90 days per default. If the message is processed by the XI adapter, the expiration period is automatically set to 90 days by the adapter.

Table 8.18 Attributes of Data Store Entries

For the entries in the data stores, SAP Cloud Platform Integration offers the following actions at the top of the details table:

- **Filter by ID**
  Filter for a specific ID. This can be very useful if the ID is specified in the Write step to be set from a unique ID from the incoming message payload. In this case, you can filter for this ID.
- **Delete**
  Remove selected entries from the data store if not needed anymore.
- **Download**
  Download selected entries. An *<ID>.zip* file is created in the download folder of your local PC containing the payload stored in the data store.
- **Reload**
  Reload the content of the details table.
- **Table Settings**
  Sort the entries and filter by the **Status** column.
- **Multi-select Mode**
  Select multiple entries at once. This option is useful when you need to delete multiple entries. Note that the *Download* action isn't available for multiple entries.

Now that you understand the data store monitor, we'll look at the variables monitor. You'll notice that several attributes are identical because the variables are technically also stored in the same data store table.

8.4.2 Monitor Variables

In some scenarios, variables are used to store configuration data, which is read and updated during message processing. Variables are used by the following flow steps:

- **Write Variables**
  The **Write Variables** flow step is used to write or update variables in the runtime. Variables can have local or global visibility, which means that a variable can be read and updated only by the same integration flow or by all integration flows deployed on this tenant.
- **Content Modifier**
  The **Content Modifier** flow step can read the value of a global or local variable and use it to set headers or properties.

The second tile in the **Manage Stores** section provides the monitoring options for the variables used in runtime. When you select the **Variables** tile, a table containing all variables defined in the SAP Cloud Platform Integration tenant appears (Figure 8.50). Table 8.19 provides a detailed description of all the columns of the table.

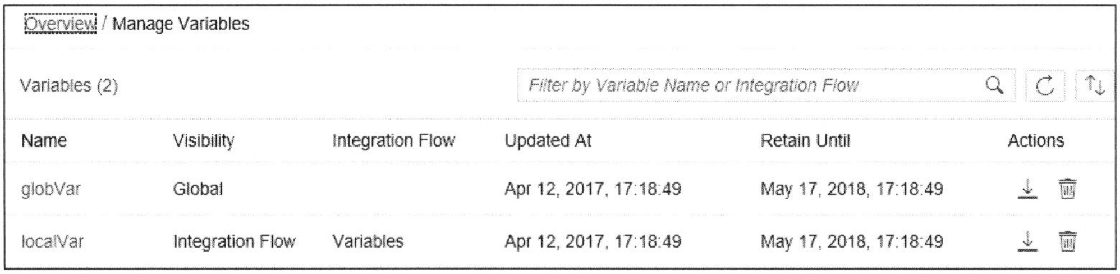

Overview / Manage Variables

Variables (2)

Filter by Variable Name or Integration Flow

Name	Visibility	Integration Flow	Updated At	Retain Until	Actions
globVar	Global		Apr 12, 2017, 17:18:49	May 17, 2018, 17:18:49	
localVar	Integration Flow	Variables	Apr 12, 2017, 17:18:49	May 17, 2018, 17:18:49	

Figure 8.50 Manage Variables Monitor

Column	Description
Name	The name of the variable as defined in the **Write Variables** flow step. The name is shown as a link. Selecting the link opens the variable in text format.
Visibility	The visibility of the variable as defined in the **Write Variables** step. The possible values are as follows: ■ **Global:** The variable can be used globally by all integration flows deployed on the tenant. ■ **Integration Flow:** The variable is used by the integration flow only.
Integration Flow	If **Visibility** is **Integration Flow,** in this column the integration flow using this variable is shown.
Updated At	The date and time the variable was last changed.
Retain Until	The date and time the variable will be deleted. This time is set to 400 days after the creation of the variable, but it's also updated along with any update of the variable. This means the variable is deleted 400 days after its last update.
Actions	Actions available for variables are as follows: ■ **Download** : This option downloads the variable as a *<variable>_<integration flow>.zip* file, which contains the variable in a *headers.prop* file, to the download folder of your local PC ■ **Delete** : This option deletes the variable.

Table 8.19 Attributes of Variables

When you select the name of the variable, which is shown as a link, a popup opens providing the content of the variable in text format (Figure 8.51). You can also download the content using the **Download** button.

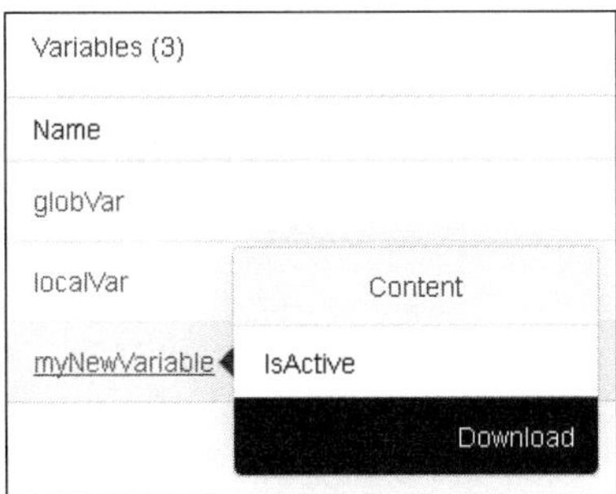

Figure 8.51 Content of a Variable

The two storage options described, data stores and variables, are based on the database of the SAP Cloud Platform Integration tenant. The third storage option for temporary data is a JMS queue based on the JMS Message Broker connected to the SAP Cloud Platform Integration tenant. For this option, the third tile in the **Manage Stores** section is important.

8.4.3 Maintain Message Queues

The **Message Queues** tile in the **Manage Stores** section shows the JMS queues used in the deployed integration flows. JMS queues are used by the following adapters:

- **JMS adapter**
  The JMS adapter is used to directly process messages to and from JMS queues: the **JMS** receiver adapter writes messages to JMS queues, and the **JMS** sender adapter polls messages from JMS queues. Refer to Chapter 5, Section 5.4, were we introduced reliable messaging using JMS queues.
- **AS2 adapter**
  The **AS2** sender adapter temporarily stores messages during runtime processing in JMS queues.
- **XI adapter**
  The **XI** sender and receiver adapter temporarily stores messages for EO scenarios, either in a data store or in a JMS queue. If storage in a JMS queue is configured in the **XI** adapter, those messages appear in the **Manage Message Queues** monitor.

Manage Message Queues Monitor Not Visible?

JMS messaging is available only with the SAP Cloud Platform Integration, Enterprise Edition, or if a JMS messaging license is purchased separately. If your SAP Cloud Platform Integration system isn't running with the Enterprise license, and no JMS Messaging is purchased, the JMS adapter doesn't appear in the list of available adapters.

Furthermore, you need to get a JMS Message Broker provisioned for your SAP Cloud Platform Integration tenant. The provisioning is triggered using a self-service in the account cockpit. Details about the provisioning of a JMS Message Broker can be found in the documentation for SAP Cloud Platform Integration (*https://help.sap.com/viewer/product/CLOUD_INTEGRATION/Cloud*) and in the "Provision Message Broker" blog in the SAP Community (*www.sap.com/community.html*).

The **Message Queues** tile is visible in the monitoring dashboard only after successful JMS Message Broker provisioning.

As depicted in Figure 8.52 and Figure 8.53, the **Manage message queues** monitor consists of two sections: the master table on the left and the details table on the right. The master table on the left side of the monitor shows all JMS queues available in the JMS Message Broker. Table 8.20 provides a detailed description of the attributes shown for JMS queues.

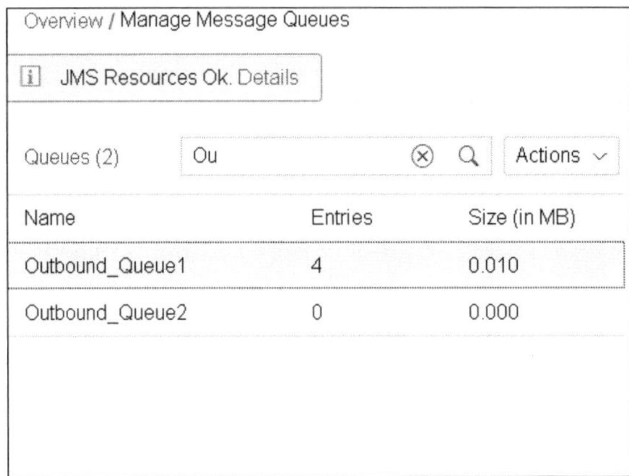

Figure 8.52 Manage Message Queue Monitor A

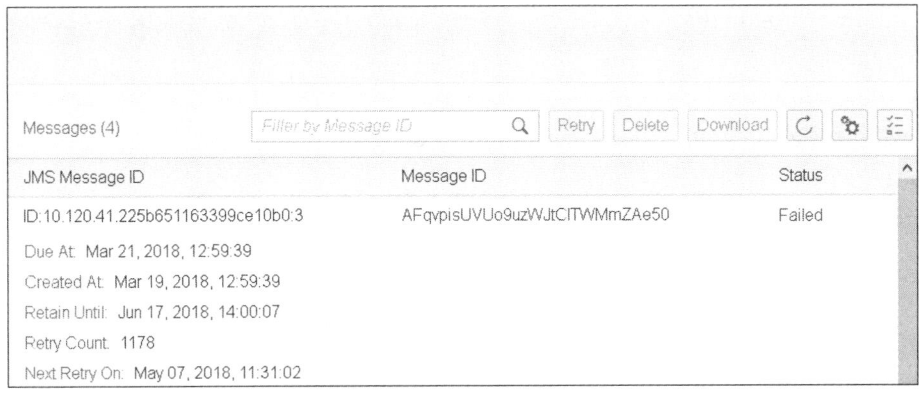

Figure 8.53 Manage Message Queue Monitor B

Attribute	Description
Name	The name of the JMS queue as configured in the **JMS** adapter. If the JMS queue is used by an **AS2** or **XI** adapter, the queue name is generated automatically as per the following pattern: `AS2_<Integration Flow Name>_<Channel Name>_<Guid>` or `XI_<Integration Flow Name>_<Channel Name>_<Guid>`.
Entries	The number of entries currently contained in the JMS queue.
Size	The overall size of all messages contained in the JMS queue.

Table 8.20 Attributes of JMS Queues on the Left Side of the Monitor

Automatic Queue Creation

The JMS queues are created automatically in the JMS messaging instance during deployment of the first integration flow using a new JMS queue name. Unlike the data store monitor, JMS queues show up in the monitor also if there are no messages available in the queue.

The actions available for queues can be accessed via the **Actions** button on top of the queues table (Figure 8.54). The following actions are available:

- **Retry**
  Restarts all messages in the selected queue.
- **Delete**
  Deletes the selected queue. Be careful with this option: it deletes the queue with all

the messages in the queue. To re-create the queue, the integration flow needs to be redeployed.

- **Where-Used**
  Shows the integration flows using the selected queue.
- **Check**
  Some consistency checks for JMS queue usage are executed; for example, it's checked if some queues aren't used by any integration flows anymore. A detailed description of the checks and the check results can be found in the "Checks in JMS Message Queue Monitor" blog in the SAP Community (*www.sap.com/community.html*).
- **Reload**
  Reloads the content of the table containing the JMS queues.
- **Sort**
  Offers sorting options for the available columns.

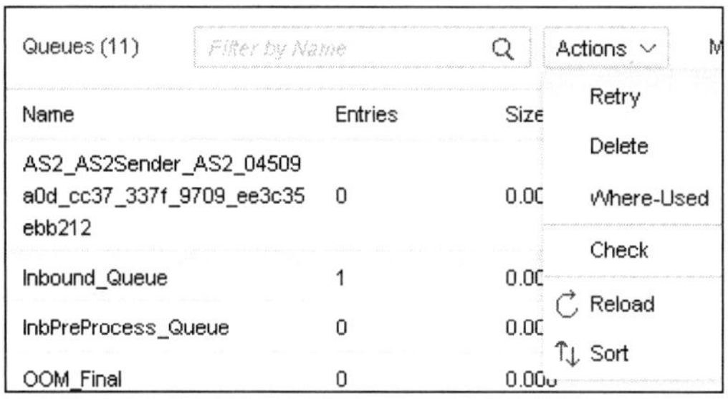

Figure 8.54 Actions for Queues

Queues Aren't Deleted Automatically

JMS queues aren't deleted automatically during undeployment of the integration flow because there may still be messages in the JMS queue, and deleting the queue would delete them as well, which would lead to data loss. Only the owner of the scenario knows if the JMS queue can be deleted with all its content or if it's still required.

Upon selecting a specific queue on the left side of the screen, all messages in this specific queue are shown on the right side in the details table. Table 8.21 describes the attributes of single messages in the JMS queue and their possible values.

Column	Description
JMS Message ID	The ID of the entry in the JMS queue. The **JMS Message ID** is a unique ID generated by the runtime when the entry is written to the JMS queue.
Message ID	The ID of the MPL. The **Message ID** is shown as a link, and selecting the link opens the MPL in the message processing monitor.
Status	The status of the message. The possible statuses are as follows: ■ **Waiting**: This is the status after the entry was written to the JMS queue. The message is waiting to be consumed by another process or integration flow. ■ **Failed**: The last processing of the message ended with an error. Follow the link to the MPL to get the details of the error. ■ **Blocked**: The message caused several runtime node outages and isn't processed anymore. The dead letter queue feature is described in detail in the "Configure Dead Letter Handling in JMS Adapter" blog in the SAP Community (*www.sap.com/community.html*). ■ **Overdue**: The message gets this status if it wasn't consumed in the due time. For such entries, the tenant administrator should check why the message isn't consumed (e.g., maybe the consuming integration flow doesn't run anymore) and solve the problem.
Due At	The date and time the message is expected to be consumed latest. This time is configured in the **JMS** receiver adapter in the configuration field **Retention Threshold for Alerting.** If the message is processed by the **AS2** or **XI** adapter, the due time is set to **2** days by the adapter.
Created At	The date and time the entry was created in the JMS queue.
Retain Until	The date and time the message will be deleted. This time is configured in the **JMS** receiver adapter in the configuration field **Expiration Period**, which is 90 days per default. If the message is processed by the **AS2** or **XI** adapter, the expiration period is automatically set to 90 days by the adapter.
Retry Count	The numbers of retries executed for this message.
Next Retry On	The date and time the message will be retried next.

Table 8.21 Attributes of JMS Queue Entries

The following actions are available on the top of the details table for messages stored in JMS queues:

- **Filter**
  Filters for a specific message ID, which can be either the JMS message ID or the MPL ID.
- **Retry**
  Restarts the selected messages.
- **Delete**
  Deletes selected messages from the JMS queue. Only use this option if the messages aren't needed anymore.
- **Download**
  Downloads selected entries. A *<ID>.zip* file is created in the download folder of your local PC containing the message stored in the JMS queue.
- **Reload**
  Reloads the content of the details table.
- **Table Settings**
  Allows sorting of the entries and filtering by the **Status** column.
- **Multi-select Mode**
  Allows you to select multiple entries at once. This option is useful when you need to delete multiple entries. Note that the **Download** action isn't available for multiple entries.

Retry of Blocked Messages

When triggering a retry for messages with status **Blocked**, keep in mind that those messages got the blocked status because they could not be processed due to the fact that the runtime node crashed multiple times. Because of this, it's very likely that the message caused the crash. Another retry may cause another runtime node crash.

JMS Resource Check

JMS resources in the connected JMS Message Broker instance are limited. Therefore, you need to monitor them carefully, especially if the load for scenarios using JMS queues increases. If the JMS resources are exhausted, you'll encounter errors during runtime processing. This needs to be avoided. Details about the JMS resources available with the SAP Cloud Platform Integration licenses can be found in the "JMS Resource and Size Limits" blog in the SAP Community (*www.sap.com/community.html*).

To monitor the JMS resources, an info bar is available at the top of the message queues monitor screen that shows the result of the JMS resource check (refer back to Figure 8.52). Three severity levels are available for the info bar:

- **Info**
  The blue info message tells you that the used JMS resources are within the purchased limits. No action is necessary in this case.
- **Warning**
  The orange message indicates that at least one of the JMS resources is in a critical state.
- **Error**
  If at least one JMS resource is exhausted, a red error message is shown.

When you click the **Details** link, the different JMS resources with the current statuses are shown (Figure 8.55). If dedicated resources are critical, the tenant administrator together with the scenario owner should take actions to bring the resources back to normal. If JMS resources are exhausted, message processing is affected, and immediate action is required.

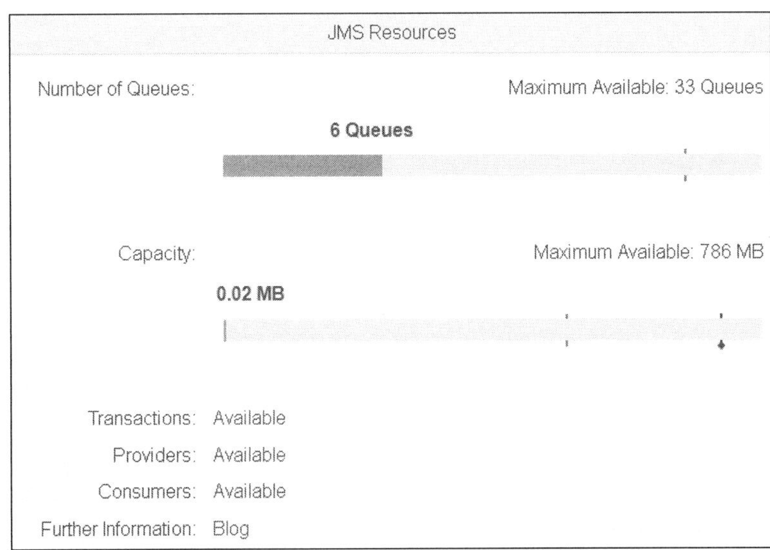

Figure 8.55 Details of JMS Resources

Let's take a detailed look at the **JMS Resources** screen as shown, what the options mean, and what needs to be done if they are critical or exhausted:

- **Number of Queues**
  This is the number of JMS queues created on the JMS Message Broker during integration flow deployment. If the limit is reached on the JMS Message Broker, deployments of integration flows using new JMS queues will fail because the new JMS queue can't be created on the JMS Message Broker. What needs to be done now? You simply have to clean up the JMS queues if new queues are required. Use the **Check** action (refer to Figure 8.54) to find out if there are unused queues and delete them. Furthermore, you can check if all integration flows using JMS queues are still required; if not, undeploy them, and delete the corresponding queues.
- **Capacity**
  There is an overall storage capacity available in the JMS Message Broker instance connected to your tenant for all the queues. If 100% of the available capacity is used, no messages can be stored in the JMS queues anymore, and the processing of the messages will end in runtime errors. To avoid this, check why there are so many messages in the JMS queues and why the messages aren't consumed. For example, the consuming integration flow might not run, or dedicated queues aren't needed anymore because they just contain messages from an old scenario. Check and correct the problem as soon as the **Critical** limit is reached to avoid downtimes in the deployed scenarios.
- **Consumers**
  Consumers are created in the JMS Message Broker from **JMS** sender adapters to consume messages from the JMS queue. For each JMS queue used in a **JMS** sender channel, as many consumers are created as concurrent processes are configured in the **JMS** sender channel in the **Number of Concurrent Processes** parameter (see Chapter 5, Section 5.4.1). If several runtime nodes are started in the SAP Cloud Platform Integration cluster, those many consumers are created from each runtime node. If the value of consumers gets **Critical**, you need to reduce the parallelism, either by reducing the **Number of Concurrent Processes** in the **JMS** sender channels or by reducing the number of runtime nodes started in the cluster.
- **Providers**
  Providers are created by the **JMS** receiver adapter in the JMS Message Broker to store messages in a JMS queue. As many providers are created as messages are send to the JMS queue in parallel. If the value of providers reaches the **Critical** limit, the parallelism of the inbound processing is too high. You need to reduce the number of parallel inbound calls from sender systems sending messages to scenarios using JMS queues.

- **Transactions**
  To consistently process messages in SAP Cloud Platform Integration, JMS transactions are required in the JMS Message Broker to roll back the processing if there are errors (see Chapter 5, Section 5.4.2, for detailed information). As many transactions are created in the JMS Message Broker as consumers and providers are under processing in parallel. If the limit for transactions gets **Critical**, you need to reduce the parallelism for the consumer and/or provider connections.

If the mentioned actions don't solve the JMS resource shortage, you may need to purchase more JMS messaging units and add them to the JMS Message Broker instance connected to the tenant to increase the JMS resources increased in the JMS Message Broker.

The last tile in this section is the **Number Ranges** tile, which was used already in Chapter 7, when we configured a complete B2B integration.

8.4.4 Maintain Number Ranges

As explained in detail in Chapter 7, Section 7.3.4, number ranges are required to define unique interchange numbers for each document for Electronic Data Interchange (EDI) processing. To do this, a number range object (NRO) can be used that defines the length of the number and the minimum and maximum value. The NRO is defined and monitored in the **Number Ranges** monitor and used in runtime when an integration flow is executed.

Selecting the **Number Ranges** tile opens the list of defined NROs in a table, as shown in Figure 8.56. Table 8.22 provides a detailed description of the available attributes of the NROs.

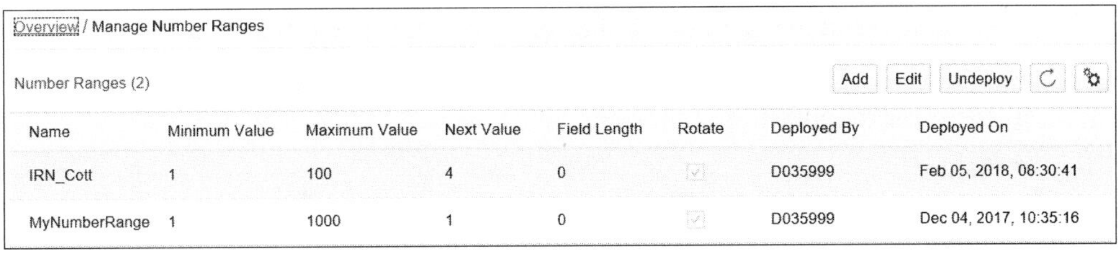

Overview / Manage Number Ranges

Number Ranges (2) Add Edit Undeploy

Name	Minimum Value	Maximum Value	Next Value	Field Length	Rotate	Deployed By	Deployed On
IRN_Cott	1	100	4	0	✓	D035999	Feb 05, 2018, 08:30:41
MyNumberRange	1	1000	1	0	✓	D035999	Dec 04, 2017, 10:35:16

Figure 8.56 Number Ranges Monitor

Column	Description
Name	Name of the NRO. This name is used in the integration flow configuration to refer to the NRO.
Minimum Value	Minimum value; should be greater or equal 0.
Maximum Value	Maximum value allowed in this NRO.
Next Value	The next value used in runtime when invoking the NRO.
Field Length	Field length of the number. Leading zeros are added to the current value to achieve a fixed field length in runtime. This means if the current value is 5, the unique number used in runtime is 0005 for a field length of 4. If **Field Length** is 0, no leading zeros are added. Maximum value allowed for this field is 99.
Rotate	If this flag is set, and the number range reaches the specified maximum value, the current value resets to the specified minimum value.
Deployed By	The user who deployed the NRO.
Deployed On	Date and time the NRO was deployed.

Table 8.22 Attributes of Number Range Objects

The following actions are available for NROs at the top of the table:

- **Add**
  Opens the **Add Number Range** dialog to define and deploy a new NRO (Figure 8.57).
- **Edit**
  Opens the **Edit** dialog to adjust the definitions of the selected NRO.
- **Undeploy**
  Removes the NRO from the tenant.
- **Reload**
  Reloads the content of the table.
- **Table Settings**
  Allows sorting of the entries and filtering by the name of the NRO or by the user who deployed the NRO.

Add Number Range
*Name: NR_for_Orders
Description: number range for Orders processing
*Minimum Value: 0
*Maximum Value: 999
Field Length: 0
Rotate
OK Cancel

Figure 8.57 Add Number Range Dialog

With this, we complete the **Manage Stores** section and start to explore the **Access Logs** section in the monitoring dashboard where access to different logs is provided.

8.5 Access Logs

As depicted in Figure 8.58 the **Access Logs** section offers access to different logs created in SAP Cloud Platform Integration. Logs get important, for example, when specific errors need to be analyzed that occur during runtime processing. Often detailed logs are requested by SAP support to analyze specific error situations. Therefore, it's important to know which logs are available and what they contain.

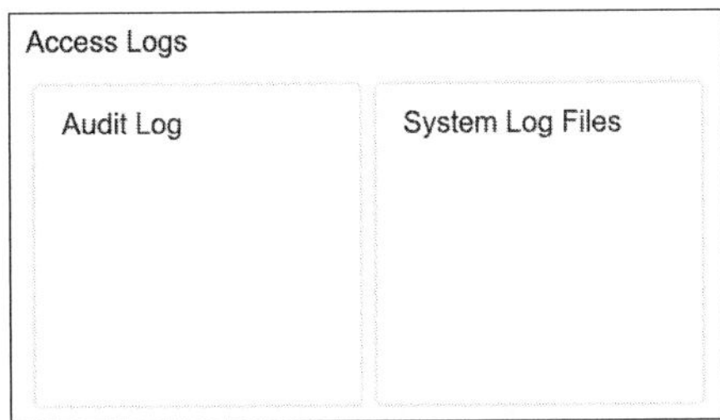

Figure 8.58 Access Logs Section in Monitoring Dashboard

There are two tiles available: the **Audit Log** and **System Log Files**. Whereas the audit log is more relevant for auditing purposes, the provided system logs are mainly required for error analysis.

8.5.1 Monitor Audit Log

Audit logs are security-relevant records. SAP Cloud Platform Integration needs to log all system changes in the SAP Cloud Platform Integration tenant. The changes logged are configuration changes, deployments, or deletions of security artifacts; log level changes; and so on. All those changes are logged in the audit log. The monitoring dashboard offers access to the audit log via the **Audit Log** tile (refer to Figure 8.58).

Selecting the **Audit Log** tile opens a table in a new screen showing all audit logs of the last hour (Figure 8.59 and Figure 8.60). However, you can adjust the **Time Range** at the top of the table to see audit logs for a longer time period. In Figure 8.59, for example, you see the audit logs for the **Past 24 Hours**. See Table 8.23 for a detailed description of the attributes for audit log entries.

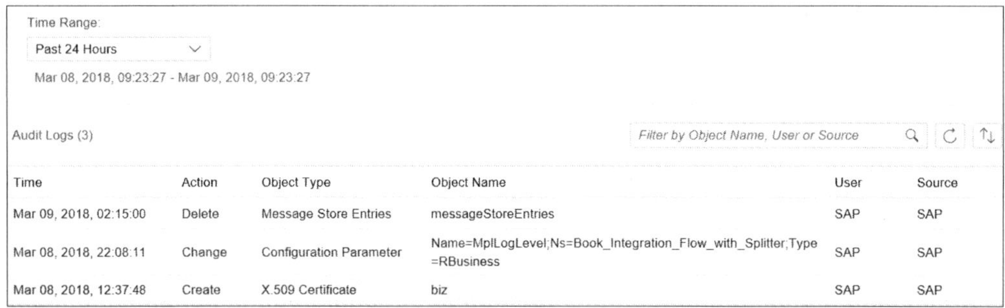

Time	Action	Object Type	Object Name	User	Source
Mar 09, 2018, 02:15:00	Delete	Message Store Entries	messageStoreEntries	SAP	SAP
Mar 08, 2018, 22:08:11	Change	Configuration Parameter	Name=MplLogLevel;Ns=Book_Integration_Flow_with_Splitter;Type =RBusiness	SAP	SAP
Mar 08, 2018, 12:37:48	Create	X.509 Certificate	biz	SAP	SAP

Figure 8.59 Audit Log Monitor A

Filter by Object Name, User or Source

Object Name	User	Source
messageStoreEntries	SAP	SAP
Name=MplLogLevel;Ns=Book_Integration_Flow_with_Splitter;Type =RBusiness	SAP	SAP
biz	SAP	SAP

Figure 8.60 Audit Log Monitor B

Retention Time

The retention time of audit logs is 30 days, after which the audit log is automatically deleted.

Column	Description
Time	The date and time the audit log entry was created.
Action	The action performed on the system. Possible values are as follows: ■ **Create: Creation of artifacts or configurations, for example, certificates in the keystore.** ■ **Change**: Changing of configuration parameters, for example, log levels of an integration flow. ■ **Delete:** Deletion of artifacts, for example, certificates, variables, or messages. ■ **Read**: Read access to artifacts, for example, to message payloads using the trace feature or to messages or variables in temporary storages.
Object Type	Type of the object that was changed, for example, **Message**, **Variable**, **Configuration Parameter**, or **X509 Certificate**.
Object Name	Name or ID of the object that was changed, for example, ID of a message, name of a X.509 certificate, or name of a variable.
User	User who triggered the change. If an SAP user triggered the change, **SAP** is displayed.
Source	IP address the change was triggered from. If an SAP user triggered the change, **SAP** is displayed.

Table 8.23 Attributes of Audit Log Entries

You can sort the entries using the **Sort** ⇅ icon or filter by **Object Name**, **User**, or **Source** using the **Filter** field at the top of the table.

Now let's look at the second tile in the **Access Logs** section, which provides access to system logs.

8.5.2 Check System Log Files

Sometimes, the error messages shown in the MPL aren't sufficient to fully understand the root cause of an error or SAP support requires detailed information for analyzing an error. In such cases, you need to have a look into the system logs written during message processing on the runtime node. The **System Log Files** tile provides access to those technical system logs.

Selecting the **System Log Files** tile opens a table containing the most important log files of the runtime nodes running in your cluster (Figure 8.61) in the **Log Files** tab. Table 8.24 provides a detailed description of the attributes of the system log files.

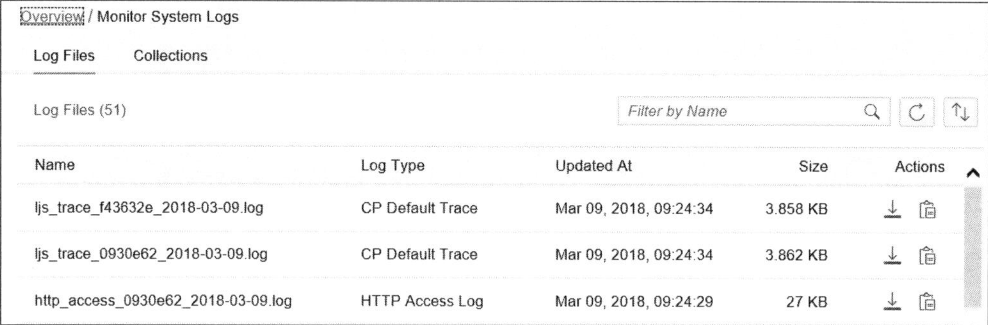

Figure 8.61 Monitor System Logs Screen

> **Retention Time**
>
> The retention time of the system log files is seven days. After that, the system logs are automatically deleted.

Column	Description
Name	Name of the log file. The name has the following pattern: *<log type>_<process ID>_<date>.log*. The process ID is shown in the message processing monitor, so that it's easy for you to identify the system log in which details about the message processing are logged.

Table 8.24 Attributes of Log Files

Column	Description
Log Type	Type of the log file. Possible values are as follows: ■ **CPI Default Trace**: System trace file. ■ **HTTP Access Log**: Log file containing the HTTP inbound requests. One log file is available for each runtime node.
Updated At	Date and time the log file was updated.
Size	Size of the log file.
Actions	Actions available for the log file: ■ **Download** : Downloads the log file. ■ **Copy Download URL** : Copies the download URL to the clipboard.

Table 8.24 Attributes of Log Files (Cont.)

You can sort the entries using the **Sort** icon or filter by **Name** using the **Filter** field at the top of the table.

In the **Collections** tab, you can access collections of the system log files (Figure 8.62). You can download the collections as an archive or copy the download URL . Downloading the collection, you get a **.zip* archive containing the latest log files.

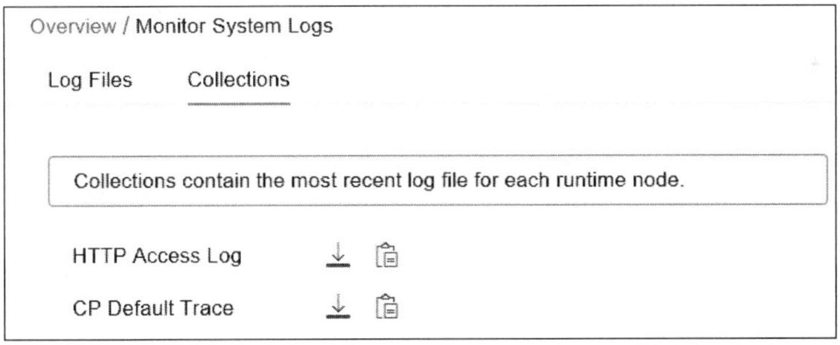

Overview / Monitor System Logs

Log Files Collections

Collections contain the most recent log file for each runtime node.

HTTP Access Log

CP Default Trace

Figure 8.62 Collections Tab in System Logs

With this, we complete the **Access Logs** section and continue with the next, very specific section that handles locks created during message processing.

8.6 Manage Locks

On the SAP Cloud Platform Integration tenant, locks are written by some components to ensure efficient and consistent message processing in the runtime. To monitor those message processing locks, you can use the **Message Locks** tile in the **Manage Locks** section of the monitoring dashboard (Figure 8.63).

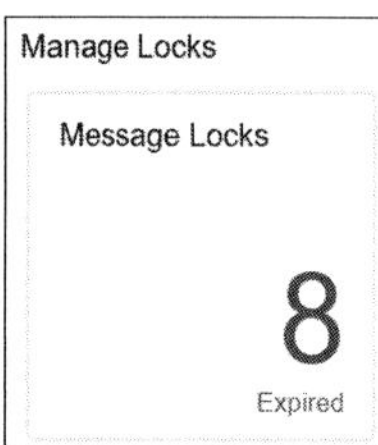

Figure 8.63 Manage Locks Section in the Monitoring Dashboard

Monitor Message Locks

During message processing in SAP Cloud Platform Integration, some adapters write entries into an in-progress repository to avoid the same message being processed multiple times in parallel, for example, by different runtime nodes, or to avoid large messages leading to out-of-memory issues on runtime nodes again and again.

The following adapters write such message processing locks:

- **SFTP sender adapter**
  To prevent double processing of files by the **SFTP** sender adapter, a lock entry is written to the in-progress repository each time a file is processed by a runtime node. As long as this lock entry exists, no other runtime node can access the file. After message processing, independent of whether the processing ended in **Completed** or **Failed**, the lock is removed by the runtime. If the runtime node crashes during processing of the message, for example, caused by an out-of-memory error, the message processing lock isn't removed, and upon restart of the runtime node, the message is retried by the adapter. If the runtime node crashes two more times during processing of this message, the message is taken out from processing, and the message lock remains in the in-progress repository. Manual action is required by the tenant administrator together with the scenario owner to check why this file could not be processed, for example, maybe it's too large to be processed by the integration flow. In this case, it should be removed from the polling directory and be split into smaller files. The lock can then be released.

- **JMS sender adapter**
  The **JMS** sender adapter uses the in-progress repository only if the **Dead Letter Queue** handling is switched on (for details, refer to Chapter 5, Section 5.4.1). If the runtime node crashes during processing of the message, for example, caused by an out-of-memory error, the message processing lock isn't removed, and upon restart of the runtime node, the message is retried by the JMS sender adapter. If the runtime node crashes two more times during processing of this message, the message is taken out from processing and marked as **Blocked** in the queue monitor (Section 8.4.3). The message lock in the message lock monitor is removed.
- **AS2 sender adapter**
  Because the **AS2** sender adapter uses JMS queues to store the message during processing, the same behavior as explained for the JMS sender adapter holds true for the AS2 sender adapter. The in-progress repository is only used if the **Dead Letter Queue** handling is switched on. The message is marked as **Blocked** in the queue monitor, and the message lock is removed from the message lock monitor if the runtime node crashed multiple times during processing of this message.
- **XI sender and receiver adapters**
  The XI adapters, both sender and receiver, can use either JMS queues or data stores for temporary storage of the messages during processing.
  - If JMS queues are used, the same behavior as explained for the **JMS** and **AS2** sender adapters holds true for the **XI** adapter as well. The in-progress repository is only used if the **Dead Letter Queue** handling is switched on. The message is marked as **Blocked** in the queue monitor, and the message lock is removed from the message lock monitor if the runtime node crashed multiple times during processing of this message.
  - If the data store is used as temporary storage, the in-progress repository is always used to avoid a message crashing the runtime node again and again; there is no configuration option available. If the runtime node crashes three times during processing of this message, the message is taken out of processing, and the message lock remains in the in-progress repository. Those entries stay in the message locks monitor until you manually release them. Before releasing the lock, check the corresponding message in the data store monitor, for example, to see if it's too large to be processed by the integration flow. In this case, you need to request the sender of this message to split the message and send smaller messages instead. The message in the data store can then be removed, and the lock in the lock monitor released.

You can monitor the in-progress repository entries in the **Message Locks** tile. When you select the **Message Locks** tile, a table containing all currently set message processing locks is shown (Figure 8.64). Table 8.25 provides a detailed description of the available attributes of the message processing locks.

Overview / Manage Message Locks
Message Locks (8)
Filter by Source or Entry
Release
Component
Source
Entry
Created At
Expires At
JMS
JMS:QueueForRetry
ID:10.120.32.173892915d361975350:1
Jul 12, 2017, 11:38:55
Jul 12, 2017, 11:55:35
JMS
JMS:QueueForRetry
ID:10.120.32.173892915d361975350:2
Jul 12, 2017, 11:56:59
Jul 12, 2017, 12:13:39

Figure 8.64 Message Locks Monitor

Column	Description
Component	Component that set the lock. Possible values are as follows: ■ **SFTP**: The lock was set by the SFTP sender adapter. ■ **JMS**: The lock was set by the JMS component; this is the case for **JMS** adapter, **AS2** adapter, and **XI** adapter when JMS queues are used for temporary storage. ■ **XI**: The lock was set by the **XI** adapter when using the data store for temporary storage.
Source	Identifies the source of the lock. Possible values are as follows: ■ For **SFTP**: `<sftp user>@<sftp server>` ■ For **JMS**: `JMS:<queue name>` ■ For **XI**: `XI_<integration flow name>.<participant name>_<channel name>`
Entry	Identifies the locked object, for example, the message or file name: ■ For **SFTP**: `directory1/dir2/test.xml` ■ For **JMS**: `ID:<JMS message ID>` (following the link opens the JMS Message in the queue monitor) ■ For **XI**: `<Entry ID from data store>`
Created At	Date and time the lock was set.
Expires At	Date and time possible retries expire. After this time, no retry is triggered anymore. The message can only be retried by releasing the lock.

Table 8.25 Attributes of Message Locks

The following actions are available for message processing locks at the top of the table:

- **Filter**
  Filters the table by specifying values for the **Source** or the **Entry** column. Using this option, you can, for example. search for a specific message ID or a file name.
- **Release**
  Releases the lock and so triggers another retry of the message or file.
- **Reload**
  Reloads the content of the table.
- **Table Settings**
  Allows sorting of the entries and filtering by the **Component** column.
- **Multi-select Mode**
  Allows you to select multiple entries at once. This option is useful when you need to delete multiple entries.

Releasing Locks Can Lead to a Runtime Node Crash

When releasing locks, keep in mind that those messages got the lock because they could not be processed due to multiple runtime node crashes. Because of this, it's very likely that the message caused the crash. Releasing the lock triggers another retry of the file or message and so may cause another runtime node crash.

With this we complete the section about message processing locks and also end the journey through all the monitors available in SAP Cloud Platform Integration. You should now feel confident to operate the SAP Cloud Platform Integration tenant and understand all the monitors available.

8.7 Summary

No one wants to build a castle that only lasts one day. After spending a lot of time building integration scenarios to help your business reach its integration goals, you'll want to ensure that the business continues to enjoy its benefits for a long time. Your castle, as such, requires regular checks and maintenance work to stay in optimal condition. The same applies for your SAP Cloud Platform Integration platform, which requires maintenance by monitoring the running integration flows and the data stored temporarily.

Given that SAP Cloud Platform Integration is a cloud-based platform, most operational tasks (e.g., health checks) are performed by SAP, as the service provider. This chapter focused on operational activities performed by customers. In the chapter, we explored the different features and monitors that can be used in SAP Cloud Platform Integration for monitoring and operational purposes. The monitors were discussed in detail and the required scenarios were outlined as well.

After reading this chapter, you should be able to monitor all integration flows deployed in the tenant and use the logging and tracing feature to analyze the runtime of the integration flows. You're now well equipped to manage the different security artifacts, such as certificates, that are needed for your integration flows. In addition, you know how to monitor temporary data, such as messages and variables, stored in the SAP Cloud Platform Integration tenant's database or in JMS queues.

With this we have covered the lifecycle of developing integration scenarios in the web designer of Cloud Integration and monitoring them in the monitoring dashboard. In the next chapter we will take you into the world of using the APIs offered by SAP Cloud Platform Integration to develop and monitor integration content.

Chapter 9
Application Programming Interfaces

SAP enables the consumption and provision of application programming interfaces (APIs) to expose different functionalities to the outside world. The chapter dives into the specifics of an API within the context of SAP Cloud Platform Integration, presents currently available features, and explores the APIs that are currently available for customers.

In today's connected world, pretty much everything is at our fingertips. From traditional desktops, mobile phones, and connected devices (e.g., watches), we're able to purchase goods, write articles, and book flight tickets. But how does data move from application A to B, for instance, when booking a flight ticket or a car? The hidden enablers in most cases are known as application programming interfaces (APIs).

An API within the context of integration is an interface through which data exchange is made possible between applications. APIs are used to expose functionalities (or programmable interfaces) to the outside world through a service path or URL.

Simply put, an API takes a request from the caller, performs a task on a server application, and returns a response to the caller. The application providing the API is known as a *service provider*. And the application or user using the API is generally called a *service consumer*.

This chapter introduces the Java and OData APIs provided by SAP Cloud Platform Integration and explains how to use them. The chapter further explores SAP Cloud Platform API Management and how to use it together with SAP Cloud Platform Integration.

9.1 Introduction

There is a lot to be said about APIs, and this topic deserves its own book. The descriptive introduction in this section is only intended to give you a brief overview.

After having read the introductory information, if you're familiar with the topic of integration, you might be wondering what the difference is between an API and a traditional web service. Table 9.1 points some differences out between an API and a web service.

Aspects	Web Service	API
Network	Needs a network connection for its operation	Can also operate offline
Protocols	SOAP, REST, XML-RPC	SOAP, REST, but can also communicate via CURL
Exposed via	XML over HTTP	JAR, DLL, XML, or JSON over HTTP

Table 9.1 Comparing Web Services to APIs

Furthermore, besides the differences mentioned in Table 9.1, all web services can be considered APIs, but not all APIs can be considered web services.

A web service is a type of API that almost always operates over HTTP (hence the **web** part of the name). However, some web services, such as the Simple Object Access Protocol (SOAP), can use alternate transports, for example, Simple Mail Transfer Protocol (SMTP). The official W3C definition mentions that web services don't necessarily use HTTP, but this is almost always the case and is usually assumed unless mentioned otherwise.

On the other hand, it can be argued that every bit of function ever created, be it in a Dynamic Link Library (DLL), Java Archive (JAR), web service, or plain code is an API. APIs can use any type of communication protocol and aren't limited to HTTP like web services are.

Now that you have a good high-level awareness of what APIs are, let's explore the Java APIs that are currently provided by SAP Cloud Platform Integration.

9.2 Java APIs Provided by SAP Cloud Platform Integration

SAP Cloud Platform Integration provides a number of Java-based APIs to access and control the processing of messages on your tenant. At the time of publishing this book, it's possible to use Groovy or Java Script as the programming language to access these APIs. Accessing the functionality provided by these APIs in a script step or while creating a user-defined mapping function can be handy (Section 9.3).

Furthermore, the APIs can be used while developing a custom SAP Cloud Platform Integration adapter (using the Adapter Development Kit [ADK]). Note, however, that if there is a custom adapter, Java is used as a development language. We discuss the ADK in Chapter 6.

The existing APIs can be classified under the following categories:

- **Generic API**
  Complete and parent set of APIs covering various features. These APIs are kept under the package `com.sap.it.api`. See Table 9.2 for a list of interfaces contained in this package.
- **Message API**
  Provides APIs to access properties of a message. These APIs are kept under the package `com.sap.it.api.msg`. See Table 9.2 for a list of interfaces contained in this package.
- **Script API**
  Provides APIs to controls scripts.
- **Mapping API**
  Provides APIs to control mappings. These APIs are contained under the package `com.sap.it.api.mapping`. See Table 9.2 for a list of some commonly used packages and their corresponding interfaces.

Package	Interface	Description
`com.sap.it.api.msg`	`ExchangeProperty-Provider`	Provides access to the properties of a message exchange.
`com.sap.it.api.msg`	`MessageSizeInformation`	Provides information about the size of a message.
`com.sap.it.api.mapping`	`MappingContext`	Mapping context object to be provided to mapping user-defined functions (UDFs).

Table 9.2 API Packages and Interfaces

Package	Interface	Description
com.sap.it.api.mapping	Output	Class used in advanced UDFs (execution type All values of Context or All values of a Queue) to return the result of a function.
com.sap.it.api.mapping	ValueMappingApi	Used to execute value mapping with the given parameters.
com.sap.gateway.ip.core.customdev.util	Message	Accesses the exchanged message. The API provides an extensive set of functionalities, including manipulation of attachment, reading and changing payload, and retrieval of message properties such as size, header, and so on.
com.sap.it.script.logging	ILogger	Performs different operations on the logs (e.g., writing message logs).
com.sap.it.public.generic.api	ITApiException, KeystoreService, SecureStoreService, UserCredential	Global API covering a wide range of functionalities, including; access key storage services, access the deployed user credentials, and access exception object.
com.sap.it.api.pd	PartnerDirectoryService	Performs different operations on the Partner Directory parameter values, the partner IDs, the alternative partner IDs, and the authorized users of a partner.
com.sap.it.api.pd	BinaryData	Container for binary data relevant for Partner Directory binary parameters.

Table 9.2 API Packages and Interfaces (Cont.)

For a full list of interfaces and classes, refer to the JavaDocs at: *http://bit.ly/2LFY6V7.*

Note

Note that the APIs summary of packages listed in Table 9.2 relates to API version 2.12.0.

To illustrate the usage of the APIs, let's next look at UDFs in a mapping.

9.3 Using the Java API in a User-Defined function

Imagine that you need a message mapping to perform a complex transformation between a source and target message. Furthermore, imagine that none of the existing standard functions can fulfill the needed logic. That is when a user-defined function (UDF) comes to the rescue.

A UDF is a custom function that is built to cater to special mapping needs that can't be expressed by the mapping functions predefined in the mapping editor. In SAP Cloud Platform Integration, a UDF can be built using Groovy or Java Script. UDF generally uses mapping-related APIs listed in Table 9.2 to transform the messages. (To see an illustration of a UDF in use, go to the example in Chapter 4, Section 4.3.)

In this section, we've built an integration flow that consumes an external OData service. After invoking the OData service, we received a response that looks like the one presented in Figure 9.1.

```
<soap:Envelope xmlns:soap="http://schemas.xmlsoap.org/soap/envelope/">
   <soap:Header/>
   <soap:Body>
      <ns1:OrderShippingDetails_MT xmlns:ns1="http://hci.sap.com/demo">
         <orderNumber>10249</orderNumber>
         <customerName>Toms Spezialitäten</customerName>
         <shipCity>Münster</shipCity>
         <shipStreet>Luisenstr. 48</shipStreet>
         <shipPostalCode>44087</shipPostalCode>
         <shipCountry>DE</shipCountry>
         <shipDate>1996-07-10T00:00:00.000</shipDate>
      </ns1:OrderShippingDetails_MT>
   </soap:Body>
</soap:Envelope>
```

Figure 9.1 Response of the Integration Flow of Chapter 4

Let's hypothetically imagine that, with regard to the consumer application, you would prefer not to have the empty spaces in the element `shipStreet` between the street name and the house number. Furthermore, the consumer requires the street field to be appended with the order number as a postfix, and the entire field should be returned in uppercase. Looking at the example in Figure 9.1, it means that the value `Luisenstr. 48` should be transformed to `LUISENSTR.48_10249` instead.

You can implement this requirement by using a combination of predefined functions in the mapping. However, for the sake of illustration, let's try to achieve this requirement using a UDF by following these steps:

1. Using the **Design** section of the SAP Cloud Platform Integration Web UI, navigate to the concerned package, and open the integration flow.
2. Click the **Edit** button.
3. Select the **Message Mapping** step that should be enhanced with the UDF, as shown in Figure 9.2.

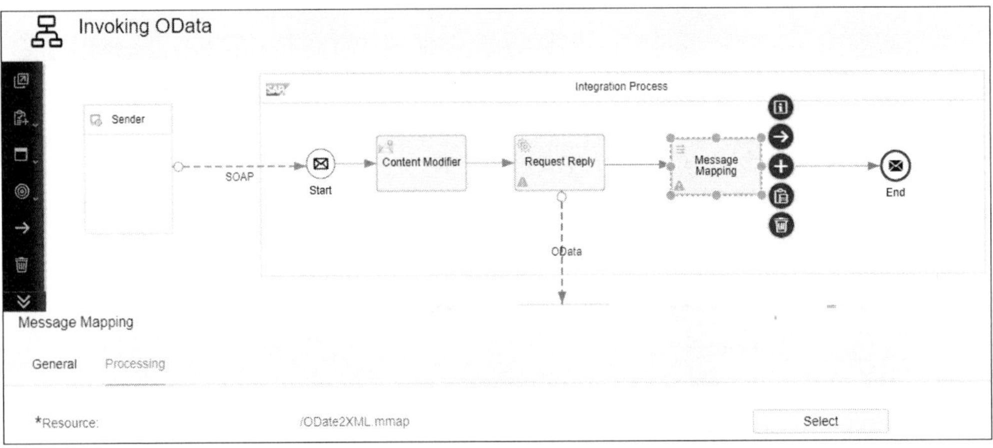

Figure 9.2 Selecting the Message Mapping Step to Be Enhanced with a UDF

4. Select the **Processing** tab, and click on the **/ODate2XML.mmap** link (see Figure 9.2) to open the mapping editor.
5. Select an element on the target message structure (e.g., the **shipStreet** field as shown in Figure 9.3). Notice that a section called **Functions** appears on the bottom-left corner of the mapping editor (see Figure 9.3).

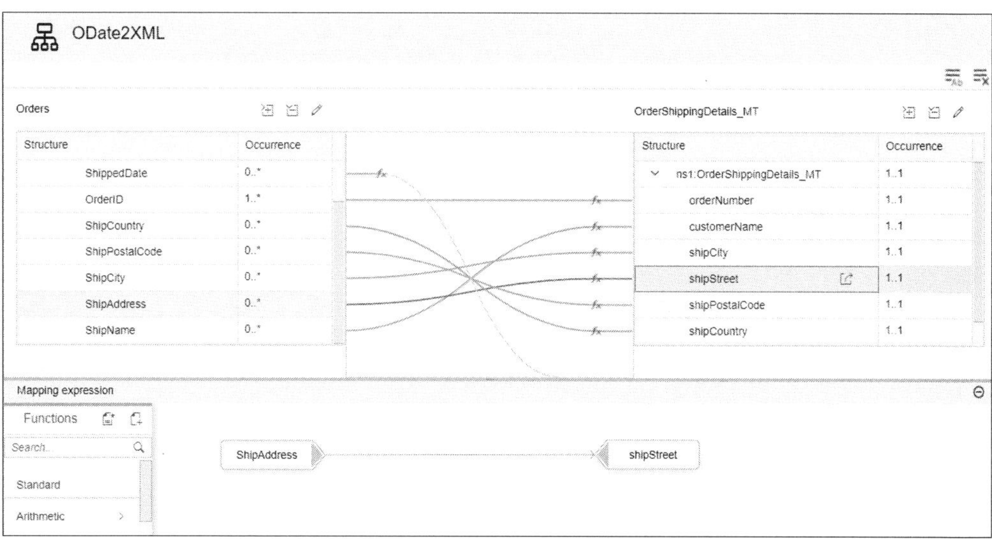

Figure 9.3 Mapping Editor with the Details of the Mapping to Be Enhanced

6. Let's now create a new UDF using the **Create** icon next to the **Functions** box in the mapping editor.
7. Specify a name for the UDF to be created (see Figure 9.4).

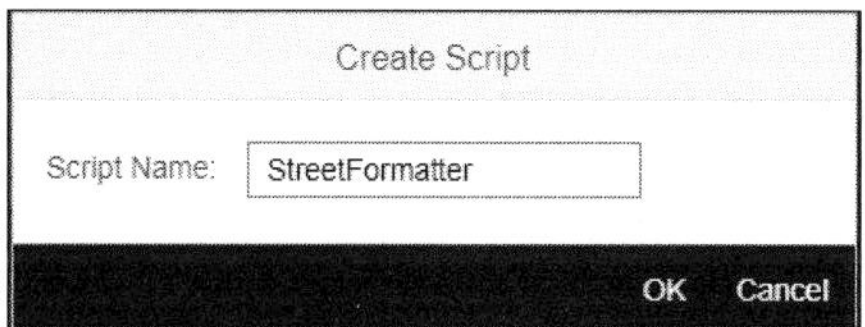

Figure 9.4 Providing a Name for the UDF

You're redirected to a UDF editor with some standard code (see Figure 9.5).

Note

As you notice on the top part of Figure 9.5, the mapping API has been imported by the statement `import com.sap.it.api.mapping.*;`. This is the same package that was discussed in Table 9.2.

Note that Figure 9.5 also has includes a sample source code to showcase what is possible. The sample code is included between the /* and */ characters.

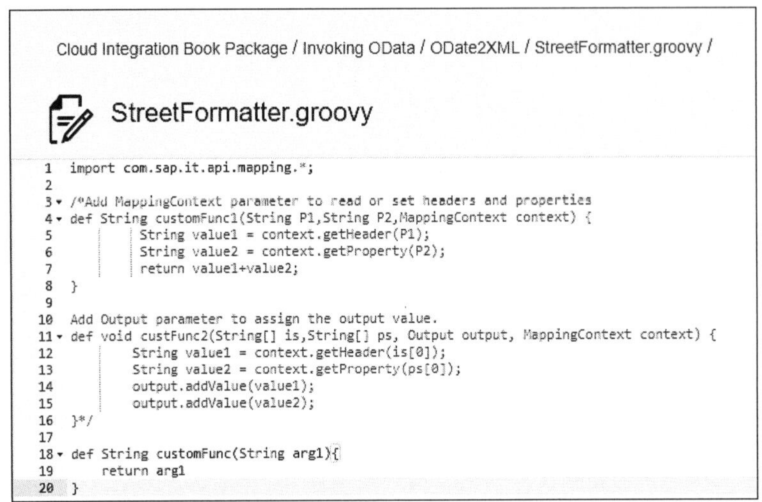

Cloud Integration Book Package / Invoking OData / ODate2XML / StreetFormatter.groovy /
StreetFormatter.groovy
import com.sap.it.api.mapping.*;

/*Add MappingContext parameter to read or set headers and properties
def String customFunc1(String P1,String P2,MappingContext context) {
String value1 = context.getHeader(P1);
String value2 = context.getProperty(P2);
return value1+value2;
}

Add Output parameter to assign the output value.
def void custFunc2(String[] is,String[] ps, Output output, MappingContext context) {
String value1 = context.getHeader(is[0]);
String value2 = context.getProperty(ps[0]);
output.addValue(value1);
output.addValue(value2);
}*/

def String customFunc(String arg1){
return arg1
}

Figure 9.5 Standard Groovy Script Code Provided When Creating a UDF

8. Rename the Groovy method (e.g., "streetFormatterFunc"), and adapt the source code to suit your need (see the example in Figure 9.6). Line 8 of Figure 9.6 indicates that the code provided is using the Java API to retrieve the `OrderNo` from the message header.

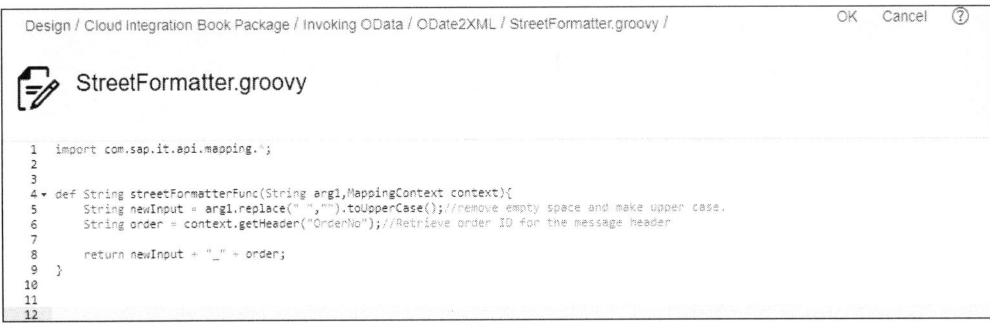

Design / Cloud Integration Book Package / Invoking OData / ODate2XML / StreetFormatter.groovy /
OK
Cancel
StreetFormatter.groovy
1 import com.sap.it.api.mapping.*;
2
3
4 def String streetFormatterFunc(String arg1,MappingContext context){
5 String newInput = arg1.replace(" ","").toUpperCase();//remove empty space and make upper case.
6 String order = context.getHeader("OrderNo");//Retrieve order ID for the message header
7
8 return newInput + "_" + order;
9 }
10
11
12

Figure 9.6 Adapted Code to Remove Empty Spaces and Turn the Text to Uppercase

9. Click on the **OK** button in the top-right corner of the screen in Figure 9.6.

10. Return to the mapping editor, and find the newly created **StreetFormatter** UDF under the **Custom** section, as shown in Figure 9.7.

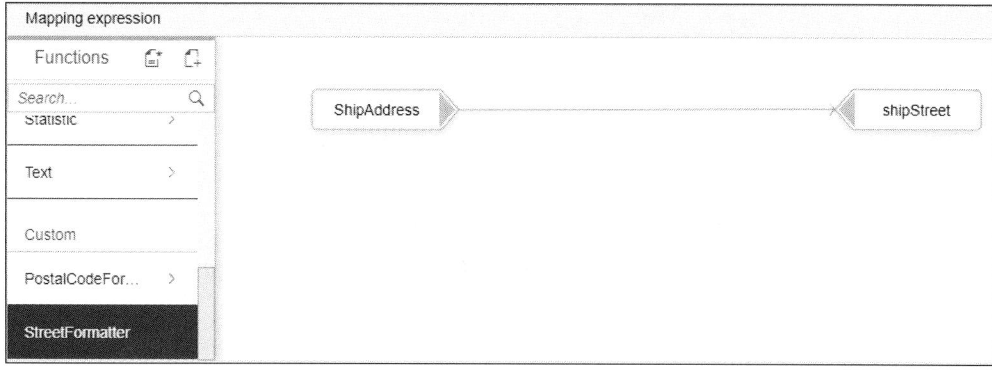

Figure 9.7 The Newly Created UDF Now Available in the Mapping

11. Click on the **StreetFormatter** UDF to see its method name. In our example, it's called **streetFormatterFunc** (see Figure 9.8). Note that the **streetFormatterFunc** comes from the name that we provided for the Groovy method in Figure 9.6.
12. Let's now use the new function by dragging it between **ShipAddress** and **shipStreet**, as shown in Figure 9.8.

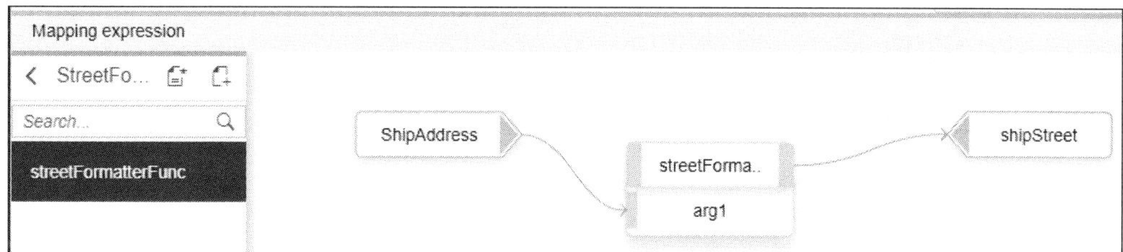

Figure 9.8 Inserting the UDF in Your Mapping Logic

13. Save and deploy the integration flow.
14. Test the service using SoapUI. You get a response with the field `shipStreet` without spaces, in uppercase, and prefixed with the order number, as shown in Figure 9.9.

```
<soap:Envelope xmlns:soap="http://schemas.xmlsoap.org/soap/envelope/">
   <soap:Header/>
   <soap:Body>
      <ns1:OrderShippingDetails_MT xmlns:ns1="http://hci.sap.com/demo">
         <orderNumber>10249</orderNumber>
         <customerName>Toms Spezialitäten</customerName>
         <shipCity>Münster</shipCity>
         <shipStreet>LUISENSTR.48_10249</shipStreet>
         <shipPostalCode>44087</shipPostalCode>
         <shipCountry>DE</shipCountry>
         <shipDate>1996-07-10T00:00:00.000</shipDate>
      </ns1:OrderShippingDetails_MT>
   </soap:Body>
</soap:Envelope>
```


Figure 9.9 Response Returned by the Integration Flow after Adding the UDF

You now know how to create a UDF that uses SAP Cloud Platform Integration Java APIs to perform transformation logic in a mapping. Let's now move to the next section where we look at using the script step in SAP Cloud Platform Integration.

9.4 Using the Script Step

SAP Cloud Platform Integration provides a script step that enables you to write different custom scripts to perform a wide range of activities and utilize the Java APIs that we explored earlier in Section 9.2. The scripting feature opens the door to the developer's imagination to do pretty much anything. Note, however, that scripting should be used with due diligence and caution to avoid unnecessary overheads and performance issues.

At the time of publishing this book, the script step supports Groovy and JavaScript. Groovy is a Java-syntax-compatible object-oriented programming language for Java platforms. To learn more about Groovy, go to *http://groovy-lang.org*.

JavaScript is a dynamic, weakly typed, prototype-based, and multiparadigm programming language for the Web. A large number of websites use it. To learn more about JavaScript, go to *www.w3schools.com/js*.

Both languages are relatively easy to learn, and there are plenty of resources on the Internet that you can use as reference.

SAP Cloud Platform Integration provides a Script API in a form of a JAR file. Using this JAR, a Java developer can easily import the library in his development tool of preference and inspect the provided methods. The Script API JAR can be downloaded from *https://tools.hana.ondemand.com/#cloudintegration*. On that web page, search for the **Using Script API** section, as shown in Figure 9.10. Then click on the **Download** link to save the JAR on your local file system.

Using Script API

The Script API enables Eclipse to display the provided methods in content assist. You need to download the Script API JAR and add it to your integration project's build path to enable usage of methods it provides in groovy scripts.

For detailed information on how to use the Script API, see Using Script API Methods in Groovy Scripts.

Script API JAR : Download

Figure 9.10 Where to Download the Scrip API JAR

At the time of publishing this book, the JAR file is called *cloud.integration.script.apis-1.36.1*.

To better illustrate the usage of the Script API, let's use a sample scenario in the next section.

9.4.1 Target Scenario

Let's reuse the example from Chapter 4, Section 4.3, to illustrate the use of the script step. In that example, we invoked an external OData service from our integration flow. Figure 9.11 shows the integration flow that was built for it.

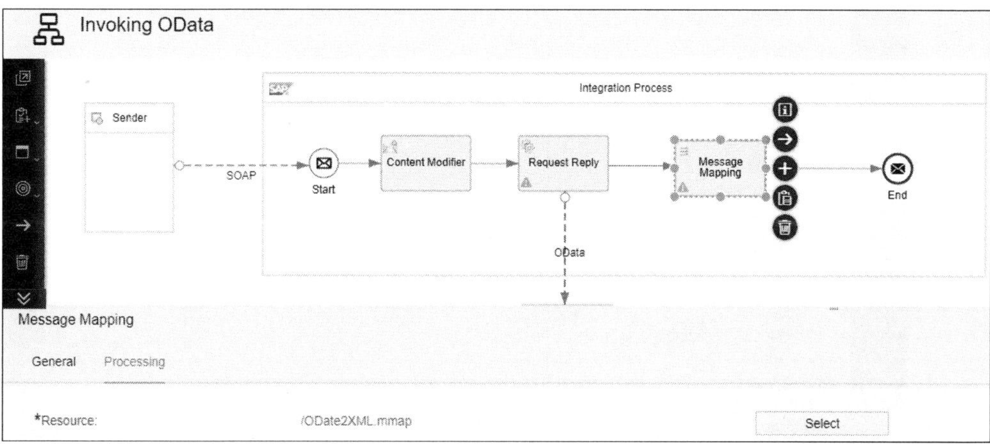

Figure 9.11 Invoking an OData Service

Imagine that the organization providing this integration flow is currently running a lucky draw on every incoming message. As an integration developer, you're requested to change the integration flow by generating a random number to be associated to each call. This random number will be used by your organization later to pick the lucky winner.

Keeping the solution simple, we can create a script that generates a random number and uses the API to save it as a message header.

9.4.2 Enhancing the Integration Flow

Let's now change our integration flow. Note that we won't detail every single step because you're already familiar with editing integration flows. Follow these steps:

1. From the **Design** section of the SAP Cloud Platform Integration Web UI, navigate to the correct package and integration flow.
2. In the opened integration flow, click on the **Edit** button.
3. Select a **Script** step from the palette (see Figure 9.12). You find this shape in the palette under **Message Transformers**.

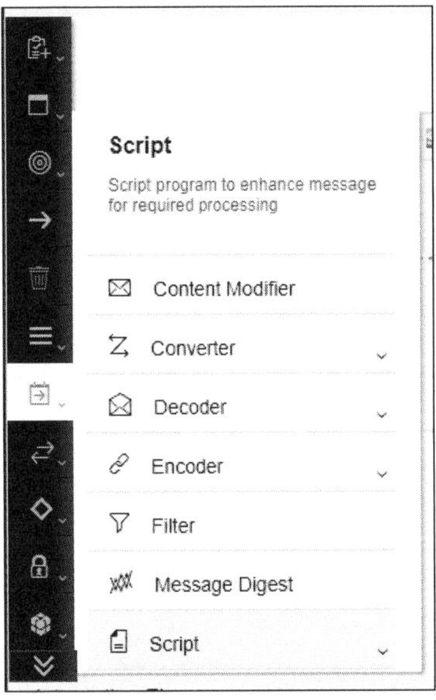

Figure 9.12 Adding the Script Step to the Integration Flow

4. Another menu appears from the palette with a choice of **JavaScript** or **GroovyScript**. Click on **GroovyScript** (see Figure 9.13).

Figure 9.13 Selecting GroovyScript from the Palette

5. Place it in your integration flow, right after the **Start** icon (✉).
6. The **Script Editor** automatically opens with some sample script, as shown in Figure 9.14. Note that this is the same editor that we used when creating a UDF in Section 9.3.

script1.groovy

Script Editor

```
/*
 The integration developer needs to create the method processData
 This method takes Message object of package com.sap.gateway.ip.core.customdev.util
which includes helper methods useful for the content developer:
The methods available are:
    public java.lang.Object getBody()
    public void setBody(java.lang.Object exchangeBody)
    public java.util.Map<java.lang.String,java.lang.Object> getHeaders()
    public void setHeaders(java.util.Map<java.lang.String,java.lang.Object> exchangeHeaders)
    public void setHeader(java.lang.String name, java.lang.Object value)
    public java.util.Map<java.lang.String,java.lang.Object> getProperties()
    public void setProperties(java.util.Map<java.lang.String,java.lang.Object> exchangeProperties)
       public void setProperty(java.lang.String name, java.lang.Object value)
 */
import com.sap.gateway.ip.core.customdev.util.Message;
import java.util.HashMap;
def Message processData(Message message) {
    //Body
       def body = message.getBody();
       message.setBody(body + "Body is modified");
       //Headers
       def map = message.getHeaders();
       def value = map.get("oldHeader");
       message.setHeader("oldHeader", value + "modified");
       message.setHeader("newHeader", "newHeader");
       //Properties
       map = message.getProperties();
       value = map.get("oldProperty");
       message.setProperty("oldProperty", value + "modified");
       message.setProperty("newProperty", "newProperty");
       return message;
}
```

Figure 9.14 Sample Code Included in the Groovy Script Editor

7. Change the `processData` method part of the script in Figure 9.14 to adapt the script to your requirements. In our case, we used the code shown in Figure 9.15. Note that the `processData` method takes a `Message` object as input and also returns a `Message`

object as an output. If you're a programmer, the script presented in Figure 9.15 is self-explanatory. It also includes comments in plain English for those less familiar with Groovy. The code generates a random number between 0 and 1000. The generated random number is then added as a message header named `LuckyNumber`. The Groovy Script in Figure 9.15 can be downloaded from the book homepage.

Cloud Integration Book Package / Invoking OData / script2.groovy / OK Cancel

script2.groovy

```
/*
 Generate a random numner and add it to the message header
 */
import com.sap.gateway.ip.core.customdev.util.Message;
import java.util.HashMap;
def Message processData(Message message) {

        //Generate a random Number
        int max = 1000;
        int min = 0;
        Random r = new Random();
        def value = r.nextInt((max - min) + 1) + min;
        //Properties
        map = message.getProperties();
        message.setHeader("LuckyNumber", value);

        return message;
}

```

Figure 9.15 Final Result of the Groovy Script

8. Click on the **OK** button in the top-right corner of Figure 9.15 to return to the integration flow. Figure 9.16 depicts the final look of the integration flow extended with the **Script** step.

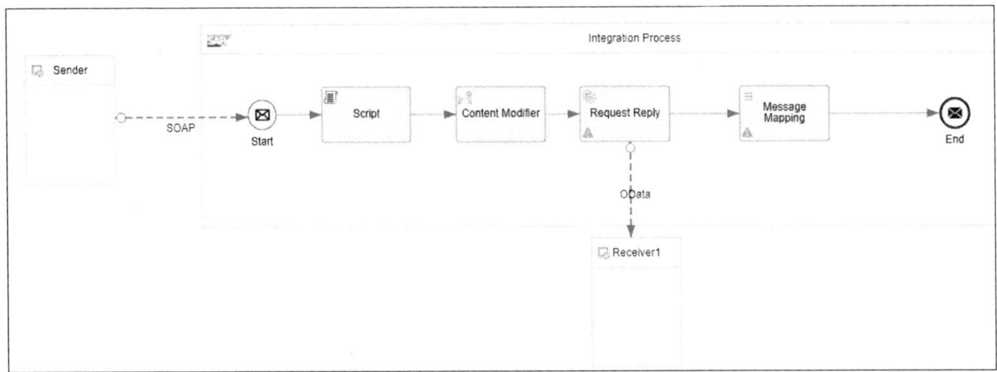

Figure 9.16 Enhanced Overview of the Integration Flow

9. Save and deploy the integration flow.

You're now ready to send a message via SoapUI. After you've triggered the message, the randomly generated number is returned in the header of the response message. Notice the `LuckyNumber` in the header section of the response in Figure 9.17 and Figure 9.18. This is exactly what we asked the script to do (see code in line 15 of Figure 9.16).

```
<soapenv:Envelope xmlns:soapenv="http://schema
   <soapenv:Header/>
   <soapenv:Body>
      <demo:OrderNumber_MT xmlns:demo="http://
         <orderNumber>10249</orderNumber>
      </demo:OrderNumber_MT>
   </soapenv:Body>
</soapenv:Envelope>
```

Figure 9.17 Returned Response Headers A

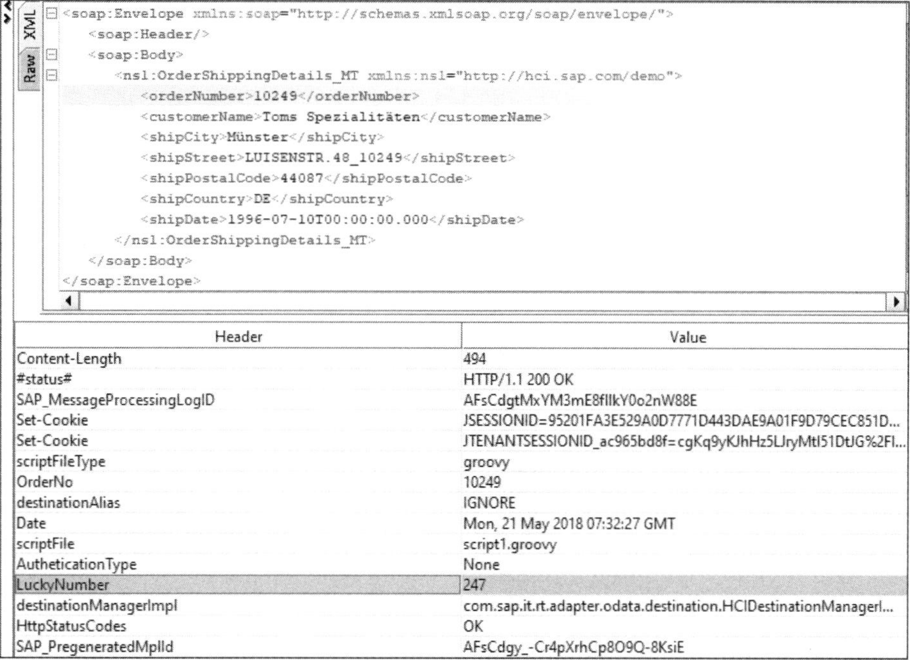

```
<soap:Envelope xmlns:soap="http://schemas.xmlsoap.org/soap/envelope/">
   <soap:Header/>
   <soap:Body>
      <ns1:OrderShippingDetails_MT xmlns:ns1="http://hci.sap.com/demo">
         <orderNumber>10249</orderNumber>
         <customerName>Toms Spezialitäten</customerName>
         <shipCity>Münster</shipCity>
         <shipStreet>LUISENSTR.48_10249</shipStreet>
         <shipPostalCode>44087</shipPostalCode>
         <shipCountry>DE</shipCountry>
         <shipDate>1996-07-10T00:00:00.000</shipDate>
      </ns1:OrderShippingDetails_MT>
   </soap:Body>
</soap:Envelope>
```

Header	Value
Content-Length	494
#status#	HTTP/1.1 200 OK
SAP_MessageProcessingLogID	AFsCdgtMxYM3mE8fIlkY0o2nW88E
Set-Cookie	JSESSIONID=95201FA3E529A0D7771D443DAE9A01F9D79CEC851D...
Set-Cookie	JTENANTSESSIONID_ac965bd8f=cgKq9yKJhHz5LJryMtI51DtJG%2FI...
scriptFileType	groovy
OrderNo	10249
destinationAlias	IGNORE
Date	Mon, 21 May 2018 07:32:27 GMT
scriptFile	script1.groovy
AutheticationType	None
LuckyNumber	247
destinationManagerImpl	com.sap.it.rt.adapter.odata.destination.HCIDestinationManagerI...
HttpStatusCodes	OK
SAP_PregeneratedMplId	AFsCdgy_-Cr4pXrhCp8O9Q-8KsiE

Figure 9.18 Returned Response Headers B

Congratulations, you can now use the **Script** step to perform different tasks using the APIs. Let's now move to discuss the OData API.

9.5 OData API

Besides the Java APIs, SAP Cloud Platform Integration also allows the developer to access various aspects of the platform using an OData API. The APIs are provided in the form of Representational State Transfer (REST) APIs that use the Open Data Protocol (OData) as a technical protocol. As a result, these APIs use the well-known HTTP methods of `GET`, `POST`, `PUT`, `FETCH`, and `DELETE`.

> **Note**
>
> Note that at the time of publishing this book, OData specification version 2.0 is supported by the SAP Cloud Platform Integration OData APIs. To read more about the OData V2 specification, go to *www.odata.org/documentation/odata-version-2-0.*

The OData APIs can be accessed using the HTTP URL of the form:

https://<host>/api/v1/<resource>?$<property1>=< property1_value>&$<property2>=< property2_value>

In this URL, note the following:

- *<host>*
  Represents the URL address of the tenant management node.
- *<resource>*
  Represents the path of the entity types to be called. Some entity resources are presented later in Table 9.4. For example, you can use the resource `MessageProcessingLogs` to address the message processing log (MPL).
- *<property1>*
  Represents the name of the property to be queried. For example, you can use the property `count` to return the total number of MPLs. It's always prefixed by the `$` symbol. Note that the property field is optional. Furthermore, you're able to add as many properties as you need by using the character `&` between them.

The OData APIs are protected by basic authentication (username and password) and require the API client to enable HTTP cookies. Furthermore, to use an API, you need to have the correct authorization group assigned to your user. Table 9.3 lists and describes the authorization groups needed for different API actions.

API Action	Authorization Group
Ability to display message overview	AuthGroup.Administrator or AuthGroup.IntegrationDeveloper
Undeploy integration content	AuthGroup.IntegrationDeveloper
Download a message	AuthGroup.BusinessExpert

Table 9.3 Required Authorization Groups and Description

The SAP Cloud Platform Integration OData APIs are structured around entity types or resources. Every entity type contains a number of properties. A property can also refer to another entity type, which means it's possible to start with one entity type and navigate to another entity type. Therefore, it's important to properly understand the entity types, their tasks, and their relationships with each other. Table 9.4 lists all available entity types and describes what they are used for.

Entity Types	Task Description
MessageProcessingLog	Reads an MPL
MessagePropcessingLogCustomHeaderProperty	Reads custom header properties of the MPL
MessageProcessingLogErrorInformation	Reads error information for a message
MessageProcessingLogAdapterAttribute	Reads adapter-specific attributes
MessageProcessingLogAttachment	Reads an MPL attachment
MessageStoreEntry	Reads a message from the message store
MessageStoreEntryProperty	Reads a header property of a message from the message store
MessageStoreEntryAttachment	Reads an attachment of a message from the message store

Table 9.4 Entity Types and Their Tasks

Entity Types	Task Description
MessageStoreEntryAttachment-Properties	Reads properties of message attachments from the message store
IntegrationRuntimeArtifact	Reads properties of deployed integration content
PartnerDirectory	Accesses the Partner Directory, creates entries, and helps manage them
LogFile	Accesses all current (nonarchived) log files
LogFileArchives	Accesses all archived log files

Table 9.4 Entity Types and Their Tasks (Cont.)

As an illustration of how each entity type relates to the others, Figure 9.19 depicts an entity model around the *MessageProcessingLogs* entity type to help you better grasp how to use the APIs related to the monitoring of message flows.

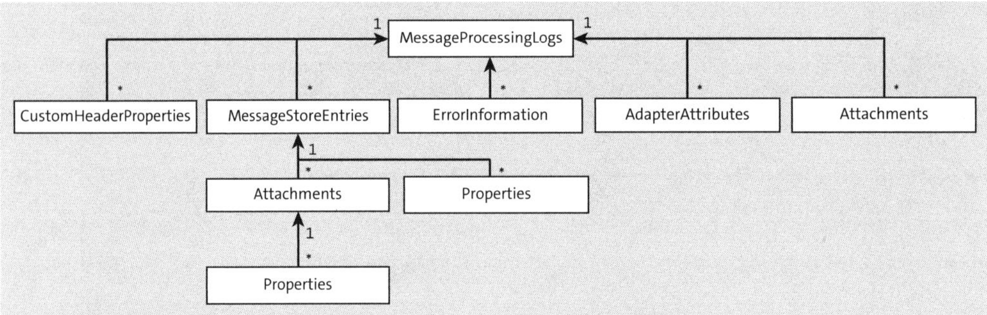

Figure 9.19 Entity Model Diagram for MessageProcessingLogs

As specified by the SAP documentation (here depicted in Figure 9.19), the `MessageProcessingLogs` contain a number of subentities, including `CustomHeaderProperties`, `MessageStoreEntries`, `ErrorInformation`, `AdapterAttributes`, and `Attachments`. Descriptions of what each subentity does are provided in Table 9.4.

Additionally, the OData APIs provided by SAP Cloud Platform Integration make use of common query options. These query options can be used on different entity types to perform specific actions on them. However, not all options are supported by each entity type. Table 9.5 describes some common query options.

Option	Description
`$filter`	Retrieves a set of entries based on the resource entity and the filter expression used in the Uniform Resource Identifier (URI)
`$metadata`	Retrieves the data model and structure of all resources
`$select`	Retrieves a subset of information on the entities identified by the resource path section of the URI
`$top`	Returns a subset of *n* top records from the resource used in the URI
`$count`	Returns the number of entries that matches the resource specified in the URI or the filter-specified criteria
`$inlinecount`	Indicates that the response contains a count of the number of entries in the collection of records identified by the resource path section of the URI
`$value`	Retrieves specific values of an entity resource specified by a Global Unique Identifier (GUID)
`$skip`	Skips *n* records in the collection returned according to the resource path section of the URI
`$expand`	Retrieves related and correlated entities for a given navigation property in line with the entities being retrieved
`$orderby`	Specifies the sorting of the returned collection by one or more values

Table 9.5 Commonly Used Query Options

Note

The OData API provided by SAP Cloud Platform Integration limits the number of entries in the response to a maximum of 1,000 entries for each call. This limitation feature protects the performance of the SAP Cloud Platform Integration runtime environment and avoids the negative consequences of queries returning huge amounts of data.

Queries with more than 1,000 entries are capped, and a **Next** link element is added to the response, which can be used to initiate the return of the additional entries.

Later in the chapter, we'll explore APIs and entities related to the following aspects:

- Monitoring MPL
- Deployed integration content
- Log files
- Message store
- Security material
- Partner Directory

The APIs listed can easily be tested and explored using the SAP API Business Hub. Let's discuss it next.

9.5.1 SAP API Business Hub

From the SAP Cloud Platform 1802 release, the OData APIs are documented in the SAP API Business Hub, which is the central catalog of all SAP and partner APIs for developers to build sample apps, extensions, and open integrations with SAP. The SAP API Business Hub landing page is at *https://api.sap.com*, as shown in Figure 9.20.

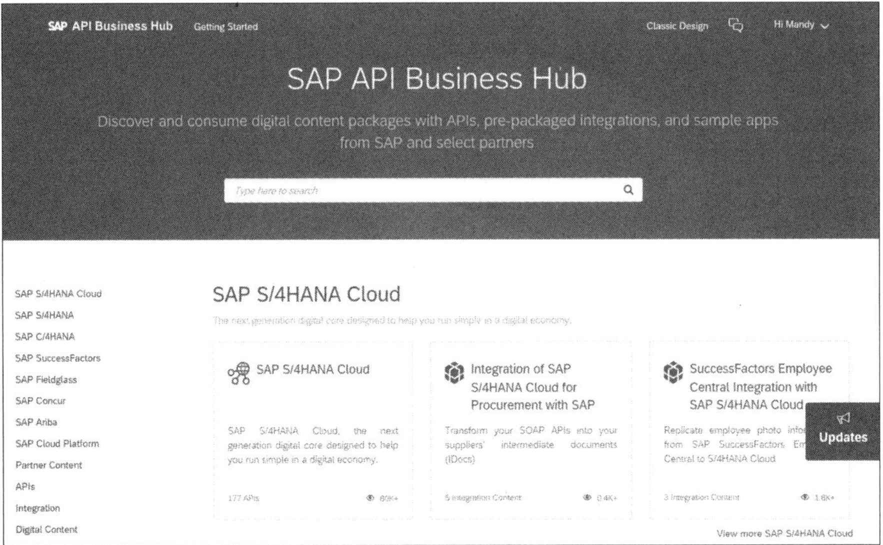

Figure 9.20 Landing Page of SAP API Business Hub

From the page presented in Figure 9.21, you can click on the **View more APIs** link to move to another page enabling you to select different packages (see Figure 9.22).

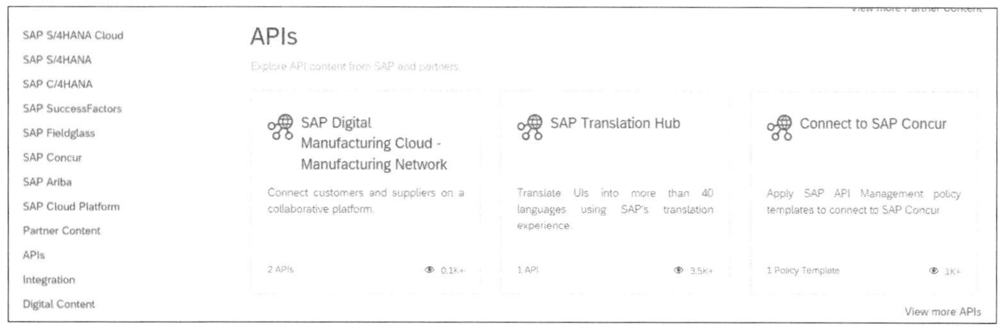

Figure 9.21 Landing Page of SAP API Business Hub, APIs Section

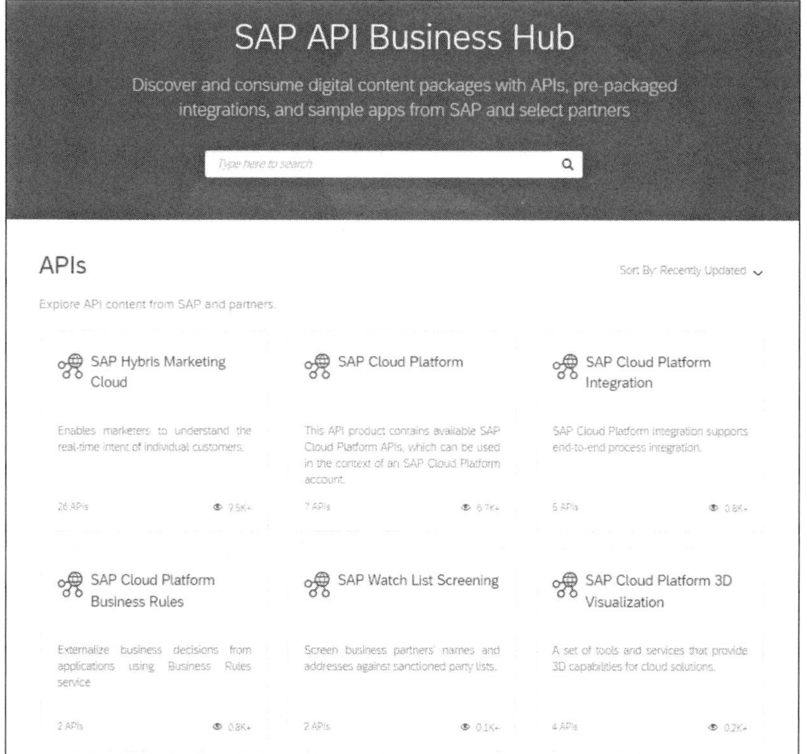

Figure 9.22 List of Available API Packages

Select the package called **SAP Cloud Platform Integration**. If you can't find it you can filter packages based on different categories to see a list of all possible APIs (see Figure 9.23).

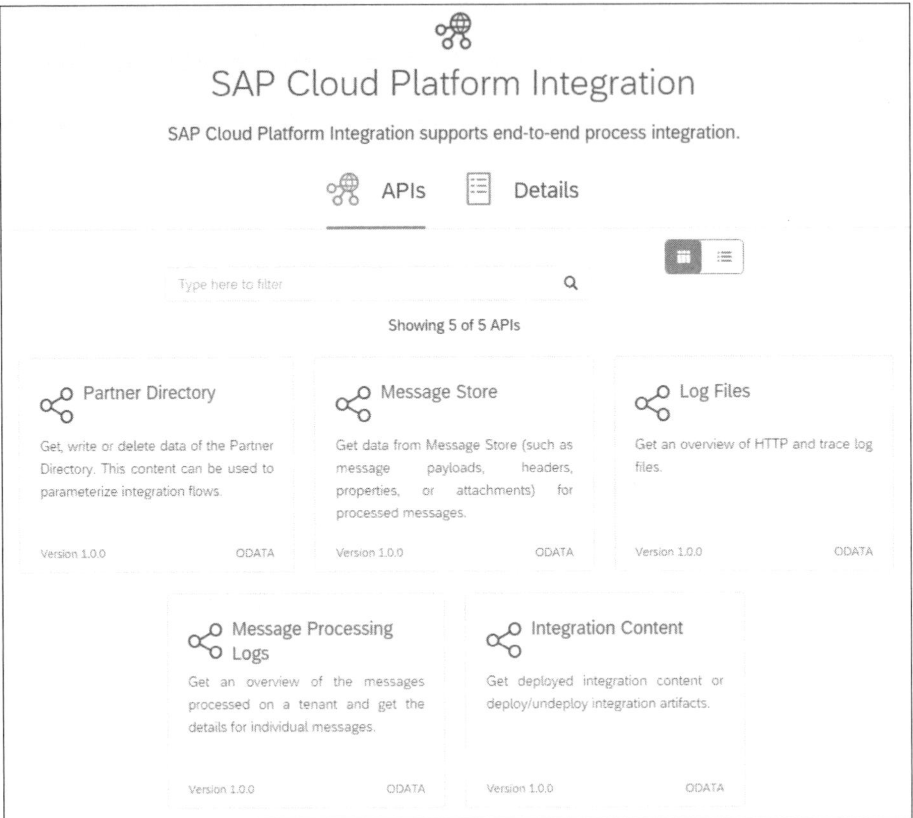

Figure 9.23 Artifacts of the OData APIs in the SAP Cloud Platform Integration Package

From the web page shown in Figure 9.23, you can explore the different APIs. Using the SAP API Business Hub, you can test and try out the different APIs directly without having to implement any code or use a third-party REST client such as Postman (*www.getpostman.com*). For APIs implementing the `GET` HTTP method, you can also use a simple browser.

The SAP API Business Hub has two different approaches to performing tests:

- API sandbox
- Your SAP Cloud Platform Integration tenant

Each of these two testing approaches are explored next.

API Sandbox

If you don't have access to a SAP Cloud Platform Integration tenant to test with, you can always use an API sandbox provided by SAP. The API sandbox is filled with test data and presents a quick way to get a feel for the way the APIs operate. Note that only operations using the GET method are supported in the API sandbox. Operations needing write access are forbidden because you need to log in before you can call operations requiring write access in the API sandbox.

For instance, let's use the Log Files API to illustrate testing using the API sandbox approach. For that, follow these steps:

1. Click on **Log Files** from the page presented earlier in Figure 9.23.
2. From the resulting page, select the **RESOURCE** tab. The page lists all operations of the API. Note that the **API Endpoint** field is automatically assigned with a sandbox-related URL.
3. Assuming we want to test the **LogFileArchives** API, we'll need to click on the **Show/Hide** link to the right of **LogFileArchives** (Figure 9.24).

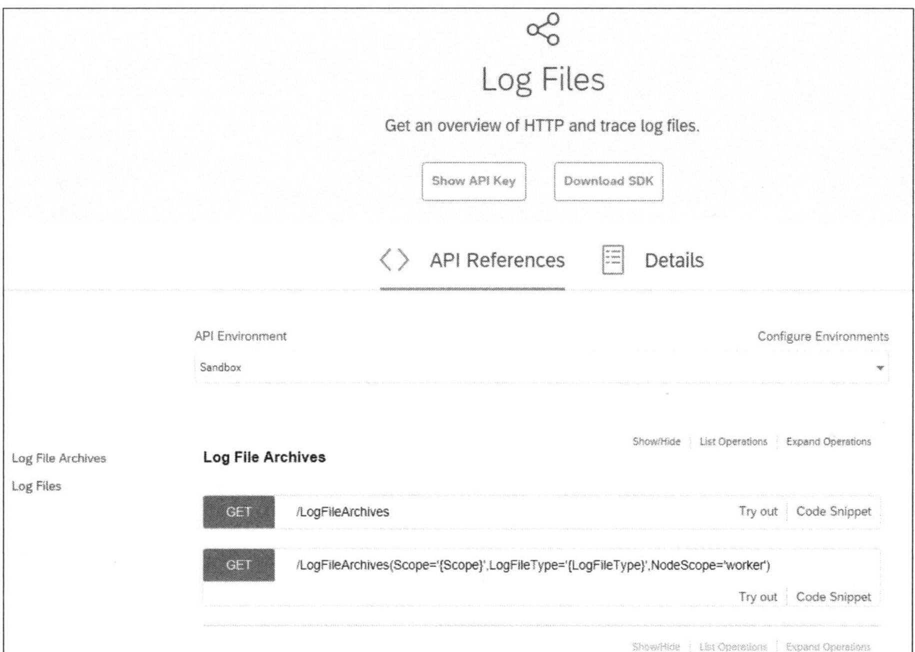

Figure 9.24 List of Entity Types Available for the Log Files API

4. From the resulting page, click on the GET button to the left of **/LogFileArchives**.
5. You get a page similar to the one presented in Figure 9.25. Click on the **Try it out!** button. Note that if your API requires input parameters, they will be listed in this page. You'll then need to fill in the required parameters as a minimum.

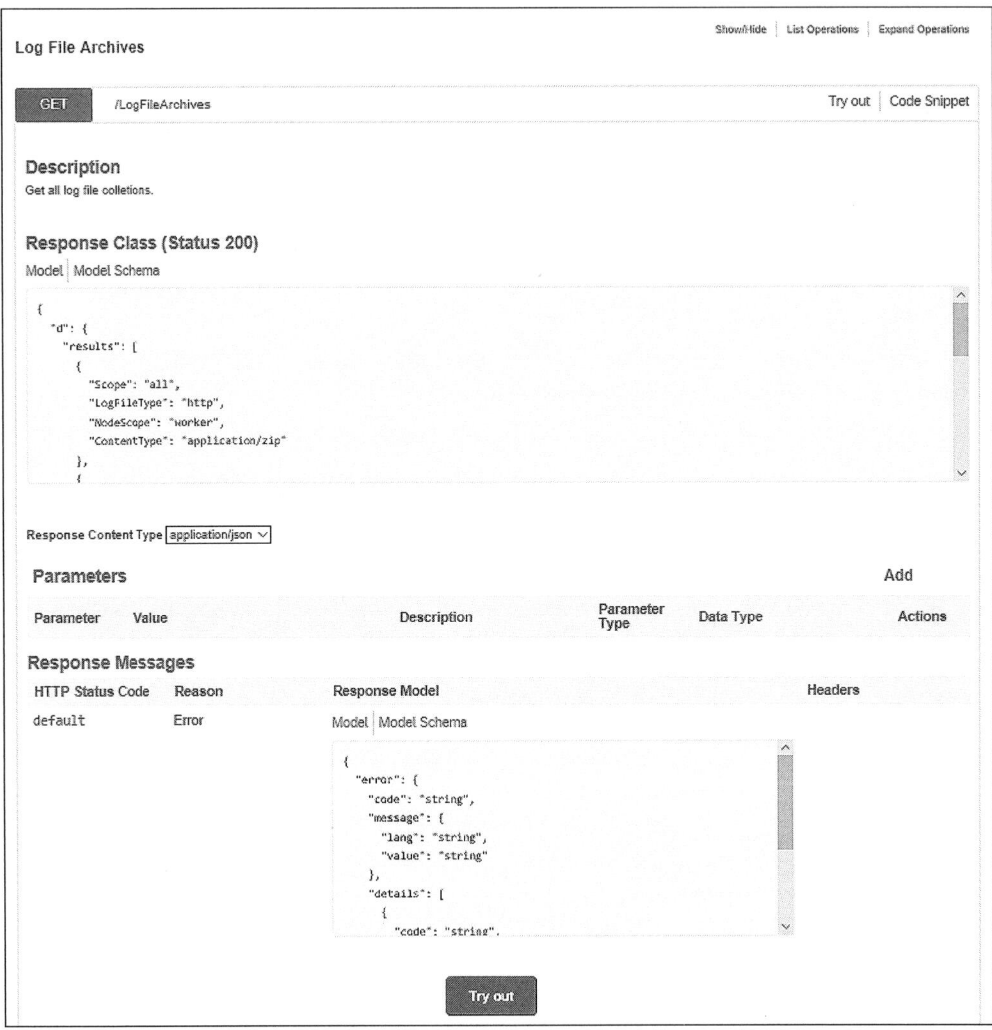

Figure 9.25 The SAP API Business Hub Try it Out! Page

From the page presented in Figure 9.25, a number of attributes and functionalities are available, as described in Table 9.6.

Properties	Description
Description	Describes the operation.
Parameters	Used to add the header or query parameters for the request message of the API.
Response Messages	Documents the possible response messages, including the different HTTP status codes and example response messages. After calling the API, both response body and response header are also returned.

Table 9.6 Properties in the SAP API Business Hub's Try It Out! Page

6. After clicking on the **Try it out!** button, a response header and body are returned on the page. Table 9.7 lists the functionalities and features available in the page shown in Figure 9.25.

Functionality	Description
Code Snippet	Retrieve the documentation and code snippet describing how to invoke this API. Currently a snippet in the following languages and technologies is supported: JavaScript, Java, Swift, Curl, ABAP, and SAPUI5 (see Figure 9.26). This snippet gives you a head start with your implementation without the need to start from scratch.
Download API	Download the API in one of the following formats: JavaScript Object Notation (JSON), YAML Ain't Markup Language (YAML), or Entity Data Model Designer (EDMX).
Show API Key	Use to retrieve the API key in the sandbox host URL to try out APIs.
Download SDK	Download a prepopulated Java Software Development Kit (SDK) for the API. Note that this is a full Java project that you can use.

Table 9.7 Functionalities in the SAP API Business Hub's Try It Out! Page

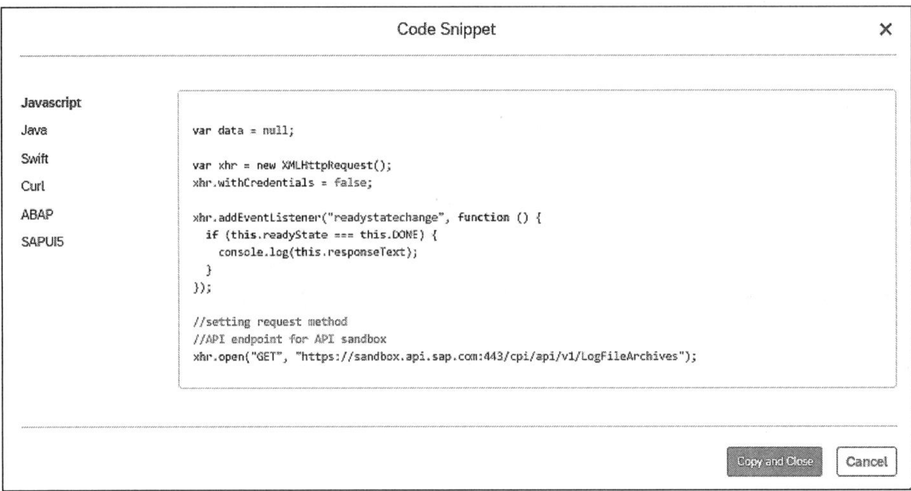

Figure 9.26 Code Snippet to Consume the API in Different Languages

Let's next look at how to configure the SAP API Business Hub to test against your own SAP Cloud Platform Integration tenant.

Your SAP Cloud Platform Integration Tenant

As previously discussed, SAP API Business Hub also makes it possible to test against your own tenant. For that, you'll need to configure SAP API Business Hub to point to your tenant by changing the API endpoint. Follow these steps:

1. Click on the **Configure Environments** link on the top-right top side of the page shown earlier in Figure 9.25.
2. If you're not already logged in, you're presented with a **Login Required** popup (Figure 9.27). Click on the **Login** button, and provide your credentials. If you're already logged in, proceed to step 4.

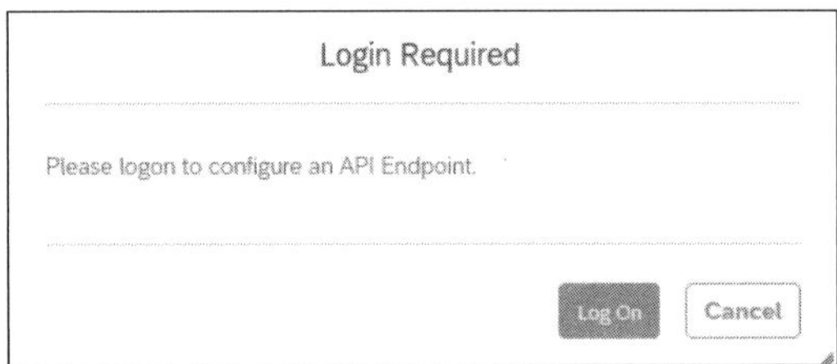

Figure 9.27 Login Page When Configuring the API Endpoint

3. You're redirected back to the main page again (refer to Figure 9.25). Click on the **Configure Environments** link one more time.
4. Select the region-specific host of your SAP Cloud Platform Integration tenant from the list presented in Figure 9.28 for the starting URL. You just need to compare your tenant URL with one of the entries presented in Figure 9.28 to find the right match.

   Enter a **Display Name for Environment**, **Account Short Name**, **SSL Host**, and your user credentials. Refer to Table 9.8 for more details about these attributes.

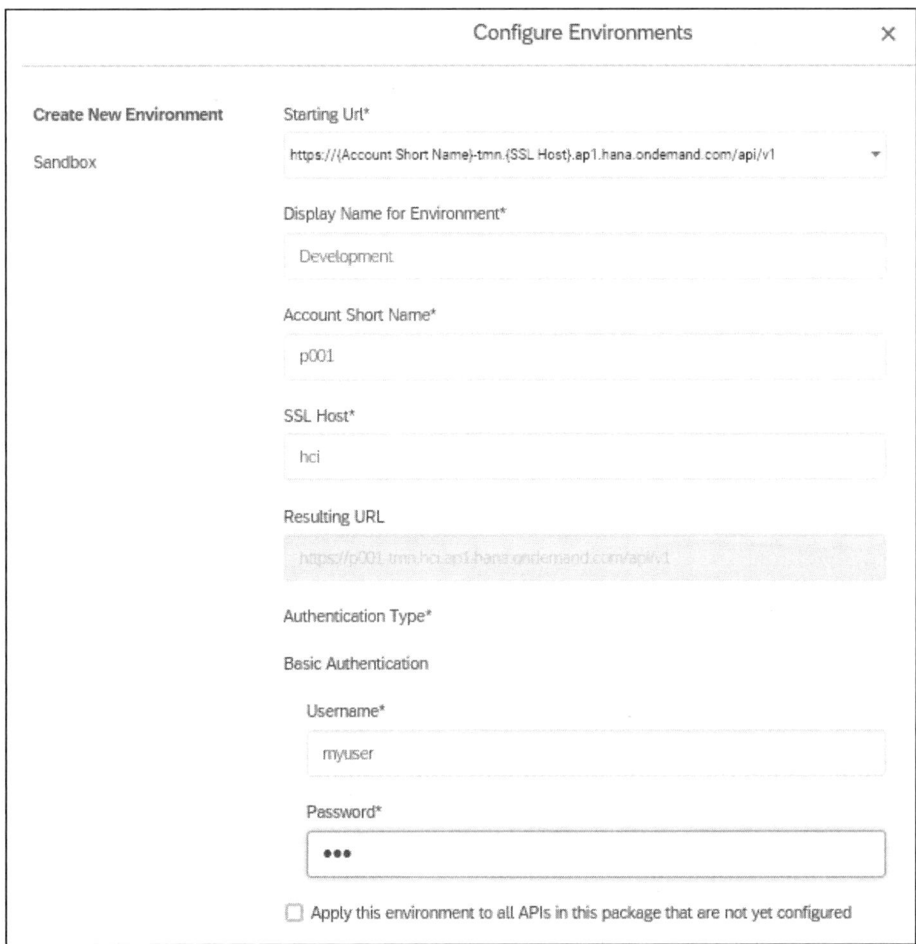

Figure 9.28 Selecting the Region of Your Tenant

Column	Description
Display Name for Environment	Enter a human-readable alias name. Example: Development, Test, or Acceptance.
Account Short Name	This is your tenant ID, which can be found between the // and `-tmn` in your tenant URL. The tenant URL is always of the format: *https://{Account Short Name} -tmn.{SSLHost}.{Region}.hana.ondemand.com.*
SSL Host	This can be retrieved from your tenant URL. The tenant URL is always of the format: *https://{Account Short Name}-tmn.{SSLHost}.{Region}.hana.ondemand.com.* Example: For *{SSL Host}*, use hci.
Username	The username of your SAP Cloud Platform Integration tenant account.
Password	The password of your SAP Cloud Platform Integration tenant account.

Table 9.8 Attributes of the Configure API Endpoint Page

And voila! From this point, you can perform the API calls against your own tenant. Let's now discuss the CSRF token handling in the next section.

9.5.2 Cross-Site Request Forgery Token Handling

Cross-site request forgery (CSRF or XSRF) is a type of security attack or malicious exploit that occurs when unauthorized commands are transmitted from a user that the web application trusts. CSRF exploits the trust that a site has in a user's browser, such as cookies associated with your bank.

Within the context of APIs, this means that a CSRF attacker can execute an action on the target application via an API without the knowledge and permissions of the consumer application. CSRF attacks have the following characteristics:

- They generally concern sites that rely on a user's identity.
- They exploit the site's trust in that identity.
- They trick the consumer application into sending HTTP requests to a target site.
- They involve HTTP requests that change application data.

To prevent CSRF attacks, some OData APIs provided by SAP Cloud Platform Integration require CSRF token validation. The CSRF token is mostly required for the APIs that need permission to write and change objects via the `POST`, `PUT`, and `DELETE` HTTP operations. There aren't enough pages in this book to go into the details of how CSRF tokens work, so for further reference, consult the many resources online, including *https://docs.spring.io/spring-security/site/docs/current/reference/html/csrf.html.*

When an API uses a CSRF token, calls made to the API without a CSRF are rejected. As a result, you need to retrieve a CSRF token first before invoking such an API. Let's now explore how to fetch a CSRF token.

You can use any API client of your choice, but for illustration purposes, we'll use Postman (*www.getpostman.com/*). You've already installed it from the scenario in Chapter 7. To retrieve the CSRF token, you'll need to use the following endpoint: *https://<TMN-host>/api/v1.*

Here, *TMN-host* represents the tenant host of SAP Cloud Platform Integration. As shown in Figure 9.29, select **GET** as the HTTP method, and specify the OData API endpoint. You also need to select **Basic Auth** and enter your credentials.

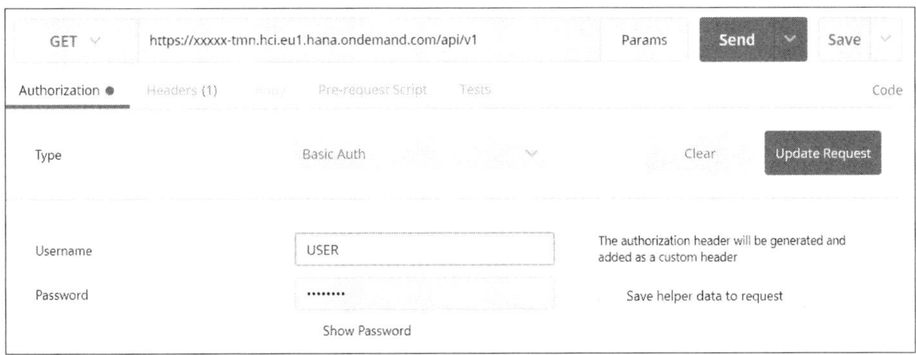

Figure 9.29 Configuring Endpoint and Authorization in Postman

In the **Headers** tab, add a new key named **X-CSRF-Token** with the value `Fetch` to request an X-CSRF token (Figure 9.30).

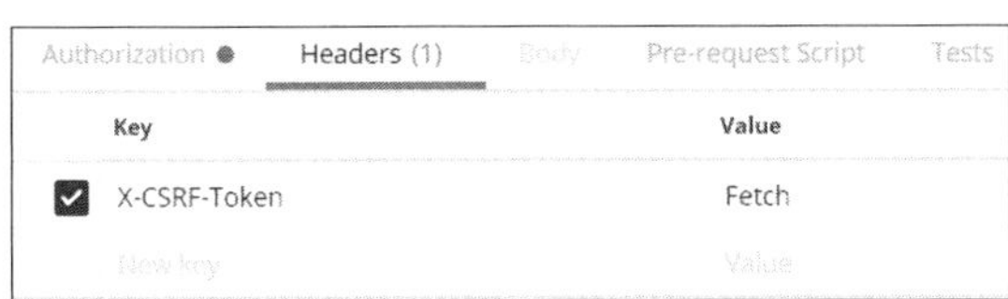

Figure 9.30 Adding the X-CSRF-Token Header

Click on the **Send** button (in top-right corner of Figure 9.29) to trigger the request. The response message includes a number of headers, including the CSRF token, which can be identify by X-CSRF-Token in the **Headers** tab (Figure 9.31).

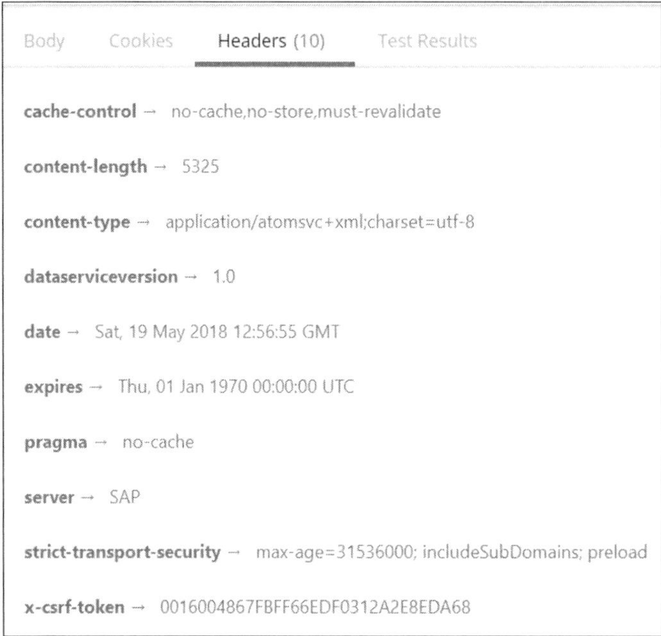

Figure 9.31 X-CSRF-Token in the Headers Tab

The value of the CSRF token can then be used in the header of your next OData API request. Furthermore, the body of the response message is filled with the list of entity types that the CSRF token can be used with. In other words, the scope of the CSRF token is limited to the entity types listed in the response (see Figure 9.32).

In the next sections, we explore the following different API categories:

- Monitoring message flows using the API
- Managing deployed integration content using the API
- Managing log files using the API
- Managing the message store using the API
- Managing security material using the API
- Managing the Partner Directory using the API.

Let's start with the message flow APIs.

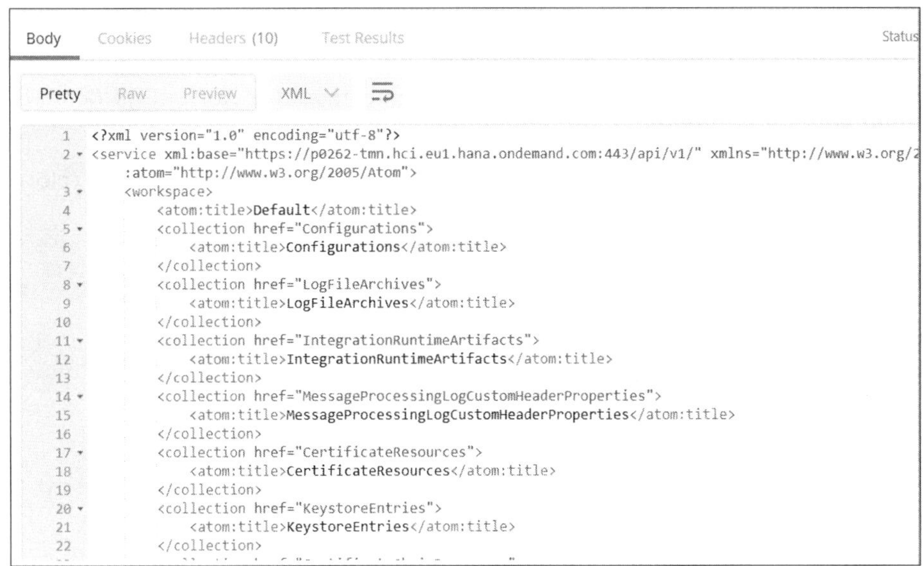

Figure 9.32 Response Body Associated with the X-CSRF Token

9.5.3 Monitoring Message Flows Using the API

When it comes to APIs related to monitoring message flows, the following entity types play a key role:

- `MessageProcessingLogs`
  Entity responsible for MPLs. This is the main and parent entity. From this entity, you can navigate to all other ones.
- `MessageProcessingLogAdapterAttributes`
  Encapsulates the adapter attributes of the MPL of a specified message entry. It includes details such as the type of adapter used in the related integration flow.
- `MessageProcessingLogAttachments`
  Contains attachments of the MPL related to a specified message entry.
- `MessageProcessingLogCustomHeaderProperties`
  Contains custom header properties of MPLs related to a specified message entry.
- `MessageProcessingLogErrorInformation`
  Contains error information for the message related to a specified message entry.

Many APIs are included in these entities. Describing all of them in detail would go beyond the scope of this chapter. However, you can find extensive details and examples in the SAP documentation at *https://help.sap.com/viewer/product/CLOUD_INTEGRATION/Cloud*. You can also explore these APIs via the SAP API Business Hub at *https://api.sap.com/shell/discover/contentpackage/CloudIntegrationAPI/api/MessageProcessingLogs*.

Figure 9.33 shows the entities and APIs available for MPLs. You can test and explore each one of them using the testing approach that was explored in Section 9.5.1.

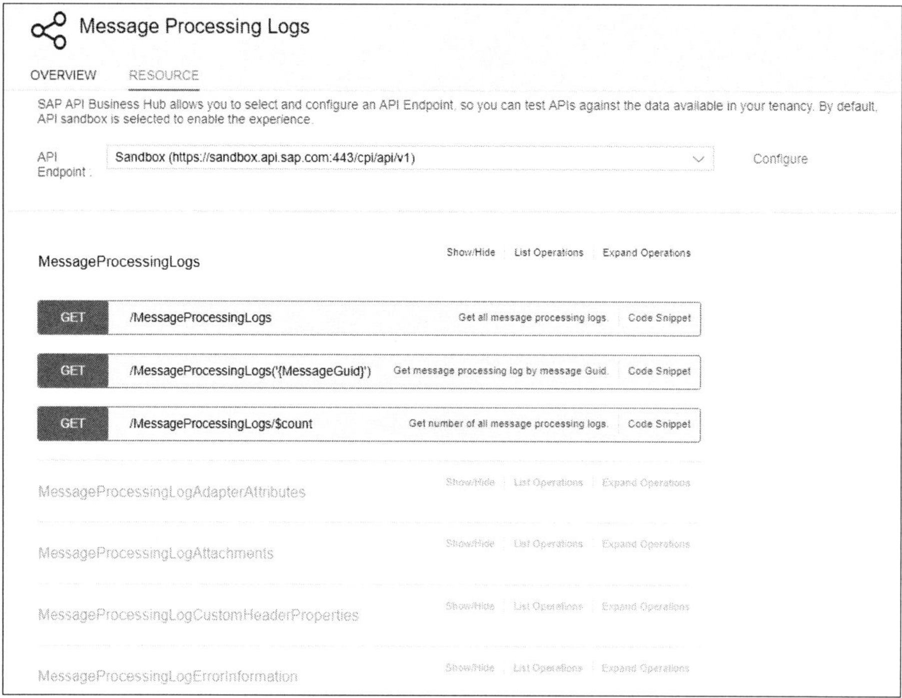

Figure 9.33 Entity Types and APIs in the MPLs

Let's use an example scenario to illustrate the usage and some of the functionalities of APIs related to the monitoring of message flows.

Assume that your organization uses many integration platforms, including SAP Process Orchestration, SAP Cloud Platform Integration, and other third-party platforms. You've been asked to build a custom dashboard monitoring solution to see, at one glance, statistics and lists of failing messages in the various integration platforms. The advantage of such a dashboard is that you don't need to log in to each of these platforms individually. You just need to log in to the custom dashboard, and you can see errors occurring in all integration platforms.

The question that comes to mind is how you can programmatically retrieve the information from the MPLs of SAP Cloud Platform Integration and find the entries with errors. This is where the Monitoring Message Flows APIs come to the rescue.

To solve this challenge, you need an API that retrieves all MPLs in error for the last hour. That requires us to use the `MessageProcessingLogs` entity. One potential solution is to use the OData endpoint:

https://<tenant>/api/v1/MessageProcessingLogs?$inlinecount=allpages&$filter=Status eq 'FAILED' and LogStart gt datetime'2018-04-29T12:00:00' and LogEnd lt datetime'2018-04-29T13:00:00'&$expand=AdapterAttributes

Let's examine this OData endpoint with the help of Table 9.9 to understand what's happening. (Note that some attributes used in Table 9.9 were also previously explained in Table 9.5.)

9

API Endpoint Element	Description	Example
`MessageProcessing-Logs`	Retrieves MPL entries.	`MessageProcessingLogs`
`inlinecount`	Indicates that the response should contain a count of the number of entries in the returned collection.	`allpages`
`filter`	Filters the result based on various criteria. As mentioned in the example columns, we're filtering all messages that have the status **Failed**. Additionally, we filter all message logs that have been created between 29/04/2018 at 12:00:00 and 29/04/2018 at 13:00:00.	`Status eq 'FAILED' and Log-Start gt datetime'2018-04-29T12:00:00' and LogEnd lt datetime'2018-04-29T13:00:00'`
`expand`	Retrieves correlated entities for a given navigation. In our case, we also want to retrieve adapter-specific attributes.	`AdapterAttributes`

Table 9.9 Attributes Included in OData Endpoint to Retrieve Entries with Errors

After calling the OData endpoint that solves our challenge, you get the response message presented in Listing 9.1.


```
<feed xmlns="http://www.w3.org/2005/Atom" xmlns:m="http://
schemas.microsoft.com/ado/2007/08/dataservices/metadata" xmlns:d="http://
schemas.microsoft.com/ado/2007/08/dataservices" xml:base="https://p0262-
tmn.hci.eu1.hana.ondemand.com:443/api/vl/">
<id>
https://p0262-tmn.hci.eu1.hana.ondemand.com:443/api/vl/MessageProcessingLogs
</id>
<title type="text">MessageProcessingLogs</title>
<updated>2018-04-29T12:58:12.413Z</updated>
<author>
<name/>
</author>
<link href="MessageProcessingLogs" rel="self" title="MessageProcessingLogs"/>
<m:count>1</m:count>
<entry>
<id>
https://p0262-tmn.hci.eu1.hana.ondemand.com:443/api/vl/
MessageProcessingLogs('Afrlv7POJUYGSI2bXJAGRQ74HMyP')
</id>
<title type="text">MessageProcessingLogs</title>
<updated>2018-04-29T12:58:12.413Z</updated>
<category term="com.sap.hci.api.MessageProcessingLog" scheme="http://
schemas.microsoft.com/ado/2007/08/dataservices/scheme"/>
<link href="MessageProcessingLogs('AFrlv7POJUYGSI2bXJAGRQ74HMyP')" rel="edit"
title="MessageProcessingLog"/>
<link href="MessageProcessingLogs('AFr1v7POJUYGSI2bXJAGRQ74tiHyP')/
CustomHeaderProperties" rel="http://schemas.microsoft.com/ado/2007/08/
dataservices/related/CustomHeaderProperties" title="CustomHeaderProperties"
type="application/atom+xml;type=feed"/>
<link href="MessageProcessingLogs('AFr1v7POJUYGSI2bXJAGRQ74HMyP')/
MessageStoreEntries" rel="http://schemas.microsoft.com/ado/2007/08/
dataservices/related/MessageStoreEntries" title="MessageStoreEntries" type=
"application/atom+xml;type=feed"/>
<link href="MessageProcessingLogs('AFrlv7POJUYGSI2bXJAGRQ74tiHyP')/
ErrorInformation" rel="http://schemas.microsoft.com/ado/2007/08/dataservices/
related/Errorinformation" title="Errorinformation" type="application/
```

```
atom+xml;type=entry"/>
<link href="MessageProcessingLogs('AFrlv7POJUYGSI2bXJAGRQ74HMyP')/
AdapterAttributes" rel="http://schemas.microsoft.com/ado/2007/08/dataservices/
related/AdapterAttributes" title="AdapterAttributes" type="application/
atom+xml;type=feed">
<m:inline>...</m:inline>
</link>
<link href="MessageProcessingLogs('AFrlv7POJUYGSI2bXJAGRQ74tiHyP')/
Attachments" rel="http://schemas.microsoft.com/ado/2007/08/dataservices/
related/Attachments" title="Attachments" type="application/atom+xml;type=
feed"/>
<link href="MessageProcessingLogs('AFrlv7POJUYGSI2bXJAGRQ74HMyP')/Runs" rel=
"http://schemas.microsoft.com/ado/2007/08/dataservices/related/Runs" title=
"Runs" type="application/atom+xml;type=feed"/>
<content type="application/xml">
    <m:properties>
                <d:MessageGuid>AFr1v7POJUYGSI2bXJAGRQ74HMyP</d:MessageGuid>
         <d:CorrelationId>AFr1v7MGmzLrpFr0xq0olvAcig5Y</d:CorrelationId>
        <d:ApplicationMessageId m:null="true"/>
        <d:ApplicationMessageType m:null="true"/>
        <d:LogStart>2018-04-29T12:50:59.723</d:LogStart>
        <d:LogEnd>2018-04-29T12:51:00.12</d:LogEnd>
        <d:Sender>Sender_SOAP</d:Sender>
        <d:Receiver m:null="true"/>
         <d:IntegrationFlowName>Invoking_OData</d:IntegrationFlowName>
        <d:Status>FAILED</d:Status>
        <d:AlternateWeblink>...</d:AlternateWeblink>
        <d:IntegrationArtifact m:type="com.sap.hci.api.IntegrationArtifact">
            <d:Id>Invoking_OData</d:Id>
            <d:Name>Invoking OData</d:Name>
            <d:Type>INTEGRATION_FLOW</d:Type>
        </d:IntegrationArtifact>
        <d:LogLevel>INFO</d:LogLevel>
        <d:CustomStatus>FAILED</d:CustomStatus>
</m:properties>
</content>
</entry>
</feed>
```


Listing 9.1 Response of the OData Endpoint Call

When examining the response message presented in Listing 9.1, you'll notice an element named entry, which represents a log entry in the message monitor. Note that if multiple entries are returned, they are sorted in descending order (with the oldest entry on the top) by default. The entries returned here can also be found in SAP Cloud Platform Integration' monitoring.

In addition, observe that the entry shown in Listing 9.1 has the MessageGuid with a value AFrlv7POJUYGSI2bXJAGRQ74HMyP. The same entry can also be found from the **Monitor Message Processing** section of SAP Cloud Platform Integration in Figure 9.34 next to the **Message ID** field. Also note that the response message has a field count, which specifies the number of returned entries. Furthermore, remember the field IntegrationFlowName, which has the value Invoking_OData and will be of use later in the chapter.

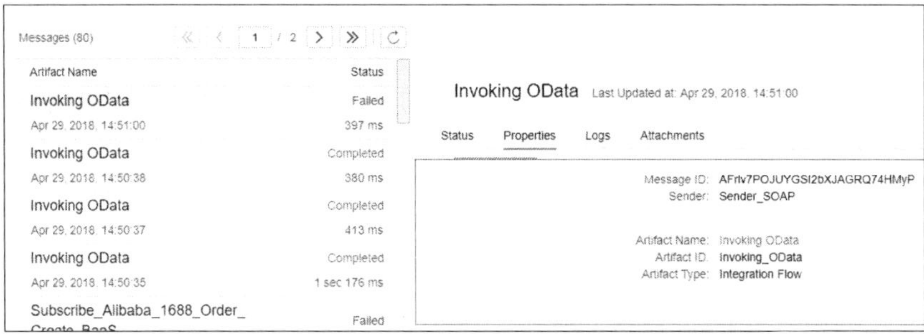

Figure 9.34 MPLs in SAP Cloud Platform Integration

The entry returned in the OData API call contains a number of properties as shown earlier in Listing 9.1. Table 9.10 lists the MessageProcessingLogs properties and their descriptions.

Property	Description
MessageGuid	GUID of the message that the processing log concerns.
CorrelationId	GUID of the correlated messages.
ApplicationMessageId	GUID specific to a particular application. Think about it as an identifier set for the sake of identification by an external application. This value can be set using a **Content Modifier** step and assigning a value to the SAP_ApplicationID header element.

Table 9.10 Properties of the MessageProcessingLogs

Property	Description
ApplicationMessageType	Property to represent a type of message as known by a business application. Use a **Script** step in the integration flow to set this property.
LogStart	Date and time that the writing of the log started.
LogEnd	Date and time that the writing of the log ended.
Sender	Identifier of the sender system.
Receiver	Identifier of the receiver system.
IntegrationFlowName	Name of the integration flow.
Status	Status of the message processing. Currently the following statuses are possible: **COMPLETED**, **PROCESSING**, **RETRY**, **ERROR**, **ESCALATED**, and **FAILED**.
AlternateWebLink	Link used to directly open the MPL on this monitoring entry.
IntegrationArtifact/Id	Technical name or ID of the integration flow.
IntegrationArtifact/Name	Name of the integration flow. This is identical to the IntegrationFlowName property.
IntegrationArtifact/Type	Type of artifact that this message processing concerns. Example: INTEGRATION_FLOW

Table 9.10 Properties of the MessageProcessingLogs (Cont.)

In the next sections, we carry on with our OData API journey by exploring APIs that relate to deployed integration content.

9.5.4 Managing Deployed Integration Content Using the API

Using the OData APIs provided by SAP Cloud Platform Integration, you can query the content of integration artifacts deployed on a tenant. The APIs that access the deployed integration content revolve around the following entity types:

- IntegrationRuntimeArtifact
  Manages all deployed integration artifacts in the tenant. It's also possible to use the POST method to deploy an artifact from the file system. Additionally, an already deployed artifact can be undeployed using the DELETE method.

- IntegrationRuntimeArtifactsErrorInformation
  Holds error information of a specific deployed integration artifact.
- CSRF Token Handling
  Holds the CSRF token for this session. The CSRF token is only required for write access (as discussed in Section 9.5.2).

There are too many APIs included in the preceding entities to discuss them all in this chapter. However, you can find extensive details and examples in SAP documentation at *https://help.sap.com/viewer/product/CLOUD_INTEGRATION/Cloud*. You can also explore these APIs via the SAP API Business Hub at *https://api.sap.com/shell/discover/contentpackage/CloudIntegrationAPI/api/IntegrationContent.*

Figure 9.35 shows the entities and APIs available. You can test and explore each one of them using the testing approaches that were explored in Section 9.5.1.

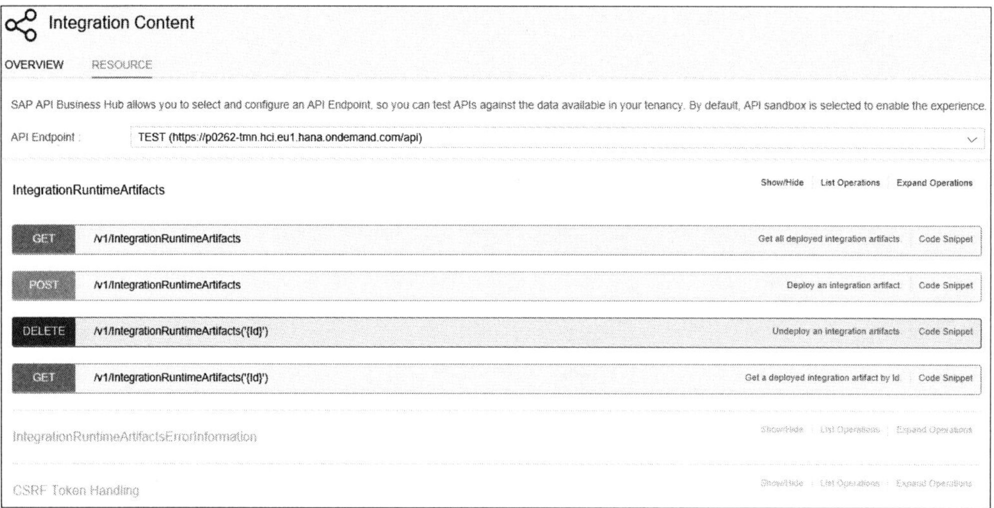

Figure 9.35 Entity Types and APIs Related to Deployed Integration Content

Let's further enhance the example scenario of Section 9.5.3 to illustrate the usage of functionalities related to deployed integration content. In the previous section, we retrieved an entry with error using the APIs of MPLs. Imagine that after retrieving and displaying the entry with error in your custom dashboard, you also want to see details of the related deployed integration content. You're interested to know the name, status, and version on the deployed content, as well as the user who deployed it and when.

To solve this challenge, you need to use the `IntegrationRuntimeArtifact` entity. One solution is to use the following OData endpoint: *https://<tenant>/api/v1/IntegrationRuntimeArtifacts('Invoking_OData')*

Note the value `Invoking_OData` was retrieved from the field `IntegrationFlowName` within the `content` node depicted in Listing 9.1.

The resulting response of the preceding OData endpoint is shown in Figure 9.36.


```
▼<entry xmlns="http://www.w3.org/2005/Atom" xmlns:m="http://schemas.microsoft.com/ado/2007/08/dataservices/metadata"
 xmlns:d="http://schemas.microsoft.com/ado/2007/08/dataservices" xml:base="https://p0262-tmn.hci.eu1.hana.ondemand.com:443/api/v1/">
  ▼<id>
     https://p0262-tmn.hci.eu1.hana.ondemand.com:443/api/v1/IntegrationRuntimeArtifacts('Invoking_OData')
   </id>
   <title type="text">IntegrationRuntimeArtifacts</title>
   <updated>2018-04-29T15:49:08.406Z</updated>
   <category term="com.sap.hci.api.IntegrationRuntimeArtifact" scheme="http://schemas.microsoft.com/ado/2007/08/dataservices/scheme"/>
   <link href="IntegrationRuntimeArtifacts('Invoking_OData')" rel="edit" title="IntegrationRuntimeArtifact"/>
   <link href="IntegrationRuntimeArtifacts('Invoking_OData')/$value" rel="edit-media" type="application/octet-stream"/>
   <link href="IntegrationRuntimeArtifacts('Invoking_OData')/ErrorInformation"
   rel="http://schemas.microsoft.com/ado/2007/08/dataservices/related/ErrorInformation" title="ErrorInformation"
   type="application/atom+xml;type=entry"/>
   <content type="application/octet-stream" src="IntegrationRuntimeArtifacts('Invoking_OData')/$value"/>
  ▼<m:properties>
     <d:Id>Invoking_OData</d:Id>
     <d:Version>1.0.0</d:Version>
     <d:Name>Invoking OData</d:Name>
     <d:Type>INTEGRATION_FLOW</d:Type>
     <d:DeployedBy>S0011540061</d:DeployedBy>
     <d:DeployedOn>2018-04-28T21:11:25.951</d:DeployedOn>
     <d:Status>STARTED</d:Status>
   </m:properties>
 </entry>
```


Figure 9.36 Response of the OData Endpoint Call

Note that every `<entry>` element returned in the response of Figure 9.36, represents an artifact in SAP Cloud Platform Integration. In our case, we only have one entry returned. The `properties` element of the response message of Figure 9.36 includes a number of attributes to describe the deployed integration content. These properties are listed and described in Table 9.11.

Attributes	Description
`Id`	Technical identification of the integration content.
`Version`	Latest version of the integration content when deployed.
`Name`	Name of the integration
`Type`	Type of artifact that this message processing concerns. Possible values include `INTEGRATION_FLOW`, `VALUE_MAPPING`, `DATA_INTEGRATION`, and `ODATA_SERVICE`.
`DeployedBy`	Name of the user who deployed the content.

Table 9.11 Properties Available for the Deployed Integration Content OData API

Attributes	Description
`DeployedOn`	Date and time that the integration content was last deployed.
`Status`	Current status of deployed integration content. Possible values include `STARTED`, `STARTING`, and `ERROR`.

Table 9.11 Properties Available for the Deployed Integration Content OData API (Cont.)

In the next section, we explore APIs that relate to log files.

9.5.5 Managing Log Files Using the APIs

Using the OData APIs provided by SAP Cloud Platform Integration, you can query log files on a tenant. Note that there are two types of log files:

- **Default trace**
  These log files include processing information of a technical nature.
- **HTTP access logs**
  These log files include information about all inbound HTTP requests arriving in SAP Cloud Platform Integration.

The APIs that facilitate the access to log files revolve around two main entity types:

- `LogFileArchives`
  Used for all archived log files.
- `LogFiles`
  Used for all current (nonarchived) log files.

These entities include a number of APIs. We won't explore them all in this section, but we'll look at a scenario to showcase what's possible. To get a full description of the different APIs, refer to the SAP documentation at *https://help.sap.com/viewer/product/CLOUD_INTEGRATION/Cloud*. You can also explore these APIs via the SAP API Business Hub at *https://api.sap.com/shell/discover/contentpackage/CloudIntegrationAPI/api/LogFiles*.

Figure 9.37 shows the entities and APIs available. You can test and explore each one of them using the testing approaches we explored in Section 9.5.1.

Let's use the example scenario to illustrate the usage of functionalities relating to log files. In Section 9.5.3, we retrieved an entry with an error using the MPL API. Imagine that you want to further troubleshoot the error from your custom dashboard. For that, you need to download a copy of all log files of type HTTP around the time period that the error occurred. Note that the error occurred around 12:51 based on the `LogStart` field shown earlier in Listing 9.1.

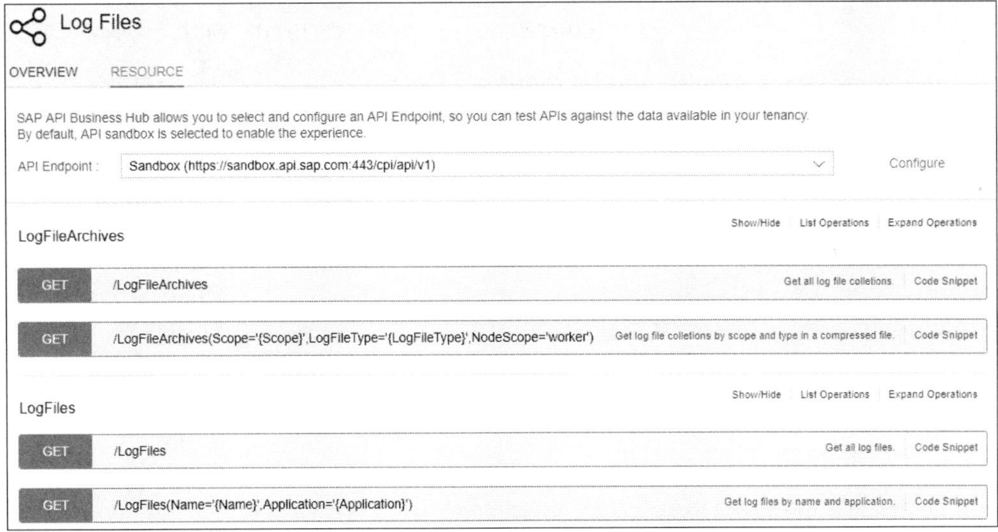

Figure 9.37 Entity Types and APIs Related to Log Files

To solve this challenge, we can use the `LogFileArchives` entity by invoking the following OData endpoint:

https://<tenant>/api/v1/LogFileArchives(Scope='all',LogFileType='http',NodeScope='worker')/$value?modifiedAfter=2018-04-29T12:50:00Z

Let's now examine this OData endpoint to understand what is happening with the help of Table 9.12.

Endpoint Attribute	Description
`LogFileArchives`	Entity used to retrieve an archived log file.
`Scope`	Indicates which scope/type of log files you want to download. Possible values include `all` to download all existing HTTP log files, and `latest` to only retrieve the latest HTTP log files.
`LogFileType`	Filters the result based on the type of log file. Possible values include `http` and `Trace`.

Table 9.12 Attributes Included in the OData Endpoint to Log Archive Entries

Endpoint Attribute	Description
NodeScope	Specifies that we're only interested to retrieve log files from runtime nodes (also referred to as worker nodes).
value	Specifies that the next parameters in the URL will contain parameter values.
modifiedAfter	Specifies the time after which the filtered log file was changed.

Table 9.12 Attributes Included in the OData Endpoint to Log Archive Entries (Cont.)

Note that you need to have the role `IntegrationOperationServer.read` assigned to your user to call log file APIs.

In the next section, we'll explore APIs that relate to the message store.

9.5.6 Managing Message Store Entries Using APIs

Using the OData APIs provided by SAP Cloud Platform Integration, we can access the tenant's message store entries. In scenarios with the requirement to persist messages, message content can be written and saved in the message store using the **Persist Message** step of an integration flow. You can then access the stored message and analyze it at a later point in time. However, note that a message is stored on the runtime node for 90 days. After this time, the message is automatically deleted.

For each entry of the message store, you can retrieve its properties, headers, payload, and attachments. The APIs that access message store revolve around four main entity types:

- `MessageStoreEntries`
  Used to manage message store entries.
- `MessageStoreEntryProperties`
  Used to manage properties of message store entries.
- `MessageStoreEntryAttachments`
  Used to manage attachments from a specific message store entry.
- `MessageStoreEntryAttachmentProperties`
  Used to manage properties of an attachment in the message store.

Referring to the entity model diagram presented earlier in Figure 9.19, notice that there is a direct relationship between a message store entry (represented by the entity type `MessageStoreEntries`) and `MessageProcessingLogs`. This relationship means that for every entry in the processing log with an attachment, you can try to retrieve its related message store entries (if available).

In this section, we're not going to explore all APIs included in the entities listed, but we'll look at a scenario to showcase what is possible. To get a full description of the different APIs, refer to the SAP documentation at *https://help.sap.com/viewer/product/CLOUD_INTEGRATION/Cloud*. You can also explore these APIs via the SAP API Business Hub at *https://api.sap.com/shell/discover/contentpackage/CloudIntegrationAPI/api/MessageStore*.

Figure 9.38 shows the entities and APIs available. You can test and explore each one of them using the testing approaches we explored in Section 9.5.1.

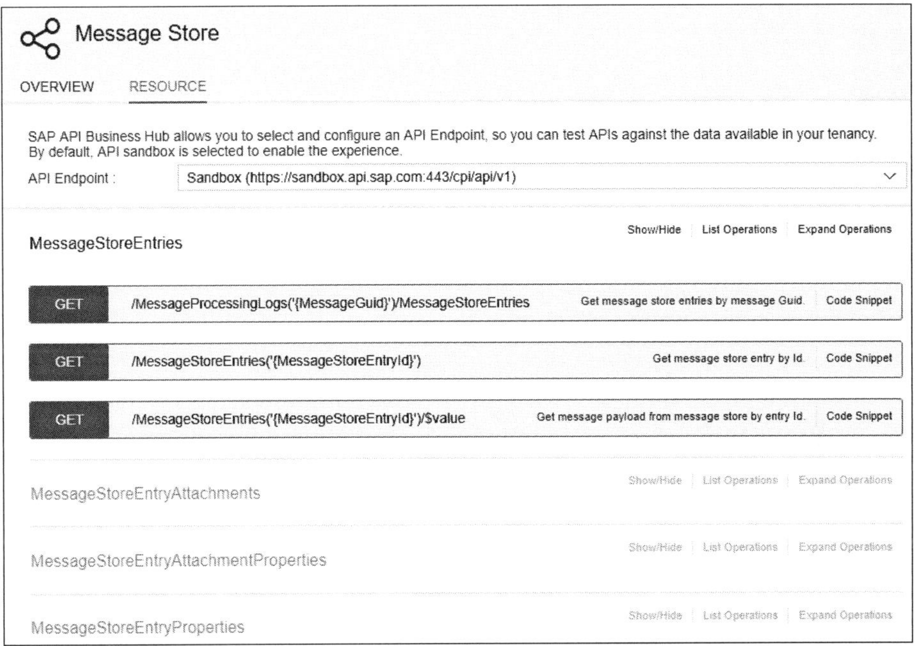

Figure 9.38 Entity Types and APIs Related to the Message Store

Note that you need to have the role `esbmessagestorage.read` assigned to your user to call message store APIs.

Consider the message aggregation scenario that we explored in Chapter 4, Section 4.6. In that scenario, we aggregated correlated messages. Imagine that after the aggregation is finished, we want to persist the final aggregated payload in the message store. We can write the payload to the message store using the **Persist Message** step to our integration flow.

To achieve that, follow these steps:

1. In the **Design** section of SAP Cloud Platform Integration, open the integration flow that you created in Chapter 4, Section 4.6.
2. Switch to edit mode by using the **Edit** button in the top-right corner of the integration flow screen.
3. Add the **Persist Message** step to the integration flow. The **Persist** step can be found in the palette on the left, as shown in Figure 9.39.

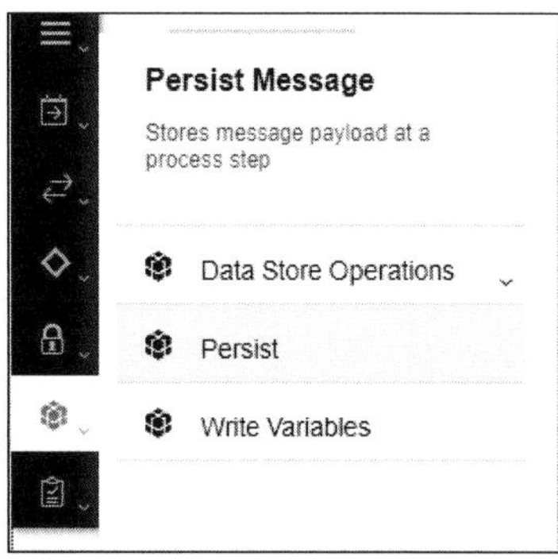

Figure 9.39 Selecting the Persist Step from the Palette

4. Ensure that the **Step ID** of the newly added step is unique. The final integration flow should look like the one presented in Figure 9.40 and Figure 9.41. Note that according to our integration flow, the message store is only populated after all messages have been collected because the **Persist** step comes after the **Aggregator** step.

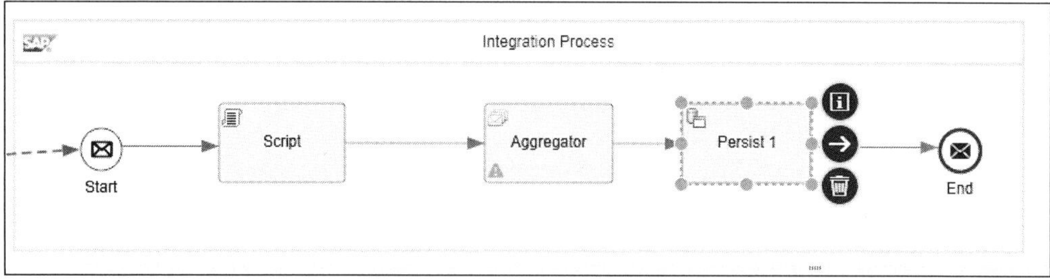

Figure 9.40 Overview of the Integration Flow Extended with a Persist Step A

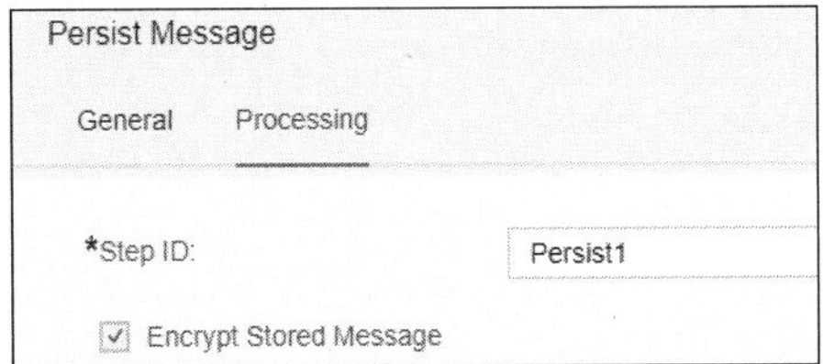

Figure 9.41 Overview of the Integration Flow Extended with a Persist Step B

5. Save and deploy the integration flow.

Now let's assume that in your custom dashboard application that you started building in Section 9.5.3, you want to be warned if a failed message flow contains entries in the message store. In such a case, you can retrieve the payload of the entry in the message store.

To retrieve the payload of the entry in the message store, you'll need to call a number of OData APIs in a particular sequence:

1. Use `MessageProcessingLogs` to retrieve the list of failing messages. You already know how to query for failing messages from our discussion in Section 9.5.3.
2. Use the message `Guid` of the message retrieved from the first call to make a second call to query if there are message store entries for messages with the specified message `Guid`. For that, the following endpoint can be used:

   https://<tenant>/api/v1/MessageProcessingLogs('<Guid>')/MessageStoreEntries

   The response of the API call is shown in Listing 9.2.

```
<content type="application/octet-stream" src="MessageStoreEntries("sap-it-
res%3Amsg%3Aac965bd8f%3Abe694f69-73a5-4430-b681-1673c963fd4c")/$value"/>
```

   Listing 9.2 Response of the OData API Call

3. Retrieve the payload of the entry in the message store. Looking at the entry returned in Listing 9.2, notice the `src` attribute of the `content` element. The value of this attribute provides details regarding how we can retrieve the payload. In this example, we can use the following link to retrieve the payload:

   https://<tenant>/api/v1/MessageStoreEntries('sap-it-res%3Amsg%3Aac965bd8f%3Abe694f69-73a5-4430-b681-1673c963fd4c')/$value

   Note that in this URL, the value between */v1/* and */$value* is copied from the `src` attribute of Listing 9.2. The API returns the aggregated payload as depicted in Figure 9.42.

```xml
<?xml version="1.0" encoding="UTF-8"?><multimap:Messages xmlns:multimap="http://sap.com/xi/XI/SplitAndMerge"><multimap:Message1>
<OrderItem xmlns:demo="http://hci.sap.com/demo" xmlns:soapenv="http://schemas.xmlsoap.org/soap/envelope/">
        <orderNumber>AA2345</orderNumber>
        <Item>
           <ItemNo>1</ItemNo>
           <Quantity>1</Quantity>
           <Unit>1</Unit>
           <LastStatus>false</LastStatus>
        </Item>
     </OrderItem><OrderItem xmlns:demo="http://hci.sap.com/demo" xmlns:soapenv="http://schemas.xmlsoap.org/soap/envelope/">
        <orderNumber>AA2345</orderNumber>
        <Item>
           <ItemNo>2</ItemNo>
           <Quantity>5</Quantity>
           <Unit>1</Unit>
           <LastStatus>false</LastStatus>
        </Item>
     </OrderItem><OrderItem xmlns:demo="http://hci.sap.com/demo" xmlns:soapenv="http://schemas.xmlsoap.org/soap/envelope/">
        <orderNumber>AA2345</orderNumber>
        <Item>
           <ItemNo>3</ItemNo>
           <Quantity>25</Quantity>
           <Unit>1</Unit>
           <LastStatus>true</LastStatus>
        </Item>
     </OrderItem></multimap:Message1></multimap:Messages>
```


Figure 9.42 Aggregated Payload Returned by the Message Store API

Now that you know how to use the message store API, let's explore the OData APIs related to security materials.

9.5.7 Managing Security Material Using the API

Using the OData APIs provided by SAP Cloud Platform Integration, we can access the tenant's keystore (X.509 certificates and key pairs). This API contains a lot of features that can't all be explored in this section.

To get a full description of the different APIs, refer to the SAP documentation via *https://help.sap.com/viewer/product/CLOUD_INTEGRATION/Cloud.*

To give you an impression of how to use them, let's work with a sample scenario to illustrate its usage. Assume that you want your keystore entries to be automatically backed up at the end of each month. Given that you don't want to perform this activity manually every month, you're looking for ways to automate the process via your custom dashboard application.

You can easily achieve this automation task by getting your custom application to call the Security Material API. To be more specific, there is an API that enables you to back up all keystore entries via the endpoint: *https://<tenant>/api/v1/KeystoreResources.*

Note that you'll need to use a `POST` method for this request. Listing 9.3 shows an example request. It's also possible to include the query option indicated in Table 9.13 on the request.

```
{"Name":"backup_admin_system"}
```

Listing 9.3 Example Request Body to Back Up Keystore Entries

Query Option	Description
returnKeystoreEntries	Possible values include true and false. When set to true, the KeystoreEntry instances that have been backed up are returned in the response. Note that this is an optional query that is defaulted to false.

Table 9.13 Possible Query Option for Renaming an Alias

Because the keystore OData API is protected against CSRF attacks, you first have to fetch an X-CSRF token before you can make this API call. We've already explored how to Fetch X-CSRF token in Chapter 7, Section 7.4.3.

Let's now explore APIs that relate to managing the Partner Directory in the next section.

9.5.8 Managing the Partner Directory Using the API

Chapter 7, Section 7.4 discussed and explained the notion of the tenant Partner Directory. We explained that during a business-to-business (B2B) project, the SAP Cloud Platform Integration owner might decide to build an application where the partners involved in the scenario can maintain their specific configuration data.

As things stand at the time this book is published, Partner Directory information can only be maintained via the OData API. The HTTP addresses required to make outbound calls to the partner systems are examples of the type of data stored in the Partner Directory.

Assuming that the Partner Directory notions are clear to you, we'll now focus on the usage of the Partner Directory OData APIs provided by SAP Cloud Platform Integration. These APIs access the Partner Directory, create entries, and help manage them. The APIs revolve around the following entity types:

- AlternativePartners
- AuthorizedUsers
- BinaryParameters
- Partners

- `StringParameters`
- `UserCredentialParameters`
- `CSRF Token Handling`

Updated details about these APIs can be found via the API Business Hub at *https://api.sap.com/api/PartnerDirectory*.

Figure 9.43 shows the entities and APIs available. You can test and explore each one of them using the testing approaches we explored in Section 9.5.1.

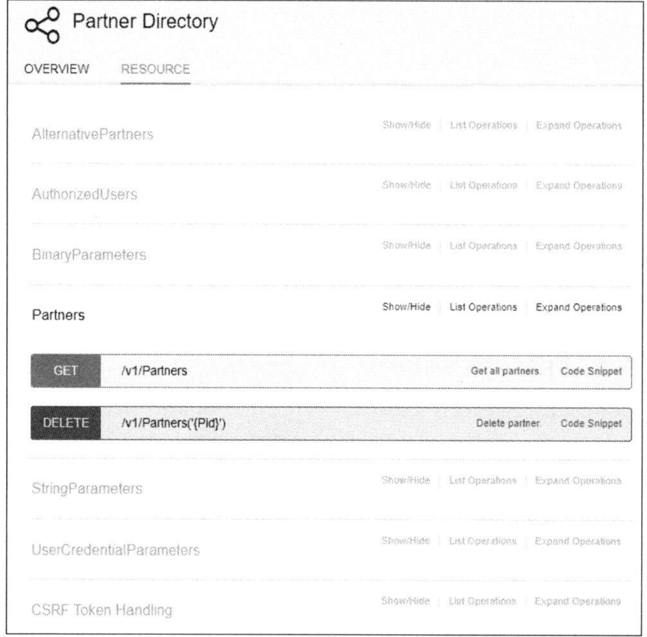

Figure 9.43 Entity Types and APIs Related to the Partner Directory

To get an impression of how to use these APIs, refer to the sample scenario in Chapter 7, Section 7.4. The scenario used the OData API to store an endpoint URL and a credential alias in Partner Directory. It's therefore not necessary to repeat it in this section.

Notes

It's important to be aware of the following Partner Directory limitations:

- The number of `AlternativePartners` in the tenant is limited to a maximum of 1,000,000.

- The number of `AuthorizedUsers` in the tenant is limited to a maximum of 500,000.
- The number of `BinaryParameters` in the tenant is limited to a maximum of 400,000.
- The number of `StringParameters` in the tenant is limited to a maximum of 3,000,000.

9.6 Using SAP Cloud Platform Integration with SAP Cloud Platform API Management

In the past, APIs were mostly only known to programmers, but in today's digital era, even business executives are aware of them and their financial impact. In a digitized world, companies are generating revenue by exposing APIs like any other service they offer to their business partners, suppliers, and customers.

Companies the likes of Amazon, Facebook, Twitter, Netflix, Uber, and Google are generating huge revenues based on their APIs. So, chances are high that APIs will play a key role in the digital transformation journey of your organization. Today, APIs are managed like traditional products!

SAP Cloud Platform API Management (referred to as SAP API Management in the rest of this chapter) can help in the digital transformation journey by providing simple, scalable, and secure access to your organization's digital assets through APIs. SAP API Management enables developer communities to consume and discover your organization's APIs. Refer to *http://bit.ly/2uLnEFV* to read more about SAP Cloud Platform API Management:

Some of its key capabilities include the following, just to name a few:

- Standardized and consistent way to provision APIs via REST, OData, and SOAP
- Real-time and historic analytics on usage, error, monitoring, and traffic of APIs
- High security standard for the APIs to prevent against attacks such as Denial-of-Service attacks (DoS), cross-site scripting (XSS), cross-site request forgery (CSRF), and so on
- Robust traffic management of APIs
- Full API Lifecycle Management

- Management, discovery, testing, subscription, and consumption of APIs by the developer community
- Monetization of APIs

Figure 9.44 depicts the positioning of SAP API Management within your landscape. As shown by the figure, different applications can consume APIs via SAP API Management, which then acts as a gateway. It also proxies the calls to the backend systems (which are either on-premise or cloud-based systems). SAP API Management connects to these backend systems via various protocols, such as SOAP, REST, OData, and so on.

Figure 9.44 shows the different personas involved with SAP API Management:

- **External applications (Mobile, Web, etc.)**
  These applications consume the APIs provided by SAP API Management.
- **Apps Developer**
  This developer is responsible to make the external applications consume APIs. This developer needs to be able to discover existing APIs and figure out how to easily consume them.
- **API Developer**
  This person is responsible to design and implement the API via SAP API Management.
- **API Admin, Owners**
  These people are responsible to administer and manage the APIs via monitoring, analyzing, and monetizing processes.

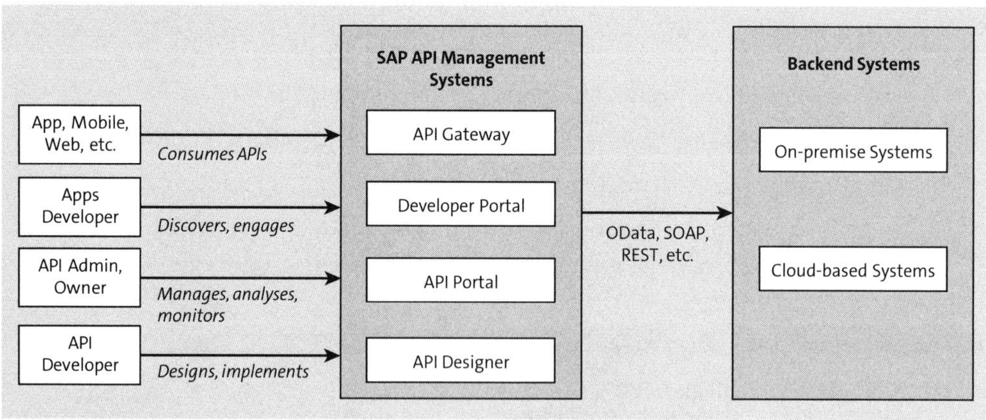

Figure 9.44 Positioning of SAP API Management and Its Personas

This positioning presented by Figure 9.44 also means that SAP API Management can proxy services provided by SAP Cloud Platform Integration, which is the main subject of this section.

SAP API Management is a big topic that deserves its own book. In the next sections, we briefly explore how SAP API Management can be used to publish APIs from services provided by SAP Cloud Platform Integration in a secure manner. To find out more about SAP API Management, follow different tutorials on the SAP community page (*www.sap.com/community.html*).

Note that SAP API Management also sits on top of SAP Cloud Platform and is included in the SAP Cloud Platform Integration, Enterprise Edition, as discussed in Chapter 1, Section 1.4. It's also possible to register for a free trial account at *https://account.hanatrial.ondemand.com/#/home/welcome*.

You might be wondering what the difference is between SAP API Management and SAP API Business Hub. SAP API Management enables any organization to expose its own APIs. It also allows their business partners to discover and consume these APIs in a secure manner. As for SAP API Business Hub, it allows you to discover, explore, and test the APIs offered by SAP.

One of the first things that needs to happen after obtaining your SAP API Management tenant is to establish a connection to your SAP Cloud Platform Integration tenant. Let's explore how that can be achieved next.

9.6.1 Establish a Connection between SAP Cloud Platform Integration and SAP API Management

Note that connecting SAP API Management to SAP Cloud Platform Integration is a one-time action. After that, this connection can be reused.

To connect SAP API Management to SAP Cloud Platform Integration, follow these steps:

1. Log in to your SAP API Management tenant via the following URL (if there is a trial account): *https://account.hanatrial.ondemand.com/cockpit*.

   The link to the productive account is given in the tenant provisioning mail received from SAP when getting a new tenant.
2. Navigate to the **Services** section on the left menu (see Figure 9.45).
3. Click on the **API Management** link under the **Integration** section (see the right panel of Figure 9.45).

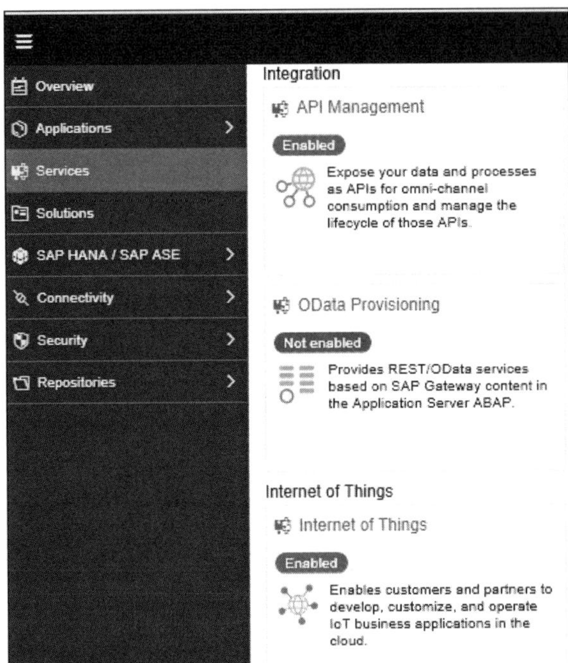

Figure 9.45 Navigating to the SAP API Management Service

4. On the next screen, select the **Access API Portal** link (see Figure 9.46).

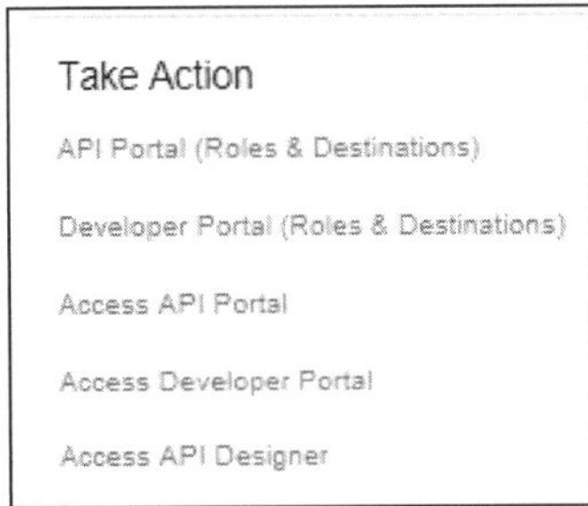

Figure 9.46 Landing Page of SAP API Management with Overview of Possible Actions

5. The next screen presents an overview of the API Portal, which contains information such as API traffic, error, usage, performance, applications, and so on. From here, select the **Develop** link on the menu located in the left panel (see Figure 9.47).

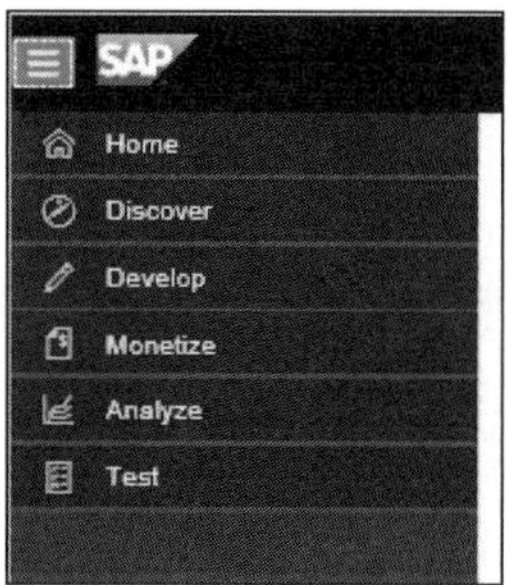

Figure 9.47 Overview of the API Portal

6. On the next page, select the **API PROVIDERS** tab at the top (see Figure 9.48). Click the **Create** button to add a new API Provider. An API provider represents the back-end system that will receive and execute the call.

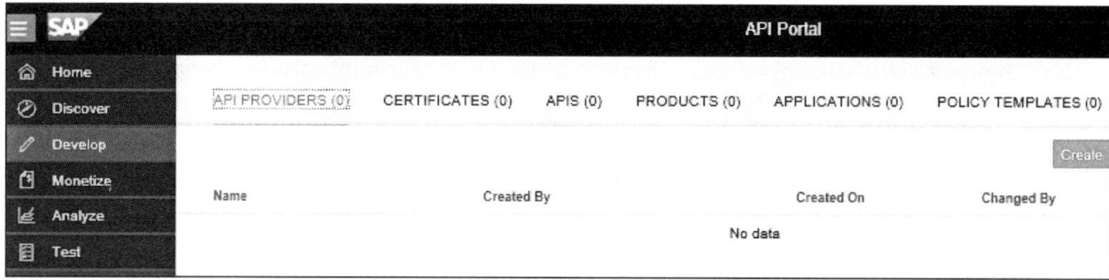

Figure 9.48 API PROVIDERS Tab

7. On the next page, provide a name and description for the new API provider (see Figure 9.49).

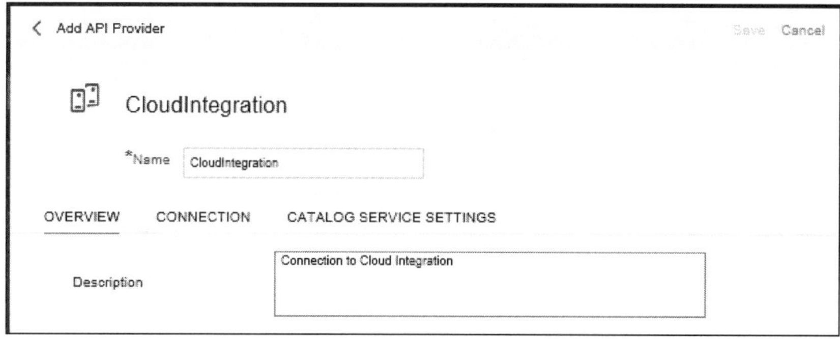

Figure 9.49 Providing a Name and Description

8. Provide the hostname, authentication, and other details related to your SAP Cloud Platform Integration tenant, as shown in Figure 9.50 and Figure 9.51.

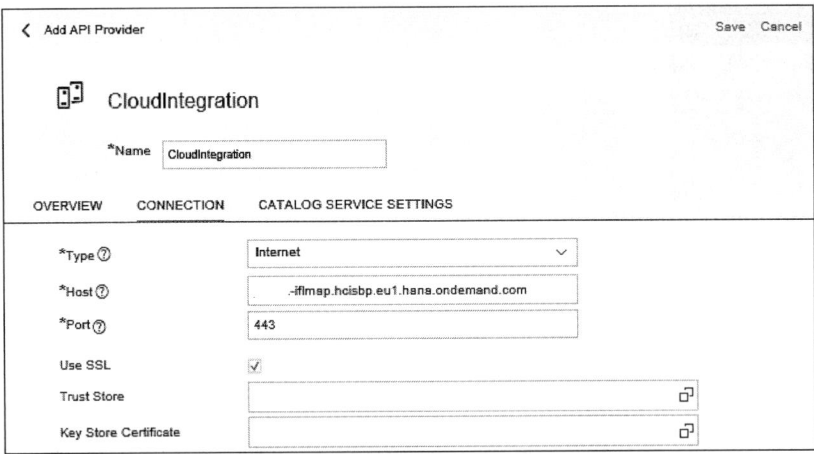

Figure 9.50 Connection Details to the SAP Cloud Platform Integration Tenant

9. Finally, click the **Save** button in the top-right corner of Figure 9.51.

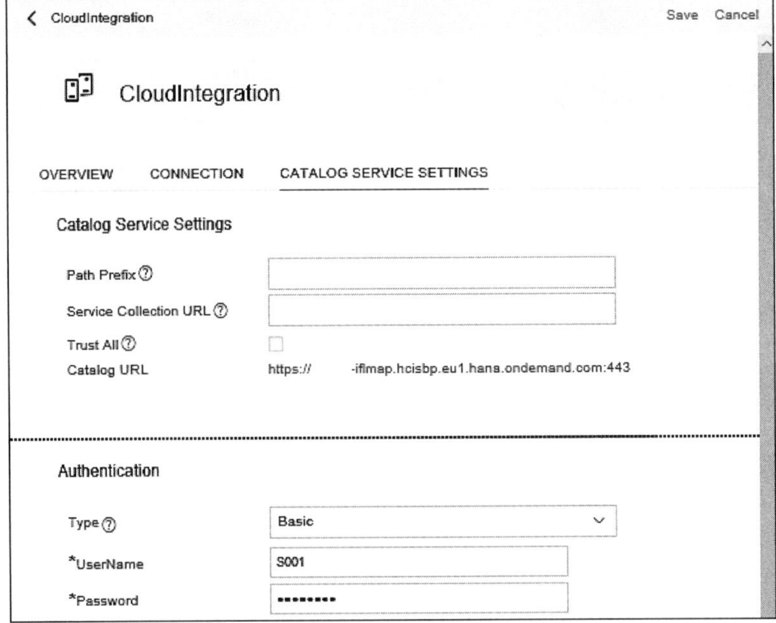

Figure 9.51 Authentication Details for the SAP Cloud Platform Integration Tenant

The connection between SAP API Management and SAP Cloud Platform Integration is now ready. In the next section, we explore how to expose an existing integration flow as a REST API.

9.6.2 Provision Application Programming Interfaces

There is a lot to learn around the topic of provisioning APIs through SAP API Management. Our intention isn't to provide a guide for SAP API Management in this section, but rather to give you a glimpse of what it can do and how it can work in combination with SAP Cloud Platform Integration to create APIs.

To illustrate the provision of an API via SAP API Management, let's once again use the integration flow example that we built in Chapter 4, Section 4.3. We already used this integration flow in Section 9.3 when exploring the **Script** step (refer to Figure 9.11). This scenario currently exposes a SOAP endpoint. Our goal will be to provide this SOAP service as a REST-based API in SAP API Management and apply restrictions to it by limiting the number of calls per minute. This approach of wrapping an existing service as an API is known as API Proxy. REST APIs can accept both JSON or XML as the payload. To simplify, we stick to XML for our scenario. The final end-to-end scenario is presented in Figure 9.52. Because the integration flow already exists in SAP Cloud Platform Integration, we only need to expose it as an API.

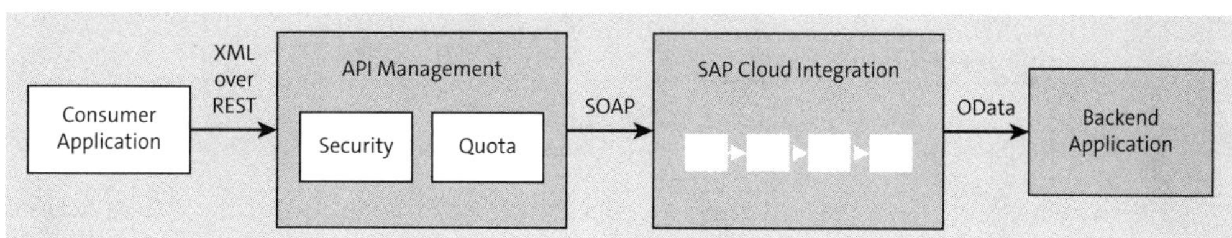

Figure 9.52 End-to-End Overview of Scenario

Let's recall from Chapter 4, Section 4.3, that the endpoint of the concerned integration flow was of the form: *https://<tenant>/cxf/CPI_Book_Demo_OData*.

We can now start the provisioning of our API by first navigating to the landing page of SAP API Management as shown in Figure 9.53 Figure 9.54. We already described how to get to this page in Section 9.6.1.

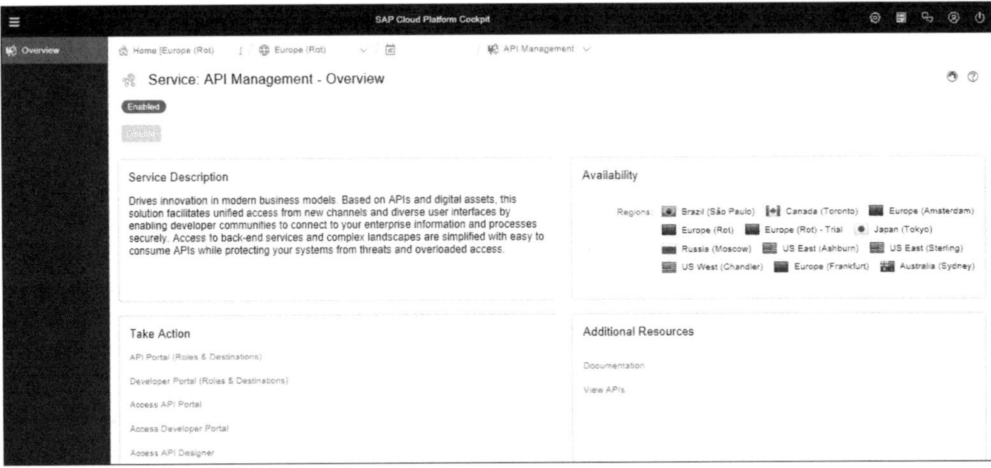

Figure 9.53 Main Page of SAP API Management

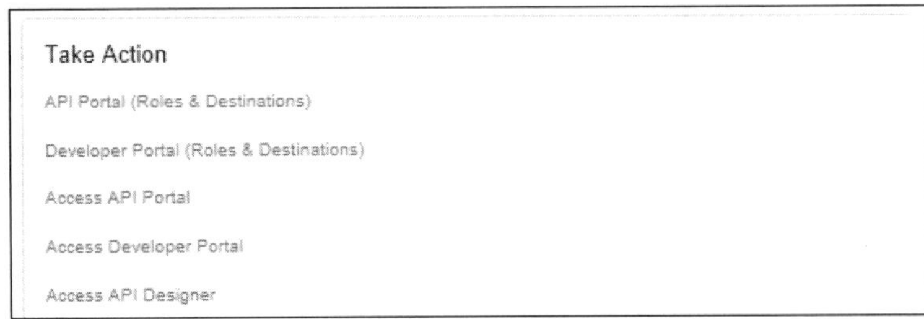

Figure 9.54 SAP API Management, Take Action Options

The page presented in Figure 9.53 includes the following options (under **Take Action**):

- **API Portal (Roles & Destinations)**
  Used to assign roles to users who are allowed to create APIs. It also enables the creation of destinations to different API providers. A destination is an object that contains connection details to a remote system or application. The connection details include the URL of the remote system or service, authentication type, and the user credentials. It's defined once and reused throughout the system.
- **Developer Portal (Roles & Destinations)**
  Used to assign roles to users interested in discovering and consuming APIs. They are also commonly referred to as developers from an SAP API Management point of view. Additionally, from this option, it's possible to create destinations to different API providers.

- **Access API Portal**
  Enables access to various monitoring matrices about APIs, applications, and products. This is also the place where you can design and create new APIs.
- **Access Developer Portal**
  Enables the developer community to access and subscribe to available APIs in SAP API Management.
- **Access API Designer**
  An API editor that includes rich capabilities to import existing open APIs, download APIs, generate equivalent HTML output views, and validate open API syntax.

From the page in Figure 9.53, click on the **Access API Portal** link. You're redirected to a page that looks like Figure 9.55.

From this page, you can access monitors and statistics about API performance, traffic, usage, and errors. Furthermore, you can create new APIs, API providers, and applications.

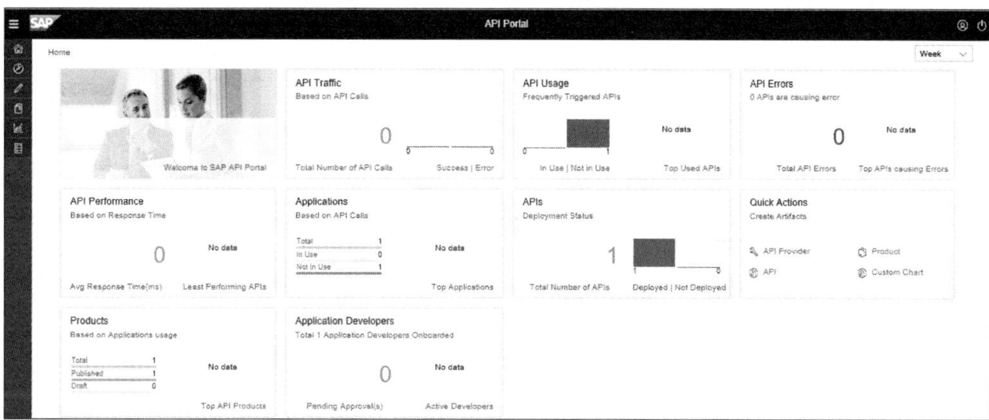

Figure 9.55 API Portal Landing Page

Let's go on and create an API by clicking on the **API** icon, which can be found on in the **Quick Actions** tile of Figure 9.55. A page pops up that allows you to fill in the details of the API proxy. The API proxy needs to point to the integration flow in SAP Cloud Platform Integration. Specify the details as shown in Figure 9.56 and Figure 9.57. Note that both Figure 9.56 and Figure 9.57 are part of the same page.

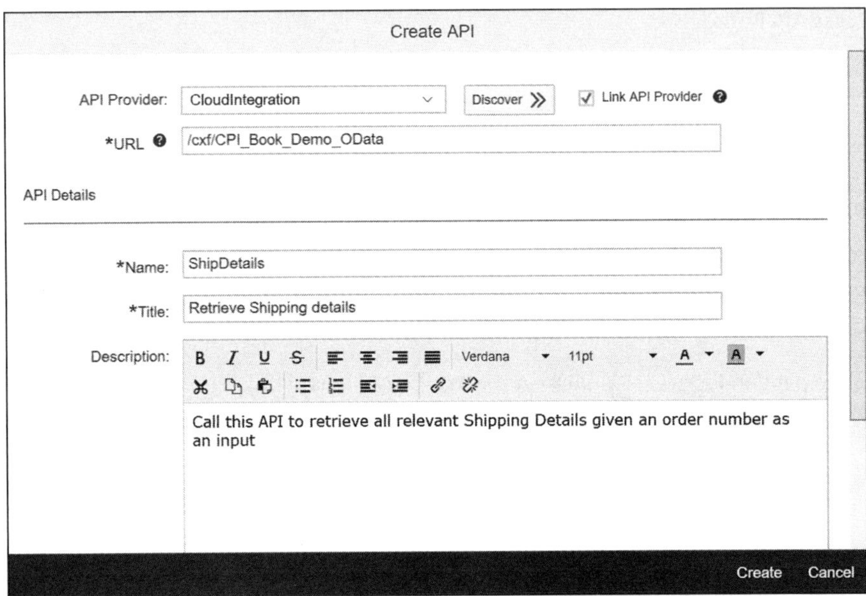

Figure 9.56 Adding Details of the API Proxy to Be Created (Top of Screen)

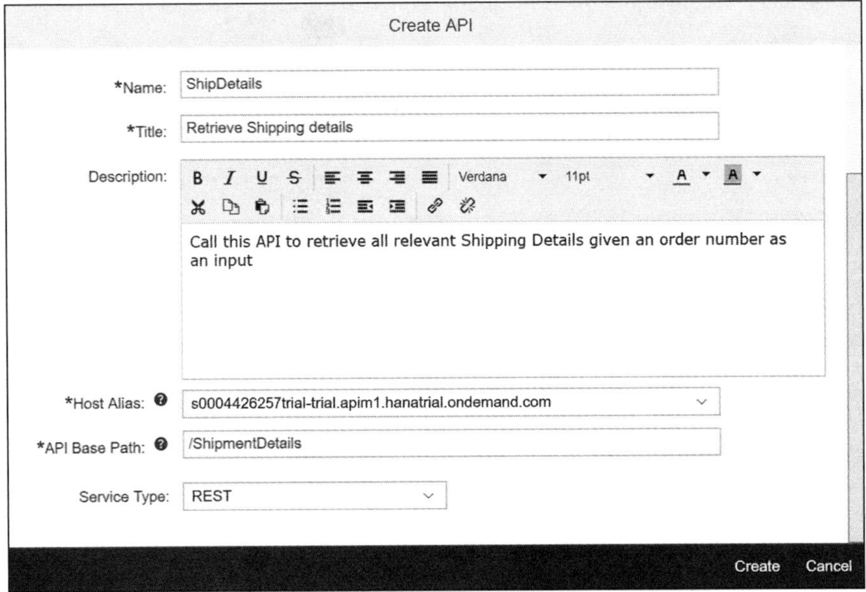

Figure 9.57 Adding Details of the API Proxy to Be Created (Bottom of Screen)

Table 9.14 provides a description of the fields used in Figure 9.56 and Figure 9.57.

Field	Description
API Provider	Specifies the API provider that we created in Section 9.6.1 to connect to the SAP Cloud Platform Integration tenant.
URL	The last part of the integration flow's endpoint, which can be found from integration artifact monitoring, as discussed in Chapter 4, Section 4.1.
Name	Meaningful name for the API.
Title	Title for the API.
Description	Description for the API.
Host Alias	Automatically populated with the host details of our SAP API Management tenant. Leave this field with its default value.
API Base Path	Specifies the base path to be used as part of the endpoint for the API.
Service Type	Possible values include **REST**, **SOAP**, and **ODATA**.

Table 9.14 API Proxy Fields

In Figure 9.58, you can add the resource by clicking on the **Add** button. An API can have multiple resources, and a resource represents an endpoint.

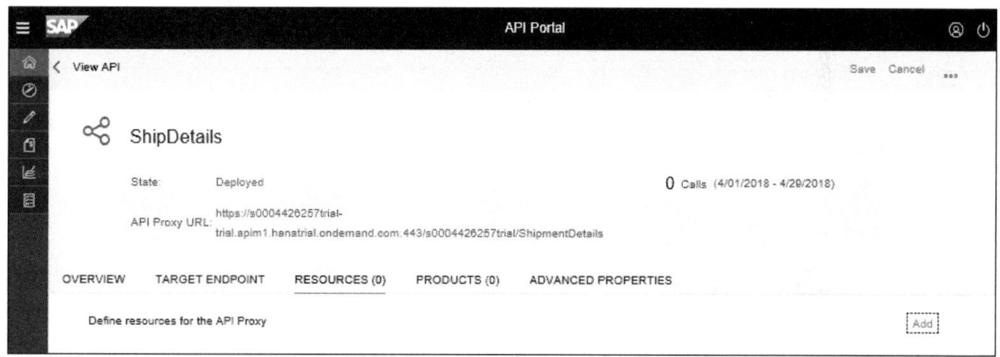

Figure 9.58 Resource Tab of the API Proxy

From the next screen (Figure 9.59), enter the name of the resource as "Shipment". Select the **POST** checkbox as the supported HTTP method, and specify a description. Then click on the **Add** button.

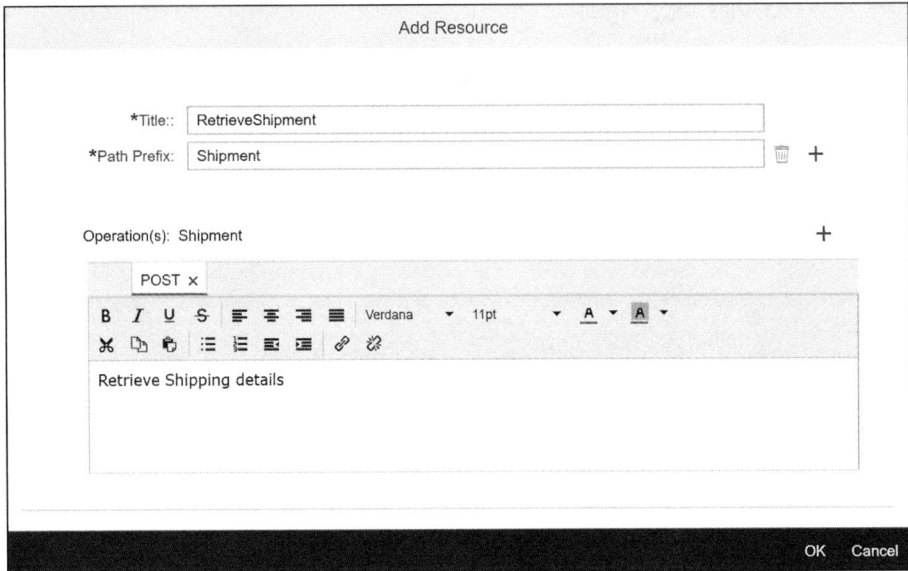

Figure 9.59 Adding a Resource to an API

Let's now add some policies to our API. An API policy is a module that implements a specific API behavior. Policies are built to let you add common management capabilities to an API such as security, rate-limiting, transformation, and mediation. You can access the policy editor by clicking the **Policies** button on the top-right corner of the screen (see Figure 9.60).

Figure 9.60 Navigating to the Policy Editor

You're redirected to the policy editor page from where a wide variety of policies can be added to fulfill your requirements (see Figure 9.61).

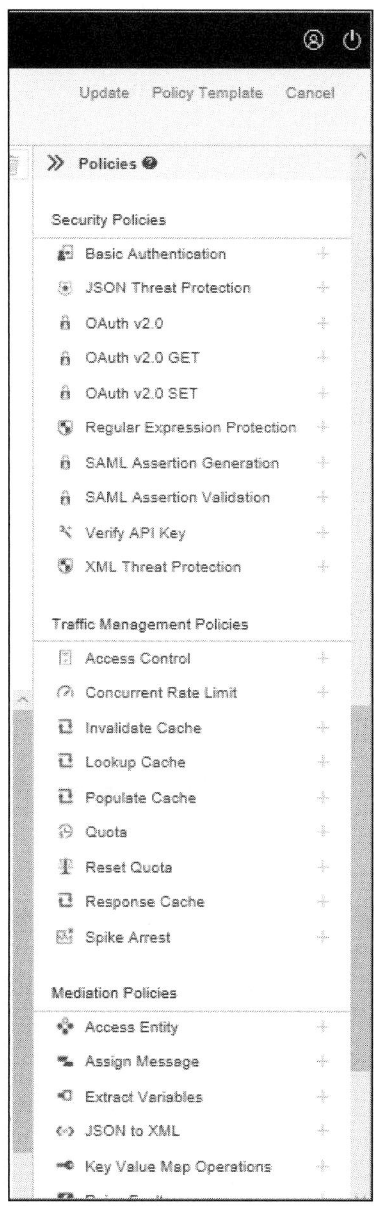

Figure 9.61 An Overview of the Policy Editors

At the time of publishing this book, the following categories of policy are included in the editor:

- **Security**
  Includes various policies aimed at protecting your API. You can add basic authentication, different versions of OAuth, SAML, XML thread protection, verify API keys, and so on.
- **Traffic management**
  Helps you regulate your API traffic using techniques such as caching, quotas, access control, concurrent rate limit, and so on.
- **Mediation**
  Actions and scripts, such as extraction of variables and conversion of JSON to XML (and vice versa), are bundled in this category.

Note that any number of policies included in this editor can be mixed together and used in combination to achieve your desired requirements. The rectangular shaped image included in the middle of Figure 9.61 represents a policy flow in SAP API Management. It defines a processing pipeline and the order of execution of the included policies.

The flow has two main execution paths: the **PreFlow** and **PostFlow**. The **PreFlow** is the top part of the rectangle and represents the actions to be executed first before the control is passed to the API provider (SAP Cloud Platform Integration in our case). The **PostFlow**, on the other hand, is the bottom part of the rectangle and represents the actions to be performed after the API provider has been called. These are, for instance, actions to be performed before sending the response back to the API consumer.

For simplicity, let's add a policy to check API calling quotas. Assuming that our backend system can only accept a limited number of calls per minute, let's use SAP API Management to limit API consumption to a maximum of two API calls per minute. This could be a good way to regulate traffic by protecting our backend system from being flooded with calls. It makes sense to add the quota policy in the **PreFlow**. Therefore, it prevents calls to SAP Cloud Platform Integration if there is a quota violation.

Let's start by selecting **PreFlow** in the top-left corner under the **Flows** section (refer to Figure 9.61). Then click on the plus icon + next to **Quota** on the right panel, under the **Traffic Management Policies** section. You are then presented with a pop-up to provide the name of the policy, as indicated by Figure 9.62.

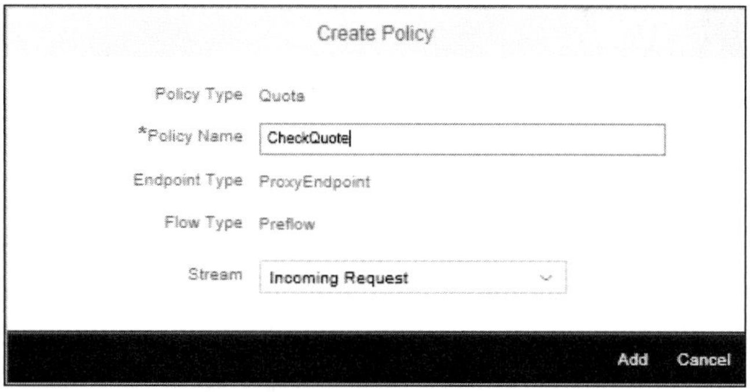

Create Policy

Policy Type Quota

*Policy Name CheckQuote

Endpoint Type ProxyEndpoint

Flow Type Preflow

Stream Incoming Request

Add Cancel

Figure 9.62 Adding the Quote Policy

Beside providing a name for the policy, select the **Incoming Request** value for the **Stream** dropdown, as shown in Figure 9.62. Then click on the **Add** button. In the next screen, specify the maximum number of allowed API calls per minute in the tag element `Allow count`, as depicted in Figure 9.63. In our case, we need to use the value `2` to fulfill our previously stated requirement.

```
<!-- can be used to configure the number of request messages that an app is allowed to submit to an API over a course of unit time -->
<Quota async="false" continueOnError="false" enabled="true" type="calendar" xmlns="http://www.sap.com/apimgmt">
    <!-- specifies the number of requests allowed for the API Proxy -->
        <Allow count="2"/>
    <!-- the interval of time for which the quota should be applied -->
    <Interval>1</Interval>
    <!-- used to specify if a central counter should be maintained and continuously synchronized across all message processors -->
    <Distributed>true</Distributed>
    <!-- Use to specify the date and time when the quota counter will begin counting,
        regardless of whether any requests have been received from any apps -->
    <StartTime>2015-2-11 12:00:00</StartTime>
    <!-- If set to true, the distributed quota counter is updated synchronously. This means that
        the update to the counter will be made at the same time the API call is quota-checked -->
    <Synchronous>true</Synchronous>
    <!-- Use to specify the unit of time applicable to the quota. Can be second, minute, hour, day, or month -->
    <TimeUnit>minute</TimeUnit>
</Quota>
```

Figure 9.63 Configuration of CheckQuota

Click on the **Update** button in the top-right corner to update the API with the added policies (see Figure 9.64).

To find more information about any policy, refer to the SAP Documentation at *https://help.sap.com/viewer/product/CP/Cloud* (and search for **SAP Cloud Platform API Management**).

In the next screen, click on the **Save** button. Well done, you're now ready to consume the API in the next section.

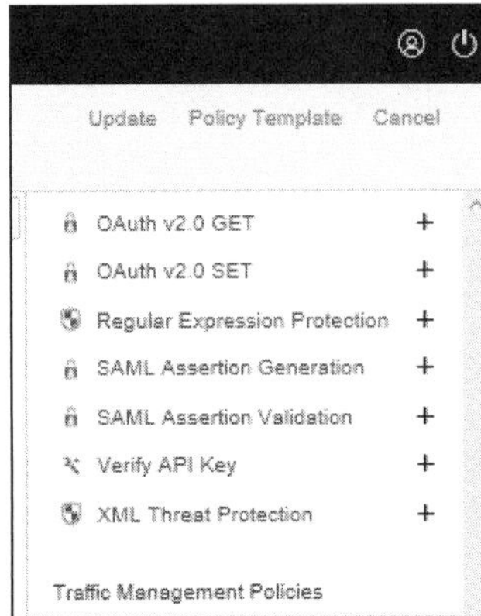

Figure 9.64 Updating the API with the Flow of Policies

9.6.3 Consume the Application Programming Interface

Now that the API is ready, we can test it using any REST client of your preference (e.g., Postman). You can also perform a test directly in SAP API Management by navigating to the test tool via the **Test** icon, as shown at the bottom of the left menu in Figure 9.65.

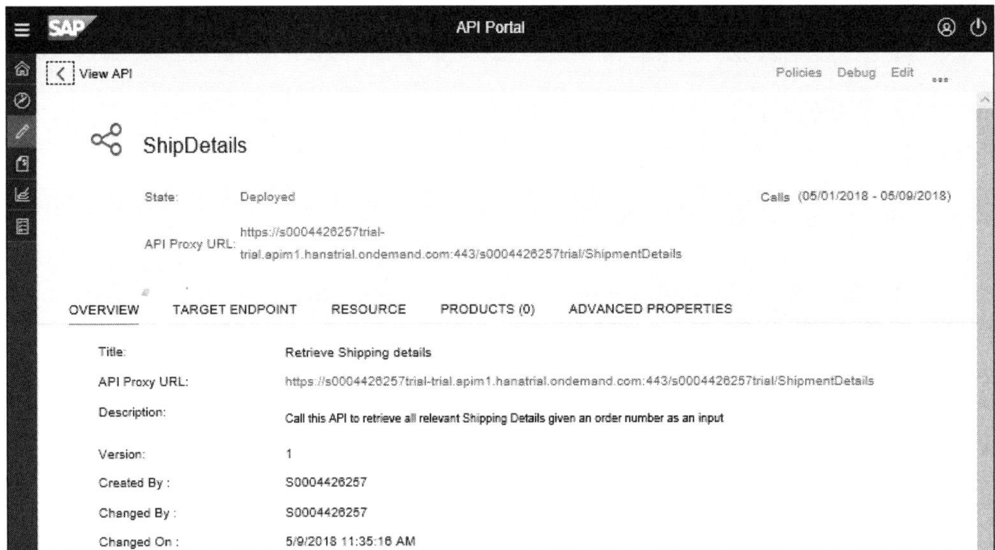

Figure 9.65 Overview of the Created API

You're then redirected to a new test page from where you should select **ShipDetails** on the left of the screen shown in Figure 9.66. Note that, by default, an endpoint ending with **/SWAGGER_JSON** is selected (see Figure 9.66). You'll need to select the other endpoint from the dropdown list. The correct endpoint will end with the prefix used while creating the resource (in our scenario, **/Shipment**).

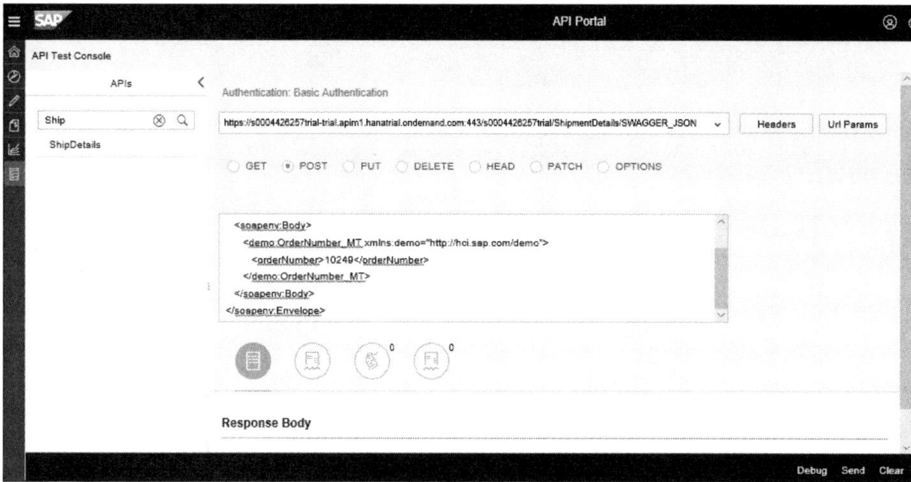

Figure 9.66 Setup of the API Test Tool

> **Note**
>
> If you're using an external REST client such as Postman, you'll need an endpoint to post the API call to. The endpoint of the newly created API can be obtained via the dropdown field in Figure 9.66.

After selecting the correct endpoint, specify the HTTP method as **POST** by selecting its radio button, provide the desired request XML payload, and change the authentication method to basic authentication. The authentication can be changed by clicking the **Authentication** link on the top-left corner of Figure 9.66.

We can now trigger the call by clicking on the **Send** button at the bottom-right corner of the screen. In the background, SAP API Management performs a check to validate whether we're still within our quota limits. Because this is the first message, the call is accepted and sent to SAP Cloud Platform Integration, which in turn returns a valid response, as shown in the **Response Body** section of Figure 9.67.

Quickly perform the same call two more times to exceed our quota limit. You'll then get a quota violation error, as shown in Figure 9.68. This error insinuates that we've exceeded the quota of two calls within the same minute.

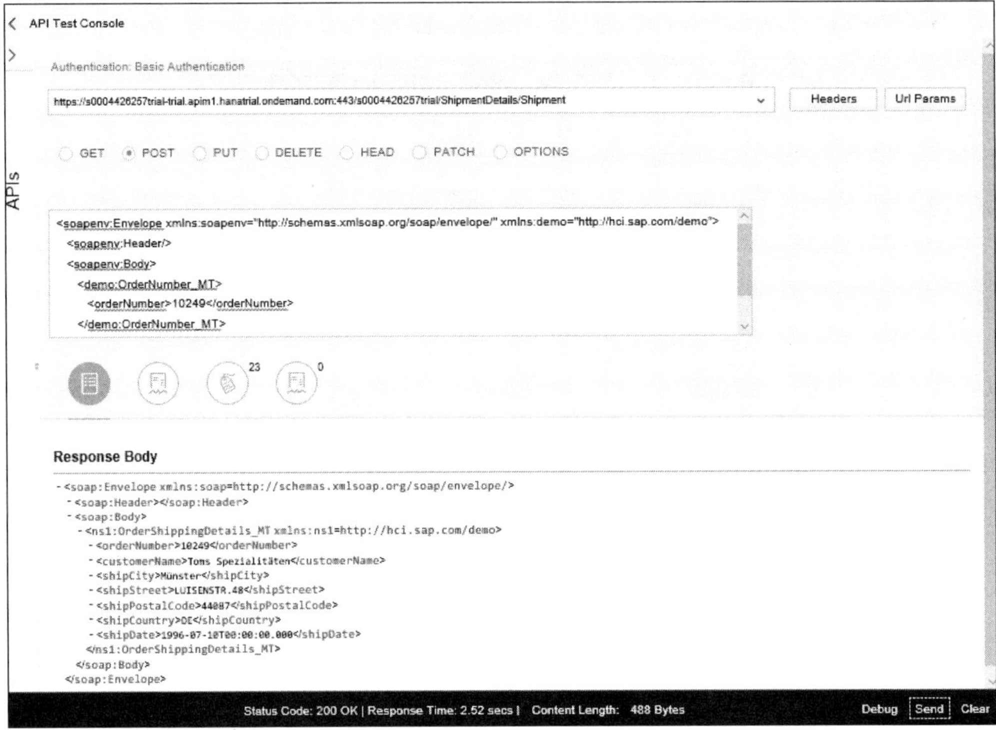

Figure 9.67 The Test Result of Our API Call

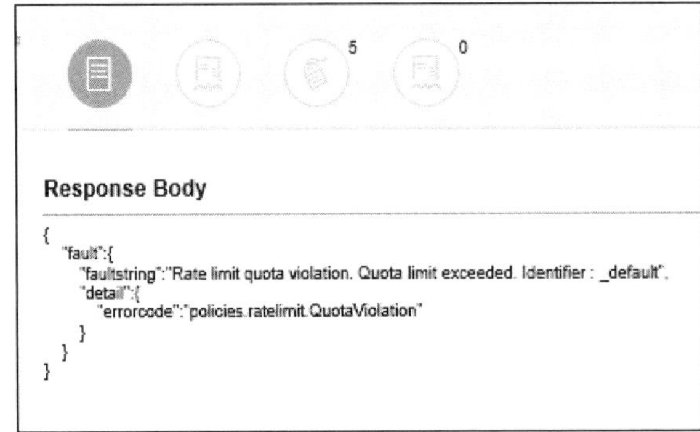

Figure 9.68 Response When Quota Is Exceeded

Congratulations, you successfully provided, called, and consumed the API. However, it's important to remember that this was a simplistic scenario. In a real-life scenario, you should consider the following additional aspects:

- **Authentication in SAP API Management**
  By default, the API exposed can be consumed without authentication. If you want to protect the API, you'll need to add the relevant policy (e.g., OAuth, API key, etc.).
- **Authentication in SAP Cloud Platform Integration**
  In our scenario, we're simply passing along to SAP Cloud Platform Integration whatever header was provided during the API call. This means that the username/password details used while calling the API are also forwarded and used for authentication in SAP Cloud Platform Integration. You could decide to use the basic authentication security policy to provide the login details for SAP Cloud Platform Integration.
- **Payload**
  Note that the sample request message used in Figure 9.66 includes the entire SOAP message. Given that we're exposing a REST API, we could decide to only use the SOAP body as input. But that will require us to perform some logic to extract the relevant data from the incoming message and construct the SOAP message to send to SAP Cloud Platform Integration. This is necessary because the service that we're consuming in SAP Cloud Platform Integration is of type SOAP.
- **Error message**
  Note that the error response returned by the API when the quota was exceeded (in Figure 9.68) is in JSON format. In a real-life scenario, you'll want to convert the response to XML before returning it to the consumer. As a hint, consider the JSON2XML policy.

These points aren't tackled in this chapter given that it falls out of the chapter scope.

You now understand how to use SAP API Management to wrap services available in SAP Cloud Platform Integration and expose them as APIs, as well as how to enforce different policies.

9.7 Summary

This chapter introduced you to the API capabilities and features of SAP Cloud Platform Integration. An overview of Java-based APIs was given, and you've also learned about how to use them in UDFs. The chapter then explored a number of OData APIs available in SAP Cloud Platform Integration and used some examples to illustrate their usage.

Lastly, the chapter explored how to use SAP Cloud Platform Integration in combination with SAP API Management to provision APIs. Even though this isn't intended to be a chapter on SAP API Management, you also learned how to add policies to the APIs using a scenario.

In the next chapter, we'll explore different security topics in SAP Cloud Platform Integration.

Chapter 10
SAP Cloud Platform Integration Security

Using an integration platform in the cloud implies that your data is processed on servers outside the boundaries of your organization and thus beyond your influence. This raises the question of how secure the data hosted by the software provider actually is and how it can be protected. This chapter summarizes the measures taken by SAP to protect your data at the highest level and shows what you can do to maximize the security level of your integration scenarios.

A fundamental characteristic of using cloud software as compared to on-premise software is the fact that you, the customer, hand over some of the responsibility for your data to the software provider. In particular, using an integration platform-as-a-service (iPaaS) implies that your data is processed on servers outside your organization. Your data is also stored on servers hosted by the software provider. Therefore, the topic of security is of a fundamental and existential importance.

This chapter will show that your data is in safe hands with SAP. It answers two questions: How secure is the data passing through SAP Cloud Platform Integration during the execution of an integration scenario, and what measures are implemented by SAP to exclude the risk of malicious actions taken on your data?

In Section 10.1 and Section 10.2, we'll cover the following:

- Security mechanisms that are already in place (i.e., inherently provided by the technical infrastructure)
- Security levels that are guaranteed by the processes associated with the development and use of SAP Cloud Platform Integration

Section 10.3 covers the topic of user management that comes first when a customer starts working with SAP Cloud Platform Integration. Here you learn how to set up dedicated permissions for people involved in an integration project.

Section 10.4 shows how you can use the tools provided with SAP Cloud Platform Integration to configure integration scenarios with the highest possible protection of the involved data. Finally, Section 10.5 explains how to manage the lifecycle of keys in the tenant keystore, a central component required to set up secure integration scenarios.

The tutorials provided in this chapter focus in the security-related aspects of the described integration scenarios. They won't repeat each step required to set up the scenario because after walking through the previous chapters, you're now already an integration expert who knows how to design various integration flows. Exceptions are those tutorials where we introduce certain security-related integration flow steps (Section 10.4.7) or adapters that we haven't introduced yet (e.g., the Twitter adapter in Section 10.4.5).

10.1 Technical System Landscape

In this section, we'll discuss the security level that is imposed by the technical system landscape. We'll first cover the security of the software architecture and the network design. Then, we provide a quick glance into the physical data security, provided by the fact that the virtual machines (VMs) that process your messages are operated at SAP data centers. Next, we discuss how data *at rest*—that is, data stored at various steps during the processing of a message—is protected by the infrastructure. Finally, we close this section by showing how data protection and privacy are ensured when using SAP Cloud Platform Integration.

10.1.1 Architecture

In this section, we'll focus on those aspects of the architecture that make SAP Cloud Platform Integration a secure cloud-based integration platform.

In Chapter 2, Section 2.1, we showed that a clustered, virtual design establishes SAP Cloud Platform Integration as an integration platform that is shared by many participants and allows flexible allocation of resources for different participants. We also introduced the basic concept of tenant isolation, which ensures that the platform resources assigned to different participants are strictly isolated from each other. Each participant has an SAP Cloud Platform subaccount and tenant assigned to it. On each tenant, an individual (virtual) integration runtime—a tenant cluster—is installed, which is strictly separated from those of the other tenants.

In other words, data and processes related to different customers are kept apart. However, in a more general sense, a customer can set up different tenant clusters for different purposes (e.g., test and production). The architecture of SAP Cloud Platform Integration makes sure that the processes and data belonging to those different use cases are strictly isolated from each other.

We'll now take a closer look at the architecture and show how tenant isolation is achieved. We'll also show which concepts are in place for secure communication between the involved participants and technical components.

In Chapter 2, Section 2.1 (see Figure 2.7), we introduced the architecture of SAP Cloud Platform Integration and provided a glance of the internal structure of the integration platform. We'll now address the following additional questions:

- How is user access to SAP Cloud Platform Integration restricted, and how is the platform protected against unauthorized access?
- How is *data at rest* (stored data) protected?
- How is *data in transit* (data exchanged between the participants and SAP Cloud Platform Integration) protected?
- How is secure communication implemented between the participants and the involved components of the cluster?

Figure 10.1 shows the high-level architecture view from Chapter 2, enriched with information on the security protocols used for the involved communication paths. In addition to this, Figure 10.1 also adds the Secure Shell File Transfer Protocol (SFTP) server for the use cases where SFTP is chosen as transport-level security (which we skipped in Chapter 2 for the sake of simplicity).

We'll walk you through this figure and explain the security-related aspects of the architecture.

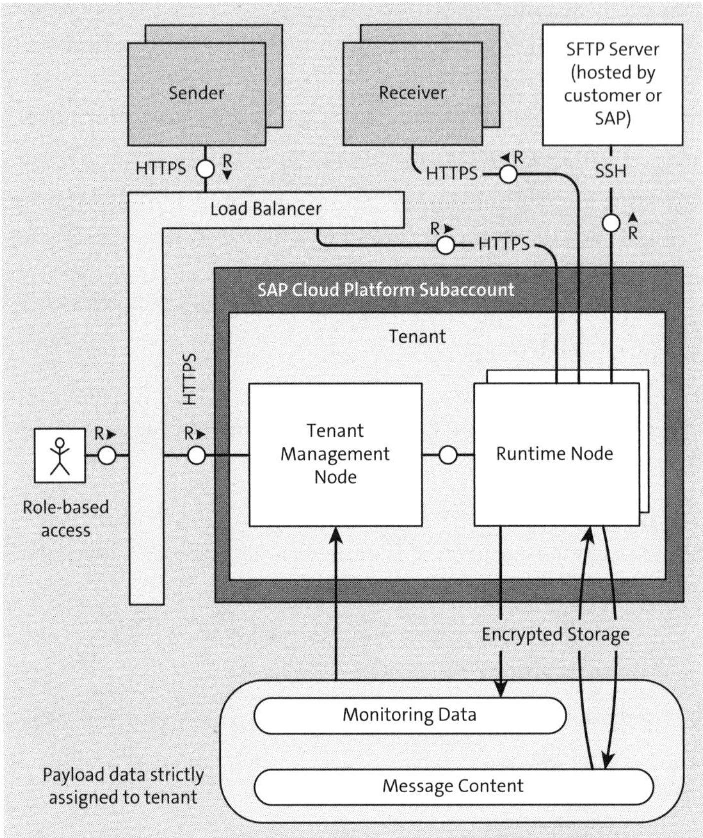

Figure 10.1 High-Level Architecture with Technical Connections, Transport-Level Security Options, and Persistence Steps

Role-Based User Access and User Management

Let's begin with the interaction points for dialog users. Access to SAP Cloud Platform Integration in the context of specific tasks (e.g., deploying integration content on a tenant) is always controlled by authorizations based on user-to-role assignments. User-to-role assignments are accomplished through the SAP Cloud Platform cockpit. You can access this application through the URL provided to you by SAP in the email informing you about the details of the tenant you requested (see Chapter 2).

With regard to user management and authorization, all platform resources are strictly isolated: in other words, a user with specific permissions on a test cluster might not have the same permissions on a productive cluster.

Each customer is given access to one or more subaccounts (by default, to one test and one productive account). The clustered design of SAP Cloud Platform Integration and the role-based access to the platform make sure that, first, each subaccount is reserved for a dedicated set of users who are completely isolated from the user setup associated with other subaccounts of the platform. In larger companies, the users assigned to a test account will be associated with persons other than those assigned to the productive subaccount.

Secondly, the SAP Cloud Platform user management allows you to assign to the users of each subaccount granular roles or authorization groups (specific groups of roles) that are tailored to the different sets of tasks that come into play in an integration project. We cover this topic in more detail in Section 10.3.

Secure Data Storage

The separation of data belonging to different tenants is based on the fact that although different tenants of SAP Cloud Platform Integration might physically share one common database, each tenant stores its data in a separate database schema or Java Message Service (JMS) queue. This ensures that data is strictly separated and isolated per tenant.

In Section 10.1.3, we focus in more detail on this aspect.

Secure Communication of the Technical Components

The separation of platform resources covers more than data storage—tenant isolation is also related to the processing of data and the way the various components involved in an integration scenario communicate with each other.

Let's take a closer look at how the connections between these components are secured. The SAP Cloud Platform Integration runtime is established as a cluster of multiple nodes of different types, with each node type responsible for specific tasks. These nodes (VMs) have various connections to other components:

- **HTTPS connections to remote components**
  A common protocol that can be used both for inbound communication (when SAP Cloud Platform Integration is addressed by an incoming request) and for outbound communication (when SAP Cloud Platform Integration sends a message to a receiver) is HTTPS. This protocol comes with Transport Layer Security (TLS).

  For inbound HTTPS requests, we first need to differentiate between requests from the user interfaces (UIs) to the tenant management node (TMN) (e.g., when a user connects to the tenant using the Web UI) and, second, requests from external sender systems (to get messages processed). In both cases, inbound communication is forwarded to the runtime node by a load balancer. As a result, the load balancer terminates incoming TLS requests and establishes new ones.

- **Intra-cluster communication**
  The intra-cluster communication (between TMNs and runtime nodes) is accomplished by a messaging service.

In Section 10.4.2, we cover how HTTPS-based on TLS works in more detail.

Additional Protocols Supported

The following additional protocols are supported by SAP Cloud Platform Integration:

- Communication between SAP Cloud Platform Integration and external components can also be secured using SFTP. When using SFTP, an SFTP server needs to be connected to the tenant (through a dedicated SFTP adapter).
- Another set of protocols (not depicted in Figure 10.1) is also supported when exchanging e-mails using SAP Cloud Platform Integration:
  - For connections using the mail sender adapter: Post Office Protocol version 3 over TLS/SSL (POP3S) and Internet Message Access Protocol over TLS/SSL (IMAPS)
  - For connections using the mail receiver adapter: Simple Mail Transfer Protocol Secure (SMTPS)

For more information, see Table 10.3.

10.1.2 Network Infrastructure

In this section, we cover the security aspects of the *network design*. We'll also expand our focus a bit and show how SAP manages the SAP Cloud Platform Integration clusters in a secure way.

Let's consider that a network is a setup of physical machines or VMs that communicate with each other in a well-defined and controlled way. A network comprises different *network segments*, and all components within one network segment are on the same trust level. The trust level determines what kind of communication is allowed, based on the implemented protocols and security settings. As such, the specific design of the network determines how the various components of the SAP Cloud Platform Integration infrastructure are arranged in a network and protected by various measures, such as firewalls.

Figure 10.2 shows the network design of SAP Cloud Platform Integration from a bird's-eye perspective. For simplicity, the SFTP use case is left out in this figure.

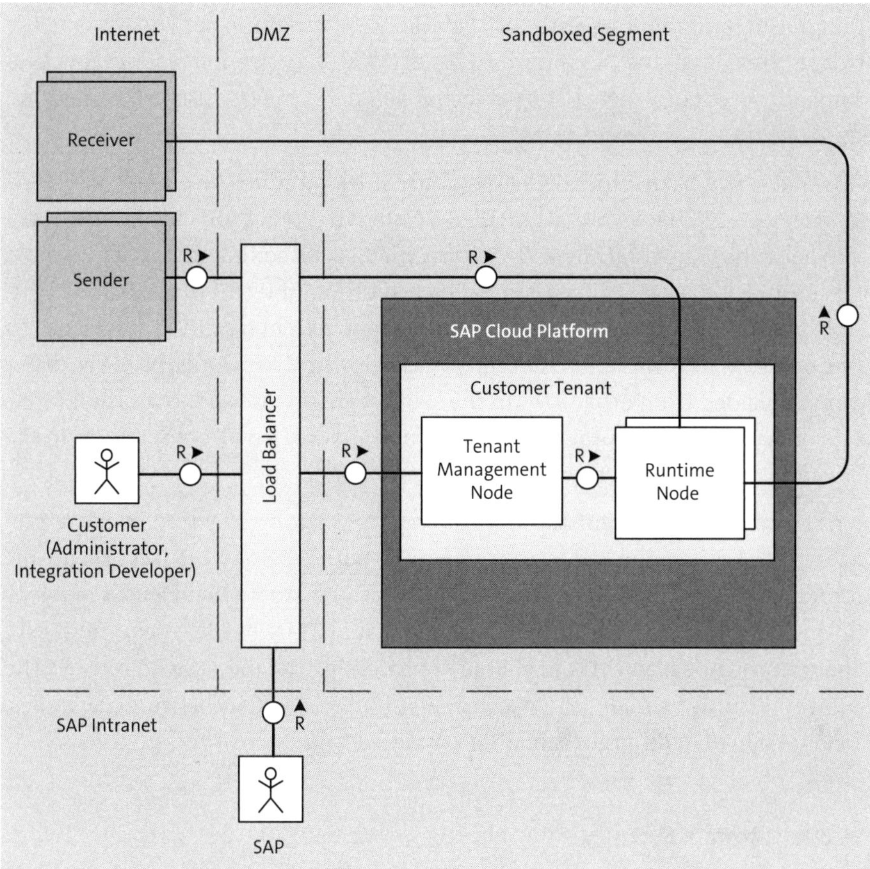

Figure 10.2 High-Level Network Design of SAP Cloud Platform Integration

As already shown in Figure 10.1, external components (sender and receiver systems as well as dialog users on the customers' side) access the SAP Cloud Platform Integration platform from the Internet. In terms of the network view, the Internet is a large and untrusted network. The components of SAP Cloud Platform Integration that process sensitive customer data can't directly be called by components from the Internet, as the load balancer is interconnected and terminates each inbound TLS request. After the load balancer has established a new TLS request, the external call is forwarded to a VM of the SAP Cloud Platform Integration cluster that actually processes the request. As you saw in Section 10.1.1, this pattern applies both for sender components that call SAP Cloud Platform Integration from the Internet and for dialog users that connect to SAP Cloud Platform Integration through a web browser (when, e.g., a user designs integration flows with the Web UI). In terms of the network design, the load balancer resides in the Demilitarized Zone (DMZ). It's common practice for organizations not to expose their external-facing services directly to the Internet and instead locate these services in a DMZ.

The VMs that process customer data aren't only shielded from the outside world. As shown in Figure 10.2, the VMs of a SAP Cloud Platform Integration cluster reside in a separate network segment: the *sandboxed segment*. Sandboxing means, in its most general sense, separating IT processes from each other. In terms of SAP Cloud Platform Integration, *sandboxed* means that, to a certain extent, each VM runs isolated from the others in its own sandbox or micro-network. In other words, each VM of the platform is shielded from other VMs in the same segment, as sandboxes can't interfere with or even "see" each other. This design makes sure that all components in the sandboxed segment are strictly isolated from each other.

We've restricted our statement above by saying *to a certain extent*: to be more precise, we have to limit and refine our consideration with regard to the fact that a TMN can interfere with those runtime nodes that are assigned to it. When a user requests monitoring data through the Web UI, the associated TMN needs to communicate with the runtime node, which is in charge of processing the message, to retrieve the data. However, runtime nodes themselves can't interfere with other runtime nodes, and nodes assigned to different tenants are isolated from each other.

10.1.3 Data Storage Security

As an integration platform, SAP Cloud Platform Integration acts like a *transit place* for data, as its task is essentially to receive, process, and forward messages. However, different kind of data associated with message processing can also be stored at various steps during message processing. In this section, we summarize by which measures *data at rest* is protected at a maximum level.

As explained in Chapter 2, Section 2.1.2, the following types of data can be stored during runtime (compare also with Table 2.2):

- **Message content**
  Integration developers can configure dedicated steps of an integration flow to store message content. The message can either be stored permanently (by default,

90 days) using the Message Store step, or temporarily (for a few seconds), to make it available for subsequent processing steps, using the Data Store step (or by using JMS queues).

- **Monitoring data**
  The message processing log (MPL) records the actually executed processing steps for a message. It can be accessed using the monitoring application of the Web UI by users that have the appropriate permission.

The tenant isolation concept ensures that data belonging to different participants is strictly isolated from each other.

Message content stored in the database can be encrypted with an encryption key, which is generated automatically and is unique for each tenant (using Advanced Encryption Standard [AES] and a key length of 256 bits). The encryption key is stored in a different database than the encrypted data. To increase security, key rotation is supported (so that keys can be changed periodically or whenever they are compromised).

In addition, with regard to access permissions, data stored in different tenants is strictly isolated: an administrator on tenant A won't have permission to access data stored on tenant B. This rule also applies to SAP internal employees in charge of setting up, maintaining, and updating customer clusters. Furthermore, SAP will have no access to data stored in customer tenants.

In the case of support, customers can temporarily grant restricted permissions to dedicated SAP employees to allow them to execute tasks such as error analysis (typically assigning read permissions using authorization group `AuthGroup.ReadOnly`; Section 10.3 for more details).

In any case, the principle of *least privilege* is always applied, which means that users are limited to the minimum set of privileges (permissions) required to perform a necessary task.

10.1.4 Data Protection and Privacy

Data protection is always related to legal requirements and privacy concerns. In this section, we first give a brief summary of where sensitivity of data is to be considered in an integration project and, secondly, provide information on specific measures taken to protect such data within SAP Cloud Platform Integration.

As a general rule, customer data processed by and stored within the SAP Cloud Platform Integration infrastructure is classified as *confidential*, in the sense that it requires (and receives) the highest level of protection.

Which Data Needs to Be Protected

Table 10.1 provides examples of which kind of sensitive data is to be considered at various steps in the SAP Cloud Platform Integration lifecycle.

Phase	Kind of Data
Message processing	Data contained in customer messages and processed on an SAP Cloud Platform Integration VM at runtime is usually business data that can contain personal information, such as names or address data. The measures to protect this data have been explained in Section 10.1.3.
Monitoring	The MPL records the executed processing steps for a message. Therefore, information about customer activities can be derived out of it (e.g., through the frequency of message processing). This data is only accessible per tenant (i.e., it's subject to tenant isolation) and for users with dedicated permissions.
Audit log	Certain events and system changes (e.g., access to message content or the deployment of integration artifacts) are logged during the operation of SAP Cloud Platform Integration. Audit logs are generated both for administrators at SAP that monitor the operations of a cluster and for tenant administrators. In both cases, the access to audit log data is protected by specific roles. For more information, see the following section.
Dialog user logs in to the SAP Cloud Platform Integration Web UI	When customers log in to their tenant through the Web UI, they register to the SAP ID Service. In this case, certain data is collected, and personal data (names and email addresses) also comes into play. SAP ID service is a special SAP Cloud Platform tenant (managed by SAP) that is used as a default identity provider (IdP) for SAP Cloud applications (see also Section 10.3).

Table 10.1 Examples of Customer Data Stored during the SAP Cloud Platform Integration Lifecycle

We'll now provide an overview of measures that are taken by SAP to protect this data.

Audit Log

To increase data protection, data accesses and other incidents are recorded in an audit log. Audit logs are generated, first, for administrators at SAP to enable them to monitor those incidents and prevent malicious usage of the same. These audit logs provide a chronological record of events such as the following:

- Data read access
- Security-critical incidents that might affect the confidentiality, integrity, or availability of the system (e.g., starting or stopping a VM, failed logins, or changes of critical system parameters)
- Configuration changes to the system (e.g., integration flow changes or content deployment tasks)

Logging such data enables SAP to perform regular audits to meet the requirements of regulatory compliance.

Audit logs are generated for each tenant, which means that log data related to different customers is separated. In addition, strict access control is imposed, and no log modifications by malicious users are possible. Logs are retained for 18 months and can be handed out to customers upon request. Components subject to audit logs are the VMs of a cluster and the load balancer.

Audit logs are, secondly, also generated for tenant administrators, and they record all security-relevant changes in their (the administrator's) tenant cluster. Such information is retained for 30 days and then deleted automatically. To display such audit logs, the user needs to have specific roles assigned. More information on how a tenant administrator can access these audit logs can be found in Chapter 8, Section 8.5.1.

European General Data Protection Regulation

SAP Cloud Platform Integration has established the necessary processes and the infrastructure to comply with the new European *General Data Protection Regulation* (GDPR) that came into action on May 25, 2018.

European customers can opt in to having their data treated according to a European Union (EU) access policy. In such a case, customer data is processed and stored exclusively at a data center located in the European Union, which is subject to European data protection and privacy laws. Back up of data is also accomplished using a data center located in the European Union.

Personal data of such customers will only be accessible to members of a dedicated European SAP Cloud Platform Integration Operations team, and not to anyone outside Europe.

Data Protection in the EU

More information about data protection in the EU can be found here:

- *http://eur-lex.europa.eu/legal-content/EN/TXT/?uri=CELEX:32016R0679*
- *https://ec.europa.eu/info/law/law-topic/data-protection_en*

10.1.5 Physical Data Security

Now that we've covered the security aspects inherently provided by the architecture, the network infrastructure, and data protection guidelines, let's take a closer look at *physical data security*. After this, we focus on how the processes related to an integration project are protected.

The VMs that process customer messages run on servers located in various regions worldwide. At the time of this book's release, SAP Cloud Platform Integration is exclusively running in the SAP Cloud Platform Neo environment. Data exchanged in the course of integration scenarios is technically stored and processed within an SAP infrastructure, namely, on servers located in SAP data centers. Customer data is also stored there for a certain time. SAP data centers are world-class and, as such, meet the highest security standards. To mention a few examples, SAP data centers rely on redundant power supplies, physical access is protected by biometric-access control mechanisms, and there is 24-hour surveillance. A security and facility support team is onsite 24/7, and locations are monitored by hundreds of surveillance cameras with digital recording. Buildings are protected against fire by ceilings, walls, and doors that provide 90 minutes of fire resistance. All of these measures are checked and audited on a regular basis.

Customers can assure themselves of the high security standards by requesting a guided tour for visitors. For more information, visit *www.sapdatacenter.com*.

10.2 Processes

In this section, we focus on various processes around the development, provisioning, and usage of SAP Cloud Platform Integration. We'll show that these processes fulfill the highest security standards.

First, SAP has certified that the development, maintenance, and operations of SAP Cloud Platform Integration comply with the requirements of standards such as SAP Cloud Platform ISO/IEC 27001, SAP Cloud Platform SOC 1 (ISAE3402), SAP Cloud Platform SOC 2, and SAP Cloud Platform: ISO/IEC 22301.

You can find the certificates at *https://www.sap.com/about/cloud-trust-center/cloud-certification-compliance/compliance-finder.html*. On this page, filter for the **Solution/Area SAP Cloud Platform Integration**.

This certification is under surveillance and renewed annually.

We'll now walk you through the security-relevant aspects of the processes that are in place.

10.2.1 Software Development Process

SAP Cloud Platform Integration software, as all SAP software, is developed in compliance with the SAP Security Development Lifecycle (SDLC), which helps build security into the software from the beginning and includes the following features:

- Test-driven development, including source code reviews, architecture audits, and security scans. In addition, quality gates have to be passed through on a monthly basis. This includes scanning the source code for security issues (checking the source code, identifying possible security issues and gaps, and helping developers fix any issues that may arise).
- Threat modeling techniques are selectively applied, which means that possible security gaps in individual components of the architecture are identified and modeled in advance. That way, possible vulnerabilities of the system can be anticipated and taken into consideration when designing the software.
- Open-source components being used are scanned for security vulnerabilities based on a risk assessment process.

The requirements imposed by the SDLC on the software development process are dynamically adapted and updated regularly based on publicly accessible sources that provide information on known software vulnerabilities (e.g., *Common Weakness Enumeration* or *Common Vulnerabilities and Exposures*).

10.2.2 Provisioning and Operating SAP Cloud Platform Integration Clusters by SAP

Let's now take a closer look at how the SAP Cloud Platform Integration platform is provided and administered by SAP. The provisioning of accounts and tenants for new customers and the setup and operation of the associated VMs is performed by the SAP Cloud Platform Integration Operations team.

SAP Cloud Platform Integration is managed and administered by software-as-a-service (SaaS) administrators from a dedicated team at SAP (these were indicated as the user icon with the title **SAP** in Figure 10.2). Members of this team are in charge of setting up and operating the individual tenant clusters of various customers. Tasks they are responsible for include starting and stopping cluster nodes, as well as performing monthly software updates.

Requests from the SAP-internal SaaS administrators associated with these tasks are again forwarded by the load balancer component. Based on the network design shown earlier in Figure 10.2, the components of the customers are also maximally isolated from the component that internally manages them.

SAP takes certain measures to minimize the risk of malicious actions on the part of SAP-internal personnel who have access to the SAP Cloud Platform Integration platform.

The SAP Cloud Platform Integration Operations team is on duty around the clock. The team members act in the role of SaaS administrator. Their tasks also include the continuous operation of the customers' VMs and monthly software updates.

Although the team is in charge of administering and operating customer clusters, and of acting on alerts (in case of unexpected system behavior), the permissions granted to these persons are reduced to the bare minimum needed to perform operational tasks—the principle of *least privilege*. SAP Cloud Platform Integration Operations team members, for example, have no permissions to access the content of messages processed on a customer tenant. Only a defined group of people has the required access rights and permissions to start and stop VMs. Monthly audits of the process make sure that the access rights of the involved persons are constantly monitored, reviewed, and strictly controlled.

All system-related activities of the team members are logged and can be checked. If a customer requires support, selected development experts at SAP can be granted temporarily restricted access to a customer cluster to debug the problem.

10.2.3 Setting Up Secure Connections between the Tenant and Remote Systems

The prerequisite of reliably operating an integration scenario is to set up secure connections between the sender and receiver systems and the SAP Cloud Platform Integration tenant.

A core task is the implementation of the required technical trust relationships between the remote systems (sender and receiver) and the tenant. In most cases, this includes the generation of digital keys and the associated configuration of the keystores of the remote systems and the tenant. Usage of public key technology always requires the exchange of public keys between the administrators of the connected sender and receiver systems and the tenant administrator (as explained in Section 10.4.1).

Whereas the provisioning and operations of VMs are always kept in the hands of SAP, the responsibility for the tenant cluster lies with the customer (tenant administrator). The tenant administrator is responsible for setting up processes and communication channels that guarantee a reliable way of exchanging security-related material with the administrators of the associated systems.

In other words, the tenant administrator is mainly responsible for managing the required security material for the tenant. However, specific digital keys are still provided by SAP. As keys have a limited validity period, they need to be updated on a regular basis by SAP. Note, however, that each change or renewal of a key pair entails the update of the associated public keys implemented in the keystores of the connected remote systems. Therefore, the keystore management functions provided by SAP Cloud Platform Integration make sure that the tenant administrator still keeps control over the activation of updated SAP keys on the tenant (as explained in Section 10.5).

10.3 User Administration and Authorization

In the architecture overview of Section 10.1.1, we showed where user management and authorization come into play in the lifecycle of a SAP Cloud Platform Integration project. In this section, you'll learn the basic concepts of user management and authorizations related to SAP Cloud Platform Integration. We'll show you how to manage authorizations for persons involved in an integration project.

10.3.1 Technical Aspects of User Management

Users and authorizations for integration project teams are managed separately for each customer account within SAP Cloud Platform. However, note that SAP Cloud Platform has no built-in user management component (as compared, e.g., to the User Management Engine that comes with the Java stack of SAP Process Orchestration). Instead, SAP Cloud Platform delegates authentication and user management to another system dedicated to managing information about user identities, also referred to as *IdP*.

By default, SAP Cloud Platform uses the SAP ID service, which is a tenant that exposes an SAP-operated IdP (see *https://cloudplatform.sap.com*). The connection and trust relationship of your subaccount with the SAP ID Service is preconfigured when you register to SAP Cloud Platform. The SAP ID Service also supports Single Sign-On (SSO), which allows users to log on once and then receive seamless access to all deployed applications.

When you initially access SAP Cloud Platform, you'll register at SAP ID Service. SAP ID Service manages users for other SAP websites, such as SAP Community. Therefore, when you have such a user (e.g., an S-user), you're already registered with SAP ID Service, so no further actions are required. You can also use a custom IdP (using an SAP Cloud Platform tenant with SAP Cloud Platform Identity Authentication service).

10.3.2 Personas, Roles, and Permissions

To manage authorizations for users involved in integration projects, SAP Cloud Platform provides predefined roles that allow you to give subaccount users permissions related to their tasks. According to the main tasks for integration projects, these roles are grouped in authorization groups shown in Table 10.2.

Authorization Group	Description
`AuthGroup.BusinessExpert`	Enables a business expert to perform tasks such as monitoring integration flows and monitoring message content stored in temporary storages
`AuthGroup.Administrator`	Enables the tenant administrator to perform administrative tasks on the tenant cluster, for example, deploying security content and integration flows

Table 10.2 Authorization Groups for Integration Team Members

Authorization Group	Description
`AuthGroup.Integration-Developer`	Enables an integration developer to display, download, and deploy artifacts (e.g., integration flows)
`AuthGroup.ReadOnly`	Enables a user to display integration content and to monitor messages
`AuthGroup.SystemDeveloper`	Enables a system developer to perform tasks required for system support (e.g., restarting subsystems of the tenant cluster, and software development tasks on VMs of the tenant cluster)

Table 10.2 Authorization Groups for Integration Team Members (Cont.)

The tenant administrator (who is the first to access the tenant and perform user and authorization management tasks) assigns the relevant authorization groups to the users that are associated with people involved in integration projects and are in charge of specific tasks (e.g., developing integration content).

In addition to assigning authorization groups to users, you can also define permissions on a more detailed level by assigning individual elementary roles. For example, to display audit log entries (as shown in Chapter 8, Section 8.5.1), the following roles have to be assigned to the user: `IntegrationOperationServer.read` and `AuditLog.Read`, whereas to display the MPL (as explained in Chapter 8, Section 8.5.1), only the role `IntegrationOperationServer.read` has to be assigned to the user.

For a detailed documentation of the roles that are available for the different tasks associated with an integration project, go to the online documentation of SAP Cloud Platform Integration at *https://help.sap.com/viewer/product/CLOUD_INTEGRATION/Cloud* and search for **Tasks and Required Roles**.

So far, we've only considered users associated to persons involved in an integration project. However, we also need to define authorizations for certain technical users (i.e., users associated with components or systems that are to be connected to SAP Cloud Platform Integration). For these technical users, a specific role needs to be assigned: `ESBMessaging.send`. Note that this role needs to be assigned to the runtime node, not, like all other predefined roles, to the TMN. You can also define custom roles for this purpose as explained in Section 10.3.3.

10.3.3 Managing Users and Authorizations for a SAP Cloud Platform Integration Subaccount

When you've requested a tenant, you'll receive an email from SAP that contains the details of your tenant, as well as how to access your subaccount (see Chapter 2). This mail contains all information you need to access your tenant cluster as well as SAP Cloud Platform cockpit. The first step after your tenant is provided by SAP is to go to SAP Cloud Platform cockpit and define the authorizations of all people in your organization that work in your integration project.

After you've logged in to SAP Cloud Platform cockpit, selected your region, your global account, and then your subaccount, and you'll get to the UI shown in Figure 10.3.

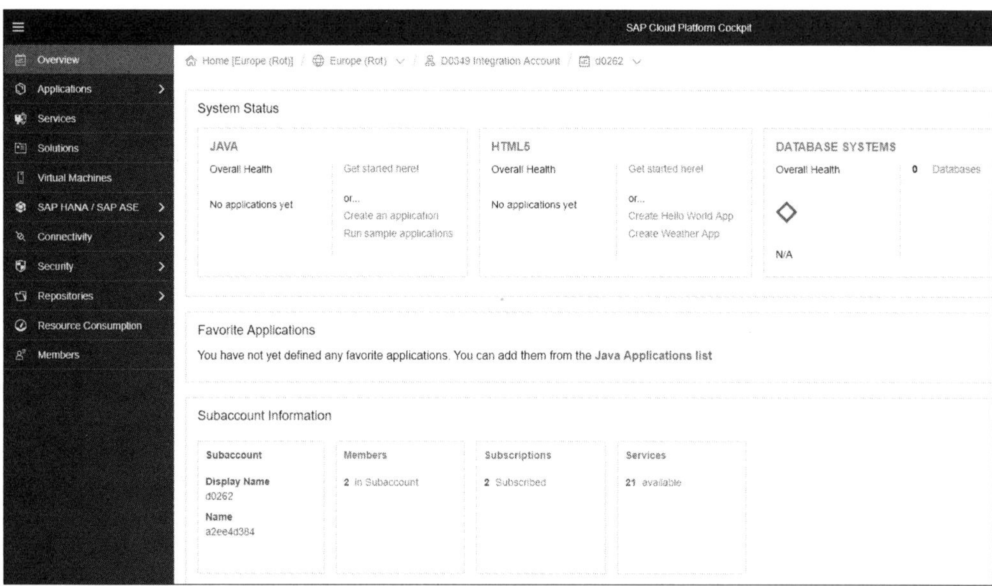

Figure 10.3 SAP Cloud Platform Cockpit When Subaccount Is Selected

As the tenant administrator, you can now start managing users and authorizations for the account. This process comprises two steps:

1. Define the members of the account. These are all people who are supposed to work as tenant administrators.
2. Assign authorization groups to the users of all (additional) persons that are supposed to perform tasks related to the tenant (e.g., integration developers).

Adding Members to the Account

In the SAP Cloud Platform cockpit navigation area of your subaccount (Figure 10.3), click **Members**, and add the users who will have the role of tenant administrator.

1. On the **Add Members** page, enter the user ID, and select the role to be assigned to the user. We recommend selecting the roles **Administrator (predefined role)** and **Developer (predefined role)** (Figure 10.4).

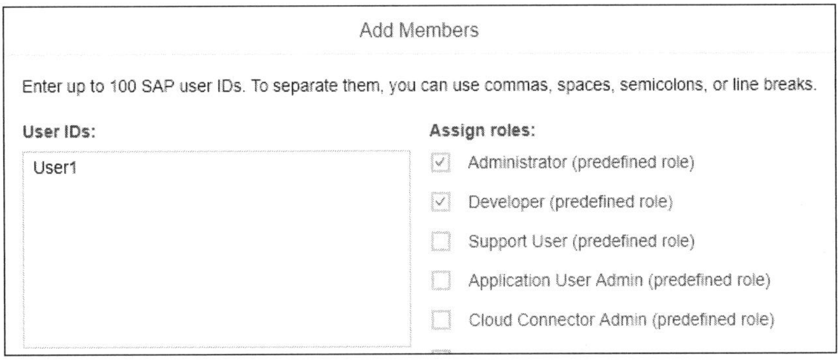

Figure 10.4 Adding Members to a Subaccount

   The **Administrator** role gives the added user ID the full permissions of a tenant administrator. It allows you to manage subaccount members, as well to manage authorizations, OAuth settings, and other tasks.

   The **Developer** role provides permissions to perform typical developer tasks such as starting or stopping applications.

   Don't use any of the other roles.

   These roles are predefined on SAP Cloud Platform and define authorizations for subaccount users. They aren't related to the authorization groups and roles that are required for specific tasks in an integration project (Table 10.2). Those are assigned in an additional step, which we'll explain next.

2. Click **Add Members**.

Defining Authorizations for Integration Team Members

After you've defined the subaccount members (tenant administrators), you'll assign authorization groups or roles to users associated with the people who are supposed to work in an integration project (e.g., for integration developers). Follow these steps:

1. In the navigation area (refer to Figure 10.3), choose **Security • Authorizations**.

2. On the **Authorization Management** page, enter the **User** for whom you want to define authorizations, and choose **Assign** (Figure 10.5).

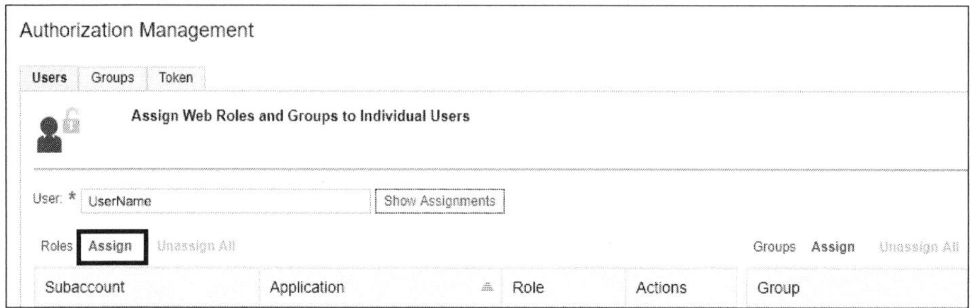

Figure 10.5 Authorization Management Page

3. On the **Assign roles to user <user name>** screen, choose the authorization group or role that is to be assigned in the **Role** field (Figure 10.6).

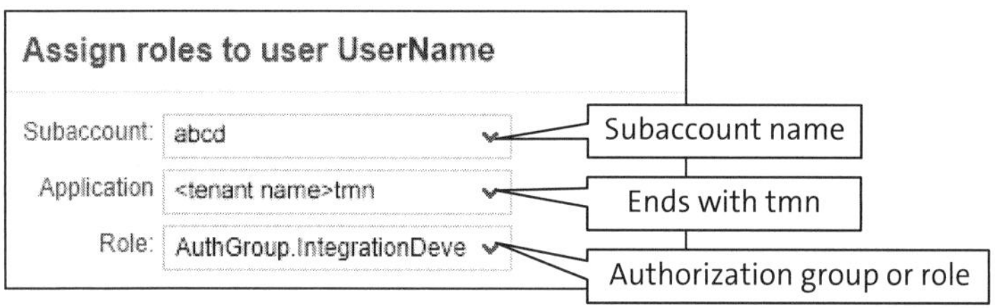

Figure 10.6 Assigning Authorization Groups or Roles to a User

Note that when assigning authorization groups or roles to dialog users associated with an integration project, you select a TMN (ending with "tmn") for the **Application** field (as dialog users access the SAP Cloud Platform Integration platform through the TMN; refer to Figure 10.1).

4. Click **Save**.
5. Repeat these steps for all users and authorization groups to be assigned.

You also can create user groups for all users who should get identical authorizations (see the right side of Figure 10.5).

Creating and Assigning Roles for Technical Users to Process Messages

To enable users associated with technical systems to process messages on the tenant, you need to define the relevant permissions on the level of the runtime nodes.

SAP provides a predefined role for that purpose, which you already learned about in Chapter 2, Section 2.3.3 (Figure 2.16), and at several other places within this book: `ESB-Messaging.send`. This role is defined on the runtime node level. To authorize a sending application to process messages on the tenant (more specifically, on the runtime node), you need to assign this role to the technical user associated with the sender. Use the same procedure as described previously for managing user-to-role assignments for dialog users, with the exception that as **Application**, you select a runtime node (ending with "iflmap"; see Figure 10.7). Remember, in contrast to dialog users, users associated with technical systems access the SAP Cloud Platform Integration platform through the runtime node (as shown in Figure 10.7).

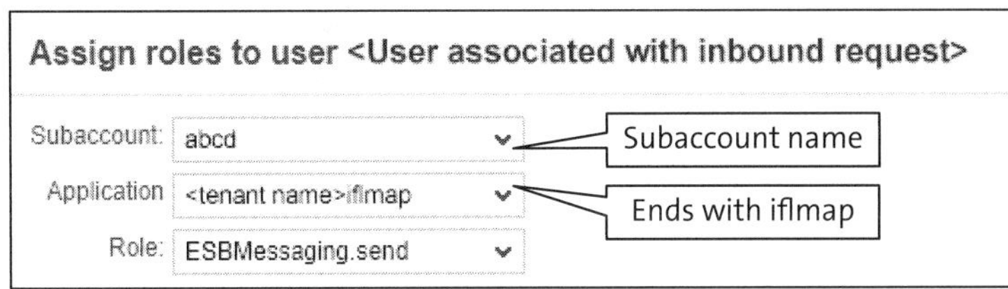

Figure 10.7 Assigning a Role to a Technical User for the Sender System

However, you can also define custom roles, for example, to specify permissions on a more fine-granular level. We'll now show how to define a new user-to-role assignment for the runtime node (to define permissions to process messages on the runtime node). In Section 10.4.4, when discussing the inbound connection, we already mentioned the option to use custom roles to define permissions for inbound calls. Follow these steps:

1. In SAP Cloud Platform cockpit, select your subaccount as shown earlier.
2. In the left navigation area, click **Subscriptions**.
3. Under **Application**, click the one ending with **iflmap** (which identifies your runtime node).
4. In the left navigation area, click **Roles**.
5. Choose **New Role**, and enter the name of your role (e.g., "MyRole"), as shown in Figure 10.8.
6. Choose **Assign**, and enter the **User ID** (of the user which is to be associated with the sending application), as shown in Figure 10.9.

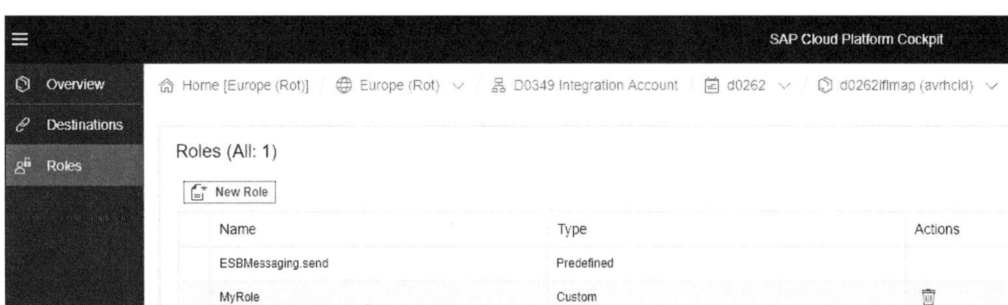

Figure 10.8 Defining a Custom Role

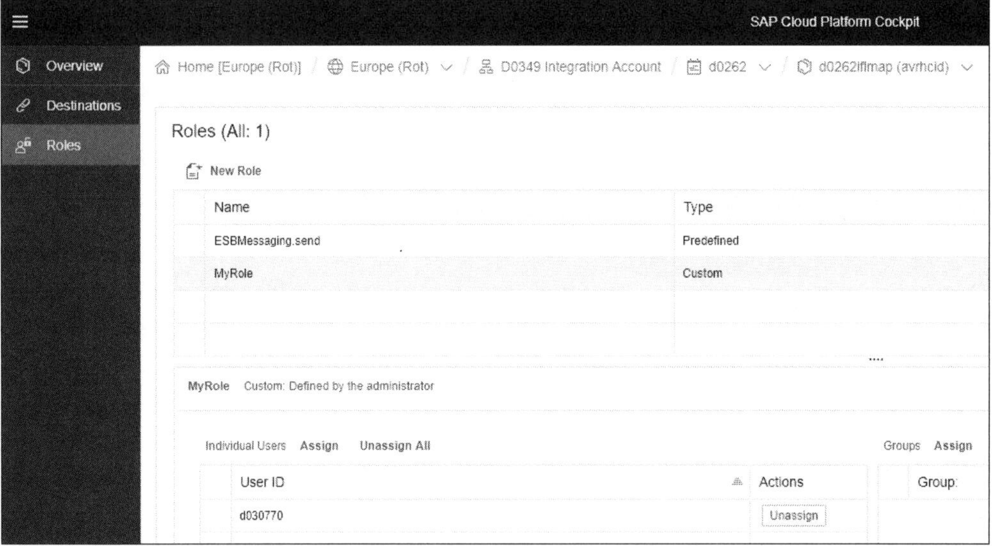

Figure 10.9 Assigning a Custom Role to a User

You've now learned how to manage users and authorizations, including how to define the permissions initially for your integration team members.

Now, from a security perspective, you can start working with SAP Cloud Platform Integration. In the next sections, we show all options of data and data flow security and how your integration team members can use the tools of SAP Cloud Platform Integration to set up scenarios with a certain security level.

10.4 Data and Data Flow Security

In Section 10.1 and Section 10.2, you learned about the security measures that are already in place when you begin working with SAP Cloud Platform Integration—given by the architecture, the network design, the processes associated with SAP Cloud Platform Integration, and other aspects. Section 10.3 introduced you to the topic of user management.

In this section, we'll discuss the options that you, as the customer, have to maximize the security of the solution by configuring the way data is exchanged between the components in the customer landscape and SAP Cloud Platform Integration. In other words, we'll focus on how *data in transit* (i.e., on its way between the involved parties) can be protected.

SAP Cloud Platform Integration provides you with a variety of options to protect data in transit on the following levels:

- **On the transport protocol level**
  Establish a secure communication channel between remote systems and the involved SAP Cloud Platform Integration components.
- **On the message level**
  Further protect the exchanged messages via digital encryption and signing.

This topic, which deals with concepts of secure communication and protecting digital data, is known as *cryptography*. In Section 10.4.1, we'll provide a brief overview of the basic terms and concepts of cryptography. Note that this is general knowledge, not exclusively related to SAP Cloud Platform Integration. Those who are familiar with the topic of cryptography can, therefore, skip Section 10.4.1 and continue with Section 10.4.2.

In Section 10.4.2 and Section 10.4.3, respectively, we provide an overview of the transport-level security options and of the authorization and authentication options supported by SAP Cloud Platform Integration. In Section 10.4.4 and Section 10.4.5, two tutorials will follow that show you how to establish secure connections between your tenant and remote systems and how to develop a simple integration flow with a specific authentication option, OAuth. In Section 10.4.6, we discuss the message-level security options provided by SAP Cloud Platform Integration. In Section 10.4.7, finally, we explain how message-level security can be implemented using SAP Cloud Platform Integration (including a step-by-step tutorial that you can easily reproduce).

10.4.1 Basic Cryptography in a Nutshell

Cryptography, in the broadest sense, deals with methods and techniques that help protect data against unauthorized access. One basic measure of protecting data against unauthorized access is to encrypt it. Encrypting means to transform a *clear text* (which is readable by everyone) into a *secret text*, prior to sending it to a communication partner. This transformation is done on the sender side by a mathematical operation (based on an *encryption key*). The dedicated receiver needs to know the inverse operation (the *decryption key*) to transform the secret text back into the clear text.

Another measure to protect a message on its way between a sender and receiver is to apply a *digital signature* so that the receiver can be sure that the message has been sent by the trusted sender (this is also known as data integrity).

The simplest and most obvious approach (which is also referred to as *symmetric key technology*) is that sender and receiver use the same key, and a critical requirement to ensure a seamless and protected communication of sender and receiver is that the key is securely exchanged between both parties prior to the actual data exchange. It's obvious that this requirement can't be met in the digital age, as the number of potential communication partners and communication paths for a given channel (e.g., email) is on a large scale and dynamically changes in the short term.

To overcome this challenge, *asymmetric* (or *public*) *key technologies* have been developed, which always require two different key types: a public key and a private (or secret) key. Both key types are generated together and are related to each other based on a mathematical operation such that the public key can be easily calculated from the private key. However, it's impossible to perform the reverse operation and derive the private key from the public key (at least, when considering computing capacities available today). Mathematically, this approach is based on one-way functions, which we won't explain further here. For more information, refer to *Cryptography and Public Key Infrastructure on the Internet* (Wiley, 2003).

For the encryption use case, the asymmetric approach works in the following way: the intended receiver of a message generates a public-private key pair and shares the public key with the sender. The sender then uses the public key to encrypt the message. The receiver then uses its private key (which is always kept with the receiver and never shared with any other party) to decrypt the message.

For digital signatures, the inverse pattern is applied. The sender signs a message using its private key (which is always kept with the sender) and the receiver (and many other potential receivers) can verify the signature by using the public key, which they have been provided with by the sender. We show how this works in detail in Section 10.4.6.

The private key must never be shared with anyone else obviously, or it would allow others to sign messages in your name or to decrypt content that is destined solely for you.

Because of the inherent mathematical concepts (one-way functions), public keys, on the other hand, can potentially be shared through unsecure channels (e.g., email). Any malicious party who receives the public key by mistake has no opportunity to decrypt or sign any message with it. Note, however, that certain additional measures should be undertaken to enable the receiver of a public key to validate the authenticity of the same, as outlined later.

Hybrid Approaches

Symmetric methods typically use simple bit operations to transform a clear text bit sequence into a secret text bit sequence. In asymmetric methods, however, sophisticated mathematical operations come into play (which use modulo mathematics). Because of this, asymmetric methods are computationally intensive and, therefore, not well-suited to operate on larger bit sequences that come along with large business messages exchanged in integration scenarios.

To overcome this issue, it's more feasible to apply hybrid approaches, which combine asymmetric and symmetric methods. In encryption scenarios, the most common pattern is as follows (see Figure 10.10).

The sender encrypts the (potentially large-volume) content of a message using a *symmetric* encryption key. Thereafter, the sender encrypts the symmetric encryption key with a public key and sends the encrypted symmetric key (along with the encrypted message content) to the receiver. Before the message exchange between sender and receiver has been initiated, the public key has been generated by the receiver as part of an *asymmetric* key pair and shared with the sender without risk. With the associated private key, the receiver, as soon as he has received the encrypted symmetric key (and the encrypted message content), decrypts it and, finally, uses the revealed secret key to decrypt the message content.

This way, we avoid applying asymmetric key operations to the whole message content.

Hybrid approaches are applied in the transport-level security option TLS, described in Section 10.4.2, as well as in the message-level security options described in Section 10.4.6. In these sections, we'll show in more detail how these approaches work.

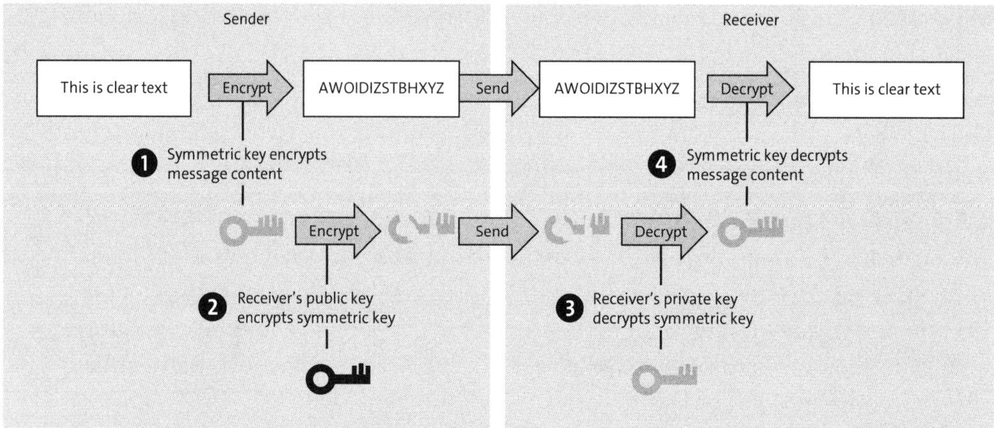

Figure 10.10 Hybrid Usage of Symmetric and Asymmetric Key Technology When Encrypting and Decrypting Message Content

Keystores

To introduce another important term, note that keys (public and private keys) are stored in *keystores* owned by the involved parties. How a keystore is implemented and its characteristics depend on the type of system that implements the services of the sender and receiver.

Figure 10.11 illustrates the setup of components for two parties exchanging encrypted messages based on public key technology. In the shown general setup, sender and receiver separately generate their own public-private key pair and import it into their keystore. In a subsequent step, both participants share the corresponding *public* key with the communication partner. Both partners also import the corresponding foreign public key into their keystores.

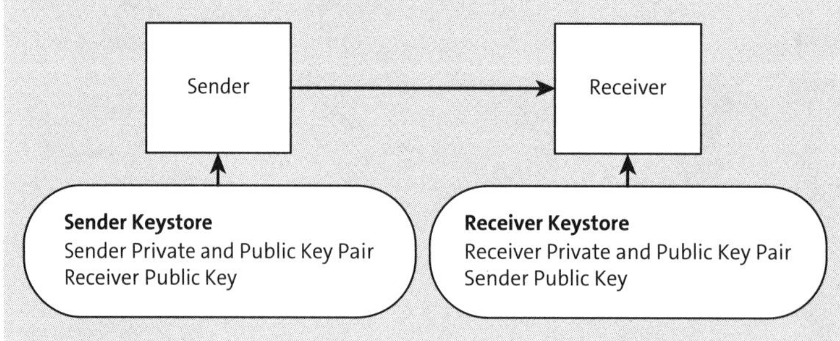

Figure 10.11 Keystores Containing the Required Key Material

Although there is no common term for the key storage of all possible kinds of systems, simplicity, we'll always talk about *keystores* throughout this book. We'll also shorten the term *public and private key pair* to *private key pair* or *key pair*.

Keystore Types for SAP Cloud Platform Integration

In scenarios described in this book, the tenant is always one communication partner. Therefore, a keystore needs to be deployed on the tenant that contains the required key material. The characteristics of the keystore also depend on the chosen security standard (as will be shown in Section 10.4.2 and Section 10.4.6).

To give an example, when you use X.509 certificates, you utilize a Java keystore, whereas when you use OpenPGP, you'll need two different "keystore" types: a PGP Public Keyring and a PGP Secret Keyring (Section 10.4.6 and Section 10.4.7).

To give an example for a remote system that can be connected to a tenant: if it's an SAP system based on Application Server ABAP (AS ABAP), the required keys are maintained with the Trust Manager in the Personal Security Environment, which takes over the role as the keystore.

Although we've stated that public keys can potentially be exchanged on unsecure channels (whereas private keys must never be shared with another party), a malicious party can nevertheless misuse this fact and send a public key to another party, pretending to be the owner of the public key. So, the question is, how can the authenticity of a public key be guaranteed to further increase security?

To answer this, we'll briefly discuss *digital certificates*. As certificates are of significant importance for the whole topic of security, we put the definition of this term and concept in an info box.

Digital Certificate

A digital certificate is a public key that is signed by a trusted authority (usually referred to as a certification authority (CA). This way, the identity and trustworthiness of the public key owner can be confirmed. Taken in short, a certificate couples an identity with a public key.

There are many options to build trust based on certificates. One example is the X.509 standard, which comes into play, for example, when two communication partners protect their communication channel using TLS (Section 10.4.2). X.509 supports the usage of PKIX-certificates (Public Key Infrastructure X.509) that allow you to build up certificate chains. These are hierarchical trust models, which include many CAs on different levels, where the CA on the higher level signs the certificate of the correspondingly lower level, and so forth. The CA on the top level is referred to as the root CA. This model is called a certificate chain.

An example of a CA is GeoTrust (*www.geotrust.com*). One root certificate issued by GeoTrust and supported by the load balancer is *GeoTrust Global CA*.

Another, alternative trust model is the *Web of Trust*. In such a model, communication partners mutually confirm the authenticity of each other's public keys, building a network of partners rather than a hierarchical structure. The Web of Trust model can be used in conjunction with the security standard OpenPGP. Figure 10.12 shows the difference between the two trust models.

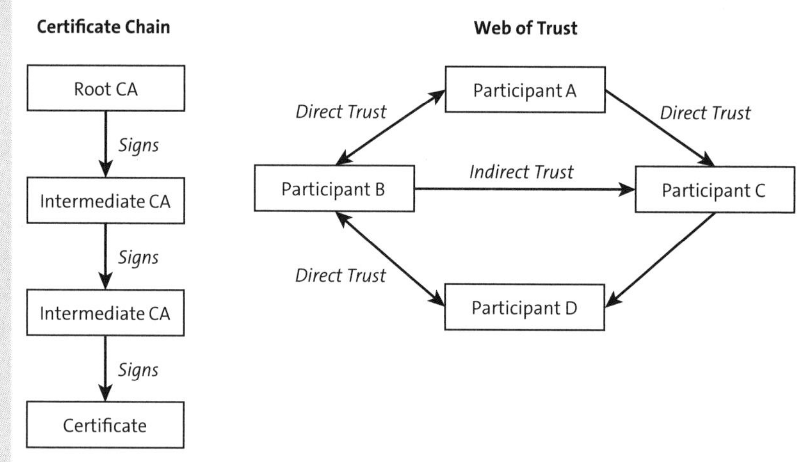

Figure 10.12 Certificate Chain (Left) Compared to a Web of Trust (Right)

X.509 Certificates

As this certificate type is the most commonly used for transport-level security, we would like to discuss a few basic concepts and terms. X.509 certificates allow you to implement trust models based on certificate chains. A set of elements is required to specify a X.509 certificate, although we won't go into detail about that in this book. We only want to point out the **Issuer** and the **Subject** field, which are required to understand the following:

- **Issuer**
  Specifies the CA (that issued and signed the certificate).
- **Subject**
  Specifies the entity that is associated with the public key of the certificate. If the certificate is used to authenticate a client calling a server, the subject usually identifies the client.

Both entries, **Issuer** and **Subject**, are uniquely defined by a distinguished name (DN), which is composed of a set of attributes such as company name, country identification, and so on. The format of DNs is defined by the specification RFC 5280 (see *https://tools.ietf.org/html/rfc5280*). That way, DNs are guaranteed to be unique, and using them ensures that, first, the certificate issuer can uniquely be identified (to make sure the certificate isn't tampered with information from a malicious party) and, second, the entity associated with the certificate certainly can considered to be the one it's intended to be.

Certificates and their management are discussed in more detail in Section 10.5.

You're now equipped with the basic concepts and terms of cryptography. In Section 10.4.2 and Section 10.4.6, we explain in detail how to apply cryptographic concepts to set up secure message exchange scenarios based on certain security standards.

10.4.2 Transport-Level Security Options

SAP Cloud Platform Integration provides various connectivity options—methods of connecting remote systems with different technical characteristics to SAP Cloud Platform Integration. The available adapters imply one of the transport protocols listed in Table 10.3, each with different options to secure the communication channel.

Transport Protocol	Description
Hyper Text Transfer Protocol (HTTP) over Transport Layer Security (TLS), also referred to as HTTPS	TLS is a protocol for secure communication over a computer network that is widely used on the Internet. As TLS is the enhancement of SSL. Note that these terms are often used synonymously. The protocol works with the following adapter types: SOAP, IDoc, SAP SuccessFactors, and HTTP.

Table 10.3 Transport Protocols and Associated Security Options

Transport Protocol	Description
SSH File Transfer Protocol: Secure File Transfer Protocol (SFTP)	This protocol has been developed for the Secure Shell (SSH) and allows secure transfer of files. SSH is a network protocol that allows you to set up a secure connection to a remote computer. This protocol works with the SFTP adapter.
Simple Mail Transfer Protocol Secure (SMTPS)	Simple Mail Transfer Protocol enables a computer to exchange emails with a mail server. With SMTPS, SMTP connections can be secured by SSL or TLS. The protocol works with the mail receiver adapter.
Post Office Protocol version 3 over TLS/SSL (POP3S)	This protocol enables email clients to retrieve emails from an email server using the Internet Protocol (IP). POP3S works with the mail sender adapter.
Internet Message Access Protocol over TLS/SSL (IMAPS)	This protocol enables email clients to retrieve emails from an email server using a TCP/IP connection. IMAPS works with the mail sender adapter.

Table 10.3 Transport Protocols and Associated Security Options (Cont.)

As TLS is by far the most commonly used transport-level security option, we'll add a few remarks on this protocol.

Transport Layer Security

TLS uses a hybrid approach of asymmetric and symmetric key technology: the asymmetrical approach is used to encrypt a symmetric session key at the beginning of the connection setup, while the latter is then used to actually encrypt and decrypt the data as long as the TLS connection (session) is active.

TLS uses a hierarchical trust model (based on X.509 certificates). During the connection setup, certificates between the client and server are exchanged, and the authenticity of these certificates is validated based on the provided signatures by certification authorities.

With TLS, SAP Cloud Platform Integration offers different options for how a client authenticates itself against the server. We'll discuss the authentication options in Section 10.4.3.

10.4.3 Authentication and Authorization

Next to measures to protect the exchanged messages by digital encryption and signature, other important aspects that impact the security of a system of components that communicate with each other are authentication and authorization.

Before presenting the options offered by SAP Cloud Platform Integration, we'll briefly clarify and distinguish the terms *authentication* and *authorization*.

Authentication and Authorization

Authentication verifies the identity of something (or someone) in a communication workflow. It checks, for example, if the person associated with a user (that connects to a server) is who he claims to be.

In information technology, authentication workflows typically relate to scenarios where a client (to be authenticated) requests access to some kind of protected resource hosted on a server. In the context of SAP Cloud Platform Integration, the term *protected resource* covers not only data but also message processing capabilities (e.g., implemented on a VM of a tenant cluster).

After authentication, an *authorization* check verifies what the authenticated entity is allowed to do in the connected server system.

In many cases, in an authorization check, user-to-role assignments of the (authenticated) user are investigated in the server system. For inbound communication (where SAP Cloud Platform Integration acts as server), the user-to-role assignments are defined by the tenant administrator (as shown earlier in Section 10.3).

Basic Authentication

This is the simplest option, where authentication is based on user credentials (username and password). When you configure basic authentication for inbound communication (where a client sends messages to SAP Cloud Platform Integration), the credentials of the technical user associated with the client are forwarded to SAP Cloud Platform Integration in the message header (through a secure channel, e.g., using HTTPS). The identity of the client is then verified based on the credentials stored at SAP.

SAP doesn't recommend using basic authentication for productive scenarios, as it's less secure than using client certificates.

Client Certificate Authentication

Using this option, the authentication step is accomplished based on digital certificates. Instead of credentials, the client forwards a digital certificate to the server. The authentication of the client is then done by checking the certificate.

Client certificate authentication is always the option of choice for productive scenarios, as certificates guarantee a higher level of security (they rely on a trust relationship, which is difficult to break, as shown in Section 10.4.1).

OAuth

Until now, we've only talked about authentication workflows that include two parties: a client (requesting access to a protected resource) and a server (that hosts the resource). In such scenarios, the protected resource is owned by either the client or the server.

We'll now talk about a different, more sophisticated authentication pattern, where the owner of the protected resource isn't necessarily identical to either client or server. Due to this, three parties (or roles) come into play:

- A user who owns the protected resources
- A client, which is typically an application
- A server (or resource server), which is typically a service provider that hosts the protected resources

That is what OAuth is about. It enables the user (as owner of the *protected resource*), to grant the *client* access to the protected resource (hosted by the *resource server*). The access granted to the client is typically *restricted*—no full access rights will be given. While doing that, you, the resource owner, can keep your credentials private. Figure 10.13 shows the basic, simplified setup of OAuth.

As an example, you can think of Twitter as a resource server and a Twitter user as the owner of his Twitter stream (which is the resource). We'll show in Section 10.4.5 how SAP Cloud Platform Integration (as the client application) can be granted access to Twitter content on behalf of a Twitter user. For that purpose, the corresponding integration flow uses a Twitter receiver adapter.

In OAuth 2.0, an additional role is added to the picture—the *authorization server*—which is the component that is finally granting access to the protected resource (and that is issuing the required access tokens, see more below). So far and in Figure 10.13, the authorization server wasn't identified. For simplicity, we assumed that authorization server and resource server (that hosts the resource) were identical, which is also a possible scenario.

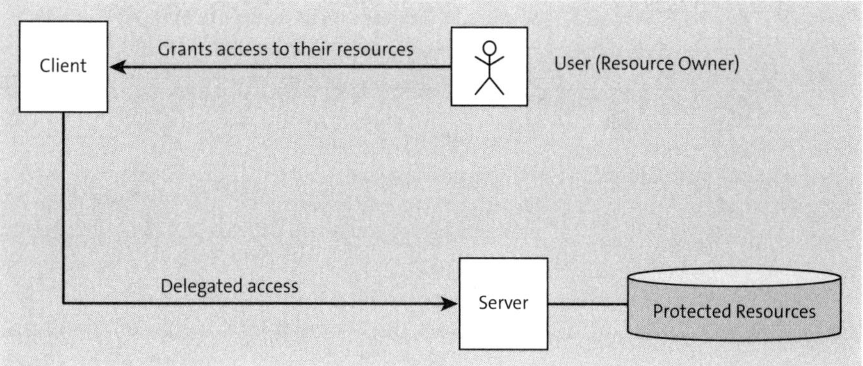

Figure 10.13 OAuth Scenario: Resource Owner Delegates Access to Protected Resources (Hosted on a Server) to a Client

To enable client access to the protected resource, the owner doesn't need to share his own credentials with the client. However, OAuth comes with a more complex setup of credentials than that used in the other authentication scenarios discussed earlier. In addition to the resource owner's own credentials (necessary to access his own resource), two additional kinds of credentials come into play. Table 10.4 provides a summary of the credentials.

Credential Type	Description
Resource owner's credentials	Enable the resource owner to log on to the resource server to access and manage his protected resources.
Client credentials	Identify the client (at the resource server's side). Client credentials are composed of the *consumer key* and the *consumer secret.* In OAuth 2.0 terminology, client credentials are a specific implementation of an *authorization grant*. An authorization grant is a credential that is used by the client to obtain an access token (see the next table entry).

Table 10.4 Credential Types Used with OAuth

Credential Type	Description
Token credentials	Authorize the client (on behalf of the resource owner) to access the resource. The token credentials identify the resource owner at the server's side. They can be revoked by the resource owner at any time. Token credentials are composed of *access token* and *access token secret*.

Table 10.4 Credential Types Used with OAuth (Cont.)

In the sets of credentials summarized in Table 10.4, the secret is a piece of information exclusively shared between the client and server. Using the two parts of a credential pair in combination helps protect those credentials from being compromised.

A characteristic of the token credentials (as compared to the client credentials) is that they can be revoked by the resource owner at any time. This allows you to adapt authorization workflows flexibly to changing requirements without the need to reconfigure the set of client credentials or to renew the resource owner's own credentials.

With these terms in mind, a typical OAuth authentication workflow comprises the following steps, now considering that resource server and authentication server are separate components. Figure 10.14 is geared to the general description of the OAuth 2.0 workflow in the OAuth 2.0 specification that you can find at *https://tools.ietf.org/html/rfc6749*.

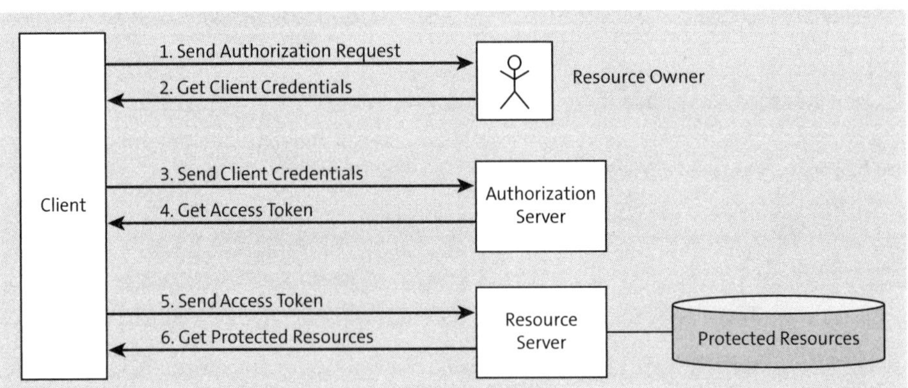

Figure 10.14 OAuth 2.0 Authentication Workflow (with Client Credentials)

The workflow comprises the following sequence of steps:

1. The client requests authorization from the resource owner to access his protected resource.
2. The resource owner provides the client with client credentials (as a specific type of authorization grant as indicated in Table 10.4).
3. The client connects to the authorization server and presents the client credentials.
4. The authorization server authenticates the client, validates the client credentials, and, if they are valid, provides the client with an access token.
5. Authenticating itself against the resource server with the access token, the client requests the protected resource from the resource server.
6. The resource server validates the access token and, if it's valid, grants the client access to the protected resource.

An important aspect of this workflow is that the resource owner at no point in time has to share his credentials with anyone.

OAuth Terminology

OAuth is available in two versions:

- OAuth 1.0 (*https://tools.ietf.org/html/rfc5849*)
- OAuth 2.0 (*https://tools.ietf.org/html/rfc6749*)

Version 1.0 uses slightly different terminology for the credentials than version 2.0 does: *consumer key* and *consumer secret* (in version 1.0) are summarized as *client credentials* in version 2.0, whereas *access token* and *access token secret* (in version 1.0) are referred to as *token credentials* in version 2.0. In other words, the terms *consumer* and *client* are used synonymously.

Note that the social media adapters of SAP Cloud Platform Integration (Twitter and Facebook adapters), which we'll discuss in Section 10.4.5, use the terms associated with version 1.0. To make it easy for you to understand how these adapters work, we mentioned both versions of the terms and set them into the proper context in Table 10.4.

This is the briefly explained OAuth authentication workflow. In Section 10.4.5, we'll show you how OAuth works together with the SAP Cloud Platform Integration Twitter adapter.

Principal Propagation

This authentication option is based on a setup where the identity of a user is transferred along all relevant communication paths of an integration scenario—from the sender to the receiver.

We show you now which authentication options are supported for HTTPS-based communication both for inbound and outbound communication. In particular, we also explain which combinations of authentication and authorization are supported by the SAP Cloud Platform Integration system when acting as server (inbound communication).

Inbound Authentication and Authorization (for HTTPS Communication)

When configuring inbound HTTPS communication (where SAP Cloud Platform Integration is to receive messages from a sender system), you'll notice that certain sender adapters that support this protocol provide the option to choose an **Authorization** option (rather than an **Authentication** option). We're talking here, namely, about the SOAP, IDoc, and HTTPS adapters. You can check this by creating, for example, a sender SOAP 1.x channel as shown in our first tutorial in this book in Chapter 2, Section 2.3.4 (see Figure 2.27). For your convenience, we show the related UI property in Figure 10.15. Two authorization options are available: **User Role** and **Client Certificate**.

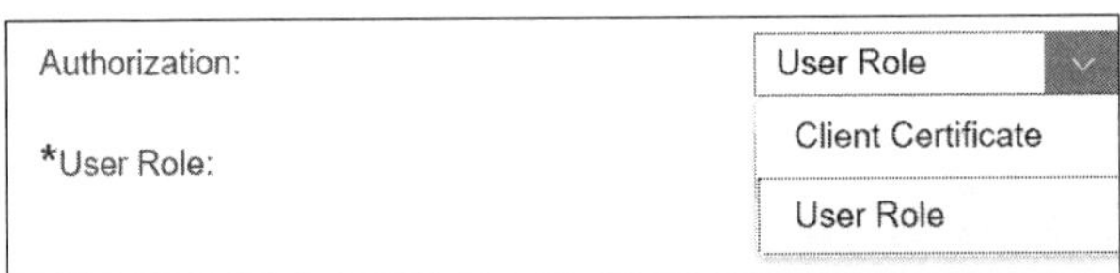

Figure 10.15 Authorization Options Offered for Certain Sender Adapters That Support HTTPS

As we're here talking about SAP Cloud Platform Integration as the server that is requested by a sender (client) system, you (as integration developer who defines an integration scenario) can specify how the user associated with the sender is authorized to "do things" on the SAP Cloud Platform Integration platform. The possible options depend on the technical capabilities of the SAP Cloud Platform Integration platform.

With the selection of an *authorization* option for inbound communication, you determine already which *authentication* option can be used along with the selected authorization option.

Table 10.5 points out the difference between the authorization options.

Authorization Option	Description
User Role	For the user associated with the sender system, the authorizations are checked based on user-to-role assignments defined for the tenant using SAP Cloud Platform cockpit. SAP recommends using this authorization option together with a *certificate-to-user mapping*. In this case, you specify the client certificates in a **Certificate-to-User Mappings** artifact (which is deployed on the tenant). In this artifact, you assign a user to the certificate. When the sender calls SAP Cloud Platform Integration, it authenticates itself against SAP Cloud Platform Integration based on the specified client certificate. In a subsequent step, authorization is checked based on user-to-role assignments defined for the user, which is derived from the certificate-to-user mapping. Already in the first tutorial (Chapter 2, Section 2.3), you learned about the role `ESBMessaging.send`, which defines permissions for a sender system to process messages on the tenant. We show how to set up such a scenario in Section 10.4.4. For certain reasons that are explained in Section 10.4.4, this is the recommended option.
Client Certificate	Using this option, you specify the required certificate in the integration flow (in particular, in the sender adapter). At runtime, the sender authenticates itself against SAP Cloud Platform Integration based on a client certificate. In a subsequent step, the permission of the sender to execute the integration flow is checked by evaluating the DN of the sender's client certificate. Note that SAP recommends that you don't use this option any longer because of certain disadvantages (e.g., that changing certificates would always mean redeployment and, consequently, downtimes of the integration flow).

Table 10.5 Authorization Options for Inbound HTTPS Communication

When you select **Client Certificate** as the **Authorization** option, you inherently determine as *authentication* method the option *client certificate*, whereas the alternative **Authorization** option, **User Role**, can be combined with different authentication options. According to Table 10.5, the recommended way to go is combining this authorization option with the usage of a certificate-to-user mapping, which comes along with *client certificate* authentication.

However, note that with **User Role** authorization, the following other *authentication* options can be used for inbound communication:

- Basic authentication, which we don't recommend to use for productive scenarios
- OAuth, which allows the configuration of specific scenarios such as principal propagation

To find out more about the supported options, check out the documentation of SAP Cloud Platform Integration at *https://help.sap.com/viewer/product/CLOUD_INTEGRATION/Cloud* and search for **Connecting a Customer System to Cloud Integration**.

Outbound Authentication (for HTTPS Communication)

The other way around—when talking about outbound communication (where SAP Cloud Platform Integration acts as client)—SAP Cloud Platform Integration can't offer any choices about how the user associated with the outbound request is authorized to execute certain actions in the receiver system.

Therefore, as integration developer, you can't specify any authorization options. This is intuitively plausible because how permissions of a calling entity are checked can only be defined by the technical capabilities of the server (in the outbound communication case, this is the receiver system). Because SAP Cloud Platform Integration (as client in this case) can't impose which technical capabilities are offered by the receiver system, it would not make any sense that the SAP Cloud Platform Integration platform allows you to specify any authorization option in a receiver adapter.

However, in a receiver adapter, you can specify the **Authentication** option supported by the client (SAP Cloud Platform Integration, in this case). You can briefly verify this by creating a receiver channel that supports HTTP communication (e.g., a receiver SOAP adapter; see Figure 10.16).

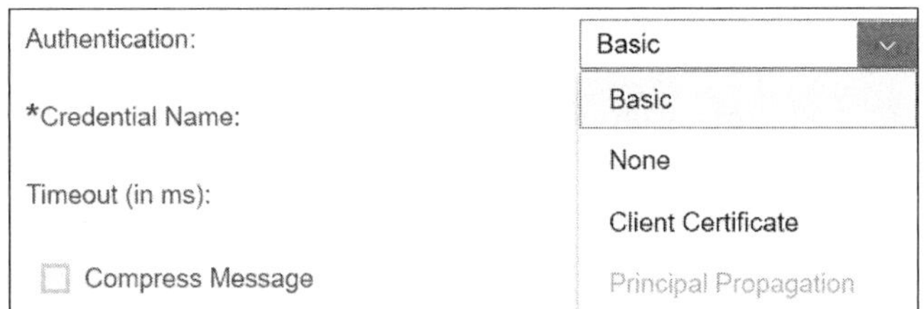

Figure 10.16 Authentication Options Offered for Receiver Adapters That Support HTTPS

Specifying an **Authentication** option is reasonable because SAP Cloud Platform Integration can provide the required artifacts for each authentication option.

Table 10.6 summarizes the different options and provides information on the related integration artifacts that are to be considered when configuring such a communication option.

Authentication Option	Description
Basic	Authentication of SAP Cloud Platform Integration against a receiver system is based on user credentials (username and password). When you configure basic authentication for outbound communication, you need to complement the related receiver adapter setting by defining a security artifact that contains the credentials (a **User Credentials** artifact as shown, for example, in Chapter 2, Section 2.3.4).
Client Certificate	Authentication of SAP Cloud Platform Integration against a receiver system is based on a client certificate. A client certificate (including public and private key) and receiver server root certificate, which is accepted by the receiver, need to be part of the **Keystore** deployed on the tenant. In the receiver adapter settings of the integration flow, the private key alias of the certificate can be specified to indicate a specific key pair to be used for this step. If you don't specify a private key alias, any fitting key in the keystore is used. For a whole setup, Section 10.4.4.

Table 10.6 Outbound Authentication Options (for HTTPS-Based Communication)

Authentication Option	Description
Principal Propagation	In this case, the tenant authenticates itself against the receiver system by forwarding the identity (principal) of the user (associated with the inbound request) to the SAP Cloud Platform Connectivity service and from there to the receiver system (which can be, e.g., an on-premise SAP system). Consequently, this option can only be selected when you've chosen **On-Premise** for the **Proxy Type** option, meaning you've configured outbound connectivity to an on-premise system through the SAP Cloud Platform Connectivity (see the upcoming info box). Setting up a scenario with this authentication option requires comprehensive configuration steps at the inbound and outbound side of SAP Cloud Platform Integration, as well as in SAP Cloud Platform Connectivity and the receiver backend system. A detailed step-by-step tutorial would go beyond the scope of this book.
OAuth (when using Twitter or Facebook adapter)	SAP Cloud Platform Integration calls Twitter or Facebook using OAuth authentication mechanisms. A **Secure Parameter** artifact is required to store the OAuth credentials. For more information, Section 10.4.5. This authentication option isn't offered for the other HTTP-based adapters and therefore is also not shown in the dropdown list in Figure 10.16.

Table 10.6 Outbound Authentication Options (for HTTPS-Based Communication) (Cont.)

Authentication option **None** (as shown in Figure 10.16) isn't considered in the table. If this option is selected, no authentication is required for the tenant when calling a receiver system.

Note that to have permission to deploy security-related artifacts, your user needs to have assigned dedicated roles, for example, the authorization group `AuthGroup.Administrator` (we covered the topic of roles and authorization groups in detail in Section 10.3).

Proxy Type

The following adapter settings are relevant in the context of configuring **Authentication** setting **Principal Propagation**.

In most HTTP-based adapters (e.g., the SOAP and IDoc adapter), you find the attribute **Proxy Type**. In the scenarios in this book, we always kept the default setting of this attribute as **Internet**, which makes sure that the tenant can connect to another system through the Internet (e.g., over HTTP).

The other option for the **Proxy Type** attribute is **On Premise**. Using this option, you enable the tenant to connect to an on-premise system through SAP Cloud Platform Connectivity.

When setting up such a scenario, you also need to install an additional component, referred to as the *cloud connector*, in your on-premise landscape that acts as proxy for those requests that try to access your on-premise system coming from the Internet.

If you use multiple cloud connector instances in your system landscape, you also need to specify a **Location ID**. With this attribute, you can identify the cloud connector instance you want to use for your connection.

You might have noticed that when you select **On Premise** as **Proxy Type**, **Authentication** option **Client Certificate** is deactivated. This expresses the fact that when using SAP Cloud Platform Connectivity, this authentication option isn't supported in the respective receiver adapter. If client certificate authentication is nevertheless required for such a connection, you need to configure this authentication option when setting up SAP Cloud Platform Connectivity.

For more information, consult the documentation for SAP Cloud Platform at *https://help.sap.com/viewer/p/CP* in the **Cloud Connector** section and the "Using SAP Cloud Platform Cloud Connector with SAP Cloud Platform Integration" blog in the SAP Community (*www.sap.com/community.html*).

10.4.4 Securely Connecting a Customer System to SAP Cloud Platform Integration (through HTTPS)

Having introduced the transport-level security options in Section 10.4.2 and authorization and authentication options in Section 10.4.3, we can now discuss how to establish a secure connection between a remote system and SAP Cloud Platform Integration. For simplicity, we'll focus on one—and the most common—option: using HTTPS over TLS and client certificate authentication. We discuss this topic separately for inbound communication (when a sender sends a request to SAP Cloud Platform Integration) and for outbound communication (when SAP Cloud Platform

Integration sends a request to a receiver) because the setup of components and the sequence of tasks differ considerably, depending on the communication direction.

For inbound communication, we show how to set up **User Role** authorization in combination with a certificate-to-user mapping.

For both directions, we first outline the target picture (setup of components and keystores) and then explain the steps required to achieve this setup.

Note that we don't provide an end-to-end tutorial on how to set up a specific integration flow. Instead, we'll focus on those steps that are relevant to set up a secure connection both for inbound and outbound direction (which are mainly certain steps in the configuration of the sender and receiver adapter). We also don't show how to configure certain sender or receiver systems in detail, as this would require a complete integration scenario and a specific technical landscape (for specific kinds of sender and receiver systems). To find more information on such a complete setup for integration packages predefined by SAP (including the configuration of certain SAP systems at the sender and receiver side), refer to the integration guides that you can find in the **Documents** section of the Integration Content Catalog for certain integration packages (see Chapter 3).

When showing the connection setup-related steps for the sender and receiver adapters, we show (as an example) how to do this for a SOAP 1.x adapter. However, the steps work also for most other adapters that support HTTP communication.

Inbound Communication

For inbound communication, the recommended option is to use certificate-to-user mappings. In Chapter 8, Section 8.3.3, we explained the corresponding integration artifact and how to manage it, and we already briefly introduced it in Table 10.5 of this chapter. Next, we'll show you how to include a certificate-to-user mapping in the connection setup for inbound communication.

Figure 10.17 shows how the components interact with each other at runtime (on top) and the required security setup to realize this behavior (bottom).

To begin the target setup, a characteristic feature of inbound HTTP connections is that the load balancer terminates each TLS request from the sender and establishes a new TLS connection to the tenant, which is then processing the request (refer to Figure 10.1). The sender system connects to the load balancer via TLS and verifies the load balancer certificate. Vice versa, the load balancer verifies if the certificate sent by the sender system is valid (as we've chosen client certificate authentication of the sender system). For the discussed security option, the certificates are stored in a keystore on the load balancer component (which is a component maintained by SAP). It's essential that the client certificate installed on the sender system is signed by one of the CAs that are supported by the load balancer. SAP has published a list of such CAs in the online documentation as shown later. If the validation is successful, the load balancer forwards the client certificate to the tenant.

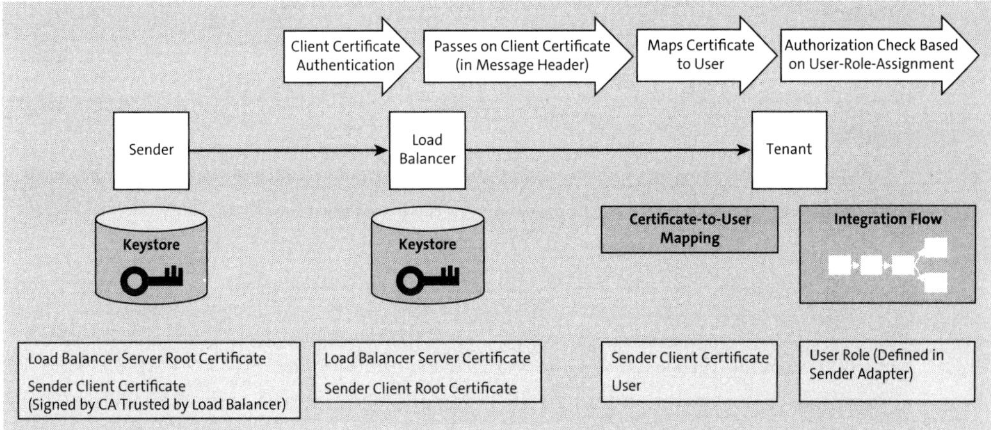

Figure 10.17 Setup of Components Required to Establish a Secure Inbound Connection Using HTTPS, Certificate-to-User Mapping, and User Role Authorization

In a subsequent step, the tenant evaluates (for the certificate) if a certificate-to-user mapping is defined (as deployed in a **Certificate-to-User Mappings** artifact on the tenant). If that is the case, the tenant checks if the sender associated with the user (as derived from the certificate-to-user mapping) is authorized to process the integration flow on the tenant by doing the following:

- Evaluating the user-to-role assignments (as defined on the subaccount for the runtime node application)
- Checking the **User Role** specified in the sender adapter of the integration flow

If the check is successful, the message is processed on the runtime node according to the integration flow settings.

You can find a step-by-step description of the required steps to set up such a connection in the "Cloud Integration – How to Set Up Secure HTTP Inbound Connection with Client Certificates" blog in SAP Community: *www.sap.com/community.html*. This blog outlines the necessary steps in detail. In the following subsections, we provide a summary of the key aspects.

Configuring the Sender System

Sender system configuration includes generating a client certificate and sending the corresponding certificate signing request (CSR) to a CA for a signature. The administrator of the sender system needs to make sure that it's signed by a CA that is also supported by the load balancer. Afterwards, he applies the CA reply and imports the signed certificate into the sender keystore.

> **Note**
>
> How the certificates are installed and the type of keystore used on the sender side depends on the kind of sender system, which isn't covered here.

Because the load balancer is controlled centrally and administered by SAP, no configuration actions are required for this component. The administrator of the sender system has to make sure that the certificates installed on the sender system are compatible with those installed on the load balancer in terms of the hierarchical trust model.

You'll find a list of root certificates actually supported by the load balancer in the documentation of SAP Cloud Platform Integration at *https://help.sap.com/viewer/product/CLOUD_INTEGRATION/Cloud* under **Connecting a Customer System to Cloud Integration • Concepts of Secure Communication • Basics • HTTPS-Based Communication • Load Balancer Root Certificates Supported by SAP**.

Configuring the Inbound Authorization in the Related Integration Flow

We assume that as the integration developer, you use a SOAP 1.x sender adapter (see Chapter 2, Section 2.3.4, Figure 2.27).

For **Authorization**, keep the setting **User Role** to make sure that for the user associated with the calling sender, the permissions are checked based on user-to-role assignments by the SAP Cloud Platform Integration framework. In the **User Role** field, you can keep the entry **ESBMessaging.send**. This role is predefined by SAP to authorize a sender (the SOAP client) to call your tenant. Alternatively, you can specify a custom role here. With this option, you can restrict access to SAP Cloud Platform Integration on the level of individual integration flows (e.g., in case certain integration flows are only to be called by specific senders).

To use custom roles, you also need to define this custom role for the runtime node and assign it to the relevant user in the SAP Cloud Platform cockpit (as explained earlier in Section 10.3.3).

When you've finished the integration flow design, deploy the integration flow on the tenant.

Defining and Deploying a Certificate-to-User Mappings Artifact

Open the **Monitor** application of the Web UI, and click the **Certificate-to-User Mappings** tile under **Manage Security**. To add a new certificate-to-user mapping, choose **Add**. In the next dialog, enter the **User Name** and click **Browse** to look for the signed certificate, which you've exported from the sender keystore prior to this activity, as shown in Figure 10.18.

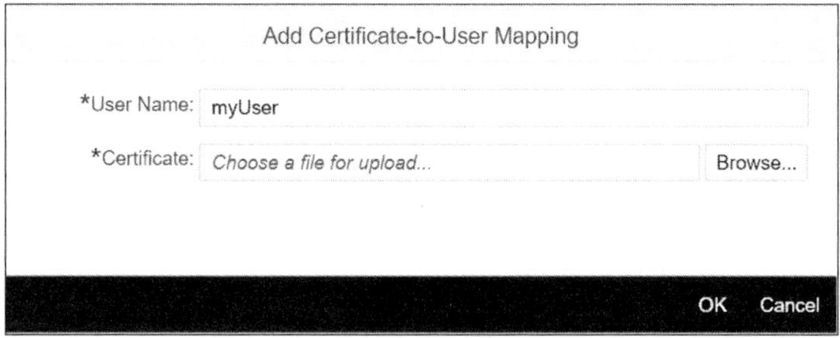

Figure 10.18 Defining a Certificate-to-User Mapping

You need to import the client certificate that the sender system uses to authenticate itself against the load balancer.

Click **OK** to deploy the newly defined certificate-to-user mapping on the tenant. For more information on the **Certificate-to-User Mappings** artifact, read Chapter 8, Section 8.3.3.

Configuring the User-to-Role Assignment

To finish the setup, you need to assign the user specified in the certificate-to-user mapping to the role specified in the sender channel of the integration flow in the SAP Cloud Platform cockpit. Only then is the sender allowed to send messages to the integration flow.

The steps when using the predefined role **ESBMessaging.send** were already shown in Chapter 2, Section 2.3.3. For your convenience, we again show the related dialog in Figure 10.19.

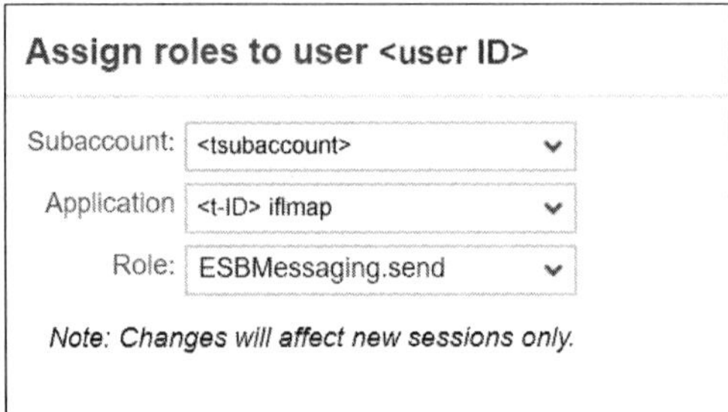

Assign roles to user <user ID>
Subaccount: <tsubaccount>
Application <t-ID> iflmap
Role: ESBMessaging.send
Note: Changes will affect new sessions only.

Figure 10.19 Assigning ESBMessaging.send to the Runtime Node in SAP Cloud Platform Cockpit

As mentioned before, you can also create your own roles in this scenario. This gives you the option to specify individual permissions for each integration flow (sender adapter).

Let's assume you define a custom role called **MyRole** for the runtime node (as explained in Section 10.3.3) and assign it to the user associated with the inbound request (let's say **MyUser**). If you use a custom role, the previously described tasks of defining the inbound authorization (in the sender adapter) and of defining the certificate-to-user mapping are slightly different:

- In the sender adapter (e.g., the SOAP 1.x channel), you define the following settings: as **Authorization**, specify **User Role**, and as **User Role**, select **MyRole**.
- In the **Certificate-to-User Mappings** artifact, you enter the user "MyUser" (to be mapped from the chosen certificate).

Having configured these settings, the integration flow can only be processed when the certificate associated with the inbound call is mapped to user MyUser and when in SAP ID service the role `MyRole` is assigned to user MyUser.

Client Certificate Authorization

In an alternative setup, without certificate-to-user mapping, inbound communication can be defined so that the permissions of the sender are checked based on the subject/issuer DN of a client certificate, which is specified directly in the integration flow.

In this case, the tenant checks if the sender is authorized to call the tenant by comparing the certificate forwarded by the load balancer with the one specified in the relevant integration flow.

This option has certain disadvantages:

- Each time you change (and redeploy) the integration flow, a brief downtime is caused by this.
- Each time when the client certificate is renewed, the integration flow needs to be redeployed (which also causes downtime).

Therefore, SAP doesn't recommend using **Client Certificate** authorization.

Outbound Communication

We now consider the outbound side where the tenant sends a message to a remote receiver system using an HTTP connection. Figure 10.20 shows how the components interact with each other at runtime (on top) and the required security setup to realize this behavior (bottom).

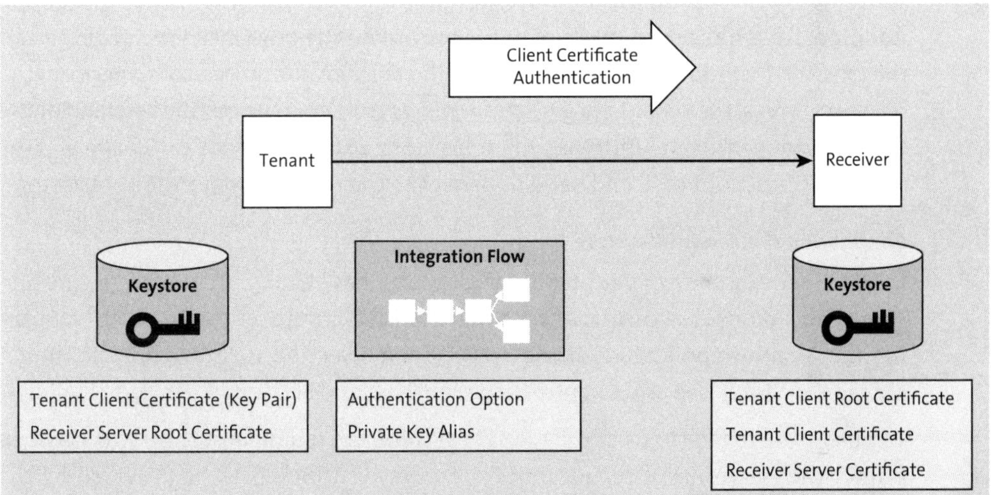

Figure 10.20 Setup of Components Required to Establish a Secure Outbound Connection Using HTTPS and Client Certificate Authentication

To begin the target setup, the tenant connects to the receiver via TLS and verifies the receiver certificate. Vice versa, the receiver verifies if the certificate sent by the tenant is valid. These steps are performed based on the installed certificates, both on the tenant and in the receiver system. For the discussed security option, the certificates of the tenant are stored in a Java keystore deployed on the tenant. Similar to the inbound case, the identity and permissions of the tenant are checked in the receiver system (based on the settings in the receiver system).

You can find a step-by-step description of the required steps to set up such a connection in the "Cloud Integration – How to Set Up Secure Outbound HTTP Connection Using Keystore Monitor" blog in SAP Community at *www.sap.com/community.html*. This blog outlines the necessary steps in detail. In the following subsections, we summarize the key aspects.

Configuring the Receiver System

Configuring the receiver system requires first creating a server certificate (private key pair) and then importing it into the receiver keystore. The server certificate can be a certificate chain where the top-level certificate is a root certificate issued by a dedicated CA. The administrator of the receiver system needs to download the root certificate from the receiver keystore and make it available to the tenant administrator.

Additionally, the receiver keystore needs to contain the tenant client certificate and the tenant client root certificate. To enable the receiver administrator to perform the necessary steps, the tenant administrator needs to export the certificate chain of the tenant client certificate from the tenant keystore, extract the root certificate and the client certificate out of it, and hand both over to the receiver system administrator.

Configuring the Tenant Keystore

With the provisioning of your tenant cluster, SAP has already provided a tenant keystore with a number of certificates. You can find the content of the keystore by opening the **Monitor** application of the Web UI and selecting the **Keystore** tile (under **Manage Security**) (see also Chapter 8, Section 8.3.2, and Section 10.5 in this chapter).

To enable the tenant to trust the receiver system, the tenant administrator needs to import the (server) root certificate of the receiver, which is to be provided by the administrator of the receiver system, into the tenant keystore.

To enable trust the other way around (so that the receiver trusts the tenant), a client certificate is also required as part of the tenant keystore (private public key pair). All tenants provided by SAP contain already a key pair. You can use this certificate to configure this step.

Figure 10.21 shows a part of the certificate list of the tenant keystore accessible in the **Monitor** application under **Manage Security** in the **Keystore** tile.

Overview / Manage Keystore
Current
Backup
New SAP keys
SAP Key History
Entries (42)
Filter by Alias
Back Up
Add
Download
Alias
Type
Owner
Valid Until
Last Modified At
Actions
addtrust external ca root
Certificate
Tenant Administrator
May 30, 2020, 12:48:38
Jan 31, 2018, 07:25:35
baltimore cybertrust root
Certificate
Tenant Administrator
May 13, 2025, 01:59:00
Jan 31, 2018, 07:25:35
certum ca
Certificate
Tenant Administrator
Jun 11, 2027, 12:46:39
Jan 31, 2018, 07:25:35
certum level iv ca (certum ca)
Certificate
Tenant Administrator
Mar 03, 2024, 13:54:25
Jan 31, 2018, 07:25:35
comodo high-assurance secure server ca (addtrust external ca root)
Certificate
Tenant Administrator
May 30, 2020, 12:48:38
Jan 31, 2018, 07:25:35
cybertrust public sureserver sv ca (baltimore cybertrust root)
Certificate
Tenant Administrator
Sep 08, 2020, 19:34:08
Jan 31, 2018, 07:25:35

Figure 10.21 Certificates Contained in the Tenant Keystore

Importing a certificate to the tenant keystore was already described in Chapter 2, Section 2.3.6. Section 10.5 will provide more details on certificate management for the tenant.

Configuring and Deploying the Integration Flow

In addition to the previous steps, you need to specify the required security settings in the related integration flow and the associated receiver adapter.

If you use an HTTP receiver adapter to connect the tenant to the receiver system, specify the following settings:

- **Authentication**
  Select the **Client Certificate** option.
- **Private Key Alias**
  Enter the alias of the signed tenant client certificate that you intend to use for authentication when connecting to the associated receiver. The alias is used to point to a specific key pair in the tenant keystore. If you leave this field empty, any valid key pair will be used for this step.

Figure 10.22 shows the authentication options that are available in the HTTP-based receiver adapters (e.g., we show the UI of the HTTP receiver adapter, **Connection** tab).

Finally, deploy the integration flow on the tenant.

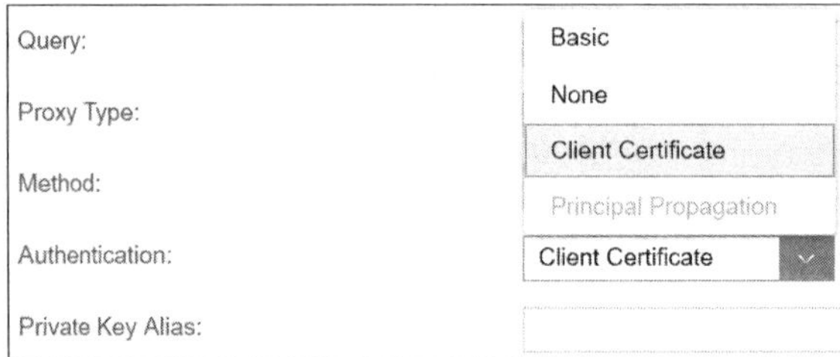

Figure 10.22 Authentication Options Available in the HTTP Receiver Adapter

Outbound Connectivity Test Tool

To test your security configuration, SAP Cloud Platform Integration provides an outbound connectivity test tool for the various protocols, among them also for HTTP connections using TLS.

When setting up the first integration flow described in this book (Chapter 2, Section 2.3.6), you already got to know this tool, in that case, for the SMTP protocol.

This tool is described in detail in Chapter 8, Section 8.3.4.

10.4.5 Setting Up a Scenario Using OAuth with the Twitter Adapter

In Section 10.4.3, we introduced the concept of OAuth, which allows a resource owner to grant client applications restricted access to his resources. Social networks, such as Facebook or Twitter, provide APIs for client applications that support OAuth.

SAP Cloud Platform Integration offers adapters to connect a tenant with Facebook and Twitter to write data to these platforms or to read data from them. Both adapter types work in the same way. In this section, we'll show you how to set up a simple integration scenario using the Twitter adapter.

The Twitter receiver adapter allows an SAP Cloud Platform Integration tenant (in terms of OAuth it's the *client*) to access Twitter (the *resource server*) on behalf of a Twitter user (the *resource owner*). After gaining access, the tenant can either read or post tweets on Twitter (via the resource owner's account). You can use this adapter, for example, to implement market analysis scenarios.

Technically, the tenant calls the Twitter API. As a prerequisite, the integration developer has to prepare the tenant so that it can call Twitter on behalf of a specific Twitter user. To do that, the integration developer obtains a set of client credentials from Twitter that will be used to authenticate the client (tenant) in the Twitter API.

In Section 10.4.3, we described a common OAuth authentication scenario in which every time the client requests access to the server, the resource owner is asked by the server to grant the client access to the protected resources. This implies a user dialog where the resource owner needs to log in to the server with his credentials. For SAP Cloud Platform Integration scenarios, this workflow isn't feasible, as each time message processing is triggered, it would require a resource owner to log on to Twitter and confirm that the required token credentials are being generated for the client.

To address this aspect, the Twitter adapter uses OAuth in a more system-centric way. The integration developer (who is identical to the resource owner, i.e., the Twitter account user) provides the tenant with all credentials (client and token credentials) when defining the Twitter adapter settings in the integration flow.

Figure 10.23 is derived from Figure 10.13, and shows the general OAuth setup adapted to the Twitter adapter scenario.

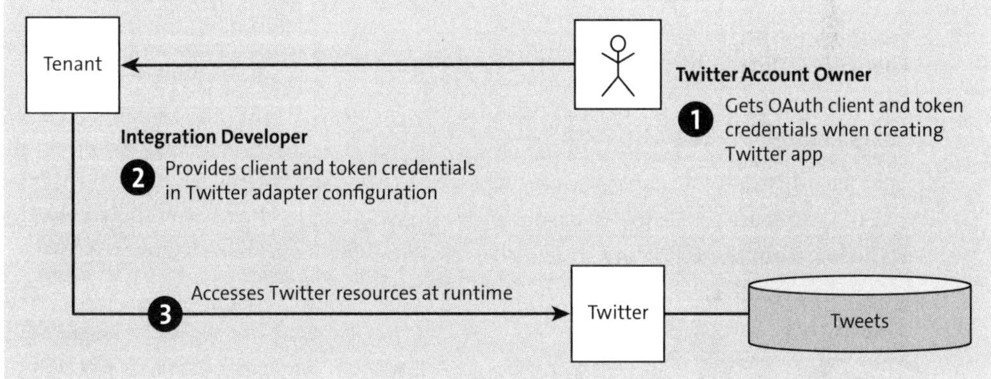

Figure 10.23 OAuth Setup of Components When Using the Twitter Adapter

Designing an Integration Flow Using Twitter Adapter

Figure 10.24 shows our target integration flow. A **Start Timer** event (introduced in Chapter 6, Section 6.1.2) starts the message flow. A **Request-Reply** step (see Chapter 4, Section 4.3 calls a receiver (**Receiver2**, which represents Twitter) and reads data from it. Finally, the enriched message is sent to an email server (**Receiver1**) using the **Mail** receiver adapter. The **Mail** receiver adapter has been used in several scenarios throughout this book, so it doesn't need further explanation (e.g., Chapter 2, Section 2.3.4). We'll keep our description short and focus on the aspects that are specific to how Twitter and OAuth come into play.

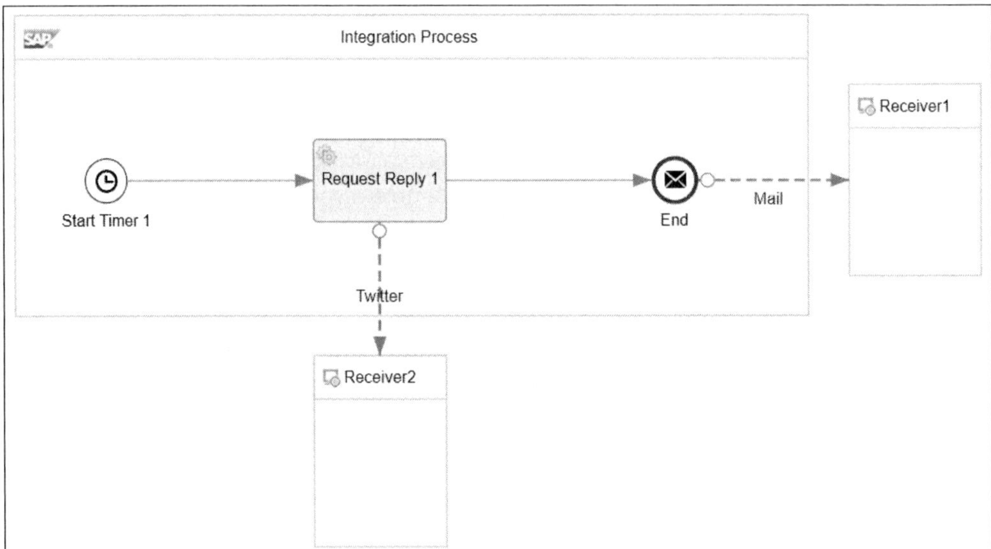

Figure 10.24 Integration Flow with the Twitter Adapter

Tasks Related to the Twitter API

Let's assume that you (the resource owner) use your own Twitter account for this scenario. To prepare to use the Twitter account in an SAP Cloud Platform Integration scenario, perform the following steps:

1. Go to *https://dev.twitter.com/apps*, and create an app by choosing **Create New App**.
2. Provide a **Name** and a **Description**. For **Website**, enter any test URL.
3. Leave the **Callback URL** field empty.
4. Confirm the Developer Agreement, and select **Create Your Twitter Application**.

   On the following page (Figure 10.25), certain information is displayed.
5. Choose **Keys and Access Tokens**.

Under **Application Settings**, you find your **Consumer Key** and **Consumer Secret**. Under **Your Access Token**, you find your **Access Token** and **Access Token Secret**.

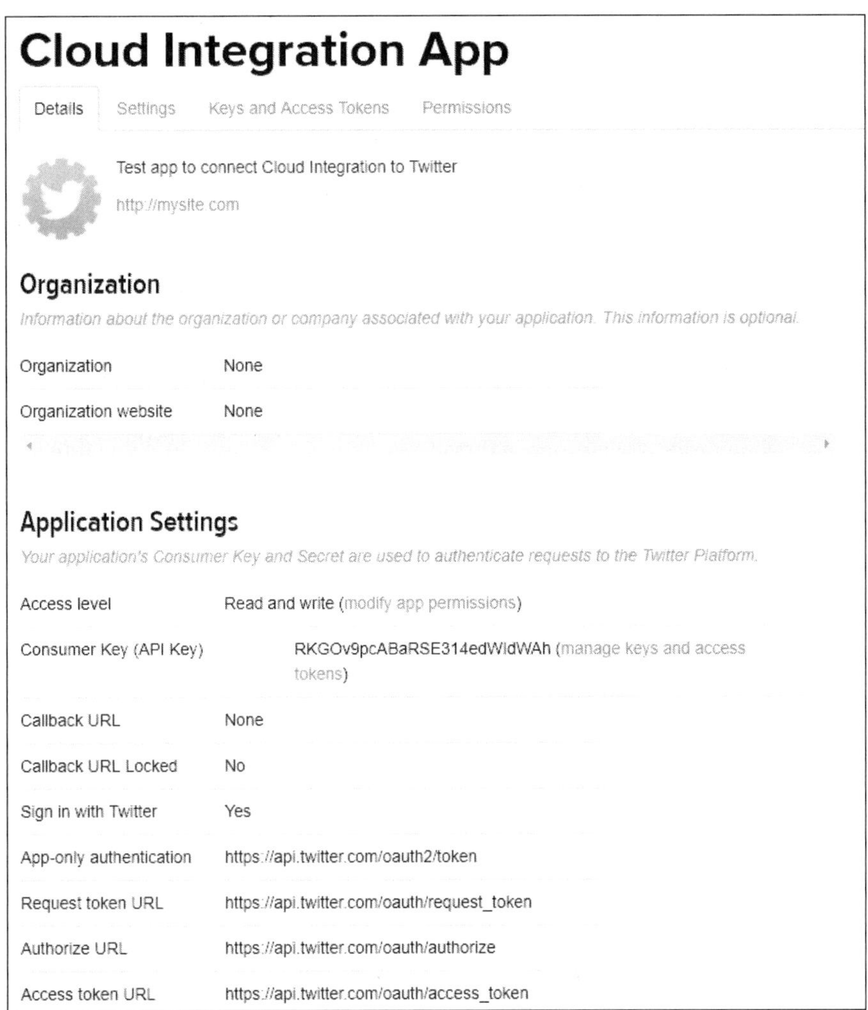

Figure 10.25 UI of the Twitter App

Now you have all four credentials that you need for further configuration of our scenario. In the next step, you'll define a separate security artifact for each of the four credentials and deploy them on the tenant. When configuring the integration flow, you'll refer to these artifacts in the Twitter adapter configuration UI.

Creating and Deploying the OAuth Security Artifacts

To provide the tenant with the credentials, you need to create and deploy an individual **Secure Parameter** artifact for each of the four OAuth credentials. It's important to point out that during this step, only you, the resource owner, can see the actual values of the keys and access tokens (when creating and deploying the artifacts). In the same way as creating and deploying a **User Credentials** artifact (see Chapter 2, Section 2.3.4), you'll give each of these entities an alias, which will be used during the subsequent integration flow configuration to complete the Twitter adapter settings. That way, no one aside from you knows the keys and access tokens. Others who use the Web UI on the same tenant will only see the credential names (aliases), keeping confidential information protected.

For the following process, we propose the aliases listed in Table 10.7 for the four credential types.

Credential	Alias
Consumer key	Twitter_ConsumerKey
Consumer secret	Twitter_Secret
Access token	Twitter_AccessToken
Access token secret	Twitter_TokenSecret

Table 10.7 Proposed Aliases for the OAuth Credentials

Repeat the following steps for each of the four credentials: consumer key, consumer secret, access token, and token secret.

1. Connect to your tenant using the Web UI, and choose **Monitor**.
2. Click the **Security Material** tile in the **Manage Security** section.
3. Choose **Add • Secure Parameter**.
4. For **Name**, enter an alias (which you later have to enter into the corresponding field of the Twitter adapter). We recommend that you use the aliases proposed in Table 10.7.
5. Paste the corresponding credential from your Twitter app into the fields for **Secure Parameter** and **Repeat Secure Parameter**.
6. Click **Deploy**.

The **Secure Parameter** artifact has now been deployed and is displayed in the table under **Manage Security Material.**

Configuring the Twitter Adapter

With the following steps, you create a receiver communication channel with Twitter adapter:

1. Using the Web UI, create an integration flow with the elements depicted in Figure 10.24.
2. For the **Mail** adapter, you can use the settings proposed in Chapter 2, Section 2.3.4.
3. For the **Start** step, use a **Timer** event. You can leave the **Run Once** checkbox selected.
4. Configure the Twitter adapter (Figure 10.26).

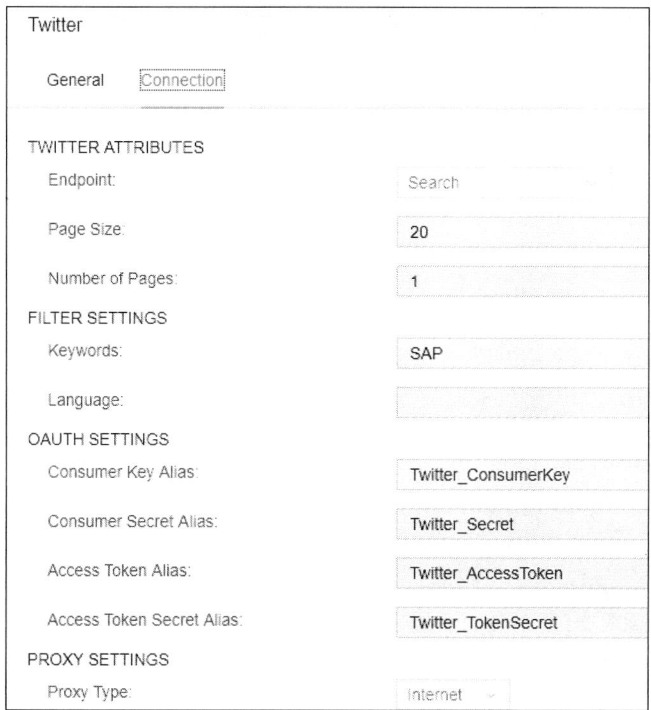

Figure 10.26 Twitter Adapter Settings

For **Endpoint** select **Search**, which enables the tenant to extract information from Twitter (based on certain criteria).

There are two other options in the **Endpoint** dropdown list:

- **Send Tweet**: Enables the tenant to send a message to Twitter (to the account of the resource owner associated with the credentials configured under **OAuth Settings**).
- **Send Direct Message**: Enables the tenant to send a message to a user who doesn't necessarily have to be identical to the resource owner. When choosing the **Send Direct Message** option, you specify this user in an additional **User** field that is hidden when one of the other two options for **Endpoint** is selected.

Select **Search** because our integration flow starts with a timer, and it makes no sense to send an empty message to Twitter.

5. **Page Size** allows you to specify the maximum number of tweets per page, and **Number of Pages** allows you to specify the number of pages that the tenant is supposed to consume.
6. In the **Keywords** field, you can either enter keywords or Twitter queries to filter Twitter content (queries are explained at *https://dev.twitter.com/rest/public/search*).
7. With **Language**, obviously, you can specify the search language (e.g., **EN** for English).
8. Under **OAUTH SETTINGS**, enter the aliases of the **Secure Parameter** artifacts deployed in the previous step (see also Table 10.7).
9. Save and deploy the integration flow.

As soon as you've deployed the integration flow, message processing is triggered (according to the settings in the timer **Start** event). Go to your email account and check if a message has been received. It should contain tweets according to the criteria you provided in the Twitter adapter.

OAuth for Inbound Connections

This tutorial showed how to set up a scenario using OAuth at the *outbound* side. There are also several options to configure OAuth for *inbound* connections (Section 10.4.3). For more information, check out the documentation of SAP Cloud Platform Integration at *https://help.sap.com/viewer/product/CLOUD_INTEGRATION/Cloud* under **Connecting a Customer System to Cloud Integration • Configuring Inbound Communication**.

10.4.6 Message-Level Security Options

On top of establishing a secure transport channel as explained in Section 10.4.2, you can further protect the messages to be exchanged with digital encryption and digital signatures. Applying these options increases the security level of your scenario because even if the transport channel is broken, the messages still can't be read by malicious parties. Signing a message allows a recipient to validate if the message has been received from the expected sender, increasing data integrity.

Why Decrypt Messages on the SAP Cloud Platform Integration Tenant?

You might ask yourself why not always pass encrypted messages through SAP Cloud Platform Integration and thus keep the exchanged message a *black box* for the integration middleware (unreadable for anyone in the unlikely case that any malicious party receives unauthorized access to the infrastructure at the software provider's side). Why is there any need to decrypt a message on the tenant at all? The reason is that various integration patterns require the runtime components to access the message content to process the message correctly.

One example for this is the content-based router (CBR) (see Chapter 5, Section 5.1). Consider a scenario where a message sent from one company is routed to one, or many, possible banks (receivers), and the actual receiver depends on the value of the bank identifier code (BIC) in the message. To process the routing step in the intended way, the message has to be decrypted on the tenant prior to the routing step to reveal the BIC.

How Digitally Encrypting and Decrypting a Message Works

SAP Cloud Platform Integration supports various message-level security standards that each work in different ways. However, there is a general pattern. All of these options use a hybrid approach of asymmetric and symmetric key technologies (Section 10.4.1). We'll briefly show this pattern for both use cases: encryption/decryption and signing/verifying.

For encryption/decryption, the process was already explained in the info box in Section 10.4.1 and illustrated in Figure 10.10, so we'll only briefly repeat the steps.

The sender uses a (typically randomly generated) symmetric key to encrypt the message content. Additionally, the sender uses the public key of the receiver (which has been provided by the receiver in advance) to encrypt the symmetric key. The encrypted symmetric key along with the encrypted message content is sent to the receiver. The receiver then uses its private key (which is associated with the public key that was used by the sender) to decrypt the symmetric key. With the recovered symmetric key, the receiver decrypts the message content.

How Digitally Signing/Verifying of a Message Works

When signing/verifying a message, the usage of public and private keys is inverted in the following way: the sender uses its private key to generate a signature out of the message content, and the receiver uses the associated public key (which has been provided by the sender in advance) to verify the signature.

As we mentioned in Section 10.4.1, the usage of asymmetric keys is, in general, computationally intensive. Therefore, applying the digital signing process on the complete content of a message can have a negative impact on overall performance because message sizes can vary from a few kilobytes to several megabytes. To overcome this problem, a *hash function* is applied to the message content prior to the signing process. A hash function allows you to calculate an expression of fixed size from an input (which can be of any size). The input, in our case, is the message content. The output is referred to as a *hash value* (other, synonymic terms are *digest*, *footprint*, and *fingerprint*). The calculation is accomplished in a fully reproducible way, which means performing the same hash algorithm on the same data will lead to the same hash value. However, the inverse operation isn't possible, which means the data can't be reproduced out of the hash value (this makes a difference to compression algorithms that allow, based on the compressed data, recovery of the uncompressed original). The resulting small size hash value is then subject to the signing process, as shown in Figure 10.27.

Here, the asymmetric key pair of the sender comes into play in the following way: The sender's private key is used to encrypt the hash value. The transferred hash value can be considered the digital signature and is sent along with the message content to the receiver. On the receiver side, the public key (associated to the sender's private key) is used to decrypt the hash value. In a separate step that is independent from the decryption of the hash value, the receiver uses the hash algorithm to calculate the hash value directly out of the message content and compares the result with the hash value that has been decrypted using the public key. If both values are identical, the signature is verified.

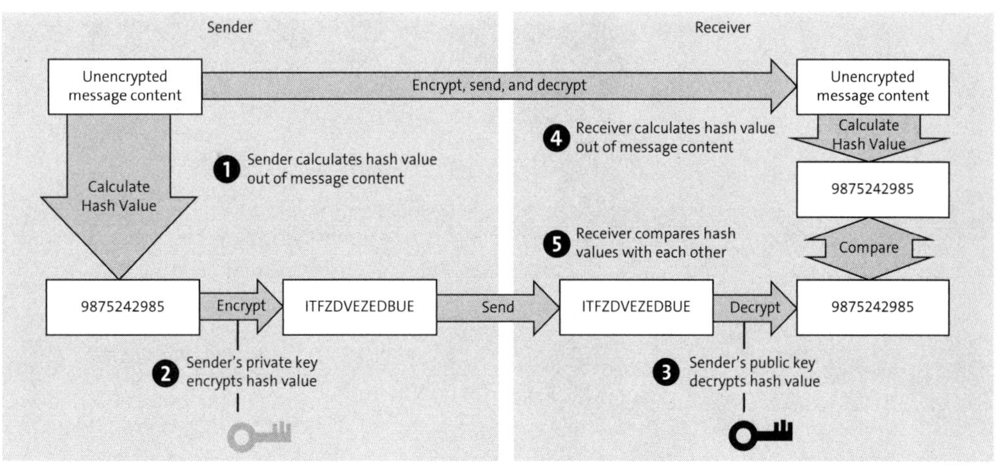

Figure 10.27 Combining Hash Functions with Asymmetric Key Usage When Signing and Verifying a Message

Overview of Supported Standards

Table 10.8 summarizes the message-level security standards supported by SAP Cloud Platform Integration and lists the supported options.

Standard	Options and References
PKCS#7/CMS Enveloped Data and Signed Data	PKCS stands for *Public Key Cryptography Standard* and CMS stands for *Cryptographic Message Syntax* (see *https://tools.ietf.org/html/rfc2315*). This standard provides the following options: ■ Encrypting the message content (and, vice versa, decrypting it) ■ Signing a message (and, vice versa, verifying it) ■ A combination of encrypting and signing a message (and, vice versa, the combination of decrypting and verifying it)

Table 10.8 Message-Level Security Options Supported by SAP Cloud Platform Integration

Standard	Options and References
OpenPGP	OpenPGP stands for *Open Pretty Good Privacy* (see *https://tools.ietf.org/html/rfc4880*). This standard provides the following options: ■ Encrypting the message content (and decrypting it) ■ A combination of encrypting and signing a message (and the combination of decrypting and verifying it)
XML Signature	XML Signature is also referred to as *XMLDSig*, *XML-DSig*, or *XML-Sig*. It's defined by a W3C recommendation (see *www.w3.org/TR/xmldsig-core/*). This standard allows for signing a message and verifying it.
XAdES	XML Advanced Electronic Signatures (XAdES) is an enhancement of XML Signature, which can be used in the context of the European Union Directive 1999/93/EC. It allows you to use signatures in electronic contracts within the European Union (see *www.w3.org/TR/XAdES/*). This standard allows for signing a message.
WS-Security	Web Services Security (WS-Security) is an extension to SOAP that allows you to apply security to web services (see *www.oasis-open.org/committees/tc_home.php?wg_abbrev=wss*). This standard provides the following: ■ Signing a SOAP body and verifying it ■ Encrypting the message content and decrypting it The following adapters support WS-Security: ■ SOAP 1.x sender and receiver adapter ■ AS4 receiver adapter
S/MIME	S/MIME allows you to securely transfer Multipurpose Internet Mail Extensions (MIME) data—in other words, emails. It's used with most common email programs (see *https://tools.ietf.org/html/rfc5751*). This standard allows you to use digital signatures and to encrypt emails.

Table 10.8 Message-Level Security Options Supported by SAP Cloud Platform Integration (Cont.)

Now you know which security options are supported by SAP Cloud Platform Integration at the transport level and the message level. In Section 10.4.4, we showed you how to set up a secure connection with SAP Cloud Platform Integration based on TLS; in Section 10.4.5, we showed you how to set up a scenario using OAuth with the Twitter adapter; and in Section 10.4.7, we'll show you how to set up a scenario that includes digital encryption (using the OpenPGP standard).

10.4.7 Designing Message-Level Security Options in an Integration Flow

In this section, we'll show you how a message can be protected on the application level by digital encryption and signatures. We've given an overview of the options and concepts in Section 10.4.6.

As we did for the transport-level security considerations in Section 10.4.4, we'll here also distinguish between two communication directions (from the perspective of the tenant):

- **Inbound communication**
  The sender sends an -encrypted or signed message to SAP Cloud Platform Integration, and this message needs to be decrypted or verified on the tenant.
- **Outbound communication**
  The tenant encrypts or signs a message and sends it to a receiver where it's decrypted or verified.

We'll summarize the key tasks of how to set up message-level security scenarios for both use cases. We then finish this section with a tutorial that shows you how to set up a simple integration flow, which includes decrypting and encrypting a message.

Before we discuss the two use cases, let's continue with some general remarks. As for transport-level security, you also need to create digital keys and establish the corresponding key storages. You've learned in Section 10.4.4 that SAP provides you the tenant already with a Java keystore deployed on it, and that to implement certain transport-level security options, this keystore needs to contain dedicated keys.

The key material for the different message-level security options must be stored in different types of key storages. Accordingly, different security artifact types have to be deployed on the tenant. In Table 10.9, we summarize the artifact types that are relevant to store keys for message-level security.

Security Standard	Related Artifact Types
PKCS#7 WS-Security XML Signature	You use X.509 keys, the same type of security material used for TLS. Therefore, you can import additional keys for message-level security into the same Java keystore that is used for transport-level security (and which you can access in the **Monitor** application under **Manage Security** in the **Keystore** tile; see Chapter 8, Section 8.3.2, and Section 10.5 in this chapter). However, make sure that you use different keys for message-level security than for securing the transport channel. Keys for message-level security don't need to be signed by a CA; they can be self-signed.
OpenPGP	You use specific PGP keys. In addition, the terminology is slightly different when compared to the other security standards. For example, in the context of PGP, *private keys* are referred to as *secret keys*. You also need dedicated key storages: ■ Use a **PGP Public Keyring** to store a PGP public key (associated with the sender or receiver system connected to the tenant). ■ Use a **PGP Secret Keyring** to store a private-public key pair associated with the tenant. You can access the corresponding artifacts in the **Monitor** application under **Manage Security** in the **Security Material** tile).

Table 10.9 Security Artifacts Required to Store Keys for Certain Message-Level Security Scenarios

Most importantly, to configure message-level security options, you have to add dedicated steps to the integration flow, which we'll discuss next.

Inbound Communication

Figure 10.28 shows how the components interact with each other at runtime (at the top) and the required security setup to realize this behavior (on the bottom).

In this use case, the components interact with each other in the following way:

- The sender does the following:
  - Encrypts the message content using the tenant's public key, which is associated with the tenant's private key
  - Signs a message using its own private key

- The tenant receives the message and then does the following:
  - Decrypts the message content using its own private key
  - Verifies the message using the sender's public key, which is associated with the sender's private key

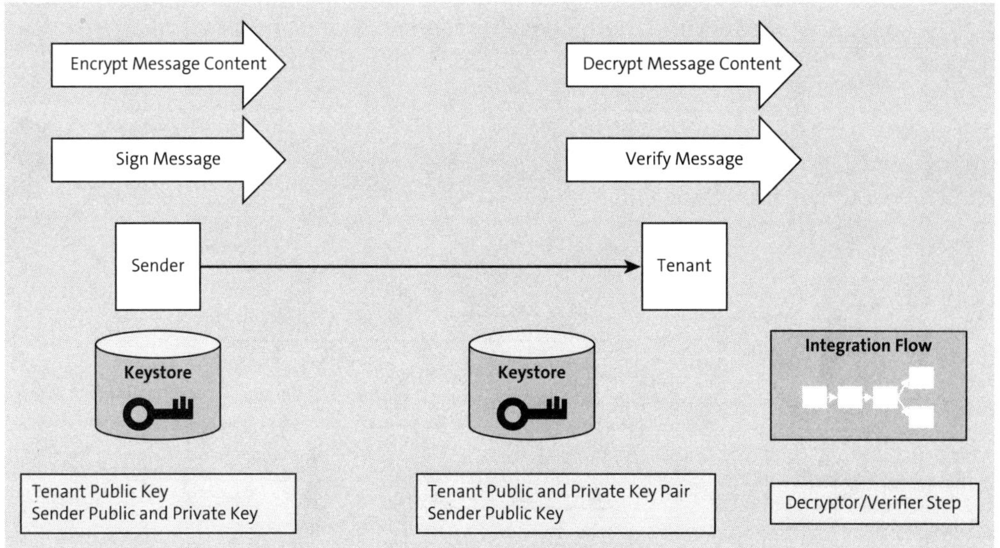

Figure 10.28 Configuring Message-Level Security for Inbound Communication

You might notice that, other than in the transport-level security case, the load balancer isn't depicted in Figure 10.28. It doesn't play a role because we consider the application level (or message level), not the transport level. The termination and reestablishment of the TLS request takes place only on the transport level. The message is encrypted on its way between the sender and tenant (across the load balancer).

To implement this setup, both on the side of the sender system and the SAP Cloud Platform Integration platform, perform the following tasks:

- Generate key pairs for both the tenant and the sender system, and set up the keystores, as shown in Figure 10.28.
- Import the tenant's public key into the sender's keystore.
- Import the sender's public key into the tenant's keystore.
- Configure the decryptor and verifier steps in the integration flow.

Note that you can also configure a combination of decryption and verification on one decryptor step for certain security standards. However, we won't cover this use case.

Outbound Communication

Figure 10.29 shows how the components interact with each other at runtime (on top), and the required security setup to realize this behavior (at the bottom).

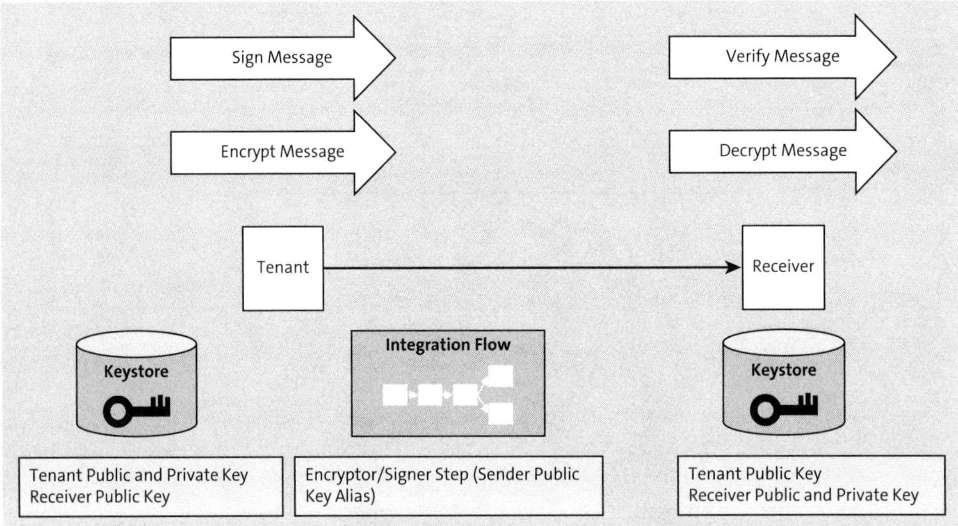

Figure 10.29 Configuring Message-Level Security for Outbound Communication

In this use case, the components interact with each other in the following way:

- The tenant does the following:
  - Encrypts the message content using a public key associated with the receiver's private key
  - Signs a message using its own private key
- The receiver does the following:
  - Decrypts the message content using its own private key
  - Verifies the message using the public key associated with the tenant's private key

To set up this scenario, you have to generate key pairs for the tenant and for the receiver, and you have to configure the relevant integration flow steps at the tenant's side.

Note that the encryptor also provides the option to combine encryption/signing.

Setting Up a Simple Integration Flow with Decryption/Encryption Steps

To complete our section on message-level security, we'll show you how to set up an integration flow that decrypts an incoming (encrypted) message, encrypts it again, and sends the newly encrypted message as an email to a receiver. A person at the receiver side then manually decrypts the received message. For simplicity, we won't consider message signing/verifying.

We'll demonstrate how this works using the OpenPGP standard. For the management of PGP keys and the manual encryption and decryption steps in the scenario, we propose you use Kleopatra, which is a publicly available software that is easy to install. Kleopatra allows you to manage PGP keys and to sign and encrypt (as well as verify and decrypt) files and text strings. You can download Kleopatra from *www.gpg4win.de/index.html*.

> **Some Remarks about OpenPGP**
>
> When used in the context of SAP Cloud Platform Integration, OpenPGP not only uses different key storages than the other security standards often use for message-level security (i.e., PKCS#7) (see Table 10.9), but it also comes with a slightly different terminology: instead of *private key*, in the context of Open PGP, the term *secret key* is used. For more information, you can go to the documentation of SAP Cloud Platform Integration at *https://help.sap.com/viewer/product/CLOUD_INTEGRATION/Cloud* and search for **How OpenPGP Works**.

Here's the scenario: As sender, we use an email server from which SAP Cloud Platform Integration polls emails (according to the mail sender adapter settings). An email that is due to be read by SAP Cloud Platform Integration contains an encrypted message (as clear text, we use the string sequence `Paul Smith`). The decryptor step decrypts the message and sends the clear text to an email account through the mail receiver adapter. The received email will contain the message as clear text.

For simplicity, we propose that in this scenario, you use the same email server and email account as sender and receiver. This means that the integration flow will poll an email with an encrypted message from the email account and send it to the same email account.

When we've executed this scenario, we'll enhance it by an additional encryptor step so that the message is encrypted again after the decryptor step and is then sent through the mail adapter to an email account. In that variant of the scenario, the receiver of the mail manually decrypts the received text using Kleopatra.

We've shown the mail receiver adapter several times throughout this book (see, e.g., Section 2.3). Therefore, we keep the related steps short and focus on the aspects of message encryption/decryption and the management of the required keys.

In this tutorial, you'll successively take over the roles of all participants: the sender, who encrypts the message; the integration developer, who creates the integration flow and deploys it on the tenant; and, finally, the receiver, who decrypts the message manually.

Figure 10.30 shows the involved components and keys.

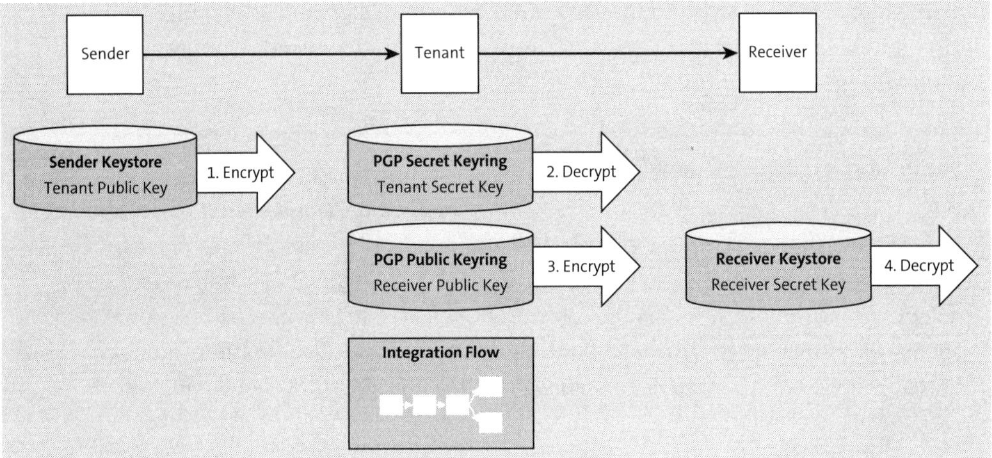

Figure 10.30 Components of the Demo Example

As already mentioned, when using OpenPGP, the required keys for the tenant are to be stored separately in a PGP secret keyring and a PGP public keyring, respectively. Both entities must be separately deployed on the tenant.

This is how it works:

- The sender uses a public key (which is associated with the tenant's secret key) to encrypt the message (manually).
- The tenant (in a **Decryptor** step) decrypts the message using its own secret key (from the PGP secret keyring), and thereafter encrypts it again (within an

Encryptor step) using the public key (from the PGP public keyring), which is associated with the receiver's secret key.

- Finally, the receiver receives the encrypted message and decrypts it (manually) using his own secret key.

As explained earlier, we start with the following integration flow that only contains a **Decryptor** step (Figure 10.31).

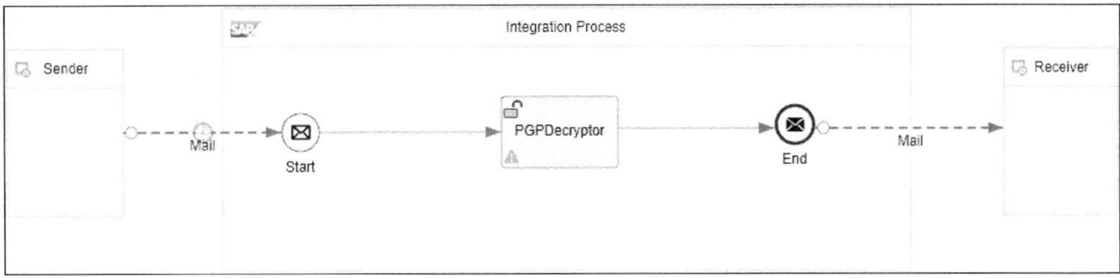

Figure 10.31 Integration Flow with Decryptor Step and Email Sender and Receiver

As a prerequisite, install the free software Kleopatra for key management. Download the software (*www.gpg4win.de/index.html*). When asked, make sure that the software package to download includes Kleopatra.

To start setting up the scenario, let's first take the role of the integration developer, who creates the private-public key pair (using Kleopatra) and deploys it as a PGP secret keyring on the tenant. The secret key is used by the decryptor step to decrypt the encrypted message.

1. Open Kleopatra.
2. Under **File**, choose **New Key Pair** (see Figure 10.32).

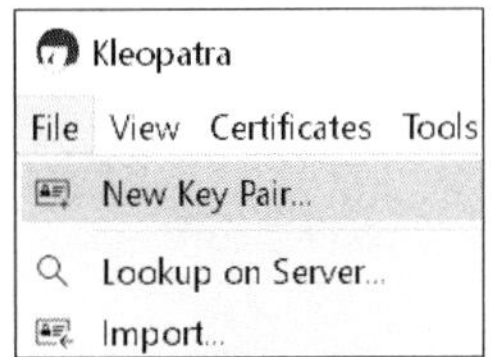

Figure 10.32 Creating a New Key Pair with Kleopatra

3. In the following dialog, click **Create a Personal OpenPGP Key Pair**.
4. Enter a name (e.g., "Tenant", to indicate that this is the tenant's key pair) and email address, and click **Next**.

5. Select **Create**.
6. Enter a passphrase to protect the key. You need to remember the passphrase for a later step when deploying the PGP secret keyring on the tenant.
7. Choose **Finish**. The newly created key pair is shown in a list (Figure 10.33).

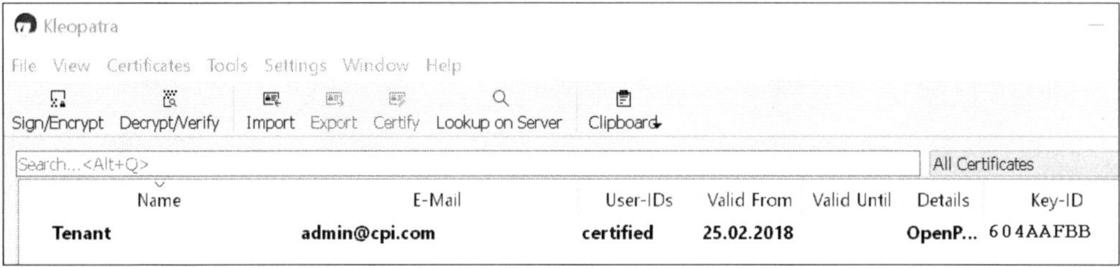

Figure 10.33 The New Key Pair Shown in a List

8. Select the key (**Tenant**), and in the context menu, choose **Export Secret Keys** (see Figure 10.34).
9. Save the key on your computer (as a *.gpg* file).

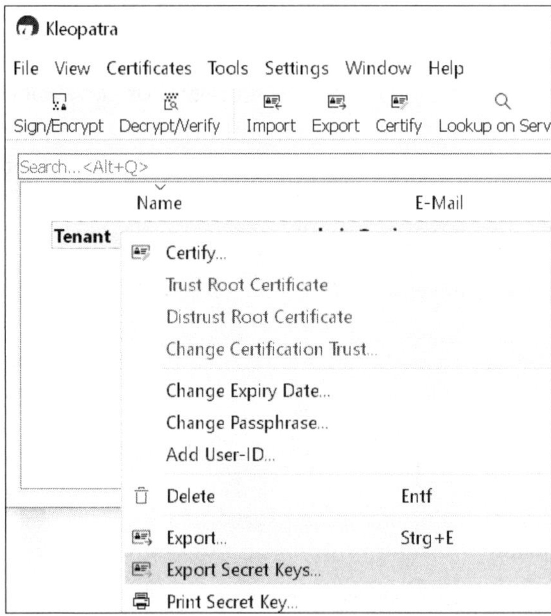

Figure 10.34 Exporting Secret Keys from Kleopatra

You now need to deploy the key pair generated with the preceding steps on the tenant:

1. Open the **Monitor** application of the Web UI, and under **Manage Security**, click the **Security Material** tile.
2. Select **Add • PGP Secret Keyring**, and choose **Next** (Figure 10.35).

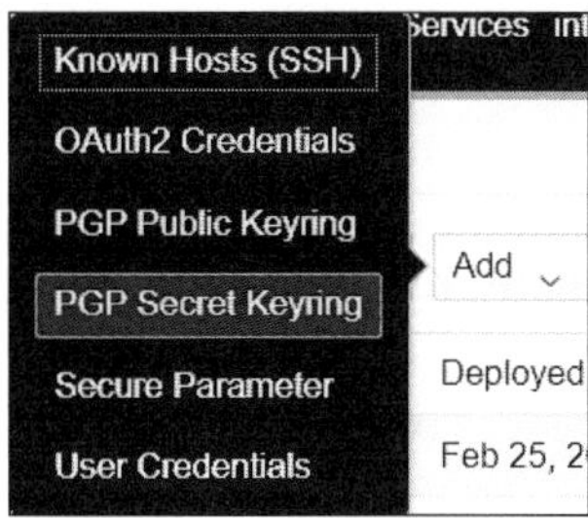

Figure 10.35 Adding a PGP Secret Keyring Artifact

3. Browse for the secret key *.gpg* file on your local disk, enter the secret key passphrase, and choose **Deploy**. The newly deployed artifact is shown in the **Security Material** overview (Figure 10.36).

Overview / Manage Security Material
Security Material (9)
Filter by
Name
Type
Status
secring
PGP Secret Keyring
Deployed
Twitter_TokenSecret
Credentials
Deployed
Twitter_AccessToken
Credentials
Deployed

Figure 10.36 The Newly Deployed Artifact Displayed in the Artifact Overview

Now switch to the role of the sender to manually encrypt the clear text with the tenant's public key. In real-life scenarios, this is performed automatically by the software deployed on the sender system. Follow these steps:

1. To encrypt your text, start Kleopatra, and then enter the clear text (e.g., "Paul Smith") in a text editor.
2. Copy the text to the clipboard.
3. In Kleopatra, choose **Clipboard • Encrypt** (Figure 10.37).

Figure 10.37 Choosing the Encrypt Option for the Clipboard in Kleopatra

4. Keep the option **OpenPGP** selected, and click **Add Recipient**.
5. Imagine that you, as a sender, communicate with many recipients who have shared their public keys with you. In this step, select the key from that recipient (the tenant, in our case) to whom you'd like to send an encrypted message (see Figure 10.38).

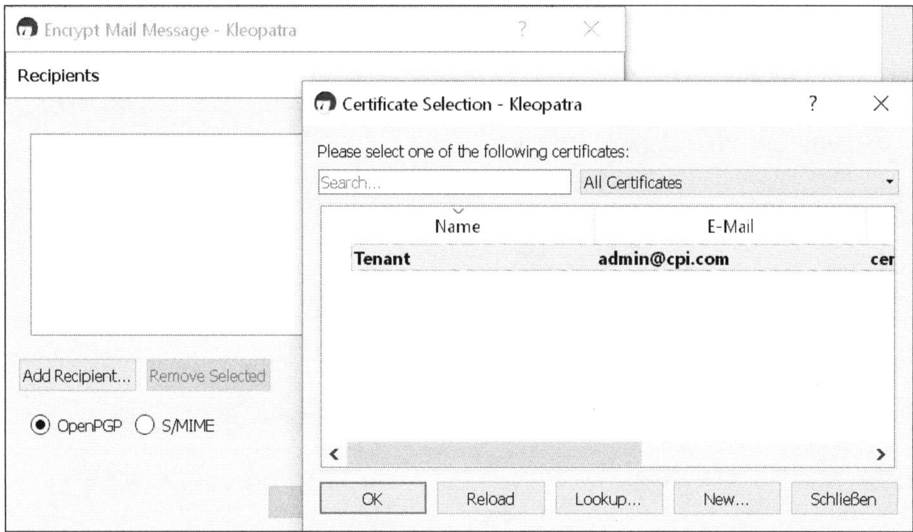

Figure 10.38 Selecting the Key to Be Used to Encrypt the Clear Text

6. Select the key/recipient, and choose **OK**.
7. When the message **Encryption Succeeded** is displayed, click **OK** (Figure 10.39).
8. Paste the text from the clipboard to a text editor. The encrypted message will look like what you see in Figure 10.40.

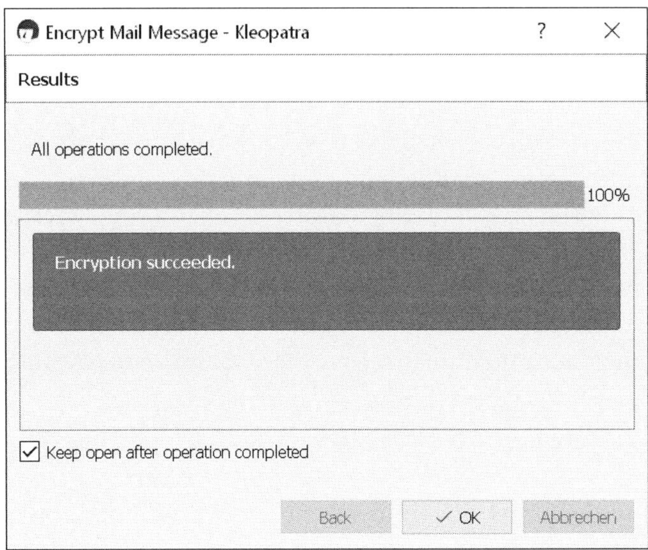

Figure 10.39 Success Message When Kleopatra Has Encrypted the Clear Text


```
-----BEGIN PGP MESSAGE-----

hQEMA8EPNLAufHwdAQf/YYGQ/J04E2lYpFQwi2v5gSdQOJFm0aLYOrmuAsfy7q6E
87xng9mMv0SlE9vnhEz/eAwUUi5DcX7ZOoVBZ6f4H9TwWaCJM7wHjMGYhYZ+Co/4
0C22E8tv+GmAUPjEW94ur0TpVyzXKHtZvELFtSB9GkrZk/sd+0nLcc+jO2YUfGpB
fAdqg3U55QIZGxfTmtiBZP3Wi6oN9IbOfHgw4n+tXmrKHmccOxTlwV0TCpYyVO8x
W0m+YwJION+ApuwSBatS+THbrUwXsMMVVUMUvI50giLXA4dfalkoXzh82AM5OZ5z
5Cxii973RNNpP931308CGZMfZxrmvRx0Td5K20ZRutJFAaJgQbCgNkXbH94hAmha
uT+lq6V+yqdpOgLfKn3i3YFmZVU1yQWZNdDDn9aYCT7Um62Ro0She6S39tHlVIWE
ACEJNmq3
=gqtZ
-----END PGP MESSAGE-----
```


Figure 10.40 The Encrypted Message (Example)

9. To finish the sender tasks, open the email account from which SAP Cloud Platform Integration should poll emails, create an email, and paste the encrypted message (the text block shown in Figure 10.40) into the email body.
10. Move the email into the folder (e.g., with the name, *CPI_DEMO*) of your email account from which SAP Cloud Platform Integration should read it (corresponding to the mail sender adapter settings as shown later).

Now let's take the role of the integration developer. We propose that you create a simple integration flow, as shown earlier in Figure 10.31.

Throughout the previous chapters, you've already become an integration development expert, and, as such, we won't go into minute detail again. We'll only briefly summarize the required steps that are specific to this demo example.

Let's propose that the **Mail** sender adapter should poll unread emails from a specific folder (e.g., *CPI_DEMO*) of the receiver email account. If you've already configured a scenario with a *Mail* sender adapter when reading Chapter 2, you can simply reuse the scenario and enhance it with the *Decryptor* step as shown in the following steps. For those who didn't (as we only showed this as a further variant of your first integration flow), we'll show how to create and configure the *Mail* sender adapter. For more information on the mail sender adapter settings, refer to the *Mail Sender Adapter* info box in Chapter 2, Section 2.3.8. Follow these steps:

1. Create a new integration flow, choose the **Edit** mode, and select the **Sender** pool (Figure 10.41).

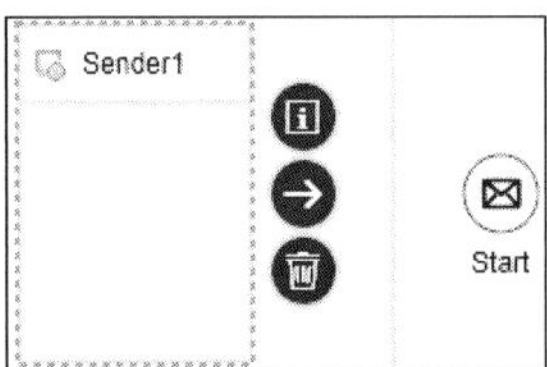

Figure 10.41 Connecting the Sender Pool with the Start Message Event to Create the Mail Sender Adapter

2. Click the arrow icon, and drag and drop the cursor to the **Start** message event.
3. As **Adapter Type**, select **Mail,** and as **Transport Protocol,** select **IMAP4**.
4. Open the **Connection** tab.
5. For **Address**, enter the host name of your email provider, followed by the port. Remember that for the mail sender adapter, when using the IMAP4 protocol, only ports 143 or 993 are allowed. We propose to use the same settings as shown in Figure 10.42; in particular, for the **Authentication** option, choose **Plain User/Password** and specify a credential name (in the example, "FirstnameLastname" as already used in the integration flow in Chapter 2, Section 2.3). We've also shown in Chapter 2, Section 2.3.5, how to create the corresponding **User Credentials** artifact, which contains the user name and password for the email account.

   Figure 10.42 shows the settings when using Gmail.

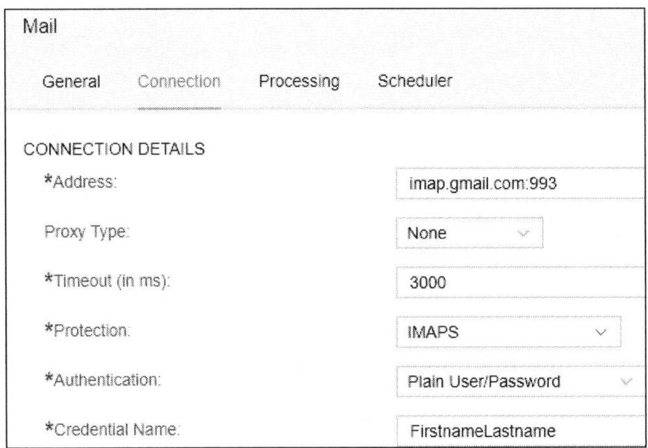

Figure 10.42 Connection Tab of the Mail Sender Adapter

6. Go to the **Processing** tab of the **Mail** sender adapter. Here, you specify how emails should be processed by SAP Cloud Platform Integration.

   Figure 10.43 shows example settings to configure the following behavior at runtime: SAP Cloud Platform Integration reads all unread mails (maximum 20 messages per poll) from folder *CPI_DEMO* of your email account. After that, the emails are marked as read (so that with the next poll they aren't read again).

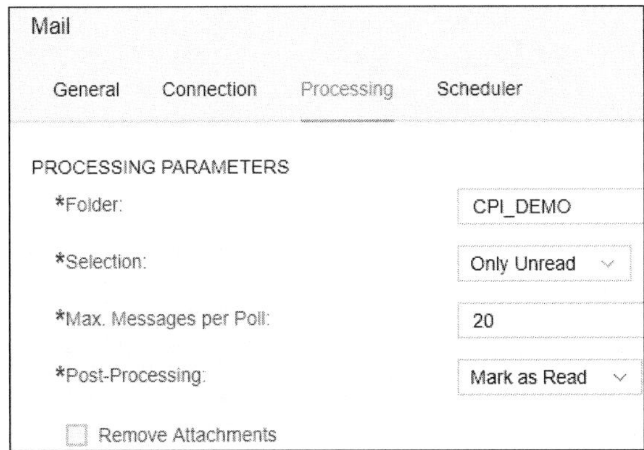

Figure 10.43 Processing Tab of the Mail Sender Adapter

7. Go to the **Scheduler** tab to configure how often emails should be polled. Note that the **Mail** sender adapter contains the same scheduler capabilities as the **Start Timer** event, which was explained in detail in Chapter 6, Section 6.1. We won't

repeat this here. However, we would like to urge you to be careful with these settings and not to spam your email account with the final integration flow. To be on the safe side, you might configure the scheduler so that emails are only polled once (as shown in Figure 10.44).

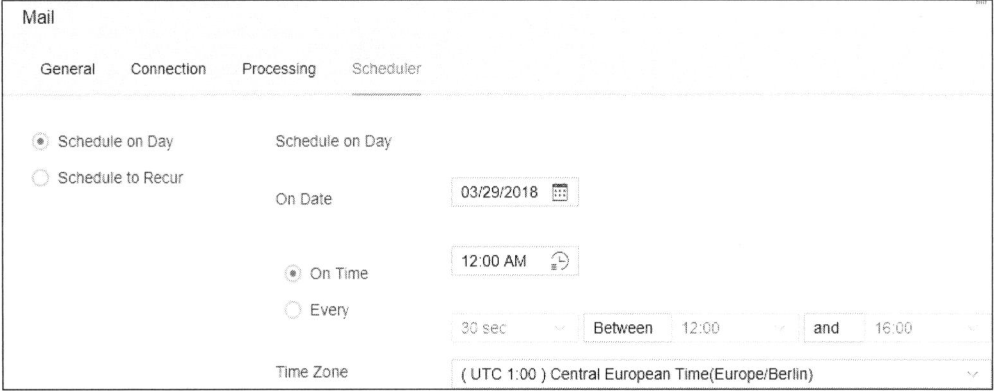

Figure 10.44 Scheduler Tab of the Mail Sender Adapter

8. To add a **PGP Decryptor** step, select the **Security Elements** icon in the palette, and choose **Decryptor • PGP Decryptor** (Figure 10.45).

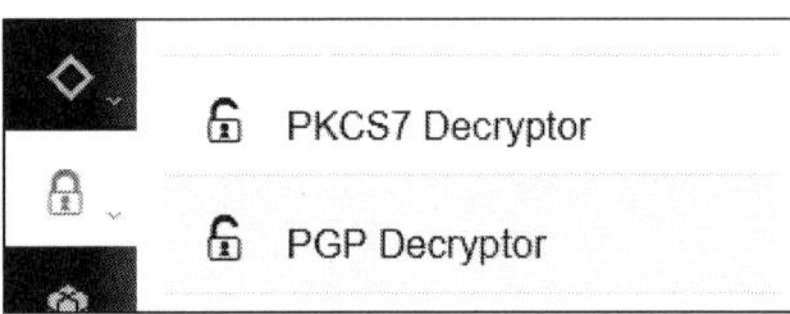

Figure 10.45 Adding a PGP Decryptor to the Integration Flow

9. In the settings of the **Decryptor** step, for the **Signatures** field, specify **None Expected**. No further entries are required (Figure 10.46).

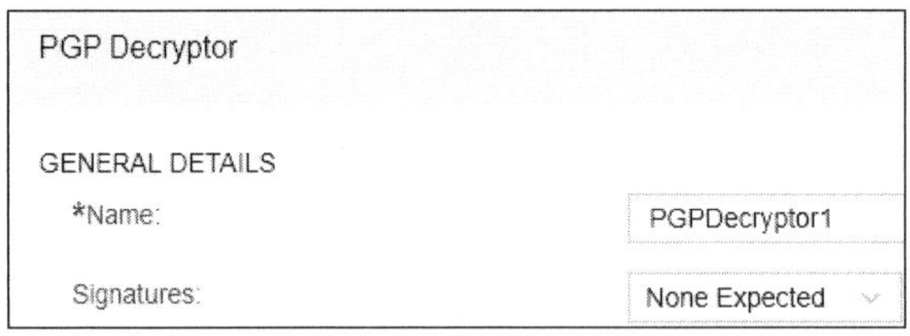

Figure 10.46 Settings of the Decryptor Step (When No Signatures Are Expected)

10. Finally, add the **Mail** receiver adapter to the integration flow.

    Use the same settings as shown in Chapter 2, Section 2.3.3.

11. Save and deploy the integration flow.

The integration flow will now poll emails as specified in the **Mail** sender adapter. Before we continue to add the **Encryptor** step, let's perform a brief check, and then deploy and run the integration flow that we've built so far.

Let's slip into the role of receiver and open the email account addressed by the mail adapter. When you've selected the appropriate settings in the **Scheduler** tab of the **Mail** sender adapter, you should have received an email with the customer name in clear text (e.g., **Paul Smith**).

To continue adding encryption to the scenario, we first need to create another key pair: the receiver's key pair. Remember that the tenant needs the receiver's public key to encrypt a message. To generate the key pair, use Kleopatra in the same way shown previously for the tenant's key pair. It makes sense to enter "Receiver" in the **Name** field (see Figure 10.47). Then follow these steps:

1. In Kleopatra, select the newly created key pair (**Receiver**), and choose **Export** in the context menu (Figure 10.48).

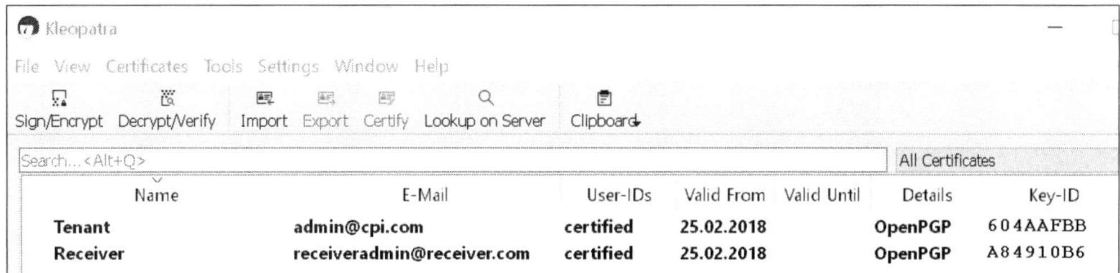

Figure 10.47 Kleopatra Key List Showing the Newly Created Receiver Key Pair

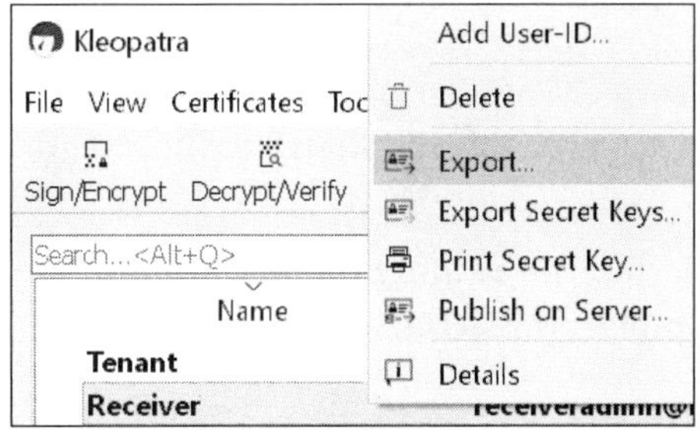

Figure 10.48 Exporting the Receiver's Public Key

2. Save the key on your computer (change the file extension to *.gpg*).

Switch to the role of the integration developer, and follow these steps:

1. Deploy the new public key on the tenant as the **PGP Public Keyring** artifact.
2. Open the **Monitor** application of the Web UI, and under **Manage Security**, click the **Security Material** tile.
3. Choose **Add • PGP Public Keyring**, as shown in Figure 10.49.

Figure 10.49 Adding a PGP Public Keyring Artifact

4. Browse for the public key *.gpg* file on your local disk, and choose **Deploy**. The artifact is added to the list of deployed artifacts as shown in Figure 10.50.

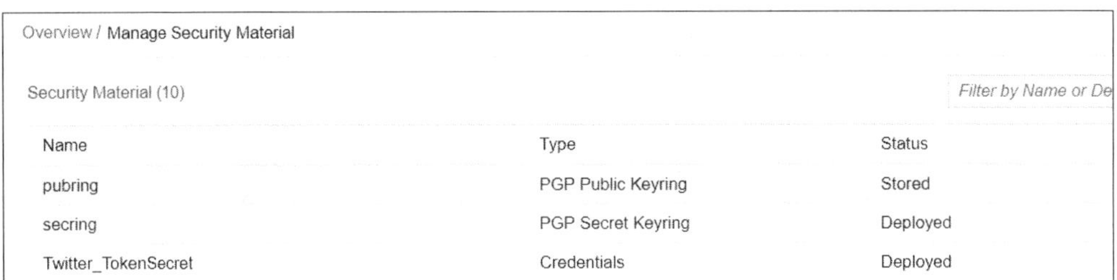

Overview / Manage Security Material
Security Material (10)
Filter by Name or De
Name
Type
Status
pubring
PGP Public Keyring
Stored
secring
PGP Secret Keyring
Deployed
Twitter_TokenSecret
Credentials
Deployed

Figure 10.50 The Newly Deployed PGP Public Keyring Shown in the List of Integration Artifacts

5. To complete the integration flow, add an **Encryptor** (OpenPGP) step to the integration flow.
6. Open the integration flow in the Web UI, click the **Security Elements** icon in the palette, and choose **Encryptor • PGP Encryptor** (Figure 10.51).

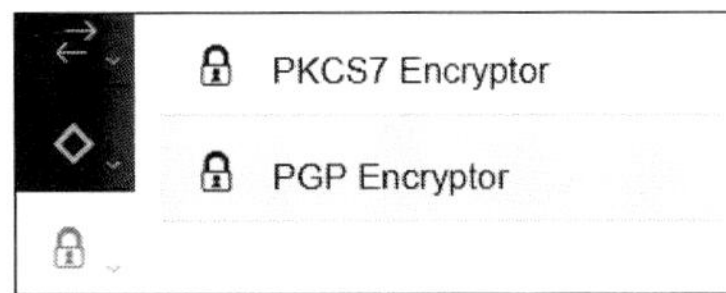

Figure 10.51 Adding a PGP Encryptor Step to the Integration Flow

7. Specify the properties of the **Encryptor** step (Figure 10.52). In the **Encryption User ID of Key(s) from Public Keyring** field, enter the user ID of the related key. To find the user ID, open Kleopatra, select the relevant key used for encryption, and check for the **Name** of the key. In our example, this is the **Receiver** key. For the other parameters, you can leave the default settings.

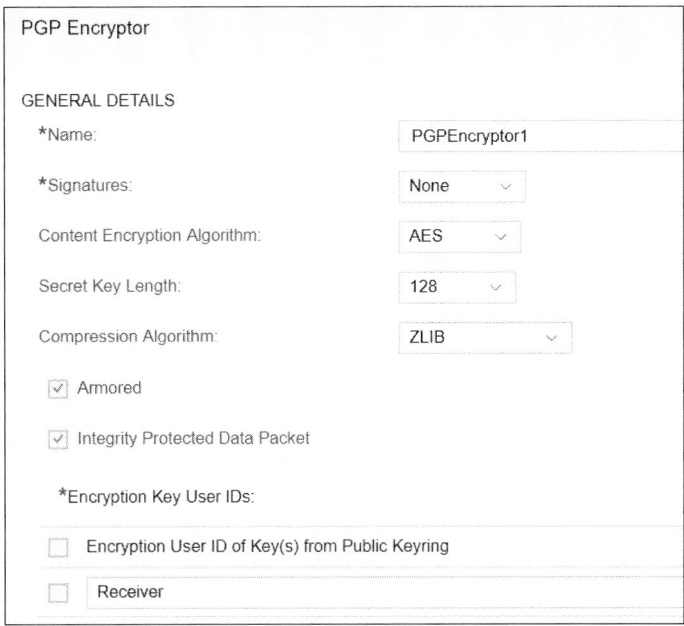

Figure 10.52 Parameters of the PGP Encryptor to Be Specified When No Signatures Are Included

8. Save and deploy the integration flow.

In the receiver mailbox, you should (depending on the scheduler settings in the mail sender adapter) find an email that contains the encrypted customer name. This looks like Figure 10.40, shown earlier, but the string sequence will be different.

To simulate the receiver's decryption step, follow these steps:

1. Open Kleopatra, and copy the encrypted mail text to the clipboard.
2. Choose **Clipboard • Decrypt/Verify** (refer to Figure 10.37).
3. As opposed to the encryption case, you don't have to select a key here (there is no **Add Recipent** option) because the receiver's private key is uniquely determined. You need to enter the passphrase for the private key.
4. When you paste the contents of your clipboard to a text editor, you should see the clear text (e.g., **Paul Smith**).

We've now shown how you can test the message encryption and decryption capabilities of SAP Cloud Platform Integration through very simple means. For simplicity, we skipped its signing and verification capabilities.

When you open the **Encryptor** step in the sample integration flow, you also have the option to include signatures (by choosing **Including** as the value for **Signatures**). In this case, you now have to specify additional parameters to define how the message is to be signed (Figure 10.53):

- **Digest Algorithm**
  This is the algorithm with which the digest (or hash value) is to be calculated out of the message content (refer to Figure 10.27).
- **Signer User ID of Key(s) from Secret Keyring**
  In addition to the user IDs that have to be specified to find the correct encryption (public) key from the PGP public keyring, in the message signing case, you need to find the correct private key from the PGP secret keyring. Remember that the tenant uses its private key to sign the message.

Figure 10.53 Additional Parameters When Including Digital Signatures

To finish this section, note that decrypting a message on the tenant (and encrypting it again before sending it to a receiver) usually only makes sense if you want to perform additional steps (e.g., CBR or mapping) that rely on the original unencrypted message. In our demo, however, we skip such additional processing steps for simplicity (see Figure 10.54).

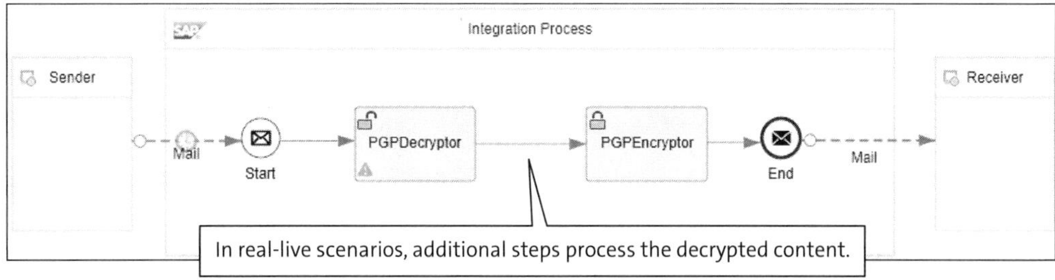

Figure 10.54 Integration Flow Steps That Decrypt an Inbound Message, Modify the Content, and Then Encrypt It Again

SFTP Adapter

Next to the mail sender adapter, SAP Cloud Platform Integration provides another polling adapter, the SFTP sender adapter.

You can modify this scenario by replacing the sender email server with an SFTP server. In this case, you need to store a file on the SFTP server with the encrypted message so that the SFTP sender adapter can poll it. For more information on how to set up a secure connection using SFTP, read the "How to Set Up Secure Connection to an SFTP Server" blog in the SAP Community (*www.sap.com/community.html*).

10.5 Keystore Management

While reading this book and this chapter in particular, you've become familiar with various kinds of security artifacts. Namely, we've shown you when you need to define **User Credentials** artifacts (Chapter 2, Section 2.3.5), **Certificate-to-User Mappings** artifacts (Section 10.4.4), **Secure Parameter** artifacts (Section 10.4.5), and **PGP Secret Keyring/PGP Public Keyring** artifacts (Section 10.4.6).

All aspects about managing these artifacts during the operation of an integration scenario were explained in detail in Chapter 8, Section 8.3.1.

We'll now elaborate on the **Keystore** artifact that was already introduced in Section 10.4.4 when talking about how to set up secure connections based on HTTP.

10.5.1 Using X.509 Security Material for SAP Cloud Platform Integration

The **Keystore** artifact allows you to manage the content of the tenant keystore. This keystore can contain key material (private/public key pairs and certificates) based on the X.509 standard (Section 10.4.1) as well as SSH keys.

SSH Keys

You can also use the tenant keystore to manage and store SSH keys that are required when configuring secure connections using SSH with the SFTP adapter, a topic which we haven't explained further in this book. For more information, read the "How to Set Up Secure Connection to an SFTP Server" blog in the SAP Community (*www.sap.com/community.html*).

Let's focus on X.509 keys. Table 10.10 summarizes in which situations you use X.509 keys and, therefore, need to consider how to deal with the tenant keystore.

Usage	Description
Certificate-based authentication of communication partners when communicating over HTTPS (transport-level security)	Certificates used in such scenarios should be signed by a trusted authority. We've explained this concept in Section 10.4.1.
Signing/verifying and encrypting/decrypting messages using the PKCS#7 standard (message-level security)	You configure these scenarios by using PKCS7 Signer, PKCS7 Encryptor, PKCS7 Signature Verifier, or PKCS7 Decryptor steps in the integration flow (Section 10.4.6). Certificates used in such scenarios can be self-signed.
Signing/verifying a SOAP body, encrypting/decrypting message content using WS-Security	Certain adapters support dedicated options to sign/verify messages or to encrypt/decrypt message content based on the WS-Security standard, which is an extension to SOAP. The following adapters support these options: ■ SOAP 1.x sender and receiver adapter ■ AS2 sender and receiver adapter To implement such scenarios, X.509 keys are also required in the tenant keystore.

Table 10.10 Using X.509 Keys in SAP Cloud Platform Integration

X.509 Keys for Transport-Level Security

As explained in Section 10.4.3, SAP Cloud Platform Integration supports various authentication options, including client certificate authentication. When you choose this authentication option for outbound connections, the tenant keystore needs to contain a client certificate, which is a signed private key pair. When you get your tenant provided by SAP, SAP provides you initially with a keystore that contains one such private key pair, which has the alias `sap_cloudintegrationcertificate` (see the upcoming info box). You can use this key pair to set up an outbound HTTP connection immediately.

As shown in the very first integration flow in Chapter 2, the **Mail** receiver adapter doesn't offer any client certificate authentication option. Instead, authentication is accomplished based on user credentials.

Recall that you had to create and deploy a **User Credentials** artifact to specify these credentials. Nevertheless, we needed to import certain certificates into the tenant keystore because the connection also needed to be protected *the other way around*: the email server needed to set up a trust relationship to the tenant. Therefore, we had to import a root certificate depending on the requirements of the email server. We referred to this certificate as the *receiver server root certificate*. When discussing the setup to establish a secure outbound connection from the tenant to a receiver system, we've already shown how the different security artifacts come into play in the whole picture (Section 10.4.4). This example showed you that the tenant keystore isn't only required to specify key pairs for client certificate authentication in outbound connections.

To find out more about the keystore content in different security setups, check out the online documentation of SAP Cloud Platform Integration at *https://help.sap.com/viewer/product/CLOUD_INTEGRATION/Cloud* and choose **Connecting a Customer System to Cloud Integration**.

X.509 Keys for Message-Level Security (PKCS#7 Standard)

As summarized in Table 10.10, the keystore can also contain keys to set up scenarios that include message-level security based on the PKCS#7 standard. As explained in Section 10.4.1, different keys are required to sign and encrypt/verify and decrypt a message. Let's briefly repeat this from the perspective of the tenant:

- To enable a tenant to encrypt a message (using the **PKCS7 Encryptor** step) and, correspondingly, to enable the receiver to decrypt the message, the receiver of the message needs to generate an X.509 private key pair and share the public part of it with the tenant administrator. The tenant administrator then imports the public key into the tenant keystore. At runtime, the tenant encrypts the message using the public key, and the receiver uses the private key to decrypt it.

- To enable a tenant to decrypt a message encrypted by a sender system (using the **PKCS7 Decryptor** step), the tenant administrator needs to generate an X.509 private key pair and share the public part of it with the administrator of the sender system. At runtime, the sender system uses the public key to encrypt the message, and the tenant uses the private key to decrypt it.

For signing and verifying messages using the **PKCS7 Signer** and **PKCS7 Signature Verifier** steps, the situation is mirror-inverted.

We've shown in Section 10.4.6 how to set up a scenario with encryption and decryption using PGP keys. The keys owned by the tenant in such a case need to be stored in dedicated key storage locations, namely, the **PGP Public Keyring** and the **PGP Secret Keyring**. When you want to set up the same kind of scenario using PKCS#7, you need to use the tenant keystore (**Keystore** artifact) to store both the private and the public keys. Besides that, the same principles apply.

To set up a scenario as summarized earlier in Figure 10.30, but using PKCS#7 keys, you need to establish the security configuration shown in Figure 10.55.

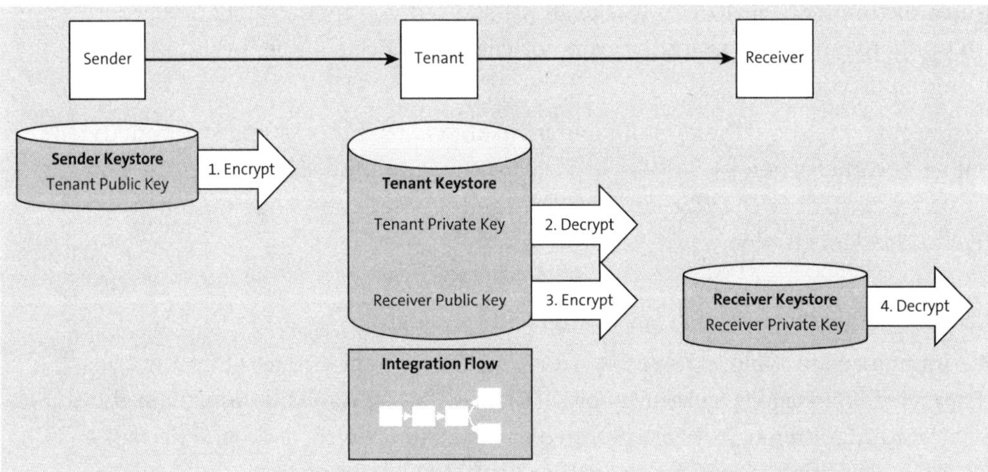

Figure 10.55 Key Setup for Encryption/Decryption Scenario Using PKCS#7 Security Standard

To set up such a scenario, the tenant keystore needs to contain the following:

- One private key pair (**Key Pair** entry)
- One **Certificate** entry that contains the public key of the receiver system (shared by the receiver administrator)

Furthermore, the integration flow uses the following steps:

- **PKCS7 Decryptor**
  This uses the private key of the tenant to decrypt the message obtained from the sender.
- **PKCS7 Encryptor**
  This uses the public key of the receiver system as specified by the **Receiver Public Key Alias** in the step.

Initial Content of the Tenant Keystore

When you get a tenant from SAP the first time, SAP also provides you with a tenant keystore that contains as initial content the following SAP-owned entries:

- Some SAP-owned CA root certificates that enable you to set up the communication with SAP cloud systems, such as SAP Ariba and SAP SuccessFactors (e.g., with the alias `sap_baltimore cybertrust root` and `sap_digicert global root ca`)
- One signed private key pair (alias: `sap_cloudintegrationcertificate`)

In Section 10.5.2, you'll learn more about how to manage keystore entries, and, in Section 10.5.3, you'll learn in particular how to deal with the lifecycle of SAP-owned keystore entries.

10.5.2 Managing Security Material in the Tenant Keystore

You get access to the tenant keystore in the **Monitor** application of the Web UI (**Keystore** tile under **Manage Security**). The basic functions have already been explained in Chapter 8, Section 8.3.2, in the context of SAP Cloud Platform Integration operations, so we won't repeat this here. However, to remind you of the content, we'll briefly summarize the most important aspects and provide additional details on the content of the keystore. In Section 10.5.3, we'll then show how to manage the lifecycle of keystore entries.

Figure 10.56 shows an excerpt of the tenant keystore.

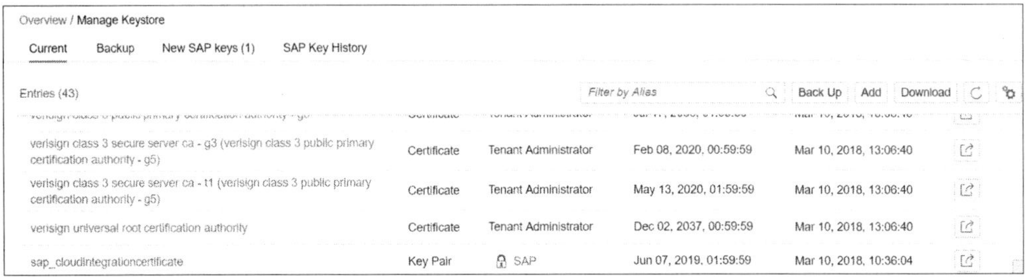

Overview / Manage Keystore

Current Backup New SAP keys (1) SAP Key History

Entries (43) Filter by Alias Back Up Add Download

verisign class 3 secure server ca - g3 (verisign class 3 public primary certification authority - g5)	Certificate	Tenant Administrator	Feb 08, 2020, 00:59:59	Mar 10, 2018, 13:06:40	
verisign class 3 secure server ca - t1 (verisign class 3 public primary certification authority - g5)	Certificate	Tenant Administrator	May 13, 2020, 01:59:59	Mar 10, 2018, 13:06:40	
verisign universal root certification authority	Certificate	Tenant Administrator	Dec 02, 2037, 00:59:59	Mar 10, 2018, 13:06:40	
sap_cloudintegrationcertificate	Key Pair	SAP	Jun 07, 2019, 01:59:59	Mar 10, 2018, 10:36:04	

Figure 10.56 Keystore Entries

The keystore can contain entries owned by SAP and those owned by the tenant administrator. Those owned by SAP are indicated by a lock icon and can't be changed by the tenant administrator. In Figure 10.56, you'll notice the key pair with the alias **sap_cloudintegrationcertificate**, initially provided by SAP as mentioned in the previous info box.

The keystore contains entries of two different types:

- **Key Pair**
  Consists of a private key pair and (commonly) an X.509 certificate chain, unless it's an SSH key, which can be identified by the alias `id_rsa` or `id_dsa`.
- **Certificate**
  Represents an X.509 certificate (in many cases, a root certificate).

As an example for a **Key Pair** entry, let's take a look at the SAP-owned key pair with alias **sap_cloudintegrationcertificate**. You can access the details of a keystore entry by clicking the link in the **Alias** column (Figure 10.57).

The left side of the figure shows the certificate chain. Note that for **Key Pair** entries, it's common to define them as part of a certificate chain. On top of the certificate chain of the key pair provided by SAP, you notice the root certificate of the CA **VeriSign**.

The details of the **Key Pair** entry are shown on the right side. Note that you can navigate to the details of the intermediate or root certificate by clicking on the corresponding nodes in the certificate chain on the left side; the details on the right then adapt accordingly. The following list describes a few of the attributes here.

Figure 10.57 SAP-Owned Key Pair Entry

> **Note**
>
> To find more information on the constituents of an X.509 certificate, check out the X.509 standard as documented in the *Request for Comments 4158* at *https://tools.ietf.org/html/rfc4158*.

- **Alias**
  The alias is the name by which you can uniquely identify a keystore entry.

> **When to Refer to an Alias (Examples)**
>
> In many cases, you need to specify the alias to tell the system which dedicated keystore entry to use for a certain integration flow step or adapter. We provide two examples:
>
> - When configuring a **PKCS7 Encryptor**, you need to specify the **Receiver Public Key** alias to select the public key that is to be used to encrypt the message for a certain receiver.

- When you configure an **HTTP** receiver adapter and choose **Authentication** option **Client Certificate**, you have the option to specify a **Private Key Alias** to point to that private key pair that is intended to be used to authenticate the tenant when calling a receiver.

- **Serial Number**
  This entry is used by the CA to uniquely identify the certificate (within the CA's organization).
- **Subject DN**
  The DN of the subject uniquely identifies the entity that is associated with the keystore entry. The DN is composed of a number of attributes that you need to specify when generating the key pair. These attributes comprise the common name (CN), which typically contains the server name of the VM associated with the tenant, and further information to identify the organization associated with the key pair such as Organization (O), Organizational Unit (OU), Country (C), and other attributes (in the example shown in the figure, information about the SAP location in Germany).
- **Issuer DN**
  The DN of the issuer of the certificate identifies the authority that issued and signed the certificate (also consisting of several entries such as a Common Name, Organizational Unit, etc.).
- **Signature Algorithm**
  This is the algorithm used by the issuer to sign the certificate.

Furthermore, the validity period is displayed (see also Section 10.5.3).

Note that as it's an SAP-owned entry, so you can only download the entry (**Download** button at the top); no further (changing) actions are possible.

Under **Fingerprints**, you find hexadecimal expressions of hash values calculated out of the public key (using different hash algorithms, e.g., SHA-1 or SHA-256). The tenant administrator can use the fingerprint to verify the trustworthiness of a keystore entry by sharing it with the related communication partner (e.g., the administrator of the connected sender or receiver system) via an independent secure communication channel such as encrypted email.

Figure 10.58 shows a **Certificate** entry owned by the tenant administrator.

Figure 10.58 Certificate Entry Owned by the Tenant Administrator

As you see on the left side, this is a root certificate as only one node of a certificate chain is shown.

The attributes have the same meaning as discussed for the **Key Pair** entry after Figure 10.57. Note, however, that **Subject DN** and **Issuer DN** are identical in this case, as the CA is both acting as certificate issuer and as entity associated with the certificate.

Figure 10.58 shows a keystore entry owned by the tenant administrator. Therefore, further actions are supported, such as deleting it or renaming it (changing the alias), as you can see from the **Delete** and **Rename** buttons at the top.

Keystore monitors have been explained in detail in Chapter 8, Section 8.3.1. We'll now focus on the aspect of lifecycle management of security material.

10.5.3 Managing the Lifecycle of Keys Provided by SAP

To increase the security level of integration scenarios, digital certificates used to protect connections have a restricted validity period. Therefore, expiring certificates need to be renewed in regular intervals—in the same way that it's a good idea to change passwords from time to time.

However, keys are a fundamental part of the setup of each integration scenario, and each change in the setup of security material might require certain adaptations in the scenario setup and might disrupt the scenario operations, unless it's done in a well-defined and orchestrated manner.

Therefore, it's of critical importance to manage the lifecycle of keys in a smart way. Namely, as tenant administrator, you need to take certain actions when a key is due to expire and replace it with a new one. You should organize such a task so that there is ideally no or, if it can't be avoided, only a minimal downtime for your integration scenarios. General guidelines of how to renew security material for the various use cases supported by SAP Cloud Platform Integration are documented in the online documentation for SAP Cloud Platform Integration (*https://help.sap.com/viewer/product/CLOUD_INTEGRATION/Cloud*) under **Operating and Monitoring Cloud Integration • Security Artifact Renewal**.

We'll now focus on the special case when SAP-owned key material is renewed by SAP.

SAP renews key pairs regularly (by default, the validity period is two years), and to enable the tenant administrator to manage renewal of SAP-owned keys, there are certain options available. What the tenant administrator is supposed to do in such a case is activate the updated key in the tenant keystore. However, this has to be done in a coordinated manner because other components (i.e., the remote systems that are connected to the tenant and that use the public part of the SAP key pair in their keystores) are affected by such a step.

Renewal of SAP-Owned Root Certificates

As already explained in Chapter 8, Section 8.3.2, there is also the option that SAP updates SAP-owned root certificates. In such a situation, there is no need for the tenant administrator to take any action. After the certificate update, the new certificate is active immediately in the keystore.

The **Monitor** application of the Web UI provides certain options to give the tenant administrator full control over the activation of keys that are updated by SAP. In particular, as already shown in Chapter 8, Section 8.3.2, the **Monitor** application provides four different tabs for the tenant keystore:

- **Current**
  Shows the content of the keystore as currently deployed on the tenant (and actively used in your integration scenarios).

- **Backup**
  Shows backed-up keystore entries (see Chapter 8, Section 8.3.2).
- **New SAP Keys**
  Shows new keys provided by SAP in case a dedicated SAP-owned key is due to expire (see upcoming discussion).
- **SAP Key History**
  Shows recently renewed SAP keys and provides the option to move a key back to the **New SAP Keys** store.

We won't go through all options of keystore management here, but you can refer to Chapter 8, Section 8.3.2. Instead, we focus on the topic of key activation and show how the tenant administrator deals with the situation when SAP updates an SAP-owned key pair. Furthermore, to illustrate the aspect that there are other components affected by key renewal, we assume (as an example) that the SAP key pair is used in a scenario where a sender sends an encrypted message to SAP Cloud Platform Integration, and the message is decrypted by a **PKCS7 Decryptor** step on the tenant. Figure 10.59 shows where the SAP key pair (the tenant private key pair) is involved.

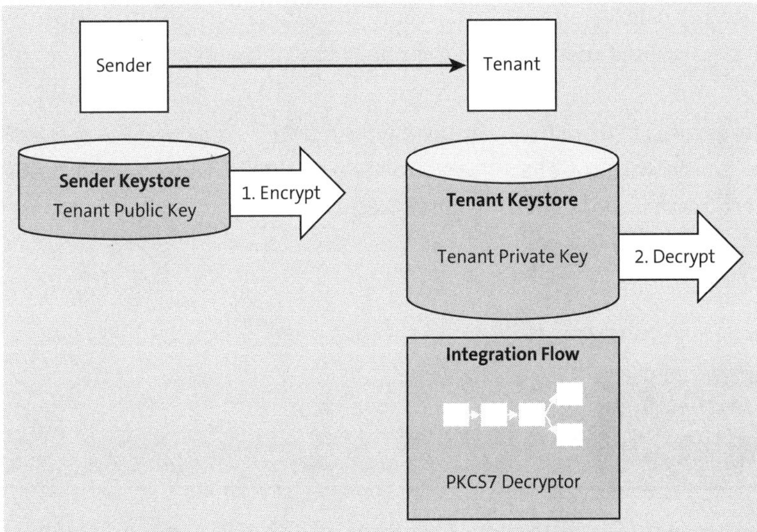

Figure 10.59 Using a Tenant Private Key Provided by SAP in a PKCS7 Decryptor Step

Such a situation requires a coordinated procedure. Let's walk through the procedure of activating the new key now:

1. SAP provides a new key pair for one that is due to expire soon.
2. As tenant administrator, you'll find the new key pair in the **Monitor** application of the Web UI under **Manage Keystore** in the **Keystore** tile in the **New SAP keys** tab (Figure 10.60).

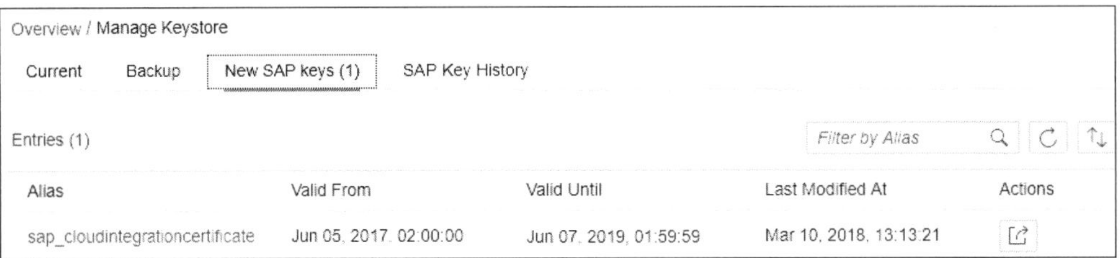

Figure 10.60 New Key Provided by SAP Visible in New SAP Keys Tab of the Manage Keystore Monitor

3. Analyze the active integration flows and remote connections. Let's assume you find out that one integration scenario uses a **PKCS7 Decryptor** step, which uses this key pair (as shown earlier in Figure 10.59). Therefore, you notice that before activating the new key pair, you need to make sure the sender system that sends the corresponding encrypted message gets the public key of the newly provided SAP key pair.
4. Download the certificate from the **New SAP Keys** monitor by selecting the new SAP key (in our example, with the alias **sap_cloudintegrationcertificate**) and choosing **Download Certificate** under **Actions** (Figure 10.61).

Figure 10.61 Downloading a Certificate from a Key Provided in the New SAP Keys Monitor

5. Save the certificate on your computer (in our example, as a file named *sap_cloudintegrationcertificate.cer*).
6. Provide the administrator of the sender system with the certificate file through a protected channel (e.g., encrypted email) and ask him to update the certificate in

the corresponding keystore of the sender system (to enable the sender to encrypt messages using the new certificate).

Key Renewal without Any Downtime

Note that until now, we've kept quiet about a critical aspect of key renewal. In the example discussed here, we didn't consider that a downtime needs to be considered under certain conditions when renewing keys in all affected systems involved in a secure communication setup.

The tenant administrator should, therefore, find out prior to the activities related to key renewal if the sender system is capable of encrypting messages with the old and the new SAP key at the same time. In such a case, the process of key renewal can be organized so that no downtime is required for the integration scenario. The administrator of the sender system can just import the public key provided by the tenant administrator into the keystore of the sender system and inform the tenant administrator when he has finished this task. The tenant administrator can then activate the new key as shown in the next step.

In the online documentation for SAP Cloud Platform Integration (*https://help.sap.com/viewer/product/CLOUD_INTEGRATION/Cloud*) under **Operating and Monitoring Cloud Integration • Security Artifact Renewal**, you'll find extensive information on this topic and also about those use cases and conditions under which a key renewal task can be organized without any downtime.

7. After the sender administrator has confirmed these actions, you can proceed and activate the new SAP key in the tenant keystore. Go to the **New SAP Keys** monitor, select the new SAP Key (in our example, with the alias **sap_cloudintegrationcertificate**), and choose **Activate** under **Actions** (Figure 10.62).

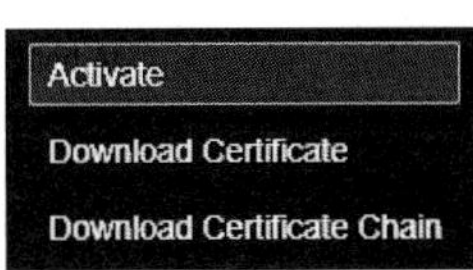

Figure 10.62 Activating a New SAP Key

8. A warning message is shown that reminds you to do the preparatory steps as explained earlier (Figure 10.63).

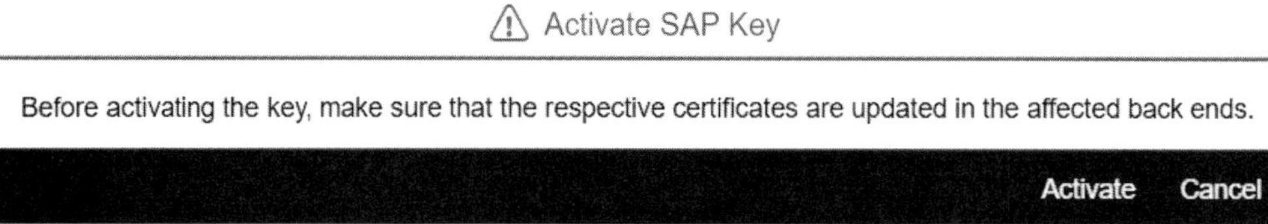

Activate SAP Key
Before activating the key, make sure that the respective certificates are updated in the affected back ends.
Activate
Cancel

Figure 10.63 Warning Message Reminding You to Update Corresponding Keys in the Connected Remote Systems

9. As you've already taken care of the required actions regarding the sender system, you can click **Activate**.

   The following happens now behind the scenes: The old key pair (with alias `sap_cloudintegrationcertificate`) is copied from the active keystore (**Current** tab) to the **Key History** keystore. Then, the new key pair (from the **New SAP Keys** keystore) is copied to the active keystore (**Current** tab) and overwrites the old key pair there. Finally, the new key pair is removed from the **New SAP Keys** keystore.

> **Note**
>
> For a detailed description of the process, check out the documentation for SAP Cloud Platform Integration at *https://help.sap.com/viewer/product/CLOUD_INTEGRATION/Cloud*, and search for **Activating a New SAP Key Pair on the Tenant.**

10. Check in the **Key History** tab to see if the old key pair has been added (Figure 10.64).

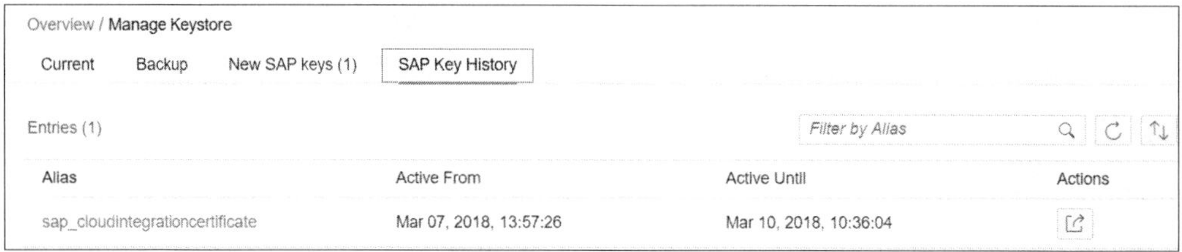

Figure 10.64 Key History Showing the Old Key Pair Replaced by the New One in the Current Keystore

The **SAP Key History** tab provides an important **Add to New SAP Keys** option, which you can use to withdraw the activation of a new key and revert back to the previous SAP key pair (as explained in Chapter 8, Section 8.3.2, Table 8.14).

11. Finally, you can verify that in the **New SAP Keys** tab, the newly activated key pair disappeared as expected (Figure 10.65).

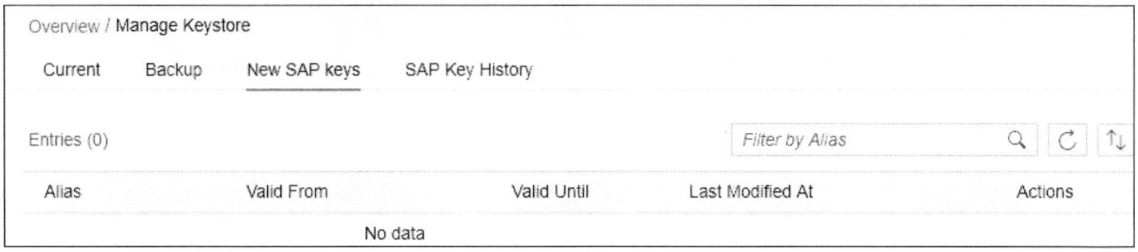

Overview / Manage Keystore

Current | Backup | New SAP keys | SAP Key History

Entries (0) | Filter by Alias

Alias	Valid From	Valid Until	Last Modified At	Actions
		No data		

Figure 10.65 Newly Activated Key Pair Finally Removed from the New SAP Keys Monitor

To finish this discussion, let's assume that the key pair to renew is also used in an outbound HTTP connection to implement client certificate authentication (in a setup as shown earlier in Figure 10.20). In this case, prior to activating the new key, download the certificate chain of the SAP key from the **New SAP Keys** keystore (choose **Download Certificate Chain** as the **Action** option), and save it as file (in our example with the name *sap_cloudintegrationcertificate.p7b*) to your computer. From the certificate chain, you finally need to extract the client root certificate and the client certificate, and make both available to the administrator of the receiver system. The receiver administrator needs to import them into the receiver keystore prior to the tenant administrator activating the new key pair.

We've only given a simple example of a situation where a key pair renewed by SAP was used in an existing integration setup. In real-life scenarios, you have to assume that expired keys need to be removed in many more *places* in an integration scenario.

In this section, we only gave a glimpse into the lifecycle management for keys. Depending on the integration scenario, there are different processes that make sure you execute key renewal on all sides of the communication in such a way that downtimes are either avoided or kept to a minimum.

We finish this section by mentioning that, in case the tenant administrator hasn't activated an SAP key pair prior to its expiration, a system job activates the key pair automatically (see Chapter 8, Section 8.3.2).

For a good introduction into how to organize key renewal, read the "Cloud Integration – Activate SAP Keys in Keystore Monitor" blog in the SAP Community (*www.sap.com/community.html*).

10.6 Summary

Security considerations often come first when businesses consider sourcing out parts of their IT processes into the cloud. This chapter provided an overview of the various measures undertaken to protect customer data processed by SAP Cloud Platform Integration at the highest level. Several security features are already built-in and available via the architecture, the network design, and the way sensitive data is protected at SAP. Furthermore, you've seen how security is taken seriously by the way processes are performed during the lifecycle of an integration project. We showed you how to manage users and authorizations for your SAP Cloud Platform subaccount. Finally, you learned what you, as the customer, can do to configure secure message exchange between your landscape and SAP Cloud Platform Integration. We've shown you, step by step, how to set up a secure connection between remote components and SAP Cloud Platform Integration and how to build integration flows that implement basic security features. We closed this chapter by providing a glimpse into how to manage the lifecycle of security material in the tenant keystore.

In the next chapter, we will provide you with an overview of some productive scenarios that use SAP Cloud Platform Integration.

Chapter 11
Productive Scenarios Using SAP Cloud Platform Integration

Now that you've undertaken a journey through the world of SAP Cloud Platform Integration, you should be familiar with the principles and concepts to begin working with it seriously. You also know that SAP Cloud Platform Integration enables you to build networks of IT applications flexibly on any scale. In this chapter, we'll show you a few examples of how this product can be used productively in real-life scenarios.

In Chapter 1, Section 1.2, we introduced SAP Cloud Platform Integration as a cloud-based integration solution that supports cloud-to-cloud integration and cloud-to-on-premise integration. We also showed that SAP Cloud Platform Integration can be used in combination with on-premise integration solutions (e.g., SAP Process Orchestration). In this chapter, we'll explain a few productive scenarios that each demonstrates one of the cloud-to-cloud and cloud-to-on-premise use cases. Additionally, we'll show you how these scenarios work in real life, in existing landscapes, with actual applications that are connected with each other.

For most of these scenarios, predefined integration content is available in the Integration Content Catalog, which you can use out of the box. That is why Chapter 3, which deals with the Integration Content Catalog, contains information about these scenarios. Therefore, we'll keep the description of those scenarios short in this chapter.

11.1 Integration of SAP Cloud for Customer and SAP ERP

SAP Cloud for Customer is SAP's cloud-based customer relationship management (CRM) solution that helps you, as an SAP customer, improve your own customer interactions.

Using a cloud-based CRM solution often requires that you replicate master data (e.g., account, product, or employee) or transactional data from a connected on-premise SAP ERP application. Transactional data may be replicated, for example, with sales orders, or may be referenced synchronously for the latest updates, such as the latest figures for a customer-specific price. Obviously, both the cloud application and the on-premise system need to be kept in sync, and, therefore, integration scenarios have to be implemented.

Figure 11.1 shows the general setup of the integration of SAP ERP with SAP Cloud for Customer.

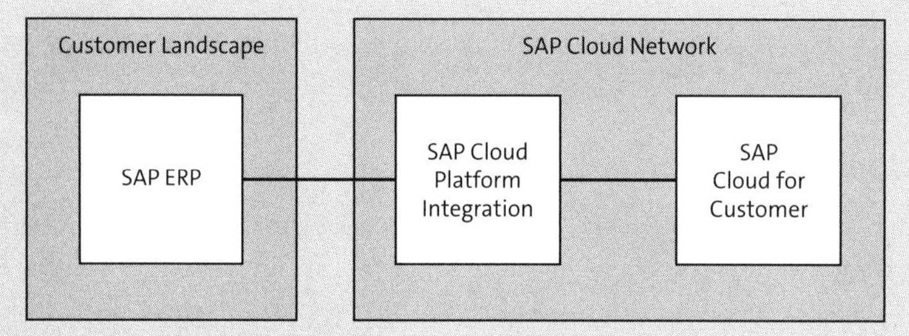

Figure 11.1 Integration of SAP ERP with SAP Cloud for Customer

SAP provides predefined integration content for the integration of SAP Cloud for Customer with SAP ERP in the Integration Content Catalog. An overview of the content and more details on the business use case of this scenario have already been provided in Chapter 3, Section 3.4.2.

11.1.1 Technical Landscape

The integration of SAP Cloud for Customer with SAP ERP is an example of cloud-to-on-premise integration. Figure 11.2 shows the commonly used technical landscape for the scenario. There are, as always, many options, but we'll briefly describe a common setup.

In the proposed setup, the SAP Cloud for Customer application and the integration middleware (SAP Cloud Platform Integration) run in the SAP cloud network, whereas the connected on-premise application (SAP ERP) runs in the customer landscape.

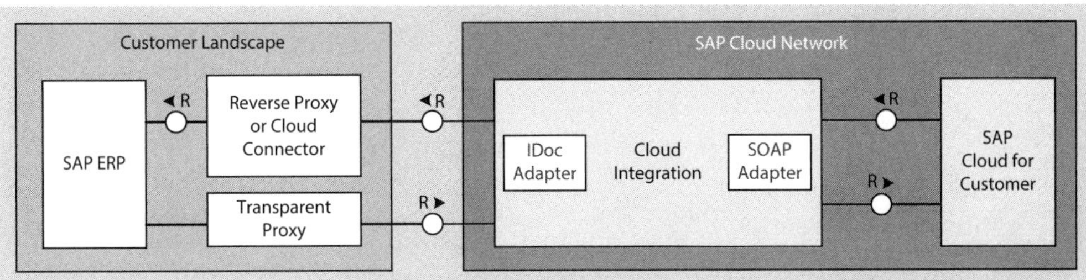

Figure 11.2 Technical Landscape for Integration of SAP Cloud for Customer with SAP ERP (Example Setup)

All components communicate with each other using HTTPS. However, note that connections between the SAP cloud network and components located in the customer landscape require particular security measures: you must ensure that the components in the customer landscape aren't directly accessible from the Internet. For this communication direction, that means when messages are sent from the SAP cloud network to the customer-based SAP ERP system, a component (either a reverse proxy or the SAP Cloud Platform Connectivity service [hereafter, SAP Cloud Platform Connectivity]) in the customer landscape terminates the Transport Layer Security (TLS) requests and reestablishes new ones. That way, it's ensured that the components in the customer landscape are shielded from the open Internet. As a reverse proxy, the SAP Web Dispatcher can be used.

The other way around, a proxy server (or transparent proxy) routes the request from the SAP ERP system to the target component (SAP Cloud Platform Integration) without terminating any TLS request.

SAP Cloud Platform Integration, as message broker interconnected between SAP Cloud for Customer and SAP ERP, typically uses the following connectivity options:

- Simple Object Access Protocol (SOAP) adapter or IDoc adapter (which also uses the SOAP protocol) for connections between SAP ERP and SAP Cloud Platform Integration
- SOAP adapter for connections between SAP Cloud Platform Integration and SAP Cloud for Customer

11.1.2 Example Adapter Configurations

To round off this section, we'll briefly show you how the connections of the scenario depicted in Figure 11.2 can be configured in a productive use case on the SAP Cloud Platform Integration side of the communication. To do this, we've provided screenshots of the four adapters that come into play at the side of the SAP Cloud Platform Integration system.

Figure 11.3 shows an example of an IDoc adapter used for the connection between SAP ERP and SAP Cloud Platform Integration (messages sent from SAP ERP to SAP Cloud Platform Integration).

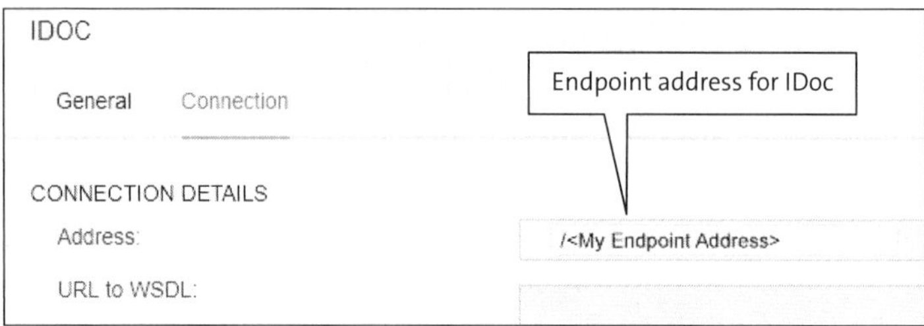

Figure 11.3 IDoc Adapter for Messages Sent from SAP ERP to SAP Cloud Platform Integration

In the same way in the first integration flow you saw in Chapter 2 for the **SOAP** sender adapter, the **Address** field should define an endpoint address so that SAP ERP can call the integration flow deployed on the SAP Cloud Platform Integration tenant. The final destination, which is to be configured in the SAP ERP system, is then composed of the URL, the runtime node (assigned to the tenant), and this endpoint address (see Chapter 2, Section 2.3.5). The field **URL to WSDL** was explained in the context of the SOAP adapter in Chapter 5, Section 5.3.1.

Figure 11.4 shows an example of an **IDoc** adapter for the connection between SAP ERP and SAP Cloud Platform Integration for the opposite communication direction (messages sent from SAP Cloud Platform Integration to SAP ERP).

In the **Address** field, you have to specify the host and port of the SAP ERP system, as well as the SAP client. The string **/sap/bc/srt/idoc** is a fixed part of the address to point to the IDoc service of an SAP system.

In the **Proxy Type** field, the **Internet** option is selected as default, which means that the connection is done via a reverse proxy infrastructure (an option used by many customers for such integration scenarios). As an alternative, you can select **On Premise** if you want to use SAP Cloud Platform Connectivity to connect to SAP ERP. For more information about this attribute, check out the "Proxy Type" info box at the end of Chapter 10, Section 10.4.3.

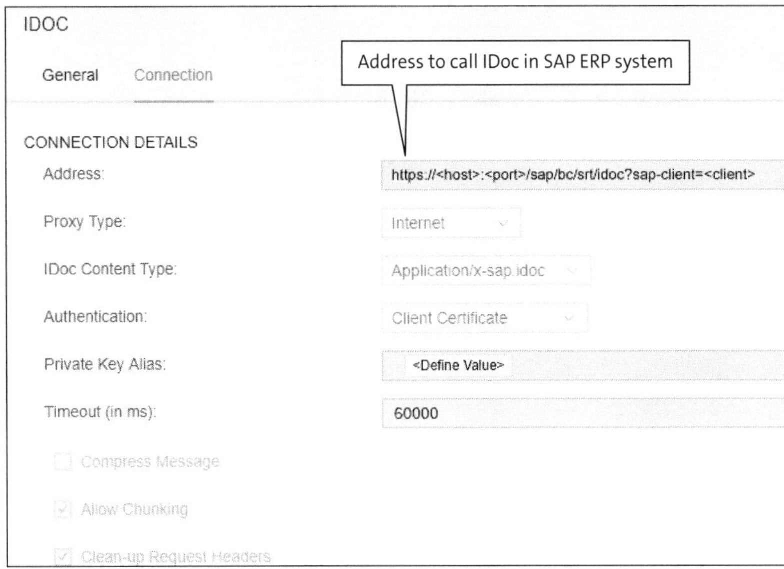

Figure 11.4 IDoc Adapter for Messages Sent from SAP Cloud Platform Integration to SAP ERP

Figure 11.5 shows an example of a SOAP (1.x) sender adapter for the connection between SAP Cloud Platform Integration and SAP Cloud for Customer (messages sent from SAP Cloud for Customer to SAP Cloud Platform Integration):

In the **Address** field, you need to define an endpoint address so that SAP Cloud for Customer can call the integration flow deployed on the SAP Cloud Platform Integration tenant.

In this example, in the **URL to WSDL** field, a WSDL is also specified, allowing SAP Cloud Platform Integration to access information contained in the WSDL to process the message (this was explained in Chapter 5, Section 5.3.1, in our example of an asynchronous message).

Figure 11.6 shows an example of a SOAP (1.x) receiver adapter establishing the connection between SAP Cloud Platform Integration and SAP Cloud for Customer for the opposite communication direction (messages sent from SAP Cloud Platform Integration to SAP Cloud for Customer).

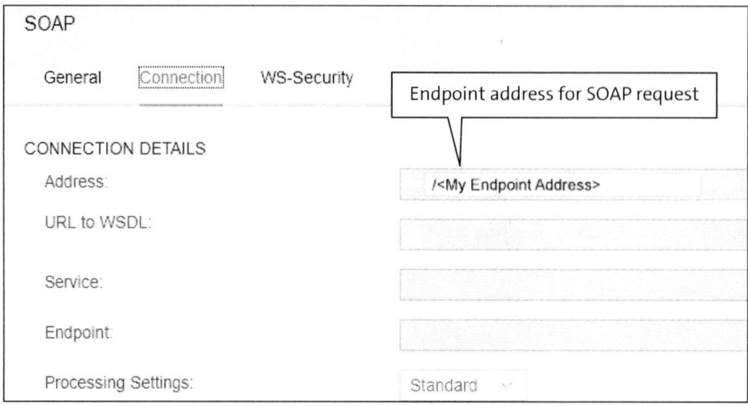

Figure 11.5 SOAP Adapter for Messages Sent from SAP Cloud for Customer to SAP Cloud Platform Integration

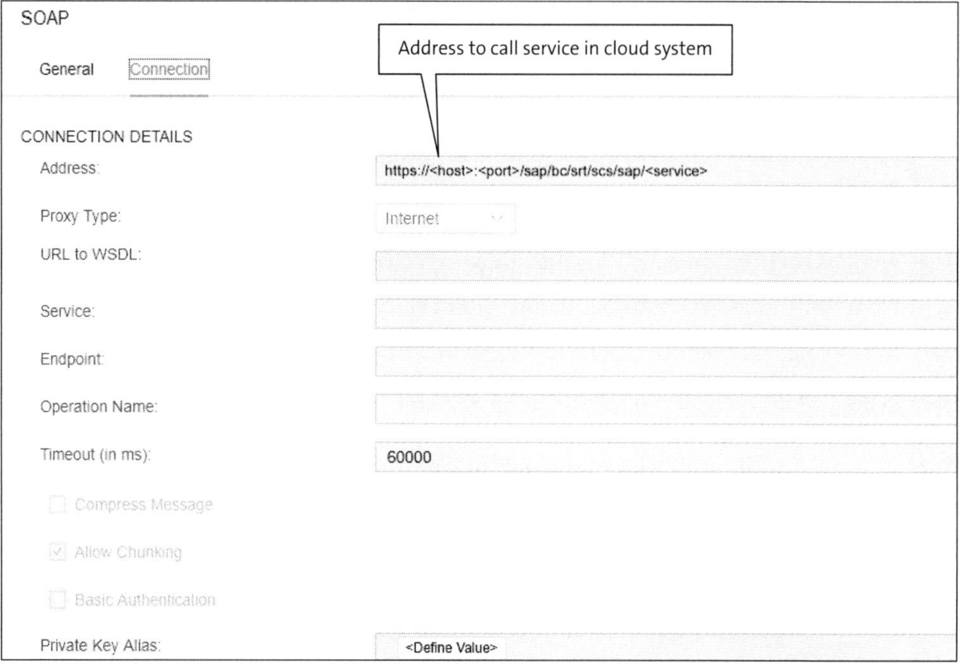

Figure 11.6 SOAP Adapter for Messages Sent from SAP Cloud Platform Integration to SAP SAP Cloud for Customer

In the **Address** field, you must specify the service address in the SAP Cloud for Customer system.

Note that the shown examples (Figure 11.5 and Figure 11.6) are retrieved from the Integration Content Catalog and reflect earlier versions of the SOAP adapter. In the meantime, updates to this adapter type have been provided so that when you create a new SOAP adapter, you'll get a slightly different user interface (UI). For more information on the versioning concept for integration flow components, see Chapter 6, Section 6.5.

11.2 Integration of SAP Cloud for Customer with SAP S/4HANA Cloud

SAP S/4HANA is SAP's next generation business suite, built on SAP HANA database technology, and providing SAP Fiori UIs. SAP Fiori is a modern UI technology that enables customers to extend the use of SAP applications to tablet computers and smartphones. You can install SAP S/4HANA in your own landscape (on premise) or use it in the public (SAP) cloud.

Customers who prefer to run the IT processes of their enterprise in the cloud can choose SAP S/4HANA Cloud. It covers the areas of logistics, accounting and financials, and sales. The integration package for SAP Hybris Cloud for Customer Integration with SAP S/4HANA Cloud, available in the Integration Content Catalog, provides a set of predefined integration flows and value mappings that facilitate the replication of objects, such as business partner and material, between SAP S/4HANA Cloud and SAP Cloud for Customer.

Compared to the integration of SAP Cloud for Customer and SAP ERP (refer to Section 11.1), this integration package deals with cloud-to-cloud integration, as illustrated in Figure 11.7.

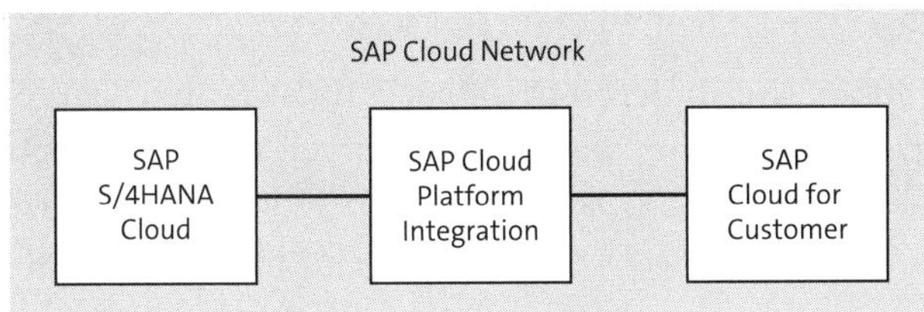

Figure 11.7 Integration of SAP S/4HANA Cloud with SAP Cloud for Customer

11.3 Integration of SAP Marketing Cloud and Various Applications

SAP C/4HANA is an on-demand product family that includes SAP Cloud for Customer (discussed in Section 11.1), SAP Commerce Cloud, SAP Customer Data Cloud, and SAP Marketing Cloud.

The available integration packages were already presented in Chapter 3, Section 3.4.3 (there, you also find a brief introduction into these solutions).

SAP Marketing Cloud is a cloud solution offered by SAP to help customers optimize their marketing activities (e.g., by developing and executing successful marketing campaigns). As already mentioned in Chapter 3, Section 3.4.3, SAP Marketing Cloud can be integrated with other components such as the following:

- SAP Cloud for Customer (e.g., for master data replication)
- Applications such as SAP S/4HANA Enterprise Management on-premise, SAP Customer Relationship Management (SAP CRM), SAP Cloud for Customer, and SAP ERP
- Social media platforms, such as Twitter or Facebook

We would like to pick out the integration of SAP Marketing Cloud with Twitter as one example for a social media platform. It's obvious that analyzing social media content is invaluable when it comes to getting to know what customers or potential customers think about certain topics. Integrating SAP Marketing Cloud with Twitter allows SAP customers to load data from Twitter into SAP Marketing Cloud and to analyze it further. For example, SAP Marketing Cloud allows you to do sentiment analysis based on Twitter content. In this context, sentiment analysis, in short, is a methodology to analyze social media content (Twitter tweeds) related to a certain topic to determine the attitude of users with regard to this topic. SAP Marketing Cloud can then use the results of this analysis to adapt and improve marketing campaigns.

Figure 11.8 illustrates the components integrated with this scenario.

In Chapter 10, Section 10.4.5, you've already become familiar with the Twitter adapter. The mentioned integration package uses the Twitter adapter to connect Twitter with SAP Cloud Platform Integration. On the other side of the communication, the HTTP adapter is used to connect SAP Cloud Platform Integration with SAP Marketing Cloud.

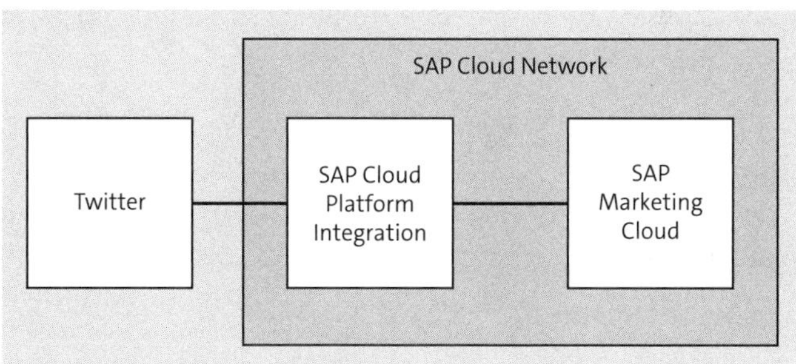

Figure 11.8 Integration of Twitter with SAP Marketing Cloud

You can find the package **SAP Marketing Cloud – Twitter Integration** in the Integration Content Catalog. When you've copied the integration package to your workspace (see Chapter 3, Section 3.2.2), you can configure the integration flow. The available integration content has been designed in such a way that you only need to configure a few parameters to set the integration scenario into operation—without any further editing and adapting any integration flow (see Chapter 4, Section 4.2, for more details on configuring externalized integration flow parameters). To finish the communication between Twitter and SAP Cloud Platform Integration, the only thing you need to do is to configure your Twitter application programming interface (API) and deploy the required OAuth credentials as **Secure Parameter** artifacts (as we've shown in detail in Chapter 10, Section 10.4.5).

You can also find a concise and easy-to-follow tutorial on the SAP website at *www.sap.com/developer/tutorials/cpi-sentiment-analysis.html*.

11.4 Integration of SAP SuccessFactors and SAP ERP

SAP SuccessFactors is cloud-based human capital management (HCM) software that provides tools for recruiting, performance management, talent management, and other employee-centric solutions. It also provides core employee management capabilities (in the Employee Central module).

In many cases, when companies plan to move parts of their HCM processes to the cloud, a phased approach might be the solution of choice. Either the company first moves only parts of the HCM processes to the cloud (e.g., recruitment) and keeps the core functions located in the on-premise landscape, or they prefer to migrate their HCM solution successively to the cloud, based on certain locations. In any case, a seamless and tight integration between the processes running in the cloud and in the on-premise environment is critical.

As an example of the separation of processes between the on-premise landscape and the cloud, a company might want to run its recruitment processes using SAP SuccessFactors in the cloud, whereas core employee management functions are kept in the on-premise SAP ERP Human Capital Management (SAP ERP HCM) application.

Figure 11.9 shows the involved components at a high level.

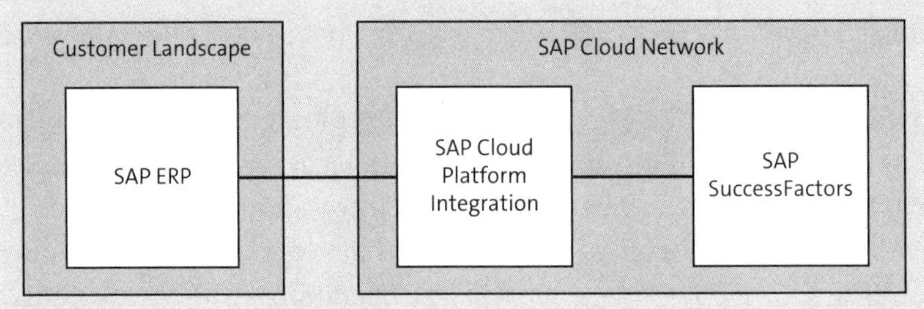

Figure 11.9 Integration of SAP ERP with SAP SuccessFactors

The integration of SAP SuccessFactors with SAP ERP is cloud-to-on-premise.

In the Integration Content Catalog, you can find various integration packages that facilitate the integration of SAP ERP-based processes with the cloud-based HCM processes of SAP SuccessFactors. An overview of the content and more details on the business use case of such scenarios has already been provided in Chapter 3, Section 3.4.1. In this section, we cover additional aspects such as the typical technical landscape setup for such scenarios.

11.4.1 Technical Landscape

Figure 11.10 shows a common setup of an SAP SuccessFactors and SAP ERP integration scenario.

An obvious option to connect the SAP ERP with SAP Cloud Platform Integration is using web services communication (through the SOAP adapter).

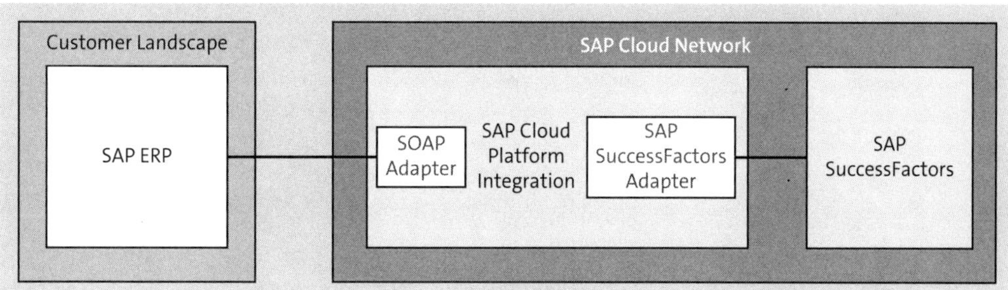

Figure 11.10 Integrating SAP ERP with SAP SuccessFactors through SAP Cloud Platform Integration

For the other side of the communication, SAP SuccessFactors offers various API options to technically integrate with and connect to other systems, including the following:

- **SFAPI**
  This is a SOAP API designed to import or export data to and from SAP SuccessFactors. It allows you to perform create, read, update, delete (CRUD) operations on SAP SuccessFactors entities.
- **OData API**
  This API allows you to access SAP SuccessFactors content using OData.

SAP Cloud Platform Integration provides an option to use these APIs in an intuitive and convenient way: the SAP SuccessFactors adapter, which is part of the SAP Cloud Platform Integration standard adapter offering.

11.4.2 SAP SuccessFactors Adapter

The SAP SuccessFactors adapter comes in several variants, depending on which API you want to connect to the SAP SuccessFactors system with (and the communication direction). Table 11.1 provides a list of these variants.

Adapter Variant	Allows You To...
Sender SOAP	Connect to an SAP SuccessFactors sender, and read data from it using web services.

Table 11.1 SAP SuccessFactors Adapter Variants

Adapter Variant	Allows You To...
Sender REST	Connect to an SAP SuccessFactors learning management system (sender), and read data from it through a REST API.
Receiver SOAP	Connect to an SAP SuccessFactors receiver to perform read or write operations on the content using web services.
Receiver REST	Connect to an SAP SuccessFactors receiver to perform read or write operations on the content using a REST API.
Receiver OData V2/V4	Connect to an SAP SuccessFactors receiver to perform read or write operations on the content using OData.

Table 11.1 SAP SuccessFactors Adapter Variants (Cont.)

Each SAP SuccessFactors adapter type provides a dedicated configuration UI to access SAP SuccessFactors entities intuitively. After you've specified an SAP SuccessFactors system to connect to, through the configuration UI of the adapter, you can easily select the entities and define certain operations on them without the need to write any line of code. When you add an SAP SuccessFactors adapter to an integration flow, you'll choose the corresponding variant by selecting a **Message Protocol**, as shown in Figure 11.11, for a SAP SuccessFactors receiver adapter.

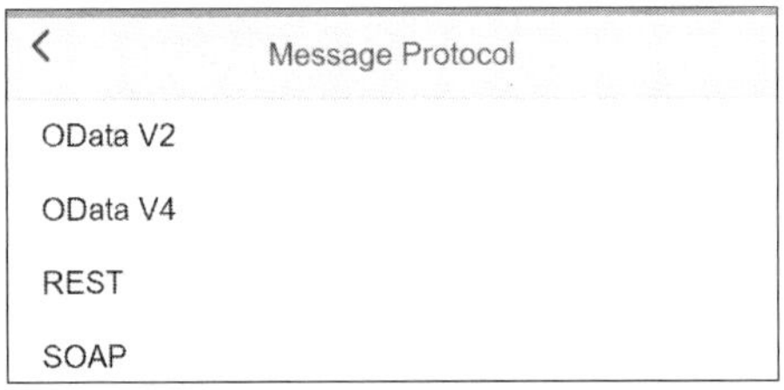

Figure 11.11 Selecting the Message Protocol to Decide Which Adapter Variant to Add (for the SAP SuccessFactors Receiver Adapter)

The detailed properties of the adapter's configuration UI depend on the chosen message protocol. Figure 11.12 shows an example for a SAP SuccessFactors adapter configuration UI for a receiver adapter when you've selected **SOAP** as the **Message Protocol**. Some key properties are indicated and explained next.

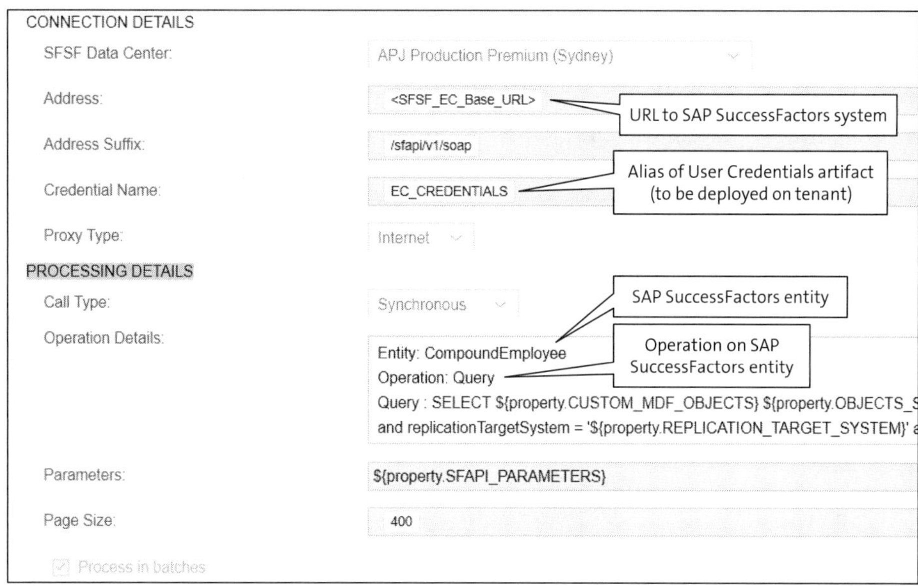

Figure 11.12 SAP SuccessFactors Adapter (Example) from the Integration Content Catalog

Note that the example shown is retrieved from the Integration Content Catalog and reflects the component version 1.1 of the SAP SuccessFactors adapter. In the meantime, updates to this adapter type have been provided so that, when you create a new SAP SuccessFactors receiver adapter (with the SOAP message protocol), you'll get a slightly different UI (with the settings now spread on two different tabs **Connection** and **Processing**). (For more information on the versioning concept for integration flow components, see Chapter 6, Section 6.5.)

When you configure an SAP SuccessFactors sender adapter (to connect to an SAP SuccessFactors sender system), you can specify only query operations. This is because the SAP SuccessFactors adapter acts as a polling adapter, reading information at scheduled intervals from the SAP SuccessFactors system (similar to how the Mail sender adapter reads emails from an email server; see Chapter 2, Section 2.3.8).

For receiver adapters, all standard CRUD operations of SFAPI (query, insert, upsert, update) are supported and can be configured (Figure 11.12).

To configure a secure connection between SAP Cloud Platform Integration and an SAP SuccessFactors sender or receiver system, you'll use the **User Credentials** artifact type, which comprises a username, password, and, specific to SAP SuccessFactors, a

11

company ID (to indicate the SAP SuccessFactors system you're connecting to). When configuring the connection, you first define a **User Credentials** artifact and deploy it on the tenant, and, second, refer to the alias of the artifact (in the **Credential Name** field) in the SAP SuccessFactors adapter. Compare this process to the one we used for the mail adapter (see Chapter 2, Section 2.3.5).

Figure 11.13 shows the properties of the **User Credentials** artifact to be deployed on the tenant to configure a secure connection between the tenant and an SAP SuccessFactors system.

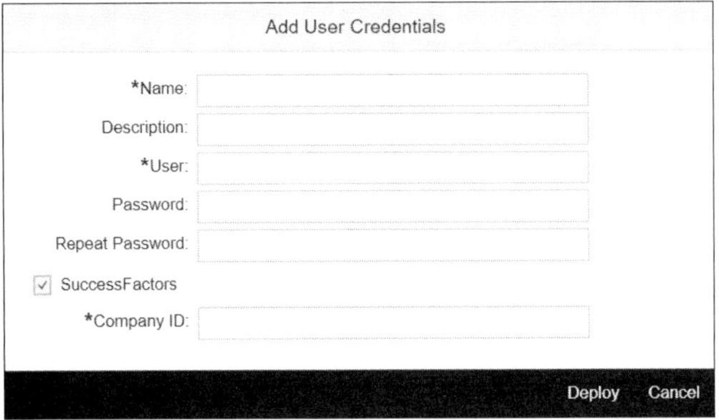

Figure 11.13 User Credentials Artifact for SAP SuccessFactors

For SAP SuccessFactors sender adapters, you can also, for example, select a scheduler to specify that the adapter reads data from the SAP SuccessFactors (sender) system at certain time intervals.

If you're interested to learn more about the integration of SAP SuccessFactors with other applications using SAP Cloud Platform Integration, check out the following E-Bite available from SAP PRESS: *Integrating SAP SuccessFactors with SAP Cloud Platform Integration (SAP HCI)* at *www.sap-press.com/4371*.

11.5 Integration of SAP Applications with the Ariba Network

The Ariba Network provides a worldwide online marketplace that brings buyers and suppliers together via the Internet and helps them facilitate their procurement processes. Interacting in this network, companies can streamline and accelerate their procurement processes, which include buying, selling, and cash management.

When you keep in mind that in the recent past, the majority of such processes still relied on the exchange of paper-based information, you can imagine that moving the processes to the network and automating them helps accelerate them greatly and considerably reduces manual errors. Both buyers and their suppliers benefit from such a shift. For example, buyers can pay earlier and may benefit from discounts because they are paying faster, and suppliers are receiving their money earlier.

The basic scenario is that a buyer (who uses an SAP ERP system to manage the procurement process) interacts with many suppliers through the Ariba Network. Each supplier is a registered member of the Ariba Network.

The Ariba Network supports different options for buyers to manage the procurement process:

- The buyer's SAP ERP system manages the ordering process, whereas the invoicing process is sourced out to, and automated via, the Ariba Network.
- The entire procure-to-pay process (including the ordering process) is automated using the Ariba Network, and the buyer's SAP ERP system only acts as a system of records.

Let's briefly focus on the first option, where the ordering process is managed by the SAP ERP system. Once set up, a typical scenario comprises the following steps at both the buyer's and supplier's sides:

1. The buyer creates a purchase order to order a product from the supplier's catalog and sends the purchase order to the supplier.
2. The supplier receives the purchase order in its inbox, creates an order confirmation, and sends that confirmation to the buyer.
3. The buyer receives the order confirmation.
4. After the article ships, the supplier creates an advanced shipping notification and sends it to the buyer to inform him that the article is on its way.
5. As soon as the product arrives, the buyer posts a goods receipt and sends it to the supplier.
6. After the goods receipt arrives, the supplier creates an invoice and forwards it to the buyer.

To integrate the buyer's SAP ERP systems with the Ariba Network, SAP provides an Ariba Network Integration for SAP Business Suite Add-On 1.0, which supports the following integration options:

- Setting up a point-to-point connection with the Ariba Network (based on web services)
- Using SAP Process Orchestration as on-premise integration platform
- Using SAP Cloud Platform Integration as the cloud integration solution

For integration using SAP Cloud Platform Integration, SAP provides predefined integration content in the Integration Content Catalog. An overview of the content and more details on the business use case of this scenario have already been provided in Chapter 3, Section 3.4.2.

11.5.1 Technical Landscape

Figure 11.14 shows the technical landscape for integrating a buyer with the Ariba Network based on SAP Cloud Platform Integration.

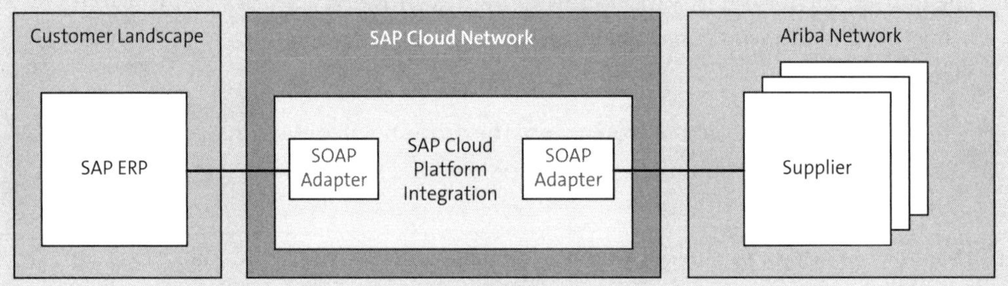

Figure 11.14 Technical Landscape for the Integration of SAP ERP with the Ariba Network

As indicated in Figure 11.14, the connectivity both for the buyer's SAP ERP system and for the Ariba Network is based on the SOAP adapter.

Note that suppliers registered in the Ariba Network can use either their own proprietary applications or an SAP application to manage the procurement process from their side, or they can use a UI provided by the Ariba Network itself.

11.6 Summary

In this chapter, we provided you with a high-level overview of a few productive scenarios that can be implemented using SAP Cloud Platform Integration. We quickly walked you through a few scenarios that allow you to integrate SAP solutions both in cloud-to-cloud and in hybrid cloud-to-on-premise landscapes. We closed this chapter by briefly touching on Ariba Network integration based on SAP Cloud Platform Integration.

With this, we close our introduction to SAP Cloud Platform Integration. In the next chapter, we provide a final outlook on the evolution of SAP Cloud Platform Integration that users can expect to see in the future.

Chapter 12
Summary and Outlook

In this final chapter, we'll briefly wrap up what you've learned over the course of this book and walk you through some of the enhancements to the SAP Cloud Platform Integration portfolio that you can expect to see in the coming months and years.

Congratulations! You've reached the end of the book, and you're now equipped with all the knowledge required to productively begin your own integration project. However, this isn't the end of your journey into the world of cloud integration: SAP Cloud Platform Integration is updated on a monthly basis, which means that you can expect continuous product improvements. In this chapter, after a brief summary of what you've learned in this book, we'll walk you through a number of key enhancements you can expect to see in the future.

In Chapter 1, we introduced you to the topic of the book by showing you how SAP Cloud Platform Integration fits into the overall cloud strategy of SAP. By outlining various use cases, we gave you an idea about how you can embed SAP Cloud Platform Integration into your own company's digital strategy. In Chapter 2, we brought you up to speed with SAP Cloud Platform Integration's basic terms and concepts and followed up with a description of SAP Cloud Platform Integration's architecture. There, you also learned how to set up and run your first simple integration flow. Chapter 3 introduced you to the Integration Content Catalog, the public show window and shop for SAP's prepackaged integration content. That chapter also introduced the Web UI. Chapter 4, Chapter 5, and Chapter 6 showed you how to use the Web UI to build your own integration scenarios, starting with the simplest integration pattern and, bit by bit, progressing to more complex ones. Each of these chapters provided a rich offering of tutorials that showed you, in detail, how to work with the tool by yourself.

In Chapter 7, we showed you how SAP Cloud Platform Integration supports business-to-business (B2B) scenarios along one end-to-end scenario. Chapter 8 introduced you to another phase of the lifecycle of an integration project: the operations phase of an integration scenario. You learned how to use the Web UI to monitor messages and integration artifacts.

Chapter 9 provided you with detailed information on how to access SAP Cloud Platform Integration based on an application programming interface (API).

To accommodate the fact that security is a key consideration when moving to the cloud, Chapter 10 introduced you to this topic in detail. You were also provided with a number of tutorials that showed you how to use the Web UI to configure secure scenarios, such as the digital encryption of messages.

Chapter 11 shared a number of examples of how SAP Cloud Platform Integration can be used productively in real-life scenarios. And, finally, you arrived here—at Chapter 12.

In this chapter, we would like to give you an overview of some areas where you can expect to see major enhancements to SAP Cloud Platform Integration in the coming months and years. However, we recommend that you view the following statements as an overview of a roadmap based on today's assumptions, without any claim to be complete. We can't give any guarantee that the mentioned enhancements will be available at a certain point in time, as SAP might change development planning without notice. If you want more reliable information to plan for your own projects and strategies, check the SAP Cloud Platform Integration online documentation, or contact SAP directly. You might also like to check out *www.sap.com/products/roadmaps.html*. If you search for **Cloud Integration**, you'll find the up-to-date roadmap.

12.1 Multi-Cloud Support

SAP Cloud Platform provides two different development environments: the Neo environment and the Cloud Foundry environment. Both environments are available in different regions worldwide. Note that such an environment to develop, manage, and run applications in the cloud is also referred to as *platform-as-a-service (PaaS)*. A PaaS usually is technically operated on an *infrastructure-as-a-service (IaaS)*, which identifies on-demand access to network, storage, and other resources in the cloud (provided and maintained by a cloud software vendor). For more information on these terms, see the upcoming info box.

We won't go into more detail. However, we would like to point out one major difference between the two environments: Neo is available on an infrastructure that is provided by SAP exclusively, whereas Cloud Foundry, which is the industry standard

PaaS—might run on an IaaS provided by various third-party vendors such as Amazon, Microsoft, or Google. Supporting both environments, SAP Cloud Platform is a *multi-cloud* enterprise cloud platform in such a way that customers can choose freely the underlying cloud infrastructure. For more information on the different environments of SAP Cloud Platform, open its documentation at *https://help.sap.com/viewer/p/CP*, and select **What is SAP Cloud Platform • Environments**. For more information on Cloud Foundry, check out the Cloud Foundry documentation at *www.cloudfoundry.org*.

You might have asked yourself why, when reading this book, we hardly touched on the topic of SAP Cloud Platform environments, in particular, Cloud Foundry. We briefly mentioned Cloud Foundry only in Chapter 6, Section 6.6.3, when showing you how to set up SAP Cloud Platform's Transport Management Service for integration content transport. Transport Management Service—a service provided on top of SAP Cloud Platform—runs in the Cloud Foundry environment (see, for example, Figure 6.82).

The answer is that at the time of this book's writing, SAP Cloud Platform Integration exclusively runs in the Neo environment. Therefore, throughout this book, we always made the assumption (without explicitly saying this) that SAP Cloud Platform Integration is used within the context of the Neo environment.

SAP Cloud Platform Integration (running in the Neo environment) is available in various regions worldwide. Physically, this means that SAP Cloud Platform Integration is deployed and operated in various data centers operated by SAP in different regions on the world. SAP continuously increases the number of data centers where SAP Cloud Platform Integration can be operated. To find out more about the actual regional availability, check out the documentation of SAP Cloud Platform at *https://help.sap.com/viewer/p/CP* and search for **Regions**.

However, that isn't the end of the story. We've stated that SAP Cloud Platform already is a multi-cloud enterprise cloud platform supporting multiple environments. Consequently, SAP Cloud Platform Integration will further evolve so that it becomes a multi-cloud service that can be used within the Cloud Foundry environment as well. This is one major enhancement that you can expect in the near future that will imply SAP Cloud Platform Integration can then also be made available on Amazon Web Services (AWS), Google Cloud Platform, or Microsoft Azure.

SAP Cloud Platform will deliver integration flow model compatibility, which means you'll be able to deploy and run your existing integration flows in any SAP Cloud Platform environment without manual adoption.

In particular, the ability to deploy SAP Cloud Platform Integration also on infrastructures provided by hyperscale cloud vendors such as Amazon, Google, or Microsoft will bring a significant increase in flexibility and scalability for the usage of SAP Cloud Platform Integration.

SaaS, PaaS, and IaaS Briefly Explained

We'll briefly shed a light on a couple of terms that often are used in the context of the multi-cloud topic.

The book you have in your hands is about software for process integration (SAP Cloud Platform Integration) that is made available in the cloud as *software-as-a-service (SaaS)*, which means it's delivered through the Internet by a software vendor (SAP) and also operated and updated by the same. By the way, that is why in Chapter 10, Section 10.2.2, we named those people at SAP who are responsible to manage and administer SAP Cloud Platform Integration as *SaaS administrators*.

SAP Cloud Platform Integration is provided as a service on SAP's enterprise cloud platform (SAP Cloud Platform). SAP Cloud Platform is SAP's cloud environment for the development, deployment, and operation of cloud applications. Such a development environment is also generally referred to as a *platform-as-a-service (PaaS)*.

Each software development platform physically runs on servers (located in various data centers in different regions on the world), requiring resources (e.g., for data storage) and access to network components. Software vendors such as SAP, Amazon, Google, or Microsoft provide such infrastructures on demand in the cloud, and such an infrastructure is generally referred to as an *infrastructure-as-a-service (IaaS)*.

12.2 Integration Content Management

With regard to the following topics introduced in Chapter 6, you can expect enhancements:

- **Integration content transport**
  As you've learned from Chapter 6, Section 6.6, integration content designed with the Web UI can be transported between different tenants. At the time of this book's writing, the cloud-based transport system, Transport Management Service, is only available as beta software. You can expect that this service will be made generally available within the next few months.

- **Versioning of integration flow components**
  In Chapter 6, Section 6.5, you learned about the versioning concept of integration flow components. As of the writing of this book, the following components can be migrated to a newer version: integration flow, integration process, and local integration process. Expect that other components (e.g., individual adapter types) can also be migrated in the future. This will provide you much more flexibility to adapt integration flows on a detailed level to new features provided by SAP.

12.3 Predefined Integration Content

In Chapter 3, you learned about the Integration Content Catalog, which is the channel where SAP provides predefined integration content that you can use out of the box.

SAP continues enhancing the portfolio of predefined integration scenarios to support the integration of different SAP solutions with applications such as SAP SuccessFactors, SAP Ariba, SAP Customer Experience, and SAP S/4HANA.

12.4 New Connectivity Options

The number of adapters provided as part of the product portfolio of SAP Cloud Platform Integration will continuously increase. As of the writing of this book, we see that you can expect the availability of the following new adapters:

- **JDBC adapter**
  SAP will make available a Java Database Connectivity (JDBC) adapter that enables you to connect SAP Cloud Platform Integration with a JDBC database and to execute SQL commands on the database.
- **OData V4**
  In various tutorials given in this book, we used the OData adapter to retrieve data from an external OData source to further process it in the subsequent steps in an integration flow. The OData adapter currently available with SAP Cloud Platform Integration supports the OData version 2.0 (as described at *www.odata.org/documentation/odata-version-2-0*). However, there is a newer version of the standard available, version 4.0 (as described at *www.odata.org/documentation*). Expect that a new adapter supporting OData version 4.0 will be made available soon.

  Note that we don't talk here about the OData variant of the SAP SuccessFactors adapter, which already supports both OData versions 2.0 and 4.0.

- **OFTP2**
  SAP will make available an adapter to support Odette File Transfer Protocol v2 (OFTP2), which is used to transfer files over the Internet and is widely adopted in the European automotive industry for B2B. Therefore, this additional adapter will significantly enhance the B2B capabilities of SAP Cloud Platform Integration.

  For more information on OFTP2, go to *www.odette.org/services/oftp2*.

12.5 Business-to-Business Support

In Chapter 7, we gave you a detailed introduction to the existing B2B capabilities of SAP Cloud Platform Integration. To name a few components, there are several B2B-related adapters and flow steps (e.g., the AS2 adapter or the EDI splitter), but there are also "larger" components, such as the Integration Content Advisor and the Partner Directory.

SAP will invest in several areas to strengthen the B2B capabilities of the platform.

12.5.1 Further Adapters

SAP will continue to provide new adapters. One example for a new planned adapter that will enhance the B2B capabilities of the platform is the OFTP2 adapter mentioned earlier.

12.5.2 Enhancements of the Integration Content Advisor

The Integration Content Advisor will be enhanced continuously. Expect the following additional features:

- **Support of additional library types**
  Integration Content Advisor will enhance its library of type systems, for example, by the additional industry standard VDA (VDA stands for the German Association of the Automotive Industry). Furthermore, SAP Cloud Platform Integration will support the VDA-specific syntax conversion.
- **Support of new formats and schemas**
  The Integration Content Advisor will enable exact schema validation based on assertions. This new capability will be supported by the SAP Cloud Platform Integration schema validator based on XML Schema Definition (XSD) 1.1.

12.5.3 Trading Partner Management

Besides these particular enhancements, SAP has a vision to provide a new service—called *Trading Partner Management*—that interested parties can use as a central hub to get connected to other trading partners to build individually defined and agreed-upon B2B scenarios with each other using an open network.

Using this service, interested companies can specify and share their own business requirements as a profile visible for other potential interested parties. This will then be the basis to create connections with new trading partners and share information with them, to invite new parties, and, finally, to deploy and run integration scenarios based on the specifications derived collaboratively.

The already available key components—the Partner Directory and the Integration Content Advisor—will be integrated technically with the Trading Partner Management service so that partner-related information (created in the context of the partner network) will be stored in the Partner Directory of a partners' tenant, and the interfaces and mappings for the agreed B2B scenarios will be created by the Integration Content Advisor.

In other words, expect that SAP will soon develop a "social-like network" for setting up B2B scenarios across trading partners.

In addition, SAP will work on archiving options as well as monitoring capabilities that allow you to monitor message flows end to end—along all parties involved in a B2B scenario.

12.6 SAP Cloud Platform Integration API

The SAP Cloud Platform Integration application programming interface (API) was introduced in Chapter 9. You can expect continuous enhancements of this API. For example, the API will be enhanced to support the management of integration content (design-time objects). Exposing such functions via an API will allow you, for example, to do mass changes in your setup of integration flows (when you need to maintain and keep up to date large numbers of integration flows).

12.7 Connectivity

As you've learned when reading this book, SAP Cloud Platform Integration comes already with a broad spectrum of connectivity options (SAP-developed adapters), which are constantly being updated. Furthermore, SAP Cloud Platform Integration customers can build their own adapters using the Adapter Development Kit (as we've shown in Chapter 6, Section 6.7).

A new SAP Cloud Platform service, Open Connectors, will allow you to extend the connectivity options of the platform in a complementary way. Open Connectors allows you to access and use a rich set of connectors that are based on REST APIs and provide harmonized access to the remote system with regard to authentication, error handling, and other aspects.

12.8 Security

The security-related features of SAP Cloud Platform Integration will be further expanded. One major part to be covered is the capabilities for the user to manage the tenant keystore. Furthermore, you can also expect SAP to continue getting certified to comply with additional security standards.

12.8.1 Tenant Keystore Management

The tenant keystore is the central component for the setup and maintenance of security material for HTTP connections. In Chapter 10, Section 10.5, we introduced you to the features that allow you to manage the content of the tenant keystore. We particularly showed you how to use the keystore monitor to manage the lifecycle of SAP-owned keys (when being renewed by SAP). The keystore monitor also allows you to add single keystore entries (in the previous releases of SAP Cloud Platform Integration, it was required to upload or remove a complete keystore and to use an external tool such as the KeyStore Explorer to manage the content of the keystore prior to deployment).

However, even with these innovations, for the creation of new keys (owned by the tenant administrator), you still rely on external tools such as KeyStore Explorer. It's planned that in the near future, you can use the keystore monitor of the Web UI to perform all tasks required to create new keys end to end (e.g., generating a new key pair, creating certificate signing requests, etc.).

12.8.2 Compliance with Security Standards

As described in Chapter 10, Section 10.2, SAP Cloud Platform Integration is certified to meet various security standards. SAP is continuously working on additional certifications. Expect that SAP Cloud Platform Integration will soon be certified to meet the requirements of the ISO27018 standard.

12.9 Harmonization of SAP Cloud Platform Integration with Other Services

SAP Cloud Platform Integration is a self-contained service that allows you to set up and operate integration scenarios without the need of any other tool. The Web UI is the main user entry point to design, deploy, and operate integration flows and to monitor the exchange of messages. However, there are certain use cases where it makes sense to combine the usage of SAP Cloud Platform Integration with other services provided on top of SAP Cloud Platform. We gave an example for this when showing how to use SAP Cloud Platform's Transport Management Service together with SAP Cloud Platform Integration to transport integration content across tenants (see Chapter 6, Section 6.6.3). Another example described in the book is the usage of SAP Cloud Platform Integration together with SAP Cloud Platform API Management (in short: SAP API Management). SAP API Management supports you throughout the whole lifecycle of an API. It allows you, for example, to publish your own APIs or to analyze the usage of APIs. In Chapter 9, Section 9.6, we showed you how to use SAP API Management together with SAP Cloud Platform Integration.

A cloud service that is related to business process integration and automation is SAP Cloud Platform Workflow. Although we haven't touched on this topic in this book, SAP Cloud Platform Workflow is an on-demand solution that helps you automate business processes by providing a graphical modeling tool that allows you to design workflows based on Business Process Model and Notation (BPMN), similar to the integration flow designer of SAP Cloud Platform Integration. Furthermore, you can use this service to manage users and tasks, and to operate, monitor and manage workflows. SAP Cloud Platform Workflow can be connected with other components based on REST interfaces. However, you can also add SAP Cloud Platform Integration to your setup to enhance the connectivity options. For more information on SAP Cloud Platform Workflow, check out the documentation *https://help.sap.com/viewer/p/WORKFLOW_SERVICE* and the E-Bite *Introducing SAP Cloud Platform Workflow* by Rohit Khan and Rajiv Pandey (SAP PRESS, 2017, *www.sap-press.com/4541*).

As there are many use cases where it makes sense to use services such as SAP Cloud Platform Workflow and SAP API Management in conjunction with SAP Cloud Platform Integration, SAP is investing efforts to provide a harmonized user experience in the long term. Therefore, expect that these services will converge in the future to provide one single entry point for users who want to access all these services.

12.10 Summary

SAP Cloud Platform Integration is already a mature integration solution with a rich feature portfolio. However, as you see from this chapter, that isn't the end of the journey. SAP Cloud Platform Integration is updated every month, and, successively, many more features will be added to its portfolio. Stay tuned, and check out the available online resources on a regular basis to be informed about new innovations. And, keep enjoying your integration journey with SAP Cloud Platform Integration!

Appendices

Appendix A
Abbreviations

Abbreviation	Long Text
A2A	Application-to-Application
ABAP	Advanced Business Application Programming
ADK	Adapter Developer Kit
AES	Advanced Encryption Standard
ANSI	American National Standards Institute
API	Application Programming Interface
AS2	Applicability Statement 2
AS4	Applicability Statement 4
ASC	Accredited Standards Committee
B2B	Business-to-Business
BIC	Bank Identifier Code
BizX Suite	Business Execution Suite
BPMN	Business Process Model and Notation
C4C	SAP Cloud for Customer
CA	Certification Authority
CBR	Content-Based Routing
CGI	Common Global Implementation Initiative
CIDX	Chemical Industry Data Exchange
Cloud Connector	SAP Cloud Platform Connectivity service

Abbreviation	Long Text
Cloud Integration	SAP Cloud Platform Integration
CMIS	Content Management Interoperability Services
CMS	Content Management System Cryptographic Message Syntax
CN	Common Name
CPU	Central Processing Unit
CRM	Customer Relationship Management
CRUD	Create, Read, Update, Delete
CSR	Certificate Signing Request
CSRF	Cross-Site Request Forgery
CSV	Comma-Separated Values
CXF	CeltiXFire
DMZ	Demilitarized Zone
DN	Distinguished Name
EAI	Enterprise Application Integration
EDI	Electronic Data Interchange
EDIFACT	Electronic Data Interchange for Administration, Commerce and Transport
EDMX	Entity Data Model XML
ERP	Enterprise Resource Planning
ESB	Enterprise Service Bus
ESR	Enterprise Services Repository
ETL	Extract, Transform, Load
EU	European Union
FSN	Financial Services Network

Abbreviation	Long Text
G&B	Generation & Build Subsystem
GDPR	General Data Protection Regulation
HCM	Human Capital Management
HL7	Health Level 7
HP	Hewlett-Packard
HR	Human Resources
HTTP	Hypertext Transfer Protocol
HTTPS	HTTP Secure
IaaS	Infrastructure as a Service
ICA	Integration Content Advisor
IntaaS	Integration as a Service
IDoc	Intermediate Document
IEC	International Electrotechnical Commission
IMAP	Internet Message Access Protocol
IMAPS	Internet Message Access Protocol Secure
ISO	International Organization for Standardization
IT	Information Technology
JAR	Java Archive
Java SE	Java Platform, Standard Edition
JMS	Java Message Service
JSON	JavaScript Object Notation
JVM	Java Virtual Machine
LDAP	Lightweight Directory Access Protocol
LMS	Learning Management System

Abbreviation	Long Text
MAG	Mapping Guideline
MDN	Message Disposition Notification
MEP	Message Exchange Pattern
MIG	Message Implementation Guideline
MIME	Multipurpose Internet Mail Extensions
MLS	Message Level Security
MPL	Message Processing Log
NRO	Number Range Object
OAuth	Open Standard for Authorization
OData	Open Data Protocol
ODETTE	Organization for Data Exchange by Tele-Transmission in Europe
OFTP	Odette File Transfer Protocol
OMG	Object Management Group
Open PGP	Open Pretty Good Privacy
OSGi	Open Services Gateway initiative
PaaS	Platform as a Service
PGP	Pretty Good Privacy
PKCS	Public-Key Cryptography Standard
PKIX	Public Key Infrastructure X.509
POP3	Post Office Protocol Version 3
POP3S	Post Office Protocol Version 3 Secure
REST	Representational State Transfer
RFC	Remote Function Call (in ABAP) Request for Comments
RN	Runtime Node

Abbreviation	Long Text
RSA	Initial letters of the surnames of Ron Rivest, Adi Shamir, and Leonard Adleman, representing a public-key cryptosystem
S/MIME	Secure/Multipurpose Internet Mail Extensions
SaaS	Software as a Service
SAP C4C	SAP Cloud for Customer
SAP CRM	SAP Customer Relationship Management
SAP ERP	SAP Enterprise Resource Planning
SAP FSN	SAP Financial Services Network
SAP HCM	SAP Human Capital Management
SAP CP	SAP Cloud Platform
SAP ID Service	SAP Identity Service
SAP MM	SAP ERP Material Management
SAP PI	SAP Process Integration
SAP PO	SAP Process Orchestration
SAP RM	SAP Reliable Messaging
SAP S/4HANA	SAP Business Suite 4 SAP HANA
SAP SD	SAP ERP Sales and Distribution
SAP SRM	SAP Supplier Relationship Management
SCA	Static Code Analyzer
SCN	SAP Community Network
SDLC	SAP Security Development Lifecycle
SFAPI	SuccessFactors Application Programming Interface
SFTP	SSH File Transfer Protocol Secure File Transfer Protocol
SHA	Secure Hash Algorithm

Abbreviation	Long Text
SMTP	Simple Mail Transfer Protocol
SMTPS	Simple Mail Transfer Protocol Secure
SOAP	Simple Object Access Protocol
SRM	Supplier Relationship Management
SSH	Secure Shell
SSL	Secure Socket Layer
SSO	Single Sign-On
SWIFT	Society for Worldwide Interbank Financial Telecommunication
TCO	Total Cost of Ownership
TLS	Transport Layer Security
TMN	Tenant Management Node
UDF	User-Defined function
UI	User Interface
UN/CEFACT	United Nations Centre for Trade Facilitation and Electronic Business
UN/EDIFACT	United Nations Electronic Data Interchange for Administration, Commerce and Transport
URI	Uniform Resource Identifier
URL	Uniform Resource Locator
VDA	Verband der Automobilindustrie (German Association of the Automotive Industry)
VM	Virtual machine
W3C	World Wide Web Consortium
Web UI	Web User Interface
WS-Security	Web Services Security
WSDL	Web Services Description Language

Abbreviation	Long Text
XAdES	XML Advanced Electronic Signatures
XI	Exchange Infrastructure
XSD	XML Schema Definition
XML	Extensible Markup Language
XMLNS	XML Namespace
XPath	XML Path Language
XSLT	Extensible Stylesheet Language Transformations

Appendix B
Literature

The following sections list the literature you may find helpful in your continued exploration of SAP Cloud Platform Integration.

B.1 Books

- Bilay, J. B., Blanco, R. V., *SAP Process Orchestration: The Comprehensive Guide* (Boston: SAP PRESS, 2017).
- Hohpe, G., Woolf, B., *Enterprise Integration Patterns. Designing, Building, and Deploying Messaging Solutions* (Boston: Addison Wesley, 2004).
- Ibsen, C., Anstey, J., *Camel in Action* (Stamford: Manning Publications, 2011).
- Schmeh, K., *Cryptography and Public Key Infrastructure on the Internet* (Chichester, United Kingdom: John Wiley, 2003).
- Stiehl, V., *Process-Driven Applications with BPMN* (New York: Springer, 2014).
- Wood, J., et al, *Getting Started with SAP HANA Cloud Platform* (Boston: SAP PRESS, 2015).

B.2 SAP Cloud Platform Integration Related Links

- SAP Cloud Platform Integration landing page
  http://scn.sap.com/docs/DOC-40396
- SAP API Business Hub containing the integration content
  https://api.sap.com/shell/integration
- SAP Cloud Platform on *help.sap.com*
  https://help.sap.com/viewer/p/CP
- SAP Cloud Platform Integration on *sap.com*
  www.sap.com/products/hana-cloud-integration.html

- SAP Cloud Platform Integration on *help.sap.com*
  https://help.sap.com/viewer/p/CLOUD_INTEGRATION
- SAP Cloud Platform Integration tools for adapter development
  https://tools.hana.ondemand.com/#cloudintegration
- SAP Cloud Platform Integration Editions and components
  https://cloudplatform.sap.com/support/service-description.html#section_11
- SAP Development Tools for Eclipse Oxygen
  https://tools.hana.ondemand.com/oxygen
- SAP Data Center Locations
  www.sap.com/about/cloud-trust-center/data-center.html
- SAP S/4HANA Cloud on *help.sap.com*
  https://help.sap.com/viewer/p/SAP_S4HANA_CLOUD

B.3 General Online Sources

- Accredited Standards Committee X12 (ASC X12)
  www.x12.org
- Anstey, J.: *Apache Camel: Integration Nirvana*
  http://architects.dzone.com/articles/apache-camel-integration
- Apache Camel:
  - Apache Camel Homepage
    http://camel.apache.org
  - Apache Camel Documentation
    http://camel.apache.org/documentation.html
  - Apache Camel Simple Expression Language
    http://camel.apache.org/simple.html
  - Writing components
    http://camel.apache.org/writing-components.html
  - List of available components
    http://camel.apache.org/components.html
- Cryptographic Message Syntax
  https://tools.ietf.org/html/rfc2315
- Eclipse
  www.eclipse.org

- Eclipse Oxygen
  www.eclipse.org/oxygen
- Enterprise Integration Patterns
  www.enterpriseintegrationpatterns.com
- GeoTrust
  www.geotrust.com
- GNU Privacy Guard for Windows (Gpg4win), including Kleopatra (a certificate manager and a universal crypto GUI)
  www.gpg4win.de/index.html
- International Standardization Organization (ISO)
  www.iso.org
- ISO 20022 standard (defines XML specifications for messages exchanged in the course of financial transactions)
  www.iso20022.org
- ISO/IEC 27001:2013 standard (provides requirements for an information security management system [ISMS])
  www.iso.org/iso/iso27001
- Mendelson AS2
  http://as2.mendelson-e-c.com
- Northwind OData service
  http://services.odata.org/Northwind/Northwind.svc
- OAuth 1.0
  https://tools.ietf.org/html/rfc5849
- OAuth 2.0
  https://tools.ietf.org/html/rfc6749
- OAuth 2.0 authorization framework
  http://oauth.net
- Oorsprong Web services
  http://webservices.oorsprong.org/websamples.countryinfo/CountryInfoService.wso?WSDL
- Open Pretty Good Privacy (OpenPGP)
  https://tools.ietf.org/html/rfc4880
- Postman
  www.getpostman.com

- RFC 5280 (format of the distinguished name [DN])
  https://tools.ietf.org/html/rfc5280
- S/MIME
  https://tools.ietf.org/html/rfc5751
- SoapUI
  www.soapui.org
- United Nations Centre for Trade Facilitation and Electronic Business (UN/CEFACT)
  www.unece.org/cefact.html
- United Nations Electronic Data Interchange for Administration, Commerce and Transport (UN/EDIFACT)
  www.unece.org/cefact/edifact/welcome.html
- Web Services Security (WS-Security)
  www.oasis-open.org/committees/tc_home.php?wg_abbrev=wss
- XML Advanced Electronic Signatures (XAdES)
  www.w3.org/TR/XAdES
- XML Signature
  www.w3.org/TR/xmldsig-core

B.4 SAP Communities

- SAP Cloud Platform Integration
  www.sap.com/community/topic/cloud-integration.html
- SAP Process Orchestration
  www.sap.com/community/topic/process-orchestration.html

Appendix C
The Authors

John Mutumba Bilay studied computer engineering and finance at the University of Cape Town, South Africa. After completing his studies, he started his career as a software engineer. He currently works as a senior software engineer and enterprise integration consultant at Rojo Consultancy B.V. in the Netherlands. With more than 14 years of international experience in information technology, he has spent the last years primarily focused on integration technologies. His SAP specialities include SAP integration- and process-related technologies, including SAP Process Orchestration and SAP Cloud Platform Integration.

In addition to his daily integration work, he provides integration-related training for SAP and for Rojo Consultancy B.V. John is the author of *SAP Process Orchestration: The Comprehensive Guide* (SAP PRESS, 2017) and one of the co-authors of *Getting Started with SAP HANA Cloud Platform* (SAP PRESS, 2016).

Dr. Peter Gutsche studied physics at Heidelberg University, Ruperto Carola. After completing his Ph.D, he joined SAP in 1999. As a technical author, Peter was involved in many knowledge management projects related to SAP's interface and integration technologies. Today, as a knowledge architect, he is responsible for the product documentation of SAP Cloud Platform Integration and works on documentation concepts for cloud software.

Peter is a seasoned technical author with wide-ranging experience in the fields of SAP Process Integration and SAP Cloud Platform Integration.

Mandy Krimmel studied engineering at Humboldt University, Berlin, Germany. In 1998, she started her professional career at a research institute of the German state of Baden-Württemberg, where she was responsible for the technical evaluation of various EU research projects. In 2001, Mandy joined SAP, working on various integration-related projects, including SAP Process Integration and SAP Cloud Platform Integration. In her current role as product owner, she is responsible for the design, architecture, and development of various cloud integration components, helping to shape the development of the SAP Cloud Platform Integration product portfolio.

Mandy is a valued mentor and an active blogger in the SAP Community on various cloud integration-related topics. She is one of the co-authors of *SAP NetWeaver Process Integration* (SAP PRESS, 2010).

Prof. Dr. Volker Stiehl studied computer science at the Friedrich-Alexander-University of Erlangen-Nuremberg. After 12 years as a developer and consultant at Siemens, he joined SAP in 2004. As chief product expert, Volker was responsible for the success of the products SAP Process Orchestration, SAP Process Integration, and SAP HANA Cloud Integration. He left SAP in 2016 and accepted a position as Professor at the Ingolstadt Technical University of Applied Sciences, where he currently teaches business information technology. His research focuses on ways to help companies benefit from digitalization using the process-driven approach.

In September 2011, Volker received his Ph.D. degree from the University of Technology Darmstadt. His thesis was on the systematic design and implementation of applications using BPMN. Volker is also the author of *Process-Driven Applications with BPMN* (Springer, 2014) and a regular speaker at various national and international conferences.

Index

B

C

D

E

F

G

H

I

J

K

L

M

Q

R

S

W

X